CLASSICAL PRESENCES

General Editors

LORNA HARDWICK   JAMES I. PORTER

CLASSICAL PRESENCES

Attempts to receive the texts, images, and material culture of ancient Greece and Rome inevitably run the risk of appropriating the past in order to authenticate the present. Exploring the ways in which the classical past has been mapped over the centuries allows us to trace the avowal and disavowal of values and identities, old and new. Classical Presences brings the latest scholarship to bear on the contexts, theory, and practice of such use, and abuse, of the classical past.

Antígonas

Writing from Latin America

MOIRA FRADINGER

Great Clarendon Street, Oxford, OX2 6DP,
United Kingdom

Oxford University Press is a department of the University of Oxford.
It furthers the University's objective of excellence in research, scholarship,
and education by publishing worldwide. Oxford is a registered trade mark of
Oxford University Press in the UK and in certain other countries

© Moira Fradinger 2023

The moral rights of the author have been asserted

First Edition published in 2023

Impression: 1

All rights reserved. No part of this publication may be reproduced, stored in
a retrieval system, or transmitted, in any form or by any means, without the
prior permission in writing of Oxford University Press, or as expressly permitted
by law, by licence or under terms agreed with the appropriate reprographics
rights organization. Enquiries concerning reproduction outside the scope of the
above should be sent to the Rights Department, Oxford University Press, at the
address above

You must not circulate this work in any other form
and you must impose this same condition on any acquirer

Published in the United States of America by Oxford University Press
198 Madison Avenue, New York, NY 10016, United States of America

British Library Cataloguing in Publication Data

Data available

Library of Congress Control Number: 2022941771

ISBN 978–0–19–289709–1

DOI: 10.1093/oso/9780192897091.001.0001

Printed and bound in the UK by
TJ Books Limited

Links to third party websites are provided by Oxford in good faith and
for information only. Oxford disclaims any responsibility for the materials
contained in any third party website referenced in this work.

To
my father Raúl and my mother Anamaría
who taught me to question everything

Contents

Acknowledgments	ix
List of Figures	xxi
Introduction: Our América, Our Antígona	1
Overture: Antigone's Death, Antígona's Birth: Juan Cruz Varela's 1824 *Argia*	54
1. "To Govern Is to Populate": Leopoldo Marechal's 1951 *Antígona Vélez*	67
2. For the People, By the People, With the People: Félix Morisseau-Leroy's 1953 Vodou *Antigòn an Kreyòl*	109
3. Brazil's Exposed Corpses: Jorge Andrade's 1957 *Pedreira das almas* and 1969 *As Confrarias*	150
4. One Hundred Years of Puerto Rican Solitude: Luis Rafael Sánchez's 1968 *Antígona Pérez*	193
5. By Way of Interlude: The Dynamics and Innovations of the Corpus in Lesser-Known Mid-Century Plays	237
6. The Incorruptible: Griselda Gambaro's 1986 *Antígona Furiosa*	261
7. Revolutionary Shame in the Year 2000: Yuyachkani's and Watanabe's Peruvian Ismene	307
8. Finale: We Are All Antígonas on the Twenty-First-Century Stage	353
Appendix: List and Diagram of Plays: Earliest Bibliographic Information Available	391
Bibliography	397
Index	435

Acknowledgments

It takes a village, they say, to go from silence to speech, from a blank page to a manuscript. In this case, it took many villages, in many countries, in many languages. It is my pleasure to express gratitude for all the support I have received over the years (some names appear more than once), though I cannot shake off the feeling that I will forget some of the names of the many colleagues and friends who are, in one way or another, embedded in this book.

I should start where it all began, as I wandered one evening in the splendid hidden worlds of the stacks in Sterling Memorial Library at Yale University. My first expression of gratitude must go to world libraries such as Yale's that allow entrance to the stacks. As I learned in the many cities where this book took me, it is rare to have that access.

Back in 2006 at Yale, I attended a stunning production of *Antígona* composed by the late Peruvian poet José Watanabe and the theater group Yuyachkani. I must thank the mesmerizing Teresa Ralli, who played all roles, for sparking my interest in modern Antígonas right then and there, and who years later would generously give of her spirit and conversation as I was writing Chapter 7 of this book.

By 2007, I had heard of five modern Hispanophone plays featuring Antígona. One evening, I stepped out of my office in the Comparative Literature department on my way to Yale's Sterling Memorial Library and ran into my colleague David Quint, to whom I mentioned what to me then was still the curious phenomenon of Antígona in Spanish. David promptly suggested, "why not a book?" I thank him for that moment of collegiality. His recommendation took a different urgency a year later.

Admittedly, in 2007 I was only thinking of a journal article, something simple, what seems now in retrospect a timid project: perhaps a conference presentation at the Latin American Studies Association (LASA) conference. I wanted something modern to wrap up my long engagement with the ancient Antigone in my first book, which had led me to devour classical scholarship on ancient Athens, fascinated as I was, as I am, by the politics of the ancient *demos* and tragic thinking. How could I not be smitten by tragedy, having been trained in psychoanalysis? I want to acknowledge my profound debt to all classicists for introducing me to that world, and especially

X ACKNOWLEDGMENTS

to Emily Greenwood, Edith Hall, Helene Foley, Barbara Goff, Lorna Hardwick, James Porter, Michael Simpson, Kathryn Bosher, Fiona Macintosh, Justine McConnell, Patrice Rankine, Andrew Laird, and Carol Gillespie for their pioneering scholarship on postcolonial reception.

The Peruvian performance had led me away from Ancient Greece and back to my native Spanish, to modern America. More so, to Peru, the country where I had spent part of my teens. A combination of Antigone, Spanish, America and my first step into a LASA conference was appealing. Curiously, my journey took me first not back to my native Spanish, but to a new language, Haitian Creole, and a new religion, Vodou, and to rehearse it all not at LASA but at one ACLA annual meeting. I picked Marechal's *Antígona Vélez* from a shelf at Sterling Memorial Library and next to it, misplaced— another glory of open library stacks—I found a dusty small book, in an old jacket, written in a language I could not read in a place I barely knew about: it was a 1973 printing of Haitian Félix Morisseau-Leroy's *Antigòn an Kreyòl*. It took me a year to understand it, but I must thank him, *in memoriam*: that play forced me to study in detail Haitian history, which radically shaped my thinking about Antígona and about the region *tout court*. And as I plowed through Haitian Vodou and Creole, I found Jan Mapou, from the Sosyete Koukouy of Miami, whom I must thank for all his work to support Haitian culture and for sharing materials with me, including a DVD of his production of the play in Miami.

Now I had three plays in hand to compare, though one of them was an unexpected discovery. Was it fate that the ACLA meeting where I first spoke about the Haitian Antigòn was held in Puebla, Mexico? I was in Spanish American territory, with a Haitian play, at an Anglophone conference, a veritable prologue for the first scene of this book. At that ACLA conference, I met Mexican scholar Héctor Taboada, whose blunt ironies about the ideological uses of the classics in Latin America not only inspired good laughs but also a reconsideration of whether I should write an article or a book. The ACLA panel on "Classicism and Latin American identity" was important, but Héctor's invitation the following year to speak at the legendary Universidad Nacional Autónoma de México (UNAM), at the heart of Mexico City, turned out to be crucial in the crafting of this book. I thank him and his colleagues, especially Carlos Tur, for their hospitality and their intellectual generosity, with which they introduced me to Mexican intellectual engagements with ancient Greece.

After that trip, the many villages of Antígona started to appear. Chance perhaps also determined that the final brushstroke that completed the last chapter written for this book—that is, the Introduction—was prompted by another conference invitation, this time to an unexpected place on the other side of the Atlantic, which would in turn lead me in a different direction but a direction that ultimately would end close to another home, Central Europe. In 2017, Ingrid Simson invited me to join a day-long workshop on Latin American Antígonas in Munich for the Deutscher Hispanistentag (the annual conference of German Hispanists). As I prepared that presentation, the final revelation that, in fact, practically all of this book's Antígonas were mothers or mothers-to-be, took definite shape. I thank the organizers, Ingrid, Anna Brüske, and Marisa Belausteguigoitia Rius, for giving me the opportunity to wrap up the book, and all the seminar participants for their exhilarating conversation, especially Suzanne Zepp, Rogelio Orizondo, Martha Luisa Hernández, and Catarina von Wedemeyer. Immediately afterwards, Héctor Hoyos kindly invited me to give an inaugural lecture at the Center for Latin American Studies at Stanford University. I thank Héctor, as well as the director and associate director of the Center, Alberto Díaz Cayeros and Elizabeth Saénz-Ackermann, respectively, for giving me the chance to add a final brush to Antígona as mother, as I headed to the West Coast.

Suzanne Zepp then had the generosity to invite me back to Germany to present my corpus at the Freie Universität Berlin; Catarina von Wedemeyer invited me to speak at the Julius Lieben Universität Guissen. There I carried with me a new precious element: a map that Yale graphic designer Mark Saba wonderfully designed with all my information about the corpus, which appears in the Introduction. The Munich group then decided to continue the conversation the following year in a seminar at LASA in Barcelona. Unexpectedly, this journey, which started in Mexico talking about Haiti in my native language in a Comparative Literature conference, came full circle and at home, in the land of another part of my ancestors, where my grandfather was born, in Austria. When María Teresa Lichem-Medeiros contacted me from Vienna, I could not have realized that thanks to her I would get a chance to organize all my photographs and to summarize my book for the Universität Wien. I am grateful to María Teresa, to Norbert Bachleitner, and the P.E.N. Club Austria, for their hospitality, for the chance to listen to questions coming from a different critical tradition about reception, and of course for allowing me an encounter with the urban geographies that appear in so many documents, photos, and paintings kept in my parents' house in Buenos Aires.

Between Mexico and Vienna, there were many stopovers, both for conferences and for archival research. I thank panelists and respondents at the

xii ACKNOWLEDGMENTS

"Virtual Caribbeans" conference in Tulane University for an enlightening conversation about Haiti. Over the years at the ACLA, LASA, NECLAS, and MLA conferences I presented various parts of this book. I am especially grateful for the invitation to two conferences in 2008, both of them crucial for this book in its early phases: the Conference "Antigone in Hispanic Studies," organized by Montserrat Roser i Puig at the University of Kent, Canterbury—the first one, to my knowledge, in the Anglophone world to be entirely focused on Latin America and Spain; and De Paul University's 2010 conference "The Year of Antigones," organized by Tina Chanter and Sean Kirkland, both of whom later invited me to write a paper for their volume *The Returns of Antigone: Interdisciplinary Essays* (SUNY Press, 2014). I owe a particular debt to Tina's inspirational scholarship in her book *Whose Antigone? The Tragic Marginalization of Slavery* (SUNY Press, 2011) and to our intellectual exchanges. Sharing this conference weekend with Erin Mee shifted my thinking about theater and Antígona. I owe her much: it was Erin who showed me the world of performance and who later introduced me to another crucial interlocutor, Helene Foley. Both of them encouraged me to write for their *Antigone on the Contemporary World Stage* (OUP, 2011) the two essays with which I began the actual writing of this book. At that same conference, I met Fanny Söderbäck who I thank for inviting me to write the prologue to her edited volume *Feminist Readings of Antigone* (SUNY, 2010), a challenge that forced me to look at world theater. My gratitude also goes to Gavin Arnall and Robert Barton for having organized my visit to Princeton for the Princeton Annual Lecture Series in Comparative Literature, and to Helene Foley for inviting me to the MLA. On both occasions I shared later stages of the book.

A turning point for the conclusion of this book was the 2017 international workshop that I co-organized upon my return from Munich, with colleagues Emily Greenwood and George Syrimis at Yale, with generous support from the Humanity/Humanities program at the Whitney Humanities Center: "*Encounters with Classical Antiquity in Latin America.*" I am eternally grateful for those intense conversations about the classics over three days with colleagues Emily and George, Aníbal Biglieri, Elina Miranda Cancela, Laura Jansen, Francisco Barrenechea, Inés de Torres, Jorge Myers, Erika Valdivieso, Isabella Tardin Cardoso, Rodrigo Tadeu Gonçalves, Brais D. Outes-León, Tiziana Ragno, and Sandro Romero Rey. I gained a wide-angled view of the classics in the region across periods and genres, covering materials from Mexico, Cuba, Uruguay, Argentina, Peru, Brazil, Colombia, Spain, and Italy. Here new friends were made and old friendships reactivated.

ACKNOWLEDGMENTS xiii

Shared projects emerged. With all of them I maintain an ongoing conversation about Latin America, as well as the future of the classics, in general.

To follow Antígona I traveled. Out-of-pocket expenses were heavy but I wanted experiential, not only academic, knowledge: I saw locations, gathered information, visited archives if available, and conducted interviews in local artistic communities. Through Yale I was supported by generous Griswold Travel Awards for my trips to Paris, Rio de Janeiro, San Juan de Puerto Rico, and Buenos Aires. In Paris, I was grateful to have Marie-Christine Muchery's help at the Site Richelieu of the Bibliothèque Nationale de France. There I found invaluable newspaper articles about the Parisian premiere of the Haitian Antigòn; for the Haitian premiere I counted on the extraordinary generosity of Pierre Moïse Célestin at the periodicals section of the Bibliothèque Nationale d'Haïti in Port au Prince, from where he sent me newspaper information otherwise impossible to get in the USA. In Rio de Janeiro, I was aided by the efficient staff at the Fundação Nacional de Artes (Cedoc/Funarte) Archive and by research assistant Carolina Cooper, who helped me to branch out my archival research about Jorge Andrade. Thanks to Alzira Agostini Haddad and Américo Nunes for last minute help with photos for Chapter 3. In Buenos Aires, I was helped by the wonderful staff at the Hemeroteca Nacional and the Biblioteca Nacional while I searched for nineteenth-century documents; at Argentores (Asociación Argentina de Actores), Karina Caruso and Eduardo Echániz spent copious amounts of time on my twentieth-century search; at the INET (Instituto Nacional de Estudios de Teatro), Susana Arbenz not only guided me but also offered me photos from her personal archive for my chapter on Marechal; at the Archivo Histórico del Teatro Cervantes, Marcelo Lorenzo took care of me by putting in extra hours to find details about the 1951 premiere of Marechal's *Antígona Vélez*; at the Goethe-Institut Buenos Aires, I was helped by Maren Schiefelbein; María de los Ángeles Marechal welcomed me at the Fundación Leopoldo Marechal and told me stories of her father's passion for Antígona. I could not be more thankful to research assistants in Buenos Aires, a city where my own time was never sufficient to deal with both the difficult state of public archives and the array of materials dispersed in private archives. I thank especially Candela Potente, Iván Fradinger, and Nathalie Goldwaser Yankelevich. Nathalie interviewed Horacio Bermúdez, who held David Cureses' personal archive, in the outskirts of Buenos Aires. I am grateful to Horacio Bermúdez for sharing otherwise inaccessible materials about Cureses with Nathalie. In San Juan de Puerto Rico, Marilí Rodríguez at the Colección Puertorriqueña of the

xiv ACKNOWLEDGMENTS

Biblioteca Lázaro at the University of Puerto Rico could not have been more welcoming; Tina Esteves-Wolff went out of her way to help me with research at the Archivo General at the Instituto de Cultura Puertorriqueña (ICP), and to interview Eugenio Monclova, whom I must thank indirectly for all the materials he shared. Tina, along with Javier Almeyda, María Rodríguez Matos, and Hilda Ayala at the ICP came to the rescue at the last minute to help me with the photos for Chapter 4. I am extremely grateful for all their help. In Bogotá I counted on the bounty opened to me at the *Centro de Documentación* of the *Teatro La Candelaria* (CDTLC), where the staff recorded materials of the theater's history for me to take back home. Through Tatiana Alvarado Teodorika, I tried to find plays in Bolivia, and through Patricio Brito, and later Patricia Gabino at the Universidad Católica de Guayaquil, in Ecuador. I thank them for their time. In Paraguay, Néstor Ruiz and Marilis Bareiro, at the Universidad Nacional de Asunción (UNA), helped me find missing information about an Antígona in Guaraní.

Without the archives many chapters of this book would not have been possible. I have a great debt to those who work relentlessly to preserve documents in Latin America; a gigantic task due to the lack of resources.

For every chapter, I conducted interviews on location and exchanged ideas with local interlocutors, playwrights, and researchers to deepen my understanding not only of Antígona plays but also of the intricacies and intimacies of political contingencies. Those were conversations about aspects of history that are not necessarily in written archives, but rather in oral ones. There are too many "Latin American" conversations embedded in this book to include them all here, but there is room to mention a few.

I owe a great debt to the playwrights and theater directors whom I was able to interview about their engagement with Antígona. Haitian director Jan Mapou, based in Miami, provided me with all materials possible about his production of the Haitian Antigòn in the USA includigng photos for Chapter 2. Puerto Rican playwrights Luis Rafael Sánchez, Rosa Luisa Márquez, Ramón Albino, and Pablo Cabrera offered me their time with unparalleled generosity. Pablo Cabrera's recollection of his direction of the 1968 premiere of Sánchez's Antígona provided details otherwise impossible to find; I thank him deeply for the Manhattan evenings. Rosa Luisa Márquez helped me imagine theater at that time in Puerto Rico, and music composer Carlos Carrillo offered me his fantastic vision for orchestra music for Sánchez's play. Puerto Rican playwright Antonio García del Toro had the courtesy to send me his version of Antígona. Colombian playwrights Patrizia Ariza and Carlos Sátizabal helped me understand not only their

ACKNOWLEDGMENTS   XV

need to see the story from the point of view of peasant victims in the context of the longest armed conflict in South America, but also provided me with a detailed political history of the Unión Patriótica (UP). I must thank them, as well as Viviana Peretti, for providing me with photos for the final chapter. In Buenos Aires, I relied on playwright Jorge Huertas' everlasting enthusiasm for all things Antígona and his unfailing support for my project including providing me with photos for the final chapter. I interviewed director Carlos Ianni at the CELCIT/Centro Latinoamericano de Creación e Investigación Teatral to understand the challenges of staging, in the very different context of Buenos Aires, a Peruvian Antígona embedded in the political process of Peru's Truth and Reconciliation Commission. I exchanged ideas also with Daniel Fermani and Jerry Brignone, who were generous with their time and sent me their plays and extra materials. I had the opportunity to learn from playwright Marianella Morena about staging Antígona with survivors of the Uruguayan dictatorship in Montevideo; the benefit of listening to details about Chile's dictatorship from playwrights Ariel Dorfman, Sebastián Morgado, who also provided me with photos for the final chapter, and Juan Carlos Villavicencio, all of whom also shared the writing process to conceive their Antígonas. Actress and writer Teresa Ralli, over the years, has answered my questions about Yuyachkani. Thanks also to her two trusted photographers, Elsa Estremadoyro and Elenize Dezgeniski, for providing me photos for Chapter 7. I thank Gabriel Núñez for confirming in personal email conversation that he was inspired by Marechal's vision of Antígona to write his Venezuelan play.

Many expert interlocutors along the way opened up unexpected historical vistas on the political avatars of the region directly related to Antígona's journeys. With Aníbal Biglieri, I shared many stories about the passion Argentines have for Antígona. To understand Puerto Rico's singularity, I benefited from conversations with Sánchez, Albino, Cabrera, Cecilia Enjuto Rangel, but especially with Héctor Feliciano, whose hospitality and intellectual brilliance in San Juan will remain unforgettable. After an evening on his terrace looking out at the ocean, while listening to his historical narration of the island's colonial fate, Puerto Rico's difference finally made sense. In Bogotá, I grasped the historical depth of the armed conflict in the intellectual company of Sandro Romero Rey, the late Luis Ospina, Rosario Caicedo, Cira Mora, and Diego Rojas Romero. I had the privilege to exchange ideas about Brazil's context for Jorge Andrade with Elizabeth Azevedo, I thank her for her precious time. I enjoyed talking to Roberto Schwarz about the legacies of Brazil's imperial history, so unique in South America.

xvi ACKNOWLEDGMENTS

It is hard for me to summarize all the help I have received from Haitian citizens over the years in understanding Haiti's history and the real meaning of the Haitian revolution for modernity. I am eternally grateful to Félix Morisseau-Leroy's family, especially to his son Alex, his daughter Maag Mitton, and his granddaughter Gina; to Paul and Claudine Corbanese, Arnold Antonin, Jan Mapou, Bob Corbett, Guy Horelle, William-Balan Gaubert; Patrick Bellegarde-Smith, and Lois Wilcken, artistic director at La Troupe Makandal, Inc. I thank David Fils-Aimé, Elizabeth St. Victor, Catherine Fox, and Paul and Claudine Corbanese for their help with Haitian Creole. Unexpectedly and unforgettably, I was contacted by Italian scholar Mario Capaldo, who, upon reading my 2011 Haiti article, shared with me a funny anecdote about how I was quoted as being "a British" academic in Italy. He also had the generosity of sending me Mossetto's article, of which I was unaware. That is the kind of companionship and collegiality one dreams of, daily, in the academy.

The Peruvian Andes are known to me from high school years, but it was only when Félix Reátegui Carrillo and Julia Urrunaga provided me with the DVDs of peasant testimonials before the Truth Commission in the Andes that I truly grasped the consequences of Peru's armed conflict in the late twentieth century. I am most grateful to have had that first-hand access to the words of surviving peasants. I owe Ponciano del Pino for a deeper historical understanding of peasant movements in the Andes. My warmest thanks must go also to Ximena Briceño for our intellectual exchange and her sharing of her unpublished text about Antígona, which enhanced my interpretation of the Peruvian Antígona. My deepest thanks to Ursula León for conducting an interview with Teresa Ralli in Lima about the group's tour to the Andean South, back in 2011. Thanks to José Cárdenas Bunsen for helping me with Quechua.

I am extremely grateful to those who took time and patience to read drafts of chapters at different stages of this book. I thank especially Lisandro Kahan, who read Marechal's chapter and the Introduction in its early stages. Guillermo Romero von Zeschau read a draft of most of the book with literary and historical eyes: I cannot thank him enough. Federico Ludueña read drafts of Chapters 1 through 4, and I am indebted to his comments. I thank Pedro Dotto, Flávia Almeida, Rodrigo Gonçalves Tadeu, and Luisa de Freitas for their comments on the chapter on Brazil. Héctor Feliciano, Cecilia Enjuto Rangel, and Tina Esteves-Wolff read the final version of Puerto Rico's chapter and offered brilliant insights, for which I am eternally grateful. It was an unexpected luxury to have the director of the 1968 play,

ACKNOWLEDGMENTS   xvii

Pablo Cabrera, read my chapter: I remain deeply grateful to him, for all his help in this project, as well as to Ramón Albino, who also read the chapter, for his unfailing support and intellectual exchange. I thank Vanessa Gubbins for the extreme care with which she read the chapter on Peru. Nils Longueira Borrego and Yelsy Hernández Zamora read with critical eyes a section on Cuba for the last chapter.

The Departments of Comparative Literature and Classics at Yale have provided me with different kinds of support over the years. I am most grateful to have counted on this vibrant intellectual community. Carol Jacobs, simply put, made my life at Yale possible; I would not know how to thank her other than in my native language. I had many early conversations about Antígona with my cherished friends Katie Trumpener, Katy Clark, Emily Greenwood, Pauline Leven, and Irene Peirano, who in different ways encouraged me to continue with this book. Emily, Pauline, and Irene gave me a treasure trove of resources when I felt the need to go back to antiquity. Rudiger Campe has been an intellectual companion and friend over the most taxing years of this project. I thank the collegiality of Jane Tylus, David Quint, Jing Tsu, Sam Hodgkin, Dudley Andrew, Hannan Hever, Martin Hägglund, Ayesha Ramachandran, and Marta Figlerowicz. Without Mary Jane Stevens' assistance and friendship it would be hard for me to imagine Yale; I owe her daily.

Yale's financial help has been constant, and I am grateful to such a supportive community. This book took its current shape in part during a year-long Associate-on-term research leave. Yale's conference funds allowed me to present this work at the conferences mentioned above. A Frederick W. Hilles Publication Fund grant from Yale was essential to cover publication costs. I am very grateful, especially, to Alice Kaplan at the Whitney Humanities Center for her support in obtaining that funding. And to Emily Bakemeier, my heartiest thanks for her unfailing support and friendship over so many years now.

I owe Helene Foley for her scholarship, and for our Manhattan conversations, but perhaps most importantly, for trusting in this project so much as to encourage me to inquire whether Oxford University Press would be interested in it. I cannot thank her enough for giving guidance through the first steps after sending the book proposal. James Porter and Lorna Hardwick, the editors of the series Classical Presences at OUP, were not only involved but also enthusiastic to see the project come to fruition. Lorna gave me crucial advice in London as to what classicists would want

xviii ACKNOWLEDGMENTS

to know; James enthusiastically read the introduction and helped me to access the grant from the Frederick W. Hilles Publication Fund. I am most grateful to all the anonymous readers who generously offered comments on the manuscript at different stages. Throughout the publication process I have counted on the expertise of Georgina Leighton and Charlotte Loveridge, whose support was vital at OUP. Thanks especially to those who at the final stage helped me see this book become real: the production manager Balasubramanian Shanmugasundaram, Jen Hinchliffe, whose unparalled skills caught the tiniest mishaps on time, and Cheryl Hunston who was in charge of the index.

At different stages of the manuscript, I have relied on the expertise of English editors. My biggest thanks must go to Gwendolyn Harper, who saw the first drafts of all chapters and not only edited language but suggested intellectual cuts. John Mackay, Vanessa Gubbins, and Janelle Gondar edited advanced drafts of several chapters; Heather Dubnick edited the whole manuscript. Kathleen Fearn deserves special thanks. She helped me polish the whole manuscript to bring it to its current book form. I have seldom had the luck of an incredible eye for detail and special care for the text such as hers. Her brilliance, patience, generosity, kindness, and sense of humor were crucial, even in last-minute emergencies. I cannot thank her enough.

Nothing would be possible without the laughter and camaraderie of intellectual companions and friends. At times I needed wise advice. I have had the luxury to count on John Beverley, Hazel Carby, Michael Denning, Carol Jacobs, Fredric Jameson, Cristina Moreiras, Laura Wexler, and Gareth Williams over the years. Immense gratitude is owed to Rosi Braidotti, who long ago showed me the way, and whose presence and solidarity are as inspiring as they ever were.

Friends and colleagues in the USA bore with me in specific moments during the writing process. They heard me complain about archives, gave me enthusiasm and fine-tuned my critical thinking: my thanks to Rafael Acosta, Francisco Barrenechea, Erik Butler, Kamari Clarke, Patrick Dove, Veronica Garibotto, Kimberley Jannarone, Erin Mee, Paul North, Ana Puga, Ignacio Sánchez Prado. I owe special thanks to friends and colleagues with whom I also share the small everyday calamities of living in between the intellectual and linguist worlds of so-called Global Souths and Global Norths: Carolina Baffi, Aníbal Biglieri, Ximena Briceño, Sean Brotherson, Rosario Caicedo, Pedro Caro, Tomás Crowder, Cecilia Enjuto Rangel, Francesca Ferrando, Eugenio García Hurtado, Gisela Heffes, Héctor Hoyos, Agnieszka Hudzik, Laura Martins, Gabriela Nouzeilles, Florencia Montagnini,

ACKNOWLEDGMENTS xix

Fernando Rosenberg, Carina Rodríguez, Fabiola Rainudo, Jenny Rodríguez-Peña, Alvaro Santana Acuña, Mariano Siskind, Carina Rosanna Tautu, Margherita Tortora, Washo Valenzuela, Claudia Valeggia, Raúl Verduzco, Caio Yurgel, Zairong Xiang, and Guillermo von Zeschau. My eternal gratitude to Seema Kazi and Elizabeth Janz for their constant presence in my life, despite geographical distances, and to my old comrade, Gustavo Guerrero, with whom I share all my poetic, not only political, attachments to Latin America. Buenos Aires is still the city of old-time, loyal friends who give me a sense of perspective, as I share the minutiae of life, and of course, the political heat of the region, with too many to cite here. Some provided special smiles during the writing of this book: my thanks to Florencia Abbate, Itatí Acuña, Miguel Alberti, Sofía Böhmer, Gustavo Badía, Mabel Bellucci, Piroska Csúri, Inés de Torres, Mercedes Etchemendi, Marcelo Ferrante, Guillermina Gordon, Gabriel Guralnik, Lisandro Kahan, Pablo Kreimer, Vivi Matta, Mariano Mestman, Adrián Muoyo, Jorge Myers, Alejandra Oberti, Daniela Oulego, Sandra Posadino, Roberto Pittaluga, Mariano Plotkin, Adriana Rofman, Claudia Salomón Tarquini, Andrea Tolchinsky, Miguel Wald, Debora Yanco. Special thanks to Mirta Clara *in memoriam*, for unfailingly warming my heart, encouraging me in dark times, sharing her knowledge and books, and enlightening my political thought in every trip I made to Buenos Aires. *Siempre estás.*

My family is embedded in this book as much as I am. They were unshakably present in every research find or mishap, in every moment of joy or misery. My father Raúl and mother Anamaría even went to archives for me, they supplied me with books and newspaper articles, they perused bookstores and libraries, they went to the theater to see Antígona productions, they read plays and translated with me. I owe them my passion for political life, my critical thinking, and my craving for intellectual challenge. I rely on my brother Erich and my sister Sonia as on no one else; my sister-in-law Cecilia, my brother-in-law Luis, my nephews and nieces Iván, Vera, Camila, and Agustín, make all the difference in Buenos Aires. With Iván I have a special debt: he helped me with archival work and bibliographic compilations as if he had been trained to do it; I praise his incredible efficiency. In Canada, I always feel the support from Betty and the late Jack, Pamela, Peter, Stephanie, and Aidan, Ian, Addison, Nick and Alex.

How difficult can it get when time comes to thank John MacKay? John reads and criticizes all I write. My thoughts are sharpened constantly by his brilliant mind. He makes me laugh to heal emotionally; he cooks to heal physically. For this book, he relentlessly brainstormed with me, suggested

XX   ACKNOWLEDGMENTS

new readings, found odd documents, picked me up at libraries, if not at airports, helped with editing. I could not imagine a better fellow traveler than him. For my gratitude to his love, I could always try English, but then again, it is not enough: *cada vez que vuelvo del mundo herida por sus extravagantes injusticias, aparece la sintonía con la que todo lo entiendes, la sonrisa con la que todo lo alivias.*

List of Figures

0.1 Patterns in the corpus, systematized up to 2015, showing number
and location of plays featuring Antígona as mother, sister, or a collective
character; routes of American vernaculars that have been rewritten;
routes of plays that have circulated among peasant communities.
This map was designed with the help of Mark Saba, Senior Designer
and Illustrator at Yale University's Information Technology Services.   6

1.1 *Antígona Vélez*. Program, May 25, 1951, Teatro Cervantes, Buenos Aires.   69
Courtesy of the INET (Archivo Documental del Instituto Nacional de
Estudios de Teatro), Buenos Aires, Argentina.

1.2 *Antígona Vélez*. May 25, 1951. Fanny Navarro as Antígona.
Teatro Cervantes, Buenos Aires, Argentina. Courtesy of Susana Arenz
of the INET (Archivo Documental del Instituto Nacional de Estudios
de Teatro), Buenos Aires.   97

1.3 *Antígona Vélez*. Directed by Oscar Ponferrada at the Theater of Nations.
Sarah Bernhardt Theatre, May 9, 1962, Paris, France. Courtesy of BNF:
Bibliotèque Nationale de France, Site Richelieu.   99

1.4 *Antígona Vélez*. Premiere May 25, 1951. Fanny Navarro and
Daniel Alvarado. Teatro Cervantes, Buenos Aires, Argentina.
Archivo Histórico del Teatro Nacional Cervantes. Buenos Aires.
Source: *Mundo Radial*, June 7, 1951.   100

2.1 *Antigòn an Kreyòl*. Sosyete Koukouy of Miami, Inc. Miami
Dade Auditorium, USA, May 10, 1998. Directed by Jan Mapou.
Courtesy of Jan Mapou.   135

2.2 *Antigòn an Kreyòl*. Sosyete Koukouy of Miami, Inc.   136
Miami Dade Auditorium, USA, May 10, 1998. Directed by Jan Mapou.
Courtesy of Jan Mapou.

2.3 *Antigòn an Kreyòl*. Morisseau-Leroy as Tiresias. Theater of Nations.
Sarah Bernhardt Theatre Paris, France, May 11, 1959. Directed by
A. M. Julien. Photographer Roger Pic. Courtesy of the
Bibliothèque Nationale de France, Site Richelieu.   137

2.4 *Time* magazine's review "Voodoo Tragedy," translated into
French and published in *Le National*, Haiti, August 16, 1953.
Bibliothèque Nationale de France, Site Richelieu.   145

xxii LIST OF FIGURES

2.5 André Rivollet's review for *Aux Écoutes*, May 15, 1959: "At the Theater of Nations, Creole Antigone and Voodoo:... from infantilism to neurosis!" Bibliothèque Nationale de France, Site Richelieu. 147

3.1 *Pedreira das almas*. Martiniano lies dead for everyone to see. Mariana and Urbana lean over him. Teatro em São João del-Rei, Minas Gerais. Directed by Marco Camarano, December 7, 1975. Arquivo Alzira Agostini H. Atitude Cultural. Courtesy of Alzira Agostini. 174

3.2 *Pedreira das almas*. Martiniano's corpse is taken to the church. Teatro em São João del-Rei, Minas Gerais. Directed by Marco Camarano, December 7, 1975. Arquivo Alzira Agostini H. Atitude Cultural. Courtesy of Alzira Agostini. 175

3.3 *As Confrarias*. Marta indicts the priests. Cia Teatro Seraphim. Teatro Barreto Júnior, Pina, Recife, Brazil. Directed by Antonio Cadengue, June 9, 2013. Courtesy of photographer Américo Nunes. 189

4.1 *La pasión según Antígona Pérez*. The multitude runs for news. Directed by Pablo Cabrera. Eleventh annual Puerto Rican Theater Festival. Teatro Tapia, San Juan, Puerto Rico, May 30, 1968. Rehearsal photo. Courtesy of the Archivo Fotográfico del Instituto de Cultura Puertorriqueña (AGPR-ICP). 198

4.2 *La pasión según Antígona Pérez*. The minimal stage: stairs, *periaktos*, and dungeon. Directed by Pablo Cabrera. Eleventh annual Puerto Rican Theater Festival. Teatro Tapia, San Juan, Puerto Rico, May 30, 1968. Rehearsal photo. Courtesy of the Archivo Fotográfico del Instituto de Cultura Puertorriqueña (AGPR-ICP). 210

4.3 *La pasión según Antígona Pérez*. The five journalists. Directed by Pablo Cabrera. Eleventh annual Puerto Rican Theater Festival. Teatro Tapia, San Juan, Puerto Rico, May 30, 1968. Rehearsal photo. Courtesy of the Archivo Fotográfico del Instituto de Cultura Puertorriqueña (AGPR-ICP). 212

4.4 *La pasión según Antígona Pérez*. Myrna Vázquez and Rafael Enrique Saldaña. Directed by Pablo Cabrera. Eleventh annual Puerto Rican Theater Festival. Teatro Tapia, San Juan, Puerto Rico, May 30, 1968. Rehearsal photo. Courtesy of the Archivo Fotográfico del Instituto de Cultura Puertorriqueña (AGPR-ICP). 213

4.5 *La pasión según Antígona Pérez*. Poster for Idalia Pérez Garay's production. Designer: Julio García. Teatro UPR, San Juan, Puerto Rico, March 20, 1992. Courtesy of the Colección Puertorriqueña of the Biblioteca Lázaro, Universidad de Puerto Rico. 214

LIST OF FIGURES   xxiii

4.6 *La pasión según Antígona Pérez*. Rafael Enrique Saldaña: white suit
and a large pendant. Directed by Pablo Cabrera. Eleventh annual
Puerto Rican Theater Festival. Teatro Tapia, San Juan, Puerto Rico,
May 30, 1968. Rehearsal photo. Courtesy of the Archivo Fotográfico
del Instituto de Cultura Puertorriqueña (AGPR-ICP).   215

4.7 *La pasión según Antígona Pérez*. Rafael Enrique Saldaña and José Luis
"Chavito" Marrero. Directed by Pablo Cabrera. Eleventh annual
Puerto Rican Theater Festival. Teatro Tapia, San Juan, Puerto Rico,
May 30, 1968. Rehearsal photo. Courtesy of the Archivo General
del Instituto de Cultura Puertorriqueña (AGPR-ICP).   231

5.1 *El límite*. At the colonial house, Delia Garcés and Enrique Fava.
Director Alberto de Zavalía. Teatro de Buenos Aires, at the
Theater of Nations, Sarah Bernhardt Theatre, Paris, France.
Premiere, June 9, 1958. Courtesy of the Bibliothèque Nationale
de France, Site Richelieu.   240

5.2 *El límite*. Another scene at the colonial house, Delia Garcés and
Enrique Fava. Director Alberto de Zavalía. Teatro de Buenos Aires,
at the Theater of Nations, Sarah Bernhardt Theatre, Paris, France.
Premiere, June 9, 1958. Courtesy of the Bibliothèque Nationale
de France, Site Richelieu.   241

5.3 *La cabeza en la jaula*. The six women at the colonial house.
Directed by David Cureses. T.E.G.E. (Teatro El Gorro Escarlata),
Buenos Aires, Argentina, June 12, 1963. Cureses' personal archive.
Photo by Horacio Bermúdez. Courtesy of the photographer.   246

6.1 *Antígona Furiosa*, Director Laura Yusem. Premiere, Goethe Institute,
Buenos Aires, September 24, 1986. The audience surrounds the stage.
Courtesy of Susana Arenz at the INET (Archivo Documental del
Instituto Nacional de Estudios de Teatro), Buenos Aires, Argentina. 263

6.2 Review of Gambaro's *Antígona Furiosa*: "Nuestros muertos insepultos,"
La Voz del Interior, Córdoba, Argentina, October 25, 1987. Courtesy
of Argentores Archive, Buenos Aires, Argentina.   264

7.1 Ismene and the mask. Teresa Ralli as Ismene, *Antígona*, Yuyachkani.
Courtesy of photographer Elsa Estremadoyro and Teresa Ralli. 343

7.2 Ismene (Teresa Ralli) grabs the mask and speaks to Antígona,
Antígona, Yuyachkani. Courtesy of photographer Elsa Estremadoyro
and Teresa Ralli.   344

7.3 Light and dust right before Ismene (Teresa Ralli) reveals
her truth, *Antígona*, Yuyachkani. Courtesy of photographer
Elenize Dezgeniski and Teresa Ralli.   350

xxiv LIST OF FIGURES

8.1 *AntígonaS: Linaje de hembras.* Directed by Roberto Aguirre.
Teatro Repertorio del Norte. La Plata, Argentina, 2002.
Courtesy of photographer Martín Hoffmann and Jorge Huertas.   354

8.2 Gambaro's *Antígona Furiosa.* Mónica Driollet, Uki Capellari,
and Sofía Tizón. Directed by Sandra Torlucci and Teresa Sarrail.
September 2011. Delborde Espacio Teatral. Buenos Aires, Argentina.
Courtesy of photographer Pablo Stubrin.   361

8.3 *Antigonón: un contingente épico.* Giselda Calero, Linnett Hernández,
and Dayse Focade. Directed by Carlos Díaz. Teatro El Público,
La Habana, Cuba, 2012. Costume designs by Celia Lendón Acosta.
Photo by Lessy Montes de Oca. Courtesy of the photographer.   362

8.4 *Antígona: las voces que incendian el desierto.* Women look for
their missing wandering in the desert. Photo taken in Samalayuca,
Chihuahua desert, Mexico, by photographer Adrián Valverde
Porras in 2004. Courtesy of the photographer and Perla de la Rosa.   368

8.5 *Antígona: las voces que incendian el desierto.* A mother caring for
her killer son. Directed by Perla de la Rosa, Telón de Arena AC.
Teatro de la Nación, Ciudad Juárez, Chihuahua, Mexico,
September 29, 2004. Courtesy of photographer Adrián Valverde
Porras and Perla de la Rosa.   370

8.6 *Antígona: las voces que incendian el desierto.* Antígona looks into
the desert. Photo taken in Samalayuca, Chihuahua desert, Mexico,
by photographer Adrián Valverde Porras in 2004. Courtesy of the
photographer and Perla de la Rosa.   371

8.7 *Antígonas: Tribunal de Mujeres.* Female collective with the same attire.
Directed by Carlos Sátizabal. Tramaluna Teatro, Corporación
Colombiana de Teatro. Poster for the 2014 premiere; photo by
Juan Domingo Guzmán. Courtesy of Carlos Sátizabal.   378

8.8 *Antígonas: Tribunal de Mujeres.* "He liked to see me with make up on,"
says the mother about her disappeared son. Directed by Carlos Sátizabal.
Tramaluna Teatro, University of British Columbia, 2017. Photo by Felipe
Castaño. Courtesy of Carlos Sátizabal.   379

8.9 *Antígonas: Tribunal de Mujeres.* Body-sized photo of Fany's murdered
father. Directed by Carlos Sátizabal. Tramaluna Teatro. Teatro Seki Sano,
Bogotá, Colombia, 2014. Courtesy of photographer Viviana Peretti.   380

8.10 *Antígonas: Tribunal de Mujeres.* Objects of the missing: the teddy bear.
Directed by Carlos Sátizabal. Tramaluna Teatro. Casa Ensamble, Bogotá,
Colombia, November 2014. Courtesy of photographer Viviana Peretti.   381

LIST OF FIGURES   XXV

8.11 *Antígonas: Tribunal de Mujeres*. A doll, depicting a woman, is
tortured and killed. Directed by Carlos Sátizabal. Tramaluna Teatro.
Teatro Seki Sano, Bogotá, Colombia, November 2014. Courtesy of
photographer Viviana Peretti.   382

8.12 *Antígonas: Tribunal de Mujeres*. Dismembered doll representing
the one that Lawyer Soraya received by mail. Directed by
Carlos Sátizabal. Tramaluna Teatro; Casa Ensamble, Bogotá,
Colombia, November 2014. Photo by Viviana Peretti.
Courtesy of the photographer and Carlos Sátizabal.   383

8.13 *Antígona Insomne*. Antígona and Child. Directed by Rubén Morgado.
Compañía Teatro Bandurrias, April 2016, Santiago de Chile, Chile.
Photo by Catalina Jara and Grupo Hormiga ONG. Courtesy of Morgado.   385

A.1 Intersections of Mothers (M), Sisters (S), and Female Collectives (FC)
in the corpus. Grafted by Mark Saba, Senior Designer and Illustrator at
Yale University's Information Technology Services.   395

All effort has been made to contact copyright holders where necessary. In some
cases, no copyright holder was found. If this information becomes available, the
author will be happy to acknowledge copyright in future editions of this book.

Introduction

Our América, Our Antígona

> I speak to you of what I speak always: of this unknown giant, of
> our fabulous America [...] The way to celebrate independence
> is not, in my eyes, to deceive oneself about its signification, but
> to complete it. [...] I work *para ella*! [for it]
>
> (José Martí, [1877] 2003)[1]

> Tupi or not Tupi: that is the question.
>
> (Oswald de Andrade, 1928)[2]

In 1824, the same year that the decisive battles to expel the Spanish colonizers from South America took place, a peculiar avatar of the ancient Antigone
appeared in Buenos Aires. It was both an incarnation of Antigone and yet
one more contingent destination among Antigone's fractal journeys across
the millennia. As part of his poetic corpus of invectives against the
Spaniards, Argentine poet Juan Cruz Varela (1794–1839) rewrote Italian
Vittorio Alfieri's two tragedies *Polinice* and *Antigone* (1775 and 1776). But,
unlike Alfieri (and Sophocles), in his *Argia* Varela killed Antigone at the
beginning of the play and made Argia, Polynices' widow and mother of his
son, the heroic protagonist.

Antigone's dramatic murder at the dawn of the liberal nation-state gave
birth to the first of multiple transfigurations awaiting the Greek myth,
Sophocles' tragedy, and its modern European versions, throughout the last

---

[1] Cuban hero of independence José Martí wrote in his "Letter to Valerio Pujol" (November
27), published in *Política de nuestra América*: "Les hablo de lo que hablo siempre: de este
gigante desconocido, de nuestra América fabulosa. [...] La manera de celebrar la independencia no es, a mi juicio, engañarse sobre su significación, sino completarla [...] ¡Para ella trabajo!"
(2003: 54; my translation). The title of this introduction refers to Martí's famous essay: "Our
America" (1891).

[2] Oswald de Andrade. "Manifesto Antropófago" (*Revista de Antropofagia* 1, São Paulo, May
1928). The phrase plays with Shakespeare's famous line; the word "Tupi," is pronounced similarly to "to be." Tupi is the general name for the approximately eighty languages spoken by the
Tupi-Guaraní kinship systems living in Brazil and Paraguay. Among the Tupi, there were
anthropophagic practices. See the manifesto introduced by Leslie Bary at http://www.corner-
college.com/udb/cproK3mKYQAndrade_Cannibalistic_Manifesto.pdf.

Antígonas: Writing from Latin America. Moira Fradinger, Oxford University Press. © Moira Fradinger 2023.
DOI: 10.1093/oso/9780192897091.003.0001

2 INTRODUCTION: OUR AMÉRICA, OUR ANTÍGONA

two hundred years in "Latin America"—a continental set of interrelated discourses, rather than a geographic location, whose polyvalent, unstable meaning I indicate in this introduction by using quotation marks alternatively around "Latin" or "America" or any of its combinations.[3] I return to this below. Not European anymore, Antigone was crafted anew into Antígona, whose first regional embodiment in the character of Argia was even stranger as an avatar of the ancient wife than of Antigone.[4] Argia was not just the wife of the unburied, but also the mother of a kidnapped son. Varela's Creon gives Argia the choice: marry him to save the child or die. At the dawn of the nation, there was a mother without a son—an ominous predicament for her twentieth-century readers, who witnessed the real-life "necropolitics" of forced disappearances during the Cold Wars, a form of politics brought by the colony, reinstated by the neocolony, and never to leave the continental political sphere.[5]

Varela's Argia-Antígona had many incarnations in twentieth-century plays, as a mother offered a peculiar deal. In 1957, Argentine Alberto de Zavalía (1911–88) placed his heroine Fortunata in a similarly impossible quandary in *El Límite* (The limit): she could save her family on the condition that she relinquish burying the impaled martyr. In 1959, Brazilian Jorge Andrade (1922–84) had his protagonist Mariana refuse to give information about her lover's hideout in exchange for assent to her brother's burial in *Pedreira das almas* (Soul quarry). Antígonas who were asked to surrender their ideals to save the life of others, not only their own, started to reveal a pattern: Antígona in "Latin" America is not a virgin but a (national) mother.

In the space of two years, in 1951 and 1953, two Antígonas from completely different nations sacrificed their life only to continue giving

---

[3] Throughout this book, I use the terms "America" and "Americanization" to refer to the continent and never to the country the United States of America. In "Latin" America's intellectual tradition, the name "America" distinguishes the continent from Europe. There is no political tradition of referring to the United States as "America"—or to the continent in the plural as the "Americas." Strictly speaking, "European" should also be in quotation marks in this Introduction, insofar as it too indicates a fiction, but my aim here is to call the reader's attention to the problem of "Latin America." Quotation marks for this political term will be used only in this Introduction, which hopefully will suffice as a reminder of the problem throughout the book.

[4] Throughout the book, "Antigone" refers to Sophocles' character and "Antígona" to "Latin American" characters. Unless otherwise specified, Anglophone spelling will refer to all ancient characters, and Spanish, French, Portuguese, and Haitian Creole to all American characters.

[5] For the term "necropolitics," see Achille Mbembe's "Necropolitics" (2003) and his account of a form of governmentality that does not manage only life but also death.

INTRODUCTION: OUR AMÉRICA, OUR ANTÍGONA 3

(national) life, but this time in death. In 1951, Argentine Leopoldo Marechal (1900–70) imagined a strange death sentence for the nineteenth-century rural heroine in his *Antígona Vélez*: sent out on a sorrel to "Indian" territory in the Argentine Pampas, she would be killed by "Indian" arrows.[6] Her Spanish-American, *criolla* blood shed on the Pampas would metaphorically fertilize what new independent Creole elites saw as an "empty" desert—a land, that is, populated by indigenous peoples. In 1953, Haitian Félix Morisseau-Leroy (1912–98) composed a Creole *Antigòn an Kreyòl* (in Haitian Creole spelling), transforming his peasant Antigòn into a Vodou goddess in the religious system of Haiti's peasant majority. Married in death to their fiancés, both Antígona Vélez and Antigòn would then give life.[7]

And the duty to give life in neocolonial times cannot avoid the dramatization of a dreaded situation: being forced to give life to a corpse, by inventing its name, identifying it, finding it. Sometimes the body is simply not there. In 1958, Nicaraguan Rolando Steiner (1936–87) imagined a heroine in his *Antígona en el infierno* (Antígona in hell) who had to first disinter Polinice, for his remains lay in a mass grave as an "NN": no name. He had been "disappeared."[8] Sometimes there is not just one body—or it is not male. In 2014, Mexican Sara Uribe (1978–) wrote *Antígona González* in response to the discovery of 196 unidentified corpses in a mass grave in Tamaulipas, where activists have to solve an extraordinary problem: how to count, how to name, how to identify corpses. Fittingly, Uribe's first section of the poem-play is titled "Instructions on how to count the dead."

As a national mother, fiancée, sister, mother-to-be, and grandmother, who had to give life to, or bury, or even find the nation's children, Antígona is often imagined surrounded by women, desiring female connection, a desire at times overtaking burial in importance or leading to the unexpected twist (for the academic, not for the audience) of the neglect of burial. In

---

[6] I place the word "Indian" in quotation marks, as it refers to the colonial ideology that assigns "barbarism" to indigenous peoples and "civilization" to European peoples. Throughout this book, I use "indigenous peoples" when not referring to this ideological construction.

[7] The words *criolla/o* (*creole*) derive, according to etymologists, from the Latin *criare* (to raise). In colonial Spanish America, *criollo/a* indicated an American-born Spaniard, in contrast to the *peninsulares* (born in Spain). Gradually, the term evolved regionally to mean local cultural traditions or demographic phenomena of mixing. To economize space, I translate the term as "Creole" throughout, thus eliminating gender, unless it is relevant to note.

[8] The term *disappeared* will be used throughout this book *without* quotation marks as a noun and a verb, as it is used in human rights social movements and law: "the disappeared" (referring to those who cannot be found) and "to disappear" (in English probably best translated as "to make disappear").

4 INTRODUCTION: OUR AMÉRICA, OUR ANTÍGONA

1982, Mexican Olga Harmony (1928–2018) imagined Cristina, in *La ley de Creón* (Creón's law), as a heroine more inclined to save the still-living rebel peasant and join the peasant women in rebellion than to bury the rebel who hangs from a tree.

Over the course of the twentieth century, whether burial is accomplished or neglected, the Antígonas gradually become collectives of women on stage. Another pattern starts to emerge: their bonding fosters interests other than the age-old violence on the male body. In 1963, Argentine David Cureses (1935–2006) multiplied the heroine by six in his *La cabeza en la jaula* (The head in the cage), in the context of the nineteenth-century Colombian wars of independence. Their purpose is to bury a male martyr, but their plan includes an unheard-of justification: their sacrifice will avenge all the women who the colonizing Spaniards have raped. In 2001, Argentine Jorge Huertas (1949–) wrote *AntígonaS: linaje de hembras* (AntígonaS: female lineage), also multiplying Antígona sixfold. Polinice's lack of burial is just one in a long list of grievances that hovers over gendered violence.

As transnational patterns take shape, the character of Antígona appears as a prism through which to catch a glimpse of similarities in postrevolutionary cultural dynamics throughout Spanish, Portuguese, and French America. By contrast, each contextualized national Antígona at the same time exposes a regional diversity, challenging any imagined uniformity we may want to assign to the spectral entelechy named "Latin America." In their relentless travels, vernacular *Antígona* plays have also followed intra-American migrations and, in the process, revealed yet more national differences—even intranational fractures.

The above examples encapsulate this book's inquiry into the circulation of Antigone's myth and its classical tragic form throughout "Latin" America. Consistent similarities or stark variations throughout the region and across time can only be seen from a particular methodological and theoretical vantage point. I chose to deviate from old colonial protocols, actualized time and again, that compare fragments of Greek culture in ex- or neocolonial territories with ancient or modern European "sources." In this book, the reader finds the construction of a vernacular corpus of American Antígonas with its own internal dynamics. The formation of the corpus follows research findings and the consideration of the colonial singularity of "Latin" America. I aim to contribute to a different understanding of "the classics" and "reception" in Latin "America." With the adjective *vernacular*, I indicate not only the locality of any given text but also a critical gesture that positions any given text with respect and in response to the (neo)colonial reading protocols that systematically abstract the local from the text in order to make it intelligible within a colonial self-referential framework. In colonial protocols, Antígonas in "Latin America" invariably become iterations of European (ancient or modern) tragedies. This book disrupts those protocols.

An Antígona corpus allows us to observe its intra-American dialogues, its historical depth, its mobilization by those Creoles who were left to their own to build new republics, and who were neither external colonizers nor the colonized, as I later explain. The corpus establishes genealogies of "cannibalizations"—to borrow from Brazilian poet Oswald de Andrade's 1928 "Manifesto Antropófago"—and of what I call "ruminations" on fragments of European *Antigones* and on "Latin" American hybrid forms mobilized by political contingencies. Thus, in this book I speak of ancient and modern fragments' circulation, cannibalization, hybridization, and rumination, more often than their reception.

Two decisions made a vernacular corpus possible: a radical historicization of vernacular plays and painstaking archival research. The latter produced an unexpected number of engagements with Antigone's myth, as well as surprising historiographical detail embedded in the texts and performances that illuminates why a fragment of antiquity may or may not have migrated at any given time. Historicization thus means both periodization and close-reading intratextual historiographical imagination. Though I have found extensive fragments of *Antigone* in legal and political discourse, novels, and poems, for reasons of space, this book limits itself to dramatic texts and performances. The research presented in this book yields seventy-nine vernacular plays, listed with the earliest available bibliographic information in the Appendix and plotted onto the regional map below (Figure 0.1).

In "Latin" America, Cuban José Martí's famous 1891 line—"our Greece is preferable to the Greece that is not ours"—could also read "our Antígona is preferable to the Antigone that is not ours."[9] The corpus in this book consists of local plays that dismember fragments of the myth rather than foreign plays adapted to new local contexts.[10] Vernacular writings are not

---

[9] I have slightly modified the English translation; the Spanish reads: "nuestra Grecia es preferible a la Grecia que no es nuestra." See "Our America" (Martí 1891). I use the phrase "vernacular writing," rather than "rewriting," to discourage the imagination of "an original" (always, "of course," European).

[10] My research also uncovered many adaptations of Sophocles' tragedy or its modern European versions. Take, for example, Carlos Maul's 1916 *Antígona* for the open air Theater of

6 INTRODUCTION: OUR AMÉRICA, OUR ANTÍGONA

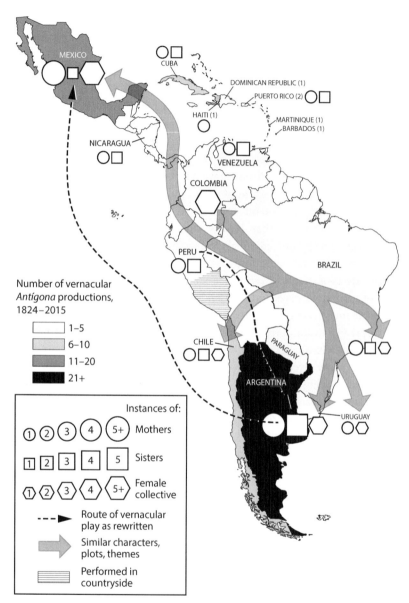

Figure 0.1 Patterns in the corpus, systematized up to 2015, showing number and location of plays featuring Antígona as mother, sister, or a collective character; routes of American vernaculars that have been rewritten; routes of plays that have circulated among peasant communities. This map was designed with the help of Mark Saba, Senior Designer and Illustrator at Yale University's Information Technology Services.

INTRODUCTION: OUR AMÉRICA, OUR ANTÍGONA   7

actualized versions of Sophocles—though this is how critics (trained in classics or not) tend to read them time and again, a problem I have been forced to engage with throughout. Antigone's "death" in 1824 haunts most vernaculars, but my decision as a critic has been to understand how and why a vernacular drama speaks of and to its audience, not of antiquity (or of European drama). In "Latin America," the vernacular *never* requires nor expects the audience's knowledge of antiquity, of tragic drama, or of *Antigone*. The vernacular tells stories about Antígona, an American character.

Of seventy-nine vernacular writings, forty-two have been published (two were written and published outside of the region and four exist in English translation).[11] Among those published, a few were impossible to find, and some have never seen the stage. Among those unpublished, some are available online, while some only exist as manuscripts. As scholars of "Latin" America know, archival research in the region sometimes presents insurmountable challenges. Access to data is costly in time and resources, and research takes longer than expected. One is inevitably bound to confront the dreaded "scenario": entering a basement with materials boxed away due to the lack of public policies in favor of preservation. There are archives I could not reach (El Salvador, Panama, Guatemala, Honduras, Ecuador, Bolivia, Costa Rica, and the French insular territories in the Caribbean). I found some archives "closed indefinitely." I am as certain that my research is not exhaustive as that the circulation of ancient Greek fragments in the region is startlingly understudied. Information in local PhD dissertations will drastically expand the corpus; nonetheless, few of those are readily accessible at the moment. Only a handful of plays in the present corpus have attracted robust criticism outside of their local venues; most have

---

Nature in Rio de Janeiro; Marechal's adaptation of Jean Cocteau's 1922 *Antigone* in 1938 in Buenos Aires; the inauguration of the theater at the University of La Habana in 1941 with Sophocles' *Antigone*, directed by Austrian Ludwig Schajowicz; Teatro La Máscara's version of the classic in 1949 in Buenos Aires; Roberto Salomón's adaptation of Eric Bentley's *Antigone, A Time to Die*, performed by Actoteatro in San Salvador in 1975. The list is long. Had I wanted to include translations or adaptations of the ancient Greek play as a didactic exercise for audiences to learn about ancient Greece or as an aesthetic choice to revive the classic, the number would have been impossible to manage, and the book's purpose would have changed.

[11] Barbadian Kamau Brathwaite's *Odale Choice* (1962) was published in Ghana and Venezuelan León Febres Cordero's *Antígona* (2012) in Spain. The four translated plays are Griselda Gambaro's *Antígona Furiosa* (1986); Luis Rafael Sánchez's *The Passion According to Antígona Pérez* (1968; unpublished translation); Ariel Dorfman's *Widows* (1987); and Sara Uribe's *Antígona González* (2014). I have translated six *Antígona* plays into English (forthcoming).

8   INTRODUCTION: OUR AMÉRICA, OUR ANTÍGONA

received little to no attention.[12] Though this book's Overture proposes the beginning of vernacular writings in 1824, I take Leopoldo Marechal's 1951 *Antígona Vélez* as the moment of Antigone's complete "Americanization" into Antígona. To my knowledge, Marechal was the first writer to give Antígona national attire. The state of the archives does not allow for a real assessment of how many more vernacular writings are underway in the twenty-first century in *relative* terms, but everything indicates that the production of twenty-first-century *Antígona* plays (mostly accessible online) is increasing at a pace that is difficult to follow. For publication purposes I stopped tracking in 2017.

To study Latin "American" *Antígonas* as a continental corpus eschews two well-trodden paths for the criticism of non-European classical traditions. On the one hand, it circumvents nation-state boundaries. On the other hand, it seeks South–South connections that would be implausible if we were to follow the colonial understanding of cultural migrations— always *from and to* Europe. Over two years, Argentina and Haiti produced two vernacular Antígonas. These two nations arguably could not be more distant in terms of history, demographics, economy, and politics. But the South–South comparison connects the two plays not simply because "Antígona" appears in the title (and thus we might at first sight suppose a common mythical inspiration) but also because both intervene in historical moments of heightened debates over those excluded from the nineteenth-century Creole liberal projects in both nations.

The case of Haitian Félix Morisseau-Leroy's *Antigòn* is methodologically paradigmatic: it re-maps routes of affinities and difference. Connections among "Latin" American *Antígonas* help redraw the maps of cultural production that only show the South under North Atlantic eyes. For scholars of "Latin" America (and for many generations of "Latin" Americans, including Morisseau-Leroy's), Haiti has always belonged in "Latin America," not least because of its independence war against France and its involvement in the Hispanic wars of independence. Venezuelan Liberator Simón Bolívar's 1815 exile in Haiti meant a Haitian donation of soldiers for his 1816 invasion of

---

[12] The Hispanophone academy, to my knowledge, has produced two panoramic monographs on versions of *Antigone* (both published in 2008): Spaniards Bañuls Oller and Crespo Alcalá's *Antígona(s): mito y personaje, un recorrido desde los orígenes* and Argentine Rómulo Pianacci's *Antígona: una tragedia latinoameriana* (Ediciones Gestos, e-book). Both books are structured with brief descriptions of plays, first through Europe and then in "Latin" America. In 2004, Spanish classicist José María Camacho Rojo wrote a state of the art list of studies of classical influences in the Spanish- and Portuguese-speaking worlds (Camacho Rojo, 2004).

INTRODUCTION: OUR AMÉRICA, OUR ANTÍGONA 9

Venezuela. In his study of the relations between Haiti and Venezuela, Paul Verna called the quintessential iconic hero of Spanish-American independence none other than *"Bolívar, the Haitian."*[13] Yet in the Anglo-American academy, Haiti's culture is studied in *French* literature departments. The reader will find irony, perhaps, in that it was French reviewers who disapproved of Morisseau-Leroy's 1959 *Antigòn* staging in Paris. On this side of the Atlantic, Cuban Alejo Carpentier lauded the play in the Venezuelan newspaper *El Nacional.*[14] Resonating with the felicitous title of Tina Chanter's (2011) book *Whose Antigone?*, *Antigòn* in Haiti poses the question, "whose Haiti?" (and by extension "whose 'Latin' America?"). For Carpentier, there was no doubt that Haiti and Antigòn were "Latin American."

This book follows Antígona's circulation across a continent inhabited by the mythical worlds of indigenous peoples, colliding with the utopian, rather than tragic, Creole imagination. Here, European notions of burial and theater did not translate easily at the time of conquest. There are regions where corpses are not to be left alone buried underground, but must be eaten by community members.[15] In other places, theater is traditionally ritual and thus does not question but rather celebrated myth. Antígona in "Latin" America must be understood within the context of what the name America implies: on the one hand, the host of European fantasies and misnomers for "a New World" (*novus mundus*) which was inhabited by millions of people organized in a myriad of social systems; on the other, the host of categories—colonial capitalism, Occidentalism, "internal colonialism,"[16] neocolonialism (rather than postcolonialism) and its "coloniality of power"[17]—that help us understand the hybrid cultural forms stemming from heterogeneous, fractured, fractal societies under regimes of colonial and neocolonial necropolitics and what I call necro*liberal* politics.[18]

---

[13] Paul Verna (1966 and 1969) wrote about the forty years of cooperation between Haiti and Venezuela and their effect on Spanish American revolutions in his study of the friendship between the two revolutionary leaders, Venezuelan Simón Bolívar (1783–1830) and Haitian Alexandre Petión (1770–1818).

[14] See Chapter 2.   [15] See Conklin (2001).

[16] Mexican González Casanova's term in (1963); revised in (2003).

[17] A phrase coined by Peruvian critic Aníbal Quijano (2000).

[18] In this book, I use "necroliberal" to refer to the unheard-of levels of capitalist accumulation in the twenty-first century and its effects in the Global South. If neoliberalism cannot but become "a *political* project to re-establish the conditions for capital accumulation and to restore power of economic elites" (Harvey 2005: 19), its application in the Global South has meant structural adjustment policies that in countries with little industry generate massive expulsion—not only exclusion—from the market. See Saskia Sassen's *Expulsions* (2014).

10 INTRODUCTION: OUR AMÉRICA, OUR ANTÍGONA

Categories, that is, forcing us out of binary thinking and its ideologies of purity.

My research has probed the intersections of comparative literature, history, classics, "Latin American" studies, political philosophy, performance history, and feminist theories. Thus, I cannot but echo Barbara Goff and Michael Simpson in their study of African versions of Greek tragedy, as they envision that before such a diverse audience they may "risk [...] satisfying none of them" (2007: 2) but see no other suitable approach to their subject matter. The rubrics below are intended to structure the exposition didactically, although, as I hope will be clear, the questions raised beneath each heading are inextricable from those raised in the other subsections.

The Classics in "Latin" America, Latin "America" in Comparative Literature

In 2005, Colombian Carlos Satizábal's (1959–) *Antígona y actriz* (Antígona and actress), staged two actresses in the role of two peasant women "watchfully" (63) entering the urban theater in Bogotá. Displaced by an armed conflict, the women walk in search of their missing. They sing an old *corrido yucateca*,[19] first in Spanish, then in *Yucateca*, indicating the heterogeneity that colonialism made inescapable: "I am so far away from the land where I was born!" the song starts (63). For the target audience, a *corrido yucateca* identifies them as Mexican peasants of indigenous descent. They sometimes speak their indigenous language to one another; they speak only Spanish to their urban audience. The two worlds they inhabit host a third one that they invoke to address the audience: "Does anyone want to know what will happen to us? Nobody? Well, while your questions start to take shape I will tell you another story, a Greek story" (64). They hear a military voice offstage, asking what they are carrying. They place stones taken out of their trunk on the stage floor: "for our burial [...] that is better than to be confused with someone I am not" (65). The peasants know they will not be heard even if they speak Spanish—the language of coloniality. But they would rather die than be confused with someone they are not—they are not armed, they are

---

[19] *Corrido* is a popular Mexican musical genre composed of a narrative song about popular struggles. During the 1910 Mexican revolution, it was used to transmit information. It originates in the mixture of oral indigenous traditions and European musical rhythms. *Yucateca* means "from the Yucatán peninsula" and is a Mayan language.

INTRODUCTION: OUR AMÉRICA, OUR ANTÍGONA 11

not Spanish. Will telling the pain of *that other* woman—the ancient Antigone, a foreign woman, just as foreign as the audience's Spanish ancestors—help the audience sympathize with them? They try. Into Antigone's story they insert their own. One of them, embodying Antigone, says, "it is my story"; the two of them in unison say, "it is our story" (65). It is—and is not—Antigone's story, just as Spanish is and is not their language, just as Antigone is and is not a universal bridge between heterogeneous audiences. Most importantly, neither for Satizábal nor for the peasant characters, Antigone's is an ancient tragic drama: it is a "story." In Spanish, the actresses use the word *historia*, which means both "history" and "story." The phrase "it is my story" is voiced individually when it refers to Antigone but by both of them when it refers to their story. They are of indigenous descent, they are Mexican and Colombian, they are fictional and historical. What fragment of Antigone's history—story is theirs? Is there any? There is a corpse, for sure. Though it is missing, and it is multiple—just as they are multiple too.

Satizábal brings cultural, historical, and linguistic heterogeneity to the lettered urban audience that most likely only speaks Spanish (or any other colonial language). Insofar as these peasant characters sing a *corrido*, their story and history includes the memory of sharing with Creoles the struggle against the Spaniards—and its consequences: Creoles betrayed indigenous peoples after independence. Satizábal's fictional peasant women prefer to die rather than to be understood in (neo)colonial terms, and thus they try translation work before the lettered urban audience. Picture the layered complexity of translation work to be done by the "Latin" American writer or scholar to take that peasant story/history to the stage of Anglophone comparative literature and classics scholarship, most likely limited by North Atlantic grids of interpretation—and their different colonial histories, in their different colonial languages.

While the two fictional peasants translate on Satizábal's Spanish stage, scholars of "Latin America," writing *from* "Latin America," translate for the stage of Anglophone comparative literature and classics "watchfully": there, Latin "America" is notably absent.[20] The difficulty of listening/reading/seeing

---

[20] Though this question exceeds the scope of this book, a search for comparative literature dissertations in the North American database *ProQuest* from 1933 to 2017 gives us a glimpse: in eighty-four years, only 11.24 percent of masters and doctoral dissertations combined engage some aspect of "Latin America." See McClennen and Fitz (2004) for statistics on "Latin" America's absence; McClennen (2004) notes that in a five-year sample period (1995–2000), the Comparative Literature Issue of the journal *Modern Language Notes* yielded only one article

12 INTRODUCTION: OUR AMÉRICA, OUR ANTÍGONA

the so-called Global South, as we know, extends across almost all types of knowledge circulation, insofar as the globalized flow of information still reproduces the colonial international divisions of intellectual labor, whereby the Global North is assigned the production of "knowledge" (science, technology, theory) and the Global South the production of "examples" (raw data, raw materials) to confirm Northern theories—both in academic and nonacademic arenas.[21] This globalized economy of knowledge does not mean that the political North and South are geographic categories: *from* "Latin America" is a political concept. North and South are political and epistemic positionalities; thus for Satizábal's fictional peasants, Bogotá's lettered middle class is the North. As much as for lettered critics in Bogotá, in comparative literature the two Colombian/Mexican indigenous peasants will most likely be two Greek Antigones.

Embedded as I am in comparative literature and its conversation with classics as established in the post-World War II Anglo-American university, my introduction of an *Antígona* corpus bears epistemic and political challenges related to Satizábal's presentation of *that other* story before the urban middle-class theater audiences in Bogotá. For the majority of critics engaged in this book, Antígona could not be other than Antigone (or an adaptation). How can Antígona speak of America, of the Colombian peasants, to her academic audience in comparative literature and classics?

In his exhaustive *Antigones: How the Antigone Legend Has Endured in Western Literature, Art, and Thought* (1984), George Steiner notices departures from the ancient plot only south of Europe, in one Turkish and one South African play.[22] Steiner follows *Antigone* in Western culture, equating the West with Western Europe, that is, without America. One of the difficulties in introducing "Latin" American Antígonas lies in what Steiner

---

about a "Latin American" author. In the following period 2000–17, I have found only four articles. From 1949 to 2017, with four issues per year, each with an average of five articles, the flagship journal of the profession, *Comparative Literature* has published approximately 1,360 articles: only fifty-seven (that is 4.1 percent) are related to the region (with sixteen on Borges) and only one issue on the Americas (eleven articles [vol. 61, no. 3, 2009], mostly pointing at invisibility). See Pollack (2009) for the "extremely low number of translated "Latin" American works in the United States," reinforcing fantasies, as she puts it, of "alterity" and readers' appetites only for "magical realism" (347). The pattern is similar in other journals, with one exception: *Comparative Literature and Culture*, which publishes five issues per year, with twenty-six essays from 2004–17, including unlikely countries such as Paraguay, only one essay on Borges, and even a category specifying "US-American" rather than "American."

[21] In this book I only use "Third World" to refer to the political project of NAM (Non-Aligned Movement) that emerged in 1955.

[22] *The Island* by South Africans Athol Fugard, John Kani, and Winston Ntshona, and *Antigone* by Turkish Kemal Demirel, both produced in 1973.

INTRODUCTION: OUR AMÉRICA, OUR ANTÍGONA   13

observed about non-European plays: they depart from the ancient tragic form. The latter becomes unrecognizable. The other difficulty lies in America's position in relation to Europe: though constitutive of the latter, America is neither European nor non-European, and thus presents a challenge for non-dialectical thinking.

With the growth of "world literature" as a subfield in comparative literature, there has been a geopolitical expansion in intradisciplinary dialogues, though new obstacles have emerged.[23] With a global circulation model framed by the center/periphery binary, the new subfield quickly placed old colonial metropolises back at the center. Pascale Casanova (2004) proposed that to enter the global market, "peripheral" texts must pass through the legitimation of European metropolises (Paris, in "Latin" America's case). As interesting as it is, in that the model takes capital value as decisive for text circulation, it also reveals that local marks of production, local markets, and local genres need to be cleansed if they are to acquire "center" legitimation. Satizábal's Colombian peasants still need to speak of Antigone's one and only dead, rather than their own countless dead. How could Antigone be imagined counting the uncountable?

The larger question in this model is *periphery for whom?* Since prevailing models for world literature are based on "recognition" in/by the world market, the neocolonial abyss is unavoidable: the North Atlantic (the geopolitical subject) recognizes and legitimizes Southern "objects" (geopolitical raw materials). The agents of recognition can never be the Colombian or Mexican rural peasants. When Morisseau-Leroy took his Haitian Antigòn outside of the "center" of Port-au-Prince in 1953, the agents of recognition he sought were in Haiti's peasant villages. Irrelevant for the periphery–center world literature market model, for Morisseau-Leroy, to be recognized

---

[23] I use the term "geopolitical" in its disciplinary sense to make an analogy between the study of foreign politics among states and the study of world literature as the cultural politics governing the circulation of national literatures. Examples of "Latin" America's slow entrance to this field abound. The Modern Language Association series "Approaches to Teaching World Literature" has issued 161 volumes: only four are dedicated to "Latin America" (Bartolomé de las Casas, Manuel Puig, Sor Juana Inés de la Cruz, and Gabriel García Márquez). David Damrosch's *The Longman Anthology of World Literature* (2nd ed., 2004) scarcely includes Latin "American" authors in the entries that qualify as standalone writers: in Volume E on the nineteenth century, two writers (out of thirty-seven) and in Volume F on the twentieth century, two (invariably Borges and, from the Caribbean, Césaire). Damrosch (2014) has also argued for the need for a paradigm shift to see the "presence of the world within the nation." For example, he chooses to read a short story by Cortázar *not* in relation to Europe but to its locality, though the latter only means Cortázar's relation to Borges (the canon of Comparative Literature). For a different perspective, see Müller and Gras Miravet (2015) and Sánchez Prado (2006).

14 INTRODUCTION: OUR AMÉRICA, OUR ANTÍGONA

meant to travel in reverse, transforming a "center" language (French) into a "peripheral" language, and a "peripheral" language (Haitian Creole), into the real center. In the "center-recognition" frame, as Francesca Orsini puts it, "nine-tenths of the world drop off the world map or appear 'peripheral'" (2015: 346).[24]

The monstrous extent of "nine-tenths" must be alarming for any rigorous academic endeavor. At stake are strategies of readings, agents who read, and the erasure of innumerable parallel worlds where literature "happens." Put otherwise, countless other "centers"—or a multi-centered world—that make the "periphery" an always-shifting relation. Publishers operating as Hispanic centers of translation and circulation (Ciudad de México, Buenos Aires, Madrid, Barcelona, La Habana) establish alternative but unnoticed routes by making some texts circulate faster in the South than in the North, for example.[25] Genres follow different patterns of circulation too: focusing on the specific case of Spanish-American poetry, Efraín Kristal (2002) challenged Franco Moretti's concept of world literature by observing that poetry was more important than the novel in Spanish America. This means that the comparison of peripheral to central novels, in a binary model, may produce knowledge about "the center" but not about the "periphery." This book tries to eschew that. It focuses on knowledge production from/within "Latin America"—always considering the latter as a political and epistemic positionality. It traces Antígona's circulation, to put it in Kristal's words, "from the center to the periphery, from the periphery to the center, from one periphery to another, while some original forms of consequence [don't move] much at all" (74).[26]

To be sure, modern and ancient dramatic texts and their performance also challenge the field of world literature from other angles. On the one hand, just as Kristal argues for the centrality of poetry in "Latin" America, Nigerian Ola Rotimi asserts the centrality of drama for African cultural

---

[24] For the idea of "literatures of the world" replacing "world literature," see also Shankar (2012).

[25] The same happens with the circulation of books throughout the so-called "Second World" (with the former USSR at its center). The newly created *Journal of World Literature* (edited by David Damrosch since 2017) has issued a number dedicated to "Latin America" (2017: 11–26) in which Nora Catelli alerts us to yet another problem: the lack of consideration of how *theory* circulates from France to "Latin" America and vice versa.

[26] See new models around "untranslatability of texts" as a critique to the Anglophone field of world literature in Apter 2013. For a Latinamericanist critique, see Ignacio Sánchez Prado's collection (2006), in which a mood prevails: Latin "America" again forced to engage with the internal contradictions of theories and methodologies created in the North for the North. See also Beverley, Oviedo, and Aronna (1993).

INTRODUCTION: OUR AMÉRICA, OUR ANTÍGONA 15

production: it cannot be compared to that of the novel.[27] This happens in "Latin" American countries with large rural populations—Haiti in the 1950s is a case in point. But on the other hand, theater has no master text that can be fixed. In 2000, a Peruvian *Antígona* written by José Watanabe and the theater collective Yuyachkani was staged in Lima, where Ismene performed a belated funeral for her brother. Audiences identified with Ismene. The play traveled the world—another world, different than the mandatory Parisian route: first from lettered Lima to Quechua-speaking peasant villages in the Peruvian Andes. Audiences identified with Antígona. Then to lettered Buenos Aires in 2006. No funeral rite was performed in Buenos Aires: the focus was punishment. In this world itinerary, which is the center and which the periphery? The localized collective memory and the cultural regimes of the visible determine meaning for different audiences: how can casting, costumes, set design, linguistic registers, become part of world literature?

In turn, classicists argue that ancient texts enter world literature only stripped of their conditions of production. Simon Goldhill pointedly reminds us that "literature" is not a category that can be applied to antiquity.[28] Edith Hall has argued that *Antigone* has undergone a process of "abstraction" of its ancient material conditions of production in order to become part of "modern" world literature.[29] To return to Satizábal's Colombian Antígonas, "Latin" American texts making their way into comparative literature and classical studies may avoid the label of "exotic, non-Western difference" (assigned as an effect of colonial ignorance, at best) if deracinated and assembled to a recognizable European text or literary genre/movement (peasants acting as Antígona, that is, as Antigone). If this is what happens with the Latin "American" text, imagine the effort needed to make visible cultural production in indigenous languages.

This book seeks to generate conditions of possibility for the "Latin" American cultural production engaging *Antigone*'s fragments to enter comparative literature and classics otherwise, that is, without being abstracted from or locked into locality. This has informed the methodological and theoretical decision to closely embed texts and performances in their historical conditions of production. Deracination reproduces a regime of ignorance about the cultures that send their texts into the "world," ignorance grants them the unreadability of "exoticism"—as if the surprise at the alleged

---

[27] Interview with O. Rotimi in Burness (1985: 11–18). [28] Goldhill (2004: 175–97).
[29] Hall (2005: 316–50).

16   INTRODUCTION: OUR AMÉRICA, OUR ANTÍGONA

marvels Columbus encountered in 1492 were still the "structure of feelings" with which "Latin American" cultures are granted access to European fields of knowledge.[30] The exotic is just a spectacle or adornment to be enjoyed—or a threat to be eliminated.

To a certain extent, "Latin" America's relative absence, or deracination, in Anglophone comparative literature, world literature, and classics, is puzzling. "Latin" American texts are written in the colonial European languages studied in those fields,[31] but they are either seen as "non-European" or transformed into "universals." One must ponder historical and, most importantly, ideological reasons for the difficulty in reading America in its difference and as part of the West. The notion of Europe as a separate entity that developed on its own (whereby large parts of America surprisingly fall into the radically Other "non-West") is the result of a symptomatic erasure of the event of 1492 as *constitutive* of European modern identity. The first European modernity depends on the Spanish and Portuguese dismantling of American indigenous empires. There is no modern Europe without America. The Eurocentric teleological narrative of European modernity as a process internal to Europe (going from the past—the appropriation of ancient Greece as Europe's origins—to the future, the French Revolution) can only be conceived if the economic world system inaugurated in 1492 (mercantilism later becoming capitalism), which displaced Spain (and then Europe at large) from the periphery, is obliterated. With 1492, the notion of a world history—not just the coexistence of disaggregated empires and cultural systems—became reality.[32] "Eurocentrism" imagines that modern European identity depends on Greco-Roman antiquity more than on the trans-Atlantic economies and cultures stemming from Europe's conquests.[33] The idea of a stark opposition between Europe and "Latin" America is better understood as an effect of Europe's internal fracture: America is constitutive of Europe in ways that Europe has "translated" into an association with ancient Greece—an interesting displacement with consequences. The very naming of the region, the Caribbean as the "West" Indies, Mexico as the

---

[30] I refer to Raymond Williams' concept developed in his *Marxism and Literature* (1977).

[31] Due to lack of expertise in indigenous languages, I engage with texts in Spanish, Portuguese, French, and Haitian Creole. As more indigenous languages are taught, we will know whether there are indigenous Antígonas.

[32] There is a vast academic production on this subject from a "Latin American" perspective, some of it in dialogue with Wallerstein's "world-systems" theory. See Moraña, Dussel, and Jáuregui (2008), Rodríguez (2001), Quijano (2000), Klor de Alva (1995), Castro-Gómez and Mendieta (1998), Beverley (1993), and A. and F. de Toro (1999). See also the classic Braudel (1992).

[33] See O'Gorman ([1958] 1961), Amin (1988), and Dussel (1995).

INTRODUCTION: OUR AMÉRICA, OUR ANTÍGONA   17

"New Spain," Colombia as "the New Granada," established enough gray areas that America never was just Europe's "Other."

How should we make legible "Latin" America, neither Europe nor its Other? The story of the Colombian/Mexican fictional peasants, in all its colonial heterogeneity, will be lost twice as it enters world literature: first, lost in the vision of the lettered Creole critic who will use an imperial language rather than any Creole mix that can include Yucateca; then doubly lost in the interpretative Anglophone traditions of comparative literature, world literature, classics, and even Spanish classics, which tend to deracinate the Creole text and identify in it only that which is considered European: the Greek Antigone found in the Colombian Antígona.

This book is framed—*haunted*—by the question "what is to be done" for Latin "American" texts to be read within classics and comparative literature's deracinating regimes of legibility.[34] Consider the two most studied "Latin" American lettered Creoles of all countries in the "Latin" region: Argentine Jorge Luis Borges and Colombian Gabriel García Márquez. Beatriz Sarlo noted how Borges, whom she called the "writer on the edge" (1993: 1), is detached from his Argentine traditions when read in the North. Sarlo's question is sharp: why was Balzac not forced to lose his French tradition to enter world literature, while Borges could not remain Argentine but had to become "universal"? García Márquez, taken as an allegory for that remote, "magical realist continent" called "Latin America," spanning from Tijuana to Tierra del Fuego, is seldom read as a chronicler of Colombian history. Roberto Schwarz (2007) noted how Brazilian Machado de Assis entered "world literature" devoid of his Brazil. How can the "Latin" American text cease being absorbed as a reflection of Europe? Can the epistemic regime of the discipline not just read itself in a "Latin American" author, but also read what they write about? Consider now Antígona: in many cases, Antígona is not the character speaking the law of burial. But without exception, the critics I engage in this book read on her lips burial laws, fearing otherwise that Antigone may disappear in Antígona.

The work we must do for the "Latin American" text is to re-embed it in its context of production. I do not see this critical task as severing the text's ties to world literature or as reinforcing the notion of "area studies": what this "region" means cannot be taken for granted and is always a political position. Rather, this book is an invitation to shift and multiply the location

---

[34] The famous question "What is to be done" refers to the title of the pamphlet Lenin wrote in 1901 about how best to develop political consciousness for change. The title was taken from the 1863 novel of the same name by Nikolai Chernyshevsky.

18 INTRODUCTION: OUR AMÉRICA, OUR ANTÍGONA

of the center, walking away, that is, from the European colonial center. If one still wanted to think (in binary terms) of a periphery, in this book, it is the colonial protocol that can still be found in the epistemic gaze of the political North. This relocation and multiplication of the center can open up the historical worlds integral to this book's "Latin" American corpus, though out of reach to Anglophone scholars who may read it only once uprooted. If Balzac circulates as "French," we must try the effect of Borges' circulation as "Argentine." Antígona's case is a prism through which to perceive the problem of the Creole text: this book does not make Antígona speak of Europe, Greece, or any mystery in the solitude of "magical realism." The Antígonas in this book's corpus "speak of what they always speak: of America," to paraphrase Martí in this Introduction's epigraph.

Mine is an epistemic gaze positioned in the political South. To dispel another mechanical association with the political South, this does not readily mean "postcolonial." The latter concept comes from a specific imperial legacy and intellectual genealogy that usually erase the "Latin" American one. Through *Antígona* plays, my hope is to entice the comparatist and the classicist to enter not only into the world of the corpus but also into the historical and cultural specificity of "Latin America" embedded in texts or performances. In each *Antígona*, the reader will find an open window to aspects of Latin "American" culture and history. I have worked *from* text and performance *to* rigorous scrutiny of the historical context embedded in the text.

It is the tenet of historical materialist theories about culture to take any text's breeding ground as central to its making. For this tradition, the illusion of a separation between art and context is nothing more than that: an illusion. As James Porter sharply puts it, in both antiquity and modernity, "claims in favor of aesthetic autonomy are logically and pragmatically incoherent" (2010b: 168). Put otherwise, they can only be understood as products of their times. A materialist interpretative tradition has a particular history in "Latin" America. This ex-colonial world of letters constituted itself in the nineteenth century as part of the political sphere of the newly independent nations. Structural economic conditions—such as the lack of full-scale industrialization and of an internal market economy—weakened the formation of middle classes in most countries of the region. This meant little room for liberal ideologies about the possibility of an autonomous sphere of art. The nineteenth-century constitution of the artistic sphere as inextricable from political power proved stronger than the timid attempts at claiming a relative autonomy among intellectuals and artists around the 1900s. The illusion that a private/autonomous artistic sphere, untouched by

INTRODUCTION: OUR AMÉRICA, OUR ANTÍGONA 19

politics, could exist never took hold. Reading "politically" is not idiosyncratic but necessary: it responds both to a predominant "Latin American" interpretative tradition and to the historical formation of its political/artistic spheres. This is why artistic production in the region is an archive for political theory. In it we can find theorizations that in the political North are mostly associated with academic production. This book asks why Antigone would be useful to local audiences, what historiography and political theory Antígona offers, and in what ways revealing Antígona's locality could help us rethink terms such as "reception of a classic" or "classics in (neo)colonial contexts."

Postcolonial Classical Reception Studies and "Latin" America

Writing *from* "Latin" America (in contrast to writing about it) also structures this book's engagement with the growing field of "postcolonial classical reception" studies. In the Anglophone academy, as Charles Martindale put it in the commemoration of the twentieth anniversary of his influential *Redeeming the Text: Latin Poetry and the Hermeneutics of Reception* (1993), "by now the battle for taking reception seriously within Classics has long been won" (169).[35] For the Latin Americanist reader, it is useful to clarify that the study of reception stands in contrast to the study of a classical tradition: to recall Martindale's words, "no final nor correct interpretation for any text; the original is lost through successive historically and culturally bounded 'chains' of receptions" (1993: 7).[36] In *A Companion to Classical Receptions*, Lorna Hardwick and Christopher Stray stress the "democratic turn" in reception studies: receptions must be studied in plural. According to the authors, "interactions with a succession of contexts [...] combine to produce a map that is sometimes unexpectedly bumpy with its highs and lows, emergences and suppressions and, sometimes, metamorphoses" (2008: 1).[37] The volume questions the superiority of ancient texts and advocates for new research into topics such as the classics and popular culture. Hardwick's editorial in the first issue of the *Classical Receptions Journal*

---

[35] Martindale (2013). Reception studies have been inspired by German scholars Iser ([1976] 1994) and Jauss (1982).

[36] See also Martindale (2006: 1–13).

[37] For "Latin" American scholars to get acquainted with the democratic turn, see Hardwick and Stray's introduction (2008: 1–11), Fiona Macintosh's (2008) "Performance Histories" (247–59), and Edith Hall's (2008) "Putting the Class into Classical Reception" (386–99).

20 INTRODUCTION: OUR AMÉRICA, OUR ANTÍGONA

(2009: 1–3) invites contributions on, for example, Arabic, Hindu, Indian, and Persian classical traditions.

Another battle has now been won within classical receptions: studies in the so-called "postcolonial" territories have dramatically expanded the field, though until recently they have remained limited to the ex-British colonies. In his entry in *The Companion to the Classical Tradition* (2007), Andrew Laird sharply articulated the absence of "Latin" America in Anglophone scholarship: "As the present chapter is the first-ever guide to the classical tradition in English to give any consideration at all to Latin America, the basic emphasis here on cultural productions *from* the countries in the region should need no justification" (228; italics in the original). A decade later, Laird coedited with Nicola Miller *Antiquities and Classical Traditions in Latin America* (2018), using "traditions" instead of "receptions" in the title and still noting that Latin America "continue[s] to be overlooked" (9).[38]

In the Anglophone academy, *Antigone* has mostly been studied in African or Middle Eastern rewritings, although, as editors Erin Mee and Helene Foley put it in their introduction to *Antigone on the Contemporary World Stage*, "*Antigone* is perhaps the only play, classical or modern, to have been (re) produced all over the world" (2011: 1). The 2015 *Oxford Handbook of Greek Drama in the Americas* (edited by Kathryn Bosher, Fiona Macintosh, Justine McConnell, and Patrice Rankine) is the first collection dedicated to America. The title uses the Anglophone construction "the Americas" to refer to the continent and the name "America" to refer mostly to the United States. Of the volume's fifty chapters, only thirteen are about Central or South America. Part VI is entitled "In search for the Omni-Americans," but only three out of thirteen chapters deal with "Latin America." Though those who write about Afro-descendant theater in the United States still refer to the USA as "Afro-American," a few authors in this section use "U.S.A." for the country or the qualifier "U.S." for a given noun. Mary Kay Gamel's felicitous title is the only one to specify both the country and the region: "Greek Drama on the U.S. West Coast: 1970–2013." Pre-Columbian antiquities—the Incan, the Mayan, and the Aztec for example—have not figured in the *Journal of Classical Receptions* as yet (2018), though modern "Latin"

---

[38] The first conference about "*Antigone* in the Hispanic world" took place at Kent University (UK) in 2008. The first panel on "Latin American classical receptions" at the American Philological Association's annual conference took place in 2010, the second in 2012 (both organized by classicist Konstantinos P. Nikoloutsos, who also edited the first journal issue about the topic [2012]).

INTRODUCTION: OUR AMÉRICA, OUR ANTÍGONA   21

America has begun to appear, with six essays published between 2015 and 2018.

Postcolonial studies coalesced in the 1990s based on the dynamics of the British Empire.[39] Anglophone postcolonial reception studies emerged with Bill Ashcroft, Gareth Griffiths, and Helen Tiffin's *The Empire Writes Back: Theory and Practice in Post-Colonial Literatures* (1989) and its model for postcolonial reception recovering the metropolis as a site of interlocution. Focused on British imperialism and English-language texts, while considering the Anglophone Caribbean and the Anglophone Americas as crucial examples, the authors read postcolonial "rewritings" of the canonical literature imparted by British education as a response to and against British colonial education.[40] In 1996, Helen Gilbert and Joanne Tompkins titled their introduction to the volume *Post Colonial Drama* accordingly: "Re-Acting (To) Empire." The classics *in English* entered into a dialectics of colonial domination and "postcolonial" resistance. An air of imperial nostalgia for being the cynosure of the ex-colony permeates this initial model (not to mention the fact that, in terms of education, in the case of the Anglophone Caribbean, it refers to British education in the metropolis rather than the islands, which were deprived of universities until the mid-twentieth century).[41]

More than twenty years on, scholars like Hardwick, Stray, Greenwood, Hall, and Goff, among others, have adjusted this initial model. Greenwood's useful expression "omni-local" emphasizes that "any given reception is

---

[39] "Latin" America is absent from the foundational Anglophone postcolonial volumes. Edward Said's *Culture and Imperialism* (1993) is based on British and French imperialism (see Hulme 1989: 3–8). Consider "Latin America's" absence in the first anthology of postcolonial texts, *Colonial Discourse and Postcolonial Theory* (Williams and Chrisman 1993) or in *The Post-colonial Studies Reader* (Ashcroft, Griffiths, and Tiffin 1995), which includes a massive eighty-six chapters, out of which only three have some relation to "Latin America": Fanon (Martinique) and Alexis (Haiti) and Rabasa with a chapter on Mercator's map. Fernando Coronil points out that in *Relocating Postcolonialism*, Jean Comaroff, in conversation with Homi Bhabha, establishes "the frame for *postcoloniality* in two periods: the decolonization of the Third World marked by India's independence in 1947 and the hegemony of neoliberal capitalism signaled by the end of the Cold War in 1989" (Goldberg and Quayson 2002: 15). Coronil wrote two articles specifically criticizing the way in which Ashcroft and particularly Robert Young (in his *Postcolonialism: An Historical Introduction* [2001]) decided to include "Latin America" (see Coronil's 2004 "Latin American Postcolonial Studies and Global Decolonization" and 1992 "Can Postcoloniality Be Decolonized? Imperial Banality and Postcolonial Power"). See Hulme (1995).

[40] In the bibliography, there is no text about "Latin" America or written by a "Latin" American author.

[41] The only pre-emancipation school was founded in Barbardos in 1743 (the Codrington Grammar School); elementary and secondary schools were founded in the nineteenth century; universities after World War II. See Braithwaite (1958).

22 INTRODUCTION: OUR AMÉRICA, OUR ANTÍGONA

'local' in relation to every other reception, while together they form part of a larger whole through their connection with a single text or work of art (another dimension of Hardwick's idea of 'classical connectivity')."[42] Nonetheless, it seems hard to break the habit of "comparing and contrasting" postcolonial "rewritings" (in contrast to writings) with the ancient European sources as they were taught in colonial education. So is the imperialist notion that the British Empire can stand in for all colonial enterprises. In the 2013 guide to postcolonial receptions on the webpage of the *Internet Archive of Performances of Greek and Roman Drama*, we read: "the literature of ancient Greece and Rome was an important part of the colonial education system. So, when writers in the twentieth century came to protest their subjugation and work toward independence, Classics was both a tool in their armory and one of the very elements from which they wished to break free. This led to fascinating reappraisals of classical texts from such places as the Caribbean, Africa, India, Australasia, and Latin America."[43] None of the above statements apply to "Latin America." Here, classics are a tool against Empire and Empire is British.[44]

In their 2015 contribution to the *Oxford Handbook of Greek Drama in the Americas*, Goff and Simpson engage the complexity of "postcolonialism" and imperial differences. They cite Greenwood's resistance to universalism as well as Laird's work on "New Spain," which shows how indigenous intellectuals in the early colony struggled with Spanish priests for (rather than against) the command of Latin.[45] However, while admittedly focusing on Anglo-America, the authors defend the analytic purchase of the category of "postcolonialism" for the continent (and disparate subalternities): when "subaltern populations of the Americas (women, the working class, but especially those of non-European descent) get a hold of Greek drama it becomes more relevant to invoke a postcolonial analysis" (34).[46] Among Spanish

---

[42] Greenwood (2013: 354–61).

[43] See http://www.apgrd.ox.ac.uk/learning/short-guides/postcolonialism-and-classics.

[44] This model raises questions even in the British context. See, for example, Hardwick's interview with Nigerian Fémi Òsófisan, for whom postcolonial theories are based on "the assumption that the focal point of cultural resistance is still defined by its relationship to the (European) colonial centers of power" (2007: 308).
See also Barbara Goff's study of Òsófisan's play (Goff 2007).

[45] See Laird (2003) Greenwood stresses the "frail connections" among representations of ancient Greece used by Caribbean writers (2010: 1).

[46] Goff and Simpson's chapter (2015, 30–50) shows a tension between questioning and accepting the paradigm of postcoloniality, perhaps symptomatic of the problems that emerge when non-British legacies are at stake. In trying to keep the paradigm, the authors risk blanket categories that lump together, for instance, "women and people of non-European descent" or

INTRODUCTION: OUR AMÉRICA, OUR ANTÍGONA   23

Peninsular classicists, reading "Latin American" vernacular writings as a subversion of the Empire's colonial canon proves somewhat tempting.[47]

It is not only a question of the model's inaccuracy for the case of "Latin" America. The model of a contestation against a colonial canon also produces the ideological effect that Greek antiquity is and always will be "owned" by imperial Europe. Thus (certain) Europeans have a "correct" (or corrective) interpretation of antiquity, what I call a "gold standard," that is, the creation of an "Ur-Antigone" in the case of this book's corpus, regardless of the fact that Sophocles himself was "cannibalizing" ancient myths for the tragic contests of fifth-century democracy.

From gold standards follow "gold standards of interpretation," influenced mostly by the Hegelian legacy.[48] For many critics that I engage in this book, "Latin American" Antígonas must fit the reified abstraction of Antigone's womanhood spanning from ancient Greece to modern Europe: an individual, born "to love," prepolitical, and caring for the biological brother. However, Latin "American" Antígonas in this book never represent a private sphere. And while critics also abstract Creon into the eternal figure standing for the "state"—although there was no such institution that monopolized violence in ancient Athens—in "Latin" America, Creon almost always represents the site of visibility of the state's monopoly of violence.

For those writing from Latin "America," using homegrown reading strategies to account for Antígona in "our" America becomes imperative. To clarify the latter, I offer a brief (and unavoidably didactic) look at the "Latin American" colonial difference that produced them.

Brief Annotations on Coloniality the "Latin" Way

Developing the full set of misencounters between Anglophone and Spanish-/Portuguese-speaking American ideas about the "postcolonial"

---

use the term "postcolonial society" with shifting valences, meaning anything from settler colonizers, to the exercise of direct rule over others, to societies that emancipate from colonial powers.

[47] See the case of Spanish classicist Lucrecio Pérez Blanco's consideration of some plays as "respectful" or "a distortion" of the Sophoclean one (1984: 143–72, chapters 1 and 4). Scholars who write about "Latin" America in the USA also face the temptation to consider the model of a contestation to colonial education. Examples are mentioned throughout this book. See also Perez Blanco (1985).

[48] See Chanter (2011) for the most enlightening discussion on the imposition of European readings on African *Antigone*s, which obscures a reading of representations of slavery.

24 INTRODUCTION: OUR AMÉRICA, OUR ANTÍGONA

exceeds the scope of this book, though it should be clear that any all-encompassing category will result in eliding "Latin American" difference all over again, given the current neo-imperial geopolitics of knowledge circulation and distribution. As Venezuelan Fernando Coronil (2000) put it, the paradigm of postcolonialism cannot account for current imperialism. The discourse of postcolonialism actually risks partaking of epistemic imperialism in not dismantling neocolonial protocols. In Laird's words, a classical tradition "can stand only awkwardly on American soil, simply because European imperialism and elitism first put it there" (2007: 227), but the word "awkwardly" also applies to the global use of the term postcolonial and its British genealogy.[49]

Just as the Anglophone postcolonial paradigm excludes Latin "America," "Latin" American scholars have been reluctant to include the master narrative of postcolonialism. More central to the debate over the region's dependence on contemporary forms of imperial global powers are Coronil's conceptualization of "Occidentalism" and the necessity for alternatives, some of which had emerged in the nineteenth century but shifted from a language of emancipation to a language of liberation with the post WWII social movements generating theories of economic dependency, liberation pedagogy, liberation theology, cinema, theater, and philosophy.[50]

Unlike Eurocentrism, Occidentalism describes the production of Western narratives of naturalized hierarchical dualisms that interpret the West in relation to the inferior "Other" in need of elimination or incorporation, or alternatively used only as a lens through which the West can understand *itself*. The Spanish Christian missions were the first to create elites in urban centers holding an "occidental" view: indigenous societies were "barbaric" and needed to be absorbed into Christianity or eliminated. For the

---

[49] Albrecht's *Post-colonialism Cross-Examined* goes beyond Anglophone postcolonialism, looking at the post-Soviet world and Afrasia. Quoting anthropologist Philip Carl Salzman, Albrecht warns that "in the postcolonial 'master narrative' [...] most of world history disappears' (Albrecht 2020: 2)." Though there is only one article connected to "Latin" America, its frame is refreshing: Gregory Jusdanis proposes to stray from the North/South axis (Europe and its "victims") to compare the siege of Constantinople in 1453 with the destruction of Cuzco in 1533, thus introducing Greece as a different type of colony than the ones studied through Eurocentric accounts of empire (Albrecht 2020: 197–216). See also Albrecht (2013).

[50] See Coronil's famous essay "Beyond Occidentalism. Toward Nonimperial Geohistorical Categories" (1996) and his engagement with "Orientalism"; for an introduction to dependency theory, see Cardoso and Faletto (1979); to liberation theology, see Gutiérrez ([1971] 1988); to pedagogy of the oppressed, see Freire ([1968] 2000); to theater of the oppressed, Boal ([1979] 1983).

INTRODUCTION: OUR AMÉRICA, OUR ANTÍGONA 25

most part, Spanish and Portuguese Americans who led the anti-imperial nineteenth-century independence wars did not discard Occidental dualism. Rather, they rephrased it, pitting "civilization" against "barbarism" to legitimize themselves as leaders of new nations. Occidentalism makes colonial regimes and independence struggles extremely complex: conquest, mixing, and education politics blur the colonizer's culture as purely "exterior," in a process whose historical depth is no less than five hundred years. The foundation of the new republics after the fall of Empire did not mean the acknowledgment of indigenous societies: just as they were for colonial agents, indigenous peoples remained "barbarians" for independent Creoles to understand themselves.

Historical depth, especially in what concerns demographic and cultural mixing, is a key factor here, in contrast to the British imperial regimes. The formation of urban lettered elites started as early as the sixteenth century. In the nineteenth century, these occidentalist elites transformed independence from Europe into a double-edged phenomenon. Brazilian historian Fernando Novais put it concisely: "the extremely complex phenomenon of independence lies in that it had to negate colonization, and at the same time, re-instate it [...] in order to claim property of the territory. [...] Those who led independence could neither culturally identify with colonizers, because they were breaking away from them, nor with the colonized, because they wanted to continue colonizing" (2008: 16). Creoles fall into a strange category, a middle layer that, according to Novais, did not exist in the African British colonies, where the struggle was between colonizer and colonized—hence the relative clarity of their cultural differences. Taking Brazil as an example, Novais describes Creoles as "neither colonizers nor colonized, because the colonizer is Portuguese and the colonized are Indians or black [enslaved peoples]."[51] Peruvian Aníbal Quijano coined the phrase "coloniality of power" (rather than its postcoloniality) to account for practices and discourses of Creole elites in the region (2000).

Because of the three-hundred-year-long slow and gradual formation of colonial Creole culture, the "Latin" American nineteenth-century wars of independence differed greatly from mid-twentieth-century anticolonialisms in Africa or India.[52] Revolts among indigenous peoples and enslaved Africans had been continual throughout the period of the colony, though

---

[51] See also Novais (1979).
[52] Coronil (2004: 8) adds that African independence should be seen similarly only if the elites recreated coloniality.

26   INTRODUCTION: OUR AMÉRICA, OUR ANTÍGONA

mostly unrecorded in colonial historiography. The colossal loss of blood that ended in the formation of independent republics in the Spanish territories, led by patriotic armies throughout the continent and enlisting indigenous and African soldiers, was not entirely an anticolonial war. It was rather an "intra-Spanish" affair. Portuguese America was even more intimately linked to Portugal since the move of the Portuguese Crown to Rio de Janeiro in 1808 made Brazil the center of Empire. Peninsular Spaniards considered American-born Creoles inferior. Creoles rebelled against the limitations imposed on them by the Spanish Crown, especially concerning the trade monopoly with Cádiz.[53]

There are many angles from which to see the formation of Creole culture in "Latin" America and understand how Greco-Roman fragments have become rooted in regional urban spaces. This local circulation is not related to the ex-metropolis and does not enter the dynamics of a "reaction" against "an external colonizer." Rather, it helps explain the local cultures that inherited the colony. It is another "intra-affair": an intra-Creole one. The Occidentalism through which both colonizers and later independent Creoles conquered and mixed with indigenous peoples does not allow for the binary lens of "the non-West" reacting to "the West," or for that matter, "local" culture reacting to "colonial education," as if colonial education were exterior to (and extricable from) the formation of new societies after 1492. In this region, lines dividing any "West" from the rest must be historicized as ideological products of their times. Occidentalism resulted in what Bolivian René Zavaleta Mercado (1986) called "motley" societies, which, to the eyes of those who see this region as "non-West," present sundry muddles of European, indigenous, and African cultural elements.[54]

Violence midwifed the motley societies of Creole culture. The Spanish, the French, and the Portuguese inaugurated an extractivist colonialism that decimated the peoples they encountered, massacred, and enslaved. Their violence also targeted culture: their evangelical and educational mission clashed against indigenous cosmologies. Theirs were, I suggest, violent

---

[53] See Chapter 2 for the special case of Haiti, where the major factor in independence wars was the role of African-born enslaved peoples leading guerrillas against the French colonizers.

[54] Zavaleta Mercado's concept *abigarramiento* or *sociedad abigarrada* (1986) is currently translated in English as "motley." It describes the modern heterogeneous assemblages resulting from the history of violence between indigenous peoples and colonizers, as well as the history of merging capitalist with precapitalist economic structures and temporalities since colonial times.

"weapons of intimacy," rather than policies of indirect rule and segregation present in most nineteenth-century British colonies. I use the word "intimacy" polysemically. Their strategies of conquest aimed at both bodies and souls. The Spanish and Portuguese took possession of the land *and* its peoples: literal, sexual possession. Men indiscriminately raped indigenous women (and later African women), so much so that rape has been seen as one of the first Spanish and Portuguese colonial technologies.[55] There were no laws forbidding intermarriages or legalizing segregation (unlike in some British colonies)—and in some cases intermarriage was fostered.

Invaders intervened intimately also in soul "correction," as they saw it. Christian missions spread widely among indigenous peoples and profoundly altered their cultures, even if sometimes their languages were preserved.[56] Syncretic cultural forms emerged by force, and at rapid pace, out of these missions. The Virgin Mary merged with indigenous or African fertility goddesses. The long history of violent mixing yielded cultural narratives, official historiographies, and in some cases public policies labeled as "*mestizaje*" as early as in the sixteenth century.[57] While in the colony *mestizaje* served the purpose of control, in the early nineteenth century, independent republics embraced its ideology as the (idealized) total fusion of cultures and races. In Mexico, there were proposals for mestizo monarchies, for the promotion of the fusion of races to avoid rebellions, and even the formulation of the "Latin American fifth cosmic race" as part of the ideology of *mestizophilia*.[58] In 1814, Paraguay's ruler Dr. José Gaspar Rodríguez de Francia decreed a

---

[55] According to statistics, sex-biased gene flow between European men and indigenous women has been the rule. Even in areas of low-density indigenous population, such as present-day Argentina, there are studies that identify at least one indigenous maternal ancestor in 50 percent of the population (see, for instance, Avena et al. 2006 and Galindo 2013).

[56] Bilingualism and preservation of indigenous languages was often observed in the Jesuits' missions until their expulsion in 1767. See, for instance, Negro Tua and Marsal (2000).

[57] *Mestizaje* is not to be confused with the English word miscegenation. The term describes a historical process of biological and cultural mixing, attempts to culturally or biologically produce mixing, and an ideology about the identity of the region resulting from those mixings. At different times, "Latin American" elites argued that mixing between Europeans, Africans, and indigenous peoples would eventually create a new race and a new culture, overcoming the "barbarism" of indigenous empires and smaller nations. The bibliography around the narratives of *mestizaje* is vast; for introductions, see Arguedas (1965), Klor de Alva (1995), Cornejo Polar (1998, 2004), León-Portilla (1975), and Lander (2000).

[58] Mexican José Vasconcelos was the so-called "cultural caudillo" of the Mexican Revolution. In his 1925 book *La raza cósmica*, he argued that "Latin" Americans were a "fifth race" that was the future of humanity (Vasconcelos [1925] 1997).

28 INTRODUCTION: OUR AMÉRICA, OUR ANTÍGONA

prohibition of marriage among Europeans to prevent the formation of a white elite, creating instead a mestizo one.

The sixteenth-century Spanish cultural penetration included higher education, establishing local literate urban elites. Ángel Rama called them "lettered cities," in contrast to the oral traditions of indigenous peoples surrounding the cities. Rama qualified the first three decades of the conquest as a "frenetic gallop [...] leaving in its wake a scattering of cities, isolated and practically out of communication from one another, while the territory between the new urban centers continued to be inhabited almost solely by the dismayed indigenous populations" ([1984] 1996: 11).[59] "Lettered" refers to institutions of education and administration, evangelization, legislation, and liberal professions (including the institution of literature) that controlled settlements across the empire, and to the corresponding individuals who run them (the *letrados*). For Rama, the urban center was modeled after the ideal of the Greek polis.

To consider how impossible it was to speak, by the time of independence, of conquering culture as "exterior," we need to take the historical depth of the lettered city seriously. The Spanish founded the first lettered city, Santo Domingo, in 1496, four years after arrival. It was the "intellectual capital" of the Caribbean until the eighteenth century and was interestingly called not the Rome but "the Athens of the New World."[60] In just four decades, the Spanish founded the first university, the Dominican Santo Tomás de Aquino (in 1538), a hundred years earlier than the first university in British America (Harvard in 1636), followed by the oldest still-active university, San Marcos in Lima, in 1551.[61] This is why Laird can speak of an innovative classical tradition starting right after the Spanish invasion. To understand the presence of European antiquity in the new mixed cultures emerging as of the sixteenth century, shouldn't we, as Jorge Cañizares-Esguerra puts it, "count the tens of thousands of youths trained for 300 years in the scholastic

---

[59] See also de la Campa (1999) and Moraña (1997). See a comparison with the Arab model of expansion in Gorman Malone (2010).

[60] Henríquez Ureña (1936: 11).

[61] Spanish universities spread across the empire throughout the 1500s and 1600s. With the exception of Harvard and William and Mary, all colonial colleges in New England were founded in the eighteenth century. The first college in a British African colony was founded in 1826 (Sierra Leone); the first college for African people was founded in South Africa in 1841; the first university in 1873. Seppo Sivonen (1995) observes that in certain British territories, colonial administrators slowed down higher education and debated the education of rural populations, given the threat of Asian nationalisms and the Bolshevik revolution. Assié-Lumumba assesses that one of the tasks after the British left was precisely to educate the people (2006: 32).

INTRODUCTION: OUR AMÉRICA, OUR ANTÍGONA   29

legacies of Greek academic philosophy and in the Justinian code of Roman Law at universities, academies and courts in Lima and Mexico, and throughout Spanish America?" (2018: 197). Add here the profound penetration of European languages. All but four "Latin" American nations developed in time a demographic majority whose *first* language is Spanish, French, or Portuguese.[62]

With Spanish colonial education came its critique, another defining feature of "Latin" American colonial difference. The Spanish conquest itself was embedded in the critique coming from within the ranks of empire. This means that both Spaniards and Spanish-Americans have debated their relation to the conquest, and politically mobilized to this end Greco-Roman fragments, for no fewer than five hundred years.[63] No other Early Modern empire debated the legitimacy of their conquest like the Spanish did: only fifty years into their colonizing enterprise, the Dominican Friar Bartolomé de las Casas (1484?–1566) and the Spanish jurist Juan Ginés de Sepúlveda (1490–1573) argued whether or not indigenous peoples were their equals in the famous "Valladolid Controversy" (1550). In 1573, the Pope declared that indigenous peoples had the right to be free and own property "even though they be outside the faith of Jesus Christ" (see Pope Paul III, "Sublimis Deus, The enslavement and evangelization of Indians").[64]

The local "American" debates over the colonial legacy heated up two hundred years ago, when the wars of independence ended and colonial territory fragmented into myriad new republics—and the ensuing civil wars. The circulation of Greco-Roman fragments depended on each new national formation, as will be evident to the reader in every chapter of this book. The Spanish colonization of what today are Peru and Mexico confronted highly developed agricultural empires, and this reality led to specific Creole

---

[62] In most countries, more than 90 percent of the population speaks Spanish or Portuguese as their first language (with the exceptions of Paraguay, Bolivia, Peru, and Guatemala), while the population that speaks English as a first language in India is around 10 percent; in Zimbabwe, 2.5 percent; in South Africa, the National Census of 2011 found 9.6 percent. Consider that due to the doctrine of indirect rule, the British colonies disseminated English only among co-governing elites, rather than the masses. See Brutt-Griffler (2002).

[63] To imagine the temporal difference on which these genealogies depend, picture where African or Indian ex-colonies will be (and who knows in what context) in the year 2150 with respect to their thinking about Europe.

[64] In the "Valladolid Controversies" Juan Ginés de Sepúlveda defended a holy war against indigenous peoples, invoking Aristotle's *Politics*. Bartolomé de las Casas argued that indigenous peoples were equal to Europeans, invoking the superiority of Christ's Doctrine over that of Aristotle. In practice, the Spanish unleashed war against indigenous peoples to expropriate land and imported enslaved Africans from the very beginning. For examples of these debates on American soil, see Laird and Miller (2018), Cañizares-Esguerra (2001), and Rabasa (1994).

30 INTRODUCTION: OUR AMÉRICA, OUR ANTÍGONA

theories about coloniality, which only translate with difficulty to areas where genocidal massacres happened immediately upon the European invasions (the Caribbean) or immediately *after* Creole independence (Chile, Argentina, Uruguay).[65]

As lettered cities gradually became modern cities with dissident intelligentsia, nationalist projects appropriated oral traditions for the consolidation of national identity.[66] The free Creole elites must be understood in their plurality, embodying the full ideological spectrum, from right to left, from the very beginning of independence. As to what to keep of the Spanish legacy in former Spanish colonial territories, the only nineteenth-century consensus among lettered elites was the unifying language across the continent, which for many brought hopes of political unification after fragmentation. And just as Spanish jurists and friars denounced the conquest from the dawn of the colony, Creole intellectuals denounced the reinstatement of coloniality from the dawn of the new republics. Argentine Esteban Echeverría's 1846 *El Dogma Socialista* (The socialist dogma) was clear: "the post revolutionary government established itself on colonial footing" (1981: 289). José Martí wrote in his 1891 "Our America": "The colony continued living in the republic." The real question was (and still is) the meaning of independence: for whom and for what purpose was it achieved? The "living colony" was the obsession of the twentieth-century intelligentsia. In the 1960s, Mexican Pablo Casanova called it "internal colonialism"; in the 1970s, Peruvian Aníbal Quijano chose "coloniality of power."[67]

For "Latin" American scholars who engage in anticolonial critique, the *post-* does not make as much sense as the *neo*colony, established by the same land-owning lettered elites who, once free from Cádiz, inaugurated a new economic dependence, first with Britain. And in some cases, imperial culture was defended. Consider Brazil, which became first the actual site of the Portuguese Crown in the early nineteenth century and then a monarchy with a local aristocracy until the last decade of the nineteenth century: what

---

[65] In Chapter 1, I explain the case of Argentina; Chile orchestrated the Occupation of Araucanía from 1861 to 1883, which led to incorporation of Mapuche land, a region that had never been conquered by the Spaniards, into Chilean national territory. Uruguay led the Campaign of Salsipuedes in 1830 against the Charrúa people.

[66] See Ramos (2003); Franco (2002).

[67] Casanova's concept is a correction to the use of "racism" as the only term to account for neocolonial continuous discrimination, a term that loses sight of the indigenous right to autonomous government and linguistic and cultural patrimony. See also Quijano (2000). Quijano's concept has been expanded, for instance, by Arturo Escobar (2004), to account for a global coloniality of hierarchies that describes imperial capitalism.

INTRODUCTION: OUR AMÉRICA, OUR ANTÍGONA   31

could it mean for the Brazilian-born aristocrats and their entourages, members of the Portuguese Empire, to rid themselves of imperial culture? At the time of independence, the embeddedness of European culture took on a new meaning: for the most part, republican elites adopted the Enlightenment narratives prevalent during the Atlantic revolutions. Thus, Spanish and Portuguese America embraced rather than rejected Greco-Roman and indigenous antiquities.[68] In the new Occidental equation of "civilization" and "barbarism," some Creole elites placed Spain on the side of feudal barbarism. Ancient Europe, appropriated freely as either part of "Latin" American Occidentalism or the substitute for Spanish obscurantism, provided symbols of democracy and republicanism. In some cases, this combined with pre-Columbian civilizations' models for unification and identity: restoring the symbols of the Inca Empire (and sometimes the idea of a monarchy) was discussed during the wars of independence. In the Overture, the reader will find fragments of antiquity in a small sample of nineteenth-century national anthems. Even in the exceptional Haitian case, French and Catholicism ended up being officially chosen to avoid what the elites feared: isolation. Each nation, in this respect, developed a particular history of expansion—or reduction—of the lettered city, generating its own channels of circulation of Greco-Roman antiquity.

The specific circulation of Greek fragments, at least in the case of "Spanish" America, may be considered anticonservative when compared to that of Latin ones. Lupher has argued (2003) that the Spanish conquest was imagined with the vocabulary of the Roman Empire, even among anti-imperialists. By contrast, Ramiro González Delgado establishes that Greek language and culture during and after Spanish colonial rule were "practically absent" (2015: 2), with the exception of Cuba. González Delgado suggests that the situation did not change drastically after independence: only in the 1830s, and in a few universities, was Greek language incorporated in the curriculum. The Greek tragedians, in turn, only appear in the first years of the nineteenth century.[69] Hernán Taboada (2014) suggests that the "disruptive" Greeks were sought to counter Latin education, perceived as more conservative. Commenting on Greek culture in colonial Spanish America, Alberto Manguel (2011) suggests: "As heirs to the Counter Reformation, for whom Greek was synonymous with heresy, Hispanic Americans in the beginning chose to translate almost entirely from Latin."

---

[68] See Bochetti (2010).
[69] See González Delgado (2015), Laird (2015), and Hualde Pascual (2012).

32 INTRODUCTION: OUR AMÉRICA, OUR ANTÍGONA

The lettered Creole elites debated fiercely what could save the new nations: the humanities (with ties to the European Enlightenment) or the sciences and industrial or technical skills.[70] By the mid-nineteenth century, classical education became the focus of yet another debate: for the Church, it seemed likely to counter the dangers of Romanticism, but soon enough the Church realized classics had been strongly associated with the revolutionary wars against empire—with freedom and equality. In the early twentieth century, lettered Creoles embraced classics again, this time to counter Anglo-American positivism, scientific racism, materialism, and utilitarianism. An iconic example was the influential programmatic publication for youth education *Ariel* (1900) by José Enrique Rodó (Uruguay, 1871–1917) and the foundation in 1909 of the Mexican group *Ateneo de la Juventud* (a strong advocate for humanistic education).[71]

The twentieth century's multiple nationalist ideologies within each nation created multiple versions of "canons," testing the possibilities and limits of the circulation of ancient texts, which were appropriated as much by right-wing nationalist movements as by populist and left-leaning movements. In "Latin" America, there is no rigorous, scholarly way to weld ancient fragments to fixed ideologies: Greco-Roman symbols circulate in every possible direction, decentered from any subversive or conservative ideology. Thus, to historicize becomes imperative.

Antígona has mostly, though not always, been mobilized in the lettered city across the continent to denounce the coloniality of power, sometimes reaching the rural peasantry. It is useful to remember that if the myth is translated into theater, *Antígona* has always already had dissident potential against the lettered city: its audience can be illiterate, as will be shown in Chapters 2 and 7.

"Latin America," Cannibalism, and Strategic Classicism

To take seriously material *from* Latin "America" means to keep the plural in mind and engage homegrown ways of thinking about the legacy of European

---

[70] Ramos (2001) studies this opposition, mainly expressed in the 1840s debate between Argentine D. F. Sarmiento (advocate of industry and science) and Venezuelan Andrés Bello (advocate for classical humanistic culture). The main debates after emancipation can be found in Luis Alberto Romero and José Luis Romero 1977 and 1988.

[71] See the fascinating study of the Mexican case in Sánchez Prado (2009). The author reconceives "occidentalism" to describe how elites also used European cultures—the classics among them—to resist nationalist projects. His thesis resonates with some analysis of Greco Roman fragments in this book.

INTRODUCTION: OUR AMÉRICA, OUR ANTÍGONA   33

culture. Even within Anglophone classical studies, Simon Goldhill has suggested that the paradigm of "reception" is "too passive a term for the dynamics of resistance and appropriation" that the cultural history of "Greekness" shows in Western culture (2002: 297). "Latin America" must be seen in its diversity, and the circulation of Greco-Roman fragments must be studied case by case in their specificity.

Throughout this introduction, I have tried to unsettle the idea of "Latin America" by marking in quotations, at the risk of tiring the reader's eyes, different words in the construct. Much like "Europe," "Latin America" is a fiction, ideologically mobilized both by left and right. This is why, in this book, the term is nothing other than shorthand for countless discourses about modernity.[72] After the European empires fell, twenty independent nation-states were formed in "Latin America" (not counting Dutch territories, nor the British territories that Cañizares-Esguerra [2006] provocatively argues should be considered as an extension of the Spanish model of colonization on account of the British model's chivalric and religious nature). However, no nation-state within the "Latin" continent that has never been "Latin" has achieved a homogeneous "imagined community" (Anderson 1993) or unified its regions. Perhaps there is more than meets the eye in the confusing separation of "Latin" from "South" America in James Porter's phrase: "German and Anglo-American perspectives have tended to predominate [...] What about reception of the Classics in Israel, or in South Africa, Latin and South America, or India?" (2010a: 476).

Zavaleta Mercado (1986) reminds us that each valley may be considered a "motherland," with its own people and customs, dresses, and dances. The memories of colonization for the indigenous Aymara peoples of the Bolivian Andes, who had lived under the Inca Empire before the Spanish invaded their land, are different from those of the Mapuche nations of Patagonia, never conquered by the Spanish and independent until the nineteenth century. The descendants of enslaved African-born fighters in Haiti had a different role during Haiti's war for independence than Creoles born in Haiti, and thus they crafted different solutions for the post-independence state. Impoverished Italian immigrants arriving in South Atlantic cities in the 1900s were seen as "white Indians," rather than "Europeans," by the landowning class descended from Spanish conquerors. In the short poems that

---

[72] See Arturo Ardao's now classic *Génesis de la idea y el nombre de América Latina* (1980). See also Dussel (1995), O'Gorman ([1958] 1961), Gerbi (1955), and Rabasa (1994). On the idea of "Europe," see Dainotto (2007). There is a vast literature on the notion of multiple modernities; see, for example, Eisenstadt (2003) and Preyer and Sussman (2016). Discussing Eisenstadt's model from a "Latin" American perspective, see Domínguez (2009) and Mota (2015).

34   INTRODUCTION: OUR AMÉRICA, OUR ANTÍGONA

comprise Japanese descendant José Watanabe's *Antígona*, a scholar of haikus may trace Japanese culture adopted in coastal Peru.

To visualize Latin "American" diversity, Brazilian Afro-feminist Lelia González coined the expression "Améfrica Ladina" preserving the European, the African, and the mestizo populations in the name (*ladino* in Central America was a colonial name for mestizo populations who spoke Spanish). This diversity is in constant flux, as it is enriched by Asian and Middle Eastern waves of migration and by indigenous cultures whose permanently evolving social forms are inextricably linked to the evolving nature of capitalism and of Creole nation-states (the latter not being a suitable category to understand them; think here of communal property, especially in Andean economies of *ayllus*).[73] It is impossible to be rigorous about the worlds emerging after 1492 without allowing oneself to be ceaselessly haunted by their heterogeneity. Cultural genealogies change drastically within nations as well as within regions.

This heterogeneity is veiled by the thick "Latin" shroud of the political appropriation of the French doctrine inspired by the 1836 chronicles of Michel Chevalier, who divided America into the Latin family (Catholic) and the Germanic/Anglo-Saxon families of the North (Protestants). The political career of the name "Latin" includes its appropriation in the nineteenth century by lettered elites as conveniently separating them from British America. At the turn of the twentieth century, when the United States became a military threat to the continent and the ideology of racist positivism peaked, the "Latinity" (read "humanism") of Latin "America" became more influential than ever. And as for contemporary activists of indigenous descent, many consider themselves from Abya Yala, rather than from any of the three "Americas"—the European, the African, and the Ladina.[74] This continent is neither Latin nor American; nor is it "the New World"; it is something unrepresented by these given names, whose imagined referents are always contested by the thunder of history.

---

[73] Literature on indigenous social forms is vast. A classic reflection on the importance of the Andean "ayllu" is José Carlos Mariátegui's 1928 *Seven Interpretive Essays on Peruvian Reality* (1971); for contemporary appraisals of indigenous cosmogonies, see Rivera Cusicanqui (2014); Viveiros de Castro's notions of perspectivism and multinaturalism (2014 and 2015); and the philosophy of *Sumak Kawsay* ("Life in Plenitude") in Oviedo (2014).

[74] The name *Abya Yala*, originally a Kuna term, is now adopted by many indigenous nations, though rejected by others, to name the continent; it translates as "land of vital blood," "land in its full maturity," or "blooming earth." What the West calls *planet*, indigenous peoples call "mother earth in equilibrium" (Pachamama).

INTRODUCTION: OUR AMÉRICA, OUR ANTÍGONA   35

The political icon of "Latin America" as a unified entity is an incomplete project, mobilized time and again as an anti-imperialist cry to foster the utopia of a continental unity, articulated mostly clearly in the *Antígona* of Chapter 4. In Spanish America, it is expressed in the notion that there are two homelands: one's own, *la madre patria* ("the father/mother land"), and "América," *la patria grande* ("the Great Father/Motherland")—what José Martí famously called "Our America," "*Nuestra América.*"

Because it encompasses both an anti-imperial message and a warning about the region's heterogeneity, Martí's call in his essay "Our América" is often quoted in debates about "our" identity. And because classicists often cite it for its allusions to Greece, it is useful here to dispel misconceptions about it. Martí asked Americans to learn how to govern "new peoples of singular and violent composition," without foreign laws that "ignore" them.[75] Martí did not call for the annihilation of European (i.e., Greek) culture in formulating a rigorous program of research into "the true elements of the country," to "derive the form of government from them, and govern along with them. Governor, in a new nation, means Creator." He could hardly have advocated for eliminating European culture: Martí was a cosmopolitan polyglot *criollo* who "cannibalized" from all the cultures and languages he knew. More than a thousand classical references to the Greco-Roman world appear in Martí's seventy-three volumes of collected writings.

Martí's "Our America" argues for a creation stemming out of all the elements of the new republics:

How can our governors emerge from our universities when there isn't a university in América that teaches […] the elements that are peculiar to the peoples of América? […] The European university must bow to the American university. The history of America, from the Incas to the present, must be taught in clear detail and to the letter, even if the archons of Greece are not taught. Our own Greece must take priority over the Greece that is not ours. We need it more. […] Let the world be grafted onto our republics, but we must be the trunk.[76]

It would be futile to disregard any of the peculiar elements of "our" America: if Martí still invokes "Greece" to name "our antiquity" ("from the Incas […]

---

[75] Here I slightly modify existing English translations. See an English version of Martí's "Nuestra América" (1891) at http://www.josemarti.cu/publicacion/nuestra-america-version-ingles/.

[76] Martí's last sentence in Spanish reads: "Injértese en nuestras Repúblicas el mundo; pero el tronco ha de ser el de nuestras Repúblicas."

36 INTRODUCTION: OUR AMÉRICA, OUR ANTÍGONA

our own Greece"), this is because, while not a priority, Europe remains one of the elements of what he thought was "our peculiarity."

Against applying "foreign laws that ignore our" peoples, "Latin" American intellectuals have accounted for the European colonial legacy as inextricable from the heterogeneity of "our American antiquity." Neither the metaphor of reception nor that of synthesis accounts for this heterogeneity. Homegrown terms are fractured mirrors; they convey the fragility of social forms and heterogeneous temporalities out of which new worlds emerged, brought forth by the colonizers' weaponry of intimate invasions.

Mestizaje as a discourse to account for "our" peculiar "mixings" gradually became the favorite of elites. Twentieth-century intellectuals contested it— arguing it erased the violence of the conquest. Brazilian Oswald de Andrade's *antropofagia*, Cuban Fernando Ortiz's *transculturation*, Argentine García Canclini's *hybridity*, Peruvian Cornejo Polar's *heterogeneity*, and Bolivian René Zavaleta Mercado's *abigarramiento* or *motley* societies, are some of the most prominent attempts to render the ways in which indigenous and non-indigenous peoples were forced to coexist, merging in contingent and incongruent forms that occlude the possibility of turning back or away from capitalist colonialism.[77] It is useful to recall here that indigenous peoples were conquered but never vanquished; heterogeneous forms of sociality easily and permanently enter into conflict within nations. Here, the circulation of any European legacy must be as intimately entrenched as it is predictably fragmentary, producing motley cultural goods.[78]

Carlos Jáuregui (2008 and 2012) argues that cannibalization is a foundational model for all subsequent twentieth-century metaphors of hybridity, which "devoured" anthropophagy to resignify its potency. Jáuregui provides the term's genealogy since colonial times. To summarize: upon arrival in the Caribbean, Columbus' crew marveled at the indigenous peoples' good will,

---

[77] See Ortiz ([1940] 2000). Ángel Rama applied the term to literary narrative (1982). It was elaborated upon so many times that critic Alberto Moreiras commented: "there is no Latin American Culture without transculturation" (2004: 149). See García Canclini (1995), Cornejo Polar (2004), and Zavaleta Mercado (1986). As mentioned above, the word *motley* emerged to describe coexisting worlds in societies with a high density of indigenous traditions, which had no possibility of escaping some form of modernity. This, of course, excludes "uncontacted" peoples in the so-called "uncontacted frontier" between Brazil and Peru.

[78] In this book, I do not engage the discourse of *créolité* generated in the 1980s in the French Caribbean by Patrick Chamoiseau (author of one *Antigone* play), Raphaël Confiant, and Edouard Glissant. Despite the fact that *créolité* responds to the previous homogenizing discourse of *négritude*, and thus could be assimilated to the Hispanic responses to *mestizaje*, the debate over *négritude* emerges much later than older *mestizaje* discourses, in the aftermath of the 1915 United States invasion of Haiti. Chapter 2 engages the emergence of *négritude*.

except when they heard a story about "cannibals."[79] In time, the latter made intelligible the otherness that the crew rejected. It provided justification for "evangelization" and protection of indigenous peoples (made subjects of the Spanish Crown) from the "cannibals," who gradually became all those "heretic" subjects who did not submit entirely to the Crown. The itinerary of this metaphor for (the incorporation of) otherness shifted from a colonial to an anticolonial meaning: the "cannibal" became one who resists being eaten (exploited) by colonizers.

Oswald de Andrade's 1928 "Anthropophagic Manifesto" was an anticolonial, anarchist text resisting interpretation and mixing languages (Portuguese and Tupí-Guaraní). But it established as the common core of "our" cultural and economic production "anthropophagia, the only thing that unites us. Socially. Economically. Philosophically." If the colonized are historically "eaten," the question of a liberated Creole consciousness becomes "to eat *or* to be eaten"—formulated by de Andrade in his manifesto as "tupi or not tupi," quoted in the epigraph to this chapter. To "be" a people—"to be tupi"—means to engage the Tupinambá ceremonial anthropophagic practice: eating the enemy.[80] Culture is that which is local after violently incorporating that which is foreign if it is useful. It implies the act of dismembering others. As de Andrade put it, the "Law of the cannibal" orders "I am only concerned with what is not mine": who is not my friend, and at the same time what is "not [my] property" (which alludes to common property, typical of indigenous societies). As Jáuregui explains, *antropophagia* was a movement for thinking how to reverse the usual assignation of Brazil (extend this to "Latin" America) as producer of raw materials and consumer of European culture: cannibalism was to produce "our" culture, neither cosmopolitan nor local—a combination, for de Andrade, of shamanic culture with skyscraper modernity.[81]

In 1940, Ortiz coined transculturation to contrast it with acculturation: he viewed marginalized groups as resignifying dominant culture through destructions and reconstructions in asymmetrical power exchanges among

---

[79] The first reference to "cannibals" appears on Columbus' journal entry of November 23, 1492. Columbus' journals are available online. See https://archive.org/stream/journalofchristo00colurich/journalofchristo00colurich_djvu.txt.

[80] See Viveiros de Castro (2014).

[81] For the Brazilian modernist movement, see the *Revista de Antropofagia* (1929–30) São Paulo, https://www.ubu.com/media/text/Andrade-Oswald-de_Revista-de-Antropofagia.pdf. The movement saw opposition, especially in the Recife group exalting Luso-African culture, in their 1926 "Manifesto regionalista" (Jáuregui 2012: 24). See also the nationalist movement Verde-Amarelismo (1926–9).

38 INTRODUCTION: OUR AMÉRICA, OUR ANTÍGONA

cultures that live together. For Cornejo Polar, Ortiz's transculturation was too close to *mestizaje*, too "syncretic," as it incorporated codes into "a more or less unproblematic totality" (2004: 117). Writing about his native Peru, densely populated by Quechua and Aymara peoples who preserve their native languages, Cornejo Polar defined his concept "heterogeneity" in 1977, emphasizing the colonial fracture: the impossibility of representing the indigenous world (mostly rural and oral) with the colonizer's episteme (mostly written and urban), resulting in "heterogeneous" texts bearing the mark of this impossibility.[82] García Canclini's 1995 metaphor of "hybrid" texts took into account the fracture but emphasized processes blurring the limits between multiple heterogeneous worlds: for him, the impurity of any cultural production and the dissolution of binaries, such as Western/non-Western, was the mark of "Latin" American production. Zavaleta Mercado refined his concept "motley societies" in 1986 also emphasizing fracture, produced by the coexistence of multiple social worlds, historical experiences, modes of production, civil organizations, and linguistic capacities in contingent, disorganized connections. These metaphors undo the illusion of a hegemonic totality. That which is hegemonic is diversity itself—with only one common link, that is, evolving colonial capitalism.

In "Latin America," these ideas constantly reappear in different forms. Consider Borges' well-known 1951 conference "The Argentine Writer and Tradition."[83] For Borges, to think that an Argentine tradition (substitute "Latin American" here) was determined only by "local color" or "by Spanish tradition" was a European (exoticizing) idea. Borges, like the Creoles of the nineteenth century, thought Argentine history "can be defined without mistake as [...] a voluntary distancing from Spain." In his eyes, "our patrimony is the universe"; South Americans, like Jews, are not attached to Western culture, nor devoted to it, nor superstitious about it, and thus can move within it with greater "irreverence."[84] In Frantz Fanon's 1952 *Black Skin, White Masks*, we find a similar feeling: "I am a man, and in this sense the Peloponnesian War is as much mine as the invention of the compass" (2008: 175). Mexican Alfonso Reyes echoes Borges: "a minuscule Greece should be born for our uses: more or less faithful to the paradigm, but always Greece

---

[82] Cornejo Polar included this concept in his speech "El indigenismo y las literaturas heterogéneas: su doble estatuto socio cultural" (at the Centro de Estudios Latinoamericanos Rómulo Gallegos, Caracas, march 1977). See Cornejo Polar (1982: 67–85). See Bueno Chávez (2004).

[83] The tradition can be seen as continental. See, for example, T.S. Eliot's 1921 essay "Tradition and the Individual Writer" (1951: 13–22).

[84] See Borges ([1957] 1997: 151–62). See also García Jurado (2005: 231–49).

and always ours," since "we have the right once we possess a module, whichever the way we acquired it, of handling it as it pleases us. What else have the tragedians of all times done, if not to retell in their own way a well-known story?" (1959: 351).[85]

As I mentioned above, writing *from* "Latin America" about Antígona's specific case, I have prioritized metaphors of cannibalization, heterogeneity, hybridity, rumination, and circulation. In a sense, vernacular Antígonas "eat" the European ones, just as Oswald de Andrade mandated, digesting what suits their needs. Cannibal teeth do not dismember the other out of hunger. Cannibals digest the enemy's best weapons; Antigone was perhaps one of them. The fractured social bodies through which *Antigone* circulates dismember the classical myth and tragedy, so that vernacular *Antígona* plays produced by the heterogeneity of any given place—a valley or a nation; a city or a region—have ceased to belong to any recognizable European category.

Throughout the book, I have engaged critics who compare vernacular *Antígona*s with their European "source." But, as I argue, the oft-posed comparative question "is the play really a tragedy?" makes little sense in the context of the social hybridity that produces these plays. *Antígona* plays are cannibalized fragments of antiquity stitched together in modern motley forms. The "Latin American" seams are visible. In most chapters, I identify what I call "quilting points": moments, figures, lines, and images that make visible the sutures binding genres, cosmologies, historical discourses, and temporalities, composing pieces that are neither European *Antigones* nor European tragedies. Quilting points do not allow us to separate the tragic from the redemptive or utopian: they reveal these plays are new, American, forms.

If anything, "reception" in this book could refer to the remainder of the European text that cannot or has not yet been "cannibalized"—that is, reception alone represents a failure in "digestion"—an *in*digestion. Some ancient fragments cannot be "digested" for any use and thus remain identifiable as "foreign"—still welcomed, but not "ours." Here, research could identify which ancient fragments are tough to crack. For example, whereas many Antígonas demand the corpses of their lost children, I have not

---

[85] Idiosyncratic and sometimes extravagant uses of the Greeks abound. Argentine Leopoldo Lugones (1874–1938) associated the *gauchos* of the Argentine Pampas with Homeric Greeks; Chilean Cesar Navarrete (1909–2003) associated the Mapuche peoples with Spartan migrations. See Taboada (2007: 229–41; 2012: 205–19). For Reyes, see Sánchez Prado (2019).

40 INTRODUCTION: OUR AMÉRICA, OUR ANTÍGONA

stumbled upon one Priam. My research on Argentine vernacular Medeas demanded a consideration of indigestion: Medeas mostly symbolize the political "others" to the nation, but many versions themselves remain iconic of foreignness.[86]

Out of the violent collision of the local and foreign fragments, we may find a text titled "Antígona" but not focused on burial. Consider a novella, not treated in this book, by Colombian cult writer Andrés Caicedo (1951–77), *Noche sin fortuna* (Night without fortune, [1976] 2009). There, Antígona is a (sexual) "cannibal" character. We can think of her as a metaphor for the way *Antigone* has been fragmented by anthropophagi: she gives pleasure and devours men she likes.[87] Daniel Fermani's 2000 "Trans Antígona Sexual" can also metaphorize Antígona's relation to Antigone's fragments, as she declares: "of each corpse I devour the part that most satiates me."[88] If anthropophagy (and all other models associated with it) is a better way to understand vernacular Antígonas, a key question for classical reception studies becomes how to identify one.

Considering that creativity lies on the "receptors"—or "Latin" American anthropophagi—poses the question whether there are any mandatory aspects of the myth or its tragic form that must remain for Antigone's story to be identifiable. What could they be? Would this not invite us to return to the gold standard that can reassure us that "Antigone, the Greek" has survived? Spanish playwright Yolanda Pollín summarizes the sentiment of many, agreeing that a classic is an "open" text, but there must always be "the idea" (of Antigone) in each version: "the writer who confronts, for instance, Antigone, has to respect certain rules."[89] However, as I see it, that would place Europe back at the center. "Ours" are fragments of Greek antiquity: we must analyze even the appearance of just a name—Antígona. In this region, it will be hard to find a vernacular that respects "certain rules": colonialism and its revivals account for that.

A vernacular Antígona may be a sister, a cousin, a fellow traveler, a friend, a listener—and an insurgent, at times, with respect to other Antígonas or Antigones. Maybe just a title or a theme. For the corpus I construct in this

---

[86] See another "case" (*Oedipus Tyrannus*) in Nelli (2015). On Argentine Medeas, see Fradinger (2020). Magdalena Bournot is writing a PhD thesis in Paris about Medeas: "Médée ou la figure de l'Autre dans le théâtre latino-américain de 1950 à nos jours." See also Miranda Cancela (2005).

[87] Andrés Caicedo also wrote a short story "Antígona" ([1976] 2009).

[88] I comment on this monologue in the Finale in Chapter 8.

[89] Quoted in Pociña and López (2010: 356).

INTRODUCTION: OUR AMÉRICA, OUR ANTÍGONA   41

book, I have considered texts with fragments or minimal references, texts in dialogue with the European ones, and texts without references to antiquity but with signposts that the scholar may recognize as part of a lineage. Ultimately, these are critics' decisions. I have prioritized the identification of fragments. More often than not, as critics look for the ancient in the vernacular, they see vernacular writings as "suited for" the popular but "caught in the impossibility of being understood by the popular, and only understood by elite classes."[90] But this is true only if the vernacular writing is read as an *Antigone*, that is, as demanding knowledge of the classic text from the audience. And this is exactly what a vernacular does not demand. A vernacular demands immersion in the political contingency of any given time and place. Playwrights have been explicit: when Argentine Sergio de Cecco (1931–86) wrote *El reñidero* (The cockpit, staged in 1962), he "wanted an Electra for the people. I wrote so that nobody really needed to know the Greek play to understand mine, which is set in the 1910s in Buenos" (1963: 10). Argentine Julio Imbert wrote a very short monologue about eternal motherhood entitled *Electra: tragedia en medio acto* (Electra: tragedy in half an act, 1957–63), clarifying in the prologue that "I did not have in mind Demeter because I did not know of her; there will always be someone who 27 centuries before us already did what we are doing; this dialogue has nothing to do with the mythology used by Sophocles or Euripides" (1963: 35). Here a meditation on motherhood, rather than the killing of the mother, takes Electra's name. The question for the researcher is not whether this is a version of the ancient *Electra* but why and how Electra may stand for motherhood in this context at this time.

Thus far, I have addressed the question of "Latin America" in Antígona. The question of the "classic" beyond the fragment of antiquity in each "Latin" American Antígona appears in this book as what I call "strategic classicism."[91] In the vernacular use of the classical fragment that counts as "our" classic—as Martí's "Greece," as Reyes' "Greece as it pleases us"—we find a political or aesthetic strategy responding to a historical contingency. As mentioned above, I have taken the opposite road to what I see as colonial protocols. For Spanish classicists Pociña and López, compilers of Antigones throughout the Hispanic world, Sophocles' character Antigone is "a point of departure [...] an intemporal prototype [...] who motivates uncountable

---

[90] See Duarte Mimoso-Ruiz (2002: 1045–59).
[91] I echo Gayatri Spivak's term "strategic essentialism" to describe the essentializing category of "woman" as a political strategy (1987: 270–305).

42   INTRODUCTION: OUR AMÉRICA, OUR ANTÍGONA

rewritings" (2010: 355). In this book, Antigone's myth and tragedy are *points of arrival*, not of origin, for playwrights: akin to Walter Benjamin's "now time," the image of Antigone "flashes" to interrupt the flow of the political present.[92] If its classicism is invoked, it is strategic. At each contingent conjuncture, unexpected cannibalizations of the myth emerge out of the intersections of different types of universality dramatized on stage for any given community.

Rather than subscribing to any "universal" identifiable in Antígona, I follow Étienne Balibar's proposal of a "threefold meaning of universality" to historicize any cultural artifact.[93] For Balibar, there is "universality as reality," which involves a single world "multiplying the interdependencies between the units—be they economic, political, or cultural—that form the network of social activities today" or what we could call global capitalism; "universality as fiction" or "the constitution of social hegemonies," based on the state's institutions, that is "the national"; and "universality as a symbol (or an ideal)," which poses "the infinite question of equality *and* liberty together, or the impossibility of actually achieving freedom *without* equality, or equality *without* liberty" (170–3; italics in the original).

Each strategic appropriation of classical fragments of *Antigone* articulates in one way or another these three types of universality when they respond to local junctures to resolve a crisis concerning political membership. On the one hand, the circulation of the classic fragments will always be marked by the real universality of the flows of global capitalism (in our particular case, colonial capitalism starting in the sixteenth century): they will always arrive abstracted from their ancient roots, in the toolkit called "universal patrimony" and enveloped in Occidentalism. An inquiry into colonial capitalism is the common denominator of all "our" Antígonas. Further, this mark of universality, as imprited by neocolonialism as it always is, has allowed for its strategic use by many theater movements in "Latin" America to rid themselves of Spanish, French, or Portuguese influence at key political moments. On the other hand, classic fragments articulate national politics (universality as fiction, or in other words, imaginary): in every chapter, the reader will find clear references to "the national," dramatized as an ideal unity of the polity. Lastly, fragments can articulate a form of utopia—a form

---

[92] In thesis XIV of his 1940 "Theses on the Philosophy of History," Benjamin explains his use of "Jetztzeit" with the example of Greco-Roman antiquity: "to Robespierre ancient Rome was a past charged with the time of the now which he blasted out of the continuum of history" (Benjamin [1940] 2007: 253–65).

[93] See Balibar (2007: 146–76).

of the ideal universal, as the utmost rebellion against the present. Post-Cold War Antígonas make this most visible. In the final chapters of this book, I convey this utopian articulation by using "universal" as a noun: those Antígonas represent an "impossible universal," a proposal for universal change formulated within socio-political conditions of impossibility. It is to articulate this type of universal that "Latin" Americans ruminate on Antígona most clearly, as I explain below. She is a figure that constantly returns to the cultural sphere as the ethico-political demand of systemic change.

Qualifying these classical appropriations as "strategic" in their articulation of different types of the universal avoids fetishizing any aspect of the ancient fragment's interpretations and rigorously historicizes each play. To be sure, the emphasis on locality is central to the structure of the ancient play's conflict: Polynices must find a place. There is no real foreigner in this story, and classicists have commented that this may be the most incestuous (i.e., radically localized) play in the extant tragic corpus. In "Latin American" *Antígonas*, the question of land recurs time and again—no doubt an aspect of the colonial legacy. Here I suggest that the translatability of *Antigone*'s conflict can be thought of in terms of a dialectic inherent in the central gesture of the play's title character. Antigone resists inclusion in the totality (Antigone's "no" to Creon) in her demand for the inclusion of someone else in the totality (Polynices' body in the polis). Recall also how she names herself "metoikos" (foreign resident) twice (lines 850–3, 867–8): she sees herself as not belonging, in spite of her lineage. As Antigone travels, it seems her gesture would be translatable everywhere. But her gesture points to something that is not translatable, to the singular irreplaceability of a name: Polynices can be no one else, and he needs to be in no other territory than his. As *Antigone* is translated into every language, Antigone performs an act that cannot be translated. *Antigone* dramatizes the imperatives of "locality": not the "universal dead" but rather "these" specific dead that must be buried "here." The borders of the local are at stake, nonetheless they can only be defined from the community's outside: Antigone can only demand the particular inclusion (of someone) as she is ousted from the community. In other words, the totality (of locality) can only be thought of as incomplete or open.

Antigone speaks of the local as soon as she is not local: she points at the need for a totality from the enunciation of its impossibility. Her act cannot be translated or replaced by any other but must be performed, no matter what, in a given setting. Yet her sacrifice signals the universality of a

44 INTRODUCTION: OUR AMÉRICA, OUR ANTÍGONA

necessity and the impossibility of totality at once. She is the paradox of any attempt at thinking about the local: it cannot be fully thought, but it must be thought. In this respect, Antígona's gesture is useful for thinking through the problem of conceptualizing "Latin America," or any given "nation," as a totality. Throughout the twentieth century, Antígona performs the gesture indicating the necessity and impossibility of totality in terms of the nation. The twenty-first century shifts toward a different totality, perhaps as unthinkable as the nation: more recent Antígona plays target the patriarchy and are thus closer to the type of universality that capitalism represents.

"Latin" American Studies: Antígona, a Case for "Our Rumination"

For the most part, "Latin" American scholars will recognize the historical discourses I tease out of the *Antígona* plays in this book, though not all the *Antígona* plays or their specific contexts. Some may be surprised at unexpected (and obscured) slices of history, or at the political thesis about the neocolony, reconstructed here in this book, as embedded in Antígona's lines. Others may discover the ubiquity of Greco-Roman fragments beyond the binary of elite and popular culture—a binary that, in this particular case, proves to be one more manifestation of the discourse of Occidentalism.[94] For Hispanophone and Lusophone classicists who study "the classical tradition" rather than the avatars of cultural cannibalization, this book may open a door to plural classical traditions.

To give a more specific account of Antígona's cannibalization in the region, this book proposes one more "digestive" metaphor that may eventually apply more widely: *rumination*. "Latin" Americans return in starkly different political scenarios to the myth and further unsettle Antígona as a foreign fragment—a foreignness still echoed in the metaphor of cannibalism. *Antigone's* moment as "foreign" culture in "Latin America" is long lost in time. Some fragments are nonetheless still being "cannibalized": the twenty-first century cannibalizes the scene of the violence upon

---

[94] Cuban Elina Miranda Cancela (2005: 70) puts it this way: "the reception of Latin American works that take tragic myth as a starting point has suffered from prejudices from some who devalue these works with a purist view [or some] who, in search of the expression of a national identity, think that in adopting a Greek myth as subject matter, the author shies away from national commitments." See also Sánchez Prado (2009).

INTRODUCTION: OUR AMÉRICA, OUR ANTÍGONA   45

Antigone's—not Polynices'—body.[95] But most fragments of the tragedy and the myth have entered a stage of what I see as cultural rumination. Antígona is *in corpore*—in the region's body: her fragments float back up into the public sphere, as if "our" cultural system were in constant need to feed itself with them.

As a metaphor, rumination alludes to both digestive and cognitive processing.[96] "Latin" America at once regurgitates and meditates on Antígona. Rumination means digestion-in-circulation: digesting as ruminants do in more than one stomach to rechew organic material, and thinking in more than one space–time coordinate. Political rumination exercises the return of Antígona's dissent time and again, akin to the insistence of the command "Never Again" to crimes against humanity: never again should politics disappear, as it does in circular waves, from the colony to the neocolony. While much has been said about Antigone as an "ethics" (of desire, of care, of humanism), Antígona's rumination dramatizes the need for the sphere of political dissensus to return, before the persistent attempt to erase it with militarization. The "good" for Antígona is utopia, rather than the Hegelian clash between "two equally good" sets of values.

The entry of "Latin" American *Antígonas* in the study of *Antigone*'s world circulation reveals an overwhelmingly political understanding of the culturally useful ancient fragments. Here is where we find an archive of theories about the neocolony, which, as I mentioned before, can be the case with art in general, and which I develop in my analysis of each case. Other than a meditation on neocolonial capitalist politics, vernacular *Antígonas* show very few stable variables. One of these is Antígona's protagonism, much as Robert Miola noted that early modern European Antigones prioritize Creon and side with Ismene (2014: 221): in "Latin America," Antígona reigns over all other characters, whether cast as an individual or as a collective of women. Creon is invariably authoritarian and sometimes secondary. Antígona is almost always—with one exception—cast as a woman (there is no hesitation as to her gender, as many classicists have argued of the ancient sister). However, there is no way to fix an interpretation always in favor of a gendered rebellion. The strict attention to locality yields particular

---

[95] See Chapter 8.

[96] My use of the metaphor follows a different genealogy than Friedrich Nietzsche's rumination as the art of reading critically (with which he famously ends his preface to his 1887 *Genealogy of Morals*). My center has been the breeding ground of regional neocoloniality, driving both the creation of local metaphors to think of European culture and the "Latin" American returns to Antígona.

46   INTRODUCTION: OUR AMÉRICA, OUR ANTÍGONA

rebellions. Consider how Anglophone critics unanimously hasten to interpret Watanabe's 2000 Peruvian Ismena as staging gendered rebellion, when, as I argue in Chapter 7, she instead stages a testimony that complies with the national political mandate of the Truth Commission, investigating crimes against humanity in the aftermath of Peru's internal armed conflict (1980–2000).

The rumination on burial is overwhelmingly present but bears characteristics that respond to historical contingency and transform the meaning of the corpse. Antígona dramatizes not only the need for burial but also the "return" of the dead: the particular impossibility inherent in the politics of forced disappearance—of corpse manipulation—that has characterized colonial and neocolonial projects. But most importantly revealing a political dynamics of the neocolony, vernacular *Antígonas* stage the event whereby a corpse is the *condition of possibility* for politics. The corpse here propels, almost as a character, a form of politics against which Antígona acts. And because it is the national corpse, sometimes plural, Antígona's recovery of the dead, sometimes even the search for or the exposure of the dead, dramatizes the return of those expelled during the colonial theft of land. Many of these plays stage the full circle of a politics of indigenous extermination that started in colonial times, continued in the republican nineteenth century, and was reinstated in the twentieth and twenty-first centuries to target other social dissidents opposed to neocolonial projects, or to extract more land under the guise of development and free-market policies. As long as "producing" corpses remains the condition for neocolonial politics, ruminating on another vernacular Antígona will continue to be an onstage or offstage political response. As long as she is there, the "disposable" are never fully untraceable. The eternal return—a rumination proper—of the unburied makes the emphasis of these plays shift from burial to utopia: the politics of disappearance must end. By the late twentieth century, utopian politics at times become more important even than the corpse and are dramatized with the formation of female collectives. Bonding among women will develop as a political theme of its own, eventually dominating the twenty-first-century stage.

But the most striking pattern of rumination, running through the entire corpus and politicizing "our" Antígonas, must be the persistent casting of Antígonas as wives, mothers, or grandmothers, making visible a particular trait of the corpse at stake. Antígona is first and foremost a national mother—or a mother-to-be. When it appears, the corpse (or the

INTRODUCTION: OUR AMÉRICA, OUR ANTÍGONA 47

corpse-to-be) is a national child. In the figure, the dramatic actions, the convictions of the Antígonas, an array of discourses about motherhood in the colonial context cross paths, from the virgin mother to the raped indigenous mother. On the one hand, as Chilean philosopher Patricio Marchant (1984) put it, while the problem of the father may be said to be European, the problem of the mother is "Latin American"—the mother who has been raped by colonizers, the mother who has lost her children. On the other hand, mother figures may have been the only way to cannibalize the Greek heroine in a region dominated both by a host of redemptive discourses (from colonial utopias of El Dorado to independentist dreams of a continental union) and by the motley images produced at the crossroads of the Christian imagination of maternal femininity and the indigenous and African cults to women's fertility. Consider the hybrid icons of motherhood permeating the region: the Mexican Virgen de Guadalupe, the Haitian Vodou *lwa* Ezili Freda, the Brazilian Virgen de Aparecida are a few examples. The icon of the Virgin Mary transforms mothers into essential participants in the economy of Christianity: the Virgin is the first to receive the promise of salvation (Jesus); her existence is necessary in order for the Truth to reveal itself to humankind (the Revelation). Even more interesting for our corpus, Mary is the image of a woman who can give life without the intervention of a human male; in other words, who can alter the natural order of things—thus, who can be political. The maternal Antígona is strategic classicism too: a cannibalization of the ancient fragment: "she wailed aloud with the sharp cry of a grieving bird, as when inside her empty nest she sees the bed stripped of its nestlings" (lines 424–5, trans. Jebb).[97]

That the cannibalizing, and subsequent rumination, of Antigone in the post-independence context has yielded a maternal character, rules out the interpretation of Antígona as an individual and enhances her politicization, visible in every internal dialogue in the corpus to this day. As a mother, she does not lend herself to critics' (almost) unanimous Hegelian expectations that she should represent the prepolitical or act across the "public/private" division. The latter has no historical or analytic relevance to "Latin American" Antígonas: theirs is the communal sphere of politics, in opposition to blood ties. Hegel's interpretative grid of the "unique" brother–sister bond—or, for that matter, its recent reworkings offering alternatives to

---

[97] See Jacobs (1996) for a reading of these lines.

48 INTRODUCTION: OUR AMÉRICA, OUR ANTÍGONA

exogamic normative forms of kinship[98]—is an obstacle to understanding Antígona. The figure of motherhood, regardless of its national coding, indicates relationality: it contains two bodies in one. Making room for another body, the mother represents an image of community par excellence. If, as Goldhill establishes, ancient tragedy "poses the question of what is shared" (2012: 241), and the ancient Antigone avoids the verbal plural, Antígona not only embraces the plural but also indexes it, just by being cast as a maternal figure. Thus cast as a mother, the "Latin American" Antígona rebels in the name of two or more. She is a figure against individuation: both as a collective (of at least two) against colonial feudal power (dramatized by many Creons on stage) and against the liberal logic of identity and individual rights that defined citizenship in the republican projects launched after independence.

I started this introduction by noting that at the dawn of the nation there was a mother without a son: Varela's 1824 Argia. Throughout the book, the reader will encounter the rumination of this pattern, out of which a theory of neocolonial capitalist politics emerges, and which I call an "Antígonal paradigm of politics." Antígona's cultural work is not prepolitical (the family) but rather a rebellion, often carried out by a collective of women, against the necro-neocolonial politics inaugurated by a special corpse: a child's corpse. In these plays, filicide, rather than parricide, is the salient feature in the project of modernity characteristic of the neocolonial order. Post-independence Creoles did not kill the king but rather their own offspring, in order to reinstate the colony and continue their conquest for land. Latin "American" Creons are akin to Hobbesian Leviathans, to the father of Roman law, to the terrible father in the Freudian myth of the "primitive horde"—worried about their offspring's violence against them.

Antígona indicts the neocolonial modernity whose only recourse to maintain power against the backdrop of the rise in democratic ideals after the Atlantic revolutions was to launch extermination campaigns. Though the plays I engage are formal mixings of tragedy and a host of redemptive narratives, whereby Antigone's sacrifice may be made to yield some meaning, by the end of the twentieth century, the corpus shows an irredeemable reminder: Antígona's sacrifice will not bring justice until the "impossible

---

[98] See Butler's incisive interpretation of non-normative sexual politics (2000). In the "Latin American" corpus, there is only one Antígona openly (though mockingly) incestuous (Reinaldo Montero's Cuban *Antígona*, 2006). In general, "brothers" are political fellow travelers.

universal" for radical change that she formulates is no longer needed. But then, of course, we may start studying happier fragments of the classics.

The Structure of the Book

This study relies on textual close and distant reading, archival research, performance analysis and history, and historical research. The construction of the corpus is an invitation to identify in the "Latin American" cannibalization and rumination of the figure of Antigone a transnational *dispositif*—a system of interrelated discourses—about politics, womanhood, motherhood, sisterhood, and, to a certain extent, burials—though burials sometimes recede in importance when compared to Antígona's utopian political mission. Historical discourses in the corpus are not footnotes to texts and performances. The historical detail the reader will find responds to the plays' thematizing history as integral to their composition, as well as to the protocol for avoiding deracination and following in the local traditions of material interpretations of culture. In each chapter, the teasing out of historical details highlights previously overlooked aspects in each play. Greek material is treated as "found footage" at a historical moment of crisis.

I have organized the main chapters with chronological, rather than national, criteria since there are observable temporal shifts in the corpus. The book comprises one overture focused on the nineteenth-century, seven chapters with specific twentieth-century cases and a final chapter treating the twenty-first century. I have chosen the specific cases on account either of their novelty or of their repercussion inside and outside their original context. Each chapter is prefaced by a short precis of the play, to facilitate comprehension of material that is, with few exceptions, unknown to the reader. Broadly, the periodization breaks down into four phases: the 1950s' focus on national identity; the 1960s' revolutionary zeitgeist; the 1980s' emphasis on postdictatorial justice; and twenty-first-century plays bringing gender politics to the fore. I preface these phases with the first appearance of Antígona—to my knowledge—in "Latin" America, in the nineteenth century, which begins the discursive matrix of motherhood, ruminated throughout the corpus.

The Overture situates Argentine Juan Cruz Varela's "killing" of Antigone in his 1824 drama *Argia* and its postrevolutionary context, right after the last historical battles to expel the Spaniards from South American territory. Argia emerges as the first mother in the corpus who is forced to decide

50 INTRODUCTION: OUR AMÉRICA, OUR ANTÍGONA

whether to save her child or defend the nation against the Spaniards. The close-reading of her motherhood allows us to counter the interpretation of this play as "an imitation" of European sources. This mother—a blueprint for many to come—takes on a different urgency if we are attentive to the Creole elites in Buenos Aires, who were concerned about maternal politics and population as they launched a genocidal campaign against indigenous peoples living in the Pampas.

Chapter 1 studies Argentine Leopoldo Marechal's 1951 *Antígona Vélez* as his critique of national liberal historiography in the context of the largest nationalist movement Argentina had seen to date. The action is set in Varela's times, and the backdrop also refers to the Creole conquest of the Pampas. A deep examination of the historical references and scenes yields knowledge that counters previous interpretations of the play as advocating the military attempt to exterminate the indigenous peoples. This Antígona is the only one in the corpus to understand the law that condemns her. But that does not redeem her death: rather, she is redeemed as a frontier mother, as her blood will fertilize the soil, giving hope for the nation's future. Marechal's irony resides in the way Antígona is killed, which suggests the everlasting presence of indigenous agency in the nation's history. The play quilts a Christian drama of redemption and Greek tragedy.

Chapter 2 focuses on Haiti's specific national quest in the 1950s, to recover its African roots against the elites' centuries-old Francophilia, through the study of Félix Morisseau-Leroy's *Antigòn an Kreyòl* (1953). The drama shows the deepest heterogeneity in the corpus: its gods are neither Greek nor Christian but belong in the Vodou pantheon; its audience was only briefly the middle class in the capital city, before the play was taken to the peasantry across the country. Antigòn here becomes a Vodou goddess and is married in heaven. The play's role was paramount in the struggle to legitimize Haitian Creole and Vodou religion as the language and culture of the African enslaved peoples who, in the playwright's eyes, made Haiti's independence possible. The play quilts a Vodou ceremony and Greek tragedy.

Chapter 3 is devoted to Brazilian Jorge Andrade's *Pedreira das almas* (1957) and *As Confrarias* (1969), with which the playwright historicized two revolts, during the mining and coffee economic cycles, respectively, in the state of Minas Gerais in colonial and imperial Brazil. The first play is based on the 1842 Liberal revolt against the concentration of power and the second on the 1789 Minas Gerais Conspiracy for independence from the Portuguese Crown. Andrade's heroines are not only mothers but also

INTRODUCTION: OUR AMÉRICA, OUR ANTÍGONA 51

innovative political strategists: they disobey by obeying orders to the letter. A true cannibalization of Antigone's funeral ritual, the characters keep the body exposed, submitting the authorities to the sight of the unburied with which they tried to threaten others. Burial recedes in importance for the first time in the corpus: Andrade's Antígonas would rather let others live than perform the burial.

Chapter 4 examines Puerto Rican Luis Rafael Sánchez's 1968 *La pasión según Antígona Pérez*, whose main character has been seen as faithful to the "original." Nonetheless, this Antígona happens not to be accused of the crime of burial, and thus could not be more different than her ancient sister. She is accused of theft. The historical minutiae embedded in the play show how it stages a unique political drama in "Latin" America: the enduring colonial—rather than neocolonial—situation of Puerto Rico as US property. Antígona Pérez is also unique in the corpus in that she rejects marriage (though she is not exactly a virgin), but her death, in the end, could not but give life, just as the other Antígonas do. The play quilts tragedy with testimony and Brechtian technique.

Chapter 5 is conceived as an interlude, to show the dynamics of the corpus as lesser-known plays come into focus and to show how patterns intensify, such as Antígona as mother and the "Antígonal paradigm" of politics, traversing the twentieth century. I briefly engage plays from the 1950s, 1960s, and 1980s that ruminate on political motherhood and exhibit a proto-feminist consciousness that develops in the twenty-first century. Two major shifts in the corpus appear in these lesser-known plays: on the one hand, the collective action whereby, under the leadership of Antígona, a group of women become heroines as they socialize motherhood, love, and widowhood; on the other, the disappearance of the corpse, in the aftermath of Cold War dictatorships, which radicalizes Antígona's politics away from the national universal and toward the formulation of an impossible universal.

Chapter 6 examines Griselda Gambaro's famous 1986 *Antígona Furiosa*, written in honor of the Argentine Mothers of Plaza de Mayo. I engage the missed encounters between criticism of the play and the historical events in which it is embedded. Gambaro's Antígona has gathered robust critical attention. Nonetheless, it is also one of the plays most deracinated by critics, seen as referring to an abstract notion of dictatorship or through the lens of ethical lessons of ancient and modern European philosophers. Its Argentine specificity refers not so much to dictatorship but rather to a precise historical split within the Mothers of the Plaza, facing the dilemmas of postdictatorial liberal democratic notions of political justice.

52 INTRODUCTION: OUR AMÉRICA, OUR ANTÍGONA

Chapter 7 studies Peruvian José Watanabe's 2000 poem-play, cowritten with the theater collective Yuyachkani, *Antígona*. Here, Ismene is a protagonist for the first time in the corpus. Similar to *Antigòn*'s itinerary, the play went from the capital city of Lima to the peasant Quechua-speaking communities of the Andean South, in the aftermath of the twenty-year armed conflict between the national army and left-wing organizations in the late twentieth century. But entering the "world," the play was deracinated as "universal." Guilt was seen as Ismene's main emotion, whereas the play ends with the word "shame," which, in the context of its Andean peasant audience, shifts the emphasis from invisible private feelings to visible feelings of communion with the other. Not even the appearance onstage of a mortuary mask can easily be deracinated here: the target audience of Andean Quechua speakers, who had never seen Greek tragedy before, had their own tradition of masks for festivities and funeral rituals. The play quilts tragedy and testimonial literary and political rituals.

Chapter 8 presents a panoramic view of the twenty-first century: a flurry of female collectives staging the struggle against gendered violence and what I call necro- neoliberalism. In the last two decades, Antígona has shared the spirit of the "gender revolution" making headlines across the globe. We even find here one Antígona who questions her gender. I identify current trends added to the continuous rumination over the politics of disappearance: a focus on Ismene, the implausible comedic version of Antígona, and a thematization of gender violence. I then analyze examples from Mexico and Colombia.

This book thus consists of a three-pronged approach to "case studies." Cases help to establish patterns that can test the assumptions with which we approach them. First, the core of the book takes the case of one fragment of antiquity—"Antigone's case." I stress here that in "Latin" American each fragment of antiquity deserves a study of its own. My findings with respect to Antigone may not apply to research on Electra, Iphigenia, or Medea. Second, the construction of an Antígona corpus takes the case to the "regional" level: the neocolonial capitalist specificity that "Latin" America represents. Lastly, the case is taken at the level of "a particular play," studying its conditions of production.

The "case" approach enhances the meaning of the "democratic turn" in classical reception studies that engage (neo)colonial capitalist contexts. The singularity of the "case" provides the plurality needed for any form of "democracy," in terms of the ways the discipline studies its objects. Finding the specificity of each case helps us avoid mechanical application of

INTRODUCTION: OUR AMÉRICA, OUR ANTÍGONA 53

categories born in other socio-historic contexts. Each case can free us from our attachment to the totalizing version of the universal. I hope each chapter in this book serves as an entry into "the case of Latin" America's heterogeneous peoples, geographies, histories, and politics. And lastly, that each rumination of Antígona in "Latin" America prompts in us, as critics, the freedom to ask whether, after the discontinuity in traditions brought about by colonialism, we can seriously say that there is any universal trait to fix to the name Antigone/Antígona/Antigòn. It is also a question of keeping the borders of the lettered cities of classics, Latin American studies, and comparative literature endlessly open.

Overture

Antigone's Death, Antígona's Birth: Juan Cruz Varela's 1824 *Argia*

Thus the fatherland is built:
Thermopylae bursting—
The constellation of Cyclops—
Its night illuminated.[1]

Mars seems to animate
The faces of the new champions.[2]

A new Rome, the Fatherland will boast
Two caudillos of valor and good name.
What rivals! Like Romulus and Remus.[3]
Those who will insult
The greatness of the Uruguayan people
Will find
The arrow of Mars, if they are enemies;
Brutus' knife, if they are tyrants.[4]

After [independence], the Creole appropriation of classical culture attempted to surpass the mediation that had thus far been carried out by Europe.[5]

---

[1] National anthem of Colombia: La Patria así se forma/Termópilas brotando/constelación de cíclopes/su noche iluminó. See the collection of examples in Gutiérrez Estévez (2004: 345). All translations from Spanish in this chapter are mine.

[2] National anthem of Argentina: De los nuevos campeones los rostros/Marte mismo parece animar.

[3] National anthem of Paraguay: Nueva Roma, la Patria ostentará/Dos caudillos de nombre y valer/Qué rivales, cual Rómulo y Remo/Dividieron gobierno y poder…/Largos años, cual febo entre nubes.

[4] National anthem of Uruguay: Del Olimpo la bóveda augusta; Y hallarán los que fieros insulten/La grandeza del pueblo Oriental/Si enemigos, la lanza de Marte/Si tiranos, de Bruto el puñal.

[5] Halperín Donghi (1987: 116).

Antígonas: Writing from Latin America. Moira Fradinger, Oxford University Press. © Moira Fradinger 2023.
DOI: 10.1093/oso/9780192897091.003.0002

An American Death for a Greek Virgin

In the winter of 1828, Juan Cruz Varela (1794–1839), editor-in-chief of the combative Buenos Aires newspaper *El Tiempo: Diario político, literario y mercantil* (1828–9), authored five articles under the heading "National Literature." A poet of the 1810 May Revolution, which started what would become the Argentine struggle for independence from Spain, Varela defended the creation of a literature for the new nation.[6] He argued that developing a robust national literature would require the purification of the Spanish language, a free press, the establishment of republican institutions, and state support for education and the printing industry. For Varela, the new American states had been consumed by war, and their institutions were "resent[ing] the impotence of their infancy."

Of the Spanish colonial inheritance, Varela wished to rescue only the language, which he believed could unite all the new republics in the region. Everything else would be created anew after 1810. For him, Spain had produced no books worth reading; in every private library in Buenos Aires, the number of French titles far exceeded the number of Spanish ones.[7] But the models for the new literature would not be French either; in Varela's view, French influences had contaminated the beauty of the Spanish language.

Unlike the elites in other new American republics, who tapped into pre-Columbian culture (especially Incan culture) to jettison the Spanish colonial past, Varela's peers embraced neoclassical forms. However, for the next generation—the Romantics of 1837—neoclassicism would hew too closely to old Europe. Twentieth-century critics would likewise see the work of the 1810 revolutionary poets as "pale derivations of European literature."[8] In his account of Varela's works, critic Félix Weinberg rightly observed: "In hearing those criticisms, the surprise [of these poets] would have reached astonishment. To have told them that their weakness was the forms [they employed]! That their poetry was closer to the old metropolis than to that fatherland in whose birth pangs they shared!" (1964: 35).

The 1837 Romantics' reaction to Varela's neoclassicism may have prompted Varela's contemporary Juan María Gutiérrez (1809–78), arguably the founder of Argentine literary criticism, to assert in 1871 that "tragedy was born and *died* at the Argentine riverbank with Don Juan Cruz Varela" (1941: 213; my emphasis). Gutiérrez thought that Varela's mastery of

---

[6] *El Tiempo* no. 36 (June 14, 1982): 2. [7] *El Tiempo* no. 36 (June 14, 1982): 3.
[8] Shumway (1991: 96).

56 OVERTURE: JUAN CRUZ VARELA'S 1824 *ARGIA*

neoclassical forms would never again be seen on the shores of Buenos Aires. Nor did Gutiérrez and later critics consider that, while inspired by ancient tragedy, Varela was probably the first "to surpass the [European] mediation," to recall Tulio Halperín Donghi in this chapter's epigraph, with respect to American engagements with *Antigone*.

Varela wrote two tragedies: *Dido* (1823), based on Virgil's *Aeneid*, and *Argia* (1824), the latter inspired by Vittorio Alfieri's (1749–1803) *Polinice* (1775) and *Antigone* (1776). Antigone's myth seems to have first metamorphosed on American soil in Varela's *Argia*, summoned for the task of building a national literature that, in Varela's eyes, would break away from the Spanish colonial legacy. Yet Varela also parted with the European classical. In a cultural cannibalism *avant la lettre*, Varela's tragedy "devoured" *Antigone* by starting the action after the Greek virgin has been killed and replacing her with a mother. Varela thus initiated "an Argentine tradition" of the myth's appropriation and later rumination, perhaps even the American tradition *tout court*.[9]

Varela's invocation of Greek antiquity for the construction of a national literature is less surprising when we consider its fragmentary presence in other contemporary cultural texts, including the national anthems for new American republics quoted in the epigraph above. This was also the height of Europe's use of Greek antiquity to construct its own cultural genealogy—"We are all Greeks…but for Greece…we might still have been savages," Percy Bysshe Shelley famously wrote in the preface to his 1822 poem "Hellas." Perhaps more surprising, a century later, *Antigone*'s fragments would be called upon once more to dramatize "national foundations." Varela's dramatic killing of the Greek virgin paved the way for a persistent rumination of antiquity for "the national" in the region.

Varela did not work directly with the ancient Greek source, instead turning to Alfieri's Italian appropriation of a Latin source: the late first-century CE version of the myth in Statius's *Thebaid*. Book 12 of the *Thebaid* depicts the battlefield encounter between Antigone and Argia, daughter of Adrastus and wife of Polynices, as they perform the funeral rites for their brother and husband. The myth is developed in Apollodorus of Athens' second-century BCE *Library*: once the war between Thebes and Argos has ended, the two

---

[9] *Antigone* also appeared in Anglophone America earlier than any other Greek tragedy. In 1845, it was the first Greek tragedy to be staged in US commercial theaters, though it followed the Sophoclean version. See Hartigan (1995).

women meet in the dark to bury Polynices; Argia eventually escapes, while Antigone is caught and killed.[10] While Alfieri had granted equal importance to the wife and the sister, Varela instead chose the mother, establishing the "matrix" for almost all characterizations of Antigone to come. The new American republics abandoned Antigone's (Greek, European) anti-procreation stance: rarely would an Antígona choose not to be a mother. The duties of burial also began to shift, as these American Antígonas, first incarnated in the character of Argia, began to produce children for the state—albeit children who would be bereft of burial rites. As if foreshadowing the fate of the new republics, these mother-heroines would carry the seed of utopia in the promise of a child. But the utopia—of the child, and of the nation—would soon collide with the historical impossibility of further growth. Tragic motherhood became dramatically linked to national politics, as new *Antígonas* would speak to the paradox of possibilities simultaneously opened and forestalled by Creole American postrevolutionary modernity.

Athens in Buenos Aires, 1810

Varela's embrace of Greece via Italy stemmed in part from the larger anti-Hispanic movement in revolutionary Buenos Aires. During colonial times, other cities on the continent had been identified as "Athens," but by 1810, Buenos Aires—less ambivalent than other cities in opposing what the revolutionaries considered the "barbarism" of Spain's *ancien régime*—carried the mantle.[11] As Gutiérrez articulated, Buenos Aires had been Sparta and was now becoming Athens (1893: 179). By the 1820s, Buenos Aires was known as the "Athens of the River Plate."[12] Although 1824 saw the military victories—at the battles of Junín, on August 6, and Ayacucho, on December 9, both in Peruvian territory—that secured independence in Spanish South America, Buenos Aires had positioned itself at the forefront of regional independence two decades prior, after expelling two British invasions (1806

---

[10] See Apollodorus and Hyginus (2007: 122). See Augoustakis (2010) for an analysis of Statius's female figures.

[11] There were many more "Athens" in the region: Santo Domingo, Lima, Buenos Aires, Bogotá, Cuenca (Ecuador), Matanzas (Cuba), and Saltillo (Mexico). To my knowledge, Arequipa (Peru) and Córdoba (Argentina) were the only "Romes." Brazilian Darcy Ribeiro (1922–97) famously called Brazil "the new Rome" in his book *O Povo Brasileiro, A formação e o sentido do Brasil* (1995: see pp. 38, 58, 65, 71, 125, 199, 265, 454 for mentions of Rome).

[12] See Sáenz Quesada (2001: 271–3).

58 OVERTURE: JUAN CRUZ VARELA'S 1824 *ARGIA*

and 1807) and successfully deposing a Spanish viceroy by popular revolt in 1810.

To reject the Hispanic legacy, revolutionary Buenos Aires embraced French, British, and Italian cultures, an approach promoted by the "Europeanizing" city's minister of government (1821–4) and the nation's first president (1826–7), Bernardino Rivadavia (1780–1845). Buenos Aires did not merely embrace non-Spanish Europe but sought to supersede it. As Domingo Faustino Sarmiento (1811–88), one of the founding fathers of the liberal nation, wrote in his now-legendary *Facundo: Civilization and Barbarism in the Argentine Pampas* (1845, hereafter *Facundo*), "Buenos Aires will realize what France could not, what the British aristocracy did not want, what the despotism of Europe lacks."[13] In Buenos Aires, Rivadavia paved the way for his vision of modernity by securing loans with Britain, making efforts to separate the church from the state, and investing in public works. By 1821, Buenos Aires boasted the region's most liberal electoral laws. Its cultural achievements included the founding of the University of Buenos Aires, the Literary Society, the Beneficent Society, the Academy of Music, the Academy of Medicine, the Academy of Law, and the Academy of Physics and Mathematics.

The 1817 creation of the Society of Good Taste in Theater, which staged English, French, and Italian productions, led to the construction of new theaters. Gutiérrez said that the Society saw itself as "founding the intellectual glory of the fatherland," a parallel to the military, which would establish the territory, and to political leadership, which would achieve peace for the nation (1941: 175). Spanish theater, deemed "gothic absurdism," was brushed aside; works by Corneille, Racine, Piron, and Molière were to be staged instead. The Society's inaugural year saw the premiere of the tragedy *Cornelia Bororquia*, the drama of a beautiful and innocent woman condemned by an Inquisition tribunal but saved at the last minute by "more humane, secular laws." The play preceded by seven years Buenos Aires' ecclesiastical reforms.[14] The city's Creole elites, envisioning an enlightened future for Buenos Aires, ignored the rest of the territory's thirteen provinces and their rural grassroots organizations, caudillos, and culture, which the elites regarded as tied to Spanish influence.

---

[13] Sarmiento ([1845] 2003: 82). Sarmiento served as president of Argentina from 1868 to 1874.
[14] Gutiérrez (1941: 178–9).

OVERTURE: JUAN CRUZ VARELA'S 1824 *ARGIA* 59

Varela was raised in an elite family possessed by patriotic fervor. His father fought against the British invaders in 1807 and was a member of the nascent mercantile bourgeoisie. Like much of his generation, Varela's father was caught between independence politics and the colonial understanding of a "good education," so he gave his son a classical education and sent him to the traditional inland city of Córdoba to pursue ecclesiastical studies. But Varela returned to Buenos Aires with an armload of love poems rather than a cassock.

In Buenos Aires, Varela quickly became a supporter of Rivadavia and joined revolutionary artistic voices. His "Oda a la Victoria de Maipú" ("Ode to Maipú victory," 1818) honored warriors in the battle that secured Chile's independence in 1818. By 1820, Varela was an acclaimed poet. His poems celebrated independence and contemporary national events, including the military campaigns to conquer lands inhabited by indigenous peoples; the war against Brazil; the construction of public works; and the founding of the all-female Beneficent Society in 1823, which assigned a political role to elite women based on their "maternal instincts."[15] As critic Ricardo Rojas would write, Varela was a "political, not a literary" subversive (1960, 4: 644). Although he only saw literary value in the classics, Varela envisioned in his neoclassical poetry a destiny for Buenos Aires that would eclipse that of Europe. He even composed a hymn, "To the glory of Buenos Aires," in which he described the city as "misting over the glory of Athens."[16]

Varela gave his first reading of *Dido* during a literary evening at Rivadavia's private residence in the winter of 1823. As Gutiérrez noted, "This spectacle was new to the nation. A poet drawing the attention of governors" (1941: 185). Varela even dedicated the play to Rivadavia. His friend Esteban de Luca (1786–1824) had already engaged in that political exercise, translating Alfieri's *Philip* (1783) into Spanish to express republican animosity toward tyranny. Varela would no doubt share those republican anxieties, while adding some of his own.

---

[15] For "republican motherhood," see Nari (2004).

[16] Rojas (1960, 4: 642). In the Caribbean, however, poets looked to contemporary events in Greece for inspiration to address their still-colonial situation. In Cuba, still under Spanish rule, neoclassical poet José María Heredia y Heredia (1803–37) praised the wars of independence in South American Hispanic countries and lauded the 1821 Greek War of Independence in his poem "Al alzamiento de los griegos contra los turcos en 1821" (initially published in 1823). See Elina Miranda Cancela, "La lucha por la independencia griega en el imaginario poético cubano del siglo XIX," at http://rialta-ed.com/la-lucha-por-la-independencia-griega-en-el-imaginario-poetico-cubano-del-xix/.

60 OVERTURE: JUAN CRUZ VARELA'S 1824 ARGIA

Though indebted to Alfieri, Varela shifted the focus of the agon from between Antigone and Creon to between the most tyrannical despot and the most suffering mother. In the prologue, he explains: "Alfieri supposes that Argia arrived in Thebes without her son, and [that] Antigone is still alive. I have supposed that Argia arrived in Creon's court after her sister-in-law's death, and bringing her son...The remoteness of these times...gives freedom to poets" (141).[17] Varela's prologue does not dwell on motherhood, instead emphasizing tyranny: "Against all *absolute* monarchs I have fired many bullets" (142). Italicizing twice the phrase "the liberty of my country," the author defended himself from any possible objection to his poetic license in presenting Creon as tyrannical. But Varela's *Argia* defines tyranny rather unconventionally: as an attack on motherhood.

The Murder of a Republican Woman, The Birth of a Republican Mother

Varela chose to dramatize freedom and civic virtue through the sacrifice of a wife and mother. Gutiérrez, in his praise of the tragedy, noted Varela's construction of the vicious tyrant: "The play is a gush of hatred and blood that boisterously clashes with characters made of granite" (1893: 240). But tyranny only acquires these monstrous proportions because Varela relates it directly to the children of the new nation. The play hinges on rendering the sacrificial heroine a mother, but not just any mother: the mother of a son kidnapped by the monarch. An ominous foreshadowing of the necropolitics to come in the next century and a half, not only in Argentina but in the region at large.

The play begins with Argia arriving in Thebes with her son Lisandro. Argia wants her husband's remains and yearns to meet that other woman who has buried her husband. Unbeknownst to Argia, this woman has already been executed. Antígona's death haunts the first scene of act 1. Varela's Creon believes that Antígona felt entitled to the crown. Creon tells Argia that her father, Adrastro, has come to the gates of Thebes to avenge Antígona's death. He even admits that his edict forbidding Polinicio's burial was a trap for Antígona, compelling her to commit a "crime" against the king, therefore providing a public pretext for eliminating her as a political

---

[17] All quotes are my translations from Varela ([1824] 1915).

rival. For Argia, Polinicio died fighting against a monopoly of power, and Antígona is an emblem of justice. The play thus aligns Polinicio, Antígona, Argia, and Adrastro as "the people" fighting for a (republican) division of power against the monarch whose only concern is to keep power.

While Antígona's death is foregrounded, her concern for burials is not. Surprisingly, Argia's quest to recover her husband's remains is quickly halted. As Creon puts it, "What did I care about burying or not burying?" (157). Much like Antígona, Polinicio becomes a haunting specter. He is invoked as a ghost in two instances: first, when Argia calls out to Polinicio in anguish, seeking advice; and again when Creon, in his only moment of fear, asks Polinicio not to show him "the undone members of a horrible rotten corpse lying unburied in the middle of the plains [Pampas]" (249). The sight of a rotting corpse in the Pampas reemerges a century later in Marechal's 1951 *Antígona Vélez*, when Polynices' burial also begins to recede in importance with respect to the politics of the living or becomes the trigger for the political imagination of the future.

Varela's Creon has something more urgent to worry about than burial: he must control Lisandro's education to prevent the child from becoming his enemy. Argia is ordered to return to her homeland without Lisandro. As the role of burial is downplayed, motherhood takes center stage, especially when Creon realizes that Argia could give *him* a new child. Argia thus undergoes a tragic fragmentation. The mother within her splits apart from the woman within her, when Creon offers to save Lisandro's life if she accepts his marriage proposal. Secretly, Creon wishes to poison Polinicio's child so that only his own progeny can inherit the throne. The ancient Antigone did not want to give a child to the city; the modern Argia already has one and can produce many more. The central question in the play is: will she reproduce for the colony or for the new republic?

The woman in Argia explodes in hatred; the mother inside her breaks down. She shouts to Creon:

Argia insults you! The one who begs is a mother.   (160)

Open your ears to the prayer of a mother; do not look at Argia; look, I ask you, at Lisandro's desperate mother…What have you done, where is my son?   (251)

After Argia, as a woman, rejects Creon's proposal several times, he decides to torture her by attacking her as a mother. He tells her that Lisandro will

62 OVERTURE: JUAN CRUZ VARELA'S 1824 *ARGIA*

die in the midst of "barbaric torture"; she will die after being "torn apart" by Lisandro's "long death in a thousand torments" (255). The mother in Argia faints.

After she regains consciousness, the woman in Argia takes the lead—albeit to be sacrificed by the nation, which could do with the child and without the woman. Creon blames Argia for preferring the role of a "heroine" to that of a "tender mother" (272). Here, Argia becomes associated with the often-mentioned heroic "people" resisting the tyrant. From Creon's perspective, *"el pueblo"*—the people—are "rebels." They are the "enemy of the crown"; their "glory" is to "humiliate monarchs" (241). For Creon's advisor, "the people" are "insolent" and "seditious" (245). These "people" are the same revolutionaries whom Varela praises in his patriotic poetry.

In rejecting Creon's advances, Argia seals her fate: death, as a woman. When Creon learns of Adrastro's threat to rescue his daughter, Creon kills Argia in front of her father, then commits suicide. Though unable to meet her, Argia will suffer the same fate as Antígona, choosing to die as a heroine. Here we witness the timid beginning of a dramatic lineage of women who wish not for a relation to the dead brother, but for a relation to other females in Latin American *Antígona* plays.

In act 5, scene 2, Argia's decision to die is presented as an almost-verbatim translation of Antigone's final stand in act 4 of Alfieri's tragedy. As Varela follows Alfieri's rendition of the famous dialogue between Creon and Antigone line by line, we hear echoes of the Italian Antigone in Argia's voice. Varela even draws the reader's attention to this dialogue in his prologue, calling it "sublime" and quoting it in French (144). The dialogue from Alfieri's act 4, scene 1:

CREONTE: Have you chosen?
ANTIGONE: I have chosen.
CREONTE: Hemon?
ANTIGONE: Death.
CREONTE: You will have it.

appears in Varela's act 5, scene 2 (268):

CREÓN: Argia, have you chosen?
ARGIA: Yes.
CREÓN: My hand?

ARGIA: My death.
CREÓN: You will die.

But since the republic needs the mother, Argia's maternal role endures. The new child is the new nation, and so the responsibility is transferred to the real savior, the republican father. Adrastro tells Creon: "I am a father and a monarch: of two such big titles, the first one is for me saintly and the greatest favor I owe to heaven" (213). Creon has been advised to fear Adrastro's paternal rage: a "father who will liberate the world from a monster," as Adrastro promises Argia (223). Once the nation has killed off its woman-warrior, the grandfather and grandson are left to construct the new brotherhood, free of tyrants.

Varela's "freedom from the ancients" became his debt to his contemporaries. He staged a discourse on motherhood that foreshadowed Antígona's life on stage in the region. Mirroring real-life revolutionary rhetoric vis-à-vis women and motherhood, Varela's drama echoed the republican ideology of mothers as simultaneously dangerous and necessary, insofar as the production of a mother depended on the presence of a woman. Tragic heroism was demanded of republican women: they not only had to give birth but also die trying. What mattered for national independence was not dangerous women, but their safe offspring: as women, they stood in for soldiers sacrificing their lives for the nation, while as mothers they sacrificed their lives during birth.

Reading *Argia-Antígona* in Buenos Aires

Varela's extraordinary interpretation of the Antigone myth was lost on critics. Reading Varela, twentieth-century commentators looked not to Varela's text and context but to his intertexts in ancient Greece and the Italian Settecento, denouncing the tragedy as useless for the didactic mission of a "national" theater. In 1944, Ernesto Morales declared that Varela had been a patriotic poet, but that "as a dramatist he leaves his native city and escapes to the past" (115). In 1947, historian Arturo Berenguer Carisomo saw Varela's tragedies as "breaking away from their vital environment" (191). In 1960, Ricardo Rojas wrote that Varela's tragedies distanced the author from "his land, his times, his people" (3: 653). Recent critics have read Varela's play as "clearly imitative" of the Greek texts via

64 OVERTURE: JUAN CRUZ VARELA'S 1824 *ARGIA*

Alfieri's versions.[18] Nicolas Shumway summarizes this view: "Unlike his patriotic verse, neither play has much to do with Argentina...the Rivadavians produced only pale derivations of European literature and society; their sense of 'good taste' encouraged imitation rather than genuine creativity" (1991: 94). Criticizing the postrevolutionary generation's dismissal of traditions such as the *sainete*—a form of popular theater with roots in early Spanish national theater—Shumway concludes, "Argentine literature is best when its writers abandon European models" (96). In a telling confusion, theatrical forms with distinctly Spanish roots do not seem to qualify for Shumway as European models, nor does he account for the fact that Varela's neoclassical education was actually what the Spanish elite schools of the colony fostered. Varela's education was, in that sense, as Spanish as the *sainete*—only it was elite, not popular.

While emphasizing the European source, critics have not explored the significance of a wife and mother (not a virgin and sister) pleading for her child at this particular time and in this particular city. Critics overlook that Varela decided to make Argia not a character in search of her husband's remains, but a mother in search of an abducted child. In other words, they performed a reading that reproduced the very Europeanizing gesture they themselves criticized.

The appropriation of classical material to mobilize an ideology of motherhood and womanhood taking shape with the birth of the republic may be understood in the context of a Catholic culture, in which a virgin can also be a saintly mother—a sanctity that Varela transfers to Adrastro's discourse on the child. But while the Catholic symbol of the Virgin Mary might help elucidate some of Varela's shift in focus from the ancient sister to the sacrificial mother, the political import of mothers in Buenos Aires at the dawn of independence is undoubtedly more relevant.

By the 1820s, the colony's Creole inheritors had already launched the political career of a national ideology of motherhood. In pursuit of territorial expansion, Creoles began sending military campaigns to conquer and populate the vast plains south of Buenos Aires, inhabited by indigenous peoples. The famous slogan, "In America, to govern is to populate"—crafted by politician and diplomat Juan Bautista Alberdi (1810–84) in 1852—captures this spirit. Alberdi established the centrality of "republican mothers" in

---

[18] See Dornheim (2000). Even Vilanova (1999c), who recognizes in passing Varela's innovative role for Argia, sees Varela as imitating the Italian. Bañuls Oller and Crespo Alcalá (2008: 421–3) confuse the plot, saying that the play centers on Creon's denial of Polinicio's burial.

OVERTURE: JUAN CRUZ VARELA'S 1824 *ARGIA* 65

laying the "foundations of the state."[19] Alberdi's declarations would influence the 1853 Argentine Constitution and its notion of the "inhabitant," rather than the "citizen," as its political subject. As written in the Constitution's preamble, freedom was for all "men of the world who want to inhabit Argentine soil," a statement that would shape immigration policies for decades to come.

In this way, the republican elite summoned women's "natural" maternal instincts to play a role in the public sphere. Sarmiento would later write: "The civilization of a people can be judged by the social position of its women."[20] The creation of the Beneficent Society in 1823 granted elite women a new political visibility (and subjectivity). Gutiérrez, praising Varela's poems to the Society, wrote, "A woman is born to be a mother, and one of her principal duties, engraved in her heart, is to educate her children. The idea behind the creation of the Society is to grant this [maternal] instinct the importance of a public function" (1893: 182). As republican mothers in enlightened Buenos Aires, elite women were to run welfare and education for the city's female population, taking that project out of the hands of the Catholic Church.

Ultimately, contemporary reviewers of Varela's tragedy were more astute than their twentieth-century successors. Recognizing *Argia* as more than a "copy," they lauded the tragedy's "high culture," in line with the other contemporary slogan pertaining to the ideology of motherhood: "To govern is to educate." Gutiérrez affirmed that Varela had surpassed his sources: in the land of the new, where only modern things were expected, it took a genius of Varela's stature to succeed in this classic genre.[21]

But Varela had done more than just surpass his sources. He placed Antigone in the midst of what would become two centuries of regional debates over the question of the Creole nation and the national discourse on women as mothers. As early as 1824, Antígona/Argia was enlisted in the army to fight on behalf of new national and against colonial literary traditions. Beginning as a symbol of elite culture, she would gradually become a mediator between the elite and the popular, an advocate for the defense of anti-essentialist notions of national literatures, and a champion of the political questioning of the national liberal projects of the nineteenth century. She would participate in the debate over the definition of the nation's constituency and its modernity. She would gradually question the Creole elite

---

[19] See Alberdi ([1852] 1923: 80).   [20] Sarmiento ([1848] 2001, 11: 87).
[21] Sarmiento ([1848] 2001, 11: 239, 213. See contemporary reviews in Aisemberg (1997, 13–24).

66 OVERTURE: JUAN CRUZ VARELA'S 1824 *ARGIA*

programs that had first summoned her to "become American," demanding that the region radicalize its modernity in order to "mist over the glories of old Europe" (to paraphrase Varela's words above). Most importantly, an ancient Greek fragment was chosen over modern romance to culturally process the nation's birth. On the one hand, the vernacular writing of *Antigone* offered a critique of colonial and neocolonial violence by focusing on the killing of the nation's children; on the other hand, it provided a myriad of "tragic ways of killing a woman."[22] Argia qua woman was a heroine for the people's liberation, but the people (Adrastro) saved her qua mother: the colonial power could only survive by killing its children—the newborn nation. Lisandro's life, rather than Argia's, was at stake. From this point on and throughout the region, the writing of vernacular *Antígona* plays would dwell on the national necessity of mothers and the disposability of women.[23] The chapters that follow show how the first true Americanizations of *Antigone* on the twentieth-century stage reassessed the nineteenth-century foundations of postrevolutionary Creole modernity.

And yet, Varela's play also revealed Argia's female desire, her yearning to meet Antígona—a desire for female companionship unlike the loving relation between mother and child. A desire that, in the nineteenth century, could only take the expression of a desire to die like the other (woman) had died. In the 1950s, another woman would desire Antígona—a real-life audience embodied by the larger-than-life female political figure of Argentine first lady Evita Perón.

---

[22] I use the felicitous title of Loraux's *Tragic Ways of Killing a Woman* (1991). For a study of romance novels and the nation, see Sommer (1991).

[23] For nineteenth-century discourses linking woman and nation, see Masiello (1997) and Barrancos (2002).

1

"To Govern Is to Populate"

Leopoldo Marechal's 1951 *Antígona Vélez*

The problem of the gaucho and the Indian are two especially controversial cores around which the oligarchic republic was inaugurated. They are the first "disappeared" of that initial generative matrix. The other [controversial core] is the European immigrant: the *gringo* from the River Plate.

—David Viñas, *Indios*[1]

It is 1820. Indigenous peoples and Christian Creoles are waging war over land in the Argentine Pampas, a region that Creoles call "the Desert" or "the South."[2] Creole Don Luis Vélez, owner of the hacienda La Postrera, situated at the northern limit of Indian land, has died fighting the Indians.[3] Don Luis' battle companion Don Facundo Galván is now in charge of the hacienda. Prior to the start of the action, Don Luis' sons, Ignacio and Martín, killed each other after Ignacio led an Indian raid against the hacienda. Don Facundo has allowed a wake for Martín but has denied Ignacio burial. Anticipating another Indian attack that night, Don Facundo prepares weapons with his men. Risking her life at the hands of the lurking Indians, Antígona Vélez ventures into the plain to bury her brother. She finds only a black thistle to mark his tomb. A chorus of witches predicts Antígona's death; a "tracker gaucho," Anselmo, identifies her as the trespasser.[4] At noon

---

[1] Viñas (2003: 160; italics in the original). All translations from Spanish are mine, unless otherwise specified.

[2] As explained in the Introduction (n. 6), I have chosen the English term Creole for *criollo/a*.

[3] Indigenous peoples are named "Indians" both in Marechal's play and in Argentine national historiography of the period. I use this term when referring to the play or to national historiography. The category originates in the colony and ideologically constructs indigenous peoples as "barbaric."

[4] A term that emerged in cattle-raising cultures in the late eighteenth century, "gaucho" designates a person of mixed indigenous and Spanish blood, who roams the plains on horseback in search of cattle and land, often in conflict with the Creole inheritors of colonial land. A "tracker" gaucho (*rastreador*) is able to identify the tracks of all animals, how much weight they

---

Antígonas: Writing from Latin America. Moira Fradinger, Oxford University Press. © Moira Fradinger 2023.
DOI: 10.1093/oso/9780192897091.003.0003

68 LEOPOLDO MARECHAL'S 1951 *ANTÍGONA VÉLEZ*

the next day, she has a romantic encounter with her fiancé, Lisandro. Unarmed and forced to dress in men's clothing, Antígona, with Lisandro following, is sent toward Indian land on a sorrel horse, only to be slain by Indian arrows. Their two corpses are found together, pierced by the same arrow. The couple are buried in the form of a cross. Facundo announces that the two are married in death.[5]

A Foundational Myth of National Liberal Historiography

Early in May 1951, Argentine first lady Evita Perón (1919–52) telephoned Leopoldo Marechal (1900–70), asking him to recreate his lost play, *Antígona Vélez*.[6] Other notables had already tried to persuade the writer to do so, among them the poet José María Fernández Unsain (1918–97), at the time the director of the renowned Cervantes Theater in downtown Buenos Aires, and Raúl Apold (1898–1980), then press secretary to President Juan Domingo Perón (1895–1974). Marechal had told them it would take too much time. But Evita's call charmed him.

After Marechal rewrote the play in a marathon two-day session, *Antígona Vélez* was staged at the Cervantes on the day for which Unsain had commissioned it: May 25, the date of one of Argentina's two annual celebrations of independence. It is difficult to conceive of a more iconically Argentine *Antígona* in the 1950s. Everything spoke to the nation's mythical foundations and its contemporary politics. At the time, there was perhaps no greater national icon than Evita herself, and few writers could have been more emblematic of Perón's political movement than Marechal.

Marechal endowed Antígona not only with her first Hispanic surname in the region but also with a claim to land—the colonial and neocolonial problem par excellence. And not just any land: *la Pampa*—the plains south of Buenos Aires. After independence from Spain, the Creole elite imagined it as a "desert," despite its semi-nomadic indigenous populations. On a hill overlooking the banks of the Salado River, La Postrera, the colonial hacienda Antígona would inherit, was situated on the southernmost limit of Creole territory. This historical frontier was constantly threatened by the *malón*: a raid by "barbaric Indians," descending upon Christian towns in

---

were carrying, or how fast they were traveling in the desert. Sarmiento's *Facundo* vividly describes this type of gaucho (see Sarmiento [1845] 2003: 32–3).

[5] All citations in this chapter are my translations from Marechal 1970. There is no complete English translation in print yet. Walter Corbella translated several pages (2008). The first edition was *Antígona Vélez* (Buenos Aires: Ediciones Citerea, 1965).

[6] See Maranghello and Insaurralde (1997: 219–20).

search of cattle, women, and, of course, the land they used to wander before being expelled by Christians.[7]

And Antígona's was not just any time either. Critics have variously located the play's action in the early nineteenth century or amid the so-called "Conquest of the Desert" (1879–83/5), the military campaign that almost wiped out the indigenous peoples in the South.[8] However, the program distributed in 1951 is decisive: "action in the Estancia *La Postrera*, year 1820" (Figure 1.1).

Figure 1.1 *Antígona Vélez*. Program, May 25, 1951, Teatro Cervantes, Buenos Aires. Courtesy of the INET (Archivo Documental del Instituto Nacional de Estudios de Teatro), Buenos Aires, Argentina.

[7] Usually left untranslated, the word *malón* indicates an "Indian gang." A famous hacienda, La Postrera is also a historical site on the banks of the Salado, approximately 170 kilometers south of Buenos Aires, which may have been known to the 1951 audience. In scene 3, after returning from his nightly search for Indians, Lisandro mentions a system of enchained lakes, one of many existing along the Salado, near the bridge: "there was no risk. We went by dry land between Las Encadenadas" ("the enchained lakes," 28).

[8] Maturo (1999: 167) situates the play during the last quarter of the century, when the treaties between Rosas and indigenous peoples fell apart. Gramuglia (2007: 41–50) locates it before Roca's campaign (42 n. 4) following Huber (1974: 150); Adsuar locates it "before 1879" (2004). Romero (1981: 232) and Vilanova (1999b: 140) also place it within the last quarter of the century; Pociña and López (2010: 359) locate it in "an imprecise moment" in the late nineteenth century. Biglieri (2009: 115), follows suit, placing the geographical frontier in the play just prior to Roca's campaign, south of the Quinto River, passing through Trenque Lauquen, Guaminí, and Bahía Blanca; but this follows the itinerary of the Alsina trench (built in 1876)

70 LEOPOLDO MARECHAL'S 1951 ANTÍGONA VÉLEZ

Likewise, the newspaper *La Nación* described the play as devoted to "acts on our land in the first years after independence, 1820, [embodying] the progressive, heroic, tragic conquest of our territory."[9]

Thus, *Antígona Vélez* inhabited the quintessential landscape—mythical, geographic, political—in which the liberal historiography of Argentina's birth set its foundational narrative: the nation's progress from "barbarism to civilization." "Civilization" meant conquering and populating "Indian" land. Antígona would perform the work of culture so famously assigned to women in the Hegelian reading of the tragedy.[10] But, for all that critics wish to see the ancient sister onstage, Marechal's Antígona does not necessarily do the cultural work of burial. The European Antigone had land for burial rites, as the Argive war ended. Her American incarnation would carry out the work of culture by participating in the war for the nation's birth. Antígona's blood would pour (Christian) life into the (indigenous) land: she would be a frontier mother.

And, as if these details did not feature enough *argentinidad*, there was Evita's involvement, along with the play's staging on May 25. While Marechal's drama frames the conflict in the context of the nineteenth-century emergence of the liberal nation, the play's production pointed to yet another nascent moment, the birth of the "popular" nation, defined by Perón's leadership. His two governments (1946–52, 1952–5) dramatically impacted Argentine politics by bringing the political voice of the working classes inside the state.[11] If May 25 stood as a mythical signifier for the nation's independence, the choice of that date in 1951 pointed to the ideology of Peronism as a refoundation of the nation. Marechal's Antígona was as Peronist as she was Argentine.

---

beyond the Salado River, rather than the location in the text, which is the Salado. Pérez Blanco (1984: 164) is the only one who locates the action squarely in 1820.

[9] *La Nación*, May 23, 1951. This is repeated in nearly every 1951 review that I have found. See, for instance, *El Mundo Radial*, May 31; and *Para Tí*, June 6 ("the pampas in the days of 1820"); *Noticias Gráficas*, May 26, which states that the 1820 stage could not have been of "more unlimited projections"; *Mundo Argentino*, June 8, also situates the action in 1820. The one exception is *El Mundo*, May 25, which locates the play around 1860. These and other newspaper titles in this chapter can be found in the archives at the INET (Instituto Nacional de Estudios de Teatro), Buenos Aires, Argentina; Teatro Cervantes Archive; and Biblioteca Nacional, Buenos Aires, Argentina.

[10] See Hegel (1962 and 2018: 259–74).

[11] Perón was elected president in 1946, supported by all provinces except one, the near unanimity of the senate, and two-thirds of the chamber of deputies. He was ousted in 1955 by a military coup.

The stories surrounding the play's production are so rife with national and popular cultural icons of Perón's time that they could be scenes written for the drama itself. Marechal had lost his only copy of the tragedy, having entrusted it to Perón's press secretary Apold or to Fanny Navarro (1920–71), the play's would-be leading actress. According to Navarro's family, it had probably been torn apart by "someone" during a fight.[12] That "someone" was none other than Evita's brother Juan Duarte (1914–53), Navarro's boyfriend at the time. As Marechal was rewriting the play, the employees of the Cervantes would bring newly minted scenes to the theater for rushed rehearsals, sometimes watched by Marechal himself. The director of the play was Enrique Santos Discépolo (1901–51), a personal friend of both Juan Domingo and Evita Perón and known as "the Philosopher of Tango." The music was arranged by Enrique Gatell and another soon-to-be world famous man of tango: Astor Piazzolla (1921–92).

The May 25 premiere was preceded by a performance of the Argentine National Anthem sung by a chorus of 150 voices; the newspaper *Democracia* reported that the audience listened "with profound patriotic fervor."[13] The Cervantes had already earned its Peronist pedigree in 1949, having hosted the first meeting of the National Assembly of the Women's Peronist Party, of which Evita was founder and leader. The theater also organized two exhibitions to accompany the May 25 performance: one dedicated to the "Achievements of the Justicialista Government" and the other to Evita herself, entitled "Eva Perón and Her Social Work."[14]

Newspaper photos of the 1951 production feature the unmistakable dress of nineteenth-century Argentine rural life: the women wear ankle-length folk skirts and have long braids, while the men wear gaucho pants, ponchos, and wide metal belts holding their traditional daggers. The play also included archetypal symbols of life on the Pampas. At the end of one battle, national songs such as *cielitos* and virile dances like "tapping *malambos*" (29) are reported outside the hacienda.[15] It is a legendary "tracker gaucho"

---

[12] See Maranghello and Insaurralde (1997: 220).

[13] *Democracia*, May 25, 1951. Perón used to write in *Democracia* under the pseudonym "Descartes."

[14] Perón's political party is officially named Partido Justicialista (PJ).

[15] *Cielitos* are Plate River dances, which became popular independence chants. *Malambos* are gaucho dances in which, to the sound of guitars, two men compete with one another by tapping their feet to display dexterity.

72   LEOPOLDO MARECHAL'S 1951 *ANTÍGONA VÉLEZ*

who finds Antígona. Set designer Gregorio López Naguil revived the use of the cyclorama to create the illusion of clouds and birds moving over the plains and employed a tilted stage to evoke the open horizon.[16] Liliana López notes that this design inaugurated an official style for Argentine theater, whereby the stage décor would accentuate the landscape and national "types" (2001: 176).

Even Marechal's experimentation with the chorus honored the Pampas. The chorus is divided into male and female sections, including a *Viejo* ("old man") and a *Vieja* ("old woman"), complemented by two additional female groups: the *mozas* ("young ladies") and the *brujas* ("witches," described as "contrary to conventions," "beautiful as evil," and their voices "ironic and prophetic" [13]). The witches anticipate the action, lending a spectral air to the play and conjuring up the folktales of the Pampas about ghostlike souls wandering in the desert (a legend explaining the phenomenon of *ignis fatuus*, or the will o' the wisp).[17] When Antígona screams in scene 2 at the sight of the unburied, the witches foresee Antígona's horse galloping toward Indian land (27).

The press applauded *Antígona Vélez*. Reviewers described it as "our" *Antígona*: "the epic aura of the struggle to conquer the desert."[18] The character of Antígona was "sublime," "pure and loving," and her sacrifice "necessary"; Don Facundo was the defender of "the most Argentine value: the land"; the conflict was between "nascent civilization and barbarism."[19] Writing for *Democracia*, Joaquín Linares observed that 1820 was the "decade of anarchy under the terror of the *montoneras* [rural militias or guerrillas]," and that the drama was set in a "barbaric ambience, with a horizon of spears, savage howls, and incendiary flames" among the "ferocious Indians who bring death to those desolate areas" (June 6, 1951).

The press thought that the play placed Argentina on the world theater map, doing for Argentina "what Alfieri did in Italy, Anouilh in France, [and] O'Neill in the United States."[20] But just as Halperín Donghi observed that

---

[16] See Maranghello and Insaurralde (1997: 221).

[17] The Spanish expression is *luz mala*, "bad light." For mythical ghosts in the Pampas see Crochetti et al. (1997). Critics have associated the witches with Shakespeare's *Macbeth*; see Romero (1981).

[18] *Crítica*, May 25, 1951.

[19] I summarize from all 1951 reviews: *El Líder*, May 27; *Crítica*, May 25; *Democracia*, May 26; *Noticias Gráficas*, May 26; the women's magazine *Para Tí*, June 6; *El Mundo Argentino*, June 8; *Clarín*, May 26. *Democracia* and *Noticias Gráficas* were Peronist; *El Mundo*, *Crítica*, and *El Líder* were Perón supporters as well.

[20] *Para Tí*, June 6, 1951.

Creoles in the 1820s needed to surpass European appropriations of the classics, we could say the same of the audience in the 1950s, who wanted to identify "our" *Antígona*, rather than the European one: the press characterized it as unlike any adaptation of the classic to date.[21] In *Democracia* (June 6, 1951), Linares wrote that Marechal had done something different from "what Goethe did with Iphigenia" in reviving Greek culture or "what Eugene O'Neill had done with Electra" in offering pseudo-scientific Freudian interpretations of the myth. The protagonist was similar to "many women of our race" and in stark contrast to her Greek counterpart, who was full of hatred, hubris, and stubbornness. The play was neither a revival of the Greeks nor that of the Europeans. In short, *Antígona Vélez* was "our" Greece.

Marechal worked with both the ancient text and modern French versions. How could these speak to the most national and popular state-sponsored movement that Argentina had ever known? Was an unburied corpse at the heart of the nation? Or was the story gripping because of the new elements that Marechal had added: Antígona's motherhood-in-death, her consciousness of the land, the haunting presence of indigenous nations? Because of Marechal's subtle critique of liberal historiography? Because Antígona had become mother of the nation, rather than sister of an (un) buried corpse?

Marechal's cultural intervention has garnered robust critical attention in Latin America. Aníbal Biglieri and Graciela Maturo identify three leading approaches: semiotic analysis, comparisons with Sophocles, and historical contextualizations.[22] Critics have alternately regarded the play as a Peronist narrative, a myth of origins, and a description of the national drama of "civilization versus barbarism."

For the most part, historicizing critics manifest their own beliefs about Peronism with their allegorical readings, viewing Peronism as national unification (thus stressing the last scene of the play, where "order" is restored) or a dictatorship (thus emphasizing the resonance between the main

---

[21] In *El Laborista*, May 25, 1951, Livio Mérico decided that Marechal's play was closer to the Greek original than Anouilh's. See also Kuehne (1975: 19–27). Kuehne does not quote the 1951 review.

[22] See Biglieri (2009: 110–22) and Maturo (1999: 170–5). For comparisons with the Greek source, see Kuehne (1975: 19–27); Arlt (1998: 201–12); Huber (1974); Romero (1981), who adds that "Marechal's tragedy does not reach the theatrical 'heights' of Sophocles or Anouilh" (244); Gramuglia (2007: 41–50); González Betancur (2010); Lambruschini (1995);Vilanova (1999b); Bañuls Oller and Alcalá (2008: 429); and Pérez Blanco (1984: 143–72). Pérez Blanco compares the play with the ancient tragedy as well as with Sánchez's Puerto Rican *Antígona*, arguing that Marechal's is "a distortion" of Sophocles in placing the land as a supreme value over the universal principle of freedom. See also Vilanova (1999a: 393–7).

74   LEOPOLDO MARECHAL'S 1951 *ANTÍGONA VÉLEZ*

character's alleged "dictatorial" actions and Perón's purported authoritarianism).[23] When critics project the tropes inherited from the classical tradition onto Marechal's text, they understand the play as a "myth of national origins" and at times invoke Mircea Eliade's concept of myth or Christian mythology.[24] When critics take the Hegelian interpretation of Sophoclean dichotomies as a model, they project them onto the larger-than-life nineteenth-century national narrative of "civilization or barbarism." Such an approach posits the play as yet another entry in the long political and literary saga of this narrative in Argentina, launched in Sarmiento's *Facundo* (1845). For Biglieri, the play expresses in the most "synthetic and eloquent way the entire foundational program of the 1880 Generation in nineteenth-century Argentina" (2009: 123).

Despite their differences, these critical approaches fail to see this play as a result of the heterogeneous cultural dynamics of the ex-colony. They share a focus on the play's Christian drama of redemption, sealed by the last scene in which Antígona's death, like that of Jesus Christ, restores order. Critics then almost invariably conclude that Marechal's play is reactionary: endorsing the conquest of the desert and the narrative of civilization versus barbarism, presenting national reconciliation as doctrine. The final scene prompts critics to ask a question that will recur in readings of subsequent American *Antígonas*: Is this play a tragedy? In her response, Laura Alonso quotes George Steiner—"Where there is compensation, there is justice, not tragedy"—and recalls that "Antígona does not die in vain" (2009: 451).

---

[23] See especially García and Cavallari (1995). For ideological readings of Peronism lacking in both historical understanding and textual evidence, see Pérez Blanco (1984), for whom the text serves Peronist ideology; Kuehne (1975), who confuses the 1940s with the 1910s: "Marechal apparently regarded the fascist-oriented state as the most expedient in confronting widespread strikes and terrorism instigated by anarchists and communist agitators" (25); Brunn (2009), for whom the play belongs in a time "when Argentina was descending further into anti-democratic, anti-liberal politics" (71); and Villaverde (1993), who writes that "the author is inclined toward governments with dictatorial tendencies" (69–70). All of these also take *Sophocles* as a gold standard.

[24] For the use of Eliade's concepts, see Alonso (2009: 439–52); for allusions to the "golden age" and a treatment of foundational rites, see García and Cavallari (1995); see also Pérez Martín (1993: 233–9). For Christian mythology (specifically, Antigone as martyr and the biblical first couple), see González de Díaz Araujo (1983: 225–8); Cicchini (1982), for whom Antígona is the daughter of God, who dies so that man can live; Romero (1981) concentrates on the symbol of the tree and the "first couple" (236); see Gramuglia (2007) for quotations from the Bible. For a reading of Antígona as a Girardian sacrificial scapegoat, see Brunn (2009), who sees the protagonist as partly an outsider to the community, marginal, and misunderstood; but this is contradicted by the text itself.

Nonetheless, the question we should ask is not whether but *where* the tragic imagination resides in this play. In other words, for whom does Antígona "not die in vain"? Only the Creole caudillo, Don Facundo, who enlisted her in the nation's war, benefits from the protagonist's death. The critics' emphasis on the redemptive ending prevents us from seeing Marechal's antiliberal critique, rather than endorsement, of this episode in Argentine historiography. Official, liberal historiography conceived of the South as a desert, bereft of inhabitants, conquered by great military men.[25] Marechal calls this ideology into question by quilting an Indian tragic drama with a Christian drama of redemption. The intratextual suture for both the Indian and the Christian drama is the frontier, at which Marechal inserts his critique of the liberal nation's political imagination concerning women and indigenous peoples. May 25 quilts the play's intratextual and extratextual histories.

Marechal's quilting of the two dramas presents two incommensurate worlds stitched together by two types of conflict. The world of Christians is agonistic: their struggle is dialectical. As a rumination on Varela's Argia, Marechal's Antígona will be a mother who must die for the new nation. But her sacrifice reveals the undialectical nature of the conflict between Christians and Indians. Antígona's death is the prism through which we see the absolute inaccessibility of the Christian world for the Indians. Between Christians and Indians there is not agonism, but tragic antagonism: "civilization" and its absolute other, "barbarism." It is in the antagonic nature of the clash that we find Marechal's tragic drama. To recall the Hegelian narrative of woman being the irony of the community—never fully incorporated into it—the dead woman is now incorporated into the community as mother of the nation, whereas the living Indian represents the irony of the community: never incorporated but always present.[26]

For all critics' insistence on Christian redemption, this redemption is only legible if it is anchored in the heterogeneous, nonredemptive story of the Indian extermination framing the play. Through the latter, Marechal criticizes the Creole redemptive epic. If Antígona's Christ-like sacrifice brings about redemption for the Christians, the Indians end up exactly where they began: removed from Creole land. As David Viñas suggests in

---

[25] The official narrative of "an empty desert" was initiated by the Creoles of the "Generation of 1837." It was translated into the military "Conquest of the Desert" in the 1880s, concealing military genocidal action and suggesting a "natural" extinction of indigenous peoples. See Mases (2002); Lenton (2008: 131–52); Briones (2005).

[26] For a commentary on the Hegelian trope, see Irigaray (1985: 214–27).

76 LEOPOLDO MARECHAL'S 1951 *ANTÍGONA VÉLEZ*

the epigraph to this chapter, theirs is the story of their disappearance. For the liberal nation, the play asserts, an Indian cannot possess the land: he *is* the land. But Marechal's last stroke ironizes this liberal nation: the Indian arrow that kills Antígona is as much inscribed in the fertile future of the nation as her maternal blood.

In fact, this Argentine vernacular inaugurates a twentieth-century tradition of cannibalizing fragments of the Greek tragedy to rewrite the epic narratives with which liberal historiographies justified their politics of population extermination in certain countries after independence, aiming at legitimizing the emergence of neocolonial politics. Since the 1950s, *Antigone* has consistently helped playwrights think through the specificity and meaning of neocolonial politics on the continent: the "necropolitics" of forced disappearance as the Creole elites' only response to rebellions against the unfulfilled promises of modernity. This theme is ruminated in the plays I treat in this book: for example, Rolando Steiner's *Antígona en el infierno* (1958), Griselda Gambaro's *Antígona Furiosa* (1986), Ariel Dorfman's *Viudas* (1981–7), José Watanabe's *Antígona* (2000), Jorge Huertas' *AntígonaS: Linaje de Hembras* (2001), and Perla de la Rosa's *Las voces que incendian el desierto* (2004) (see the Appendix of this book for a comprehensive list of plays).

Don Facundo's lines condense the reasons of state that justify the politics of disappearance. His reasons are none other than those legitimizing the foundation of the modern state as theorized by the early modern European school of political realism in the sixteenth and seventeenth centuries. This modern political imagination invokes the logic of survival—made imperative by an imagined ever-present background of war—as the origin of the idea that state violence is legitimate in order to protect the community. Constitutional historians in Latin America have discerned parallels between the eighteenth- and nineteenth-century wars of independence from Spain and the sixteenth- and seventeenth-century formation of states in Europe. While the French Revolution was underway in Europe, aiming to restrict sovereign power, the American continent by contrast was facing a similar predicament to that of early modern Europe: the establishment of sovereign power.[27] Marechal's Christian drama resonates with early modern narratives of the foundation of the state, whereby politics becomes the logic of survival that can solve the (imagined) background of war. Neither a heroic

---

[27] See, for example, Chiaramonte (2001).

myth nor a civilizing mission, the raison d'être of the early modern state is akin to the vision of the law of Marechal's Facundo, as bringing the end to war by "taking possession of the land" (24).

But perhaps the most interesting thesis that emerges in the play, and reemerges in subsequent regional *Antígonas*, is that through Marechal's critique we see the inherent impossibility of the modern genocidal enterprise, insofar as the latter is carried out against the specific imagination of the premise of universal equality inaugurated by the age of Atlantic revolutions. Neocolonial politics collapses two types of modernity: that which needs the foundation of state power and that which establishes citizenship in terms of equality. This is why citizenship, in the written foundational constitution of the Argentine nation and in the play, rests on the "inhabitant"—he who takes the land. Marechal inscribes the dead Indian in the body of Antígona Vélez, establishing the problem of the new republic's unburied as those who cannot truly disappear. Because two types of modernity overlap at this time, a modern genocidal enterprise aimed at establishing the nation-state cannot but encompass an ominous future brought about by the universal premise of equality in modern states: the disappeared are bound to return to haunt the nation.

Marechal's appropriation of the classic source further develops two latent possibilities in the ancient text, an enhancement for which neocolonial necropolitics likely provided inspiration: first, the question of land; second, the question of the unburied as the disappeared. Land was key to colonial expansion, which, in neocolonial nineteenth-century Argentina, came to define the new nation. Antigone's ancient burial site also refers to land. The messenger conveys to Eurydice: "Lastly we heaped a high-mounded tomb of *his native earth*" (l. 1205; my emphasis). Antigone ties her brother's name to a specific land: Polynices needs to be buried in Thebes. Antigone claims a right to land for her brother; Creon leaves the brother landless in death. And, while the kind of modernity that developed in the colonial Americas was necropolitical, Creon's ancient prohibition of burial may be seen as incipiently necropolitical in that he aims to disappear a name from the community. Polynices' corpse has not disappeared, but the tomb with his name has. His name returns as both the contaminating plague and as Antigone's politics. A threat to the living, a woman; the territory marked by the ritual; and a rotting corpse that resists disappearance at all costs are ancient fragments that allowed Marechal to translate the ancient excess into his version of a modern excess: neocolonial national history.

78 LEOPOLDO MARECHAL'S 1951 *ANTÍGONA VÉLEZ*

Marechal's Literary and Political Universals

"Vanguardist, Catholic, Peronist": critic Jorge Lafforgue's words paint a succinct portrait of Marechal.[28] He was a thinker of "the national," someone who, as Juan W. Wally (2008) put it, "thought and loved Argentina with a passion." The classics, especially *Antigone*, were part and parcel of Marechal's lifelong passions. His youth found him in the company of such contemporaries as Jorge Luis Borges and Ricardo Güiraldes in the 1920s' avant-garde circles of national writers. Marechal had acquired what he termed "ontologies of the South" during childhood summers spent in the southeast Pampas of the province of Buenos Aires at his uncle's house in Maipú, a low, swampy plain area whose main economy was cattle raising. Just as his Antígona discovers the meaning of Don Facundo's law when she encounters the South, Marechal first discovered *la patria* ("the motherland") in the plains south of Buenos Aires.[29] In the 1930s, he embraced Christian existential humanism with a transcendental vision of humankind.[30]

Marechal envisaged a new Argentina, first in Christian nationalism, and then in Peronism. He became a militant as well as an organic intellectual (in the Gramscian sense) of Peronism, occupying public offices from 1943 to 1955. After 1955, when Perón was ousted from power, Marechal was ostracized to such a degree that he called himself "el poeta depuesto" ("the deposed poet") and became so reclusive that he was presumed dead.[31] Marechal's intellectual horizon was a combination of the classics with the political project of third-world nonaligned nationalism and revolution. His vision for Argentine literature was based on the ecumenical, universal impulse of Christianity, though he believed the only way to achieve it was to embrace the local. If Argentine literature was to be Argentine, it had to "go deeper into the autochthonous and thus transcend to the universal."[32] The challenge was to "produce a universal expression of what is ours."[33]

---

[28] See his notes in http://www.lamaquinadeltiempo.com/algode/marechal1.htm.

[29] I translate *patria* as "motherland" instead of "fatherland" for two reasons: first, to be consistent with the poet's work, whereby the homeland is imaged as female, and second, because *patria* in Spanish is often articulated with the image of motherhood, as in the expression *la madre patria* ("the mother fatherland").

[30] For Marechal's complete intellectual biography, see Maturo (1999).

[31] See his "El poeta depuesto," written in epistolary form presumably to his friend José María Castiñeira de Dios, Marechal (2008: 147–65). The text originally appeared in *Nuevos aires*, vol. 1, no. 1 (1970): 55–60.

[32] *La poesía lírica: Lo autóctono y lo foráneo en su contenido esencial*, conference held on June 23, 1949: quoted in Maturo (1999: 59).

[33] Quoted in Maturo (1999: 163).

Becoming poet laureate in Argentina in 1940, Marechal thought a poet should express the "essence" of a people. He returned incessantly to the literary themes of *la patria*, his childhood in rural Buenos Aires, and his ontologies of the South. His writing is permeated with quasi-mythical motifs of the Pampas—its winds; its dryness; its ears of corn; horseback riders, colts, sorrels, mares, cows, and bulls; fires; gauchos and their guitars; witches and healers—motifs that comprise the imagery of *Antígona Vélez*. His first ode to the homeland, "De la patria joven" ("Of the young motherland," 1929), heralds the recurring metaphor of birth or its impossibility: "the motherland is a suffering that our eyes have not learned to cry for."[34] In his 1937 collection on the South, *Poemas australes*, the recurrent figure of the "tamer of horses" (*el domador de caballos*) in his corpus first appears as the great harmonizer of the elements. In 1950, Marechal composed his famous epic ode to the motherland, *Cantata Sanmartiniana*, resonant with Greek choruses, in praise of the Liberator General José de San Martín (1778–1850) in the year officially chosen to honor the great general. Both Perón and Evita attended the premiere in the province of Mendoza, where the *Cantata* was performed to inaugurate a Greek amphitheater in the Andes on the Cerro de la Gloria.[35] In Marechal's 1966 book of poems, *Heptamerón*, his "Discovery of the Motherland" and "Didactics of the Motherland" return to unborn motherland: "the motherland is a suffering that does not yet know its name" (303); "it is necessary to dress her in the metals of war" (306).

In 1948, Marechal published his first "total" novel, *Adán Buenosayres*, canonized after his death as "the Creole *Ulysses*." As in his *Antígona*, the Greek myth and the Bible join the local to describe the poet Adán's pre-death odyssey through the literary and popular myths of Buenos Aires in the 1920s and 30s. In the first chapter of book 3, the main characters discuss national myths: Indians, gauchos, European immigrants, Jews, urban lowlifes, the British, and tango. None ends up representing the nation. The conversation takes place in the Saavedra neighborhood, on the northern edge of Buenos Aires: a frontier space, like the one in *Antígona Vélez*—a "zone where the city and the desert join in a combative embrace, as two

---

[34] *Poesía*, 112. The Spanish reads, "La patria es un dolor que nuestros ojos no aprenden a llorar" in *Poesía* (1924–50), ed. Barcia (1984: 112–13).

[35] This is the Hill of Glory, which houses a monument commemorating the trail followed by San Martín's Army of the Andes to liberate Chile and Peru from the Spanish.

80   LEOPOLDO MARECHAL'S 1951 *ANTÍGONA VÉLEZ*

giants involved in a singular battle" (183).[36] Faithful to the national imagination of the frontier, Marechal includes the Indians in an acid but melancholic page on their "final destiny" (212), a destiny that recurs in *Antígona*:

> [Bernini]: Were they not the natural owners of the pampas? [...] [W]hat right did the whites have to invade Indian land and exterminate them like ferocious beasts? [...]
>
> [Schultze:] Sentimental. [...] If you knew something of history or meta-history, you would not lament that violent clash of two races, one already without a destiny, one with a mission.
>
> [Bernini:] That is pure militarism!...
>
> [Franky:] You are a Teutonic barbarian!
>
> [Schultze:] The world is renewed with the spear of Mars [...] the spear that destroys to reconstruct.
>
> [Bernini:] Poor Indians! We exterminated every last one, here, on this very land where we now stand.   (213)

After this dialogue, an Indian "returns" in an act of surreal appearance and disappearance. Arriving on his horse, he demands that the men pay for their safe passage; the men offer the "magic bottle" of alcohol to the Indian, and the Indian departs. One of the men thinks about the always-already present Indian blood that, instead of disappearing, has impregnated the next national type—the gaucho:

> Del Solar did not justify Bernini's anachronistic lament for the extinction of a race that, in the end, concerned more the prehistory than the history of Argentines. But (*ahí estaba la madre del borrego* [*there was the mother of the stray child*]), that Indian root, right before dying, had left in the pampas a sprout in pain, a heroic prolongation of its blood, a crucial type, flower of war...The Gaucho!   (215; my emphasis)[37]

---

[36] Significantly, Saavedra is associated with foundations: its name honors the first president of the revolutionary 1810 junta, and it is the only neighborhood in Buenos Aires actually "founded" by declaration. Quotations are from Marechal (1948).

[37] In Spanish *borrego* literally means "lamb," but here it is used as slang for the gauchos, who, for the elite, were vagabonds and simpletons.

As in *Antígona*, the novel features an Indian root that would become national legend. Indian agency is associated with the "mother," just as the Indian arrow is associated with the mother-Antígona. Everything in the novel and in the play indicates the violence of "the combative embrace" that bred the hybrid new cultures of the nation—as it bred with violence its mixed population, "flowers of war." In the novel, Marechal manifests admiration for the true rural *criollo* of the Pampas, Liberato Farías (Lisandro Farías in his *El banquete de Severo Arcángelo* [1965]). Liberato embodies the mythical tamer of horses, that vivid memory of Marechal's childhood that symbolizes the tamer of the world. In *Antígona*, Lisandro becomes a man by taming a horse, while Antígona looks on. In the novel, Adán watches Liberato as he tames a horse. In his four *Austral Epitaphs* (1954), Marechal dedicates one to the herdsman of the plains, giving him a name that resonates with *Antígona*—Facundo Corvalán. He dedicates another epitaph to the tamer of horses Celedonio Barral. Echoing Sophocles' first "Ode to Man" in *Antigone*, the epitaph's opening line reads: "In the pampas he tamed all the horses, except for one."[38]

Marechal's vision of tragedy was that the audience would "really experience the risk of tragic passions [...] and thus be inclined not to repeat them."[39] He profoundly admired Sophocles' *Antigone* and had translated it in 1938 for the Amigos del Arte stage, working from Jean Cocteau's French version.[40] Recalling the smell of rotting animals on the plains and the stench of human corpses, in his *Adán Buenosayres* (1948) the poet exclaims: "venerable Antígona! Wrangling with crows and men over her brother's corpse, carrying out the funeral rite at midnight, her soul alone between the dust storm and the stench with which the flesh screams its defeat" (420).

The highly lyrical language in *Antígona Vélez* reworks metaphors and themes of Marechal's early poems and novels. Lisandro Farías is now the fiancé Lisandro, a man taming a horse; Facundo Corvalán the herdsman is now Don Facundo, the man in charge of the hacienda. In Marechal's poem "Second Elegy to the South" (1953), the South is described as "a fruit that I was biting and that has turned bitter on me"; the lyrical "I" laments, "you

---

[38] "Domó en la pampa todos los caballos, menos uno," *Poesía*, 306.

[39] Quoted in Maturo (1999: 165).

[40] Amigos del Arte existed in Buenos Aires from 1924 to 1942. In 1949, the theater group Teatro La Máscara staged Sophocles' *Antigone*. Alejandra Boero played Antigone; in 1982, she performed a loose adaptation of the tragedy called *La ciudad es del que manda* (The city belongs to him who commands). For more on Teatro La Máscara, see Asquini (1990). See also the entry for Boero in Zayas de Lima (1996: 56).

cry [...] for the harvest of men that death gathered on the plains."[41] Similarly, in the play Antígona's South "is bitter because it does not yet give flowers" (46); for Facundo, the men and women in the South "will harvest the fruit of so much blood" (58). In his poetry, the *patria* is a feeling of suffering that "does not yet know its name"; for the female chorus in *Antígona Vélez*, it is "another suffering [...] born to the plains, and we don't yet know its name" (50). And, just as Marechal titles an early poem "Niña de corazón encabritado" ("Child of a bucking heart," 1929), he has Facundo describe Antígona as having a heart that is both "mañero" ("wild," 21) and "enredado" ("snarled," 23).

Threads of National History for the Theatrical Loom: *Caudillo* and *Indian* Wars

Marechal's play is steeped in Argentine historiography. The play's references to the "caudillo wars" and the "Indian wars" depicted in foundational national historiography and renovated in nationalist narratives were part of the culture of Marechal's generation. The Indian *malón* was no longer threatening the elites, but a new figure was—the "gringos," as Viñas reminds us in the epigraph above, impoverished Europeans arriving in the port of Buenos Aires since the mid-nineteenth century, but especially after the "Indian wars" had ended.

The importance of May 25, expressed in the "patriotic fervor" of the audience at the 1951 premiere, stemmed from that date's significance for Argentine citizens from all sides of the ideological spectrum: revolution, popular sovereignty, independence, republican politics, freedom, and transparency. Argentine anxiety over the nation's political origins underlies all this imagery and is reflected in the country's record number of national holidays celebrating independence: May 25 celebrates the 1810 Buenos Aires revolt that ultimately led to independence; July 9 commemorates the actual declaration of independence in 1816 in the northern city of Tucumán; and since 1938, June 20 has honored the national flag and August 17 is dedicated to the Liberator José de San Martín.[42] Marechal's play is about both

---

[41] "El Sur es una fruta que yo mordía y se me ha vuelto amarga"; "Lloras...por la cosecha de hombres que la muerte levantó en la llanura" (*Poesía*, 302).

[42] In 2010, a fifth date was added: the Day of National Sovereignty (November 20), commemorating the triumph against the Anglo-French navy in the Battle of Vuelta de Obligado (1845).

May 25 and July 9. Because May 25 and its symbols recur in other Argentine *Antígona*s, it is worth mentioning here that the date is widely regarded as signifying the popular rejection of the Spanish Crown. During the week of May 18 to 25, 1810, the residents of Buenos Aires deposed the Spanish viceroy Baltasar Hidalgo de Cisneros by gathering at the square that today takes the name of that month: Plaza de Mayo, a major arena for national politics that reappears in later *Antígona*s. On learning that the Primera Junta (First Junta) they had elected had not complied with their May 22 vote to expel the viceroy, the citizenry shouted, "The people want to know what this is about."[43] Historians agree that the crowd sought transparency as much as freedom.

May 25 may remind us of Antigone's rebellion, but July 9 resonates with the ancient fratricidal war: on that day, Creole leaders from most provinces in the territory gathered in the city of Tucumán to declare independence and seal their alliance with a national constitution. Nonetheless, after defeating the royalist armies in 1824, the alliance disbanded amid full-scale armed conflicts known as "the caudillo wars," which lasted until the early 1860s.

Marechal's play is set at the very beginning of these wars. The caudillo leaders of *montoneras* (rural militias) had a following among gauchos and indigenous nations. The conflict centered on whether to form a federation or a centralized government. The Federalists pursued provincial autonomy, while the Unitarians sought centralized power in Buenos Aires. The two caudillo leaders most relevant to Marechal's play are Facundo Quiroga (1788–1835) and Juan Manuel de Rosas (1793–1877). To an Argentine audience, Marechal's Don Facundo immediately evokes Quiroga and, as I argue below, Rosas.

Ruler of the territory of the North (more precisely, La Rioja), Quiroga had legendary courage, earning him the nickname "tigre de los llanos" (tiger of the plains). A Federalist, he was both admired and feared. He lived intermittently in Buenos Aires, during which time he befriended Rosas, the caudillo who controlled the territory surrounding the city. Rosas was also admired and feared. A son of landowners in the province of Buenos Aires, he was raised in the area where Marechal's play is set: the Salado Hacienda, near the banks of the Salado River, the natural border with the indigenous peoples in the province until the 1810s. Land was Rosas' business: he accumulated land

---

[43] In Spanish: "El pueblo quiere saber de qué se trata."

84 LEOPOLDO MARECHAL'S 1951 *ANTÍGONA VÉLEZ*

during his reign, confiscated it from his opponents, and gave it to his supporters. His first official duty was to defend the borderlands of the province against indigenous attacks in 1818; this is Don Facundo's role in *Antígona* in 1820. From 1829 to 1832, Rosas was governor of Buenos Aires; in 1835, he was reappointed, going on to rule for seventeen years with the *Suma del poder público* (extraordinary powers) and the title "Restorer of the Laws and Institutions." Marechal's Don Facundo likewise restores the law with extraordinary powers. A staunch Federalist, Rosas ruthlessly eliminated all his enemies, obtaining de facto national unity. He was demonized as an opponent of democracy but revered by his followers as a nation builder who forged alliances with the masses.[44] Marechal's Don Facundo mercilessly eliminates the enemy Ignacio (and tries to do the same with the Indians), and he achieves Christian "unity" (among Creoles) at the end of the play.

The historical war among the caudillos was "fratricidal." The liberal nation regarded it as a war of "barbaric men." Sarmiento's *Facundo* portrayed caudillos as threats to the "civilized" social contract. But for the elites, "barbarism" was not restricted to caudillo warlords. Just as numerous critics describe Marechal's *Antígona Vélez* as a story of fratricide perpetrated by the Creole brothers Ignacio and Martín, many liberal historians narrate the formative first decades of the nineteenth century emphasizing only the caudillo wars. But while at war with each other, the nineteenth-century "brothers" were waging a parallel war against the indigenous peoples whose help they had enlisted in their fight for independence from Spain. Marechal's play suggests that this parallel war shaped the nation even more than the caudillo wars.

Creole politics with regard to the "Indian question" were in flux during the early decades of the nineteenth century, but critics of the play bypass this history. The 1951 program situates *Antígona Vélez* in 1820, the year when the governor of Buenos Aires, Martín Rodríguez (1771–1845), signed the Pact of Miraflores, establishing the southern border of the province of Buenos Aires south of the Salado River, right where Marechal set his *Antígona Vélez* and where the caudillo Rosas had been raised. But 1820 was also the year that the treaty was broken by a war among "Creole brothers," which Marechal may have intended to echo in the play. For this war involved not only Creole brothers but also "Indians": Federalist Chilean caudillo José

---

[44] On Rosas and Quiroga, see Myers (1995); Halperín Donghi (1965: 121–49).

LEOPOLDO MARECHAL'S 1951 *ANTÍGONA VÉLEZ* 85

Miguel Carrera (1785–1821), who, according to legend, was nicknamed Pichi Rey (little king) among his indigenous followers in the Pampas, led the "*Malón* del Salto" against Unitarians, bringing with him indigenous chief Yanquetruz, two thousand "Indians," and five hundred deserters to attack the Creole frontier with "Indian" territory near the Salado. Marechal's Ignacio likewise brings the Indians to attack La Postrera.[45]

Frontier commander Rosas spent the 1820s signing pacts with, and waging wars against, indigenous peoples, whom he classified as either "friends" or "enemies." Like Antígona's father, Rosas grew up dealing with indigenous peoples, speaking their language; like Antígona's father, Rosas' grandfather died during an indigenous attack in 1793. Rosas' 1833 expedition was such a success that in 1834 he was welcomed back in Buenos Aires as "Hero of the Desert." He had rescued some six hundred captive Creoles, signed a peace pact that would last twenty years (though it would at times be broken), and befriended the great Mapuche chief Calfucurá (?–1873), known as the "Napoleon of the Desert," as well as other famous chiefs who saw him as "the white Indian."[46]

Marechal's play evokes the 1820s and the Indian question, along with the names of military commanders Rodríguez, Rosas, and Quiroga. The Indian question was of vital concern for the new elites, who prepared for the expansion of livestock production for the British market and aspired to create a "modern homogenous nation."[47] When the Miraflores pact was broken in 1820, Martín Rodríguez initiated the military campaigns that foreshadowed the Conquest of the Desert in the 1870s, led by Julio Argentino Roca (1843–1914), the general who would twice serve as the nation's president (1880–6, 1898–1904) and used the military language of "the absolute cleansing" of the territory for a "real conquest." Gradually, indigenous peoples became the first "disappeared of the nation," as Viñas put it.[48]

In Marechal's time, the "Indian question" arose initially amid the possibility of reparations during Hipólito Yrigoyen's democratic government (1916–30) and in the 1940s, when Perón began giving indigenous peoples property titles addressing them as "workers" with work benefits. Marechal

---

[45] Carrera was executed in 1821. Historians Joaquín E. Meabe and Eduardo R. Saguier have described the life of his sister Javiera as an "Antígona of the River Plate." I thank them for providing me their unpublished manuscript about Javiera Carrera's life "Una Antígona Americana en el Río de la Plata (1817–1821)." See https://er-saguier.org/.

[46] When Rosas fell in 1852, his indigenous friends attacked Buenos Aires; see Bernal (1997).

[47] See Lenton (2010: 15).

[48] Viñas (2003: 160). See Halperín Donghi (1963). The ideology of cleansing had already been developed in the writings of the 1820s; see Martín Rodríguez's diary, published in 1969.

86   LEOPOLDO MARECHAL'S 1951 *ANTÍGONA VÉLEZ*

must also have witnessed the 1946 *Malón de la Paz* (Raid of Peace), the first march of indigenous peoples into downtown Buenos Aires to claim their right to the land. Perón received them, only to expel them after learning their demands.[49]

Whereas the caudillo and Indian wars constitute the backdrop for, and textual focus of, Marechal's play, Marechal's life unfolded more broadly amid political and cultural developments that comprised a déjà vu for the Creole elites. As Viñas put it, by the time Marechal was born, the elites were facing another threatening *malón*, again calling into question the definition of *argentinidad*.[50] In the nineteenth century, indigenous peoples referred to the military arm of the elites as "white *malón*" (*wingka aukan*). At the turn of the twentieth century, the Creole elites were seeing their own white *malón*: the European "gringos" (mainly Italians) escaping famine and war. The period of the 1880s to the 1940s witnessed an uninterrupted influx of European immigrants, eager to "make it" in America. Marechal himself was a product of this migration: French on his father's side and Spanish on his mother's. In "El poeta depuesto," Marechal recalls,

> it is said that Roca, looking from the window of the [Government] House at a column of recently disembarked immigrants, asked himself what would happen when the sons of those men reached the government [...] [there was] a minority [the "oligarchy"] that saw this novelty first with proud disdain, then with anxiety, and finally with a fear that today borders on panic. (158)

While initially welcomed, the European immigrants soon threatened Argentine national identity. In 1905, there were more foreigners and children of foreigners in the city of Buenos Aires than native inhabitants. Among these immigrants were Spanish and Italian socialists, anarchists, and communists, including Parisian Communards. In Viñas' words, it was "a red *malón*" that soon transformed "any frustrated settler into an urban anarchist" (2003: 124). Roca's classmate and minister of education, Eduardo Wilde (1844–1913), laughingly referred to the immigrants when he said, "The cows turned out to be bulls for us."[51]

Around this time, a nationalist revision of history, in its conservative as well as democratic forms—a right and left wing of "national"

---

[49] See Valko (2007); Lenton (2010: 85–113).   [50] Viñas (2003: 125).
[51] "Las vacas nos salieron toros," quoted in Viñas (2003: 124).

LEOPOLDO MARECHAL'S 1951 *ANTÍGONA VÉLEZ* 87

thought—emerged with newfound vigor. Historical revisionists busily recast the "barbaric" caudillos, such as Rosas and Facundo, as "builders of national sovereignty."[52] The discourse of "civilization and barbarism" became the war between "Buenos Aires and the interior." The nationalist right wing reawakened the neo-Hispanist discourse of the Conquest of the Desert. This generation inverted Sarmiento's dichotomy: the true Argentina now resided among gauchos and caudillos, not among foreign "gringos."[53] Marechal's play could not have resonated more intensely with his political times.

War: Barbaric National Foundations

The historical context outlined above shows how densely "Argentine" Marechal's *Antígona* was. But how exactly did *Antígona Vélez* intervene in the national narrative of "civilization or barbarism" that Sarmiento's book immortalized and Marechal's generation revisited? Critics have identified differential markers between the civilized and the barbaric in Marechal's language, which Biglieri eloquently summarizes as the "cultural incompatibility" between Indians and Creoles in the face of "an ontological frontier."[54]

Nonetheless, because this is a play framed by the violence of the beginning of war, it highlights the instability of such categories. The text signals the beginning: "*a* combat" (*un combate*, 55) has been won by the end of the play, although critics mistakenly read "*the* combat" instead. The epilogue indicates the war's continuation: Lisandro mentions a certain Captain Rojas and his *blandengues* (frontier cavalry defending haciendas against "Indian" attacks); Anselmo specifies that Rojas seeks to wage war "beyond the frontier of the Salado" (55).[55] Around this time (in 1823), the real-life Rodríguez was able to advance with his military expedition beyond the Salado. As the female chorus says in the epilogue, "[t]he plains are a war that does not

---

[52] National thought developed into popular nationalism, Catholic nationalism, and republican nationalism. Historians of every stripe devoted either a book or an essay to Rosas; see, for instance, Ibarguren (1933); Rosa (1970); Gálvez (1974); Ansaldi (1984).

[53] See Viñas (2003: 117–25); see also Svampa (1994).

[54] Biglieri (2009: 121–2). Most critics devote extensive space to identifying the dichotomies that organize the play and that differentiate "civilization versus barbarism." Pérez Blanco (1984: 148–65), has the most complete version.

[55] The reference to the *blandengues*, considered among the first Argentine patriots, connotes the beginning of the century. These were colonial volunteer militias incorporated in 1816 as "frontier militias."

88 LEOPOLDO MARECHAL'S 1951 *ANTÍGONA VÉLEZ*

know how to sleep" (55). In the context of war, moral debates would become irrelevant: the Creole hacienda is under threat of dissolution.

Consider the surprising (and overlooked) dialogue in scene 1 concerning the community's preoccupation with Ignacio's corpse. The Old Man from the chorus utters the law of burial well before Antígona: "That a brother is here, between his four honored candles, and the other one outside, thrown on the ground like garbage: There are Laws that nobody has written on paper but that nonetheless command" (11).[56] Nobody will dare bury Ignacio, but not because they fear Facundo. Rather, as a man in the chorus explains, "Who will take [a cross] to him? We cannot leave the house: the infidels have surrounded the hill" (12). Facundo has directed his cannons toward the hill; his foreman tells him that the Indians might attack at dawn (20). The men and women stand between the "civilized" (Christian) violence of the waiting cannons and the threatening (Indian) "fury" of the desert.

We first see the slippage between barbarism and civilization in how they both produce excess violence. As the witches state in the epilogue, the deaths of Antígona and Lisandro "*sobraban*" (54): they were excessive. Even if one argues that Sarmiento's narrative of civilization and barbarism is tragic—because barbarism bears the irreversible fatalism of "nature" (as do the gauchos, tyrants, and Indians associated with it)—for him "nature" is nonetheless a fatality reversible by the work of culture. Sarmiento's narrative is a drama of redemption: there was a happy ending for the desert's solitude, despair, evil, and ruggedness. The desert would be redeemed by roads, trains, schools, ports, and, especially, European immigrants raising their peaceful, disciplined children, without violence.

But for Marechal, violence remains the frame of the Pampas—and of the nation—without redemption. Marechal quilts Christian redemption to Indian tragedy to show the surplus of death (of both Creoles and Indians) paving the way for Sarmiento's trains. It is not a war of two different "cultures," civilized and barbaric, but of means—of incommensurate technologies of violence, spears and bullets—over the same desired object: the land. To read Marechal's drama, we may reframe the Hegelian reading of tragedy as the clash between two equally valid ethical substances as the clash between two equally valid violent substances.[57] I have argued elsewhere that *Antigone* involves a confrontation between two forms of politics; in

---

[56] I have found only one article that observes this remarkable line: see Alonso (2009: 446).

[57] See Hegel's *Phenomenology of the Spirit*, chapter 5 ([1807] 2018) and *Aesthetics. Lectures on Fine Art* ([1818–29] 1975).

LEOPOLDO MARECHAL'S 1951 *ANTÍGONA VÉLEZ* 89

Marechal's play, we see a confrontation between two equally barbaric technologies of violence over land.[58]

On the slippery substance of violence, rather than the landscape of the desert confronting two cultures, the map of civilization and barbarism is drawn. Metaphorizing the monopolization of violence on which the notion of the Western state relies, one technology of violence is "civilized" because it is centralized: a single gun shoots many bullets.[59] The other technology is "barbaric": a single spear. Spears need as many men as spears, while many bullets can be shot by one man—a metaphor also for the historical struggle between Federalist and Unitarian Creoles whose difference was the advocacy for or against a centralized power. In scene 1, the two brothers are contrasted in terms of the one and the multiple: Martín is "like a tree: firm, straight, and silent"; Ignacio is "like laughter: he danced on one's body" (14).

While Indians and Creoles share in the violence, their opposition lies not only in their weapons but also in the institutions through which they produce the violence. In the indigenous "irrational" South, violence is natural. Its symbols are duly noted by critics: the "ugly face of the desert" (21); the "fury of the South" (43); "the dust storm" (61); the animals like "demons" (45); "the bitter South" that "does not let love grow" (56); the Indians eating "their mares raw" (18). Creole violence is cultural. The imagery of the furious desert is opposed to the patient, almost painstaking training and socialization of violence at the hacienda. As one of the men in the chorus explains: "We spill our blood [...] thus we have been *taught*, from the time we *learned* how to ride a horse and handle a spear" (21; my emphasis).

The slippage between civilization and barbarism is likewise seen in the play's historical location, period, and names, all of which immerse us in the logic of survival as the only politics possible at the hour of the nation's birth. War is the nation's midwife. Critics usually reference proper names as mere indicators of the play's distance from Greece. They only cite, in passing, Facundo's name as Marechal's invocation of Sarmiento's narrative and the fearless caudillo Facundo Quiroga. Some suggest that Marechal uses that name in accordance with the revisionist history of his era, which vindicated

---

[58] Fradinger (2010: 33–86).
[59] My comment is metaphorical. To be historically precise, the revolving gun was not really in circulation until Samuel Colt's 1836 patented invention. Nonetheless, revolver-type weapons had been known since the sixteenth century in China and Germany.

90 LEOPOLDO MARECHAL'S 1951 *ANTÍGONA VÉLEZ*

caudillos as civilized "authority."[60] However, Marechal criticizes both liberal historiography for situating civilization in the city and nationalist revisionism for linking civilization to the caudillos. In Marechal's play, the two can only be understood amid the backdrop of indigenous extermination. Indeed, "Facundo" is a name pregnant with meaning for the Argentine national imaginary, conjuring up the caudillo against the civilized city. Sarmiento's Facundo stands for "bestial" violence (*hombre bestia*, 63): the passion for evil. Sarmiento opposes Rosas to Facundo only spatially, insofar as Rosas is inside, and not outside, Buenos Aires: Rosas is as barbaric as Facundo, but he is the cold calculation of "evil without passion" (3), a savagery that has coopted the city.[61] For Sarmiento, Facundo's lust for freedom had become the brute force of government in Rosas. Argentine Ezequiel Martínez Estrada put it thus in 1947: the name Rosas signified the "institutionalized caudillo" and the "caudillo-ed institution."[62] Sarmiento's liberal plan for the nation—"to be or not to be savages" (7)—was the elimination of both types of tyrannical caudillos. But Sarmiento had to admit that civilization and barbarism were intimately related: "time will consolidate the work of unitary organization that [Rosas'] crime had initiated" (171).

Marechal takes up Sarmiento precisely where the latter realizes his dichotomies only work in dialectical relation. Marechal's Don Facundo condenses the two caudillos Facundo Quiroga and Rosas into "Don Facundo's reason."[63] With Marechal's pen, Sarmiento's "to be or not to be savages" becomes Facundo's "the land is or is not man's land" (21), the necessary preliminary to civilization. Marechal's Facundo does not antagonize but rather defends the city (or Christian fortress). The words of Sarmiento's Rosas—"he who is not with me is my enemy" (160)—are those of Marechal's Facundo: "the enemies of La Postrera are my enemies" (12).

In turn, Don Facundo's last name, Galván, evokes the mythical gaucho Facundo Corvalán of Marechal's poetry, as well as the neocolonial conquests of the Pampas.[64] There are twin lakes named Galván in 25 de Mayo

---

[60] See Martínez Cuitiño (1982: 38–9); Vilanova (1999b); Adsuar (2004); Lambruschini (1995); Alonso (2009); Romero (1981: 236); Brunn (2009); see Gramuglia (2007: 46–7), for the argument that Don Facundo is both Facundo Quiroga and Perón, who are enlightened despots.

[61] I quote from Sarmiento ([1845] 2003).

[62] "El caudillo institucionalizado y la institución acaudillada," Martínez Estrada (1974: 17).

[63] The Spanish reads: "mi razón" (literally, "my reason"). This connotes "authority" rather than "logic." It also echoes the idiom "tener razón" ("to have reason" or "to be right") and, of course, in the context of the play, the "reason of state."

[64] Adsuar (2004) also notes this name. She interprets it linguistically: in Spanish close to "to galvanize" or "to cover with steel." I thank Ana Puga for suggesting a resemblance to the

County in the province of Buenos Aires, and there is also the Creole Lieutenant Colonel Cándido Galván (1824–1907), who had received a concession to conquer Patagonian lands. Rosas' "Indian" friend, Chief Calfucurá, wrote a letter to president Bartolomé Mitre (1821–1906) alerting him that Galván, "supplier of Bahía [is] very rich and a thief."[65]

While Facundo Galván defends the landowning Christians, the name Ignacio is reminiscent of Rosas' historical enemies. It calls to mind a legendary indigenous chief of the Pampas, whom Chief Calfucurá identifies in his correspondence as another "thief": Ignacio Coliqueo, whose name means "The Blond One." The historical Ignacio (1786–1871) had settled in 1820 in the area of Salinas Grandes, near Bahía, in the province of Buenos Aires. He had refused Calfucurá's invitation to defend Rosas and instead befriended Rosas' enemies. In 1861, Mitre gave him land in Los Toldos, the eventual birthplace of Evita Perón.

Marechal's Martín, Ignacio's brother, is reminiscent of another indigenous chief, Martín Toriano, allied with Rosas and Calfucurá in the defense of the frontiers against other indigenous peoples. The name Martín also recalls the national liberator San Martín (who appears in Marechal's *Cantata*, mentioned above); consider also the connotation of the word *San* (Santo/Saint), which resonates with Martín Vélez's death "like Jesus," as the chorus states.[66]

This sketch aligns Facundo-Rosas-Galván-Martín (Toriano, San Martín) and Calfucurá (allied with Rosas) with the Creole landowners, represented in the play by Facundo Galván. In opposition, Ignacio stands with the enemies of the landowners (Ignacio Coliqueo, Marechal's Antígona, and Evita Perón, at different levels of analysis). Facundo Galván embodies the Creole

---

Spanish noun for a bird of prey, *gavilán*. Marechal wrote a poem about this bird: "Fábula" (1932), in *Poesía* (1984: 122).

[65] Viñas (2003: 100). Bahía Blanca is in the South of Buenos Aires province, near the salt lakes, Salinas Grandes. In the twentieth century, a port named Galván was built there. Chief Calfucurá invaded Bahía in 1859 with three thousand indigenous warriors.

[66] Along with Sarmiento's Facundo, critics associate Martín with another national mythical figure, the gaucho Martín Fierro, immortalized in José Hernández's poem (1872); see Adsuar (2004); Romero (1981); Villaverde (1993: 59). This lacks consistency with the text: Fierro is an outlaw who has left to live among "Indians," and thus is closer to Ignacio in the play. Whether Fierro is the bad outlaw (a liberal version) or the good one ("the people," in the nationalist version), he is dispossessed (unlike Marechal's Martín, who owns the land). Fierro figures in Marechal's world as a symbol of the oppressed nation that has lost its land and rights to the cattle-raising oligarchy; see, for instance, Marechal's 1955 conference *Symbolisms in Martín Fierro*, Talleres Gráficos de Correos y Telecomunicaciones, Buenos Aires. Nonetheless, I agree with Biglieri (2009: 119–22) that there is an intertextual reference to the famous poem in terms of its portrayal of the "Indian."

92 LEOPOLDO MARECHAL'S 1951 *ANTÍGONA VÉLEZ*

landownership required for the "civilized" order that precedes any liberal legal institution. As Facundo puts it in his first confrontation with Antígona, the first "law" is the "law of the plains," which commands Creoles to "take possession of this land and not let it go" (24).

While Facundo Galván is the caudillo-owner associated with the strong executive hand of Rosas, the name Vélez links Antígona with the historical figure who drafted the legal framework to safeguard Creole land: Dalmacio Vélez Sarsfield (1800–75), Sarmiento's friend and contemporary, and lawyer for the legendary caudillo Facundo Quiroga. He crafted the Civil Code that was in place until 1871 and created the first national institute of agronomy in an effort to modernize livestock production. In the play, Antígona's father defends the land not only with the sword but also with the law. She tells Facundo, "My father knew how to pass laws," and "instead of shouting laws, he died for them!" (24). Two modes of action—violent (Don Facundo) and lawful (Antígona's father Vélez)—are used toward the same end: putting indigenous land in Creole hands. And this is precisely what Antígona "understands" when she yields to Facundo's death sentence: the land must be populated.

Marechal's choice of names maps the Creole solution to the problem of landownership in the early nineteenth century: technologies of violence. Historically, though, there had been nonviolent alternatives, one of which was embodied by the Miraflores hacienda itself, the location of the 1820 treaty between governor Martín Rodríguez and indigenous peoples. In 1811, Creole landowner Francisco Hermógenes Ramos Mejía (1773–1828) bought this land from indigenous inhabitants and allowed them to live on his property, showing them how to cultivate the land. In 1814, Ramos Mejía presented a plan to dispense with military intervention and peacefully integrate indigenous peoples and Creoles, granting equal rights to all. When the Miraflores pact was breached, Martín Rodríguez raided Ramos Mejía's hacienda in 1821, accusing him of "befriending savages." Rosas imprisoned Ramos Mejía, his peaceful proposals having become "heretical."[67]

Marechal's tragic frame recasts Sarmiento's fundamental conflict not as a confrontation between Facundo and the (civilized) city, Facundo and Rosas (the Creole brothers), or Ignacio and Martín, but as one between all these and their most radical enemy, the Indian, the ultimate "Other" with whom there can be no negotiation, for he is not a rebel but a heretic—not just because he does not yield to acculturation, but because of a more egregious

---

[67] He was also seen as religiously heretical. See Yunque (1969: 116–17); Ricci (1923).

LEOPOLDO MARECHAL'S 1951 *ANTÍGONA VÉLEZ*   93

failure: Indians will not yield their land. In scene 3, Captain Rojas announces that he will "wipe out the Indians from the desert" (29); in the epilogue, the chorus explains Rojas' wish to go "beyond the Salado" (55). In 1822, Governor Rodríguez declared in his diary that "the war against the Indians must be carried out to the point of extermination" (in 1969: 67). In 1833, Rosas wrote to Facundo: "we will [...] do away with all Indians who are hostile to our frontier" (quoted in Viñas 2003: 61). And in 1880, General Julio A. Roca promised naval officer Dardo Rocha: "we will seal with blood and will smelt with swords, once and for all, this Argentine nationality."[68] Roca had written in his personal notebook: "*La Pampa* has to be occupied, after the destruction of the nests of Indians."[69]

Marechal's critique of the violence upon which Argentina's map was redrawn indicts the surplus of death produced by the "combative embrace" of barbaric arrows and civilized bullets at the heart of the nation—traversing the flesh of Martín, Antígona, Lisandro, and Ignacio. If historically this violence was intended to wipe out the Indians, in the play it does not accomplish its goal: Indians remain inside the nation's Creole body. While Antígona and Lisandro die by an Indian arrow, this is the result of the "civilized" law of Facundo. Critics note that Martín dies with an Indian arrow traversing his chest as if he were Christ, but Ignacio dies with a bullet "starring" his forehead (10–11). Just as the arrow-cross on Martín's chest may refer to Jesus' death, the bullet-star (of epiphany) on Ignacio's forehead may allude to Jesus' birth. The bullet of civilization gives birth to Christ; the arrow of barbarism leads to Christ's redemption. For Marechal, if the sacrifices redeem the conflict for the Creoles, it is only because they carry the imprint of Indian agency—and, what is worse, on the body of the nation's mother.[70]

An Antígona for an American Problem: Frontier Motherhood

Faced with such an urge to survive, under what circumstances and for whom can proper burial rites be a matter of overriding importance? Eager

---

[68] Quoted in Viñas (2003: 107).   [69] Quoted in Schoo Lastra (1937: 188).

[70] As well as the Star of Bethlehem, of course, the Star of David could be considered here. I have not found any analysis of Ignacio's "star," though there are many references to Martín's death; see Romero (1981: 229); González de Díaz Araujo (1983); Cicchini (1982); Romero (1981: 236); Gramuglia (2007); Brunn (2009: 49). Huber (1974) notes the way in which both brothers die but does not analyze the field of signification opened here.

94 LEOPOLDO MARECHAL'S 1951 *ANTÍGONA VÉLEZ*

to revive the Sophoclean text, critics often read this Antígona as defending burial, defiant of Facundo's law. Her confrontation with Facundo is frequently seen as "total, because they both defend two irreconcilable absolutes."[71] But neither burial nor defiance fully characterizes this American heroine. Her interaction with Facundo begins, but does not end, with classical defiance. Rather, the context of war described above transforms this Antígona into what I call a "frontier mother." And while some critics hastily identify Antígona as the Virgin Mary—the *mater dolorosa*—this mother-Antígona does not die as the biblical Virgin does but instead becomes something closer to the figure of a warring Jesus. This Antígona seems to be neither purely Greek nor Catholic: she is heterogeneously American.

As stated above, the community first voices the law of burial. In scene 1, a woman in the chorus asks, "will he not have a cross on his headstone?" In scene 2, the men ask, "what should we do with a dead man lying on the plains? [...] it is an ancient law that commands us to hide our misery beneath the earth" (26). We only see Antígona's classical defiance in scene 2, but by scene 5 this defiance is tamed by her confrontation with the rugged "desert." In scene 2, Facundo justifies his law as "the law of the plains" (24), to which Antígona replies, "What law, sir?"

Facundo's law is to "take possession of this land and not let it go" (24). Antígona concedes this law to be "just," though "they wave a sad banner over it" (24). Since the choruses have already announced the law of burial, Antígona focuses instead on Facundo's use of death. Facundo's punishment is addressed to all living men "who go about wanting to disobey the law of the plains" (24). Antígona's appeal to the godly command for burial comes rather late in this dialogue: "God has mandated burial for the dead" (25).[72] At this moment, she sees indignity in the unburied body; she also sees the "law of the plains" and Ignacio's "betrayal" of this law (24), and finally Facundo's betrayal of the laws that her father would have defended (25). Nonetheless, summoning ancient courage, she goes out into the desert.

But where does her courage really come from and what happens to her for embracing this courage? In scene 2, after confronting Facundo, Antígona leans on the cannon aimed at the desert and stares at the Pampas. Left alone,

---

[71] Gramuglia (2007: 44). This absolute opposition appears in all criticism mentioned above; see this argument as central in López Carmona (1986).

[72] See Gramuglia (2007) for a reading of biblical references in this dialogue, especially Judas' treason in Mark 14:21; see Pérez Martín's description of the "Calvary of the Argentine Passion" (1993: 238). For the play's sources in the colonial period and Golden Age Spanish theatre, see Dubatti (2001: 171–3).

she calls out to Ignacio in motherly despair: "Antígona will look tonight for her lost child [...] over there they have forgotten that Antígona Vélez was the mother of her little siblings. Why doesn't the moon arise against such evil! She would understand how a woman cannot forget the weight of a child when he returns afraid of the darkness with two silver stirrups in his trembling hands!" (27).

First a mother, then a woman, then a man: these are the stages of Antígona's metamorphosis at the frontier, mapped onto the strict, gendered law of the land, which equates women with motherhood. Gendered divisions organize all aspects of life at the hacienda. Men speak of becoming "men" when they ride or tame horses, while women talk of weeping and feelings. Men bleed to death on behalf of the Pampas, and women cry for them. Although Facundo would like to cry and grieve for the unburied, he can't: "It hurts her? It hurts me too! [...] this piece of land will be softened with blood and tears. Let women do the crying! We have to give our blood" (21). Men's relation to the land is also gendered. For Facundo, "The land is or is not man's land. It is not man's land when one has wooed the land as one would woo a fiancée and then has to leave her" (21); "the land is man's land when one can be born and die for her" (22); "I will not let this land go even if women cry and men bleed" (22).[73] Facundo dreams of a land of "men who do not bleed and women who have not learned to cry" (22). Agricultural imagery accompanies the dream: the task is to plant seeds. For Facundo "to bury [Martín] is like planting a good seed" (20). The women's tears will water plants: as Antígona puts it, "to weep is like watering; where we have wept, something will have to flourish" (46).

The law of the land has made Antígona a mother since childhood. She did not become a mother; she was born a mother, to tweak Simone de Beauvoir's famous phrase.[74] Critics lose sight of motherhood, emphasizing instead Antígona's manly transgressions. As María del Carmen Bosch puts it, "Antígona forgot the chores that are proper to her sex: weeping and praying, as the women of the chorus remind her" (1999: 272). However, Antígona is neither a girl nor a boy: rather, she grew up mothering. As she states, "[I had] a duty in these pampas [...] people say that Antígona Vélez never had dolls because she had to be the mother of her siblings" (41).[75]

---

[73] Marechal's words here are all grammatically feminine: *tierra*, *llanura*, and *loma*.

[74] "One is not born, but rather becomes, a woman" is Simone de Beauvoir's iconic phrase ([1947] 1972, 330); the original reads, "On ne naît pas femme: on le devient" (2:267).

[75] Consider, for example, Pianacci's statement: "she does not mention tasks proper to her gender" (2008: 85); López Carmona (1986): "she is the Amazon who wants to substitute man

96 LEOPOLDO MARECHAL'S 1951 *ANTÍGONA VÉLEZ*

Her lack of dolls signifies not boyhood, but her responsibility for real children over toys, as recalled by the chorus: Antígona was the "mother" of her two siblings (34). In scene 2, when Antígona calls out for Ignacio, she says she used to be "the mother of her little siblings" (27). In scene 4, Antígona describes the consolation of her burial rite to Lisandro as the "cry of a newborn" (41). Speaking to the women's chorus, she realizes she "was a mother before being a bride" (48).

Antígona will remain a mother throughout. Though she is surrounded by women—a female chorus, three young ladies, three witches, and her sister Carmen—none of them accompanies Antígona to the desert. They are all too busy with their men. Antígona yearns for a connection with the women around her, but she is only heard when she expresses herself as a mother. Her first address, in fact, is to a nonhuman mythical woman-mother: the moon can illuminate the desert for her search, as it would understand her search "for a lost child" (27). When Antígona is caught, the female chorus splits; some wonder why she did not stay to cry with them—as a woman would do—while others understand Antígona's motherhood: she had to go out because one of Antígona's "children" was lost in the night. And if Antígona briefly feels (patriarchal) womanhood, this is nothing but a passing regret. Before her death, she engages in a long dialogue with the female chorus. Antígona speaks of her regret at not having died the night she buried Ignacio, because after hearing Lisandro's declaration of love at midday, she realizes she had forgotten what love is.

At the frontier, Antígona is most fittingly perceived through the lens of an American problem. Her role is not to limit the powers that be, as it was for Antigone in democratic Athens, but to aid in the establishment of a new political constituency. Her sacrificial blood will be at once manly and motherly, much as her native language's construction of the nation is multi-gendered, the *madre patria* ("the mother(father)land"). The clearest dramatization of Antígona's American problem is her desert epiphany. Just as the European encounter with the "wilderness" of America is revelatory in so many narratives of conquerors and settlers, Antígona's experience of the land's ruggedness makes her understand Facundo's law. And, just as in Varela's *Argia*, the individual brother cedes in importance to the urgency of the greater cause: the nation. At noon, having been condemned and dressed as a man, Antígona tells the female chorus (Figure 1.2):

when he is required by the pampas" (38); Romero (1981: 233) is the only one who comments on motherhood, albeit in passing.

Figure 1.2 *Antígona Vélez.* May 25, 1951. Fanny Navarro as Antígona. Teatro Cervantes, Buenos Aires, Argentina.

Courtesy of Susana Arenz of the INET (Archivo Documental del Instituto Nacional de Estudios de Teatro), Buenos Aires.

> Women, have you not already discovered the true face of the South? The South is bitter, because it still has no flowers to give. This is what the man who condemns me today learned a long time ago. I learned it last night, while I looked for a flower for Ignacio's grave and could only find the thorns of a black thistle. (46)

And:

> The man who now condemns me is harsh because he is right. He wants to conquer this desert [...] so that children can play without fear [...] he wants to populate the South with flowers! And he knows that Antígona Vélez, riding dead on a bloody sorrel horse, could be the first flower in the garden that he seeks. (47)

Antígona's contact with the desert at midnight teaches her "what could blossom" with her death (47). The plains are infertile. There are no flowers to bury one's dead. If the "universal" Antigone who defends burial in times of peace can exist in this land, a previous Antígona must first exist: an Antígona of war. She must first secure the land; then, only then, burial.

In Christian cosmology, there is only one mother who can conceive without male participation, and Antígona is as far from the Virgin Mary as she is from the Greek virgin. Thus, before being dressed as a man, Antígona will also require another epiphany: a man, to whom she will be married in death.[76] In scene 4, a midday romantic encounter takes place between Antígona and Lisandro under an *ombú*—a tree characteristic of the Pampas— that stands on the hill. Stage directions indicate "a biblical image: the first couple beside the first tree" (40; Figure 1.3).

Lisandro reminds her they are not just "siblings," that they became a man and a woman when they were fifteen. Blood and water, the two fluids signifying gender throughout the play, mark the entrance of the two lovers into adulthood. Lisandro narrates how he had to tame a horse and dismounted with bloody wounds on his hands. Antígona had been watching him the whole time, and he could only think of her eyes as he rode. Antígona, crying, washed and kissed his hands. Now under the tree, Lisandro makes her realize that "he who mounted the horse was a child, he who dismounted was a man [...] and she who followed him with her eyes began her crying as a child and ended up crying as a woman" (43; Figure 1.4).

As a mother who has now realized the (patriarchal) difference between motherly and womanly love, Antígona is now ready to ride the horse into Indian land. For Facundo, "everything will be decided by the legs of a horse. Between her law and mine, let God be the judge" (39). Antígona tells her fiancé the same: "God will speak in the legs of that horse" (40). Antígona will die bleeding, like a man, but fertilizing, like a woman. Thus, she must not ride alone: at the last minute, Lisandro rides along with her, toward his own death.

Facundo's last line resonates with Antígona's: the bloodshed will yield a future. As the play closes, a melancholy clarinet sounds. A sergeant and his soldiers appear at La Postrera carrying the dead bodies of Antígona and Lisandro, both pierced by the same Indian arrow. Following Facundo's order to bury them, the bearers arrange the bodies to form a cross on the ground under the same *ombú* tree under which they stood as lovers in the previous scene. For the witches, "together they formed, against hatred, one heart, broken" (55). For Facundo, "they are married" (58). A man from the chorus

---

[76] Love (rather than the rugged desert) is usually cited as the source of Antígona's transformation; see, for instance, Bañuls Oller and Alcalá (2008: 429–30).

LEOPOLDO MARECHAL'S 1951 *ANTÍGONA VÉLEZ* 99

Figure 1.3 *Antígona Vélez*. Directed by Oscar Ponferrada at the Theater of Nations. Sarah Bernhardt Theatre, May 9, 1962, Paris, France.
Courtesy of BNF: Bibliotèque Nationale de France, Site Richelieu.

Figure 1.4 *Antígona Vélez*. Premiere May 25, 1951. Fanny Navarro and Daniel Alvarado. Teatro Cervantes, Buenos Aires, Argentina. Archivo Histórico del Teatro Nacional Cervantes. Buenos Aires.

Source: *Mundo Radial*, June 7, 1951.

tells him they won't give him grandchildren. Facundo corrects him. Their children will be "all the men and women who one day will reap the fruits of so much bloodshed" (58).

Marechal's Facundo is neither excessive nor wrong, but a necessary evil. It is not only Antígona's dutiful understanding of the law of the land but also her predestined motherhood that transforms Facundo into a needed political figure for the future: the landowner who is now also the priest-father, who has carried out the sacrificial rite that founds the nation, to conquer, to civilize, to populate the Pampas once they have been emptied. When Facundo hears that Captain Rojas will "wipe the plains clean of Indians" (29), he is pleased: "May God desire it. There is not a single rose or ear of corn to the South" (29). By the end of the play, Facundo has planted the roses of Antígona's motherhood, having carried out the landowner and the military's evangelical mission to bring Argentina into liberal modernity. This was the goal of the historical "Second Conquest" of the so-called desert: a remake of the first one by Spanish conquerors accompanied by the Church. On the altar of the land, however, the liturgy has needed more than Antígona's white chalice; the rite is not complete without the Indian arrow-cross: Indian agency, once again in play.

Crossings on the Dramatic Frontier: "Indian" Noise

At the heart of Marechal's quilting of the Indian and the Christian dramas are two mysteries that critics have not solved. These mysteries encode the text's marks of colonial hybridization, formally and thematically. They cipher Marechal's critique of an era's neocolonial imagination about "Indians" and their relation to land, women, and civilization. First, Antígona is killed as a man: Why does she cross the frontier in male drag? Second, Ignacio leaves the hacienda to go with the Indians: Why does he return with the *malón*?

Indian agency is invisible onstage. It can only be tracked in the words of Creole characters, through whom we know that Indians do not want to be seen. In scene 1, the Creole men say, "They are outside with an open eye" (12). In scene 2, Facundo asks, "Have you seen anything outside?" The men reply that they have not: the Indians will not light a fire at night, for that would make them too much of a target (20). Indians are cast as a ghostly threat, as Christians anxiously await the confrontation. In scene 1, the men imagine the Indians in action during the night; the women wonder, "What

102 LEOPOLDO MARECHAL'S 1951 *ANTÍGONA VÉLEZ*

if they attacked during the night?" (13); the men will remain by their cannons, waiting, just in case.

But even more than in words, Indian agency may be discerned in how Antígona (and by extension Lisandro), Ignacio, and Facundo (metaphorically) cross the frontier. Marechal makes these crossings symptomatic of what the Creole elites imagined (or could not imagine) about Indian agency: an Indian, by definition, could not claim the land, could not impregnate a white woman, and could not offer any political alternative other than embodying the enemy that would justify the unification of the Creoles into a state. A frontier is not just a spatial partition.[77] It is also the limit of an era's imagination.

Throughout the twentieth century, historians and anthropologists have reconfigured the frontier (geographical, ideological, political, or cultural) as a space for the production of difference. The Argentine Pampas of the nineteenth century have been reconceived as a frontier of dynamic and fluid negotiation between cultures—not just confrontation.[78] This does not contradict the perception of frontier literature as Viñas put it: "an elementary drama. Pure war" (2003: 54). Rather, it endows the frontier with complexity: a site for the production of new subjectivities, hybrids, subversions, and reversals. Marechal's frontier is one such space of subversion.

The three crossings at the frontier that I referred to above are hybrids that blur dichotomies, illuminate fantasies of purity, and conceal other possibilities that may have been revealed by frontier exchanges. Facundo's metaphoric crossing transforms him into a "barbarian" because of his decision; the Christian Ignacio's willful crossing turns him into an "Indian enemy." Antígona's forced crossing is the most paradoxical: it transforms her into a man in the eyes of the Indians and into a real mother in the eyes of the Creoles (it also transforms Lisandro into a feminine man, for he is guided by love, which in the play belongs to the feminine). Antigone's "cannibalization" here is complete.

These crossings, dismantling dichotomic thinking, render Facundo an "enlightened dictator," Ignacio a "white Indian," and Antígona both a "male woman" and a "virgin mother." The "enlightened dictator" undoes the imaginary opposition of a nondictatorial "enlightened government" and an unenlightened "dictatorship." The "white Indian" unravels the imaginary

---

[77] Although Arlt (1998) identifies the play as belonging to the corpus of Argentine "frontier literature," she refers to the geographic and historical border at stake.

[78] On the Pampas, see Mandrini (2006) and Mandrini and Paz (2002).

racial purity of "white" and "Indian." The same goes for gender: the "male woman" and the "virgin mother" reveal "woman and man" to be constructions positing the terms as clearly distinct.

Antígona significantly refers to Facundo's "barbaric" decision as crossing a frontier: "God has erected his frontier at death. And even if men mounted all the horses of their fury, they wouldn't be able to cross that frontier and reach Ignacio Vélez to inflict upon him another wound" (23). Facundo's crossing into "barbarism" partakes in the modern philosophical imagination of the nature of the state, for which thinking outside of monopolizing violence implied savagery. His "enlightened dictatorship" unveils the Western exclusion of civic organizations other than the state. The plains were historically replete with alternative indigenous organizations.

But there is something special about Ignacio's and Antígona's crossings: they are metatheatrical. Ignacio's crossing deceives Christians in the realm of culture and politics; in terms of blood, he will be seen as Christian, which is why his decision appears to be willful. At first glance, the deception functions so that he may be left unburied: he is a "traitor." But Ignacio's "Indianness" speaks to a specific national imagination about the Indian in relation to land.

Ignacio is the white man who "crossed sides": in scene 1 the Spanish reads, "*se pasó a los indios*" (11, "he went with the Indians"), a common nineteenth-century expression for Creoles living in Indian territory, having crossed frontiers under duress as captives, or willingly, or simply because of the harshness of frontier living conditions. Historians describe willing Creoles crossing the frontier as "renegades," "refugees," "transculturites," or "allies."[79]

The play is vague about why Ignacio has "gone with the Indians." A man from the chorus says that Ignacio, "*un Cristiano de sangre*" (11, "a full-blooded Christian"), had returned to the hacienda by night with the *malón*, wanting to be the "owner of this house, this land, and its 10,000 red head of cattle" (11). The terms are irreversible: Ignacio's Christianity is a "blood" fact. He has only become an Indian temporarily, by dint of using their weapons. Another man puts it more politically: Ignacio had "*deserted* and returned as an *enemy*" (12; my emphasis). But, as another chorus man explains, he is also likely rebelling against Facundo's control of the hacienda, which is not based on kinship: "[Facundo] stayed on this hill, with Don

---

[79] See Villar, Jiménez, and Ratto (1998); and Operé (2001).

104 LEOPOLDO MARECHAL'S 1951 *ANTÍGONA VÉLEZ*

Luis' sons [...] His goal was to remain on this land with the cattle until Ignacio and Martín could handle the sword against the southern rabble, and the plow on this barren, cropless land" (12). Facundo did not own the land; should he have handed over the property to the brothers but has not done so? Another chorus man asks whether anyone denied Ignacio the land. Facundo claims that "it is and will be Vélez land" (12), but also gives no hint of stepping down.

Ignacio returns with the Indians as the only "Indian" with a name. Ignacio has become a barbarized white—or maybe an "Indianized white"— rather than a "white Indian," as the mestizo children of white women and Indian men would be called. While nameless Indians travel "from the South to rob females and horses" (22), Ignacio, the Indian with a name, comes with a different, more radical purpose. He arrives as the owner of the house, the land, and the cattle. An Indian only claims goods; Ignacio claims the land. He illuminates the relationship between the Indians and ownership for the Creole imagination. He is not a full-blooded Indian, because for Creoles an Indian, by definition, cannot claim the land. Rather, an Indian is the land—to be claimed by whites. (The political memory of the colonial *encomiendas*, whereby land would be granted to colonizers *with* whomever inhabited it, surfaces here).

Like Ignacio's, Antígona's crossing is a theatrical disguise. Male drag, however, is forced upon her, and so we must assume that it conceals something more disturbing for the Creole imaginary than Ignacio's disguise or, for that matter, Lisandro's sudden "feminization" as he is overcome by passion. Both Ignacio and Lisandro act willfully: because Christianity is a bodily fact—a blood rite—they will not become Indian, despite their actions. Women present a different challenge for the Creole imaginary: their blood can become Indian in the form of their offspring.

Historical research shows that a white woman, like Antígona, riding a horse, would most likely not have been killed but instead would have been taken captive by Indians. In his study of intertextuality in Marechal's play, Biglieri references Esteban Echeverría's epic poem "La Cautiva" ("The captive," 1837), but does not connect it with Antígona's clothing. Narratives of captive men and women constitute a continental genre of a New World literary tradition; however, these formalized accounts are curiously absent from the Argentine tradition. In an attempt to recover this memory, Susana Rotker includes the white captive women of the Pampas among the nineteenth-century disappeared from the nation (the Indian and the gaucho). As Rotker (1999) reminds us, the captive woman in Echeverría's poem conveniently dies with her "honor" unsullied by Indian hands. So, too, must Antígona. In real life, rescued captive women were shunned by society, to the point that some would choose to remain a captive of the Indians rather than "be servants to the Federalists."[80]

Antígona's cross-dressing rules out her becoming the mother of an Indian. Like the land, a white woman and a child are to be taken by Creoles. Facundo himself makes this connection between a woman and the land, which once courted should not be left (21). Alberdi's dictum "to govern is to populate" had meant to populate with white immigrants rather than "white Indians" (children of white women and Indian men) or "Indian whites" (children of white men and Indian women).[81]

For Facundo, it is better to see Antígona's death than witness the horror of her Indian pregnancy. But Antígona reminds her audience that such "horror" did in fact occur at the nation's birth. Recall Marechal's *Adán Buenosayres*: there *had* been a "mother of a child" (a stray child), an "Indian root" leaving a "heroic prolongation of its blood, a flower of war" (215). A mother-warrior, Antígona must die giving birth to flowers that will make the desert grow. But Marechal's irony lies in the technology that impregnates Antígona: an Indian arrow. She is joined in "marriage" by the Creole caudillo to a Creole son. But whose children are Antígona's? Those of the caudillo that gave the order to kill her, or the Indian who executed the order? The nation, ironically, results from a tacit pact between the caudillo who commands and the Indian who shoots the arrow.

The *Antígona* of Los Toldos and Greek "Universals"

Antígona Vélez fits seamlessly into the cultural politics of 1951 Buenos Aires. Critics tend to interpret Facundo as a stand-in for Perón, identifying the two leaders as authoritarian.[82] But Facundo's "reason" is a reason of war, akin to a "reason of state," in line with the Western tradition of political realism concerning the state's monopoly on violence rather than with a

---

[80] Unitarian general Manuel Baigorria's female companion says these words when he takes refuge with indigenous peoples and she decides to do the same; see Baigorria (1975: 74).

[81] Juan Bautista Alberdi ([1852] 1923: 80).

[82] Official Peronist discourse did not associate Perón with Facundo or Rosas, but rather with the Liberator San Martín, and designated 1950 the "año Sanmartiniano." The association between Perón and Rosas arose with 1960s revisionism. See Halperín Donghi (1996).

106   LEOPOLDO MARECHAL'S 1951 *ANTÍGONA VÉLEZ*

specific historical regime. Parallels are more easily found in Antígona Vélez as a rumination of Varela's Argia, in the connection between Antígona and the real-life Evita, and between Marechal's "nationalist classicism" and the "strategic classicism" of Peronist cultural politics. It is more accurate to say that Facundo embodies Marechal's reading and criticism of the Peronist hopes for any pure construction of the "national."

The opposition of national–foreign was central to Peronist politics. Appropriately, the ultimate frontier dramatized in Marechal's play is the performance itself: the contact between the nation and the world. What joins and separates the pairings of "woman–man," "Indian–Christian," and "barbarism–civilization" is subsumed in the dichotomy of "national" and/or "foreign" literature and the particular resolution to that dichotomy offered by Marechal's play. The cultural frontier between "Greek" (foreign) and "Argentine" (national) solved a problem for the real-life cultural politics at stake, for the dichotomy in question vanished: the "Greek universal" and "Argentine national" at the frontier produced a concrete (not abstract) "Argentine universal."

For Marechal, Peronism was "the only popular revolution" granting Argentines national sovereignty and social justice.[83] The goal was to make "culture" accessible to workers, resulting in a massive "symbolic takeover of the city" by the popular sectors of society, as Ballent puts it (2004: 318).[84] Peronism, in turn, had a complex national cultural politics aimed at "homogenization" through education, theater, sports, and the media. Nonetheless, despite conceiving a national culture in opposition to the "foreign," this politics soon proved unsustainable. Peronism had to contend with the colonial, neocolonial, and anticolonial mix of Argentina's intellectual worlds, and particularly those of Buenos Aires, intimately linked to (certain) European countries. Thus, cultural politics took an interesting turn during this period: not quite national and not quite foreign.

In the theater, this meant both making "universal theater" accessible to the people and rescuing national theater. In 1949, the Argentine Society of Authors established that 50 percent of national and international playwrights should be staged.[85] Laura Mogliani describes it as a question of both "popular and traditional art, [and] the adaptation of 'classical' texts," to the popular sectors. We must understand in this context the staging of Sophocles' *Electra* and Shakespeare's *The Taming of the Shrew* at the Law

---

[83]   See his "El poeta depuesto" ([1970] 2008: 150–1).
[84]   See also Chamosa and Karush (2010).   [85]   See López in Pellettieri (2001: 174).

LEOPOLDO MARECHAL'S 1951 *ANTÍGONA VÉLEZ* 107

School of the University of Buenos Aires for the First Festival of October 17, 1950, celebrating the Day of Peronist Loyalty.[86]

One may see the classics as legitimizing Peronist cultural politics, but in the context of this study, I suggest we see here the drama of a Creole impossibility epitomizing the problem of postrevolutionary national culture: fixing national cultural frontiers in the neocolonial nation. Here would be the inevitability, for any attempt at the construction of a modern "national literature," of a disarticulation of the opposition between national and foreign, which could happen with the third category of "the universal"—the universal always cannibalized by the local. The cultural work of "the universal" is to help displace "the national" crafted by elites, offering instead the possibility of the emergence of various points of view, as different constituencies cannibalize "the universal" and incorporate it into the "motley" national.

Marechal's *Antígona Vélez* is the first American *Antígona* in which we can fully sense the ambiguity established in José Martí's expression "Our Greece." Martí used the phrase as a contrast between the Amerindian and the Greek antiquities. Marechal turned the Greece lingering in Martí's rhetoric into something "American"—enhancing, via cultural rumination, Varela's initial gesture of 1824. Greece was not a "found antiquity" for Americans (for elites to discover their "Western origins") but a cluster of fragments available to construct "our" alternative, modern, "antiquities"—remnants of the colony that could be transformed by the popular revolution in which Marechal believed.

Antígona Vélez condensed every possible world of 1951 Buenos Aires: it belonged to the classical, universal world as much as to the local, traditional Argentina. It made Greece part of Argentina as much as it made Argentina part of the universal. It was equally steeped in national history, national liberal historiography, and nationalist revisionism; it was as much surrounded by icons of the neo-Hispanist nationalism of Peronism's military wing as it was by the icons of Peronism's most popular wing. Evita Perón's aura hovered above it all.

As for Evita, the woman who desired Antígona as much as Antígona desires a relation to all the women around her onstage, 1951 was Evita's sacrificial year. She announced her decision to resign her candidacy for vice president in a massive gathering at the Plaza de Mayo, marked by references to 1810: "[these are] the people of 1810 who gathered to ask what it was all

---

[86] Mogliani (2006: 3). See also Mogliani (2005a: 25–8; 2005b: 201–8). The "Day of Peronist Loyalty" commemorates the workers' demand for Perón's liberation in 1945. For Marechal, both May 25 and October 17 were "national popular revolutions" (see his "El poeta depuesto"). Marechal, Discépolo, Fanny Navarro, and Evita herself were involved in these productions. See López in Pellettieri (2001: 173–81).

108 LEOPOLDO MARECHAL'S 1951 *ANTÍGONA VÉLEZ*

about"; to Christianity: "here the 2,000-year-old miracle happens again: the humble [are those who believe]"; and to sacrifice. Historian Fermín Chávez (1924–2006) called Evita "the Antígona of Los Toldos." Interestingly, Los Toldos, her hometown, was the place where the Indian Ignacio Coliqueo settled after he was given land. Evita was born with the assistance of an indigenous midwife, and close to Coliqueo's land (the word *toldos* is a colloquial way of describing Indian dwellings).

Critic M. Dolores Adsuar (2004) suggests that Antígona's sacrificial lines echo Evita's speeches. Argentine anecdotes and iconography of Evita's sainthood abound. The poet José María Castiñeira de Dios, Marechal's close friend and, by then, Undersecretary of Culture, recounts witnessing a poor woman, with a hideous sore on her face, approach Evita at the Ministry of Labor, intending to kiss her. Castiñeira de Dios heard that the wound could be syphilitic and tried to prevent the woman from getting too close to the first lady. But Evita brushed him aside and let the woman kiss her. This inspired Castiñeira de Dios to write a poem comparing Evita to the mythical pelican that nourishes its young with its own lifeblood.[87]

In cannibalizing *Antigone*, Marechal imagined the beginnings of the nation's foundational war. If Marechal's generation dreamed of brotherly reconciliation—San Martín, Facundo, Rosas, and Perón—his *Antígona* transformed it into a tragedy. His play asked if the Indians, Antígona, and Evita were the necessary sacrifice for the new pact among brothers. At the time, reviewers responded with a resoundingly unanimous yes; both Peronists and anti-Peronists saw the play as "our *Antígona*." The play won the First National Theater Award in 1954. Since then, the play has been regularly staged across the country. On May 9, 1962, director Juan Oscar Ponferrada staged it at the Theater of Nations in Paris. André Camp wrote in *France Inter* of its "undeniable lyrical air."[88] It might have been the lyrical air of being in-between everywhere, neither here nor there, at the frontier: both Greek and Argentine, elitist and popular, universal and local, rural and urban, tragic and dramatic, popular and neo-Hispanist Peronist—an unstable frontier that, most of all, exposed cultural anxieties regarding the impossibility of fixing the meaning of mother (a female child caregiver who, as an adult, has to dress as a man to avoid impregnation with the wrong seed) and by extension, the meaning of motherland.

[87] See Navarro (2005: 271).

[88] "Soirées de Paris," May 16, 1962. An innovative production was directed by Pompeyo Audivert in 2011, once again staged at the Cervantes Theater (with references to the disappeared of the 1976–83 dictatorship).

2

For the People, By the People, With the People

Félix Morisseau-Leroy's 1953 Vodou *Antigòn an Kreyòl*

"Thank you Dessalines/ It is you who taught us to say NO"
("Mèsi Papa Desalin"/"Thank you Papa Dessalines")[1]

In the Haitian peasant village of Teb, the rural chief Créon has prohibited the burial of Polinice after quashing the rebellion. At Créon's house, Antigòn and Ismène quarrel over Antigòn's decision to bury their rebel brother. At the request of Ismène, their godmother Marraine calls on the Vodou spirits for help. Papa Legba is heard first but cannot help. Tiresias asks Créon to undo his edict, but Créon instead orders Tiresias to call on the Vodou spirit Ezili Freda. She feels she is not respected. Antigòn buries her brother and is imprisoned. Hémon sides with her. Créon tries to turn her into a zombie, summoning the Vodou spirits of the dead for help. He places a knife in a bowl of water, and the water turns red. Ezili returns to the house and,

---

[1] Félix Morisseau-Leroy, "Thank you Dessalines" (1953), translated into English in *Haitiad & Oddities* (1991). The English version has "Dad" for "Papa." In this chapter, I have kept the French spelling of the author's name, honoring the request of his heir Alex Morisseau-Leroy, who kindly granted me permission to publish my English translation of the play separately (forthcoming). In Haitian Creole, the playwright's name is spelled Feliks Moriso-Lewa; he was popularly nicknamed "Moriso." All quotes are from the Haitian Creole edition *Antigòn an Kreyòl* (*Antigone in Creole*, 1970). I have not obtained an English translation by Mary Dorkonou that exists in Ghana; there is a mimeographed French translation at the Bibliothèque Nationale de France by Edris de Saint-Amand (used at the Paris premiere of the play). All translations from Haitian Creole into English in this chapter are collaborations between David Fils-Aimé, Elizabeth St. Victor, Catherine Fox, Paul and Claudine Corbanese, and myself. I thank all of them for their assistance. Throughout the chapter, I have opted for the standard Haitian Creole spelling of Vodou (instead of the French or English versions) and its pantheon of deities (for instance Danbala [the serpent, spirit of life] instead of Damballah). Since Creole was an exclusively oral language, its orthography has been submerged in ideological debates to this day, although the orthography proposed by the Institute Pédagogique Nationale became official in 1980. All translations from French reviews or texts in this chapter are mine.

Antigonas: Writing from Latin America. Moira Fradinger, Oxford University Press. © Moira Fradinger 2023.
DOI: 10.1093/oso/9780192897091.003.0004

110   FÉLIX MORISSEAU-LEROY'S 1953 VODOU *ANTIGÒN AN KREYÒL*

attempting to save Hémon's life, "mounts" Marraine. Hémon, however, has gone to save Antigòn. Suddenly, a rainbow appears: Antigòn and Hémon have been rescued by the spirit of life, Danbala, and his wife, Ayda Ouèdo. They are now dead but deified. In the village, Créon's wife Euridice commits suicide, and the rivers overflow. People protest, and Créon orders his servant to announce a prohibition on yelling. The servant obeys.

A Haitian Point of View

The Haitian "father of Creole," Félix Morisseau-Leroy (1912–98), staged his *Antigòn* in 1953 in Port-au-Prince and in 1959 in Paris. In both cities, Antigòn dramatized what Jacques Rancière calls "politics": an antagonism where one party speaks "out of place" insofar as the other does not believe the two speak the same language or have the same right to speak and thus the same right to be heard.[2] Antigòn spoke out of place to the Haitian elite, but she was heard. In the ex-metropolis, the French were reluctant. As with all things Haitian, since Haiti's historic expulsion of the French, Antigòn's success in Port-au-Prince was exactly what made for her cold reception in Paris.

Curtain rises in Port-au-Prince. As part of his struggle to create a national literature in Haitian Creole, in less than two months Morisseau-Leroy taught the ancient Antigone to speak the Haitian Creole language and to practice Vodou rites. For the première of *Antigòn an Kreyòl* on July 15, 1953, at the "quasi-aristocratic" Theater Rex in the capital (*Haiti-Journal*, July 20, 1953), Antigone would become Haitian. The play ran at the Rex for two nights; on the third, it was performed in the open-air garden of the College of Agriculture at Damiens, eight kilometers from the city, for a peasant audience. For the first time, a classical text was performed in Creole and with Vodou rituals—that is, in the languages of the 90 percent excluded from Haiti's polity, who formed the poorest peasantry of the hemisphere, or what today we would call the "subaltern."[3] In theater, Creole and Vodou were used solely in comedy, as they were considered respectively to be "bad French" and superstition. By then, only an elite 10 percent of the population spoke French fluently. But in 1953, Morisseau-Leroy proved to this elite "that Creole is apt for the expression of the most serious, the most nuanced,

---

[2] Rancière (1999).
[3] For "Latin American" debates about this term, see Beverley (1999) and Rodríguez (2001).

FÉLIX MORISSEAU-LEROY'S 1953 VODOU *ANTIGÒN AN KREYÒL* 111

the highest sentiments."[4] It was one step toward the self-legitimation of practically an entire country. For the elite, Creole was not a language; taken to its logical extreme, this meant that 90 percent of Haiti simply could not properly speak.

Curtain rises in Paris. Invited to the stage in May 1959, Morisseau-Leroy's *Antigòn* made French reviewers laugh. Critic Léon François Hoffman put it mildly in an encyclopedia entry for Morisseau-Leroy: "[the] somewhat perplexed French public [...] was unaccustomed to classical tragedies in voodoo settings."[5] At the Théâtre des Nations, the French heard the "bavardage gazouillé" ("babbling chatter") of the Creole language (*Aux Écoutes*, May 15, 1959). Robert Kemp, member of the Académie Française, wrote for *Le Monde* (May 13, 1959) that for this "plantation drama" he would have liked to translate Créon's language—unfaithfully, he confesses—into "sugar cane is not good this year, next season will be better." Kemp did "not receive one single shock of grandeur or majesty," but was nonetheless compelled to express how impressed he was at *physical* majesty: "Mlle. Odette Wiener [Antigòn], nonetheless, has a noble silhouette." *Paris Journal* (May 12, 1959) noted the presence of Kemp at the theater, though the reviewer missed the country by misplacing the first three letters: M. Kemp "did not seem to find the *Tahitian language* at the level of French" (my emphasis).[6]

Sophocles imagined that the utmost rebellion against power had to (literally) wear the mask of a woman—a rebellion unthinkable in a world of men. And yet, where Antigone managed to speak to Creon in *his* political language on *her* own terms, Creon saw instead only a madwoman in his agora. Morisseau-Leroy did not need to mask womanhood. But he needed to reconfigure Antigone so as to express a comparable utmost rebellion: to speak out of place in Haiti, Antigòn simply needed to be able *to speak*. Morisseau-Leroy dared, masking Creole and Vodou with only the thinnest of veils: Greek names, which in post-independence nations were not an oddity. Antigone's difference—claiming political equivalence—inspired Morisseau-Leroy to make his Antigòn enter the "world republic of letters"[7] as equivalent, not identical, not even similar, both to her ancient Greek sis-

---

[4] *Le Nouvelliste*, July 16, 1953. All Haitian newspaper reviews were generously sent to me through digital archives by Moïse Celestin at the National Library of Haiti. My deepest thanks to him.

[5] See Hoffman in Smith (1997: 1050–2).

[6] I found all Paris reviews at the Site Richelieu of the Bibliothèque National de France; I thank Marie-Christine Muchery for her help.

[7] I refer to Pascale Casanova's *The World Republic of Letters* (2004).

112 FÉLIX MORISSEAU-LEROY'S 1953 VODOU *ANTIGÒN AN KREYÒL*

ter and to all Creons. Antigòn took a stand to speak on equal terms to the national and the international stages in their (most venerable) theatrical language: tragedy. But she did it on her own terms—Creole and Vodou. The international theater in Paris heard only a Caribbean madwoman. As in ancient Athens, in modern Port-au-Prince and Paris Antigòn was doing politics, from the position she occupied in the political structure of both cities. Like her ancient sister, the Haitian Antigòn was still a niece to power, but to what power? The Haitians saw her speaking up to the peasant chief and understood her Creole; the French saw her speaking as one formerly enslaved person to another and still babbling. At home, it was the story of the excluded subaltern. In Paris, it was the story of the ex-colonial South: of the Haitian elite and its subaltern population viewed in light of what Haiti had done to France—the tiny slave island that defeated the great Napoleon. We might even call this disparity the "location of subalternity":[8] trying to represent a Haitian peasant in Haiti was not the same thing as in Paris.

Indeed, for Morisseau-Leroy it had all started with a political act, much as it had for Marechal just two years prior and Varela a century before that. The play and production were not about politics; they *were* politics. This was, after all, how Morisseau-Leroy had always read *Antigone*: "as far as I was concerned it was always political" (1992: 667). By all accounts, *Antigòn* established a veritable turning point for the emergence of a national literature in Creole—a full 150 years after independence.[9] Inspired by Morisseau-Leroy's success, fellow traveler Franck Fouché (1915–78) adapted two other classics, one of them Greek: Sophocles' *Oedipus Rex* in 1953 and Federico García Lorca's *Yerma* in 1954. Tragedy offered the perfect dramatic structure that could grant all oral expressions (and Creole was an oral language) the same majesty. It was the Western theatrical language par excellence, legitimized by two millennia, five hundred years of colonialism, and two hundred years of the highest humanistic enterprise possible: European philosophical appropriations. Therein lay Morisseau-Leroy's "strategic classicism."

But there was more. It couldn't be just "tragedy," for there was the question of the nation's history and of "national culture." For Morisseau-Leroy, Antigone spoke both quintessential *Haitian* languages: that of sovereignty

---

[8] I echo Homi Bhabha's (1994) expression "the location of culture," which questions where to identify "culture."

[9] See Laroche (1978: 131).

FÉLIX MORISSEAU-LEROY'S 1953 VODOU *ANTIGÒN AN KREYÒL* 113

and that of Vodou. Central to the 90 percent of Morisseau-Leroy's chosen audience, Vodou lore depends on burial rites, which prevent corpses from being reused as "zombies" and thus have political and historical import: the metaphor of "zombification" conjures up Haiti's enslaved past. The ritual roots of theater helped the playwright craft a Vodou ceremony; Antigone's concern for burial helped him address the nation's ominous nightmare of a return to slavery. This specific tragedy could legitimize both Creole and those who spoke it—those who, in Morisseau-Leroy's eyes, had revolted to make Haiti possible in the first place.

With three radical gestures—the play was not in French, its gods were neither Greek nor Catholic, and its performance did not stay indoors— Morisseau-Leroy transformed Antigone into a Creole-speaking Vodou goddess. He put on stage the drama of the enslaved peoples that postrevolutionary mulatto elites excluded to jump on the bandwagon of modern liberal "progress," when, after independence, Haiti adopted French and Catholicism, instead of Creole and Vodou. Morisseau-Leroy changed the Greek princess into a Haitian ancestor, into one of the people's own, not only making her autochthonous to Haiti but also having her speak the language of the radical difference that gave birth to the black nation of Haiti.

Antigòn was, thus, not a European drama in Haitian Creole for the peasant audience to acquaint itself with elite "universal culture"—a common move in inaugural moments of vernacular literatures. It did not "translate" *Antigone* into Creole either. It was not a Haitian "adaptation" of a Western "classic" made palatable for local or international audiences. Nor was it was an adaptation of a European adaptation of *Antigone*. Morisseau-Leroy used neither Anouilh's nor Cocteau's interpretations, both of which he considered adaptations for elite audiences; he chose instead to read Leconte de Lisle's French translation, available in Haiti.[10] He went beyond Fouché's idea of retaining the "classic essence" and integrating "masterpieces to the national patrimony."[11] Morisseau-Leroy's choice was for a "*Haitian* point of view"[12] that would make the tragedy part of the Haitian tradition.

---

[10] "Une interview de Morisseau-Leroy, L'auteur d'*Antigone en Creole*," *Le Matin*, Port-au-Prince, July 24, 1953. Morisseau-Leroy did not read Sophocles in Greek either (though he knew the language).

[11] Fouché (1955: 21–33). Nonetheless, Fouché clarified that, for his adaptation of Lorca's *Yerma*, he transformed Lorca's peasants into citizens: a story of infertility would not be credible among Haitian peasants, whom he qualified as too prolific.

[12] *The Miami New Times*, May 2, 1996.

114   FÉLIX MORISSEAU-LEROY'S 1953 VODOU *ANTIGÒN AN KREYÒL*

With his "Haitian" point of view on a Greek text, Morisseau-Leroy intervened in the question of the national. In both Haiti and Paris, reviewers criticized him for not choosing something "closer to Haiti's temperament." But, like *Antígona Vélez*, *Antigòn* showed that "the national" was not necessarily "the autochthonous content." Rather, it was the heterogeneous text marked by colonial and postrevolutionary politics, demonstrating the impossibility of fixing cultural national borders in neocolonial contexts. For Morisseau-Leroy, something "closer to their temperament"—whatever that might have meant—was not necessarily a "point of view." A point of view does not emphasize what is viewed, but rather the (collective) subject that is viewing—that is, it emphasizes history. And for Morisseau-Leroy, at stake was the historical struggle that informed the views of the collective he chose as audience.

A Haitian point of view meant taking the Greek text not as a starting point, but rather as a point of arrival. Morisseau-Leroy identified what he needed to dramatize for his audience—theater always being for him an event for raising political consciousness—and then looked for Antigone's help. Like Marechal, he questioned inherited forms of tragedy as universally fixed. The Haitian point of view needed to shift the emphasis from theater to ritual and from the tragically irreconcilable to the possibility of metamorphosis. Just as Marechal found a quilting point between Christian drama and Greek tragedy, Morisseau-Leroy quilted Vodou ritual with Greek tragedy by giving Antigone a Vodou death. Antigòn died in the Western sense but obtained eternal life in Vodou cosmology. Morisseau-Leroy displaced the tragic conflict between Antigone and Creon—now a Vodou drama of metamorphosis—onto the tragic antagonism between Haiti's revolutionary past (represented by Antigòn) and political stasis (represented by Créon's servant).

Morisseau-Leroy and His Generation: A Call to Recover Africa

Morisseau-Leroy's Vodou goddess is inscribed in the call of an entire generation for whom the stakes went beyond the struggle against the dictatorship at the time, the pro-US regime of Paul Magloire (1907–2001), who in 1950 had ousted peasant-born Dumarsais Estimé (1900–53), the first pro-black left-wing president after the US occupation (1915–34).[13] Morisseau-Leroy's

---

[13] Paul Magloire made the cover of *Time Magazine* for February 22, 1954.

intervention spoke to long-standing political debates in Haiti, whose reemergence was spawned by almost twenty years of US occupation from 1915 to 1934. Known as the "generation of the occupation," Morisseau-Leroy and his peers saw their intellectual mission calling for a revival of Haiti's African roots. During the 1930s, they split into two distinct camps. Morisseau-Leroy belonged with the Marxists, who emphasized class; the *noiristes* focused on race.[14] The Marxists, following Communist party founder Jacques Roumain (1907–44), accused *noirisme* of replacing class with race. But for both, the question of Haitian culture was crucial, especially the reevaluation of Vodou as the strength, rather than the "underdevelopment," of the people.

The US occupation was widely seen as a national trauma, forcing Haitian intellectuals to find domestic causes for the fall into neocolonial hands. In his influential 1919 *La Vocation de l'élite*, Haitian ethnographer, writer, and politician Jean Price Mars (1876–1969) had argued that the Francophile mulatto elite suffered from "collective bovarysme."[15] Price Mars and fellow ethnographer Odette Mennesson-Rigaud summarized the recovery of Africa with their famous 1958 assessment that the 1804 declaration of Haiti's independence was a product of Vodou, rather than of the French Revolution.[16] For this generation, the nation's birth had its source in the cohesive force that Vodou granted enslaved peoples fighting against the French. In 1990, theater director Robert Bauduy (1940–2008) located the birth of Haitian theater in the legendary Vodou ceremonies at Bois-Caïman in the nights of August 1791.[17] The latter became the symbol for the last stage of the revolutionary uprising that expelled the French from Haiti.[18] The lessons of this generation soon served to guide the international 1950s pan-African movement of *negritude*.

Morisseau-Leroy was active against the US invasion from early on. Born to a prestigious middle-class mulatto family in Grand Gosier, a rural village

---

[14] See Smith (2009). The dictator François "Papa Doc" Duvalier (1907–71), who seized power in 1957, was part of the intellectual movement of the "Griots," the voice of *noirisme*, made state policy during his rule. Morisseau-Leroy would only address Duvalier's dictatorship in his two 1978 plays, *Wa Kreyon* (*King Creon*) and *Pèp La* (*The People*), the former centered on Kreyon's demise after Antigòn's death.

[15] Price Mars was also a leader internationally in the Pan-African movement. His 1928 *Ainsi Parla L'Oncle* (*So Spoke the Uncle*, 1973), was a landmark recovery of Haiti's African roots.

[16] See Price Mars ([1928] 1973: 100–10) and Mennesson-Rigaud (1958: 43). The elites were ambivalent: see François Dalencour's and Jean Fouchard's doubts in Hoffman (1992: 265–6). See also Geggus (2002b), Dayan (1995), and Dubois (2004a).

[17] Robert Bauduy's statement appears in both his 1990 (43–8), 1974, and 2002 (26–7) publications.

[18] The historical data is controversial (see Hoffman 1992: 267–301). See the most complete historical account in Geggus (2002b: 81–99).

116 FÉLIX MORISSEAU-LEROY'S 1953 VODOU *ANTIGÒN AN KREYÒL*

east of Jacmel, and son of a general in the Haitian army, the young teenager was already defending his nation at age fourteen, when he wrote a letter to Jacques Roumain expressing his protest against the US occupation. At age seventeen, Morisseau-Leroy organized a "peace walk" in his town. For him, national identity was built on the history of the war of independence and the sovereignty brought by the revolution.[19]

An avowed Marxist, Morisseau-Leroy adhered to the ideology perhaps best summarized in *Coumbite*, the Haitian journal of the National Society for Dramatic Arts, with the phrase: "to be rational is, first and foremost, to be people" ("être rationnel, c'est avant tout être peuple").[20] As he once put it, "I choose as spectators the 90% of the population, and a whole class of people, for whom the *real drama* unfolds" (1955b: 130; my emphasis).

Creole: The Will to Exist

An "irascible advocate" of Creole and Creolophile "in the most prodigious and audacious sense," Morisseau-Leroy became the father of "Creolophonie" in contrast to Francophonie.[21] In 1986, he expressed his absolute commitment to Creole thus: "Haitian literature will be Creole or will not be" (1986: 57). George Lang frames his comparative study of Caribbean Creole literatures in those terms: Creole literatures have to be "willed into existence" (1997: 43). Lang finds that "adaptations of European language masterpieces are quintessential Creole strategies" in the Caribbean (34), just as they were for vernacular European languages and their "conscious reaching back for remote reserves," as Ernst R. Curtius put it, of Greek and Latin masterpieces to adapt into French and English.[22] When Morisseau-Leroy's colleagues asked him what could possibly be translatable into Creole, he said, "everything must be written in Creole, even *Antigone!*"[23] And indeed, for Morisseau-Leroy, it was not a question of translating, but of writing.

To assess the impact of Morisseau-Leroy's linguistic decisions, we must understand the extent to which Creole had to be willed into existence. In 1986, Morisseau-Leroy estimated that from the nineteenth century until the

---

[19] *The Miami New Times*, May 2, 1996.
[20] Quoted in Claude Innocent's "La SNAD de 1956" (2002: 22).
[21] Dumas (1985: 65–7; 2000: 364). [22] Curtius ([1952] 1990: 392).
[23] *The Miami New Times*, May 2, 1996.

FÉLIX MORISSEAU-LEROY'S 1953 VODOU *ANTIGÒN AN KREYÒL*   117

1950s there were not even ten poets who wrote in Creole.[24] In his 1986 speech in defense of Creole, Morisseau-Leroy responded with conviction to the elitist complaints that Creole literature was "a literature of records and cassettes" due to the high illiteracy rate in Haiti: "I have nothing against records or cassettes; they participate in what I call the oral revenge."[25]

In July 1954, exactly a year after *Antigòn*'s success, the journal *Optique* published a special issue devoted to Haiti's peculiar linguistic situation, describing a Kafkaesque situation. French was the official language of all government documents, education, and literary writing, but only 10 percent of Haitians—an urban mulatto elite—could speak it. In the transcription of a roundtable titled "Creole and the Law" (41–8), Price Mars recounted what he considered a "tragic" anecdote: during a trial for murder, some peasants were condemned to death in French, but they only spoke Creole. In her article in the issue, "Creole against French" (19–37), Edith Efron gave examples of the "two Haitis tragically separated by language" (20), from the entire education system being conducted in French to simple private issues, like marriage proposals written in French sent to parents and suitors who did not understand them. Efron's comments on priests' sermons in French are the most ironic: "[they] could be pronounced in the most pure Latin, for all that the believers understand" (26); "the average Haitian has as clear a comprehension of the official religion as he has of the official language, which is to say none" (27).

For the urban mulatto elite, Creole was a "false" language, incapable of abstractions. For the nineteenth-century literate elite, Creole might have been enough to lead the revolution but not to communicate it: they set to "naturalizing French," as the generation of writers of 1836 put it, even as they voiced their preference for "an indigenous literature."[26] Efron quotes Dantès Bellegarde, minister of education from 1918 to 1921: "the specific language of Haiti [is] French" for "our country is too small [...] for us to create an original civilization, that is to say, purely Haitian" (30).[27] Abandoning French would mean the isolation of Haiti.

---

[24] Morisseau-Leroy (1986). Though Morisseau-Leroy specifies that there was a Creole theater during colonial times, for him the tradition was lost after independence. See Morisseau-Leroy (1992: 667–70). See the same estimation in Charles (1984: 152–7). See also Fouché (1964).

[25] Morisseau-Leroy (1986).   [26] Charles (1984: 154).

[27] See Hoffman's "Francophilie et nationalisme culturel" (in Hoffman 1992: 17–44) for a compilation of quotes on the elite's francophilia.

118 FÉLIX MORISSEAU-LEROY'S 1953 VODOU *ANTIGÒN AN KREYÒL*

Nonetheless, Creole had historically enabled communication among enslaved peoples so efficiently that they led the only successful slave revolt in the modern world. If anything, Creole had been emblematic of clarity and communicability. Efron shows Creole proverbs depicting French as the "false" language: "a language associated with lying, camouflage, mystification, incomprehension, duplicity, and even treason" (35). Haitian Creole had been a lingua franca, as Lucien Daumec reminds us, created by "approximately fifty-four ethnic groups from Africa" to organize against planters.[28] Creole carried the historical aura of a threat to power.

Morisseau-Leroy's article for *Optique*, titled "Why Do They Write in Creole?," was one of his two fierce defenses of Creole. His anxiety concerned the educated writer's isolation, not from France but from his own people. For Morisseau-Leroy, Creole would prompt the translation of Haitian literature into other languages (51). Next to Morisseau-Leroy's article, *Optique* published beat generation poet Herbert Gold's "...And why we will translate them": "we, foreigners will learn Creole [...] or pay translators to put their work in our own languages. Long live the Villon of Haiti! Long live the Chaucer of Haiti" (62).[29]

The August 1955 issue of *Panorama* announced the creation of the Institute of Creole Language in Port-au-Prince. Its president, David Odnell, wrote that the history of Creole was nothing more, nothing less than "the history of the *Haitian people*" (1955: 226; my emphasis). That year Morisseau-Leroy wrote his "Defense for a Creole Theater": in a country where "the spectators and the writers are all poor [...] the theater in Creole is the only genre that addresses the generality of the Haitian people without class distinctions" (1955b: 131).[30] His urgency to write in Creole aimed at "valoriz[ing] a heritage which is inseparable from the colossal legacy of Independence" (1955b: 56).

The Colossal Legacy of Independence: The War within the War and Tragedy's Metamorphosis

What was the "colossal legacy" that Morisseau-Leroy's generation was busy recovering, and how did Antigone help, other than by speaking Creole and

---

[28] Daumec poetically narrates the origins of Creole in "Odyssée d'une langue" (1954: 38–40).
[29] See Morisseau-Leroy "Pourquoi ils écrivent en créole," *Optique* 5 (1954: 48–59) and Herbert Gold, "...Et Pourquoi nous les Traduirons," *Optique* 5 (1954: 59–65).
[30] "Plaidoyer pour un théâtre créole"; see also Morisseau-Leroy (1983: 19).

FÉLIX MORISSEAU-LEROY'S 1953 VODOU *ANTIGÒN AN KREYÒL* 119

prophesying Vodou?[31] As historians unearth what Michel-Rolph Trouillot calls Western "formulas of silence"[32] that have disavowed Haiti's revolutionary challenge to Western universalism, they also unveil the divisions among enslaved peoples that determined the rebellion's aftermath. These are foundational divisions that have proven fertile soil for both historians and writers to cannibalize the genre of tragedy.[33] The two linguistic Haitis were also tragically divided during the revolution, between enslaved Creoles and enslaved African-born peoples, called *bossales*. Beyond Antigone's burial rites, the ancient story of a fratricidal war for power dealt the playwright another hand.

Trouillot briefly describes the last revolutionary phase as a set of transitions from "mass insurrection (1791) […] to the proclamation of Haitian independence with Dessalines (1804)" (1995: 89). This story is usually told from the perspective of three famous Creole leaders with different visions for a post-slavery world: Toussaint Louverture (1743–1803), who was betrayed by Napoleon and died imprisoned in France; and Louverture's two lieutenants: Jean-Jacques Dessalines (1758–1806), who declared independence in 1804, named himself emperor, and was assassinated two years into his rule; and Henri Christophe (1767–1820), who declared himself the first king of Haiti in 1811 and committed suicide in 1820.

Morisseau-Leroy was most attracted to Dessalines—the radicality of Antigòn's "no" to power can be seen as one of the playwright's homages to Dessalines that appear in many of his poems. It is not difficult to understand this preference: born into slavery, Dessalines was the least "French" of the three great leaders and was even pejoratively referred to as a "congo"—a generic word meaning "African"—in French correspondence.[34] The point of contention among the Creole leaders was Haiti's relation to France. Whereas Toussaint thought Haiti could not survive without France, Dessalines made

---

[31] For recent historiographies of this legacy, see Geggus (2002a, 2001), Geggus and Fiering (2009), Dubois (2006, 2004a, 2004b), Dubois and Garrigus (2006), M.-R. Trouillot (1995), Dayan (1995), Buck-Morss (2009), Fick (1990), Munro and Walcott-Hackshaw (2006, 2009), and Nesbit (2008). See also Julia Gaffield's website with a wealth of documents from the revolution at https://juliagaffield.com.

[32] See Trouillot (1995).

[33] For theatrical represenations, see Aimé Césaire ([1963] 1970), James ([1934] 2013), Walcott ([1950a] 2002, 1950b), Edouard Glissant ([1961] 1986), Hénock Trouillot (1967), Coicou ([1907] 1988), Métellus (1991, 2004), Vincent Placoly (1983), and Eugene O'Neill ([1920] 1988). Vèvè Clark (1992a) included the word "tragic" in the title for an essay on the theatrical representation of the Haitian revolution (the essay lists sixty-three plays about the topic from 1796 to 1975).

[34] See Thornton (1993).

120 FÉLIX MORISSEAU-LEROY'S 1953 VODOU *ANTIGÒN AN KREYÒL*

his way into history as the ferocious, inexorable, and merciless avenger whose motto was "kill and burn everything" French. Dessalines declared that all Haitian citizens were black (regardless of skin color) and ordered the massacre of the French colonists remaining on the island after the final battle was won. He famously expressed his victory on April 28, 1804: "I have avenged America."

Dessalines also advocated freedom of worship, while both Toussaint and Christophe were devout Catholics and against Vodou. Dessalines wanted a redistribution of land among formerly enslaved peoples, whereas Christophe imposed strict labor regulations that yielded revenues from the system of "fermage" previously put in place by Toussaint (where the land belonged to the government). And it was Dessalines who adopted the Taino name *Haiti* for the new nation; he named his army "the army of the Incas," identifying his soldiers with the Amerindian past.[35] For Laroche, Dessalines' utopia was to erase in one stroke the colonial rule from 1492 to 1804.[36] In the 1970s, Laroche framed Dessalines' legacy concisely by quoting Louis Mercier's declaration that "on n'est pas haïtien si on n'est pas dessalinien" ("one is not Haitian if one is not Dessalinian") (1978: 108). The Haitian national anthem, adopted in 1904, was composed in Dessalines' honor and called "La Dessalinienne."

Despite their differences, the leaders confronted a common problem: a fratricidal war that Trouillot calls "the war within the war" among Haitians (1995: 37). Creole enslaved peoples (and mulatto freedmen) were pitted against African-born enslaved peoples. Trouillot exemplifies the "war within the war" with an early revolt, before the declaration of independence. Colonel Jean-Baptiste Sans Souci, an African-born enslaved person from Congo who rose as a leader of guerrilla tactics, did not surrender to the French in 1802—unlike the main leaders, Toussaint, Dessalines, Christophe, and Pétion. Christophe eventually murdered Sans Souci, very near the place where he constructed his palace, also called Sans Souci.[37]

---

[35] See "The Naming of Haiti" in Geggus (2002a: 201–21); Geggus argues that the revolutionary elite of the nineteenth century, especially the mulatto elite, identified with ancient Arawak and Taino indigenous fighters against the Spaniards to differentiate themselves from Europeans.

[36] See Laroche (2005).

[37] This provides Trouillot with a powerful example of what he calls the "silences" of history (1995: 31–69). Eurocentric readings interpret Christophe's construction of the palace as an imitation of the German palace of Sans Souci at Potsdam. Trouillot looks closer to home at the enmity between the Creole Christophe and the African-born enemy, Sans Souci, and the Dahoman stories of vengeance that Christophe might have known, as sources for the construction and the naming of the palace after the enemy.

FÉLIX MORISSEAU-LEROY'S 1953 VODOU *ANTIGÒN AN KREYÒL* 121

At the time, 50 percent of Haiti's enslaved peoples were born in Africa. In the north, where the final revolt started, 60 percent of enslaved peoples were from the African Kingdom of Congo. Scholars now assess their African guerrilla tactics as crucial to victory. Many enslaved peoples in Haiti had served in Congo's eighteenth-century civil wars.[38] Nonetheless, Geggus notes that not one of the thirty-seven officers who signed the declaration of independence was African; two-thirds were of mixed race (2002a: 209). Creoles saw the revolution as a transfer of French power to them. This was not the ideology of those who brought with them not only African war tactics but also African political philosophy. Bossale people aimed at ending the plantation system completely and defended democratic ideas of leadership.[39]

At the moment of revolution, there were Creole armies, instructed in European warfare and arranged on a hierarchical basis, and Bossale independent gangs, organized with guerrilla tactics, local leadership, and along the lines of nations that in turn formed secret societies. A history of *marronage* had also contributed to these independent organizations, which prepared the revolution "from below," as Carolyn Fick puts it, "in spite of, and not because of, their [Creole] leadership" (1990: 228).[40]

Disproportionately constituted by previously freed men, the new post-revolutionary ruling class had to solve the problem of the island's economic production. They struggled to impose new forms of the old plantation system on formerly enslaved peoples who would not work for new "masters." For Fick, the wish for an egalitarian society and a preference for subsistence economy showed "the implacable resistance to forced labor [...] the beginning of a consciousness that later [formed] a class of small, more or less self-sufficient, peasant producers, [...] the very antithesis of the plantation regime" (180).[41]

The form and idea of Greek tragedy were mobilized to account for these dilemmas of the new republic, both in theatrical and historical texts. Tragedy has been successfully used to critique Enlightenment principles by

---

[38] See Thornton (1991, 1993) and Thornton and Heywood (2007).

[39] For the influence of African political philosophy on the Haitian revolution, see Thornton (1992).

[40] The Creole leaders even complained to the French about untamable Bossale organizations. Leaders Jean-Francois and Biassou told the French commissioners in October 1791 that their slaves "would not surrender": "They were 'entirely subject to [...] a multitude of *nègres* of the coast [of Africa] who [...] were accustomed to fighting [*à guerroyer*] in their country'" (Thornton 1993: 202). See also Fouchard (1981) and Fick (1990).

[41] For details about independent farmers' republics and peasant rebellions, see Nicholls (1985).

122   FÉLIX MORISSEAU-LEROY'S 1953 VODOU *ANTIGÒN AN KREYÒL*

showing their negative dialectics—for instance, freedom's development into its opposite, slavery. And in its staging of the avatars of contingency, tragedy has served to counter teleological philosophies of historical progress that model reality upon reason. But in light of Morisseau-Leroy's original cannibalization of the tragic form for the staging of a Vodou ceremony, it is relevant to ask here, *who* needed to counter these teleologies of progress with European tragedy? Was it the peasant audience?

Most famous among Caribbean uses of tragedy against a romantic vision of the Haitian revolution is C. L. R. James' 1963 appendix to his 1938 *The Black Jacobins*. There, James framed anew the heroic Toussaint: his fall was not a result of his mistakes, but of his "tragic" dilemma. France had enslaved him and his people but also generated the principles of universal equality; nonetheless Toussaint miscalculated revolutionary France. David Scott's 2004 study of C. L. R. James follows James' idea that tragedy has an enlightening function that the romantic narrative lacks and sees tragedy as the best response to postcolonial questions: if Toussaint was a product of modern slavery—and as such could not "choose *not* to be modern" (129; italics in the original)—we must contend with the legacies of the modern colonial project. If romanticism was useful for understanding the moment (and movement) of resistance to the colony, it was not useful for understanding its legacies.

Not only Toussaint but also Dessalines has appeared as a tragic hero. Haitian Hénock Trouillot's 1966 essay *Dessalines ou la tragedie postcoloniale*, which he adapted for the theater as *Dessalines ou le sang du Pont Rouge* (Dessalines or the blood of Pont Rouge) in 1967, framed the reasons for Dessalines' assassination as tragedy rather than failure.[42] Trouillot suggested that the class of ex-colonial *anciens livres* (mulattoes, in contrast to the black *nouveaux livres* freed by the revolution) had inherited land and fiercely resisted Dessalines' proposals for agrarian reform (78). Trouillot qualified both the reactionary revolt against Dessalines and historians' interpretation of it as the result of the empire's inefficiency, or as "what Aimé Césaire could call the Tragedy of Dessalines."[43] In Trouillot's view, Dessalines miscalculated—as did Toussaint—but with respect to his Creole fellow travelers.

The above uses of tragedy share an implicit approach to history as enacted by "great men" and written by intellectual elites. The form of tragedy is

---

[42] For a description of eight plays that treat Dessalines' history, see Coates (1996).
[43] H. Trouillot's reference to Césaire's 1963 play *The Tragedy of King Christophe* (1966: 79).

mostly preserved, but the effect is somewhat ironic. On the one hand, tragedy produces a form of knowledge about modernity that counters heroic romantic narratives and about the predicament of postcolonial intellectuals—whether embodied by political leaders such as Toussaint, or political writers such as Césaire, who must deal with the burden of the colonial past. On the other hand, tragedy, as enlightened practice, performs an Enlightenment "lesson" that supersedes the tragic experience.

But this circularity is less urgent than the fact that the agents of the revolution did not share the tragic vision of the European-educated writers of their history—nor the romantic heroism with which their leaders were portrayed. They were, rather, steeped in a different cosmology: Vodou. So, in a society where Vodou prevails, who profits from the knowledge produced by the European tragic form? If history is narrated from a different point of view—not that of its leaders—is tragedy (and its "lesson") still the most illuminating frame? Morisseau-Leroy's originality lies in his answer to this question.

Laroche exposed the problem when he criticized Césaire's view of Christophe's history as "tragedy" in *The Tragedy of King Christophe*. Laroche's question was also a Haitian point of view with respect to the European form of tragedy. If Césaire's Christophe makes tragic mistakes, Laroche's Christophe makes the mistakes of any free man—not those of one enslaved by his past: "the King Christophe of Haiti's history, unlike the character in Césaire's drama, probably had this conviction, [he gave] himself the symbol of the phoenix and the motto 'I am reborn out of my ashes' [...] no temporary error could mortgage his future, that is, that of his people" (1978: 106).

If the tragic is understood as the irreconcilable confrontation between two goods (only redeemable in aesthetic experience), Laroche writes "one would have to start by asking if the history of King Christophe, such as that imagined by Césaire [...], would be considered as tragic with regards to the history of Haiti, for what is at stake is knowing *whether the history of Haiti accepts the hypothesis of a tragedy. I don't think so*" (104; my emphasis). Laroche briefly considers the lyrics of enslaved people's chants during battle as an example of a nontragic worldview: for them, at stake was not individual death but collective immortality. Laroche explains the "Haitian conception of time" (104): "the death-as-fatality that characterizes the Greek tragic is not found in Haiti. Whether it is about the zombie (death kept alive) or the Kanzo (the living who does not know how to die), Haitian mythology does not propose death except as images of a metamorphosed life [...] it is

124 FÉLIX MORISSEAU-LEROY'S 1953 VODOU *ANTIGÒN AN KREYÒL*

not tragic in the Western sense" (105). For Laroche, Christophe's "tragedy" is really the drama of free men: "no Haitian is ready to admit that Haiti's history is a tragedy and to think that the independence of this heroic little country became a lamentable tragedy. The avatars of History are nothing but lessons for the free man who shapes his own destiny" (105).[44]

Laroche also criticizes the idea of a "lesson": which Haitians need lessons? And what can tragedy's lesson offer them? Both for Laroche and for Morisseau-Leroy, a Haitian point of view was that of the heirs of the enslaved peoples who chanted at the battlefront: the agents of the revolution "from below." In their appeal to Greek tragedy, Caribbean intellectuals target the limits of the heroic romantic narratives of teleological progress. But this type of heroic narrative is not hegemonic among those whose cosmology emphasizes metamorphosis.

For both Laroche and Morisseau-Leroy, at stake were the staging of and the meditation upon transformation. For his audience, Morisseau-Leroy would need to quilt into *Antigone* not so much a remembrance of the limits of reason, but rather, the limits that the revolution from below had put on slavery: the transformative power of a non-negotiable "no." A Haitian concept of time provided a lesson about change: any return to slavery needed to be seen as a possible metamorphosis into freedom again. If there was a lesson from the past, this was not about how the colony limited the possibilities for enlightened modernity, but rather, about how this very same past had *opened up* the future. For the makers of the revolution, the past meant slavery. For the enlightened leaders and intellectuals, the past meant the failure of the *liberal* nation. In both cases, the real issue was to give historicity back to what had been "naturalized"—be it the condition of slavery or the fixed and inexorable path to progress through reason. For the grandsons of the men on the battlefield against slavery, the past always referred to the perils of slavery's naturalization.

Interestingly, if one can say that Greek tragedy and Vodou stage the temporality proper to historicity, both do so in a manner that seems to be the experience of political modernity par excellence: human *contingency*—so well abbreviated in the famous formula from the *Communist Manifesto* "everything that is solid melts in the air." For the modern narrative of heroic control—exercised by our conquering reason—tragedy stages contingency as warning: the antidote against the illusion of calculation. Vodou is itself

---

[44] Trouillot's quotation refers to Kesteloot's analysis of Césaire's tragedy (Kesteloot and Kotchy 1973).

based on contingency, staging it as hope. Morisseau-Leroy's originality was to test whether the theater of Vodou would accept the hypothesis of tragedy. He proceeded to quilt both visions, making a drama of transmutation confront a tragedy of stasis.

Vodou: A Historical Cosmology Transformed into Political Theater

On stage, the quilting point between tragedy and Vodou is Antigòn's death: her Haitian "no" to slavery transforms her into a Vodou goddess. For Morisseau-Leroy's generation, just as Creole was the idiom of the Haitian revolution, Vodou was its theatrical language, resulting from some syncretism between West African and Christian rites and from the material conditions of slavery and slave resistance.

Slave resistance included the "Maroon societies" where Vodou was a central practice. Morisseau-Leroy's play registers a legendary entry in the history of the relation between resistance and Vodou: that of the African-born one-armed sorcerer Makandal (?–1758), probably a Vodou initiate when he was captured in West Africa. Makandal has become part of the nation's lore as the first Maroon enslaved person known to have planned a revolution and foretold the end of slavery. He escaped from slavery around 1746 and led guerrilla attacks against the French, such as the so-called "great fear of 1757," when Makandal and his followers caused widespread poisoning by introducing local herbs into the water and food supply in the northern plantations. In 1758, he was bound to the stake and escaped, only to be captured and burned alive before an audience of enslaved persons. Legend has it that he escaped once again, having metamorphosed into a butterfly.[45] In the play, Tiresias informs Créon that he saw a butterfly arrive at his house, only to swiftly fly away.

But the most legendary of all entries in the relation between Vodou, resistance, and theater is Vodou's direct role in the revolution, epitomized in the much-debated 1791 Vodou ceremony at Bois-Caïman, mythically considered the engine of the revolution's final phase. In the ceremony, all participants drank the blood of a sacrificial black pig, and the priestess Cecile Fatiman, while possessed by Ogou, the spirit of war, selected Boukman

---

[45] For accounts of this legend, see Boyce Davis (2008: 646), Weaver (2006: 91), and Fick (1990).

126 FÉLIX MORISSEAU-LEROY'S 1953 VODOU *ANTIGÒN AN KREYÒL*

Dutty, Jean-François Papillon, Biassou, and Jeannot to lead the uprising that would soon become the revolution.[46] Morisseau-Leroy's choice of Vodou was risky. Associated with historical revolt, it was consistently persecuted by authorities and at times officially forbidden as "superstition."[47]

Vodou gave *Antigòn* a specific political resonance. To understand how Antigone could be incorporated as a goddess into the Vodou pantheon, we need to consider how Vodou's malleable belief system is inflected by the everyday experience of its devotees. There is no Vodou orthodoxy transmitted by a hierarchical institution. Vodou varies from country to country, within regions and between households. Unlike the Christian God, Vodou's unifying source of universal power, *Bondye*, does not interfere in human affairs. Vodou practitioners interact with deities called *lwas* (spirits), intermediaries between the living, the dead, and *Bondye*. Vodou is a historical cosmology, a dialogue with ancestors. It is often described as democratic because its pantheon is enriched by members of the community whose spirits have been deified after death—just what happens to Antigòn at the end of the play. In 1983, artist and Vodou initiate Maya Deren (1917–61) put it succinctly: each Vodou spirit can be seen as "a deposit" of history.

Vodou practitioners serve the spirits with gift-giving, ritual ceremonies, and spirit possession, or what has been called "possession performance," given its highly theatrical composition (the behavior of the spirits is well known; they personify familiar character types). As happens with humans, and as will happen to Antigòn on stage, spirits are also subject to transformation. There may be one warrior spirit (Ogou), but it manifests itself in various forms of aggression (the drunkard or the heroic soldier, for instance).

The play stages interactions with the *lwas* from the first scene onward. The two most important Haitian families ("nations") of *lwas* are called to help with the disharmony brought about by Antigòn's rebellion: the Rada (originating in Dahomey) and the Petwo pantheons. These nations express different modes of relationships that their spirits represent, their hegemonic domains in life, their ethos, and the way their devotees relate to them. Some Petwo spirits are said to originate in Congo and the Caribbean plantations, though many are considered a product of the history of slavery: in ceremonies, their manifestation is usually welcomed with the crack of whips,

---

[46] See Geggus (2002b) and especially H. Trouillot (1970).

[47] Morisseau-Leroy witnessed one of the harshest campaigns against Vodou (known as "rejeté") during 1941–2; see Hurbon (1993).

FÉLIX MORISSEAU-LEROY'S 1953 VODOU *ANTIGÒN AN KREYÒL* 127

whistles, and knives. Though many Rada spirits have inverted Petwo versions, in general the Rada spirits are "sweet," while the Petwo are "hot" and violent.[48] Morisseau-Leroy breaks the pattern that Vodou ceremonies usually follow. The play unfolds at Créon's *péristile*. The latter is an open space where Vodou ceremonies are carried out, where the devotees gather under a roof around a *poto mitan* (central pillar). Priests (*houngans*) and priestesses (*mambos*) lead the rites; in the play, the sisters' godmother initiates the ceremony, and later Créon plays the role of *houngan*. Ceremonies start with prayers, drums, and songs to the spirits—songs for the Rada spirits are first, then come those for the Petwo spirits. Since spirits do not speak in the language of the living, the first to be called for the ceremony is Papa Legba, the god of crossroads, who opens the gate between the two worlds and usually stays throughout the ceremony. In the play, Legba departs shortly after he appears, indicating a communicational disturbance in Créon's house. Spirits are expected to "mount horses" (possess participants) and speak through them. In a Vodou ceremony, a complete "theatrical set" emerges not only from the stage, the music, songs, chorus, dance, costumes, and audience but also from the impersonation of the spirits.[49] Nearly everyone present can be "mounted" by a spirit, thus acquiring the spirit's personality and highly coded behavior. A "crisis of possession" happens in the play when Antigòn's death is imminent.

Morisseau-Leroy exploited to the maximum the theatrical set built into Vodou rituals. As much as he was a "Creolophile," he was a "theatrophile," devoting his life to popular theater as the great educator of the illiterate masses. To better reach peasants, he advocated for itinerant theaters to tour rural villages. He thought of Haitians as people who had "theater in their blood": "in Haiti everything is put on stage, from official to Vodou ceremonies."[50] In 1955, Morisseau-Leroy declared to the audience at the International Club of Commerce that "each time there is an evolution in theater, there is progress for the people."[51]

---

[48] For introductions to this cosmology, see Métraux (1958), Herskovits (1971), Rigaud (2001), Hurbon (1995), Michel and Bellegarde-Smith (2006), Desmangles (1992), and Deren (1983).

[49] See Price Mars (1946) for a detailed comparison between Vodou ceremonies and dramatic aspects such as plot, character, thought, and action; see also Saint-Lot (2003) and Kremser (1990).

[50] In Künstler (1955: 67).

[51] Quoted in Montas (1955: 737–5). See Künstler (1955), Montas (1955), and Cornevin (1973) for an account of how the 1948 foundation of the Société Nationale d'Art Dramatique (SNAD) meant a renaissance for theater.

128 FÉLIX MORISSEAU-LEROY'S 1953 VODOU *ANTIGÒN AN KREYÒL*

Morisseau-Leroy's generation understood Vodou as a theater stemming, as other ancient theaters, from religious festivities. The roots of a theater with, for, and by the people would be found in collective peasant cultural forms, such as the "*cumbite*" or "*société*" (work societies), the "*Rara*" festivals (carnivals), and the rites of Vodou.[52] In the 1940s, Haitian psychiatrist Louis Price Mars had already identified Vodou rites of possession as the origins of many popular religions around the world and a theatrical performance in their own right.[53] He named Vodou an "ethnodrama": "a dramatic religion, whose gods [are] faithful mirrors of man's desires, needs, and ambitions" (1981: 183); "the *stage* is the ceremonial environment, the *stage manager* is the body of popular traditions [...] the *actors* are the believers" (187; italics in the original). In studying "possessions," Price Mars saw "many models of incarnation, each with a complete set of body features that new generations learn through traditions, in accordance with the original meaning of the Greek word 'poiein'—to do" (185). In 1959, French actor Jean-Louis Barrault associated the Brazilian version of Vodou ceremonies (*candomblé*) with Greek theater: "The scene I attended in Rio de Janeiro in which the spirit 'rides' the adept, struck me because it took place exactly the same way as the scene in Agamemnon where Apollo 'rides' Cassandra" (Price Mars 1981: 187).

But Morisseau-Leroy's generation also identified something else in Vodou: its historical political force, its power to create a countermovement to elite European theater. In 1976, Morisseau-Leroy's contemporary Franck Fouché put the thoughts of a generation down on paper, dedicating an entire book to the issue: *Vodou et Théâtre*. Fouché called for a transformation of Vodou rites into a popular theater, which he associated with "a guerrilla theater" (112) such as the *Living Theater* in New York City and Cuban revolutionary theater. For Fouché, Vodou rites were already "*pre-theater*" (19), just as the ancient Greek rites contained the matrix of tragedy, and the *péristile* resembled the space of ancient Greek theater. By his account, the recovery of the theatrical elements from their ritualistic context would transform pre-theater into theater, in other words, would produce the "secularization" of sacred Vodou rituals (23). The new theater would speak the language of the people and demystify Vodou beliefs, inviting the spectator/

---

[52] See Vèvè Clark (1983, 1986). On the "*Rara*" festivals, see McAlister (2002).

[53] See Price Mars: *La crise* (1946); *Témoignages 1 (essai ethnopsychologique)* (1966); *Les maîtres de l'aube* (1982); and "Ethnodrama" (1981: 183–9). See also Louis-Jean (1970). Michel Leiris (1958) linked theater with African ancestral religious rites.

FÉLIX MORISSEAU-LEROY'S 1953 VODOU *ANTIGÒN AN KREYÒL* 129

actor/participant to interrogate his living conditions without recourse to gods (113). If Vodou was about transformation, then Vodou itself could also be transformed into theater and by theater. Neither barbaric nor an opiate for the masses, Vodou was instead a "theater history" inscribed, like all ancestral religions, in the social praxis of its people. Thus, Vodou could become part of the struggle for liberation (85).

In 1956, Fouché called Morisseau-Leroy a "sublime madman" (30) for having built, "armed with hammer and sickle," his own popular experimental theater, Théâtre d'Haïti, on his property in Morne Hercule (Pétion-Ville). For the two-hour performances, he would recruit actors from the nearby Vodou temples. He trained peasants to dramatize their own problems. At the Théâtre d'Haïti, Morisseau-Leroy declared, "a dramaturgy was born where the *griots* and the traditions of commedia dell'arte shook hands."[54] Tragedy helped Morisseau-Leroy secularize Vodou rites. If Vodou could stage historic contradictions, tragedy had done the same in a different context. It was a question of quilting the two.

The Play: Minimalist Vodou

Antigòn is a Vodou ceremony on a theater stage. Displacing the ancient tragic antagonism between Antigone and Creon, it dramatizes the historic Haitian antagonism between autonomy and slavery.[55] Antigòn's "no" to power clashes against Créon's (and his servant's) "yes" to destiny. To this tragic antagonism, Morisseau-Leroy quilted Vodou metamorphosis to deify humans by adding them to the pantheon of Vodou *lwas*. The tragedy thus acquires the utopian redemption of Vodou lore and the Vodou theater, a tragic tone. This is how the virgin Antigòn, as much as Antígona Vélez, becomes a mother-in-death. Antigòn does not give children to the nation,

---

[54] See Morisseau-Leroy (1983: 87; 1994: 85–7).

[55] My analysis of the play is based on the text and four productions: in Port-au-Prince at the Theater Rex in 1953, in Paris at the Théâtre des Nations festival in 1959, in New York at the Sacred Heart Auditorium in Queens in 1976, and at the Miami Dade Auditorium in 1998. My archival information is drawn from Haitian and French newspaper reviews. I have only found three articles where the play figures beyond a passing mention: based on the Creole edition, Shelton (2000) and Dominique (2002); and based on the French translation, Mossetto (2003). I thank Italian scholar Mario Capaldo for drawing my attention to Mossetto's article, which describes the play scene by scene. See also Cornevin (1983) for this play in the context of Haitian theater, though understood only as an adaptation keeping the formal structure of Greek tragedy. Bañuls Oller and Alcalá (2008: 432–3) follow this understanding in their two-page comment on the play.

130 FÉLIX MORISSEAU-LEROY'S 1953 VODOU *ANTIGÒN AN KREYÒL*

but eternal life to revolution. Like Marechal, Morisseau-Leroy found in Antigone's death the possibility for redemption and tragedy: while Antigòn lives in heaven as a goddess, Créon (with his servant) remains on earth, a slave to his destiny.

Prologue and Overture

The narrator's prologue conveys the plot, and a sense of fatality pervades as he tells the audience that this story has been told again and again, everywhere. The tragic looms: "the family has been cursed" (8). In the 1959 Paris performance, the heterogeneity of Morisseau-Leroy's text appeared already in the prologue, which was recited by three masked actresses to the rhythm of a Yanvalou dance belonging to the Vodou rites of Rada.[56] A Yanvalou dance represents the undulation of waves as well as the spirit of Danbala, the serpent spirit of life, water, and fertility. After the movements symbolizing transformation, the audience heard a "universal" tragic story:

> It is a story told in every country and in every language. I added to it Haiti's sun, and I added to it the way Haitian people understand life and death, courage and pain, luck and bad luck. I added to it saints, the dead, mysteries, the spirit that watches over the long road, the cemetery, the gate, trees, gardens, the sea, the river that commands the rain, the wind, the thunder in Haiti; all of which are very similar to what they call Greek gods. (8)

And:

> It happened in Greece, but it is so universal that it could happen today in a rural district in Haiti that is also called Thebes, at the house of a chief of a rural district who has a big *péristile* and believes himself to be the state...Anywhere, anytime, there could be an Antigone who says No, a King Créon who didn't want to listen to advice. (9–10)

---

[56] In the absence of exact data about the first production in Haiti in 1953, I am using information about the production at the Théâtre des Nations in Paris in 1959, courtesy of the Bibliothèque Nationale de France, Site Richelieu. Because Morisseau-Leroy's Théâtre d'Haiti company staged the play in the two cities, we may assume that there were similarities in the production.

FÉLIX MORISSEAU-LEROY'S 1953 VODOU *ANTIGÒN AN KREYÒL*   131

It is a story told everywhere that belongs to everyone, as the narrator says: "I'm not responsible for what happens to them. I'm just like all of you here" (9). The narrator only helps the audience understand the story by setting it in the Haitian cultural and physical landscape. Like an African *griot*, the narrator suggests that the story's origin does not matter. It partakes of oral lore. What matters instead is its contingent nature: the fact that it *can* happen. Crucial, then, is *the form* of an accident. The writer's address to his own people is the postcolonial liberating shift in consciousness illustrated by Frantz Fanon's attention to the strategic change of the formula "'once upon a time' to 'what you are now going to hear happened somewhere, but it might happen here, today or tomorrow'" (1959: 92). The story is a warning: if it is an accident, it may not be destiny. Thus presented, it echoes Laroche's vision: Haiti's "no" does not accept the hypothesis of a tragedy.

The curtains rise, and we see the setting of a specific part of Créon's house, surrounded by trees, and a space with two small chairs, a big armchair, and a table: the open space of the *péristile* (stage directions). In the Miami production, the Vodou altar of the house has offerings to the *lwas* and Vèvès[57] painted on the backcloth of the set. What follows gradually unveils loyalties between humans and *lwas*, weaving the Greek myth into the tapestry of Haitian history.

First, we hear Antigòn's strong "no." The "universal no" that Morisseau-Leroy rescues from the ancient tragedy resonates with the foundational Haitian "no" to France. The "rural chief" (*chef de section* in the original) who "thinks of himself as the state" refers to an existing political structure in rural areas, whereby a man chosen from among peasants is appointed by the Army to control the rural section. This chief is technically a member of the Army and the only real link in Haiti between the state and the peasantry, in charge of everything from guns to medicine. Anthony Maingot specifies that this is a French-style institution, more than two hundred years old; chiefs are often allied with landowners and become almost feudal lords when left on their own to rule their small territory.[58] Much of the violence in rural sections stems from confrontations between peasants and the armed rural chief (during Duvalier's regime, chiefs were de facto members of the Tonton Macoutes). According to Laroche (2005), rebellion against abusive armed power is one of the founding myths of the nation.

---

[57] Ritual diagrams of the astral forces that attract the spirits to earth; see Rigaud's collection (1974).

[58] See Maingot ([1994] 2018), Comhaire (1955), and Lahav (1975).

132 FÉLIX MORISSEAU-LEROY'S 1953 VODOU *ANTIGÒN AN KREYÒL*

Yes and *no* appear throughout the play with unstable meaning until the latter is settled: Antigòn's opening "no" (to Ismène, but indirectly to Créon) and Créon's servant Filo's closing "yes" (to Créon) posit the two attitudes toward the armed authority with whom no negotiation is possible. The drama of listening structures the relation among characters and will help display the opposition between autonomy and slavery. Antigòn and Créon reject voices, but different ones. While Antigòn does not listen to the military chief, Créon does not listen to his people or to the disembodied voice of the spirits' "law" (*lwa* in Haitian Creole is pronounced like *loi* [law] in French). In the Vodou imagination, listening to the spirits is an essential moral quality.

The first scene is an act of listening: Antigòn's refusal to listen to Ismène:

ANTIGÒN: I tell you: no
ISMÈNE: But, Antigòn, you have to listen.
ANTIGÒN: I don't want to listen.

When the godmother Marraine enters, the "no" and "yes" switch speakers, but the irreconcilable opposition remains. Ismène complains: "Antigòn wants to do something, and I told her no. She said yes." Later in the scene, Ismène recapitulates:

ISMÈNE: I am going with you.
ANTIGÒN: No.
ISMÈNE: No? Why?
ANTIGÒN: When I told you about burying Polinice you said no, no is no. (15)

Antigòn's "no is no," which refers to action, and in this case rebellion, has a strong resonance in Morisseau-Leroy's poems, whereby what makes a black man a man is his capacity to say "no." In the same year that he staged *Antigòn*, the playwright also published his now legendary poem for Dessalines, titled "Mèsi, Papa Desalin" ("Thank you, Papa Dessalines") and quoted in my epigraph above:

> If I am a man
> I must say: Thank you, Dessalines.
> [...] It is you who taught us to say: NO
> We are told some Negroes say: Yes, Yes!

FÉLIX MORISSEAU-LEROY'S 1953 VODOU *ANTIGÒN AN KREYÒL*   133

> Some others say: Yes, sir!
> You taught us to say: NO!
> Dessalines teaches all Negroes on earth how to say: NO.[59]

Dessalines appears in many of Morisseau-Leroy's poems. In "God is good," he is a godly figure: "It is HE/ Among valiant men, HE is Dessalines" (1991: 44). In the poem "Sa m di nan sa, Depestre," Morisseau-Leroy complains to "his little brother" René Depestre: "stop helping others ridicule Dessalines."[60] Following this thematic thread in Morisseau-Leroy's corpus, from *Antigòn*'s very first line we intuit a link to the Haitian revolution. Morisseau-Leroy's choice to write poems in honor of Dessalines—and not Toussaint Louverture or Christophe—is the radical choice for an American (not French) Haiti. It is the founding "national" choice. Echoing Mercier's dictum that to be Haitian is to be Dessalinien, Dany Laferrière refers to Dessalines as an "un-exportable" entry into history:

> As for Dessalines, he is the strongest Haitian figure but the least known abroad. He is *not exportable* […] I met a bookshop owner in Martinique once and he said to me: Édouard Glissant does this, Aimé Césaire does that, but they will not talk about Dessalines. So I asked him why they don't and he replied that if they were to talk about Dessalines, they would have to make Martinique independent. […] He is the appalling animal, the *national monster* […] A monster is against everything, just like Dessalines was. We hear talk about this monster and he was on our side. He was a monster to defend us.   (2005: 199; my emphasis)

Antigòn's "no" is as radical as Dessalines', and to judge from Morisseau-Leroy's Parisian experience, *Antigòn*'s Vodou performance may have turned out to be equally un-exportable. I return to this later.

The Vodou Ceremony: Créon's "Left-Handed?" Sorcery

After Antigòn and Ismène's quarrel, we see the quilting of tragedy and Vodou. From the start, something develops against the usual Vodou ritual:

---

[59] In Marie-Marcelle B. Racine's translation for the compilation *Haitiad & Oddities*, the last line reads "Dessalines, please teach all black people/ All blacks on this earth to say: No" (1991: 35–6). The line "Yes, sir!" is in English in the poet's original version, though with Creole spelling.
[60] *Optique* 19 (1955c: 7).

134 FÉLIX MORISSEAU-LEROY'S 1953 VODOU *ANTIGÒN AN KREYÒL*

the breaking of the burial rites has its correlative in the breaking of ceremonial rites. Marraine skips the songs and incantations that usually open ceremonies and, with her *canari* (clay pot), calls for help. In a Vodou ceremony, the *canari* is used to invoke the spirits only in the case of an urgent matter.[61]

And, indeed, the order of life and death has been altered, but following Vodou cosmology rather than Greek tragedy. In tragedy, life and death antagonize one another. In Vodou, life and death are transformations of life: the dead live among us in different forms, but only if they have been buried properly. The antagonism that organizes the ceremony is between two forms of life. One comprises life and death in the Western sense, and another one comprises the *living dead*, a type of death-in-life created by the lack of burial and later symbolized by Créon's aim at Antigòn's "zombification." On the side of life, the Vodou spirits of life and beauty join the two humans who will become Vodou spirits: Antigòn and Hémon. On the side of the living dead, Créon, helped by the spirits of the dead and his servant Filo, conveys the most ominous metaphor for slavery, bringing national memory onto the stage: death-in-life stands as the death of autonomy—the life of a "zombie." As rural chief and later *houngan*, Créon will have abused power in trying to make Antigòn a zombie.[62] The spirits of life gradually abandon Créon as he and his servant Filo come to represent enslaved life. In the play, this form of life will not find redemption—hence the tragedy.

The polarity between the gods of life and those on the side of zombification emerges as soon as the ceremony begins. The spirits called in are Papa Legba, Ezili Freda, Danbala, and Baron Samedi and his wife, Granne Brigitte. I add here a *papillon*—a butterfly that appears fleetingly. The first three (alongside the *papillon*) abandon Créon explicitly. And while the Baron and his wife decide to help him, Tiresias interprets this as abandonment: the gods have not protected Créon from his cruel intent.

In keeping with Vodou ceremonial order, Papa Legba is called in first. Coming out of the *canari* and addressing Marraine as *mambo*, Legba's disembodied voice opens a different entryway to memory: he announces the familiar ancient story but confesses that he can't be of help and departs. Legba's unusual decision to leave inaugurates a rich symbolic field of references that remain constant throughout the play: it signals that the communication between Créon's house and its ancestors is broken. Thus, we have

---

[61] See Métraux (1958).

[62] In rural Haiti, a *chef de section* could also be judge, notary public, or prosecutor, or serve as *houngan*.

misgivings from the start regarding Créon's decree. Unlike Marechal's Facundo, or for that matter, the ancient Creon, there is no justification for the Haitian Créon to have banned burial. We are given no details of the war between Haitian brothers, aside from Créon's assertion that Polinice died "in rebellion" (21). Créon will later say he went "with the enemy" (29). To follow my association between Antigòn's "no" and Dessalines' foundational "no," the rebellion "against a brother" echoes what Trouillot calls the "war within the war" at the hour of the nation's foundation.[63] Polinice might have even rebelled against Créon; the text only allows us to speculate, though the paintings and photos used in the productions indicate that it is the time of the Haitian revolution (Figures 2.1 and 2.2).[64] If nothing will justify Créon,

Figure 2.1 *Antigòn an Kreyòl*. Sosyete Koukouy of Miami, Inc. Miami Dade Auditorium, USA, May 10, 1998. Directed by Jan Mapou. Courtesy of Jan Mapou.

---

[63] Clark speculates the same: "In 1953, this particular text must have resonated in the minds of Haitian intellectuals accustomed to the history of civil wars among blacks and mulattos during the nineteenth century and well into the twentieth throughout the Marine Occupation" (1992b: 784).
[64] The Miami Creole performance has Ismène speak of a "civil war." The Miami set has walls decorated with a picture of a military leader wearing a round hat with feathers that looks like Toussaint's and a photo of ruins that could be the Citadel Laferrière, the military fortress built by Christophe's 20,000 men. This photo is placed high above other wall decorations, as if overlooking the rest of the set. Créon wears military attire, as he does in all four performances on

Figure 2.2 *Antigòn an Kreyòl*. Sosyete Koukouy of Miami, Inc. Miami Dade Auditorium, USA, May 10, 1998. Directed by Jan Mapou. Courtesy of Jan Mapou.

Créon's action also seems impermeable to any kind of advice. Already at this point in the play, there is no Vodou transformation in sight for him.

After Papa Legba has left, Tiresias, played by Morisseau-Leroy, both in the première in Port-au-Prince and in Paris at the Théâtre des Nations, tries to convince Créon to undo his action (Figure 2.3).

In Tiresias' speech, there is a bad omen: in the morning, a *papillon* perched on a column of the *péristile*. Tiresias thought the butterfly would bring good luck if it remained. But the butterfly left "with the speed of the North Wind" (23).[65] As I have mentioned, a butterfly may indicate the presence of the legendary one-armed sorcerer Makandal, who "jumped out" shouting "Makandal sauvé" ("Makandal saved") when bound to the stake and told his followers he would return transformed into a mosquito or butterfly. Makandal is also believed to have appeared to warn Dessalines of his assassination. I have also mentioned one Jean-François Papillon among the four revolutionary leaders present at the Vodou ceremony of Bois-Caïman. Tiresias' omen

which I base this account. I thank the director of the play, Jan Mapou, for facilitating a DVD and photos of the performance in Miami.

[65] The north wind blows in December and briefly interrupts the dry season, which runs from November to January.

Figure 2.3 *Antigòn an Kreyòl*. Morisseau-Leroy as Tiresias. Theater of Nations. Sarah Bernhardt Theatre Paris, France, May 11, 1959. Directed by A. M. Julien. Photographer Roger Pic. Courtesy of the Bibliothèque Nationale de France, Site Richelieu.

comes from indomitable, ancestral, and revolutionary African Maroons. The butterfly-Makandal-Jean-François who dreamed of freedom has departed.

Ezili Freda comes next, called in by Tiresias at Créon's behest, since she is the guardian of Créon's house. Like Legba, Ezili is a spirit of the *Rada* rite, of the female family of symbols for charm, love, beauty, and imagination. She protects and is served by men rather than women and is known to be jealous and demand exclusive attention; when one speaks to her, flattery is the strategy. After her disembodied voice is heard in this *péristile*, she leaves dissatisfied, arguing that today "people do not listen to the adults" (27). Instead of listening to her, Créon complains out loud: "where were they" when the time came to save the village Teb or Polinice from the war—"why didn't *maitresse* Ezili take Polinice away from the enemy?" (29).

Now everything seems in place for Créon's act of sorcery. Impermeable to the gods of life, Créon calls on the spirits of the dead to perform a job with "his left hand." The spirits of the dead protect the cemeteries, led by the father of the family, Baron Samedi ("*Séclé- Quitté*" in the original)[66] and his

---

[66] In the original edition, the name of the spirit who protects the dead is "*Séclé- Quitté*" instead of Baron Samedi (*Sèkle-Kité* in Dominique [2002]; *Sèkle, kite*, in Bayeux's reproduction of this passage for his *Anthologie de la Littérature Créole Haitienne* [1999: 204]). In Saint-Amant's translation for Presence Africaine: "*Secle-Quitte*, mon loa protecteur. Secle-Quitte, toi qui gardes les morts, mon grand loa" ("Secle-Quitte, my protector spirit. Secle Quitte, you who guard the dead, my great spirit"). The spelling of this name changes from edition to edition;

138 FÉLIX MORISSEAU-LEROY'S 1953 VODOU *ANTIGÒN AN KREYÒL*

wife, Granne Brigitte. These spirits are Legba's counterparts in death. No violent sorcery is performed without first calling on the spirits of the dead, who determine the dead's entrance into the cemetery. The Baron and (especially) Brigitte are also powerful sorcerers, at times in charge of vanquishing enemies.[67]

Créon's decision to call the Baron and Brigitte reveals his interpretation of Antigòn's defiance. This becomes more evident when Filo, in his report to Créon, identifies Antigòn as a *djab*, which further aligns her with the Haitian revolution. In the Vodou imagination, *djab* are wild, individualistic, insatiable, supernatural spirits, whose function is magical protection or injury. They were believed to guard revolutionaries against white colonial bullets. Legend has it that during the 1791 Bois-Caïman, Mambo Marinette was possessed by Ezili Dantor, a hot *lwa* and mother figure sometimes referred to as a female *djab*, to perform the sacrifice of a wild hog. *Djab* belong to neither the Rada nor the Petwo pantheons and are often "chained" in ceremonies to control them. In their female form, the *djab* are said to be condemned to walk the earth for dying while still virgins.[68] An echo of Antigone's age-old virginity? We should not rush to a conclusion: Antigòn will marry in heaven, that is, in a different form of life.

From Créon's point of view, Antigòn is the utmost (and magically dangerous) expression of freedom. The burial scene that Filo reports indicates that spirits protect Antigòn: it does not rain where she goes; she walks on air, and she has many disembodied arms helping her. Créon is at first baffled: "I must be dreaming...What have I done to the *lwas*, to the dead?" (46–7). He talks to Antigòn, but to no avail; infuriated, he calls Antigòn *djab*. Now it is clear that, for him, Antigòn's indomitable spirit will only be tamed by assassination.

Bayeux transcribes it with a comma and without capitalization, which in turn renders his French translation "Cerclez, quittez," to convey not a spirit but rather an order to "encircle" and to "leave" the place. After a year of research, I found no consensus as to what Séclé-Quitté means: it does not appear in the Vodou pantheons, and Vodou experts have given me suggestions that range from a rare name for Papa Legba to a spirit of the pantheon of Kita spirits of Congo. For this chapter, I follow the usage I found in journals contemporary to Morisseau-Leroy's *Antigòn*, such as the formula to invoke Baron Samedi in Marcelin: "Au nom de Baron Samedi, gardien du cimetière, vous seul qui traversez le purgatoire par l'intermédiaire de M. Guédé-ronsou-mazaka. Nègre guide-di wélo, *Nègre séclé-quitté*, balai-rouzé, Nègre cume sur l'avalasse, trois-houes, trois-pinces, trois-piquois, trois-gamelles, Nègre cocoyer méyer, à l'envers, alovi, Ago, ago-ci, ago-là" (1955: 49; my emphasis). The same formula appears in Rigaud (1974: 330) though with a different spelling: "Nègre cèclez quittez."
 [67] See Marcelin (1955).   [68] See Dayan (1995: 54).

FÉLIX MORISSEAU-LEROY'S 1953 VODOU *ANTIGÒN AN KREYÒL*   139

The *papillon* (Makandal) having left the *péristile*, Antigòn—just as legend says Dessalines did—will miss the warning. Créon asks Brigitte to help him trap Antigòn's soul in a vase full of water. Créon has told Hémon that he will only find Antigòn's "zombie" (54), and this is what he aims at with his sorcery. Antigòn's initial "no" here acquires its full significance: her "no" to Polinice's lack of burial prevents his "zombification."

For the Vodou imagination, a zombie is one of the living dead. It is a haunting image in folk belief and an extreme metaphor for national consciousness: it represents the enslaved's loss of will, a body whose soul has been robbed with black magic and can be used to serve a human master, rather than a Vodou spirit. This mythical image responds to Vodou's cosmology: the spirits of the dead can populate the world of the living. Burial rites are essential to properly separate the soul from the body and keep good relations between the living and the dead. The zombie, then, remains among the living with no memory and no consciousness of its state.[69] This is the type of death feared in Haitian Vodou. For Laroche, it is the "image of a feared destiny that needs to be combated [...] both a collective and individual destiny" (1978: 193).

Créon thus summons the feared accident—which can happen anywhere and must be resisted—the most nightmarish image of the enslaved colonial past. Now performing as a *houngan* on stage, Créon introduces a knife into the vase, and the water turns red:[70] Créon has killed Antigòn's soul, as he says to Tiresias, holding the vase in his hands, "with the permission of the gods" (55). Tiresias warns him that the spirits have not protected Créon from committing murder. Tiresias attempts to secularize the gods: like historical events, the gods too can be seen from different points of view. But the scene had such a strong impact on audiences that Morisseau-Leroy felt compelled to speak about the gods' ambiguous relation to power:

> When Créon called the gods and asked them for the authorization to kill Antigone, they gave him that authorization...I am very different from Sophocles and Anouilh in that respect. Gods are made by men and they act exactly like men. So he killed Antigone with the [...] power of the gods. He didn't use a gun. He didn't use what Sophocles used. [...] In my

---

[69] See Métraux's classic account (1958).

[70] In the Miami production, he turned to face the wall and put a red cape around his neck; when he turned back to the audience, the lighting was dimmed as he held a vase with a doll inside and plunged the knife into it.

140 FÉLIX MORISSEAU-LEROY'S 1953 VODOU *ANTIGÒN AN KREYÒL*

play, I use the entire power of the gods! Wherever the play was performed no one laughed during that scene....It is a very serious affair that the gods are on the side of the chief. (1992: 669)

Morisseau-Leroy's use of the gods presents the most challenging element for interpretation. The gods' loyalties are in conflict at the climax of the play, which coincides with that of any Vodou ceremony: the crisis of possession, the most emblematic intimacy between Vodou and theatrical performance. If the spirits of the dead have "helped" Créon, the spirits of life intervene to save Antigòn. Protesting Tiresias' interpretation, Créon asks Tiresias to call Danbala, to prove that the gods of life are with him. Danbala has gone instead toward Antigòn. Ezili comes, but neither for Créon nor as a disembodied voice: she "mounts" the "horse" of the godmother, outraged at the glass of red water. Acting of her own accord, Ezili wishes to save the handsome Hémon, who she says will soon die. We later learn that Hémon had come "like the wind" (65) to take Antigòn out of her cell. This associates him with Makandal's wind: the butterfly Tiresias saw earlier fly away may be now returning. Ezili, in the body of the godmother, makes Tiresias call Antigòn's soul by ringing the clay pot. But Danbala has already mounted (and thus protected) both Antigòn and Hémon.

The young couple's voices are heard from offstage: they are crossing to a place where they cannot die. Antigòn's voice recalls and continues Hémon's earlier speech, when he challenged his father. After a heated discussion, Hémon leaves the *péristile*, linking Antigòn to revolution: "I am leaving. I am going to Antigòn [...] I am entering a place [...] where there are no hungry people, where there aren't people who are afraid of others [...] Antigòn and I are entering a country where people live *freely* [...] *drums are beating*" (52; my emphasis). Antigòn follows his lines: they will not return to earth, for they are now married in a place where there is no time, misery, or death. Créon sees two rainbows appear in the courtyard: the symbol of Danbala and his wife Ayda Ouèdo. Antigòn and Hémon have become their children.

The transformation of Antigòn and Hémon inserts the Vodou symbols of colonial history in the European form of tragedy. Créon has worked with his "left hand" and will have no redemption. Antigòn and Hémon have been deified within the terms of Vodou cosmology because they have been true to their mission on earth: to say "no." From a secular point of view, we may see this, as Max Dominique puts it, as a "negative utopia" (2002: 44) in the tragic future of no misery—tragic because it is the kind of future from

FÉLIX MORISSEAU-LEROY'S 1953 VODOU *ANTIGÒN AN KREYÒL* 141

which the dead sorcerer butterfly-Makandal operates. From a Vodou point of view, we may see in it the "metaphor of a world where everything is to be written and re-invented," as Shelton puts it (2000: 28).[71]

In Vodou, Antigòn will stay among the living forever, worshipped as a goddess: she will have her own altar like other *lwas* and will "mount" the horses when needed. This is how Morisseau-Leroy envisioned her: immortal. In an interview with Lucien Balmir for the newspaper *Le Matin* (July 24, 1953), Morisseau-Leroy said: "initiated in the cult and daughter of the gods, Antigone is [...] charged with personalizing that which is eternal." In his later poem "Antigone," published in *Diacoute 2*, Antigone is the "girl who knows how to die" yet on stage, the poet tells her: "listen to me well Tigone; you shouldn't be the one who dies all the time [...] tonight won't go like that; tonight we'll take the lash out at King Créon" (1972: 13).

Morisseau-Leroy indeed lashes out at King Créon. As Antigòn stands protected by Vodou for having said "no," with Ezili's act, the spirits have abandoned Créon for the second time. Ezili has sided with Hémon, that is, with Antigòn. Although Créon seems to believe that no god understands "men of rule" (73), he will stand in the opposite end of autonomy, by confessing that instead of imposing power, power has been imposed upon him. Créon's crisis comes after the news of Euridice's suicide. As Filo reports, Euridice has thrown herself into the river, a traditional dwelling place for the Vodou spirits. The river overflows, showing the spirits' anger. The people won't stop yelling, and Créon orders them to shut up (69). Créon wants to cry for the death of his son, but restrains himself: as King, he needs to provide an example for others. In his last attempt to exercise power, he orders Filo to forbid the people from crying (74). In a final confused speech—one in which he relinquishes full responsibility—he realizes he is cursed: "it is my fault but it is not my fault [...] there was no way for me to understand what they were telling me. There was something holding me back" (73). The play's opening line—Antigòn's "I tell you: No"—finds its opposite in Filo's final bow to Créon's power: as Filo obeys Créon's new order, the last line reads "Yes, King Créon" (74).

The alignment of the gods triggers Créon's doom: there is no possible transformation for him. Créon is servant to "something" other than himself,

---

[71] Shelton emphasizes Haitian culture and history but at the same time argues for the "easy" link between ancient Thebes and Haiti, taking the Greek text as a starting point: "a legend that opposes in inexorable fashion the blind power of the State and the need for rebellion. The link that exists between the Haitian context and the events of Sophocles' Thebes is certainly not forced" (2000: 28).

much as Filo is servant to Créon. If Antigòn's miraculous transformation into an immortal being grants the drama a redemptive touch, Filo and Créon's stasis reminds us of wherein lies the tragic for the nation: the loss of autonomy. The ancient tragic antagonism has become that of transformation and stasis, which can be rephrased as autonomy versus slavery. The gods of life have voiced their preference: autonomy. And while the spirits of the dead might have sided with Créon, for Filo there is only the tragedy of the black man who says "yes." A black man is a man only when he says "no."

A Revolutionary Present for a Revolutionary Past

Antigòn no doubt forms part of the Haitian movement both toward the legitimation of Creole as a language in its own right and toward a theater history that would secularize Vodou as a consciousness-raising force (showing the struggles among humans reflected among *lwas*). *Antigone* eased Morisseau-Leroy's secular dialogue with Vodou's sacred traditions in two ways.

On the one hand, Antigone's ancient passion—burial—served to dramatize a central concern in Haitian lore: the need to avoid the circulation of corpses or body parts in ceremonies performed by priests who practice with the "left hand." As in other places, in Haiti, funeral rites have been endowed (on stage and off) with a necropolitical dimension. When, years later, Morisseau-Leroy recalled that "people said that Duvalier did what Créon did" (1992: 670), he did not bring up just any anecdote to illustrate Duvalier's abuse of power. He brought up funeral rites: "Duvalier stopped a funeral in the middle of the street. That was in April 1959. I watched it […] The soldiers disappeared with the body, as they did in *Antigone*" (670). Of course the audience did not need Duvalier to be reminded of the importance of funeral rites. It sufficed for the playwright to make Créon speak of Antigòn as a "zombie," echoing in one stroke the Vodou warning about tampering with funeral rites and about slavery.

On the other hand, *Antigone* was an ideal vehicle for his view of Vodou's political role. To recover Vodou was not to recover "African tradition," but rather, a radical version of modernity's ideals propelled by African traditions in historical context. For Morisseau-Leroy's generation, Vodou had been crucial in the making of a specifically Haitian modernity. More than a result of French ideas, Haiti's independence stemmed from the strength of Africans and Creoles unified by language and Vodou. For many Haitians,

FÉLIX MORISSEAU-LEROY'S 1953 VODOU *ANTIGÒN AN KREYÒL*   143

Petwo Vodou rites, in particular, founded Haiti, Vodou, and Creole.[72] To recover Vodou at the most elite of urban theaters reminded the elite and the historians who read the Haitian revolution as "the daughter of the French Revolution" that the historical agents who fought for emancipation had been excluded by neocolonial masters.[73]

Morisseau-Leroy's Créon embodies those elites. As I have linked Morisseau-Leroy's Antigòn with Dessalines, I am now bound to strengthen that link, as well as considering the possibility that Créon may be the playwright's version of the first self-declared king of Haiti, Henri Christophe. Looming large in Caribbean literature, Christophe is suspected of having been involved in Dessalines' assassination in 1806.[74] Dessalines was the only one of the three revolutionary leaders who openly relied on Vodou. Legend has it that he ignored Makandal's spirit's warning before his departure to Pont Rouge, the site where he was killed. Of all three national heroes, he is the only one who has been, like Morisseau-Leroy's Antigòn, deified in Vodou. In the people's consciousness, he is the Creole Vodou *lwa Ogou Dessalines*, who walks along with the African *Ogou* spirit of war (Dayan 1995: 30).

But perhaps more telling than these legends is the strange fact that history seems to have given Dessalines his own Antigone. Might this history have also inspired Morisseau-Leroy? Once assassinated, Dessalines' corpse was mutilated and left unburied. According to written and oral history, a horrified Dédée Bazile, nicknamed Défilée-La-Folle ("Défilée the madwoman"), collected the leader's remains in a bag and was then helped to bury them properly. Défilée had been born a slave. She marched with the revolution, giving soldiers provisions, and was said to have gone mad. Dramatic representations of Défilée have her recover her reason at the sight

---

[72] See Dubois' comment, based on his conversations with Paris-based *houngan* Erol Josué, in his epilogue to *A Colony of Citizens* (2004b: 432–7).

[73] This trend continues. For efforts to recover the African roots of the Revolution, see Thornton (1993), M. Trouillot (1995), Nesbit (2008), Geggus (2001, 2002a, 2002b), and Fick (1990). Eighteenth-century France perceived African enslaved peoples as "inspired" by French ideals (see Sala-Molins 2006). See also Buck-Morss (2009) (though in the end Buck-Morss measures the revolution back against the parameters of the French one: Haiti "surpassed the metropole in actively realizing the Enlightenment goal of human liberty, seeming to give proof that *the French revolution was not simply a European phenomenon but world historical in its implications*" [39; my emphasis]).

[74] Contemporary to *Antigòn*, see Carpentier (1949), Walcott ([1950] 2002), and Césaire ([1963] 1970). In Haiti, the tradition goes back to the nineteenth century; see especially Chanlatte ([1818] 1918), Romane (1823), and Leconte ([1901] 1931).

144   FÉLIX MORISSEAU-LEROY'S 1953 VODOU *ANTIGÒN AN KREYÒL*

of Dessalines' dismembered corpse. She knew what she had to do: she had to bury her black brother.

In 1906, for the centenary of Dessalines' assassination, the poet Massillon Coicou wrote the national drama *L'Empereur Dessalines* (Emperor Dessalines). He portrayed Défilée carrying the leader's bones in the folds of her dress and asked: "isn't she the most beautiful incarnation of our national consciousness, this madwoman who moved amidst those who were mad but believed themselves sane?"[75] In 1967, Hénock Trouillot showed Défilée's grief at the sight of the corpse in his *Dessalines ou le sang du Pont Rouge*. She cries in despair that her countrymen have accomplished what the French could not: killed the "titan," the "father of the nation" (121). Grieving, she collects Dessalines' remains: "This blood, oh the blood of a just one! The blood of the black Christ! The blood of the Emperor!" (121). But her grief "is so true that Défilée has regained reason" ("repris sa raison," 130).

Morisseau-Leroy's Créon may have been Christophe, the man involved in Dessalines' murder. His Antigòn embodies every gesture of "national consciousness." Like Dédée Bazile, she needed to bury the brother, and like Dessalines, taught the nation to say "no." Antigòn, at once Antigone-Dessalines-Dédée, represents the antislavery and anticolonial revolutionary consciousness of the nation. Perhaps, even, Morisseau-Leroy's effort to render the message of the un-exportable Dessalines (to recall Laferrière) "exportable."

Back to the World: "To Be or Not to Be" Exportable

Haiti's urban press and peasant audiences recognized Antigòn as their own and lauded Creole as a real language. In fact, things at home went better than expected. The *Haiti-Journal* (July 20, 1953) warned of "tumultuous incidents" expected with this premiere: protests from those who did not want to "enthrone our vernacular language in our salons." But the review's complaint was related not to Creole but rather to Morisseau-Leroy's stand regarding the contested meaning of "national" consciousness. The reviewer agreed that Morisseau-Leroy's use of Creole was a masterstroke but asked the author to further convince the unconvinced elites that Creole was a literary language by translating *Haitian* plays, such as Massillon Coicou's *L'Empereur Dessalines*, into Creole. Interestingly, even if "Haitian" meant the

---

[75] Quoted in Dayan (1995: 41). Dayan cites Coicou's now lost second part of the play *Emperor Dessalines*, drawing from sources such as Duraciné Vaval, Ghislain Gouraige, and Timoléon Brutus. See also Braziel (2005).

history of the republic, the reviewer still associated it with the French language: the question was to know whether the moving words of Dessalines, Pétion, and so on, would be "as magic[al]" for the audience in Creole as they were in French. The elites would rather remember the national monster Dessalines with the "magic" of the French language. The reviewer for *Le Nouvelliste* (July 16, 1953) also warned that the play risked "two big dangers: vulgarity and ridicule," but asserted it nonetheless had escaped both: Creole "is capable of expressing the most profound and noble sentiments." *Le National* (July 27, 1953) complained of an excessive interest in Vodou, but also asserted that the new language seemed almost natural, to the point that "our emotion was so great in certain passages that we completely forgot the vehicle that transmitted messages that had so much pathos" (Figure 2.4). *Time* magazine announced the "Voodoo Tragedy" in the second week of August 1953 and made a point about Creole's simplicity and profundity, comparing it to the English language.[76]

Figure 2.4 *Time* magazine's review "Voodoo Tragedy," translated into French and published in *Le National*, Haiti, August 16, 1953. Bibliothèque Nationale de France, Site Richelieu.

---

[76] The review was translated into French for *Le National*, August 16, 1953: 9.

146 FÉLIX MORISSEAU-LEROY'S 1953 VODOU *ANTIGÒN AN KREYÒL*

Peasants saw the performance three days after the urban elite, out in the open air, eight kilometers away from the city. Morisseau-Leroy recalls: "Everyone sat on the grass; they were people from the country, from outside Port-au-Prince. It was an audience of peasants. And that was one of my proudest moments. Because it is for them that I write, not for all of those other writers. I write for the peasant. I write for the people of Haiti."[77] For him nothing confirmed his success more than an exclamation he heard from one of the spectators sitting on the grass: when Créon called Danbala, the spectator shouted out a prescient, if ill-timed, prediction: "Danbala won't reply!"[78] After Port-au-Prince, the play went to Saint-Marc and Cap Haïtien and many rural villages, where it played in improvised open-air theaters for peasants who sat on cushions on the ground.

Paris provided the lesson in "exportability": could the Haitian drama enter world theater? Paris hesitated about everything: Creole as language, Vodou as theater, and, of course, an Antigone who was neither Greek nor French. The play was staged from May 11 to 15, 1959, at the Sarah Bernhardt Theater for the Théâtre des Nations festival. In the French reviews, the play did not measure up to the "depth" of the "original" Greek tragedy—which, of course, amounted to nothing more than its French adaptations. Black, Haitian, Vodou, Creole *Antigòn* was not tragic enough, nor was her language a language. At stake was not the text, the acting, the direction, or the *mise-en-scène*, all of which were more or less praised. But to whom did Antigone's tragedy belong—whose tragedy was Greek?

For French reviewers, the attempt to transport the "universal depth" of Greek tragedy to the "simplicity" of the tropics was a failure. In the program of the Théâtre des Nations (May 11–15, 1959), Jean Cathelin presented the show as "a re-creation" whose "naiveté and 'meridional' flavor of Creole" gave the old story "a simplicity of dramatic movement that our intellectualized versions do not know how to grant anymore." The French press proceeded to elaborate on Haitian simplicity and French complexity.

For *L'Aurore* (May 12, 1959), the play "disconcerted" Parisians, and Creole made people "laugh." *Les Arts* (May 20, 1959) thought of it as "a mistake," all the more regrettable because the audience would have preferred a play "closer to Haiti's temperament." Georges Lerminier, writing for *Le Parisien Libéré* (May 13, 1959), found only the French-sounding names of the actors worth hearing. Creole was not a "tragic language"; *Antigòn* was the

---

[77] *The Miami New Times*, February 5, 1996.
[78] Morisseau-Leroy (1983); see also *The Miami New Times*, February 5, 1996.

"infantile" version of "Uncle Créon's Cabin" (he would have preferred a more "Caribbean story"); but he had to welcome "this troupe, whose names all sound so French, and who live of our culture and for our culture." *France Soir* sought confirmation of all the above in black spectators: "for the black audience that understands Creole the piece is excellent, but for the French, Morisseau-Leroy should have adapted a topic more specifically black and folkloric." *Le Figaro* (May 12, 1959) could not see Haiti: this *Antigone* had evoked the "French influence in Haiti." *Lettres Françaises* (May 28, 1959) expressed that "the profound drama escapes us, is it there at all? [...] we would like a play inspired more distinctly in the life of the Antilles."

Perhaps summarizing it all was André Rivollet's extreme title for *Aux Écoutes* on May 15, 1959: "Au Théatre des Nations, Antigone créole et le Vaudou:...de l'infantilisme à la névrose!" ("At the Theater of Nations, Creole Antigone and Voodoo:...from infantilism to neurosis!") (Figure 2.5).

Admiring only the "muscular training" of the actors and dancers, Rivollet concluded that the show was of "difficult export"; the dances were "beyond hysteria, dementia becomes mechanic, without being, at all, contagious," and the tragedy was a "babble," "a disservice to Sophocles," "laughable," "full of anachronisms and caricatures." To top it all, Rivollet no doubt missed

Figure 2.5 André Rivollet's review for *Aux Écoutes*, May 15, 1959: "At the Theater of Nations, Creole Antigone and Voodoo:...from infantilism to neurosis!" Bibliothèque Nationale de France, Site Richelieu.

148 FÉLIX MORISSEAU-LEROY'S 1953 VODOU *ANTIGÒN AN KREYÒL*

French—"one French word emerges sometimes from the torrent of phrases"—and complained, "where is the purity of blacks, rewriting the Bible their way in that unforgettable film *Green Pastures*?" Antoine Golea followed suit in his review of the dances that preceded the play, with a title "Monotones Hystéries: Danses de Haiti" for *Carrefour* (May 20, 1959): Vodou dance was "a crisis that owes as much to hysteria as to epilepsy." There were more cautious reviews that warned the French of their own limitations. After a caption that described Haiti as "keeping the effort of French culture intact" and the phrase "they speak Creole, we see nannies," critic Paul Morelle (*Libération*, May 13, 1959)[79] asked whether the French were not victims of their imagination associating Vodou with dementia and Creole with *Uncle Tom's Cabin*. Dominique Nores in *Les Lettres Nouvelles* (May 13, 1959) agreed that the "Creole dialect seemed naïve" and "hurt" the possibility of a tragic feeling, but asked the audience to "surpass this discontent" and discover the interest in setting the tragedy at a place "intimately in agreement with its ideology," given that "Haiti is the land of gods more than of men." Nores, nonetheless, failed to find Créon's speeches tragic.[80]

The ancient Antigone had dramatized the need for "locality," insisting that Polynices be buried in Thebes. Antigòn dramatized the same urgency for locality. Ironically, most of the French press, while asserting Antigone's universality, could only think of the universal as having one locality—France—and of tragedy as having one locally specific form—Greek (which the French could rightly imitate). Antigòn's exportability proved limited.

Back in the Caribbean, Cuban master of letters Alejo Carpentier (1904–80) had heard of a Haitian Antigòn while living in Caracas in 1953. He understood the stakes. In his review "Antígona en Creole," he considered Morisseau-Leroy's attempt "without precedents on the world stage"; he criticized Anouilh's *Medea* for its artificial faithfulness to the classic *Medea*

---

[79] An earlier incarnation of the *Libération* founded by Sartre (et al.) in 1973, it appeared from 1944 to 1964.

[80] Jacques Lermarchand's most favorable account in *Le Figaro Littéraire* (May 12, 1959), places *Antigòn* closer to the Greeks than the French, praising Morisseau-Leroy's decision to begin with Antigone's "No," warning the readers that "no familiarity" is in her spirit when she says "Tonton Créon"; he complains about modern versions of Creon, which help us "understand" him. *Aurore* (May 13, 1959) and *Humanité* (May 13, 1959) write about the "sweetness" the play brings to the Greeks. In *Nouvelles Littéraires* (May 21, 1959), René Jonglet emphasizes a local adaptation of the political concept of the reason of state; Emile Vuillermoz for *L'Intransigeant* (May 14, 1959) was touched by simplicity, sincerity, and humanity, unveiling how all the rest is "of the domain of university rhetoric." Only Jean Sel found "a powerful novelty" in this Antigone's combination of "realist language" and "magical events" in *France Observateur* (May 21, 1959).

FÉLIX MORISSEAU-LEROY'S 1953 VODOU *ANTIGÒN AN KREYÒL* 149

and stated that he preferred Morisseau-Leroy's *Antigòn*, which he imagined surrounded by the real vultures of the Haitian mountains, much more suited to express the tragic feeling than the measured civilized versions of France, Belgium, or Scotland.[81]

For all her lack of success in the metropolis, Antigòn managed to export Dessalines to the ex-colonial South. Morisseau-Leroy lived in Africa for twenty-one years, and the play was staged in Nigeria, Ghana, and Senegal. Then it was staged at the National Theater Festival in Jamaica when Morisseau-Leroy lived there. In 1981, Morisseau-Leroy settled in Miami, where he died. Since then the play has been staged in Miami, Boston, New York, and Washington, DC.

As she traveled, Morisseau-Leroy's Antigòn whispered to her audiences of her eternal survival. Housed in the Rada pantheon, she continues to give life, exporting the Dessalinean message: universal equality and emancipation. If modernity means anything, Antigòn says, it is the radical stance against "zombification" of any kind everywhere: a story that needs to be told by everyone.

---

[81] *El Nacional*, Caracas, August 18, 1953. See both the review on Medea and on Antígona in Carpentier's *Letra y Solfa*, 1959: 130–4. Carpentier had done the sound for the first adaptation of *Antigone* in Cuba (May 20, 1941) inaugurating the University Theater at the University of La Habana, Plaza Cadenas. Directed by Austrian émigré Ludwig Schajowicz, who used Juan M. Dihigo's translation, Antígona was adapted to celebrate the thirty-ninth commemoration of the birth of the Republic of Cuba in 1902—by now a familiar gesture to the reader. Carpentier also wrote a review in *El Tiempo*, entitled "Antígona de Sófocles en la universidad" (May 25, 1941).

3
Brazil's Exposed Corpses

Jorge Andrade's 1957 *Pedreira das almas* and 1969 *As Confrarias*

[...] in the middle there was a hillock from which, here and there, human remains would be revealed when it rained enough and there were many corpses on the soil that had not been buried yet [...][1]

Pedreira das almas (1957)

In the small town of Pedreira, in the state of Minas Gerais, the mines are exhausted.[2] People cannot cultivate the land; neither can they bury their dead nor pay taxes. The 1842 Liberal Revolt is taking place. Gabriel, one of the leaders of the revolt, wants his fiancée, Mariana, and the people of Pedreira to abandon the town in search of new fertile lands in the Planalto (São Paulo state). Mariana's mother, the matriarch Urbana, opposes leaving behind the town's dead. Mariana's brother, Martiniano, has joined the revolution with Gabriel. The action begins when Gabriel returns to Pedreira, defeated by monarchic forces, and seeks shelter in the mountain caves. The military soon lay siege to the town; Martiniano has been taken prisoner. With the condition that Mariana stays in Pedreira, Urbana promises not to

---

[1] G. W. Freyrreis, describing the Cemetery of the New Blacks, Rio de Janeiro, 1814. Cited in Júlio César Medeiros da Silva Pereira's *À flor da terra: cemitério dos pretos novos no Rio de Janeiro* (2014). The book describes burial "just below the surface," with the example of a Catholic cemetery built next to a slave market in Rio de Janeiro, operating between 1772 and 1830 as a shallow mass grave into which approximately three corpses per day were tossed, naked and without burial rites.

[2] The *Encyclopedia of Latin American Theater* (Cortés and Barrea 2003: 66) translates the title of the play as *Quarry of Souls*. *Pedreira* could also be "pit" or "mine." The play was first published by Ahambi editora in 1958. I use the 1960 edition by Agir Editora in Rio de Janeiro. Esther Mesquita translated the play into French. All translations from Portuguese in this chapter are mine.

Antígonas: Writing from Latin America. Moira Fradinger, Oxford University Press. © Moira Fradinger 2023.
DOI: 10.1093/oso/9780192897091.003.0005

JORGE ANDRADE'S *PEDREIRA DAS ALMAS* AND *AS CONFRARIAS*   151

report Gabriel to General Vasconcelos, who is looking for him. Vasconcelos offers to release Martiniano in exchange for information about Gabriel. Before Urbana can decide, Martiniano is shot. Vasconcelos forbids Martiniano's burial. Urbana takes his corpse into the church and embraces it for three days until she dies of grief. Mariana demands that the General see the exposed corpses if he wishes to find Gabriel. He and his troops enter the church and exit in horror at the sight (and smell) of the decomposing bodies. The soldiers rebel against Vasconcelos, who declares Gabriel dead to his superiors. Gabriel and his followers leave. Mariana remains with her dead.

As Confrarias (1969)

It is 1789, the time of the "Inconfidência Mineira" in Minas Gerais.[3] Marta's son José, suspected of participating in the conspiracy against the monarchy, has been killed. Gold mining is at its height, destroying fertile lands and leaving peasants without property. With José's lover, the black courtesan Quitéria, Marta transports José's rotting corpse on a hammock from confraternity to confraternity, the only possible places for burial at the time. She visits the four confraternities in town: the Ordem Terceira de Nossa Senhora do Monte Carmelo (only for white members); the black confraternity of Rosário (only for blacks); the Irmandade de São José (only for *pardos*),[4] and the Ordem Terceira das Mercês (only for liberal merchants). Each one rejects the corpse because José does not fit into any of their identity categories. Engaging the priests in each religious order, Marta unveils their economic interests, prejudices, and injustice. Flashbacks provide a second temporal place of action in the past, through which we learn of Marta's life with her husband and her son. José was an actor; in the flashbacks, we see him performing. Marta's husband, Sebastião, was a farmer. He was hanged from a tree while defending his land from gold miners. In the end, José is buried but not in a confraternity.

---

[3] The title of the play could be translated as *The Confraternities* (or *The brotherhoods*). In this chapter, I quote from Andrade's *Marta, a árvore e o relógio* ([1970] 1986: 25–70). For an introduction to colonial fraternities in Minas Gerais, see Boschi (1986).

[4] *Pardo* indicates mixing (*mestiços*, of Indigenous-European descent; *mulatos*, of African-European descent; *cafuços*, of African-Indigenous descent). In 1500, Portuguese Pêro Vaz de Caminha wrote an official letter about the first landing on Brazilian coasts, describing indigenous peoples as "pardos." Over time, the term became one of five official census categories. I use it because it appears in Andrade's text; current Brazilian critical race studies are questioning all colonial racial categories.

152 JORGE ANDRADE'S *PEDREIRA DAS ALMAS* AND *AS CONFRARIAS*

Obeying to the Letter

To leave the body exposed: to use the enemy's own weapon against him. Does the tyrant want a body rotting in the city, in the church, in the plaza, for all to see? Let it rot then. To shift the location of the spectacle: let it rot for *all* to see, including the tyrant. Let the tyrant be part of his own audience, rather than just command it. "May my brother's body remain exposed... it will be a living remembrance of your sin," says Mariana to the General in *Pedreira das almas*. "May the smell of his corpse make life in the city intolerable!" says Marta to the priests, in *As Confrarias*. The Brazilian Antígonas bring to the stage a new political strategy. This shift in the treatment of the corpse is so radical that Jorge Andrade's particular *antropofagia* of Antigone's ancient burial can be seen as the creation of another myth: that of a woman whose courage lies not in disobeying man's law by invoking a superior law, but rather in disobeying it by actually following its command to the letter—we may even call it a Socratic solution.

Jorge Andrade (1922–84) knew *Antigone* well. In São Paulo, he had taught theater to high school students, examining modern "problems" through the lens of Henrik Ibsen's *An Enemy of the People*, Shakespeare's *King Lear*, and Sophocles' *Antigone*.[5] Obsessed with the history of his country, he wove national history and *Antigone* into a story about national mothers. While *As Confrarias* did not see the stage when it was written, *Pedreira das almas* successfully began a theatrical career when the renowned theater company Teatro Brasileiro de Comédia (TBC) chose it in 1958 to celebrate its tenth anniversary. Reviewers celebrated the choice: "national" theater at the TBC—for once! As Arantes writes (2001: 68), it was a "turning point for both the playwright and the TBC" in their search for *brasilidade*. It staged Brazilians as agents of their own history, highlighting the nation's rural roots.[6]

The TBC was probably Brazil's most professional artistic company, but its productions were mostly European dramas.[7] For their tenth anniversary, they decided that *Pedreira* be accompanied by Arthur Miller's *A View from the Bridge* and William Shakespeare's *Macbeth* (although the latter was not

---

[5] See Andrade's interview with *Visão* (1966).

[6] All archival materials are from FUNARTE in Rio de Janeiro, where I was assisted with excellence: newspaper reviews, interviews, journals, and critical works on Andrade's plays have no page numbers. In 1966 and 1977, the play was produced in São Paulo and then in many cities in Brazil in 1967, 1978, 1980, 1983, 1984, and 1987.

[7] *O Estado de São Paulo* (1958). For the history of the TBC, see Guzik (1986).

JORGE ANDRADE'S *PEDREIRA DAS ALMAS* AND *AS CONFRARIAS*   153

staged). Reviewers noticed the fragment of antiquity immediately—at least "to a certain extent" they viewed the play as "reminiscent" of *Antigone*.[8] But the latter was not seen as "foreign": it was a renovation of Brazil's *national* theater. Like Marechal and Morisseau-Leroy, Andrade's "strategic classicism" was to deploy Antigone's burial to speak about the nation's foundations. The press applauded Andrade's statement about history: "two generations struggling: one wants to evolve and the other wants to keep the status quo"; "the eternal conflict between the new and the old."[9]

Literary critics went looking for a "complete tragedy."[10] Critic Décio de Almeida Prado settled the debate in 1964: "it is and it wishes to be a tragedy, in the traditional sense of the word [...] Greek reminiscences are innumerable [...]." Andrade's tragic frame had managed to translate the death of Brazilian historical cycles into the "universal" experience of the human capacity for change and to escape from the didactic political theater in vogue in the 1960s.[11] The tragic conflict was seen successively displaced from one pair of adversaries to the next: first, in the confrontation between Gabriel and Urbana; then, Urbana and Vasconcelos; later, Mariana and Vasconcelos; followed by Mariana and her mother Urbana; and, finally, between Mariana and Gabriel. Mariana is a constant presence in all these pairings.[12]

While critics and reviews were warm, the 1958 audience was cold.[13] The production ran for less than two months. The play was so laden with historical detail that it was difficult even for the local audience to follow. Some reviewers questioned whether it could reach contemporary audiences at all.

---

[8] Rosenfeld (1962: 110).

[9] See, respectively, *A Gazeta Esportiva*, November 13, 1966; *O Estado de São Paulo*, November 18, 1966; and *A Gazeta*, São Paulo, November 30, 1966.

[10] Azevedo (2014: 91).

[11] See Almeida Prado (1998), Maciel (2005), Pontes and Miceli (2012: 241–63), Guidarini (1992), Magaldi and Vargas (2001), Azevedo (2014), Sant'Anna (1997). See also critical comments in Andrade's collection, *Marta, a árvore e o relógio* (1986), from writers including Anatol Rosenfeld, Décio de Almeida Prado, Antonio Candido, and Sábato Magaldi.

[12] See Rosenfeld (1962), Mazzara (1997: 3–16). Clark (1981) relates the debate over the play as "tragedy." For a comparison with the Sophoclean text, see Nuñez (1986); for a comparison with the Greek theme of burial, see Garavello Martins (2012). See also Rosario Moreno (1997) and Vilanova (1999b: 141–2). See a brief note in Bañuls Oller et al. (2008: 438–41), although this commentary includes plot mistakes, considers 1842 a "decolonizing process," associates Vasconcelos (with no textual evidence) with US control of countries in South America, and refers in a note to the military coups of Chile (1973) and Guatemala (1954). See Pianacci (2008: 106–9) for another brief summary of the plot.

[13] Arantes quotes Guzik's research on "the cold reaction" of the audience. Guzik considered that 140 people per show was not a success, given the expenses of the show's production (Guzik 1986: 171 in Arantes 2001: 89).

154   JORGE ANDRADE'S *PEDREIRA DAS ALMAS* AND *AS CONFRARIAS*

In press interviews, Andrade repeatedly found himself explaining that the dead bodies the press associated with *Antigone* were Brazil's dead: Brazilians needed to appropriate their roots and bury and redeem the past.[14] In addition to the distant setting, the audience struggled with the form: to quilt national history with a Greek tragedy was too innovative, and the language was too lyrical.

Andrade got the message. He rewrote the play three times (in 1958, 1960, and 1970). First, he replaced the Greek-inspired female chorus with four female characters. Elizabeth Azevedo contrasts the 1958 version, with its choral voices speaking simultaneously and fragmentarily, creating the impression of "a beehive" at their mass exit, with the "restrained" 1960 version, where the new individual female characters speak clearly and without interrupting one another (2014: 89–91). In both versions, the women wore long shawls, making them look ghostly. They were differentiated by dress color and voice pitch: the women who would leave the town were dressed in white and had "clear" voices, while those who stayed with their dead were dressed in gray and had "dark" voices—a performative way of quilting utopia with tragedy. Whereas some reviews of the 1958 premiere spoke of the "epic" character of the play, there was nothing Brechtian in the first version. The second version, however, included a didactic twist at the beginning: Mariana and her best friend, Clara, stand at the church entrance, narrating the backstory to the audience, as if Andrade felt that the audience really needed help.

Much like Marechal's "lyrical" theater, Andrade's *Pedreira* was so richly poetic that translating it to the stage proved cumbersome. Critic Paulo Mendonça attended performances of both the 1958 and the 1966 productions of the play in São Paulo. His almost one-page-long review of the 1966 production in *Folha de São Paulo* dwelled on the difficulty of Andrade's poetry:

> With a marked influence of Greek tragedy, [...] it is important [...] to project its *áspera poesia* [rough poetry], the *densidade mineral* [mineral density] of its text. [...] the strength of the play depends on the way in which the original [text] reaches the audience with all its rustic violence [...] I insist. It is the words that basically count [...] what gives a strange and obscure magnetism to the play is the harsh beauty of its language. Without its valorization the production sinks.   (January 12, 1966)[15]

---

[14] *O Estado de São Paulo*, November 5, 1958.
[15] Andrade's language was an issue for most reviewers. In 1966, while Mendonça was criticizing the student production at the University of São Paulo, Gilberto di Pierro suggested

JORGE ANDRADE'S *PEDREIRA DAS ALMAS* AND *AS CONFRARIAS*   155

The TBC booklet presenting the 1958 premiere featured director Alberto D'Aversa's comments on the difficulties of producing "the first proper tragedy on the Brazilian stage."[16] D'Aversa had found obstacles in both the novelty of its language and what he saw as its "extreme Brazilian-ness." He coined the phrase "theater of expression" (contrasting it with expressionism) to describe the play: "an epic theater entrusted to poetry and not to method."[17]

In the same booklet, the TBC clarified details for spectators. The director of the company wrote that the real message of *Pedreira* was for Brazilians "to love the past but not to remain fixated on it, to reach for new lands, new rivers, new wealth [...]" (5). Renowned literary critic Antonio Candido inadvertently referred to the quilting of tragedy and utopia. He wrote that Gabriel and Martiniano inverted the Sophoclean order: Gabriel is the living dead buried in the hiding place, needing to be above ground, and Martiniano is the dead living, who lies unburied, exposed in the open air of the town. But at the same time he stressed the play's Brazilian roots and compared the "new lands" imagined by the youth of Pedreira to the Guaraní indigenous narratives of a mythical "land with no evil" (1958: 284).

As the play was restaged after the military-civic coup in 1964, reviews highlighted its "national" character, though the history lesson shifted from "the rural roots" of *brasilidade* to the people's "cry for liberty." The law school students who produced it in 1966 at the University of São Paulo expressed that the play was "*o nosso grito de reforma*" ("our shout for reform"); the *Gazeta Esportiva* qualified the students' choice of Andrade's play as "*história atualíssima. Uma história universal*" ("the most contemporary history. A universal history"). In 1977, the major newspaper *Folha de São Paulo* wrote: "*Pedreira no momento certo*" ("*Pedreira* at the right moment"), aligning the play with other denunciations against the dictatorship, such as Chico Buarque and Paulo Pontes' 1975 Medea, *Gota d'Água*, and Gianfrancesco Guarnieri's 1976 *Ponto de partida* (on the murder of journalist Vladimir Herzog). Critic Hilton Viana noted in *Diário da noite* that Andrade's play had premiered nineteen years previously, but "the

---

doing without the text and choosing a "plastic production" emphasizing the corporeal performance (*Diário Popular*, São Paulo, November 30, 1966). See also *A Gazeta* and *Jornal da tarde*'s reviews.

[16] The booklet included music composer Diego Pacheco's choices to convey the spirit of the town and the "poetic roots of the play": folk songs from São Paulo and Minas Gerais, especially from folklorist Rossini Tavares de Lima.

[17] See Arantes (2009: 91). The Portuguese reads: "um teatro épico confiado à poesia e não ao método."

156 JORGE ANDRADE'S *PEDREIRA DAS ALMAS* AND *AS CONFRARIAS*

audience of new generations may think it was just written yesterday" (1977). Sábato Magaldi wrote in *Jornal da Tarde* "*Um passado de candente atualidade*" ("A past of burning topicality," 1977) and directly mentioned Sophocles: "*Mariana é quase uma* Antígona" ("Mariana is almost an Antigone").[18] If *Pedreira* presented difficulties in terms of its historical detail, its lyrical, and theatrical language, *As Confrarias* was complex to the extreme. It required such an exorbitant budget that it failed to see the stage until 2013. Andrade was certain the play would not pass the dictatorship's censors, so he did not concern himself with translation to the stage.[19] Critics of *As Confrarias* dwell on the spectacular and grandiose scenic description of colonial society and its pillars, the confraternities, as well as its metalanguage. Andrade's dead living in this play is the actor José: the skill of wearing a mask could better unmask colonial society.[20]

While critics and reviewers were busy looking for Andrade's tragic frame, Andrade, just as Morisseau-Leroy and Marechal had done, transmitted hope. The *brasilidade* of Andrade's plays lies in his reflection on a particular political language and strategy for change. Andrade's Antígonas quilt tragedy with redemption, the quilting point being in both cases the exposed corpses. Thanks to these corpses, a utopian vector appears on these stages: in *Pedreira*, he who needs to lead the town out of its misery will live to do so, and in *As Confrarias*, he who needs burial will find it by teaching the town a lesson. To be sure, for the exposed corpses to quilt the tragic and the utopian, Mariana and Marta have to become mothers who will make a sacrifice for the life of others. And just like Varela's Argia, and Marechal's Antígona Vélez, Mariana and Marta also share the desire for female exchange.

---

[18] See also Jairo Arco e Flexa for a comparison with Sophocles' *Antigone* (*Veja*, *São Paulo*, January 6, 1977: 79).

[19] Catarina Sant'Anna writes: "according to Andrade's widow, the author purposely constructed *As Confrarias* and *O Sumidouro* as complex works, almost as if enjoying his freedom, because he deemed them unfeasible according to the criteria of the censors and the dire financial straits for theater at that moment" (1997: 78–9). The Student Theater Group Vicente de Carvalho in Cidade de Santos (São Paulo) staged *As Confrarias* on July 13, 1972, with Andrade's assistance at Teatro Radio Clube. On June 5, 2013, a theater company, Companhia de Teatro de Seraphim, finally took up the complete project in Recife, directed by Antonio Cadengue. When the play was published in the collection *Marta, a árvore e o relógio*, Mendes reviewed it for the journal *Palco +Platéia* (1971).

[20] For analysis of metatheatricality, see especially Sant'Anna (1997), Azevedo (2014), Arantes (2001), Oliveira (2003, 2005), Patriota (1992), and Nosella (2012).

JORGE ANDRADE'S *PEDREIRA DAS ALMAS* AND *AS CONFRARIAS*   157

But their extraordinary originality lies elsewhere. Mariana and Marta bring to the stage a different exercise in politics: a praxis of the literal, we could say—a political praxis of citation. On the one hand, they interpellate authority personally, making the rotting bodies impart a sensory lesson rather than pontificate about abstract ideals. The subtext for this lesson rests partly on the religious model of the exposure of Christ's tortured body: the symbol of Saint Thomas the Apostle, who needed to see with his own eyes in order to believe, hovers over *Pedreira*. It is, of course, part of Andrade's penchant for the metatheatrical: seeing makes the audience "believe." But most importantly, the lesson in a politics of citation is part of what made Andrade's theater "national": as I explain below, foregrounded in *As Confrarias*, the exposed tortured body of the eighteenth-century rebel "Tiradentes" (Joaquim José da Silva Xavier, 1746–92) is the nation's icon for revolt. The women in Andrade's plays risk their lives by thwarting the sacredness of burial and exposing the corpse's smell and decay. If the condition of possibility for colonial necropolitics is a corpse, these Antígonas use that very same corpse for a politics of the living—just as the Brazilian Republic did by transforming Tiradentes into a hero.

On the other hand, Andrade's women mimic the language of those who use the corpse as a catalyst of politics. Rather than opposing the law or presenting an alternative to it (the corpse "should" be buried due to divine law, human rights, and so on), the women demand radical consistency from those who issue the commands. Mariana and Marta ask the tyrant to become a "true" believer in what he has done, to face the ultimate consequence of his edict, just as both heroines face the ultimate consequence of their decisions. Their rebellion is to take the edict to its paroxysmal extreme. The women act on the exception that proves the rule: the tyrant commands that everyone see, except for him. Followed to the letter, the burial ban includes those who issue the command. It is their intervention on the "unsaid" of the edict that allows these women to demand radical consistency and to remain alive, for Andrade bets on life. As for Varela's Creon, as for Marechal's Antígona, for Andrade's heroines the brother's burial recedes in importance with respect to their lesson for living.

On and off stage, a politics of citation became a strategy for women in search of their missing relatives during and after the continent's Cold War militarization of politics. Chapters 6 is devoted to this political strategy. But Andrade's inspiration for his particular cannibalization of the ancient burial came from his vision of Brazil's colonial history, its Christian imagination, and the great thinkers who reinterpreted Brazil's history in the early

158 JORGE ANDRADE'S *PEDREIRA DAS ALMAS* AND *AS CONFRARIAS*

twentieth century. The latter argued that bourgeois liberal representative politics, based on the liberal institution of impersonal, abstract laws, was impossible in Brazil. Brazil's public space had developed through the influence of powerful landowning (and slaveholding) family groups, strong regionalisms, and a political sphere dominated by personal alliances. Andrade's Antígonas are "Brazilian" in that they pursue the "politics of the personal" that Andrade thought characterized Brazil's roots. Unlike the ancient sister, they aim at transforming their political audience, on and off stage, through citation and experience—affective, emotional, sensory experience.

Jorge Andrade: *"eu fui à história procurar, eu estudei, sim, eu estudei"*

When revisiting Brazilian theater in the 1960s, Latin American scholars first think of the experimental "theater of the oppressed," led by legendary Augusto Boal (1931–2009) and associated with other theater collectives, such as Teatro de Arena and Teatro Oficina. In 1967, the latter revived Oswald de Andrade's concept of *antropofagia* by staging his 1937 play, *O Rei da Vela* (*The Candle King*), for the first time.[21] "Committed" art was everywhere: the world famous revolt of Cinema Novo (Glauber Rocha, Nelson Pereira dos Santos, Ruy Guerra, Leon Hirszman, Ivan Cardoso), Bossa Nova's second generation of musicians (Nara Leão, Marcus and Sergio Valle, Edu Lobo), and the Tropicália movement (Gilberto Gil, Caetano Veloso, Maria Bethânia). In politics, the famous CPCs (Centros Populares de Cultura/Popular Cultural Centers), liberation theology (Hélder Câmara, Leonardo Boff), and the northeast *ligas camponesas* ("peasant leagues," helped by the Communist Party), illuminated the roads to be taken. Culture and politics were gunpowder, even after the 1964 military coup—until its worst crackdown started in 1968.[22]

A playwright of "Brazilian roots," as Luis Humberto Martins Arantes calls him (2001: 82), Andrade is neither a name that immediately traveled abroad nor one associated with any of the internationally renowned

---

[21] The translation of Andrade's phrase in the subheading reads: "I went looking for history; I studied, yes, I studied" (interviewed in *Istoé* April 19, 1978, p. 45). For an introduction to Brazilian theater from the point of view of performance studies, see George (2014). For militant theater groups in Brazil during the 1960s, see Silvana Garcia (1991) and Mostaco (1982).

[22] For a general introduction, see Schwarz (2014: 7–47).

JORGE ANDRADE'S *PEDREIRA DAS ALMAS* AND *AS CONFRARIAS*   159

Brazilian cultural movements of the 1960s. Yet in Brazil, Andrade is considered one of the greatest playwrights ever, part of the 1950s movement for theater modernization and "nationalization." Brazilian critics usually place the birth of socially conscious art in the northeast part of the *sertão*[23] and in the genre of the novel, at the turn of the twentieth century, championing peasant struggles (written by José de Alencar, Jorge Amado, Graciliano Ramos, Rachel de Queiroz, and so on). For Brazilian critics, Andrade is to São Paulo (that is, to the modern metropolis) what the northeast novelists are to the *sertão*. Andrade's historical dramas earned him the label of "*O homem-memória* [the memory man] [...] of the modern stage."[24] His contemporaries in the 1960s were discarding the past and, with it, classical artistic genres—think of Boal's rejection of Greek tragedy as a reactionary form.[25] Andrade saw the mission of his theater elsewhere: he set out to recover forgotten pasts elided from official historiography, buried in shallow graves. His eyes were on the historical corpses haunting the twentieth-century political scene, just as the unburied slave corpses, in G. W. Freyrreis' epigraph to this chapter, disturbed the dwellers of early nineteenth-century Rio de Janeiro.

Because of his historical vision, his contemporaries saw Andrade as "nostalgic," "reformist," and "sulista" (a "southerner").[26] Because his theater was first staged by the traditional TBC group, following the principles of the Italian *commedia dell'arte*, it was considered more elitist than the popular groups influenced by Brecht (Teatro de Arena) or by the living legend José Celso Martinez Corrêa (Zé Celso, Teatro Oficina), who had spent time at the Berliner Ensemble. And because of his dialectical vision of history, Andrade was accused, by contemporary right-wing and left-wing groups alike, of doing "intellectual" theater, too nuanced to express the shining energy of utopian rhetoric. He was seen as not didactic enough, not direct enough, and too resistant to the (then) preferred "right or left" explanations that could mobilize people into action. He was censored by the right-wing military but also ostracized by the left. Nonetheless, Andrade confronted his contemporaries with his oft-repeated statement: "*Teatro não é palanque*

---

[23] The *sertão* is a semi-desert subregion that occupies part of (but is not limited to) the northeast of Brazil. It is considered the "backlands" to the coastal towns in which the Portuguese first settled. It has a mythical status in the national political imagination, especially for its millenarian nineteenth-century religious movements.

[24] J. P. Pinto, as quoted in Arantes (2001: 19).   [25] See Boal ([1979] 1983: 1–50).

[26] See Arantes (2001, chapter 2) for the reception of Andrade's plays in Brazil in the 1960s; see also Rosenfeld (1996).

160 JORGE ANDRADE'S *PEDREIRA DAS ALMAS* AND *AS CONFRARIAS*

e muito menos púlpito" ("Theater is not a political podium and much less a pulpit").[27] Andrade thought "all theater [was] political," though never "party politics."[28]

Andrade was born and educated in the oligarchy of São Paulo. He was the son of *fazendeiros* (landowners), whose ancestors were the famous Junqueiras—one of the most traditional centuries-old landowning families in Brazil, having been given land by 1750 in the mining region of Minas Gerais, where Andrade's two Antígonas take action. When mining production ended in the early nineteenth century, the Junqueiras emigrated toward the São Paulo region, where they started coffee plantations—this is the drama in *Pedreira*. Haunted by his memories of his family's plantations (*fazendas, cafezais*), Andrade was forever marked as a boy by the economic recession of 1929, after which his family lost their land and migrated to the city. During the recession, he spent his childhood working in the plantations from dawn to dusk, eating with workers and not returning home except to sleep. When the loss of family land became real, he saw his beloved grandfather lose his mind, insulting an invisible enemy with a gun in his hand and his face "spitting words as weapons: 'In no way will I give my land. [...] if the [lenders] come here I will receive them with bullets, bullets!' "[29]

"Roots," "the past," "real life" are keywords in most of Andrade's plays. As he put it, "I find it difficult to believe that a literary work does not have its roots in real facts [...] nobody invents anything [...]."[30] He devoted himself to the large library his family owned at the *fazenda* and tried to stage the historical drama of Brazilian—not European—men and women: "future generations will want to know how they lived, how they thought, how they fought [...] I thought of documenting São Paulo's 400-year history [...] I organized my theater in cycles: the cycle of gold, of coffee, and of industrialization. You can only explain the present by looking into its roots. I went looking for history."[31]

Andrade's early theater can be seen as an epic saga of Brazil, especially of the southwest, from colonial times to the mid-twentieth century.[32] Brazil became an indigenous monarchy when, in 1808, the Portuguese Crown moved to Rio de Janeiro, making Brazil the site of the Portuguese Empire.

---

[27] *A Tribuna*, Vittoria, November 19, 1975.
[28] "A TV é tão válida quanto o teatro," *A Tribuna*, November 19, 1975.
[29] From his memoir, *Labirinto*, Andrade (2009: 79).   [30] Azevedo et al. (2012: 31).
[31] *Istoé*, April 19, 1978, p. 45.
[32] For a synthetic vision of Andrade's first ten plays, see Rosenfeld, "Visão do ciclo," in Andrade ([1970] 1986: 559–617).

JORGE ANDRADE'S *PEDREIRA DAS ALMAS* AND *AS CONFRARIAS*   161

The Portuguese king remained until 1821 and left his son Pedro I in power, later succeeded by Pedro II. In 1822, Pedro I declared himself Emperor of Brazil, solidifying an already-entrenched local aristocracy. The monarchy survived until 1889. Slavery, a recurrent theme in Andrade's plays, lasted until 1888 and was crucial first for the sugar plantations in northern Brazil, then for the eighteenth-century gold rush, the nineteenth-century coffee plantations, and the twentieth-century rubber industry. Andrade's plays portray the economic "cycles" of sugar, gold, and coffee, which determined the circulation of wealth among landowning elites tied to the monarchy. His concern was to register the decline and emergence of elites. His dramas became stories about forced migrations to the cities after the exhaustion of rural resources; the loss of economic grandeur; the mixing of Europeans, indigenous, and African populations; and the very early violent encounter between the Amerindian peoples and the Portuguese who discovered gold mines. For Andrade, the roots of modern Brazil were rural: what needed explanation was urban development. Later in his life, Andrade divided his work into "rural" and "urban" plays.

Theater became for Andrade a way to position oneself vis-à-vis the discovered history. His ultimate thesis was that his country had not processed its own history and, therefore, could not explain its present; theater would/could help finally bury the past. As he put it in 1973: "I fought against my dead and theater made me accept them."[33] It may seem less surprising now that he chose Antigone twice, and indeed Antigone appears often in his 1978 memoir, *Labirinto*, when he meditates on Brazil's unburied past. His theater can be seen as a grand but shallow burial site, where unburied corpses are made to speak to the living—with a lesson.

Brazil's Intellectuals, *Antigone*, and the History Andrade "Went Looking For"

Andrade's choice of Antigone also becomes clearer when we consider how Antigone was deployed to explain Brazil in the early twentieth century. Andrade was inspired by the towering intellectuals who revolutionized how Brazilians interpreted their past: São Paulo historians Sérgio Buarque de Holanda and Caio Prado Júnior (1907–90), cultural critic Antonio Candido

---

[33] From the interview with Anatol Rosenfeld for *Revista Argumento* in 1973 (compiled in Azevedo et al. 2012: 52).

162 JORGE ANDRADE'S *PEDREIRA DAS ALMAS* AND *AS CONFRARIAS*

(1918–2017), his own theater professor, Décio de Almeida Prado (1917–2000), northeastern sociologist Gilberto Freyre (1900–87), and legendary novelist Érico Veríssimo (1905–75).[34] Through a different genre, Andrade dealt with the same questions as his contemporaries: What was Brazil—a nation, or just a country? Which roots could explain its present? Had modernization really happened?

For Andrade's contemporaries, the development of Brazilian life had depended on the patriarchal family (keeping land, property, and political elites in place). This type of social bond responded directly to the demands of a capitalist plantation economy for the external market rather than the internal one; the permanent supply of enslaved labor made the development of the internal market irrelevant.[35] In Brazil, individuals with no family were seen as a marginalized periphery. Thus the often-quoted complaint that "Brasil não tem povo, tem público" ("Brazil does not have a people, it has a populace/spectators"),[36] which alludes to the nineteenth-century semifeudal relations in rural latifundia, whereby peasants could not organize easily— hence "no people"—because they were coopted by the benefits given to them for following the political will of the landowning families. For Andrade, the dramatization of family relations was as crucial as rescuing the voices of the "people," which he saw mostly absent from national literatures and theaters.

In his *Raízes do Brasil* (*Roots of Brazil*, 1936), Buarque de Holanda transformed *Antigone* almost into a symbol for the political sphere as it was developed in Brazil's plantation economies—certainly one more reminder, in the context of this book, of how Greek fragments were mobilized to understand the national. Buarque de Holanda did not read Antigone as a freedom fighter but followed the Hegelian interpretation of Antigone as a defender of family values against the city-state. In a chapter titled "Antigone and Creon," he proposed that one of Brazil's contributions to civilization was the social production of what he called *o homem cordial* ("the cordial man"). "Cordial" must be understood etymologically: *ex corde*, from the heart. The cordial man was not necessarily agreeable. He was the man *ruled* by the heart: "enmity can be as cordial as friendship, in that both come from

---

[34] See Freyre ([1933] 2002), Buarque de Holanda ([1936] 1973), Prado Júnior ([1942] 1965), and Candido ([1959] 2000). These names appear often in Andrade's memoir *Labirinto* ([1978] 2009).

[35] See Botelho et al. (2001).

[36] "Público" can be translated also as "audience, spectators". Coined by Afro-Brazilian writer and journalist Lima Barreto (1881–1922), the phrase refers to the end of the monarchy and the paradox that people remained recipients of decisions made by the elites.

JORGE ANDRADE'S *PEDREIRA DAS ALMAS* AND *AS CONFRARIAS*   163

the heart, proceed from the sphere of the intimate, the familiar" (*Roots*, 137). For Buarque de Holanda, family relations and values of loyalty and reciprocity had cemented the Brazilian social pact. Rather than imported liberal ideologies, depicting abstract collectivities ruled by lay work ethics and formal law, Brazilian society was bound by what, according to him, Antigone represented: "Creon embodies that abstract, impersonal notion of the City, in a struggle against the concrete, tangible reality of the family" (141); "[…] in Brazil it is possible to see, throughout our history, the predominance of singular wills […] of the uncontestable, absorbing, supremacy of the family—the sphere of so called 'primary contacts', of blood and emotional ties […] always provided the compulsory model of any social unit among us" (146).

Antigone was a metaphor for the country's public sphere, remaining loyal to the community in her proximity. Bourgeois political representation could not bind people as strongly as the intimate bonds forged by friendship or enmity; political relations in Brazil had emerged from personal ones. As long as the "cordial man" must be loyal to his associates, he acts like Antigone rather than Creon: he forgoes the general good and cares instead for those with whom he has a personal relationship. Ironically, for all the Hegelian imagination about Antigone that inspired Buarque de Holanda, his reading of Antigone was not exactly Hegelian: the family values he saw in Antigone did not represent the "family" against the city, but rather the "city as family." Antigone's defense of the family was the defense of the rural political sphere. Hers were not only blood relations but rather personal relations: political alliances. This illuminates Andrade's *Antígonas*, as they are made to choose a tangible presence—the stench of a corpse—to personally affect their people in the public space.

Like his intellectual peers, Andrade saw Brazil's capitalist enterprise, from the time of conquest, as the production of raw materials for external markets. Andrade's two plays are set in the state of Minas Gerais, where, in the early eighteenth century, *bandeirantes* (explorers) from São Paulo discovered the first gold mines.[37] The gold economy determined the economic importance of the state and was characterized by the formation of small towns with a short life cycle around exploratory activity: Pedreira is one such town. Once mineral resources were exhausted, the towns would be abandoned; for mining to occur, the fertile lands were destroyed. Marta's

---

[37] *Bandeirantes* were first- and second-generation of Portuguese settlers in the São Paulo area, who sought treasure and kidnapped Amerindians during the seventeenth century.

164 JORGE ANDRADE'S *PEDREIRA DAS ALMAS* AND *AS CONFRARIAS*

peasant husband complains about this in *As Confrarias*. The end of the gold cycle meant the beginning of "the coffee cycle" in the neighboring region of São Paulo, represented at the end of *Pedreira das almas*. Andrade's characters circulate between both plays. Marta is mentioned in the 1970 version of *Pedreira* as the woman who inspires Gabriel to search for fertile lands; Martiniano is the young miner who is leaving the exhausted mines of Morro Velho to buy land in Pedreira. In *Pedreira das almas*, Martiniano becomes Gabriel, the father. The son Gabriel leaves Pedreira for the land that starts the economic coffee cycle.

Andrade's Antígonas act in the context of two historical rebellions in the state of Minas Gerais, led by the middle classes and aristocrats against Crown taxation.[38] *Pedreira das almas* is set during the 1842 Liberal Revolt against the Conservatives in Brazil's indigenous monarchy, near the end of the economic cycle of gold that had dominated Minas Gerais for over a century. *As Confrarias* is set during the 1789 revolt for independence against the Portuguese Crown, known as "Inconfidência Mineira" ("Minas Gerais Conspiracy"). Both plays mention the 1720 revolt of Vila Rica, considered embryonic of the 1789 revolt and led by Portuguese-born Felipe dos Santos Freire, whose quartered corpse was left exposed as a tactic of intimidation. In the 1960s, the 1789 "Inconfidência" was in vogue, celebrated in the arts because the conspiracy group included many Arcadian poets with neoclassical inclinations, who are well recorded in the history of Brazilian letters— though Andrade would say that the real reason for such celebration was that the revolt was not really popular.[39]

In *As Confrarias*, Marta's son is assassinated after going to a secret meeting to convince an audience to join the legendary leader of the 1789 conspirators, Tiradentes, who was finally hanged in Rio on April 21, 1792. Like

---

[38] There were many famous revolts led by enslaved people too: consider the "Sabinada" in Bahia (calling for the abolition of slavery, 1837–8); the "Malê Revolt" (inspired by Muslim teachings) in 1835; the separatist movement of the Grão Pará in the North (1835–40); the revolt in Maranhão with an army of three thousand Maroon enslaved people (1838–41).

[39] In 1967, Guarnieri and Boal wrote their legendary play *Arena Conta Tiradentes*. For an anthology of the poets who participated in the Inconfidência rebellion, see Grünewald (1989). For artistic works thematizing the revolt before the 1960s, see Cecília Meireles' novel ([1953] 2005), Castro Alves' play (1867), Viriato Correia's play ([1939] 1941), and Paulo Ariano and Perassi Felice's *Tiradentes ou o Mártir da Liberdade* (1917). As to films, see Renato and Geraldo Santos Pereira's *Rebelião em Vila Rica* (1958); Joaquim Pedro Andrade's *Os Inconfidentes* (1972), and Geraldo Vietri's *O Mártir da Independência: Tiradentes* (1977). For documentary films, see Humberto Mauro's *Os Inconfidentes* (1936) and Victor Lima Barreto's *Painel* (1950). For a study of how the conspirators and Tiradentes were constructed as national heroes, see Fernandes Toledo (2016).

JORGE ANDRADE'S *PEDREIRA DAS ALMAS* AND *AS CONFRARIAS*   165

Felipe dos Santos' body, Tiradentes' was dismembered, and the pieces were sent to Vila Rica, where he had begun propagating revolution. Brazilian historians generally agree that Tiradentes' hanging became legendary due to the horrific spectacle engraved in the memory of generations to come, and to the way in which the Republic made Tiradentes an independence martyr (his execution day is a national holiday in Brazil). The entire plot of *As Confrarias* hinges upon the horror of this rotting body: Marta's exposed son is the corpse embodying the nation's brutal history.

The Liberal Revolt of 1842 that inspired Andrade's *Pedreira das almas* was closer to Andrade's home. To write *Pedreira*, Andrade spent over three years in the family's estate archive in São Paulo. The revolt, an internal affair among Liberal and Conservative elites over the question of the centralization of power, included in its ranks Andrade's Junqueira ancestors. In the play, Andrade has every character remember repeatedly one massacre in this revolt: Bela Cruz. In historical accounts, when the Imperial Army arrived, the rebels took refuge in the *fazenda* Bela Cruz, owned by Gabriel Francisco Junqueira: from here departed the famous armed *coluna Junqueira*, led by Gabriel Junqueira and Francisco José de Andrade, illustrious citizens and the playwright's ancestors. Imperial forces pillaged the Junqueira *fazendas* and also armed the enslaved people to kill the families left behind as the insurgents marched to the battlefront. In the play, Andrade's young Liberal rebel Gabriel is haunted by having witnessed his family's massacre in his father's absence.[40] Andrade's Gabriel represents the defeated Liberal youth, which returns to Pedreira once the town of Baependi has fallen (in real life, Baependi's defeat signaled the end of the revolt). Andrade's military character, Vasconcelos, is a representative of the victorious Imperial Army.

Pedreira das Almas: Exposure of a Corpse, Lesson 1

Two Corpses: The Father and The Son

If Antigone was, for Buarque de Holanda, a metaphor for the "roots" of Brazil, Andrade's stage conveyed just those roots: rooted in the quarry town, Mariana and Urbana are surrounded by images of stones, earth, and

---

[40] Real-life episodes like this appear in José Antônio Marinho's massive 500-page memoir of this revolt (written in 1844 and newly published in 2015).

166   JORGE ANDRADE'S *PEDREIRA DAS ALMAS* AND *AS CONFRARIAS*

graveyards. When Andrade's 1970 collection came out, *O Estado de S. Paulo* wrote of *Pedreira das almas*: "few works are able to recreate so greatly the environment [...] of the desolation of the stones that mould it, the nostalgia for the green of trees, and for a fertile and beautiful land, without the dead asphyxiating the living" (October 23, 1970: 12–13).

Stage directions in act 1 indicate that the action happens entirely in front of a stone church. Having no land for burials, people engrave the names of the deceased on the stone stairs leading to the church. There are also two stone statues. Everything is ash, white, or gold. On one side, the stage is framed by a single tree at the entrance of a grotto and a path leading to a valley; on the other, by the front of a colonial house and a path to town. As the curtain rises, Mariana reminds Clara that gold mining has ended: "Stones, flagstones, tombs…and only one tree, not a single corn cob! Gold remains in the images and the altars!" (22).

Death lurks like a ghost character on this stage. The lovers' first encounter has Gabriel inform Mariana that the revolutionaries were defeated. But he asks her "not [to] think about the dead" (27). Mariana cannot but think of the dead: "How not to think of death if death is there, dominating the thoughts of everyone" (27). Gabriel is fixated on rebirth: when Mariana tells him that his father is dying, he interprets it as the chance for renewal. Gabriel, the son, will finally be able to leave the dead town. He plans to take his father's corpse with him to bury him in the new valley, almost as if it were a foundational corpse.

This initial tension between the two lovers runs through the play. One is fixated on the death of the father and, thus, on new futures, and the other on (what will become) the death of the son, and thus on the historical roots of the present. As much as Marechal had gendered the communities in the plains, Andrade thoroughly genders the two political paradigms at stake, visible also in stage props. The tree, the grotto, and the path to the valley symbolize the road to the new: the death of the father signifies that the sons will live. The front of the colonial house and the path to town symbolize another, primary, political paradigm: the death of the sons, the Antígonal paradigm of politics, preceding any promise of modernity that would follow the death of the father and making the mourning of the sons the subtext of any neocolonial modernity.

The women, led by Urbana and Mariana, represent the stone town and its colonial paradigm: here, (colonial) fathers kill sons; Urbana and Mariana protect sons. But, while Urbana has always been the rooted matriarch, immovable like a rock and symbol of the permanence of family bonds,

JORGE ANDRADE'S *PEDREIRA DAS ALMAS* AND *AS CONFRARIAS* 167

Mariana only becomes motherly once she sees her brother die. A singular mother at that: not the simplistic mother figure that critics see in her. Mariana is a strange mother, without biological children, without a husband, and with a female chorus backing her. Hers cannot but be a political motherhood: her mission is to deal with the corpse in order to save Gabriel's life. She will not give Gabriel a child; rather, as a political mother, she delivers him to the future and gives history its child. Since she safeguards the memory of the town and at the same time propels history forward, critics see her as a figure for history itself.[41] But what does this say about history in monarchic Minas Gerais? Even if Mariana is central to the movement of history, nothing is there for her other than female sacrifice: the woman in her dies for the political mother of history to emerge. She is one more national mother, like her predecessors.

There are, then, two unburied corpses in this play: that of the son, a monarchic political paradigm (in the context of Brazil's indigenous monarchy), and that of the father, which Gabriel sees as the promise of modernity. In the monarchic/colonial paradigm, other national unburied bodies perform foundational work too—enslaved people in shallow graves of the sugar and gold cycles. Andrade's first allusion to enslaved people—and their possible liberation—is the real city upon which Pedreira is modeled, which Andrade visited during a trip to Minas Gerais: the historic city of São Tomé das Letras.

São Tomé, a small town entirely built of stone above a large quartz mineral deposit, is considered "a mystic city" due to several mysteries, including a religious apparition that helped an enslaved person obtain his freedom. Its legend involves Andrade's ancestors, the Junqueiras. By the end of the eighteenth century, a runaway slave allegedly found an image of Saint Thomas, or Saint Thomas himself, in a grotto. Impressed, the landowner João Franciso Junqueira purportedly freed the enslaved person and built a church by the grotto (today in the town center). Gabriel Francisco, João Francisco Junqueira's son, is said to be buried beneath the altar of the church. With the decline of mining activity in the nineteenth century, the city was abandoned.

In the play, when the people following Gabriel are planning on leaving Pedreira, the matriarch Urbana recalls the saintly legend of São Tomé. She reminds the priest about the heroic deeds of her father, whom she compares

---

[41] See Almeida Prado (1998), Maciel (2005), Pontes and Miceli (2012: 241–63), Guidarini (1992), Magaldi and Vargas (2001), Azevedo (2014), and Sant'Anna (1997).

168 JORGE ANDRADE'S *PEDREIRA DAS ALMAS* AND *AS CONFRARIAS*

to the colonial *bandeirantes*: "these stones remember the exemplary deeds of *bandeirantes*, Father Gonçalo. [...] It was in this grotto that my father had, for the first time, a vision of his city. [...] They found strange signs on the stones and an image of São Tomé in a stone niche. 'This is the place for the city. São Tomé will protect us, as he protected us from the storm.' They discovered gold in the grotto" (35).

The symbol of Saint Thomas in this play is telling, and not only because of the legend that Saint Thomas preached in Brazil, Paraguay, and Peru among indigenous peoples in ancient times.[42] Saint Thomas was transformed by the vision of an exposed (resurrected) corpse. In John's Gospel, we read: "Except I shall see in his hands the print of the nails, and put my finger into the print of the nails, and thrust my hand into his side, I will not believe" (20:24–9). Mariana's aim is to transform people as they see the corpse—also an echo of the republican politics of vision that made of Tiradentes' exposed corpse a symbol for freedom.

Saint Thomas indicates a "conditional" utopia: change happens with a sensory experience. Urbana represents the official historiography that conveys the legend of Saint Thomas while eliding the enslaved, recognized by Andrade's Liberal ancestor. While Urbana defends order and monarchy, Gabriel and Martiniano have seen the world of enslaved people. It is fitting that the grotto where Saint Thomas' image was found now shelters Gabriel upon his arrival in Pedreira. Mariana suggests that he hide "behind the stone of São Tomé" where "nobody will find you" (54). The grotto is a saintly place, a reminder of one whose change came about upon seeing Christ's exposed body, but also a reminder of the work of an enslaved person, who made the landowner see an image and managed to effect change in him: he was freed.

Gabriel's political paradigm depends on the protection he receives in the sacred grotto, thanks to which he will live, find burial for the father in the new town, and establish a new pact among brothers.[43] But for the new beginning to materialize, the sacred grotto had to exist, the enslaved laborer had to find Saint Thomas' image, and the women will have changed the town by exposing the son's rotting corpse, citing the exposed saintly image

---

[42] See Jesuit missionary Antonio Ruíz de Montoya (1585–1652): *Conquista espiritual hecha por los religiosos de la Compañía de Jesús en las provincias de Paraguay, Paraná, Uruguay y Tape* (especially chapters 21 to 26), published in Madrid in 1639. The Inca Guamán Poma de Ayala (1535–1616) also mentions the legend.

[43] Arantes sees in Gabriel the ideology of "the new man" in Latin America (2009).

JORGE ANDRADE'S *PEDREIRA DAS ALMAS* AND *AS CONFRARIAS*   169

and also the military orders banning burial. A stark, gendered difference is posited around the two rotting bodies.

Two Types of Mothers, Two Types of Offspring

There would be no survival for Gabriel if this weren't a story about women and their socialization of the unburied corpse. Fathers, Vasconcelos in this case, would continue killing the nation's sons. Critics associate Urbana and Mariana with Antigone because Martiniano's corpse is a major factor in their decisions.[44] In turn, they tend to locate the "real" tragic conflict only in Mariana. Clark (1981) summarizes: Mariana is tragic because she has to choose between *her lover* and *the dead* (the dead brother, the dead mother, the dead town); Urbana is "torn between handing over Gabriel to the troops and obtaining her son's release [...] rather than assuming any tragic proportions in the conflict, [she] dies spiritually" (24).

But unlike the ancient corpse, Martiniano's corpse belongs to *all* women in the town. Andrade's quilting point between the tragic and the utopian is this corpse: change comes about when it is seen, not buried. Interviewed by *A Gazeta* in 1977 about her role as Urbana in São Paulo's Teatro Alfredo Mesquita, actress Cacilda Lanuza said that though "not exactly 'feminist,' it was a play about women's suffering in war because they remain to see their dead men, they [...] unite the people in order to defy authority in the face of death."[45]

Andrade's women indeed "see" the dead, literally, and they gather to face death. Female desire for relation permeates this play well before the corpse's appearance. Mariana has never been alone: the female collective precedes Gabriel's entrance on stage and has a tinge of religious communion. Mariana and Clara share their dreams, as they explain the background story to the audience. When the curtain rises, we hear chants to a female saint (Saint Lucia in the edition I use here, Saint Marta in others): "she would make waters clearer/ such a beautiful lady" (21). Expressing this female religiosity,

---

[44] This comparison is almost unanimous; see Magaldi and Vargas (2001), Rosenfeld (1962), Clark (1981), and Mazzara (1997).

[45] "Um personagem bem marcante para a atriz Cacilda Lanuza" (*A Gazeta*, São Paulo, July 19, 1977); see also her interviews "Um desafio para mim," in *Popular da Tarde* (July 11, 1977), and "Os últimos dias desta Pedreira das almas," in *Folha da Tarde* (July 21, 1977); "Pedreira das almas: eis os conceitos de Cacilda Lanuza sobre seu último trabalho no palco," *Diário Popular* (July 11, 1977); and "Pedreira das almas," *A Gazeta*, July 5, 1977.

170 JORGE ANDRADE'S *PEDREIRA DAS ALMAS* AND *AS CONFRARIAS*

Mariana dresses in white with a black veil. Mariana and Clara mention "Marta" as the spokeswoman for the future; she has convinced Gabriel to leave town. Marta reappears later as a catalyst for change when Urbana mentions that Marta used to visit Gabriel's father.[46] When Clara and Mariana are speaking of the new lands, they sound as if they are praying in communion. Mariana says: "strange names that sounded like the goods of a distant paradise" (23). Both women take turns in exclaiming "Invernada!," "Cajuru!," "Indaiá!," "Monte Belo!"; "Gabriel's descriptions became almost prayers…" (24). Clara dreams: "in the small cemetery made of land, only of land, there will not be Barons and Baronesses. All the tomb inscriptions will be the same: arrived in 1842, died in…!" (22).

Around the corpse, the women's communion gathers its full strength and performs in full force in act 2. Vasconcelos has imprisoned the men and dictated a curfew for the women; the townspeople have to stop bringing stones from the valley to build a new cemetery.

The chorus hesitates: either the town turns Gabriel in or ceases constructing the cemetery. After Vasconcelos has captured Martiniano, and a soldier shoots him as he tries to escape, his unburied corpse is left for everyone in the town to view. When Martiniano lies wrapped solely in Urbana's arms inside the church, a woman of the chorus, Genoveva, shouts to Vasconcelos: "Make Martiniano live and Urbana will speak!" (35). Vasconcelos hears literally: how could a dead man "live"? (81). Slowly, the women of Pedreira appear on stage, one by one, in an ominous number, breaking the curfew. In chorus-like fashion, they torment Vasconcelos: "where is my son? […]," "where is my father" […] "and my fiancée"? (81). Genoveva refers to Urbana's fate as that of all the women in the town qua mothers: "we are all crying for Urbana […] the men come out of our wombs, Sir!" (81). The women warn Vasconcelos and his soldiers that Martiniano's soul remains in the air, unable to rest. When Vasconcelos is about to take Mariana prisoner, Clara "sees" Martiniano's soul, and the chorus of Graciana, Elisaura, and Genoveva, with their horrified expressions and movements, convince the soldiers to let Mariana go (87).

And yet the story that women weave has consequences for our reading of the tragic, especially if we see the conflict through the lens of motherhood. The difference between Urbana and Mariana does not lie in the meaning of

---

[46] Present in the first edition, the dialogue is not in the edition used here. Urbana tells the priest that each time Marta showed up to visit Gabriel's father, something would happen in Pedreira.

the word "tragic" (in the common sense of "catastrophe" for Urbana and in the literary sense of "tragic genre" for Mariana). In reality, the women's tragic decisions relate to competing notions of womanhood and motherhood. Urbana represents a biological notion of the family, whose predicament becomes a public affair due to the militarization of the town. But this idea of motherhood, in a militarized context, is not useful for political change: it needs to die for Mariana to emerge. Mariana represents a different, but equally tragic, motherhood conflict.

It is easy to bypass Urbana's real conflict while looking for the ancient Antigone in the text. Urbana's conflict is between two equally compelling personal loyalties, rather than with the authority that takes her son prisoner. In fact, she agrees with the forces of order and has expressed this to everyone in the play: "government must be respected" (41). The really tragic choice Urbana faces (for a brief moment, only to then be deprived of it) is between her two biological children, rather than between turning Gabriel in and getting her son back.

Urbana's traits as a matriarch were readily available for Andrade in the real-life Dona Josefa Carneiro de Mendonça. During the 1842 Liberal Revolt, Josefa was imprisoned aged sixty for hiding the Liberal rebels when imperial forces invaded the town of Araxá in Minas Gerais.[47] As in the historic Araxá, imperial forces in the play unleash repression when they invade Pedreira. Urbana's predicament starts when she is forced to concede that Mariana is hiding the rebel Gabriel, whom Urbana sees as an enemy taking her daughter away from Pedreira.

Things go awry for Urbana at the sight of Martiniano as a prisoner. Indeed, an example of metatheatrical language but also of the principle driving the play, that "seeing produces change": Urbana first declares herself "the only one responsible" for Martiniano's departure with the rebels. She then lies: "it was me who hid Gabriel" (62). But to everyone's dismay, she pauses and asks: "what guarantee would I have if [...] Gabriel shows up?" (62). Graciana (in the chorus) encourages Urbana: "speak, he is your only son" (63). Martiniano shouts: "do not speak mother [...] I would have no respite"; Clara screams at Urbana "we cannot live here" (63). Vasconcelos insists: "choose, my lady, your son is my prisoner" (63). Urbana is in anguish (stage directions).

---

[47] See Marinho ([1844] 2015); see also Schumaher and Vital (2000). Dona Josefa acted along with other women; she was also the great-great-grandmother of critic Antonio Candido, Andrade's fellow traveler.

172   JORGE ANDRADE'S *PEDREIRA DAS ALMAS* AND *AS CONFRARIAS*

Urbana's is a mother's anxiety: she needs to be loyal to both of her children. She has promised loyalty to Mariana, if Mariana stays in Pedreira (56). But if Urbana keeps her promise to Mariana, her son will die. If she protects her son, she betrays her daughter. Urbana tries to bring her daughter into her own internal conflict: "don't you see what will happen?" but Mariana retorts: "it will be a choice that does not depend on us, mother" (64). Urbana insists: "but would I not be choosing if I remain silent? Where is the love for your brother? Do you only think of that man?" (64). Mariana, indeed, at that moment only thinks of "that man"—quite unlike the choice that the ancient Antigone made.

Mariana's certainty that the choice is not theirs soon becomes fact. In the heat of the mother–daughter discussion, Martiniano is killed, to the surprise of Vasconcelos, who is left with no leverage to force the mother's confession. Urbana is thus robbed of her son and of her agency to decide between her two children. She slowly enters a path of no return and never speaks again. She has not denounced Gabriel, she has let her son die, and her life will also be inadvertently sacrificed for the revolt.

Although both Urbana's and Mariana's predicaments are those of a mother, Mariana's is a sacrificial maternal act for the community. Mariana's decision was never entirely between Gabriel and her mother, and even less so by the end of the play, when she sacrifices her chance of happiness with Gabriel. As in Urbana's case, critics have missed this nuance by focusing on Mariana's decision between lover and mother. But Mariana never doubted her decision for Gabriel's life. She made it before the drama with the unburied corpse unfolds; and, at the sight of the unburied brother, her decision is only radicalized. Mariana has always chosen Gabriel: she undergoes this self-revelation when she sees her brother die. She knows now more than ever that she has to let Gabriel live—and thus, save "the people."

What Mariana does not know is the cost of her sacrifice: an internal split between her womanhood and motherhood—a familiar, tragic predicament for Latin American Antígonas since Varela's 1824 crafting of Argia as the mother who must decide whether to marry Creon and protect her child or to die. While Urbana is all mother, Mariana's feelings are initially those of a woman in love: her womanhood is defined as happiness with Gabriel. But she realizes that she most loves his ideas. By the end of the first scene of act 1, we learn that Mariana and Gabriel are, in fact, cousins. Hearing Gabriel's dreams about the future, she says, "I don't know what I love the most: you or the image of you working in the distant lands" (50). From the first conversation between Clara and Mariana, "distant lands" mean freedom and equality

JORGE ANDRADE'S *PEDREIRA DAS ALMAS* AND *AS CONFRARIAS*   173

for all. While Mariana makes decisions as a woman of ideas, while she is not a biological mother, she can't be a free woman either in the town and times of Pedreira: the siege of the town leaves her with only one possible role, enabled through her self-sacrifice: political motherhood.

At the beginning, it seems Mariana is divided between Gabriel and her mother. After hiding Gabriel in the grotto, Mariana begs her mother: "I don't want to leave without your blessing" (48). But no critical attention has been paid to the fact that Urbana replies to Mariana with a threat: "if you leave without my blessing, the government will know where Gabriel is" (48). The priest is outraged at Urbana's apparent cruelty: "Urbana! Do you forget the commandment of God to forgive others?" (48). Things rapidly change for Mariana: she first warns Gabriel: "without the consent of my mother, we would always be under threat" (49). Then she transforms her fear into resolve: in scene 2, once Gabriel's father has died and he feels free to leave, Mariana gets ready to leave with him anyway: "I will go with you, nothing will make me change my mind" (52). Mariana is free from Urbana's grip well before Martiniano's arrival, and she will remain so throughout.

Critics have seen Mariana's final decision to stay in Pedreira as the result of Urbana's influence, again having her decide between Gabriel and Urbana. But it is not exactly Urbana who makes her stay. Almost alone in the end, Mariana enters the church to bury her mother and brother. She tells Gabriel that he never belonged where she belongs, in Pedreira. But this does not mean she has chosen her family. Rather, she has chosen to accept the consequences of her actions—of having become an agent of history. In fact, Mariana's transformation shows that she becomes as political as Gabriel. When Mariana refuses to denounce Gabriel, she starts by speaking a language that Urbana never spoke. To Vasconcelos, Urbana speaks like a biological mother: "he is just a kid! […] he is my son!" (64). Mariana uses Gabriel's political language: "nobody has *the right* to demand a betrayal from us, not even in the name of an official order" (61; my emphasis).

But Mariana's radical transformation comes with the sight of her brother's corpse. Andrade's penchant for metatheatrical devices prompts the question: what is politics other than the theater of politics—and what is theater other than a sensory experience that can transform us? Mariana is transformed by the sensory, just as she wants Vasconcelos to be transformed, and just as Andrade wants the spectator to be moved by his idea of theater. Vasconcelos' theater of the visible is to expose the body. Mariana responds by "citing" this visual strategy. She is not radicalized by lofty ideas of freedom, impersonal principles that could be claimed as a universal,

Figure 3.1 *Pedreira das almas*. Martiniano lies dead for everyone to see. Mariana and Urbana lean over him. Teatro em São João del-Rei, Minas Gerais. Directed by Marco Camarano, December 7, 1975. Arquivo Alzira Agostini H. Atitude Cultural. Courtesy of Alzira Agostini.

although she believes in them. Like Urbana, Mariana is changed by the material presence—the actual vision, touch, smell—of a part of her own circle of relations, that is, those tangible personal relations that Buarque de Holanda theorized as "the political" in rural Brazil, or that same transformation of the self that Saint Thomas represents (Figure 3.1).

After seeing her dead brother, Mariana transforms his death into a corporeal sensation for the authorities to experience—she makes it political in the sense that Andrade's contemporaries viewed politics in rural Brazil. Mariana aims to involve Vasconcelos personally. When Vasconcelos says, "he will not remain without burial, this only depends on you" (67), Mariana reacts with her politics of citation: "Well, then, let him remain exposed" (68). By repeating the order banning burial, Mariana has seized the power to give orders. Mariana is "transfigured" (stage directions, 68) as she commands that the body be moved inside the church (Figure 3.2).

Critics do not see Mariana's radicalization as a political strategy, but rather as Mariana's "transfiguration" into Urbana.[48] Stage directions

---

[48] Clark (1981: 28).

Figure 3.2 *Pedreira das almas*. Martiniano's corpse is taken to the church. Teatro em São João del-Rei, Minas Gerais. Directed by Marco Camarano, December 7, 1975. Arquivo Alzira Agostini H. Atitude Cultural. Courtesy of Alzira Agostini.

indicate, indeed, that her similarity to Urbana "increases" by the end: she is dressed in mourning, and her walk is "almost identical" to Urbana's (84). But unlike Urbana, Mariana launches a tirade against the government as the wide-eyed soldiers look at her with admiration (stage directions, 69): "laws! I don't accept them. Neither do the people of Pedreira accept laws,

176　JORGE ANDRADE'S *PEDREIRA DAS ALMAS* AND *AS CONFRARIAS*

other than those of God's [...] Open the prisons and bring on the torture instruments [...] May my brother's corpse remain exposed...it will be a living memory of your sin, of your indignity! [...] you have swords. We [have] respect and freedom. That is what Gabriel represents for us" (69–70). Mariana's role as the new "matriarch" is opposite to Urbana's: her motherhood is political rather than biological.

As act 2 opens, Urbana has been agonizing for three days in the church at the sight of her son's putrefaction (91). Speechless, Urbana has already departed with the dead. Mariana has witnessed this process. She leaves the church, transfixed and walking stiffly, confused by the intense chorus of women harassing Vasconcelos with their "vision" of Martiniano's soul wandering. The scared soldiers want to leave. Vasconcelos cannot understand: "you would sacrifice the people of Pedreira for a man?" (92). Prompted by the female chorus to come back "from the dead" to fight (92), Mariana launches another political speech, urging Vasconcelos to see his victims' faces inside the church:

> you say they are no more than corpses? So, then you must have the courage to insult them with your presence" (94) [...] Enter the church and see! (96). You will never have Gabriel because you killed Martiniano...and I...because I let Martiniano and my mother die! [...] Governments like yours only execute impious laws, with subordinate arms or slave hands. They *never see the true image* of their victims. If you enter the church [...] in that disfigured face [...] *you will see* what the Province was reduced to due to your justice! That way *you will know* what Gabriel means to us. Go inside, and Gabriel will be yours!　(96; my emphasis)

Only when asked to have the courage to personally relate to the catastrophe does Vasconcelos hesitate: he peeks into the church, but he turns around with "horror in his eyes" (stage directions, 97). He declares Gabriel dead to his superiors. Azevedo rightly asserts that Mariana uses the corpses as "weapons [and] helped by the women [...] frees the community" (2014: 91). Nothing has been solved with an appeal to higher principles—on either part, we should add, because in this incarnation of Creon, Vasconcelos is just a military man following orders.

In the final dialogue between Gabriel and Mariana, Gabriel reminds her of their love pact. He blames her mother's hatred for destroying their lives. But, for Mariana, it is the cost of her political decision that now grips her heart: "two people lost their lives. Don't you understand? [They were]

JORGE ANDRADE'S *PEDREIRA DAS ALMAS* AND *AS CONFRARIAS*   177

my family. How do you want me to be the same?" (104). Mariana does not "choose" the dead: rather, her political strategy to free the town has had the tragic—incalculable—consequence of her participation in her family's death.

We may see a strange parallel here indicating one of Andrade's major concerns: the burden of the past on the shoulders of children. Both Gabriel and Mariana have lost their families. Gabriel reminds her of this: she had promised him a family instead. This is the new pact, upon the death of a father, for which Gabriel had to wait patiently: the end of the gold-mining cycle, the new fertile lands, respect guaranteed to everyone, as his father had taught him (44)—a new pact in which Mariana would certainly become a dutiful biological mother. Critics tend to side with Gabriel and his anger at Mariana's decision. In Gabriel's eyes, she makes a pact with the dead when she utters her mother's words—"our dead cannot be abandoned." Gabriel blames the dead for her staying behind: "I left [...] Bela Cruz to grow up among the dead, waiting for my father's death to live. I don't love them because they did not let me live in peace [...] and now they destroy my hope" (104). He asks Mariana why she let him live, only to tie "him up forever to those dead" (104).

But Mariana is now a different woman, and her pact has changed: it is no longer a pact with a man, but rather a pact among women, who found political agency by exposing—on the rotting faces of corpses—the cost of Brazil's monarchy. Mariana encourages the women who accompanied her to go with Gabriel. She tells them her sacrifice is enough. She alerts Gabriel that he also became political at the sight of death: seeing the attack on the family in Bela Cruz, seeing the death of the father, having the image of Martiniano alive, as a fighter beside him. For the women, and for her, the pact came about at the sight of the dead son: "it was from Martiniano's agony that the image of the distant land sprung [...] Martiniano died so that you could leave [...] you will take with you Martiniano's true image. His other [image] belongs to Pedreira and is mine. It was only me who saw it. After that [...] life is not free anymore" (105).

The son's death frames Mariana's political paradigm, but she does not die like Urbana. Rather, she does what Urbana could not do. Mariana imagines herself a free woman, standing up to authority. By the end of the play, she is not Urbana nor the biological mother of Gabriel's children nor a free woman: she is a strange matriarch, a woman without a man, a mother with no children: as Pinto says, she has "invented" a new tradition (1998: 57). She may stand in for the figure of the narrator/author who remains to tell

178   JORGE ANDRADE'S *PEDREIRA DAS ALMAS* AND *AS CONFRARIAS*

Pedreira's story. But most of all, Mariana is a figure for the political pact among women that makes possible any future pact among the brothers.

Enslaved People: The Other Exposed Corpses

"With subordinate arms and slave hands," says Mariana to Vasconcelos. Genoveva (in the chorus) says, "with our husbands, fiancés, sons and fathers *acorrentados* [chained] in *senzalas* [slave settlements] we have the same fate as Urbana's" (81).[49] In Andrade's plays, the nation's unburied are always the poor: workers and enslaved people, those whom Andrade believed to be true agents of change. *Pedreira* is full of references to slave history and abolitionist revolt. Its traces begin with the real town upon which Pedreira is modeled, São Tomé das Letras. But they appear most dramatically in the dialogues that refer to Gabriel's and his father's history. Gabriel's dreams of freedom constantly refer to his witnessing the massacre in Bela Cruz, the *fazenda* where he was born. For Mariana, this was the inception of Gabriel's radical ideas: she shouts to Vasconcelos, "this is a government that governs with massacres. You started with the one at Bela Cruz! It was from there that Gabriel came, to liberate Pedreira" (95).

We hear about Bela Cruz in the words of practically all the characters. As the curtain rises, Clara explains: "after Martiniano knew of the massacre at Bela Cruz, Gabriel became for him […] an example" (24). Thinking of Gabriel's father, Mariana says, "after Bela Cruz, he has only suffered" (26). When Gabriel and Mariana meet, Gabriel urges them to depart because imperial forces could repeat what they did before: "twenty years ago they gave weapons to slaves, and now!" Mariana doubts: "what happened at Bela Cruz cannot happen again" (26). Desiring Urbana's blessing, Mariana urges her: "do you forget of Bela Cruz?" (33). To Urbana's accusation that he does not have any respect for the past, Gabriel retorts with anger: "I witnessed the destruction of my family, Dona Urbana. I was inside a basket and saw everything without being able to do anything […] I saw those slaves drunken and infuriated […] I have few memories […] they all come down to my family's massacre" (46). Father Gonçalo warns Urbana: "we forget our guilt […] what was our attitude when Gabriel's family was assassinated?"

---

[49] *Senzala* ("dwelling place") is a Bantú word, used in contrast to the *casa grande* (main house of the slave holders).

JORGE ANDRADE'S *PEDREIRA DAS ALMAS* AND *AS CONFRARIAS*   179

(38). When Urbana is about to turn Gabriel in, Clara shouts: "Urbana, remember what happened in Bela Cruz!" (63). Right before being shot, Martiniano yells out: "not for me mother! Remember what happened to [Gabriel]." Mariana had similarly warned her mother before: "remember what they did to [Gabriel's] family, they would do the same now!" (63).

With this insistent reference to Bela Cruz, to my knowledge overlooked by critics,[50] Andrade revisits official historiography with his own historical thesis, just as Marechal and Morisseau-Leroy had done in their plays. Bela Cruz was the most important slave revolt in Minas Gerais in the first half of the nineteenth century, and Andrade's inclusion of it may be attributed to the fact that the 1833 massacre at Bela Cruz was painfully recorded in the documents of the Junqueiras, Andrade's ancestors. Andrade sides with historians who argue that enslaved people were instrumental in a conservative plot against Liberal abolitionists. Andrade has Mariana accuse Vasconcelos of having enslaved people do the dirty work for the Crown. He also has his characters accuse Conservatives of using enslaved people to kill Gabriel's family—that is, Andrade's family.

Brazil's conservative elites resisted all foreign pressure, especially British, for abolition, seeing in it a threat to Brazil's imperial sovereignty. Bela Cruz happened in the context of abolition debates in the Constituent Assembly, of British pressure for abolition, and of the 1831 law against slave trafficking, a law "both an outcome of British pressure and a cynical strategy of the great slave-holders who supposedly controlled Parliament—*uma lei para inglês ver* [a law for the British to see]."[51]

The *fazenda* Bela Cruz, belonging to the Junqueiras, was attacked on May 13, 1833 by enslaved people, who killed all the white people present. They also killed Gabriel Francisco Junqueira's son, Gabriel. It is as if Andrade had revived the murdered son, Gabriel, for the fictional *Pedreira* to offer a different outcome. Instead of the real-life father (Gabriel Francisco) mourning his child—the political paradigm of colonial violence against the dangerous children of the colony—the fictional Gabriel would mourn his father, as the cycle of life might command—at the expense of women, of course, who, in the figure of Mariana, will mourn the children. But this is what all our Antígonas thus far convey.

---

[50]   Almeida Prado (1964) appears to be the only one who mentions it in passing.
[51]   Marquese et al. (2016: 136). See also Alencastro (2000).

180　JORGE ANDRADE'S *PEDREIRA DAS ALMAS* AND *AS CONFRARIAS*

The real-life father in question, Gabriel Francisco Junqueira, was born in São Tomé das Letras, the town that inspired *Pedreira*. In 1831, he defeated the conservative imperial candidate for the Constituent Assembly. Revolts linked to taxation, abolition, and burial grounds were in the air. That year, just two years before the massacre at Bela Cruz, Conservatives had gathered enslaved people to support the Revolt of Arraial de Santa Rita do Turvo against the regency in Minas Gerais.[52] And two months before Bela Cruz, in March 1833, the Revolta do Ano da Fumaça took place, in which the conservative military, in the name of the return of the Emperor, took the capital of Ouro Preto, liberated military prisoners, lowered taxes, and allowed for burials outside of the confraternities.[53] In a plantation economy like that of nineteenth-century Brazil, where there were no public cemeteries, enslaved people were the most exposed to being deprived of proper burial, as the epigraph of this chapter suggests.

Historians debate reasons for alliances in Minas Gerais between Conservatives, who wanted the Emperor restored, and popular sectors, including enslaved people—especially because the province had the highest concentration of enslaved people in the first half of the nineteenth century and also sought secession. Some historians see the event in Bela Cruz as a slave revolt. Others believe that Gabriel Junqueira's Conservative opponents orchestrated the revolt. Slave depositions unanimously expressed the intention to exterminate the entire families of the Andrades, Junqueiras, and Machado e Penhas, to take over their land and give money to the "Caramurus," that is, advocates of the return of Pedro II, known as a Liberal. Archives indicate that Conservatives would have spread rumors among enslaved people that the white revolt of "Caramurus" in Ouro Preto (previously Vila Rica) was to exterminate all proslavery whites. Thus, the white revolt needed to be supported by a black revolt: enslaved people would be free if Pedro II returned to power.[54]

Critics read Andrade's play as the internal conflict among elites. But Andrade presents a thesis about how elites instrumentalized enslaved

---

[52] See accounts by Prado Júnior (1985).　　[53] See, for instance, Silva (1998).

[54] See Ferreira de Andrade (2008; see also 1998–9). See testimonies on the CD: "Processos dos Junqueiras Assassinados praticados pelos escravos da Freguesia de Carrancas, em 13 de Maio de 1833"; PROCESSO-CRIME/homicídio dos Junqueiras. Ano 1833, Caixa 03–23, Museu Regional de São João Del Rei. See Ferreira de Andrade's introduction to the CD: "Negros rebeldes nas Minas Gerais: a revolta dos escravos de Carrancas (1833)"; there are 474 pages of testimonials of the massacre and criminal processes. See also Pascoal (2008).

JORGE ANDRADE'S *PEDREIRA DAS ALMAS* AND *AS CONFRARIAS*   181

people in the organization of their revolts. As Mariana says to Vasconcelos, the elites did not do the killing: their black soldiers did. As it articulates two corpses and two forms of motherhood, *Pedreira* also articulates two forms of oppression and two revolts. Andrade's Gabriel says Conservatives used slave power to kill his family. In the play, even the priest Gonçalo is unsettled by the possibility that what Gabriel says may be true. Urbana could not be less concerned; for her, the revolutionaries are "troublemakers," and as for the enslaved, it was "just a revolt," and they were all executed, as should have happened (41). But Gonçalo remembers Bela Cruz and thinks things are murkier: "it was not proven who gave weapons to the slaves, and many affirmed that it was the agents of the absolutist party who did" (38). Urbana still does not understand: "Padre Gonçalo, [what] was the interest of the government in that massacre!" (38). But Gonçalo has an answer: "the hatred Gabriel's father had for the absolutists was known. He was a man of advanced ideas! [...]. He understood the slaves [...] the extermination of his family was the beginning" (38).

It is no doubt a story about fathers and sons, and mothers and daughters: the teleological time of progress, wherein the son mourns the father's death and is free to live, versus the circular time of the colony and its impossible exit, as the mother mourns the child's death once again, just as in real life, Gabriel Francisco had to mourn his child. It is a story about Conservatives versus Liberals, as it is a story about plantation owners and enslaved people. As the father did, Gabriel and Mariana see slavery. To Clara, Mariana says "Gabriel fights against the Absolutists who used slaves to exterminate his family and the Liberals" (5); to Mariana, Gabriel says: "Twenty years ago they armed the slaves [...] and now! [...] they are doing the same in all of the valley. They destroy and confiscate the *fazendas*" (7). Foundational to Pedreira was the work of the enslaved man who discovered the image of Saint Thomas; foundational to Gabriel's struggle for freedom is the emancipation of the enslaved.

By the end of the play, as Gabriel leaves the village, he murmurs that "the past is a monster that accompanies us wherever we go" (109). Gabriel's past rests on his father's abolitionist values, for which he must continue fighting. Gabriel's father's past was also the story of a young man who left grueling work in the mines to find a new life. Before leaving his town, he sought the blessing of one unburied son, who only found burial after a mother's long journey. As with Gabriel, the young traveler seeking economic renewal depended on the mother's mourning of a son. This is Marta's story in *As Confrarias*, to which we now turn.

182 JORGE ANDRADE'S *PEDREIRA DAS ALMAS* AND *AS CONFRARIAS*

As Confrarias: Marta, the Mother of Humanity, or Exposure, Lesson 2

In 1968, Andrade's rumination over colonial motherhood had him once again structure a play around the exposure of a rotten corpse, quilting tragedy and redemption. At the end of *As Confrarias*, an impoverished young man approaches the site where a small hillock covers "that" unburied corpse—so he thinks. He finds Marta as she sits on the ground talking to her dead son, who is finally buried, after having been exposed throughout the play. Now the burial mound is exposed rather than protected inside a confraternity. The young man asks with eager curiosity: "is it *here* that they buried him?" He kneels to pray to the dead to bless his trip. Marta is outraged: "pray? Why? Tell me your story; that is a better prayer." She sits on top of the burial mound. Now the young man is furious: "you are sitting on top of the grave!" Marta convinces him to sit too: "tell me about your work." The sacredness of the burial mound overcome, the man tells her he has a "horrible" job in the mines of Morro Velho (67–9).[55] Near his house there was one tree: "there I hid the gold that I found [...] I am going to buy land in the valley of Pedreira das almas" (69). Surprised, Marta asks his name. He answers "Martiniano." She tells him: "I thought it was Sebastião [...] could that be the name of your father?" (69).

For Marta, whom we will come to see as the mother of the people, Martiniano could be her and her husband Sebastião's son. As she hears Martiniano, she thinks of the tree by which she had to leave Sebastião unburied. Bringing her back to reality, Martiniano responds that his father's name is Gabriel. That will be his son's name, he adds. Marta invites him to walk so that she can tell him—and "whoever wants to hear"—the true story of the buried man at whose grave Martiniano sought a blessing (70). The young Martiniano in *As Confrarias*, who leaves the mines behind, will have a son, Gabriel, in *Pedreira*.

As Confrarias and *Pedreira das almas* are tightly connected, though *As Confrarias* opens and thus chronologically orients the reading of the collection published as *Marta, a árvore e o relógio*. *As Confrarias* situates us in the town of Vila Rica, site of the 1789 Revolt Inconfidência Mineira, with gold mining at its height, destroying all fertile lands occupied by small farmers—just like Marta and her husband. As always, Andrade sought out history: he

---

[55] This mine is still in use; gold was once found there in the eighteenth century, and rural farmers were ousted by British capitalists who entered to exploit it.

JORGE ANDRADE'S *PEDREIRA DAS ALMAS* AND *AS CONFRARIAS*   183

spent a year in the archives of Ouro Preto's confraternities and months in old Vila Rica to best recreate that society. He also read the ten volumes of *História da Companhia de Jesus* (History of the Society of Jesus). In the eighteenth century, the dead could only be buried in church confraternities. Thus, finding a burial place during one's life was almost an obsession in colonial Minas Gerais.[56] Marta links the lack of burials to the capitalist enterprise of colonial Brazil. As she says to one of the priests: "where they find gold, the land contracts leprosy and falls apart, it covers itself with unburied bones"; the priest responds that if it were not for gold, there would be no churches; Marta retorts: "but also, the bodies wouldn't be sick" (40). In *Pedreira das almas*, the priest voices Marta's message when discussing with Urbana: "[men] only dreamed of gold […] Easy gold, on shallow earth, brings God's punishment" (39). Easy gold also brings shallow graves.

As the people's wife-mother par excellence, Marta helped Andrade rewrite official historiography from the point of view of those who lacked burials. Andrade saw them as the real agents of history, much as Marechal had seen the "Indians" and Morisseau-Leroy the Africans who led the revolution. For Andrade, the 1789 Inconfidência Mineira was "fake": "to investigate history is to escape the perspective of the winners. Why is Tiradentes the martyr of independence and not one of the mulattoes of the revolution of Alfaiates, in Bahia? The Inconfidência Mineira was a fake revolution, idealized by historians; the Alfaiates Revolt was a social revolution, a revolution of the people. Theater can evoke that history."[57] Alfaiates, also known as the "Inconfidência" or "Conjuração Baiana," was a revolt led by the popular classes from 1796 to 1798.[58]

As the newspaper *O Estado de S. Paulo* put it, "Marta is the author's fixed idea, he puts her in every play […] and must write especially for her."[59] Rosenfeld describes her best: "Marta imposes herself as one of the great figures of Brazilian drama. A woman of the people, malicious, malleable but inflexible, pure and sensual to the point of obscenity, brutal and tender, impious and maternal, realist but also capable of dreaming, […] she is mysterious and undefinable" (1996: 114). Rosenfeld compares her to Gorki's "mother" (Pelageya Vlasova) and considers her both "*real mas ao mesmo*

---

[56] See, for instance, Boschi (1986).   [57] *Istoé*, April 19, 1978, p. 45.
[58] The Bahia conspirators are sometimes called the "black Jacobins"; see Ruy (1942) and Mattoso (1969).
[59] March 7, 1971, p. 254.

184 JORGE ANDRADE'S *PEDREIRA DAS ALMAS* AND *AS CONFRARIAS*

tempo grande demais para ser real" ("real but at once too larger than life to be real," 114). Andrade thought of her as the "true revolutionary," "the real 'inconfidente'": "she believes that the dead are not useful, and she will put his son to use because he fought for freedom; she is a woman of the people, a washing lady, a bread maker, the mother of all humanity […] she is not my favorite character but perhaps the origin of all others."[60] Critic Catarina Sant'Anna (1997) and historian Rosangela Patriota (1996) see it that way: with Marta, Andrade unveiled the Inconfidência Mineira as merely a conspiracy of poets, unable to achieve popular support. In the play, Andrade is self-conscious about his own erudite art, as he has Marta criticize poets who write "beautiful things but they are paralyzed before the ugly ones […] struggle, blood, death […]!" (61). By the end of the play, Marta despairs "watching" her son in a flashback, as he goes to the conspiratorial meeting. As she says to the priest of the merchant confraternity: "when he needed the most to live his character well […] he was the worst actor ever!" (65). As she "listens" to her son José on stage delivering a speech with the lines of Marcus Brutus and Cato, she shouts: "this type of language they don't understand, son! […] talk about the *derrama*, not about rights, José! […] talk about Barbacena, not about Caesar!" (66).[61] José, we could say, was just performing classicism, rather than Andrade's "strategic classicism."

We can reconstruct Marta's own life story as she provokes the priests, performing just like her son did, trying to convince them to bury him, revealing their hypocrisy. She was profane: abandoned at a Franciscan convent and raised to be a nun, she escaped and married instead. In several flashbacks, she "talks" to her husband and her son, as we see them appearing on stage in different forms, with a special light effect indicating the flashback. At the blacks' confraternity, we hear her husband's story: the image of Sebastião is illuminated, and landscapes of corn and wheat blowing in the wind are projected onto the background screen. Her husband brought the news that they had found gold in their farm and in the river: "we will lose the land, Marta" (41). She wanted to leave; he wanted to stay. He warned Marta that gold mining destroys every land, so leaving did not make sense. He had to fight (41). Soon after gold mining started in Morro Velho, dead mine owners appeared—strangled and with no hands (42).

---

[60] Andrade interviewed at the rehearsal with the student group; archived at Rio's FUNARTE with the presentation booklet of the student's performance (July 13, 1972).

[61] The "derrama" was a special taxation of the Crown; Luís António Furtado de Castro do Rio de Mendonça e Faro, Count of Barbacena, was the Governor of Minas Gerais at the time of the Inconfidência.

JORGE ANDRADE'S *PEDREIRA DAS ALMAS* AND *AS CONFRARIAS* 185

They found the hands under Sebastião's tree and came to hang him from it. Before dying, he asked Marta not to bury him: his bones would be best scattered on the shallow grave of his land. At the confraternities of *pardos*, we hear her "speak" to José: she never knew who her parents were, thus her son cannot trace his "true" blood.

It is hard to overlook how the play about the 1789 Revolt—with the popular tinge that Andrade added to it, as he was thinking also about the 1798 slave revolt Inconfidência Baiana—was in dialogue with 1969. Andrade was certain it would be censored. Brazil's 1964 dictatorship, which until then had been relatively tolerant, was hardening.[62] *As Confrarias* was written right after the military promulgation of the so-called "AI-5" in December 1968. The AI (Atos Institucionais/ Institutional Acts) were decrees that increasingly militarized politics, culminating in AI-5, which closed parliament indefinitely, suspended the right to *habeas corpus*, and unleashed a massive wave of repression of revolts and strikes. It was based on the Doctrine of National Security, which spread throughout the Cold War dictatorships in Latin America.

How not to see the story of a mother who presents to the authorities the body of her rotting son in dialogue with the 1968 suspension of *habeas corpus*? And how not to see the exposed body in a dictatorship as those exposed in the aftermath of the Inconfidências of 1789 and 1798, taken to be republican "martyrs"? *As Confrarias* is as much the story of the exposed corpse that republican elites claimed as foundational as it is the story of the disappearance of *habeas corpus* in 1969—the story of a political mother who ends up convincing the authorities that killed her son that *they* need to bury him.[63]

---

[62] While *As Confrarias* was not staged in 1969, João das Neves' Greek *Antigone* was staged in Rio de Janeiro as a political protest, performed by the left-wing theater company Grupo Opinião (1964–84). Das Neves used Ferreira Gullar's poetic translation. The production had Ismene rebel after Antigone's death. Costumes were modern; speech was popular. People who went to the shows felt they had participated in an act of resistance to the military. See an interview with actress Renata Sorrah, who played Antígona: "Renata Sorrah: Antígona, Tragédia Clássica nos Anos de Chumbo—Ocupação João das Neves," September 29, 2015 at http://www.itaucultural.org.br/explore/canal/detalhe/renata-sorrah-antigona-tragedia-classica-nos-anos-de-chumbo-ocupacao-joao-das-neves/. Earlier, in 1962, *Antígona América*, written by legendary political activist and philosopher Carlos Henrique de Escobar Fagundes (1933–), had premiered in São Paulo. Darcy Penteado was the scenographer and designer, just as he had been for *Pedreira*. See Magaldi and Vargas (2001). I have not been able to obtain this text.

[63] Two years later, in 1971, an international scandal broke out as well-known fashion designer Zuleika Angel Jones' son was kidnapped and killed by the military. She led a campaign to bury him, which reached Henry Kissinger's ears. She was murdered in 1976.

186   JORGE ANDRADE'S *PEDREIRA DAS ALMAS* AND *AS CONFRARIAS*

As Marta exposes the corpses of those who have no representation, she is almost a composite of Buarque de Holanda's notion of Brazilian politics and Jacques Rancière's 1999 reworking of the ancient Greek notion of radical democratic politics. On the one hand, her strategy (like Mariana's) is metatheatrical: to establish a spectacle of the tangible for authorities so that they may change. On the other hand, she voices the interests of those who cannot be heard, the unburied dead, and is thus akin to those who can make politics happen by forcing their voice into the existing order, per Rancière's account of "the political." Rancière's analysis takes into account Aristotle's and Plato's reasons for excluding some from the sphere of the political: the kind of activity and the space and time in which this activity is done. Enslaved people, artisans, and women are associated with those activities that prevent individuals from having a part in the political order.[64] Marta carries on her shoulder those who have no part: literally, the corpse of her son, and symbolically, the corpse of her husband. Marta and these corpses represent those whose work (the time and place of work is implied here too) prevents them from participating in politics. Marta has no profession; she is a mother who makes bread. Her husband was a farmer who knew how to plant but lost his land. Her son is everyone and no one: as an actor he cannot belong in any confraternity. As she puts it: "if we weren't given the means to make enough for a living, how could we pay for dying?" (40).

Marta's quest to represent those who have no part is vividly dramatized, not only with the theme of work but also with the theme of racial purity. She starts her *via crucis* to bury her son in the racialized confraternities. Marta herself cannot clearly trace her bloodline. Through her visits to the confraternities, Andrade exploits what he saw as the hypocrisies of racial divisions in colonial Brazil. His irony was to leave the son's race unknown: as an actor, he is a "mulatto," regardless of his color, as all actors were in eighteenth-century Brazil, due to their ignoble profession. Actors were neither enslaved nor free citizens, but rather strangers. As Marta tells the priests of the *pardo* confraternity: "he had a lot of 'pardo' in him. Maybe [a lot] of those who are strangers in their own home" (48). And José comes to see himself as a

---

[64] In *The Politics of Aesthetics*, Rancière expands as follows: "Aristotle states that a citizen is someone who *has a part* in the act of governing and being governed." But before that the polis has to determine "who have a part in the community of citizens. A speaking being, according to Aristotle, is a political being. If a slave understands the language of its rulers, however, he does not 'possess' it. Plato states that artisans [...] *do not have the time* to devote themselves to anything other than their work. They cannot be *somewhere else* because *work will not wait*" (2004a: 8; emphases in the original).

JORGE ANDRADE'S *PEDREIRA DAS ALMAS* AND *AS CONFRARIAS*   187

nomad: "I felt like someone who had crossed a border, without knowing where he was coming from or where he was going, in a nation with no geography."

Neither the white Confraria do Carmo, nor the black Confraria do Rosário, nor the *pardo* Confraria do São José accepts the son: he is racially ambiguous even for the racially ambiguous confraternity of *pardos*. José is not even seen as "pure" *pardo*. Purity of blood is what counts, as Marta unveils at each confraternity playing her "game" of provocation (stage directions). At the black confraternity, she tells the black priests that the whites "suspected my son had black blood" (39). The priest retorts: "looking at you, it is easy to prove that he only had white blood" (39). To Marta's objection that her son could have had a black father, the black priest reminds her that "mulattos and pardos are not blacks [...] beneath their black skin their blood is white" (39). At the black confraternity, one priest accuses the minister of exploiting blacks also: "in the mine you enslave blacks from other nations!" But the minister replies they are "from enemy tribes" to which the priest responds "in Africa, not here. They should all be free" (37). In turn, at the white confraternity, Marta overhears the reason for rejecting a servant whose skin is white: even though his wife looks white they have found documents of mixed origins, indicating the presence of black blood. In the Confraria da São José for *pardos*, the minister and the judge complain that whites demean them and blacks reject them (46).

In Marta's representation of the voiceless, symbolized in the unidentifiable blood or skin color of her son, there is a universal claim, which Marta states loudly and clearly to the priests in the confraternity of merchants. She is told there that "neither you nor your son will have salvation!" but she answers: "salvation is for everyone or it will be for no one" (67). Like Mariana, Marta believes in equality and freedom. But, like Mariana, she will not lift those banners to justify the need for burial. She will follow Mariana's political strategy of citation, as the burial of the corpse recedes in importance with respect to the lesson for the living.

To Use or Not to Use the Body: That Is the Question

In each confraternity, Marta is invariably asked: "what do you want at our church?" Her response seems simple: burial. But by the end of her visit the impatient and irritated priests realize that there is something more elusive about her wishes and yell: "what do you really want now?!" As she leaves

188 JORGE ANDRADE'S *PEDREIRA DAS ALMAS* AND *AS CONFRARIAS*

each confraternity, she addresses the priests with some version of the phrase, "you'll bury him too" or "you will go to his burial too." Marta's secret plan is to let everyone see how her son decomposes "until his bones become apparent. From his vigorous body only his hair shall remain. The smell of his body shall make life in the city unbearable! It is my way of burying him where it is necessary," as she shouts to one of the *pardo* priests (58). To expose a body in a church must recall the tortured body of Christ. Marta accuses the Church: "for centuries you have exploited an exposed body, confusing life and death!" (56). At the confraternity of *pardos*, a priest attempts to bribe her: she can bury the body if she reveals how he died— which means unveiling the conspiracy in which José was involved. Marta inquires about the Church's use of the body: "what do you want to use my son for, mister priest? To obtain a canonry? And you? For the royal favor?" (57). The priest retorts: "and you? [...] to avenge your husband? [...] to destroy our church? [...] to protect a sedition?" (57).

Indeed, everyone uses, abuses, exposes, and overworks bodies in this play. For Andrade, also at stake is the use of the corpse as an extension of the living body abused through manual labor. Those who do manual labor only possess their own body. They are, for Andrade, those who sacrifice themselves while working for others. And the mother's body giving life is the subtext of all manual labor involved—in this performance, staged as the inverted mirror of pregnancy, as Marta does not carry José inside her but on her shoulders in a hammock, helped by a correspondingly different "midwife," José's lover.

We can trace bodily use as what defines the main popular characters in the play. Marta's husband works the land with his hands and, when he needs to fight for justice, severs the hands of those who exploit him. José's lover Quitéria, as Marta describes her to the priests, "was a slave" until she "discovered the force she had between her legs [...] she seems to have been made to feed humanity with those breasts" (53). In a flashback conversation, José, Marta, and Quitéria sit at the bed, and Quitéria, "slapping between her legs," says: "it was with this that I got my freedom" (63). Both Sebastião's and Quitéria's bodies are ultimately motherly: they manually feed, one with crops, the other with breasts. An extension of Marta's body, these are bodies that work for freedom.

Marta speaks of the body as her "language," as she repeatedly reminds the priests while she talks about bodies. Of her labor pain, she says to the white priests: "my son was born, making me suffer, breaking my body into *torrões da dor* [lumps of pain]...(*pausing for effect*) when his head came through between my legs" (30). Outraged, the priest exclaims: "you are not an animal!" [...] maternity is a sacred thing! You can't talk like this!" (30). To the Virgin's icon in the first confraternity, she says: "this night our steps will sound like groans of agony and birth pangs" (35). Of her son's sexuality, she tells the *pardo* priests: "in bed he did things that many do and lie about doing [...] he loved whites, blacks and pardas" (50). Stage directions depict her "watching" as her son and his lover are in bed. During the flashback scene, when she kisses her son goodbye before he goes to the conspiracy meeting, she says to a priest: "(*intentionally debauched*) I like to watch... when they are making love!; Cleric: You watch? Your own son?; Marta: Don't I watch him eat, drink and dream?" (64). Scandalized, a *pardo* priest asks, "do you think everything is permitted?" and she replies, "for me God exists exactly because everything is permitted" (50).

While the main characters expose their bodies as producers—even when dead—the churches usurp the result of this labor, mainly in the form of gold. The play's stage directions depict lavish furniture and artistic icons inside the churches, as well as the church processions and the priests' lust for gold. Marta exposes that materiality as sinful, whereas the material existence of the body is godly (Figure 3.3).

Figure 3.3 *As Confrarias*. Marta indicts the priests. Cia Teatro Seraphim. Teatro Barreto Júnior, Pina, Recife, Brazil. Directed by Antonio Cadengue, June 9, 2013. Courtesy of photographer Américo Nunes.

190   JORGE ANDRADE'S *PEDREIRA DAS ALMAS* AND *AS CONFRARIAS*

When Marta decides to shatter an icon on the altar at the merchants' confraternity, she yells: "this God is already dead. Can't you feel the smell of his decomposition? [...] you [...] killed him, with the knife of disaffection. Only the *sweat of your bodies* will be able to wash the blood on this knife" (67; my emphasis). To Martiniano, who wants to pray in front of José's tomb, Marta says that "work" is prayer (69). Coming from the mines, Martiniano ironically says, "if working is prayer... I have prayed a lot" (69).

José condenses best how the body is put to work in this play: as a maternal body. Now a rotting corpse that serves the cause of freedom, while alive José was a maternal body of sorts, encompassing all humanity. He was Marta's—and the playwright's—extension. His body permeates the play not only because it is rotting and visible everywhere Marta takes it, but also because his body "appears" in the flashback scenes when José "talks" with Marta or with Quitéria, or when he performs his roles. It is not until Marta understands her son's bodily labor that she comes to terms with his acting, and this is only because she understands acting as the bodily labor giving birth to others.

At first, we know through flashbacks that Marta blames her son for being only a character on stage and a lover in bed, without noticing the groans of enslaved people, the poverty, and the injustice in the city where he works. Compared to his father, who fought for justice with his own hands, José embodies characters who are not majestic. José can only respond: "I cannot exist without my body. I am what my body is [...] [the body] of a character, of a philosopher, of myself [...]?" (52). He has been "acting" since he was a child: in the first flashback, we hear Marta admonishing her son to stop moving like a plant and start planting: "instead of imitating plants make some of them grow, like your dad" (30). For José, this is not about "imitating": "each and every one has their own meaning of what it is to plant" (31).

When "speaking" in flashbacks, we see José as a young actor in three roles conveying the same idea: freedom. Marta's metatheatrical show at every confraternity echoes the metatheatricality of José's performances, which include a dialogue between Cato and Marcus Brutus from the Portuguese tragedy by Almeida Garrett; a monologue from the character Figaro (by Beaumarchais); and several paragraphs from the *Cartas chilenas* by Tomás Antônio Gonzaga.[65] Sant'Anna argues that the play short-circuits

---

[65] Sant'Anna (1997: 314) observes that Portuguese Almeida Garret's *Catão* was performed for the first time in Lisbon on September 29, 1821, in the aftermath of the 1820 revolution. For her, the tragedy was to educate the audience: it is about the [younger] Cato who resisted Caesar and killed himself and Marcus Brutus, who instead decided to fight against Caesar. João

JORGE ANDRADE'S *PEDREIRA DAS ALMAS* AND *AS CONFRARIAS* 191

texts from "Brazil's military dictatorship, the time of the Inconfidência Mineira (with Tomás Antônio Gonzaga), pre-revolutionary eighteenth-century France (with Beaumarchais), first century A.D. Rome (with Luculus by Brecht and Catão by Garrett), and Sophocles' Athens" (1997: 269).

But while José's characters embody freedom, Marta's understanding of her son is an insight of *maternal* imagination. As she says to the black priest, her son was a man who "had the color of mankind [...] *que nascia no corpo dêle*" ("that was born [daily] in his body," 35). To the minister who asks her "where did you finally find your son?" she responds: "(*waiting for the effect*) I found him in the body of the other [...] sometimes in the body of a woman" (43). Before we see José performing one of his four acting speeches—a dialogue between Marcus Brutus and Cato—Marta explains at length: "Those who transform themselves into blacks, men, women, Jews, Muslims feel everyone as they really are. They abandon their bodies for another body. They forget their feelings and give birth to other feelings. [...] They find in themselves feelings that belong to all" (43).

If José was a man whose feelings belonged to all, because he was everyone, of every color, of no particular belonging, of no geography, of no identity, a sign for the universal, he had to be properly buried in a site that belonged to all, not hidden under any of the exclusionary identities represented by the confraternities. Marta leaves the corpse exposed in the churchyard of the last confraternity she visits and runs away: "the body will remain in the churchyard, waiting for an answer from the Province...or until he is buried. I only know how to fight for the living" (68). The brothers of all confraternities despair: Marta's lesson, as Mariana's, is for them *to see* the consequences of their refusal to bury. When stage directions indicate that altars disappear and we see a mound in the middle of the stage, Marta comes back and "talks" to her son: "they all got together to bring you here" (68).

Like Mariana, Marta has imparted a lesson with the exposure of a corpse. And like Mariana, Marta has not been alone. Marta has the constant company of José's lover, who helps her carry the heavy hammock in

Baptista da Silva Leitão de Almeida Garrett, Viscount of Almeida Garrett (1799–1854) was a participant in the 1820 revolt. The *Cartas Chilenas* is a series of poems that circulated anonymously in Vila Rica at the time of the Inconfidência Mineira. A citizen by the name Critilo writes to one Doroteu, accusing the governor of corruption, providing information that would have been known by his contemporaries but changing all referents to Spain instead of Brazil: the letters read as if the corruption was in Spain and Chile. Both Sant'Anna and the historian Affonso Ávila support the idea that the author was Garrett (see Avila 1967); Oliveira gives other possible names (2003: 201).

192 JORGE ANDRADE'S *PEDREIRA DAS ALMAS* AND *AS CONFRARIAS*

peregrination through the town. The two women praise each other and in every confraternity work together to offend the priests. Andrade's mothers have the female company that Varela's Argia was seeking and Marechal's Antígona desired. For Mariana and Marta, the corpse has generated a living bond among women.

Marta and Mariana manage to bury those who lie in shallow graves with citational political strategies that belong in Brazil's rural public sphere of personalized relations. Their politics precedes any burial, and burial precedes any pact among the brothers who may have the luxury of seeing their fathers' death, not their children's death. But Marta and Mariana also expose Andrade's thesis about the colony: the unburied sons are in shallow graves, like the enslaved people in the makeshift cemetery in Rio that Freyrreis documented (in my epigraph), because the roots of Brazil were capitalist—in spite of its semi-feudal relations of production.

The epigraph of *Pedreira das almas*, from Carlos Drummond de Andrade's poem "Os bens e o sangue" ("The goods and the blood," from his 1951 collection *Claro Enigma* [Clear Enigma]) reads: "and everything will turn to nothing, and dried out of gold, iron will be drained, and hills dried out of iron will cover the sinister valley where there will be no more privileges." The colonial capitalist enterprise left workers dead on the ground, as the gold extracted for the external market or the churches stole their lives. The Brazilian Antígonas invented a political strategy to deal with the scattering of bones in the grounds of the nation's plantations. Their female bonding around the dead son is the Antígonal paradigm of resistance to colonial necropolitics. Their citational politics will be ruminated historically, on and off stage, during and after America's Cold War dictatorships.

4

One Hundred Years of Puerto Rican Solitude

Luis Rafael Sánchez's 1968 *Antígona Pérez*

> The [US Supreme Court] decision in the case *Commonwealth of Puerto Rico v. Sánchez Valle* could be the beginning of a new narrative that answers genuinely the question "who are we?" instead of the question that Puerto Ricans have been trying to answer for more than a century: "who are we in relation to the United States?"[1]

Antígona Pérez, imprisoned for twelve days in the dungeons of the Presidential Palace in the imaginary Latin American Republic of Molina, will soon be executed and wants to tell her story. After the Tavárez brothers, Héctor and Mario, failed to assassinate Generalísimo Creón Molina, Antígona placed a decoy bomb in a library and stole their exposed corpses from the plaza, burying them in secret. During the two acts (seven and five scenes, respectively), Antígona receives six visits in prison. Three types of chorus intervene outside the palace: five journalists with press reports and two "multitudes" divided by gender. The choruses alternately encourage or dissuade Antígona. Antígona refuses to disclose the burial location. Her mother, Aurora, is her first visitor. Next is Creón, who tries to convince her to live. After this, prison guards rape Antígona with a bottle in an attempt to make her confess. Creón and his wife, Pilar Varga, meet with Monseñor Bernardo Escudero, the representative of the Catholic Church, who then descends to the dungeons to convince Antígona that salvation is possible. Next, her best friend, Irene, visits to tell her that Fernando Curet, Antígona's

---

[1] Font-Guzmán (2015); court case: *Commonwealth of Puerto Rico v. Sánchez Valle* 579 US (2016). Puerto Rico could not prosecute the accused because the US Supreme Court established that the authority to govern Puerto Rico derives from the US Constitution. On Puerto Rico's colonial status, see Font-Guzmán (2015) and Font-Guzmán and Alemán (2010).

Antigonas: Writing from Latin America. Moira Fradinger, Oxford University Press. © Moira Fradinger 2023.
DOI: 10.1093/oso/9780192897091.003.0006

194   LUIS RAFAEL SÁNCHEZ'S 1968 *ANTÍGONA PÉREZ*

fiancé, has accepted a government post and has become Irene's lover. Lastly, Pilar Varga tries her luck at convincing Antígona to save herself. Antígona never confesses. Creón visits once more and finally orders her execution. Amid a flood of other trivial news, the journalists report that Antígona "confessed."

Antígona's *Hic et Nunc*

It is May 30, 1968. *La pasión según Antígona Pérez: crónica americana en dos actos* (The passion according to Antígona Pérez: an American chronicle in two acts) is the last play showing at the eleventh annual Puerto Rican Theater Festival at the traditional Teatro Tapia in downtown San Juan. The action is set contemporaneously. The theater rests in complete darkness before the blinding light of a follow-spot illuminates two or three spectators. The sounds of police sirens and street noise filter into the theater. The beam finds Antígona Pérez on stage. She blinks and adjusts her eyes in reaction to the harsh light. The beam slightly shifts to illuminate her surroundings. We now see that she is imprisoned in the lower part of the stage, below a large staircase with platforms, a space that represents the palace dungeons. Throughout the performance, Antígona barely steps out of this space.[2]

Under an intense cone of light defining her figure, Antígona stares at the audience, breaking the fourth wall and establishing an intimate testimonial bond to begin her story. The prologue says the play is the "chronicle of her own passion, occurring in the imaginary Hispanic American Republic of Molina" (11): "Let us begin where one always begins. Name: Antígona Pérez. Age: Twenty-five. Continent: America. Color...(She smiles.) It doesn't matter. I bring a story for those who have faith [...] poetry! Of course, it's poetry! I am twenty-five years old and I will die tomorrow" (13).[3]

---

[2] I owe details of the 1968 premiere to Luis Rafael Sánchez (whom I interviewed in May 2012 in New York); to theater director and playwright Pablo Cabrera, who directed the play's premiere in 1968; and to theater professor and producer Ramón Albino Rodríguez (both of whom I interviewed in New York during 2015).

[3] All quotations of *La pasión según Antígona Pérez* [1968] 1983 are my translations. Obregón translated it into French (1998). Hilda Quintana de Rubero translated the play into English as part of her dissertation "Myth and Politics in *The Passion According to Antígona Pérez* by Luis Rafael Sánchez" (1983); Robert Cardullo offers his version in *Antigone Adapted* (2010); Charles Pilditch worked on it for the New York Studio Duplicating Service for the 1972 New York premiere in Spanish (held at the New York Public Library); Gregory Rabassa was the translator for this premiere. Here is an example of why I do not follow the existing unpublished translations and instead did my own for this chapter. Prologue stage directions indicate that on the *periaktos* (a revolving device to display and change theater scenes) one of the political slogans should

LUIS RAFAEL SÁNCHEZ'S 1968 *ANTÍGONA PÉREZ* 195

However, this is not necessarily a common place to "always begin" when one desires to speak: "Yes. I want to speak. About those of us who grew up in a harsh America, a bitter America, *una América tomada* [an America taken over]. About generations painfully strangled. The press has invented an untrue *historia* [story]" (14).[4] She begins her story by role-playing a citizen and a police officer, theatrically set by the sirens and spotlights. Her first "no" to Creón is a contesting act of self-identification, asserting her identity despite the labels with which the press identifies her throughout the play: "a terrorist," a "miscreant," a "conspirator." And it is an act of warning to the audience that both her story and (her republic's) history need correctives: the Spanish word *historia* means both story and history. America, Antígona's abode, has been taken over—*tomar* in Spanish means to grab, seize. Joan Corominas speculates that the etymology of that Castilian voice comes from the frequent Latin verb *autumare*, which in legal parlance meant "to claim right of ownership over an object," "to take away something from someone."[5] Antígona will soon tell us both her story and the history of a particular claim to ownership, for she is, after all, a "student of history" (42).

She wears what would have been fashionable for middle-class young women on the island at the time: a black leather skirt and black leather boots. But, more importantly, her audience would have easily associated her attire with the independentist Nationalist Party of Puerto Rico (PNPR), founded in 1922.[6] Soon after its foundation, the legendary mulatto Pedro Albizu Campos (1891–1965) joined the PNPR. Albizu's rhetoric was that of faith and passion, *patria* or death. Sánchez's title for Antígona's passion was borrowed three decades later by Puerto Rican critic Arcadio Díaz Quiñones for his article about Albizu in *El Nuevo Día*: "La pasión según Albizu" ("The passion according to Albizu"): "Albizu Campos, the chosen one, gave his life to politics in the form of Passion and Death. He has been maybe the only saint that Puerto Rican culture has produced in the twentieth century, with his martyrdom, canonization, liturgy, sacred texts, fanatics and heretics"

---

read: "lo harán los descamisados" (13; "the shirtless will do it"). Cardullo translates "What will the dispossessed do?"; Quintana de Rubero, "the Underdogs will do it." Both miss the field of reference entirely—not only the French revolutionaries but, most importantly at the time, Argentine Peronism and, in particular, the use that Evita Perón made of the word "shirtless" to refer to the grass roots of Peronism; Pablo Cabrera's 1968 production based the character of Pilar Varga on Evita Perón.

[4] It would be more accurate to say "America taken over" here. "América tomada" resonates with one of the most studied short stories written by Julio Cortázar, "Casa tomada" ("House taken over," 1946).

[5] *Diccionario crítico etimológico castellano e hispánico* (1980).

[6] I owe this association to professor Ramón Albino.

196 LUIS RAFAEL SÁNCHEZ'S 1968 *ANTÍGONA PÉREZ*

(September 20, 1998: 16). The association between Albizu, Antígona's attire, and her nationalist passion is reinforced as the play unfolds. Yet, according to her self-identification, she seems to have no nation other than "America." Nationalist in costume, continental in feeling: she has no state. Race? Antígona reassures the audience that her skin color is irrelevant. Stage directions cast her as typically multiracial, "summariz[ing] in her physique the race-crossing in which the Hispanic American existence resides" (13).[7] In Puerto Rico at the time, driver's licenses included the category "color," following the racial logic of segregation in the United States.[8] Other American nations do not usually include racial labels on official documents. The casting indicates what Antígona has said with words. Her abode, then, follows the logic of a place where race is written in the law: the United States. She lives in a seized "continent" and wears nationalist attire in an imaginary republic where color matters.

Gender? She is a woman of "angular anatomy with no curves" (stage directions, 13). Her androgynous young body may represent every youth at twenty-five in 1968 America—in contrast to all clichés of hypersexualized "Latinas." A sexualized Antígona is what others want. Her mother thinks she should marry and have a "beautiful, respectable, prosperous family" (28). Creón wants her alive not to ruin her "possibilities as a young woman" (40). Rape as torture is chosen because Creón sees her as a woman.

Antígona's abode is both nationalist and continental; she is in her twenties; her gender appearance is neutralized; she is alive in 1968. In her self-presentation, her name and her age matter the most. Antígona foresees her critics saying: "Some will think I am too young to say something worth listening to" (13). She is just a rebel student, like so many other rebel students in 1968. Stage directions indicate, nonetheless, that the audience should give her credit: "an old age behind her eyes possesses her at times" (13)—the old age of her name, no doubt, but also of those who decide to risk death for a greater cause. She claims there is "poetry" in that her "youth has been cradled by the sad ageing of the soul" (13). Antígona Pérez is one more soul who "will die tomorrow" after carrying the weight of the world's freedom on her shoulders. She renews the fearless old rhetoric of "patria o muerte,"

---

[7] Quintana de Rubero translates "she is the racial mixture typical of Spanish-Americans" (71); Cardullo elides this sentence. Even if it sounds odd in English, my choice conveys the sentence's existential tone: "el cruce de razas en que se asienta el ser hispanoamericano" (13). It keeps the literal "cruce de razas" as "crossing" since other common translation alternatives (i.e., *mestizaje*) are hotly debated in Latin America.

[8] I owe this rich detail to Puerto Rican theater director Rosa Luisa Márquez.

LUIS RAFAEL SÁNCHEZ'S 1968 *ANTÍGONA PÉREZ*   197

echoing Che Guevara's speech before the 1964 United Nations Assembly, but also—most importantly for my analysis—the American radically anticolonial and revolutionary consciousness that started with the Haitian Revolution.

Antígona's abode is the continent in 1968, effervescent as all the other youth who, like her and like the ancient Antigone, undertook the sacrifice of their lives with the prospect of death as a future. After Antígona's speech and her mother's visit, journalists announce Nixon's expansion of the war into Cambodia (17), Sartre's rejection of the Nobel Prize (17), Dean Rusk's support for US intervention against the threat of communism (18), and, most importantly (as indicated by the emphasis on the word "extra" and shouted by each journalist in succession), a series of deaths (or ends) of leaders known for their transformational politics: "Extra. Extra. Martin Luther King is assassinated. [...] Extra. Extra. Che Guevara is gunned down [...] Extra. Extra. Pope John XXIII dies. [...] Extra Extra. Charles de Gaulle resigns [...] Extra. Extra. John F. Kennedy is assassinated" (35–36).[9] The "multitude" runs "disturbed" toward each journalist, to finally "freeze" at the impact of the last line (stage directions, 36) (Figure 4.1).

On that evening—May 30, 1968—Antígona will be executed. Ernesto "Che" Guevara was assassinated ten months earlier, on October 9, 1967, in La Higuera, Bolivia—offstage, we may say, since it was done clandestinely. Che's corpse, like the corpses of Antígona's fictional compañeros, the Tavárez brothers, was exposed for public viewing then buried in secret. King was killed on April 4, 1968, less than two months before our Antígona meets her end. Che and King also died young, both only thirty-nine years old.

By the 1960s, three circum-Caribbean neighbors had raised high the hopes of the continent's youths: other young people were busy toppling dictators and making it out alive. In May 1957, a civic uprising overthrew Colombian dictator Rojas Pinilla; in January 1958, a rioting crowd ousted Venezuelan dictator Pérez Jiménez; and in January 1959, Fidel Castro's guerrillas took La Habana by storm, toppling dictator Fulgencio Batista. And, in the Dominican Republic, on May 30, 1961—seven years earlier and

---

[9] Dean Rusk was Secretary of State under presidents John F. Kennedy and Lyndon B. Johnson, from 1961 to 1969, and publicly defended the intervention in Vietnam; Sartre rejected the Nobel Prize in 1964; the reference to Nixon was probably added in later editions since historically he only took power in January 1969, well after the premiere of *Antígona Pérez*; Pope John XXIII died in 1963; De Gaulle resigned in 1969, Kennedy was shot in 1963.

Figure 4.1 *La pasión según Antígona Pérez*. The multitude runs for news. Directed by Pablo Cabrera. Eleventh annual Puerto Rican Theater Festival. Teatro Tapia, San Juan, Puerto Rico, May 30, 1968. Rehearsal photo. Courtesy of the Archivo Fotográfico del Instituto de Cultura Puertorriqueña (AGPR-ICP).

on the same calendar day that *Antígona Pérez* took the stage—a group of young officers assassinated dictator Rafael Leónidas Trujillo Molina (1891–1961). There was a momentary breath of air for the Dominican Republic when socialist Juan Bosch was democratically elected in 1963, only to be overthrown in 1965 as a civil war broke out and 42,000 US marines intervened to prevent "another Cuba." Trujillo's successor, Joaquín Balaguer, won the elections: the Dominican Republic (America) was taken over, again.

Antígona lives in the "imaginary republic" of Molina, where Creón Molina declares "there is no universe for heroes" (45). Juan Bosch's name is relegated to a swift appearance in the "news." Antígona's end is not glorious: at the finish of the play, the journalists transform it into a banality. The audience hears the execution shots; two of the five journalists report Antígona's "confession"; the others fill the air with trivial updates on Jackie Kennedy's vacations, Pierre Cardin's new fashion show, and the filming of *Who's Afraid of Virginia Woolf* (122). The curtain falls.

LUIS RAFAEL SÁNCHEZ'S 1968 *ANTÍGONA PÉREZ* 199

Antígona's abode is the turmoil of 1968, and yet she fights alone; her abode is the continental utopia, her name mythical, her age emblematic; and yet she studies history, her name is Hispanic, her age is precise—Pérez, dead at twenty-five. She lives in an imaginary "Hispanic American Republic," and yet it is named after the historical Dominican dictator Trujillo Molina. The imaginary republic "freezes" at the historical news of Kennedy's assassination. Kennedy had felt "at home" visiting Puerto Rico in 1961; six years later, future Puerto Rican governor Luis Ferré would launch the campaign for US statehood.

Antígona dies for and with the continental rebellion of 1968, but unlike the youth of other nations, Antígona is onstage during a politically unique historical context offstage: Puerto Rico is one of two archipelagos in the continent de facto owned by an imperialist power (the other is the British colony of the Malvinas Islands,[10] which Antígona's speeches will include). Both Puerto Rico and Cuba had been under US occupation at the outbreak of the 1898 Spanish–American War,[11] but after the 1901 Platt Amendment, the United States withdrew from Cuba, and a republic was established in 1902 (albeit with concessions to the United States). Puerto Rico became—and still is—a colony.[12]

Antígona's abode is her university's history department, in 1968, in the Republic of Molina, property of Creón Molina; onstage, in Puerto Rico, legal property of the United States. And yet, critics systematically settle the tension between the mythical and the historical in this play by erasing the historical: the Republic of Molina is invariably understood as an allegory for an eternal entelechy named time and again "dictatorial Latin America." The Republic of Molina is Latin America, is dictatorship, is Puerto Rico. In 1997, Spanish critic Lucrecio Pérez Blanco wrote "[the play gives] life to a fact that had been, was and is still felt in Hispanic America: dictatorship" (132); in 1984, he summarized it as "Molina, even if it makes us think of the Dominican Republic under Trujillo's dictatorship, can be any Hispanic American republic" (176 n. 37).[13]

---

[10] Known in the UK by their British colonial name of the Falkland Islands.

[11] When the United States provoked the surrender of Spanish forces, they established a military regime, transforming the agricultural system into a sugar plantation economy and imposing English in schools, where children had to pledge loyalty to the US flag.

[12] Puerto Rico is a "Free Associated State" to the US, but its territory is US *property*. The UN Decolonization Committee has asked the United States repeatedly to allow Puerto Rico full self-determination.

[13] Pedro Bravo Elizondo calls it "an X-ray" of dictatorship, the "endemic evil" (1975); González Barja writes "a harsh critique to military dictatorships in Latin America" (1972). See a good compilation of this type of criticism in Waldman's bibliography (1988).

200 LUIS RAFAEL SÁNCHEZ'S 1968 *ANTÍGONA PÉREZ*

There is no sophisticated allegorical *mise en abîme* here, whereby Molina would be an allegory of another allegory ("dictatorial Latin America"), pointing at some truth about the lack of reference of any linguistic construction. Instead, when critics take the Republic of Molina to signify "Dictatorship" (capital D), they attempt to unify disparate historical examples under one umbrella. Beltrán Valencia (2014), while offering a more nuanced approach of the fight over meaning production between Antígona and the state-controlled media (which refers to dictatorship), reminds us of the standard reading to this day: "Antígona Pérez is seen as [...] an American symbol of freedom and the Republic of Molina the sum of many Latin American dictatorships" (38). In a long footnote, Beltrán Valencia lumps together sixteen examples of twentieth-century Latin American dictatorships, half of them happening after the play's appearance in 1968 or successfully brought down.[14] Angelina Morfi (1982) compiles a long list of disconnected abstractions to account for American "dictatorship": "the alliance of the US with dictatorial governments; controlled press; participation in undeclared wars; the Church as unconditional ally of the government."[15]

History is also purged when critics view the conflict as an "ideological clash between two characters" (Gómez Aponte 2012) or as a confrontation of "different personalities" (Fiet 2004). Exceptional are critics like Alyce de Kuehne (1970) and José Luis Ramos Escobar (2012), who zoom into *some* historical specificity. Ramos sees real-life dictator Trujillo as Sánchez's main inspiration, and Kuehne takes the play as an allegory for Puerto Rico, identifying Aurora, for instance, with the Puerto Rican Partido Popular, and Antígona's rape with that of the island.[16]

The extirpation of history is primarily argued with an essentialist reading of the Greco-Christian symbols and existentialist undertones, which allegedly comprise a universal language. Critics are fascinated by the "universal" name: Antigone. In their eyes, Greek mythology would "purify"

---

[14] The note mentions: "a predominance of dictatorial regimes [...] or certain types of family dynasties: Argentina (1976–83), Bolivia (1970–82), Brazil (1964–85), Chile (1973–90), Colombia (1953–8), Cuba (1952–9), Dominican Republic (1930–61), El Salvador (1931–79), Guatemala (1954–86), Haiti (1957–90), Honduras (1963–71), Nicaragua (1936–79), Panama (1968–89), Paraguay (1954–89), Peru (1968–80), Uruguay (1973–85)." Of the sixteen countries above, only eight were actual right-wing dictatorships in 1968—all of them of different natures.

[15] Javier del Valle's 2011 review of a production of the play repeats the gesture: "during that agitated year of 1968, the majority of [countries] in America lived under military dictatorship" (*El Nuevo Día*, April 13, 2011).

[16] The Partido Popular Democrático stands for the status quo: it was founded by the father of the "Estado Libre Asociado," Luis Muñoz Marín.

LUIS RAFAEL SÁNCHEZ'S 1968 *ANTÍGONA PÉREZ*   201

Sánchez's play from the flaws of "insular theater" or political theater in the 1960s. For Ben-Ur, one of the play's "merits" is its "[pitch] at a fairly abstract level, with the Greek myth acting as cloak and shield, though it is directed towards the present historical hemispheric contingency [...] classical and Christian myths grant immunity to the playwright from the 'soiled hands' of the dramatist who opts for narrow, sentimental commitment" (1975: 20). The epigraph by Albert Camus, in turn, fostered existential readings. For Francisco Arriví, Kuehne, Gloria Waldman, and others, "it aims to speak [...] to men of the whole world."[17] In this view, morality replaces not only politics but also the ancient tragic religious world: Antígona's decision to die fulfills "the most rigorous existentialist requirement; at no time is she inauthentic" (Waldman 1988: 275). In turn, Efraín Barradas wrote that the Greek myth allows Sánchez to reveal essences: "the essential *americanidad* ('American-ness') of the Puerto Rican" (1979: 15).

When it comes to the other "universal" language, Christianity, even the Christian rhetoric of Antígona's "passion" is denied historical context. Beltrán Valencia and Ben-Ur see the play as an empty parody of the "universal" values of tragedy and of Christianity, presenting a world with "no gods." Brunn rightly associates Antígona's martyrdom with "the curious fusion of a Christian framework and Marxist revolutionary ideology [that] characterized some of the innovative Latin American theater in the 1960s and 1970s" (2012: 39)—only there was nothing "curious" in that fusion, a social movement that took the globe by storm on many fronts. The Catholic rhetoric in the play situates God on earth, not in heaven: liberation theology first swept the continent—and then the world—after the Second Vatican Council (1962–5) and the 1968 Bishops' Conference of Medellín (Colombia). With its core principle of "the preferential option for the poor," liberation theology radicalized the ideology of martyrdom already present in American left-wing movements of the 1960s.[18] Antígona explicitly refers to liberation theology when she considers whether there is "salvation" in this life (81). In act 1, along with the deaths of Che and King, we learn about the death of Pope John XXIII, who called for the Second Vatican Council. Historically, Catholicism in the Latin American sixties was profoundly divided, with the emergence of the "popular Church," which organized

---

[17] Arriví (1967: 20), Kuehne (1970), and Waldman (1988). The epigraph is from Camus' The Plague: "for nothing in the world is it worth turning one's back on what one loves." See also José Luis Ramos Escobar (in López, Pociña, and Silva 2012: 429–35).

[18] For an introduction, see Gutiérrez ([1971] 1988).

202 LUIS RAFAEL SÁNCHEZ'S 1968 *ANTÍGONA PÉREZ*

peasants and mobilized masses alongside left-wing militants. Sánchez has Monseñor Escudero impersonate the Church's right-wing discourse, and Antígona the left.

The reference to Antígona's passion is Christian; her last name is Spanish; and her first name is, indeed, Greek—another instance, in this book's corpus, of cultural heterogeneity. Sánchez frames this hybridity with historical—rather than mythical—temporality. Antígona's name is "the beginning" of her story (14)—not her eternity. As she says throughout, the eternal in her is an idea: freedom. The Greek origin of her name helps her understand her life on this earth: "My [truth] is simple. It starts with my name, *este Antígona tenso* [this tense Antígona], with which my father satisfied his penchant for the heroic. His friends, military men like him, admired me [...] I did not know that Antígona was the young woman who decides to die" (14). The tension in her name is that between the mythological—the ancestral woman who decides to sacrifice herself—and the historical—the modern woman who understands her father's wishes, for him and for her, in Creón's regime. Like his brother Creón, Antígona's father was a low-ranking military officer who "married up." For Creón, the heroic name and spirit have no place in the republic. But, for Antígona's father, they exist in (his own deadly) rebellion against Creón. For Antígona, however, the name boils down to a class difference and, in the context of 1968, a class ideology. In contrast to the honorable Greek name, she chooses her father's local surname, "Pérez": "leave me with the common and mistreated Pérez, that way I feel my feet more on earth" (71), she says to Monseñor. The sacrificial rhetoric she is to inhabit is as ancient as it is modern: the 1960s rhetoric of the "new man."[19] As to the Christian "passion," Sánchez historicizes this too. There are only twelve scenes reminiscent of Christ's *via crucis*, rather than fourteen. Without the eternal redemption, Antígona's life is framed by human, not godly, temporality.

Proper names create a tapestry of historical references throughout the play. The "imaginary republic" takes the second last name of the Dominican dictator Trujillo Molina. Antígona Pérez's assassinated friends carry the surname of Dominican guerrilla fighter Manuel Aurelio Tavárez Justo, who was executed in 1963 while trying to regroup the 1J4, the Movimiento

---

[19] Che Guevara's 1965 legendary letter to Carlos Quijano, published in the Uruguayan journal *Marcha*, was titled "El hombre nuevo" ("The new man"). Its ode to sacrifice and passion reads: "the true revolutionary is guided by great feelings of love. [...] Our freedom and its daily support have the color of blood and are filled with sacrifice" (March 1965).

Revolucionario 14 de Junio. The guerrilla group was formed after a 1959 international expedition to Dominican shores failed to topple Trujillo. Tavárez Justo was thirty-two when he died. The character of Antígona may have been inspired by female fighters, some Dominican, some Puerto Rican. Among them are the Dominican Mirabal sisters, members of the 1J4, killed by Trujillo on November 25, 1960: Minerva (Tavárez's wife) was thirty-two; Patria was thirty-six; and María Teresa was twenty-five.[20] María Teresa allegedly expressed in prison that "one risks one's own life without thinking of personal benefits [...] maybe what we have closer to us is death, but this idea does not frighten me."[21] Antígona Pérez often expresses an intimacy with death; the line she addresses to Monseñor Escudero echoes María Teresa's: "To die is the least serious thing in one's life" (81).

Puerto Rico's own historical Antígonas, enlisted as freedom fighters, attracted international attention in the 1950s. Blanca Canales Torresola, at age forty-four, led the 1950 Jayuya uprising, "liberating" the town for three days until the US military squashed the revolt. Lolita Lebrón, at age thirty-five, led the 1954 attack on the House of Representatives in Washington, DC. When arrested, she shouted, "I have come to die for Puerto Rico!" Olga Viscal Garriga,[22] at age twenty-one, refused to recognize US authorities while on trial for participating in a 1950 revolt in San Juan. Antígona Pérez is a composite of Blanca, Minerva, Patria, María Teresa, Lolita, and Olga.

My emphasis on history in this chapter serves not just to balance the allegorical readings that this play has thus far produced, but rather more to account for the oddities in plot, performance, and stage directions that remain unresolved by critics—in other words, to account for that "tension" in the name Antígona that the main character stresses and the plot enhances. For it is in that tension that we find Sánchez's quilting point between the tragic myth and a historical narrative with the undertone of a testimony: Antígona is the girl who will always die, and she is the one who testifies, learns, and teaches history. Sánchez's play is a "tragic testimony"—a quilt of forms that reappears in Peru in 2000.[23] In this chapter, I find answers

---

[20] The world commemorates them on November 25, the International Day for the Elimination of Violence Against Women.

[21] See José E. Marcano."Patria, Minerva y María Teresa Mirabal Reyes: Las Hermanas Mirabal," *Mi país*, at http://www.jmarcano.com/mipais/biografia/mirabal1.html.

[22] Pablo Cabrera remembers that while she was a student at the University of Puerto Rico in the 1950s, Olga Viscal's sister, Sonia, played the leading role in Rafael Acevedo's student directorial project of Jean Anouilh's *Antigone*.

[23] Testimony emerged as a literary genre precisely at this time to give voice to the oppressed, with Cuban Miguel Barnet's 1966 *Biography of a Runaway Slave*.

204 LUIS RAFAEL SÁNCHEZ'S 1968 *ANTÍGONA PÉREZ*

by following in Antígona's footsteps: by being, like her, a student of history—a student of Puerto Rico in the historical 1968.

Collective Action: The "Now" of 1968

The *hic et nunc* of this Antígona was the "long '68." Latin America in the 1960s was not the land of dictators—and even less so of Trujillo-style dictatorships.[24] No other Latin American nation was ruled by another in the way that Puerto Rico was. In no other nation had the struggle for independence (both in the nineteenth and twentieth centuries) failed to produce an official narrative of the nation-state's birth. Rather, Latin America in the 1960s was a land of massive social movements, ripples of the successes of the 1950s, and leading, of course, to massive political repression orchestrated transnationally in the context of the Cold War.

Antígona speaks the rhetoric of those massive movements, of an ideological kinship among the American youth of 1968: a "continental feeling" of "la patria grande" ("the great fatherland"), a narrative dream of commonality, resurfacing the age-old narrative of the nineteenth-century Bolivarian dream of continental union.[25] In his 1815 "Jamaica Letter," Simón Bolívar even referenced Greek antiquity when writing about his dream of "consolidating the New World into a single nation [...] or a confederation. How beautiful it would be if the Isthmus of Panamá could be for us what the Isthmus of Corinth was for the Greeks."[26]

Cultural expression in the 1960s celebrated that utopian horizon of commonality. In 1966, the youth of eighty-two countries from Asia, Africa, and Latin America gathered for the first "Tri-Continental Conference" in La Habana. By 1968, Uruguayan Eduardo Galeano was busy researching European exploitation since the conquest, which would lead to his 1971 book, *The Open Veins of Latin America: Five Centuries of the Pillage of a Continent*, whose title, echoing Antígona's reference to "American blood" and bloodletting, soon became a popular bible of left-wing activists in the

---

[24] Trujillo's oddity was associated with Creón in 1963 by Dominican Marcio Veloz Maggiolo, who wrote, before Trujillo's fall, a short one-act piece titled "Creonte," indirectly portraying Trujillo.

[25] This narrative is still active; its latest version was Argentina's 2006 "Plan Patria Grande," which granted Argentine permanent residence to any migrant with a Latin American passport. See http://www.migraciones.gov.ar/pdf_varios/estadisticas/Patria_Grande.pdf.

[26] See the "Jamaica Letter" at http://faculty.smu.edu/bakewell/bakewell/texts/jamaica-letter.html.

region. The Tricontinental journal published revolutionary art and film manifestos; the political music movement "Nueva canción" ("New song") spread like wildfire, celebrating "American kinship." Argentine César Isella first sang in Chile what later he and Tejada Gómez would publish as "Canción con todos" ("Song with everyone," 1969), which became the continental hymn of unity, the background music on Radio La Habana for eleven years, and was declared the "Latin American Hymn" by UNESCO in 1990. Engraved in the hearts of that generation and generations to come was its world-famous chorus: "all blood can become a song in the wind, sing with me, sing, American brother."[27]

And yet, the dissonance between Antígona Pérez's American spirit and her solitary death remains striking. Onstage, there appears no strong collective of women or men. Antígona in Puerto Rico is slowly but surely abandoned by every character in the play. She is a lone bird singing continental kinship in the corpus of Latin American Antígonas and remains alone to this day. Her solitude is akin to the solitude of Puerto Rico's unique political situation in the region. I trace the continuity the play proposes between the Dominican Republic, Puerto Rico, and the imaginary frontiers of the Republic of Molina to investigate Antígona's solitude as Puerto Rico's solitude: a hundred-year-old cry for freedom. Antígona is the memory of the 1867 "I swear you will be free," pronounced by Puerto Rican father of the independence movement, Ramón Emeterio Betances (1827–98).[28] She commemorates the first freedom revolt in Puerto Rico in 1868, remembered as "el Grito de Lares" ("the Lares Revolt") and considered a founding moment for the nationalist movement that Betances then led in Spain's colonial island. In the 1930s, the incorruptible, radical icon of nationalism, Pedro Albizu Campos, took up Betances' legacy, leading two decades of resistance until he was defeated in 1950. Antígona's rhetoric onstage is reminiscent of Albizu's. In the 1960s, Puerto Rican armed resistance championed Albizu's struggle. Antígona places a bomb in the library to distract authorities, so as to "hide the corpses in the trunk of a Peugeot, and bury them" (107).

---

[27] The Spanish reads: "toda la sangre puede ser canción en el viento, canta conmigo, canta, hermano americano."

[28] This is part of Betances' 1867 Proclama de los Diez Mandamientos de los Hombres Libres (Proclamation of the Ten Commandments of Free Men). Betances was known as "the Antillean," traveling throughout the Caribbean with the message to free Puerto Rico and create an "Antillean Confederation."

206 LUIS RAFAEL SÁNCHEZ'S 1968 *ANTÍGONA PÉREZ*

Puerto Rico is among the handful of archipelagos in the world still considered colonial property. As critic Daniel Zalacaín has observed, Antígona Pérez's passion is "Puerto Rico's passion in its struggle to preserve its identity against the North American avalanche to which it is submitted" (1981: 118). She is less concerned with burial than with the Puerto Rican anticolonial situation. In fact, this is the first play in the corpus where the receding in importance of the burial, which I mentioned in previous chapters, becomes clear: burial is secondary to her act of possession of the corpses, and by extension, of the land where she has put them to rest. In the eyes of power, Antígona's true crime is robbery. Creón Molina rules a republic that belongs to him: it carries his name—the Republic is "of Molina" ("de Molina"). In Creón Molina's eyes, the question is, to whom do the corpses belong: to the ruler, metonymically associated with Empire, or to the freedom fighters (Antígona and all her "siblings")?[29]

Lumping the history of the continent's nations into a seamless narrative about "dictatorship" and excluding Puerto Rico's singularity not only eliminates the tension and quilting between history and myth that gives the play its Brechtian air but also overlooks that this quilting is present right in the play's subtitle: a "chronicle." It overlooks Antígona's passion for history. It ignores that throughout the play, Antígona refers to "local manufacture" (45) to describe the Tavárezes' assault on Creón, who instead blames foreign ideologies. It overlooks that the only character who makes an atemporal equivalence between America and dictatorship is her treacherous friend Irene, who tells Antígona: "América is the land of perpetual men" (109). It overlooks Antígona's response to Irene: "*history* is inevitable" (109; my emphasis). It overlooks Antígona's rhetoric that invokes America as the idea of eternal resistance. Near the end, after the multitude divides into women and men, both parties exhort Antígona with eight phrases: "Antígona, do not give up [...] do not suffer [...] do not lose [...] do not die [...] go on [...] easy [...] wake up [...] alert" (104). Antígona uses these phrases in her monologue addressed to the men, but substitutes her name with "America": "I will also start to shout America do not give up, America do not suffer..." (104). For Antígona, America means resistance, not dictatorship.

Like Marechal in Buenos Aires, Morisseau-Leroy in Port-au-Prince, and Andrade in São Paulo, Sánchez quilted the "world language" of Antigone,

---

[29] Nevertheless, the vast majority of criticism "compares and contrasts" the ancient Antigone and Antígona Pérez in terms of the importance of burial. Recent examples include Ford (2013) and Brunn (2012).

tragedy, and Christianity (a language of faith, fate, integrity, sacrifice, resistance, and dignity) with the local language of the colony and the problem of the national, rendering Molina meaningful to his audience. In the play, Antígona's real crime quilts everything up: her robbery speaks the language of the colony, not of universal rights to burial. Vélez and Pérez belong, indeed, to the same Hispanic family. But they are not twins. As Ramos Escobar puts it, Antígona Pérez is merely Antígona Vélez's "distant cousin" (2012: 430). While the previous national Antígonas questioned the borders of already-conformed nation-states, Antígona Pérez never had a nation-state. She is different in that she wants a nation-state. An American nation-state.

Assessing the play's historical context illuminates Antígona's specific, Puerto Rican, anticolonial struggle and her American spirit as closer to their nineteenth-century expression than to that of the continental 1968: her cry of freedom is closest to Varela's Argia against the Spanish Empire. The tensions between the Greek and Christian myths and their historicity in the play articulate this temporal dislocation: the return of Puerto Rico's failed 1868 revolt in the global language of 1968. Antígona's anticolonial struggle in a world convulsed by the utopia of socialism helps us understand her solitude on stage.

The Passion According to Luis Rafael Sánchez: National and Popular

Associated with the Caribbean "new novel" and the generation of the 1960s, profoundly marked by the deaths of Puerto Ricans in the Vietnam War, and obsessed with the "national" question, Luis Rafael Sánchez is a towering figure in Latin American letters. Born in 1936 to a working-class family in the small town of Humacao, Sánchez traveled to San Juan, New York, and Spain for his education. His international reputation emerged with the publication of his novel *La guaracha del macho Camacho* (*Macho Camacho's Beat*, 1976), reviewed in Puerto Rico as "a chronicle of the spiritual impoverishment of all social classes violated by the worst of colonialisms."[30] Although he conceived it as a parody of the Hispanic American novel,[31] readers of Puerto Rican newspapers initially qualified it as "bragging of vulgarity and bad taste."[32] Sánchez's novel incorporates Caribbean musical

---

[30] Juan Manuel Rivera in *Claridad*, June 3, 1976, p. 8.
[31] Interview, cited in Calaf de Agüera (1979: 75).   [32] Pagán (1976: 6).

208 LUIS RAFAEL SÁNCHEZ'S 1968 *ANTÍGONA PÉREZ*

rhythms and humor, street expressions and slang, and innovative techniques of fragmentation, plurivocality, intertextuality, and cinematic and theatrical elements. Sánchez has a penchant for portraying marginality, distancing himself from realism with an aesthetic of the grotesque and vulgar. He writes from and against realism, the tradition of national theater launched by Emilio Belaval's 1938 manifesto: "Lo que podría ser un teatro puertoriqueño" ("What a Puerto Rican theater could be").[33] The latter set the agenda: the island and its people became the center of "almost every play written and produced in Puerto Rico since 1938."[34]

Sánchez expresses his political and aesthetic commitment to Puerto Rico as the advocacy of cultural survival under the threat of Anglophone culture: "Puerto Rican theater has been essentially nationalist and should be; because Puerto Rico has an unresolved political problem [...] the disappearance of our personality as a people [...] the participation of Puerto Ricans in the conflicts that tie them to the United States."[35] Sánchez's passion for Puerto Rican sovereignty was made publicly clear in his speech at the March 2016 VII International Congress of the Spanish Language (CILE) celebrated in San Juan.[36] He dedicated his words to two of his intellectual icons: Puerto Rican nationalist activist Óscar López Rivera (1943–) and Spanish poet Federico García Lorca (1898–1936). A Vietnam veteran, López Rivera was imprisoned in the United States for over thirty-five years, accused of seditious conspiracy against the US government. He was the leader of the clandestine armed group FALN (Armed Forces of National Liberation of Puerto Rico) and has remained an international icon for anti-colonial struggle.[37] An "Antigone figure," one may say, he was offered clemency in 1999 but refused it because it did not extend to other Puerto Rican political prisoners partaking in his cause. He was released on May 17, 2017.

Opening his speech with López Rivera was its own political statement. Dedicating the entire speech to the defense of Puerto Rico's cultural identity was an indictment. Sánchez qualified the relation with the United States as

---

[33] See Arriví (1967 and 1972: 6–7). For the 1938 manifesto, see Belaval (1948: 9–24).
[34] Jordan Blake Phillips, quoted in Waldman (1988: 101).
[35] Interview with Waldman (1988: 36).
[36] Available online at https://www.youtube.com/watch?v=N6yFQkP9rvs.
[37] The FALN operated until 1983, leading to the formation of the Boricua Popular Army, active to this day. It was part of "la nueva lucha" ("the new struggle"); several organizations went underground after the defeat of Pedro Albizu Campos in 1950, among them the Movimiento Pro Independencia formed in 1959, the Movimiento Independentista Revolucionario Armado, Organización de Voluntarios por la Revolución Puertorriqueña, and Los Comandos Armados de Liberación (CAL). See González Cruz (2006), Paralitici (2011), and Morejón Flores (2016).

"the obsession, the one and only theme, with which we have had to live together all Puerto Ricans for a century."[38] With the king of Spain in the audience, he pointed out that the Royal Academy of Spain (RAE) had not accepted the word *puertorriqueñidad* while it had accepted other expressions of Hispanic nationality (such as *argentinidad*). Consistent with his beliefs, in 2006 Sánchez adhered to the Panama Proclamation of 2006 for the Independence of Puerto Rico, approved unanimously by twenty-two nations at the Latin American and Caribbean Congress for Puerto Rico's Independence. The Congress took place in Panama to commemorate 180 years of the Amphictyonic Congress of Panama, summoned by Simón Bolívar in 1826 (the name of the congress honored the ancient Greek Amphictyonic League), a congress that had discussed Puerto Rico's independence.

The 1968 Production: The Spectacular Duo Sánchez/Cabrera

The 1968 premiere of *Antígona Pérez* in San Juan was a smashing success. Critics and audiences agreed that Puerto Rican director Pablo Cabrera (1931–) knew what he was doing at the traditional Tapia Theater. Cabrera's grand cinematic and operatic spectacle revolutionized theater in Puerto Rico. His direction of *Antígona Pérez* secured his status as master of mise-en-scène. Cabrera's career as a director started upon his return from Italy, where he was supposed to study medicine but was captivated by theater (and by towering opera figures such as Maria Callas). He trained at the famous Centro Sperimentale di Roma, a point of arrival for many Latin American artists in the 1950s and 1960s. Back home, Cabrera joined the Puerto Rican "new theater," which echoed the 1960s theater movements throughout the continent—a "guerilla theater" outside of the high-class experience of the grand Tapia—an "Off Tapia theater," as Lowell Fiet puts it (2004: 243). Cabrera knew Sophocles' *Antigone* well. As a student at the University of Puerto Rico in Rio Piedras, Cabrera had read the classics in the Western Civilization course curriculum. But, as he notes, upon reading Sánchez's text, "at no point did I recall Sophocles. This was an entirely different text."[39]

---

[38] See Alemany (2016) at http://www.elmundo.es/internacional/2016/04/03/570005a626 8e3ed9718b45fb.html.

[39] All information about Cabrera's career comes from my 2015 interviews with him and Ramón Albino Rodríguez.

Cabrera's vision for the production in 1968 was majestic. As he says, "el teatro entra por los ojos" ("theater gets in through the eyes"): you see first, then you hear. The state-run Division for Community Education in San Juan had granted him a generous $27,000.[40] No fewer than forty extras were hired, many of them student actors at the University of Puerto Rico Drama Department. The stage had at its center a gigantic spiral staircase with several landings to represent either the interior of the palace or the outside world. The staircase reached down to the orchestra pit. The props were minimal; there was no furniture. Lighting effects defined the atmosphere of the different spaces (Figure 4.2).

Figure 4.2 *La pasión según Antígona Pérez.* The minimal stage: stairs, *periaktos*, and dungeon. Directed by Pablo Cabrera. Eleventh annual Puerto Rican Theater Festival. Teatro Tapia, San Juan, Puerto Rico, May 30, 1968. Rehearsal photo. Courtesy of the Archivo Fotográfico del Instituto de Cultura Puertorriqueña (AGPR-ICP).

---

[40] In 2017, approximately $186,000, according to the Inflation Consumer Price Index calculator on the website of the US Bureau of Labor Statistics: http://www.bls.gov/data/inflation_calculator.htm.

The music was perfectly coordinated with the lights, intensifying the visual carvings of space and, occasionally, individual character's lines. The actors sat on the landing of the stairs, rather than on chairs. The widest part of the staircase had three *periaktos*, consisting of a total of nine gyrating panels covered with posters featuring headlines taken from contemporary newspapers all over the continent and "all that noise from propaganda" (14) from consumer products (soda, beer, cigarettes).[41] The moving panels even had traffic lights.

Cabrera's production placed the *periaktos* in front of the cyclorama. Cabrera recalls that during the 1968 premiere, Sánchez would update the titles on the panels with breaking news. Two wind fans were used to lift dozens of newspapers into the air, creating the impression that they were falling from the sky. The extras ("the multitude" in the stage directions) would run to catch loose papers falling on the ground, hungry to consume whatever they were fed. Sánchez's stage directions featured grandiose numbers: "a hysterical multitude of 200 heads after those newspapers [...] reading voraciously the few pages that they have managed to grab" (14). Five strong, flexible men were cast as the journalists, each carrying a light camera. They identify themselves by the newspaper they represent, reading the news with a mechanical "official" attitude, and produce their own lighting effects to emphasize their entrances and exits: "when they finish their last news report they flash their cameras. The lighting is magnificent" (stage directions, 18; Figure 4.3).

Cabrera remembers using the journalists' camera flashes for metatheatrical commentary along with Antígona's Brechtian gestures. A journalist would focus his camera on an actor upon their entrance; the actor would stop and "freeze" when the journalist released the flash and "took" the photo.[42] The audience was thus repeatedly made aware of theatricality, of the artificiality and performativity of public life in the "Republic of Molina," and of the frames with which the media captured the characters' stories. Antígona would be locked at the end of the staircase, only able to move a few steps; but from her position, she could see and comment on palace events and address the audience. Reviewers identified the latter as a

---

[41] The use of "propaganda" in Spanish refers both to commercial advertisements and to ideological messages.

[42] See Juan Luis Márquez's review on Cabrera's direction for *El Mundo* (in Waldman 1988: 287).

Figure 4.3 *La pasión según Antígona Pérez*. The five journalists. Directed by Pablo Cabrera. Eleventh annual Puerto Rican Theater Festival. Teatro Tapia, San Juan, Puerto Rico, May 30, 1968. Rehearsal photo. Courtesy of the Archivo Fotográfico del Instituto de Cultura Puertorriqueña (AGPR-ICP).

Brechtian technique, though we can also view in it the frame of Antígona's testimony before the audience about her life in Molina.[43]

Cabrera cast Myrna Vázquez (1935–75, then thirty-three years old) to play Antígona: he found her fragile and beautiful. Her body had to contrast with the towering figure that Cabrera imagined for Creón, who had to be someone as grandiose as the immense "United States eagle" (Figures 4.4 and 4.5). The aim was to give the impression of an ominous threat to little Antígona, symbol of the small island of Puerto Rico for Cabrera. The massive number of extras that Sánchez imagined enhanced this contrast.

The costumes were designed by Gloria Sáez, Zuckie Cruz, and Piri Fernández (1925–2003)—the last an independentist fighter, daughter of the only woman who renounced US citizenship when it was granted to Puerto Ricans in 1917, and president of the UN's anticolonial congress in the 1960s,

---

[43] Benigno Trigo sees Brechtian techniques and the use of platforms as Sánchez's comments on the colonized psyche, a set of oneiric scenes: "the play is a dream remembered by Antígona: a space divided into upper and lower platforms, into light and dark areas" (2016: 18).

Figure 4.4 *La pasión según Antígona Pérez.* Myrna Vázquez and Rafael Enrique Saldaña. Directed by Pablo Cabrera. Eleventh annual Puerto Rican Theater Festival. Teatro Tapia, San Juan, Puerto Rico, May 30, 1968. Rehearsal photo. Courtesy of the Archivo Fotográfico del Instituto de Cultura Puertorriqueña (AGPR-ICP).

which discussed Puerto Rico's situation. Vázquez cut her hair short to play Antígona. Rafael Enrique Saldaña was cast as Creón: Cabrera and Sánchez had the Dominican dictator as model. The real-life Trujillo was legendarily pompous and majestic, dressed in white suits adorned with so many medals that he was nicknamed "Chapita" ("Bottlecap"). Sánchez's stage directions say: "The Generalísimo is dressed always in impeccable white color; gabardine, cashmere, linen, drill, all white. The lapels are covered with orders, medals, honors" (37). Saldaña accordingly wore a crisp white suit and a large pendant that resembled the decoration that Trujillo received in 1938 during his first government (the "Order of Trujillo") (Figure 4.6).[44]

---

[44] Amaury Veray Torregrosa (1922–95) composed the music arrangements for Mexican Silvestre Revueltas' concert for percussion, with the drums bringing a military air to the theater. Artist Rafael Rivera García did the grafitti. For a brief comment on Cabrera's direction of this play, see Gómez Aponte (2012: 123–8).

Figure 4.5 *La pasión según Antígona Pérez*. Poster for Idalia Pérez Garay's production. Designer: Julio García. Teatro UPR, San Juan, Puerto Rico, March 20, 1992. Courtesy of the Colección Puertorriqueña of the Biblioteca Lázaro, Universidad de Puerto Rico.

Even the stage's smallest details presented a regal majesty. Cabrera's entire proposal for the stage design can be seen as representing the Spanish Crown, rather than a modern "dictatorship." The presidential palace members, residing upstairs and descending for one scene, donned lavish dresses and exuberant jewelry. Cabrera recalls that a goldsmith friend of his from

Figure 4.6 *La pasión según Antígona Pérez*. Rafael Enrique Saldaña: white suit and a large pendant. Directed by Pablo Cabrera. Eleventh annual Puerto Rican Theater Festival. Teatro Tapia, San Juan, Puerto Rico, May 30, 1968. Rehearsal photo. Courtesy of the Archivo Fotográfico del Instituto de Cultura Puertorriqueña (AGPR-ICP).

the famous jewelry store Joyería Riviera in San Juan was escorted nightly by an armed security guard, bringing jewelry worth $250,000 for the actress playing Pilar Varga, a character Cabrera imagined as regal as Evita Perón, who was known for her penchant for designer European clothing and jewelry. Every glamorous detail for "Pilar" was carefully considered. She primped herself at the mirror in the upper landing wearing a robe, while domestic servants sprayed perfume from pump-spray glass bottles, not onto her skin, but around her, so she would walk into a misty, scented cloud. She descended to visit Antígona while thumbing the pages of *Burda*, the legendary Brazilian fashion magazine of German origin (first published in Brazil in German).

The play has since seen nothing but success. In 1971, *Antígona Pérez* left the island for the mainland and was staged at the Hispanic theater of the University of Texas. On May 18, 1972, the Puerto Rican Traveling Theater (PRTT) performed it at the theater-minded Cathedral Church of St. John the Divine in New York City. Cabrera directed another majestic production there, with Miriam Colón, founding director of the PRTT, as Antígona. Tony-winner Karl Eigsti, scene and lighting designer, was able to make use of the high altar. Howard Thompson reviewed it twice for *The New York*

216 LUIS RAFAEL SÁNCHEZ'S 1968 *ANTÍGONA PÉREZ*

Times, first on May 20 and again on August 25: "last night, the play, the players and the church merged no less than hauntingly" (May 20, 1972: 20). It was a hit: a thousand people every night, international and national press, community leaders. The PRTT then toured neighborhoods in New York.[45] The play may be one of the most staged Puerto Rican plays on the island. Among the many later productions, three are often mentioned. José Luis Ramos directed the first in 1976, in Mayagüez and then in San Juan at the Sylvia Rexach Theater;[46] the second, in 1992, was directed by Idalia Pérez Garay with Alba Nidia Díaz as Antígona at the University of Puerto Rico Theater in San Juan (Figure 4.5). Gilberto Valenzuela directed the third in 2011–12, with a cast of sixty. In *Claridad's* review, there is a catchy subheading: "The Two Antígonas" (February 30, 2011, *sic*). But the reviewer does not compare the "first" Sophoclean source and the "second" Puerto Rican production, as an academic critic, trained to see the Greek as "original," might expect. Rather, the reviewer compares one Puerto Rican production to another: Valenzuela's production is contrasted to Cabrera's original production in 1968. Antígona Pérez is so local that in a page-long interview with the actors, the Greek text is never mentioned. The actors speak of the "bible" (Sánchez's text) and of the historical events surrounding 1968. Cabrera's production turned the play into a Puerto Rican classic.[47]

Both Sánchez and Cabrera became part of the larger Caribbean movement of theater modernization, which quilted Brechtian technique with the

---

[45] Anthony Mancini wrote in the *New York Post* that "it was good theater, free of charge, for the people" (August 10, 1972, quoted in de La Roche 1995: 69). On August 21, 1972, Colón performed a scene of the play in the Street/Community Theater Festival at the Lincoln Center (*The New York Times,* August 22, 1972: 52). Two days later, they performed the whole play in the Lincoln Center Mall. Howard Thompson's second review in *The New York Times* on August 25 praised the "scathing, often gripping drama" with which Sánchez "updated" the ancient version (17). The following Monday they went to Boston; audiences identified with Antígona. See Thompson (1972: 17). See The New York Public Library Archives (Billy Rose Theatre Division for the Performing Arts, Dorothy and Lewis B. Cullman Center) for the PRTT archival records of this tour.

[46] Reviews were consistently negative. In *Claridad,* González harshly criticized the *mise-en-scène,* though he praised Sánchez's text (February 7, 1976). In *The San Juan Star,* Collins faulted José Luis Ramos' direction but also the playwright himself for the "melodramatic pathos": Creón is "too bad to be true, and Antigone too good to be true" (February 5, 1976). In *El Vocero,* Ramón Porrero considered that the production almost misinterpreted the play (February 16, 1976, p. 20).

[47] So much a classic that its latest incarnation will become an opera. In 2003, Puerto Rican composer Carlos Carrillo wrote a twenty-minute opera fragment for the play, and in 2015, he was completing a musical score "La pasión según Antígona Pérez: for soprano and orchestra." When the emblematic Latinx Hostos Community College paid homage to the playwright on May 1, 2012 by staging the play at the Teatro Pregones in New York, Carillo's fragment was part of the music score.

LUIS RAFAEL SÁNCHEZ'S 1968 *ANTÍGONA PÉREZ*   217

Greek classics: therein lay the duo's "strategic classicism" against nationalist realist theater.[48] Sánchez's Brechtian "distance," as well as his inspiration in Sartre and Christianity (and García Lorca), drew the most critical attention. Brecht had been influential in street theater but was now entering professional theater with premieres such as that of *Antígona Pérez*.[49] Writing for the *San Juan Star*, Ani Fernández considered the chorus of five newsmen as the perfect Brechtian touch.[50] Throughout the play, the history-student-turned-teacher Antígona quilts tragedy with historical lessons by breaking the fourth wall to address the audience, eliminating any sense of mystery.

Whenever Antígona steps out of her limited space, she comments on another character, explains something to the audience, or interprets the words of her interlocutors. In scene 6, Monseñor Escudero, back from the Vatican, visits Creón's palace. Creón explains that the Tavárezes' attack called the attention of multitudes "who concentrated in front of the palace all day in spontaneous support for me" (69). Antígona looks at the audience: "Multitudes that were obliged to come under threat" (69). Creón then explains to Monseñor that the Tavárezes' "public wake" at Plaza Molina was "for the relatives to identify the terrorists." Antígona looks at the audience: "Creón's mandate was that the corpses rot in open air after serving as punitive example for the people" (73). The beginning of act 2 repeats Creón's movements at the end of act 1: he walks toward the dungeons and says "Lights"—and "the illumination is extraordinary" (stage directions, 88). Creón is in command of what is seen and not seen.

Antígona also teaches the audience about the art of theater: "The second part will really start when Creón says to me: Antígona, you look like me. The second part is shorter than the first. It is logical. The conflict has already been laid out. The motivations, also. What is missing is for the rest of the characters to understand that there is no alternative for me. I want to live. [...] But not if the price is to mutilate my own self-esteem" (88). Creón then appears before her and says verbatim: "Antígona, you look like me" (88). Creón's wife Pilar Varga is introduced in stage directions as: "The first lady starts to put on her skirt. Antígona slides to the right, but signals

---

[48] See Ramos Escobar (2012), Márquez (1979: 300–6), Morfi (1980), Ramos-Perea (1989), Meléndez (1992: 151–67), and Waldman (1988).

[49] See Waldman (1988), Ramos Escobar (2012), Fiet (2004), Dávila-López (1989, 1992), and Colón Zayas (1985).

[50] See Dauster (1971), de Kuehne (1970), Morfi (1982), and Waldman (1988). Ben-Ur (1975) and Santos Silva (1981) associate the Brechtian techniques with the ancient chorus; Ford (2013) compares the multitude and the journalists to the ancient chorus.

218   LUIS RAFAEL SÁNCHEZ'S 1968 *ANTÍGONA PÉREZ*

emphatically toward the platform" (53) and says "Pilar Varga, First Lady of the Republic of Molina, Creón's girlfriend since the times when the now Generalísimo was only a military apprentice [...] she has polished his social manner [...]. She has polished his ambition too [...] in a moment we shall see her [...] remind[ing] him what he would want to forget: that he is in power thanks to force. Pilar Varga, First Lady of the Republic of Molina" (54).

At times, and much like Antigone did with the ancient uncle, Antígona simply reclaims the meaning of words. Pilar Varga says to her, "give life, love, not death," and Antígona replies, "the first lady says Antígona's lines" (118). Monseñor says "nobody has asked us to visit you but our desire to speak to you. Believe it, Antígona" (79). Antígona "proudly" (stage directions) responds: "I believe, Monseñor. I am in these dungeons because I believe" (79).

Given the above, and as with previous Antígonas, critics raised again the question of what is "proper tragedy."[51] For all Cabrera's Brechtian twists, some critics were still nostalgic for the label of "tragedy." As Dauster wrote: "Antígona is a tragic character in the most rigorous sense [...] she undergoes a progressive and inevitable self-discovery" (1971: 85).[52] The audiences identified systematically with Antígona's struggle, rather than with her ironic analysis of Creón's world. As with every Antígona in this book, Sánchez's quilting of forms produced something unclassifiable by European categories. Antígona, *because she is Pérez*, struck an emotional chord among Puerto Rican audiences. As she puts it to her mother: "The dead belong to their living" (27).

What's in a Chronicle? 100 Years of Puerto Rican Solitude: From 1868 to 1968

In 1968, Sánchez was writing "An American Chronicle" about his dead, who were buried in the motherland, for his living.[53] This play premiered and was set in 1968, with references to the world news of 1968. As much as Greek tragedy, Sartrean existentialism, and the passion of Christ are part of the Western lexicon, so is "1968." And while one may disagree about its results,

---

[51] For comments on the mixing of myths, genres, and historical reality see Ben-Ur (1975), Morfi (1980), Woodyard (1973), and Waldman (1988); see Ben-Ur (1975) and Waldman (1988) for a comment on García Lorca's lyricism in this play.

[52] For the play as tragedy, see also Ben-Ur (1975) and Pérez Blanco (1984).

[53] Personal interview, May 1, 2012.

when it comes to politics, there is one feeling we do not associate with 1968: solitude.

Sánchez's 1968 Antígona acts alone. Not even the ancient Antigone was so lonely. The brief appearance in act 2, scene 2 of an encouraging female multitude does not balance Antígona's solitude: the multitude is immediately followed by Irene's betrayal. On stage, the number of extras and the lights enhance her loneliness. After Antígona's imprisonment, stage directions indicate the appearance of a "200-head multitude" (19). As the multitude murmurs "the country is back to normal" and "peace is ours," Antígona's voice interrupts at the sound of the word "peace," and the conical light beam falls on her to contrast her body with the multitude: "let's not talk about order to avoid confusion" (19). Just as one voice stands against "200" heads at the beginning, in act 2 during the palace reception for Monseñor Escudero, Antígona's Brechtian voice contrasts with Creón's "500 military" escorts.

Antígona is first abandoned by her mother, Aurora, who expels her from home out of fear (31). During Aurora's visit, Antígona unveils the mother's solitude, even if the mother now follows the regime: "What did you have to lose? […] had they killed you, they would have broken for you the knot of solitude […]" (32). When Irene breaks the news that Antígona's fiancé Fernando has accepted Creón's job offer, Antígona realizes she thought he would have "more integrity"; but for Irene, integrity means the loneliness of dissidence and ostracism (110). Antígona responds that, just as the solitude of fear has a limit, the solitary danger of dissidence also has a limit: the limit of imprisonment, torture, and death. When Irene tells her that Fernando is now controlling her visits, "Irene sees her breaking down but does not decide to help her" (stage directions, 107). Antígona's suffering is first performed in solitude: Irene wants to hug her goodbye, but Antígona rejects the embrace. She breathes in "the air of the whole universe" and says "goodbye" (stage directions, 107). It is a universal goodbye, as absolute and total as the air she breathes.

By the end of the play, Antígona looks at the audience and reflects that while both Irene and Fernando courageously helped her, now "finally, Fernando and Irene also leave. If faith did not emanate from one's own self, how difficult it would be to live" (113). And at last, when Pilar insists that if she has someone who loves her she should live, Antígona answers: "I do not have anyone who loves me" (118). Pilar says that giving life and love is the most important thing; Antígona rebuts: "to die is to give love, the most complete love" (119). Existentialist messages? Yes. But there is more.

220 LUIS RAFAEL SÁNCHEZ'S 1968 *ANTÍGONA PÉREZ*

When one thinks of 1968—worldwide—what comes to mind is collective action: mass demonstrations, guerrilla movements, workers' strikes, grassroots movements, popular protests, and anti-imperialist struggles. Before Antígona Pérez, none of her American sisters were entirely alone: in 1824, Argia has her father rescue her child; in 1951, Antígona Vélez dies with her lover; in 1953, Antigòn is rescued by a Vodou *lwa*. Andrade's 1959 Mariana has the women of the town supporting her, and his 1969 Marta is unfailingly accompanied by her son's lover. Contemporary plays that I briefly mention in the upcoming Interlude stage female connections for Antígona. Four people help Zavalía's 1958 Antígona character with the corpse. In 1963, Cureses' wives act together in what becomes the first real female collective in the corpus; Steiner's 1958 Antígona ends with Ismene calling for revolution; Rengifo's 1966 Antígona Sellers has her friend Peggy and her lawyers. The seemingly solitary Antígona in Fuentes Mares' 1968 play willingly distances herself from collective action. Female collectives will become prominent in Antígona performances in the twenty-first century.

Where in the American continent, then, can we imagine Antígona Pérez's solitude in 1968? To put it differently: how can we understand the national theater of "Antígona against Creón" staged in a country with no national army (and thus defended, or left alone, by other countries)? Can we read an Antígona that has no nation-state in the same way as one who speaks to her nation-state? Some may still want to identify a political resonance in Antígona Pérez's phrase "Continent: America" (13): Che Guevara's nickname was "Comandante de América." Che's country was every country and no particular country. But because Antígona Pérez quilts myth with history—in fact, studies history—the fact that she inhabits both the imaginary Republic of Molina on stage and a historical colony offstage takes on a different urgency.

The "imaginary Republic of Molina" refers to a unique historical dictatorship in Hispanic America, and Sánchez's nation, Puerto Rico, is a solitary case among the Hispanic American nations. Critics bypass the histories of both the Dominican Republic and of Puerto Rico. A testimonial fragment from Puerto Rican revolutionary nationalist militant Edwin Cortés poignantly summarizes the "history question" in Puerto Rico, recalling how, in Chicago, "in high-school I understood what it meant to be Puerto Rican [...] I asked a teacher why Puerto Rican history was not taught and she answered that Puerto Rico did not have a history."[54]

---

[54] Edwin Cortés (1955–) joined armed struggle in the 1970s and was arrested in the United States in 1983; he was liberated in 1999. I quote from González Cruz's compilation

LUIS RAFAEL SÁNCHEZ'S 1968 *ANTÍGONA PÉREZ* 221

In Brechtian manner, Antígona teaches history. Her own life story follows a historical narrative: it is a "chronicle." It is not simply the newspaper "chronicle" with which the five journalists interrupt the flow of events on stage seven times in a twelve-scene play. The chronicle also harks back to the colony, paying homage to the first literary tradition in America, the *Chronicles of the Indies*. Born as a colonial genre, the *Chronicles* were "versions of the truth": letters, diaries, and travelogues written by Spanish conquerors, missionaries, and explorers. Addressed to the Spanish Crown, these chronicles offered individual perspectives on their experiences, with specific goals such as obtaining money from the Crown to continue an expedition.

As Antígona explains, "newspapers have invented a story that is not true [...] a story with the aim of destroying my name, my reputation. There will be, thus, two versions of the same truth. Mine. Theirs. Mine is simple. It starts with my name" (14). Antígona's "version of the truth" is framed with historical temporality; the regime's "truths" are framed ahistorically. Aurora's "dangerously majoritarian" (23) position is that "the world is only one world, Antígona. Main characters, secondary characters, choruses. This is how it always was, this is how it always is, this is how it will always be" (22). Listening to Antígona's hopes for the "transfiguration of the republic," Irene says: "how long do you think that will take, Antígona? Ten, twenty, thirty years? América is the land of perpetual men" (109). Antígona's version of the truth is that the "inevitable" is history (109). "Transfiguration" will never cease. Creón also sees history in Antígona. He believes that he is doomed, and she is not: "Give up. I *do not know* how to go back. You still can learn it" (92; my emphasis).

Antígona's chronicle starts with her name; Sánchez's chronicle starts with the name of the republic, unveiled in the first line of the prologue. In Spanish, the imaginary Republic "of" Molina is polysemic: the preposition "of" (*de*) can be appositive (a description: the "Republic of Panama"), but also possessive. "Of Molina" can mean that it belongs to Molina. No historical Republic of Molina existed, though there was a real city "of Molina": the Dominican dictator Trujillo Molina decided to rename the capital of the Hispanic island after himself. Santo Domingo is the oldest city in America, the site of the first university, first cathedral, first castle, first monastery, and first fortress in America. In colonial times, it was also called the "first Athens of America." In 1936, it became "Ciudad Trujillo" and remained so until

---

(2006: 70). Carmen Valentín's testimony, in the same collection, speaks of a similar school story (González Cruz 2006: 83).

222 LUIS RAFAEL SÁNCHEZ'S 1968 *ANTÍGONA PÉREZ*

Trujillo was killed in 1961. The name "Molina" thus conveys both the historical city of Trujillo Molina and the imaginary Republic of Molina. Consider all the references to the island's colonial status thus far. Now recall Antígona's crime. Critics hasten toward the Greek. Ford summarizes: "the premise of Sánchez's Antígona Pérez is similar to the ancient Greek text—Antígona is jailed and condemned for burying the bodies of her 'brothers'" (2013: 86). But nowhere in the play is Antígona accused of unlawful burial. In fact, Creón is less concerned with the burial itself than with its location: his land. We see here one more instance of the brother's corpse receding in importance, just as in previous chapters. Antígona's crime is not even that which critics like Ben-Ur add to the burial: "collaborating to assassinate the tyrant" (1975: 19).

Antígona's charges are uniquely framed in terms of private property: from Creón's point of view, she is a thief. No other Antígona in Latin America had been accused of theft thus far nor in the decades that follow. Consider that the Republic of Molina "belongs" to Creón Molina, that the historically existing Dominican Republic was "owned" by Trujillo Molina, and that the historically existing Puerto Rico is owned by the United States (a country that actively backed Trujillo Molina until just before his end). Antígona explains the "local manufacture" of the Tavárezes' assault by referring to another solitary colonial situation: the Malvinas Islands—a British colonial property. A real-life, locally manufactured attempt killed Trujillo in 1961, while another real-life, locally manufactured attempt failed to take possession of the Malvinas in 1966 (I return to this later).[55]

There is an irony in the use of the word "American" in this play, for colonialism is at the center of Antígona's textual, performative, and historical solitude. Where in America, exactly, was this play written? In a country in Hispanic America, or in that country misappropriated as "America" in English usage? Perhaps Thompson's review on May 20, 1972, of the New York premiere captures it best, expressing how the same name is the site of ideological confusions. Thompson's use of "American" reveals Puerto Rico's odd place in America: the reviewer comments on "the *American* premiere" of a play in "a republic somewhere in *the Americas*"—and I add, whose title was "an *American* chronicle" (my emphasis). Thompson's English usage of "America" unveils this confusion: the name is simultaneously one and multiple. The singular America (the United States) does not correspond with

---

[55] Locally manufactured urban guerrilla actions in San Juan, from the 1950 Jayuya revolt to "la nueva lucha" ("the new struggle") emerging in the 1960s, also failed.

the Americas (the rest of the continent), as if because it is singular, it is excluded from the multiple Americas. And where exactly is Puerto Rico in America/the Americas? The play is American, both in the English and Spanish use of the term: it was written by a US citizen, for an audience of US citizens who speak the Spanish language, performed in a US territory, portraying the identity of this place as Hispanic American, with a name referring to a Hispanic man who owns a Hispanic country and is a composite of two actual Caribbean dictators, one Hispanic and one Haitian, both referenced in the play. It is "an American" chronicle in the anti-Spanish (anti-European) sense; it is a Hispanic Américan chronicle in the anti-Anglophone sense of the name "America" as it was appropriated for the country with no name (the USA).

Puerto Rico both is and is not part of the United States: it is the United States' Hispanic property. Justice Edward Douglass White (1845–1921) invented the concept of "unincorporated territory" to describe Puerto Rico in the Insular Cases, a series of US Supreme Court decisions between 1901 and 1922 that legalized the US annexation of Puerto Rico (and other territories): "while in an international sense Porto Rico [sic] was not a foreign country, since it was subject to the sovereignty of and was owned by the United States, it was foreign to the United States in a domestic sense, because the island had not been incorporated into the United States, but was merely appurtenant thereto as a possession."[56]

Despite having been granted US citizenship in 1917, and despite the creation of the ELA (Free Associated State) in 1952, Puerto Ricans are still subject to US federal laws without the power to vote for the US president; they defend the US flag; they have no embassy. In 2016, after the court case *Puerto Rico v. Sánchez Valle* cited in the epigraph of this chapter, the US Congress passed the Puerto Rico Oversight, Management, and Economic Stability Act to ensure that Puerto Rican debt gets paid, citing Clause 2 of the US Constitution: "Property Clause: The Congress shall have power to dispose of and make all needful Rules and Regulations respecting the Territory or other Property belonging to the United States." In talking to Luce López Baralt about what it means to publish in Puerto Rico versus, say, in Barcelona, Sánchez ironically asked, "Can you imagine the United States Embassy promoting the Cervantes Award for Luis Rafael Sánchez?"[57]

---

[56] The Supreme Court case is known as *DeLima v. Bidwell*, 182 U.S. 1 (1901). See its imperialist logic in Venator-Santiago (2015).

[57] López Baralt (2016).

224   LUIS RAFAEL SÁNCHEZ'S 1968 *ANTÍGONA PÉREZ*

How, then, can Puerto Rico's Hispanic tradition be narrated? Certainly not as the continental narrative tradition, starting with the nineteenth-century wars of independence, that depicted the birth of Hispanic nation-states with heroic bloodshed. Sánchez poetically plays with this fact. In his 2016 speech at the Spanish Language Congress in San Juan, he described the island as *"Huérfana de gestas, aunque colmada de gestos,"* shifting one vowel in "gestas/ gestos," translated, literally, as "orphan of heroic deeds but overflowing with gestures." Unlike all other American nation-states, Puerto Rico lacks a constitutive official (made mythical) narrative of revolutionary imagination with the rhetoric of *patria o muerte* ("fatherland or death") that portrays a people in arms recognizing itself as a unified agent of history and provides a retrievable ideology of heroism and literary accounts of a military victory against a colonial regime or an enemy invasion.

In Puerto Rico, to sacrifice one's life "for one's country" means to fight for the official narrative of another country that speaks a different language. Sánchez thought of Antígona upon seeing Puerto Rican coffins returning from Vietnam, covered with the US flag.[58] Toward the end of the play, right before the female multitude expresses brief support for Antígona, one of the journalists reports: "International. The number of young Puerto Ricans that refuse to join the North-American Army grows" (102). The Puerto Rican difference can be summarized thus: Puerto Rican soldiers were fighting a colonial war in Asia in the 1960s, defending the US flag, while Cuban filmmaker Santiago Álvarez was filming Vietnam's resistance against the US Army, which Puerto Ricans were forced to join and for which they were forced to die.[59] In the play, Antígona reframes the question of where the Tavárezes' corpses belong; for whom or what they fought; to which flag they pledged allegiance.

Antígona's cry for freedom in Puerto Rico exceeds the continental cry for social justice in the 1960s. It is the cry in every national anthem of nineteenth-century America. There were many isolated "gestures" of "local manufacture" for the independence of Puerto Rico, but none that unified "the nation"—except the Spanish language itself, a most unique (and

---

[58] Personal conversation in New York, May 1, 2012.

[59] Sánchez's play echoes José Luis González's well-known short story about Puerto Rican soldiers drafted to Korea, "Una caja de plomo que no se podía abrir" ("The lead box that could not be opened," 1954), adapted for theater by Lidia Milagros González as "El entierro" ("The funeral") in 1971. A mother receives a lead box that supposedly contains the remains of her son (drafted for the war in Korea) but has to bury "him" without really knowing what is in the box, since it cannot be opened.

LUIS RAFAEL SÁNCHEZ'S 1968 *ANTÍGONA PÉREZ* 225

solitary) form of anticolonial battle in Latin America. Puerto Rico's struggle for Spanish is a continuous national independence saga, *the* anticolonial gesture against the imposition of English.

National sovereignty appears even in the prologue with "the absolute historicity" (11) of the news collage covering the *periaktos*. Photos of Creón Molina in military attire, and of Antígona struggling against the guard in the palace, mix with the slogans:

> Christian Democracy; The *Descamisados* [shirtless] will do it; *Patria* or Death; July 26; Bosch for President; Yankees go home; The *Canal* [channel] belongs to Panamá; Bolivian Mines for Bolivians. (11)

The "absolute historicity" of this prologue alludes to a socialist national sovereignty against twentieth-century imperialism. It starts with the Catholic social doctrine: Christian Democracy was a key political actor in the 1960s in Chile, Venezuela, and—importantly—the Dominican Republic, where Juan Bosch, the leader of the exiled opposition to Trujillo, had been the first freely elected and anti–US-intervention president after Trujillo's fall. Puerto Rico closely followed Bosch's return to the island: the governor of Puerto Rico was present when Bosch took power. Bosch was toppled by a coup, exiled again in Puerto Rico, and his return to the Dominican Republic demanded by insurgents in April 1965, when the United States intervened with Marines. While Bosch represents, on the *periaktos*, a social revolution in the Dominican Republic, the "Descamisados" represent the working class of Argentine Peronism, positioned after World War II as "neither Yankee nor Marxist"—one of Peronism's slogans. The July 26 Movement, created by Castro and Guevara, means victory in Cuba; Panamá and Bolivia stand for struggles against foreign appropriation of the canal and the mines; the classic independence motto expressing willingness to die for the nation and the motto against US foreign intervention in the region ("Yankees go home") share the same anti-imperialist tone.

This initial tapestry of "news" happening in Latin America hardly fits the allegorical blanket statement by critics about Molina as "any Latin American dictatorship." Rather, it points to social and political struggles. Where can we situate the singularity of Trujillo Molina as a dictator, the inspiration for Sánchez's Creón and his republic of "Molina"? Could this historical model explain Creón's mysterious charge against Antígona? González Barja writes a curious line in his review of Ramos' 1976 production for *Claridad* (July 2, 1976: 7): "one never really knows why Creón wants to know where the

226   LUIS RAFAEL SÁNCHEZ'S 1968 *ANTÍGONA PÉREZ*

bodies are," concluding that this is the plot's "defect." Waldman sees it as an act to show "that only she is free" (1988: 273). But a closer look at Antígona's "crime" sheds better light on Creón's odd insistence on location, beyond his show of power.

Here, it is crucial to see how little Trujillo's singularity among US-backed dictators is understood. Because the country was semifeudal when he came to power, Trujillo managed to personally own 60 percent of the industrial property of the country and almost 70 percent of agricultural property on the most fertile land. During Juan Bosch's exile, he was invited to give a talk at the Universidad Central in Caracas on February 27, 1959. Complaining that Latin Americans did not understand Trujillo, Bosch titled the talk "Trujillo: Reasons for a Tyranny without Precedents."[60] Bosch explained how Trujillo remained in continuous power amid the political uprisings in the Caribbean during the 1950s: the country was Trujillo's personal property. The lack of capitalist development gave Trujillo the chance to transform the country into his own capitalist enterprise. In trying to understand his country, the rest of America made the typical mistake of "applying the situation of other Latin American nations" to that of the Dominican Republic: "Argentina, Colombia and Venezuela were victims of political tyranny, but the Dominican Republic is not a political tyranny. [It is neither] a nation, nor are its inhabitants a people [*un pueblo*], nor can those in power [*el poder*] be said to form a government. [It] is an impious capitalist enterprise [...] and the power is in the hands of the master [*amo*] of the enterprise" (10); "only bankruptcy will produce rebellion" (11); "Trujillo is not a political tyrant in the traditional manner in our America. He is the owner of the land, of the banks, of the factories, of men" (12).[61]

Creón's odd phrases now appear in a different light: "in my Republic there is no universe for heroes" (45). To Antígona, he proclaims: "The Republic is mine"; "The Army is mine" (120). Antígona is quick to mock his colonial ownership: "The world, the universe are yours. Where will you go, Creón, dethroned? To play the drums of Papa Doc or get political asylum in some European country [...]? Ridiculous ex-emperor of America" (120). In turn, Antígona knowingly says to her mother, "if I only knew the crime they accuse me of"; Aurora responds, "you *stole* some corpses that were *property*

---

[60] See Bosch ([1960] 2009).

[61] Trujillo's megalomania can also be explained by the economic grip he had on the island. Among the self-declared honorifics Trujillo accumulated were the Boss, Generalísimo, the Benefactor, the Father of the New Fatherland, His Excellency, First Medical Doctor of the Republic, and Restorer of Financial Independence.

of the Republic" (26; my emphasis). Antígona reacts: "The dead belong to their living" (27). In his first visit, Creón tells her: "We have demanded that you return the bodies that belong to no one, neither to Antígona, nor to Creón, because they belong to the State, whose head is its Generalísimo" (38). For Antígona, the brothers' bodies belong to the land, and the land to them: she says she buried them "in *their* land" (40–1; my emphasis).

At the palace, Monseñor Escudero inquires into the exact nature of Antígona's crime. "To have *stolen* the Tavárez corpses" (72; my emphasis), replies Creón. Monseñor asks: "where did she *steal* them from?" (72; my emphasis). Monseñor finds their public display at the Plaza Molina somewhat strange: "it was the purview of the family to carry out the posthumous rituals" (73). But Creón claims the corpses: "No, the corpses belonged to the State as evidence" (73). All too strange now for Monseñor, he asks what the penalty is "for the crime of stealing" (72), only to receive the extreme answer "sentence to life or death" (72). Monseñor visits Antígona to voice Creón's opinion: when she says she is accused of "that elemental gesture of compulsory fraternity, compulsory love," the bishop tersely responds: "your crime is robbery. The trial will be made on that singular reality" (80).

In the Western imagination, the death penalty for stealing belongs in the Middle Ages. "Life or death" in the context of the play's political rhetoric seems more suited for political crimes such as treason—unless we consider the dialogues around robbery and possession in relation to a different type of possession: *of the land*, of the nation, that "monothematic and one-dimensional" artistic obsession with "the colonial question," as Sánchez would say.[62]

Creón tells his people that the burial of the bodies revealed the influence of "terrorist ideologies" coming from a "far away continent" (49) and were motivated by Antígona's love affair with one of the brothers: against foreign ideology, "it is important to save [...] this civilization that I have created" (49). During Creón's second visit, Antígona warns Creón of "possession": "the night will come when all of Molina discovers that no people *belongs* to any man, that no man *belongs* to any man, that everyone *belongs* to their freedom" (98; my emphasis). For Creón, the Tavárezes' "only purpose was to cede the nation to foreign powers" (27). For Antígona, nothing is foreign in Molina except Creón's US military support: "you'd call for the intervention of foreign troops [...] for the landing of 20,000 Marines. But no, Creón. The assault was of exclusively local manufacture" (45).

---

[62] Galich (1975: 4), quoting Sánchez.

Local Manufacture It Is: But Is It Right or Left Nationalism?

When Antígona says to Aurora, "[the Tavárezes] were convinced that Creón's death would provoke the crisis that would lead to something less useless than this dictatorship" (27), she refers not to any foreign ideology but to a very local "theory of crisis," launched by the Puerto Rican MPI (Movement for Independence) in the early 1960s. The theory declared that a combination of an armed assault and an economic crisis would force the US to concede independence.[63] When Creón inquires about the arms used in the assault, Antígona mentions three types of weapons, insisting on their "local" manufacture: "an Halcón made in Argentina, a Stern made in Great Britain, a ridiculous arsenal of old weapons from old plans that never materialized" (48).[64] While "old weapons and old plans" may sound local—dating back to the Lares Revolt in 1868—we may ask, what is "local" in a weapon from Argentina and one from Britain? In the news report cited above, Journalist 5 redefines *local* and *foreign* along Antígona's lines: he shouts, "a group of Argentine students has taken over the Malvinas Islands challenging England's colonial mandate" (50).

Argentina, England, and the old colonial question: much like the archipelago of Puerto Rico, the Malvinas Islands are among the isolated colonial scenarios in America. Sánchez honors once again "absolute historicity." On September 28, 1966—two years before *Antígona Pérez*—a group of eighteen Argentine youths executed the first landing on the Malvinas since the last official Argentine presence in the islands 133 years prior. "Operation Condor," as it was called, highjacked a Douglas DC-4 that brought them to Stanley Airport, where they displayed seven Argentine flags, baptizing the airport with the name Antonio Rivero, the gaucho leader of the revolt against British occupation in 1833. They were eventually forced back to the mainland.

We may identify the parallels between these attacks: the Tavárezes' fictional attack, the assassination of Trujillo, the landing in the Malvinas, and the attacks occurring in Puerto Rico in the 1950s and 1960s.[65] Where

---

[63] See Morejón Flores (2016) and the "crisis thesis" in Movimiento Pro Independencia (1969).

[64] The Stern was a family of cheap British submachine guns; the Halcón was similar but made in Argentina.

[65] The parallel between Creón Molina and Trujillo Molina is seen also in how the Tavárez brothers ambushed Creón and shot at his car with machine guns, exactly as Trujillo was killed in 1961.

LUIS RAFAEL SÁNCHEZ'S 1968 *ANTÍGONA PÉREZ* 229

Creón sees "foreign ideologies" at work, Antígona sees the fight for independence from foreign ideologies. She is one of the independentists honoring one hundred years of solitary struggle for sovereignty since 1868. The 1960s' "new struggle" in Puerto Rico picked up the 1868 cry for independence. In 1967, following the "theory of crisis," the CAL (Comando Armado de Liberación) urban guerrillas launched clandestine armed attacks in San Juan. In 1968, at the annual commemoration of the 1868 revolt in Lares, the CAL publicly claimed responsibility for all bomb attacks. They specifically targeted the Condado tourist area. According to a previous *comunicado*, their goal was "to end the US monopoly of industry and commerce in Puerto Rico and expel all US companies from the island."[66]

Both onstage and off, everyone talks about property. The language of the CAL and the "theory of crisis" are about national sovereignty and national property. Creón refers to the dead as his property, accusing Antígona of theft. The Tavárezes and Antígona speak of "crisis" and claim property from the US-backed usurper Molina. While the language of property in this play has been overlooked, there is a particular unnoticed oddity articulating the foreign and the national with the political left and right, pointing to the singular problem of nationalism in the colonial context. In Latin America, nineteenth-century Creole anticolonial discourses focused on sovereignty decoupled from social justice. In the 1960s, nationalist discourse emphasized sovereignty and wealth distribution.

This peculiarity occurs during the "pagan" (stage directions, 64) reception for Monseñor Escudero at the presidential palace: wine bottles, laughter, and delights, including a 1955 Chilean wine, which Monseñor wants to try. Antígona describes it as "an effervescent, rumba, exuberant party" (65). Creón talks with Monseñor, who is lenient with Creón's polishing of his official version of the events. Although Monseñor Escudero seems to come from the Vatican Council—"the Vatican Council respects us," he tells Antígona—he embodies the corruption of the Church (accepting gifts from Creón for Church matters). The performance details of scene 6 convey Sánchez's perspective on the Church and the army. Lavishly dressed priests surrounding Monseñor Escudero at the palace wait to see Creón. The stage directions add "500 military men entering the stage from the side passages"

---

[66] I cite from Morejón Flores (2016: 6) the *comunicado* on February 22, 1968, announcing the existence of the clandestine armed group CAL ("Armed Commandos of Liberation"), which operated from 1963 to 1972. See also González Cruz for the Lares commemoration (2006: 32). López Rojas (2004) suggests that the tourist Condado area was targeted because exiled right-wing Cubans had settled there. See also Irizarry (2010).

230   LUIS RAFAEL SÁNCHEZ'S 1968 *ANTÍGONA PÉREZ*

(59)—the perfect contrast with Antígona's solitude, and by extension the island's solitude in the face of US control. It is indeed strange that Monseñor would want to taste this specific 1955 Chilean wine. But it is even more striking that his wish arises from having heard card-carrying Communist Chilean poet Pablo Neruda in London asserting the incomparable value of Chilean wines (61). That Monseñor Escudero, a representative of the Church allied with the right-wing military, would be inspired by Communist Neruda is strange enough. But that the conversation between Monseñor and the palace couple would then veer not toward the (pagan) quality of the wine but toward nationalism is even stranger. This shift reveals that nationalism is as "tense" in the play as the "tense" name of Antígona.

Hearing Neruda's praise, Monseñor thinks the wine in question is "that temptation from hell" (61). For Monseñor, hell is a mixture of wine and communism. For Pilar, there is too much nationalism in Neruda's phrase (61): her hell is wine, communism, and nationalism. Neruda, in Pilar's eyes, is a communist nationalist. But Monseñor gives the wine of communist nationalism its merit. Or is it just the wine of nationalism—conservative or bourgeois nationalism, the type that prevailed when the new Hispanic republics gained their independence in the nineteenth century? Rather than disputing Pilar's suspicions, Monseñor pronounces: "Nationalism is the only chance given to man to possess the universe" (62). Pilar thinks she has "heard such commentary before," and the bishop responds: "it is a commonplace that no sensible man discards" (62). It is "commonplace" to convince passive spectators that they can possess the universe. Creón and Monseñor share the meaning of nationalism: Creón's soul and Monseñor's wine are interchangeable during their conversation. Monseñor inquires after Creón's "soul," and Creón wants to know how his "wine" is doing (62–3). They ironically agree that a "public confession" would not be advisable and that Creón's soul will remain "calm" so long as Monseñor believes it to be calm, and Monseñor's wine "is sinful, a bit treacherous and tasty" (63). Monseñor asks for more of Creón's wine. The right-wing allies enjoy the tempting pagan party of tasty nationalism—as long as it is in their power to define it (Figure 4.7).

But wine turns things "red." For Monseñor, wine is sinful. The red "wine/blood" that the churches in Latin America were sipping from their chalices in the 1960s led to liberation theology or Christian Democracy. What was so tempting about Chile? Recall the slogan on the *periaktos*: the road taken in Chile was the Social Doctrine of the Church—in political terms,

LUIS RAFAEL SÁNCHEZ'S 1968 *ANTÍGONA PÉREZ* 231

Figure 4.7 *La pasión según Antígona Pérez*. Rafael Enrique Saldaña and José Luis "Chavito" Marrero. Directed by Pablo Cabrera. Eleventh annual Puerto Rican Theater Festival. Teatro Tapia, San Juan, Puerto Rico, May 30, 1968. Rehearsal photo. Courtesy of the Archivo General del Instituto de Cultura Puertorriqueña (AGPR-ICP).

Christian Democracy. By 1968, Chilean Frei's Christian Democracy was paving the way for the first democratically elected socialist government in Latin America (that of Salvador Allende in 1970). Wine production and wine workers in Chile in the 1950s were notably "red." Inspired by the "red" (Communist) Jesuit Alberto Hurtado, and helped by Christian Democracy, peasants unionized and led the 1953 winery strikes. With Christian Democracy in power, Chile saw the first attempt to carry out agrarian reform in 1962.

While a 1955 Chilean wine may mix Christian Democracy, nationalism, and social justice, Pilar's comment about "nationalism and the universal" is yet one more reference to the Church's embrace of nationalism. Monseñor Escudero would fit in well with the Puerto Rican party of conservative Catholics (Partido de Acción Cristiana/Christian Action Party) that formed in 1960 by attracting nationalists within the independence party. The

232 LUIS RAFAEL SÁNCHEZ'S 1968 *ANTÍGONA PÉREZ*

progressive Social Doctrine of the Church had also embraced nationalism as a sensible articulation of the "vital tension" between the singular and the universal for all humanity. Its icon, Monseñor Antulio Parrilla Bonilla, was summoned in 1967 by independentists and socialists to unify all activities commemorating the centenary of the 1868 Lares Revolt.[67] The commemoration happens every year in Lares, but in 1968, 30,000 patriots came from across the island and even from New York. At the 1968 commemoration of the 1898 US invasion in the town of Guánica, an independentist nationalist act declared its plaza "a liberated plaza."

All roads in this play lead to nationalism. Creón Molina views himself as having "reconstruct[ed] the republic" (57) after a dangerously left-wing government (58). Pilar identifies the "truth": "Do not reduce yourself to a democratic man [...] you imposed yourself by force; you will remain in power if you preserve force [...] the same as virtuosos tune their instruments constantly, the *conquerors* [*conquistadores*] tune their power constantly" (58; my emphasis). Pilar unveils Creón's "national reconstruction" as an old colonial scene, this time backed by US marines. As with all conquests, in music as in government, an initial success does not suffice: it needs constant exercise. Creón wants Antígona to see him as benevolent, but even in the minor tiffs with the prisoner, he tunes the instrument of force: when Antígona accuses him, he grabs her arm and says "there is a privilege that gives me absolute advantage: force" (91).

The conversation between Creón and Monseñor ties up nationalism with the social doctrine of Christianity. For Monseñor Escudero, the ideas of the real-life Monseñor Parilla may have been the temptation of Hell—like the Chilean wine—but they nonetheless seem to be worth a taste. Does the play ask its audience if nationalism within colonial struggle should be more than just an anti-imperialist struggle for sovereignty, that is, an anti-imperialist socialism? Was the tragic frame for the Tavárezes' assault a warning that urban guerrillas in the 1960s needed more than just a "theory of crisis"? Morejón Flores cites the debate about the internal tension between "the national" and "the social" among the CAL guerrillas and the independentist movement of the 1960s, asking if the CAL were not simply favoring the local national bourgeoisie, rather than the masses (2016: 10–13). Did the

---

[67] See 1967–8 Puerto Rican major newspapers (*El Mundo, El Imparcial, San Juan Star*) for stories about the 100th anniversary of the Lares Revolt. With respect to Parrilla, see "En su centenario Monseñor Parilla preside Comité Conmemora El Grito de Lares," *El Mundo*, July 18, 1968.

call for armed struggle to expel all US companies suffice? Was it about recuperating property for the local bourgeoisie or for popular distribution? Were Sánchez's Tavárez brothers seeking conservative or socialist nationalism? We know little of the Tavárezes. We know more of Antígona's *via crucis* without redemption. As the black leather skirt and boots she wears may bear an association with the Nationalist Party at the time, her rhetoric of a (secular) passion for national freedom may echo Albizu Campos, that icon of Catholic nationalism who inspired "la nueva lucha." His form of struggle for independence was as incorruptible as Antígona's resistance. Like Antígona, Albizu taught Puerto Rican history, correcting false official stories before an open-air audience; he was nicknamed "*el maestro.*" Like Antígona, Albizu was imprisoned and tortured—in his case, for more than twenty years, both on the mainland and the island.

If we compare Albizu's speeches with the play's heroic ethos and political will, we may hear a call for all Antígonas. Consider his May 8, 1950 speech: "the heroism of only one woman, and the heroism of only one man, can make the most powerful empire tremble […] Courage does not need physical strength, the weakest woman can bring down an empire! If she has courage. Let her grip her rosary! Let her be inspired by the eternal. […] we have to bring down the US despotism, I have spoken!" Albizu's nationalism, unlike Antígona's, was Catholic, and his ideas were controversially conservative in social aspects. They were anti-imperialist, rather than socialist.

In 1933, Albizu planted a tamarind tree at Lares Plaza to honor the martyrs of 1868. The tree was brought from Simón Bolívar's estate in Venezuela and planted with soil from nineteen Latin American nation-states. In 1952, after the declaration of the ELA, Albizu gave an impassioned speech in Lares, qualifying time and again the United States as "tyranny" and Puerto Ricans as "slaves," instigating a revival of the 1868 Lares Revolt: "[we are only] US citizens to be drafted to fight in Korea […] this has to be defied only as the men of Lares defied despotism: with the revolution."

In 1968, Antígona's cry for self-determination stands in continuity with the 1868 Lares Revolt. In 1868, Betances' cry for freedom shared the spirit and action of the nineteenth-century independence revolutions. One hundred years later, Antígona's cry bears the weight of a lonely, unique history of Latin American anticolonial struggle. She could be Albizu's "one woman," daring to bring down "US despotism." She is socialist nationalism's passion for the red wine, not just conservative nationalism's pagan fun. Sánchez's Antígona in 1968 is the sole island desiring to end its isolation: to become an American nation-state among others.

234 LUIS RAFAEL SÁNCHEZ'S 1968 *ANTÍGONA PÉREZ*

Coda: No Latina Curves, but Future Mother at Last

Antígona does not love a man, but rather, a land. Critics have read the play as portraying women as leading the liberation struggle. In her final speech, Antígona warns Creón, "you will have to kill all the young irresponsible women who will confront you risking their lives, Creón" (120). Seemingly echoing the ideology of *marianismo*, Santos Silva writes: "Antígona augurs that it will be the women who confront [Creón] [...] due to [their] traditional and acknowledged psychic strength" (443). Barradas (1979), Ford (2013), and Peña-Jordán (2003) also praise the female multitude.[68] Other critics hesitate: for Waldman, Antígona has no exit (1988: 320). Brunn (2012) sees Sánchez as reproducing gender hierarchies, though this misreads the historical context and the text: disregarding that Antígona has no blood brothers in this text, Brunn says Antígona "is obliged to resort to familial bonds as the only ground from which she could stage political resistance [...] she has to allude to symbolic kinship, to their 'obligada fraternidad' ['obligatory brotherhood']" (2012: 80); she cannot escape "the old script" of familial duty—a "space traditionally identified as feminine" (43); she erases her subjectivity and is "transformed into a redemptive image of a martyr for humanity" (45).

Nonetheless, if women are the hope for the future, the critics above would need to account for the ambitious Pilar Varga, for whom "weakness has nothing to do with governance" (118), and whose role is to tame Creón's fear of losing power—he thinks fear is part of the job description, it belongs to rulers. As to Antígona's sacrificial narrative as "an old female script," where does that leave Che Guevara's speeches about sacrifice and love for the revolution? Why would we need to compare Antígona's "obligada fraternidad" with that of her ancient Greek sister, rather than with the dominant political narrative of sacrifice and kinship in Latin America, embraced by both men and women in the 1960s?

Nothing in Antígona's rhetoric is out of sync with her times and her land. She follows the era's imagination of liberation theology, Marxism, and the political project of the Third World Non-Aligned anti-imperialist movement. Latin Americans called themselves *hermanos/as latinoamericanos/as* ("siblings"). They were to sacrifice "to create one, two, three, many Vietnams," as Guevara famously said at La Habana's Tri-Continental Conference on April 16, 1967. Antígona's final speech to the male multitude includes: "Salvation is [to] question one, two, many times, whether they are

---

[68] See also Peña-Jordán (2003: 377–88).

LUIS RAFAEL SÁNCHEZ'S 1968 *ANTÍGONA PÉREZ* 235

not ousting us from ourselves" (104). A discourse of "fate" was in vogue: "we are led to pursue this struggle" (Guevara's same speech) meant that imperialism had imposed it. And for that struggle, individual subjectivity was a nuisance of old bourgeois times.

For telling gender constructions in this play, we need to look elsewhere. Antígona Pérez's character cannot fully escape the ideology of motherhood belonging to practically all twentieth-century American Antígonas. Antígona makes room for a man in her moment of weakness. Gender ideology lies there, rather than in sacrificial rhetoric, kinship, or strength—all qualities shared by her generation. Marriage as a woman's future is what breaks Antígona's spirit—albeit for a split second. What remains when she recovers is what must remain: the possibility of the maternal work of reproduction, if not of real-life humans, then, at least, of ideas.

Like the ancient virgin, Antígona herself is not concerned with femininity—she "has no curves." At stake for her is her inviolable "spirit": "they will violate my body with the hope that they will violate my spirit [...] but they will leave my heart immaculate. The heart is what matters" (47). She stoically resists rape and is unfazed by Creón's attempt to soil her reputation as a woman and by her elders' advice to marry. Creón attributes her secrecy to her "sexual relation" with one of the Tavárez brothers (43). Antígona does not deny it. Aurora reminds her: "If you returned [...] you could build a beautiful family [...] You are nothing else but a woman" (27–8). Pilar Varga visits Antígona "for a conversation among women" (116): "Antígona, if you have someone who loves you, just live" (117).

Antígona's spirit is expressed in the play's epigraph, from Camus' *The Plague*: "For nothing in the world is it worth turning one's back on what one loves." Rieux's sentence in Camus' text continues: "Yet that is what I am doing, though why I do not know" ([1974] 1976: 170). Camus' Rieux stays with his cause instead of returning to his wife. Antígona does the same. The self-doubt hidden in the epigraph's reference surfaces for Antígona only for a moment, near the end: it comes almost as an instance of self-revelation. It needed to be so in a play where self-revelation is reserved for women rather than men—as if only women could answer the "why" in Rieux's question. These moments of self-revelation are strictly relational: they are a woman's question, in women's dialogue, with hints of a female desire for relation.

Aurora's self-revelation is that she does have faith—in fear. She defends, as Andrade's Urbana, biological motherhood: she wants to save her daughter. "The others" are "not [my] children" (33). When Antígona asks her what she could have lost, Aurora understands: "Maybe, (revealing this to herself) fear. (as if a powerful truth came to her). Loyalty to fear. (Loudly)" (32).

236 LUIS RAFAEL SÁNCHEZ'S 1968 *ANTÍGONA PÉREZ*

Irene's self-revelation is conformity. She had tried to live up to the (cruel) ideals of sacrifice, hiding Antígona in her house. During her visit, the moment of revelation occurs in both women simultaneously. Upon hearing that Fernando has accepted a position in the palace, "for the first and only time in all her passion, Antígona Pérez breaks down," her "head and arms" down, and her "chest compressed" (stage directions, 107). Antígona tells Irene that she has never lost her calm until now: not when she placed the bomb in the library, not when she hauled the corpses into the trunk of the car, not when she buried the corpses (109). Irene, in turn, finds herself suddenly shouting, "no! I do not want Fernando to die!" (110). There is love in that scream: "the two women gasp at realizing it" (111). Antígona asks, "do you love him?," Irene admits: "we got close during your captivity […]. We don't aspire to change the world even if it is despicable for us. […] we conform ourselves" (111).

Fear. Love. Weakness. These emotions are reserved for women, with the exception of Pilar. As for the multitude of women, we know nothing of them other than their chorus in act 2, scene 2: out of 110 print pages, they occupy just three. They are undifferentiated voices that suddenly split from the multitude to encourage Antígona before the final three scenes (Irene, Pilar, and Creón's visits). Witnessing Antígona's complete solitude, the female chorus tells her, "Do not give up; Clean, Antígona, Pure, we need you" (103). Like a midwife during birth, the chorus encourages Antígona's reproduction—not of a child, but of ideas. As she says before her execution—and as the 1960s generation believed—ideas "do not succumb to bullets […] To kill me is to make me alive again, to make me new blood for the veins of this bitter América […] Fast, Creón, fast, kill me. Give me death" (121).

Antígona Pérez cannot truly die. Nor can our other Antígonas. Pérez will not be a biological mother but will bleed to make her ideas live. Her "distant cousin" Antígona Vélez reproduced by bleeding, fertilized by Indian arrows. Antígona Pérez will bleed from bullets traversing her body upon Creón's orders. The ideology of reproduction that has served the construction of Antígona thus far still shows its metaphoric power for utopian politics—even in the case of the loneliest Antígona in twentieth-century Latin America.

5

By Way of Interlude

The Dynamics and Innovations of the Corpus in Lesser-Known Mid-Century Plays

From Patriarchal National Sacrifice toward a New Female Bonding

The true meaning of an "American Antígona" can only be grasped with a panoramic view of the map of the corpus. It is only in the avenues, streets, and roads connecting *Antígona* plays that we can fathom how the mobilization of ancient fragments is part and parcel of "our" local topography: of a shared imagination about the neocolonial political bond. In the majority of lesser-known plays listed in the Appendix, the scholar can find traces of the transnational *dispositif* about womanhood, motherhood, sisterhood, and burials that appear in the preceding chapters. At times, lesser-known plays foreshadow new cannibalizations of the myth, to be ruminated on later. Two of these new cannibalizations appear in the second half of the twentieth century: Antígona cast as a collective of women, and the corpse shifting from being identifiable (and exposable) to unrecognizable or missing. This sets the stage for Antígona's *national* universal to become a *utopian* universal—what I called in the Introduction, an "impossible universal."

Varela's 1824 Argia gave Antígona a patriarchal platform for heroic motherhood in the nineteenth century. Born mothers or mothers *in potentia*, Argia and her mid-twentieth-century sisters, Antígona Vélez, Antigòn, Marta, Mariana (and, symbolically, Antígona Pérez), secured future lineages in America. While in antiquity the lineage ended with Antigone's sacrifice, in America, the postrevolutionary imagination elicited maternal sacrifice. As Antígona-the-mother—the female iteration of the warrior—is split between the mother of her child and the mother of the nation, her fate was sealed with a nation-founding mission. For the newly born patriarchal nation, Argia produces a son; Antígona Vélez bleeds seeds in the plains; Antigòn gives eternal life in heaven; Mariana births the son of history; Marta buries the martyr of the new republic; and Antígona Pérez gives new blood for "the veins of America."

Antígonas: Writing from Latin America. Moira Fradinger, Oxford University Press. © Moira Fradinger 2023.
DOI: 10.1093/oso/9780192897091.003.0007

238 THE DYNAMICS OF THE CORPUS IN LESSER-KNOWN PLAYS

As a woman, Antígona was disposable once her reproductive labor was complete. While in antiquity Antigone is split between her symbolic and her physical death (she is "already dead" before burying the brother), in America, Antígona undergoes a split between being a woman and a mother. The woman with autonomous interests apart from the patriarchal contract, whereby she gives a child to the nation, must be sacrificed if the totality of the (closed, territorial) nation is to be imagined. The debiologization of her motherhood in early plays did not result in Antígona's reinscription as an autonomous woman. The latter will only happen in the twenty-first century. In the beginning, she had no other option than to be born a biological mother and die a republican mother.

As a mother, Antígona posited the promised but impossible exit from the neocolony, and thus her revolt must ride a utopian wave: she represents the nation to come, the community that could come about but never arrives. Its future lies dead at the site of Antígona's revolt. Thus, her tragic rebellions must be quilted with utopian narratives. Antígona-the-mother fights to give birth to the new: there is an impending sense of gestation, of a radical change that must occur through her body, her action, or sacrifice. Antígona's embodiment of the maternal creates symbolic worlds, debiologizes motherhood, and deprivatizes love. In spite of biological traces in early plays (Antígona Vélez bleeds; Antigòn dies as Creon makes her "bleed" into a vase; Argia and Marta have their own child), Antígona-the-biological-mother must veer away from biology: she must decide politically. Throughout the twentieth century, there is not one single Antígona defending her biological offspring. As the twentieth century advances, the debiologization of motherhood becomes increasingly prominent.

Lesser-known plays show the persistence of the initial nineteenth-century template of political motherhood at work. Consider the versions of Argia and Antígona Vélez in Argentine Alberto Zavalía's (1911–88) *El límite* (The limit) (1957–8) and Venezuelan José Gabriel Núñez's (1937–) *Antígona* (1977), as well as the "motherly virginity" of Sánchez's Antígona Pérez that is echoed in Mexican José Fuentes Mares' (1918–86) *La joven Antígona va a la guerra* (Young Antígona goes to war, 1968) and Argentine Juan Carlos Gené's (1929–2012) *Golpes a mi puerta* (Knocks at my door, 1983).

Zavalía ruminates on Argia as a sacrificial mother and on Marechal's ironic take on Sarmiento's narrative of "civilization and barbarism." He sets the play just two decades later than Varela's and Marechal's 1820s, during the 1840 caudillo wars, which, for Zavalía, were an expression of "barbarism." Zavalía's mother-Antígona originates from an oral legend about the

THE DYNAMICS OF THE CORPUS IN LESSER-KNOWN PLAYS 239

real-life aristocratic widow Doña Fortunata García de García (1802–70) from Tucumán, seat of the 1816 pact of national independence. In 1841 in Tucumán, General Oribe (1792–1857), ally of Rosas, ordered the killing of the enemy Marco Avellaneda (1813–41; ex-governor of Tucumán). His impaled head was exposed in the Independence Plaza. According to legend, Fortunata buried the martyr's head.[1] Zavalía's prologue positions "Fortunata and Oribe [...] manipulated by the same forces that influenced Antigone and Creon" (10).[2] But the play actually positions Fortunata as another Argia. The dramatic encounter between General Oribe and Fortunata happens at her colonial house. Oribe offers to keep Fortunata's children alive and save her gravely ill husband if she gives up her wish to bury the impaled head. She refuses. The nation's freedom—as expected in this book's corpus— becomes more important to Fortunata than her family, just as it was for Argia (Figures 5.1 and 5.2).[3]

Marechal's imagination shapes Núñez's *Antígona* (1977).[4] In a coastal town, a war against guerrillas has ended. Before Antígona is killed there is a love scene between her and her fiancé Gabriel. Pianacci suggests that Núñez makes "the same mistake of many authors who do not know how to rejuvenate the structure of the myth [...] and infallibly end in [...] melodrama" (2008: 301). For Pianacci, Núñez's love scene is unnecessary. But within the context of this book's corpus, the scene perfectly echoes Marechal's love scene. Antígona will help with "so many people to bury!" (51), but her real task is to give birth to the future. This is why, before burying her brother, Núñez's Antígona—like Antígona Vélez—tells her beloved that she has been a mother since she was little: "I only had my siblings and I played with them and at the same time raised them" (53). Antígona asks Gabriel why he did not "make her a woman" in their first dance: now she only "feels like" a mother, while remaining a virgin (54). Echoing the end of Marechal's play,

---

[1] Tomás Eloy Martínez (1999) discovered that Fortunata seems to have actually kept the head with her, in her bed, until she died.

[2] The epigraph is a Spanish translation of Sophocles' line 91: "*Renunciaré cuando me falten las fuerzas*" ("I shall give up when strength runs out"). I use the 1959 edition by Publicaciones El Teatro de Buenos Aires. In 1958, it premiered at The Theater of Nations in Paris and was reviewed by Robert Kemp for *Le Monde* ("Le Theatre: Le Carrose et El Límite"), *Libération*, *Le Figaro*, *L'Aurore* (all on June 11, 1958). On June 4, 1959, it premiered at the Teatro Presidente Alvear in Buenos Aires.

[3] For criticism see Morais (2015), Bañuls Oller and Crespo Alcalá (2008: 442–4), Pianacci (though he confuses the date of the premiere) (2008: 93–5), and Biglieri (2016).

[4] I thank Gabriel Núñez for confirming in personal email conversation that he was actually inspired by Marechal's vision of Antígona (as well as by Anhouil's play and texts by Venezuelan Arturo Uslar Pietri).

240 THE DYNAMICS OF THE CORPUS IN LESSER-KNOWN PLAYS

Figure 5.1 *El límite*. At the colonial house, Delia Garcés and Enrique Fava. Director Alberto de Zavalía. Teatro de Buenos Aires, at the Theater of Nations, Sarah Bernhardt Theatre, Paris, France. Premiere, June 9, 1958. Courtesy of the Bibliothèque Nationale de France, Site Richelieu.

Figure 5.2 *El límite*. Another scene at the colonial house, Delia Garcés and Enrique Fava. Director Alberto de Zavalía. Teatro de Buenos Aires, at the Theater of Nations, Sarah Bernhardt Theatre, Paris, France. Premiere, June 9, 1958. Courtesy of the Bibliothèque Nationale de France, Site Richelieu.

Núñez's chorus laments Gabriel's death at Antígona's side, invoking the children whom they will bring to life in death: "two tombs must be dug to bury two spouses [...] as if they had been married, as if they had given us children [...] hundreds of children! Thousands of children! [...] because their blood is like a rose that teaches us" (63) about freedom.

The corpus presents very few cases in which Antígona is not a mother, and even in some of those cases virginity is politically motherly. José Fuentes Mares staged his *Young Antígona* just a few months after Sánchez's *Antígona Pérez* saw the stage in 1968. Fuentes Mares seemingly imagined the exact (ideological) opposite of Sánchez's heroine. Just like Antígona Pérez, Fuentes Mares' character participates in a clandestine guerrilla cell in any given present-day revolution.[5] Quilting tragedy and Brechtian technique, Fuentes Mares gives Antígona a difficult choice between her ideals and an anonymous child's life. The guerrilla cell entrusts her to plant a bomb on a train, but at the last minute, and unlike Antígona Pérez, she

---

[5] The play premiered at the University of Chihuahua on October 10, 1968, eight days after the Tlatelolco Massacre at the Plaza de las Tres Culturas in Mexico City.

242 THE DYNAMICS OF THE CORPUS IN LESSER-KNOWN PLAYS

refuses to execute the attack when she sees the child smiling inside the train. What has happened here, other than imagining Antígona as a mother again?[6] Though ideologically different, both virgin heroines are mothers. The maternal dilemma is so pervasive in the corpus that there is even a motherly scene in the only play in the corpus wherein Antígona is cast as a nun. Gené's *Golpes a mi puerta* centers around the conflict faced by two liberation theology nuns hiding a *guerrillero* during a civil war.[7] The religious sisters Ana and Ursula have a mother–daughter relationship of sorts. Ana is told that if she signs a declaration stating that she was forced at gunpoint to hide the man, Ursula will not be executed. However, this would also mean breaking her faith by lying about the rebel and betraying her liberation theology oath to be a woman no different from the others. She should die, protecting others. She waits until Ursula signs the document before calmly tearing it apart and facing execution. Before execution, while praying together at dawn to the Virgin Mary, Ana asks Ursula if she ever thought of having a child. For Ana, this is the real sacrifice to the Lord: "we celebrate Mary's motherhood offering our frustrated motherhoods" (79). But when they look at the *guerrillero* asleep, they both confess that it hurts to have renounced love and procreation (81).

Antígona's political motherhood never leaves the Latin American stage. But new themes tag along the way. Two of them are first staged in mid-twentieth-century lesser-known plays and determine later developments in the corpus at large: (1) an autonomous relationship among women as Antígona becomes multiple on stage, and (2) the disappearance—or multiplication—of the corpse. It is worth noting that the 1960s also produced the first example of what seemed implausible: a comedic cannibalization of Antigone. *Antígona Humor* (1961, written by Dominican Franklin

---

[6] In the twentieth century, the only plays in which motherhood does not play an important role are: Joel Sáez's *Antígona* (Cuba, 1993); Tomás González Pérez's *El viaje en círculo* (Cuba, 1989); Valeria Folini's *Antígona la necia* (unpublished, Argentina, 1998); Patrick Chamoiseau's *Une Manière d'Antigone* (Martinique, 1975); and *Antígona*, produced by Alberto Ure (Argentina, 1989). I cannot assess José Triana's inaccessible text *Detrás Queda el Polvo* (Cuba, 1968) or Héctor Santiago's *Antígona Antígona* (Cuba, 1994 written in New York). According to Bosch (1999), Triana's play is housed at the National Library in La Habana, Cuba. Per my conversation with Elina Miranda Cancela, not even the playwright has a copy. Bosch sees this Antígona as a revolutionary who decides not to bury her brothers against the order to do so. See Pérez Asensio (2009) and Miranda Cancela (2006, 2008).

[7] The play premiered in Caracas in the small residential theater house, Sala Juana Sujo, before going to the national theaters; it was later adapted for the screen as *Knocks at My Door* (1994) by Alejandro Saderman. See Boling (2013) and the summary in Bañuls Oller and Crespo Alcalá (2008: 472–4).

THE DYNAMICS OF THE CORPUS IN LESSER-KNOWN PLAYS   243

Domínguez [1931–])[8] interestingly thematizes women's relationality, but the comedic will only find its full development in the twenty-first century (see the list of comedic versions in the Appendix).

The First Female Collectives: The Novel Gender Turn in Antígonal Politics

Could the immense creative energy devoted to cannibalizing Antigone express a postindependence urgency (and failure) to inscribe women as political subjects, to symbolize the difference(s) between a mother and a woman, and among women? Could Antígona fulfill the command to "surpass" her European sisters by entering the political using a language beyond the two forms of negative difference in which women are inscribed in Western cultures—woman as the negative of man (or the negative of the same) or as the complement of man? Was her motherhood an exact match to patriarchal motherhood? Varela's Creon judges Argia for rejecting maternal "sweetness" and choosing instead the nation. Fighting for the republic was doubtlessly yet another patriarchal version of motherhood. Nonetheless, a fascinating subtext emerges then and there, with Argia in 1824 entering the city with the urge to meet another woman, Antígona. This desire runs through the Antígona corpus but becomes more visible from the 1960s onward.

Here, the multiplicity implied in the figure of the mother starts to expand: the relational desire of the mother (two bodies in one) to protect the nation's child sometimes morphs into a relational desire of women for women—a female desire for sharing, friendship, solidarity, complicity, love. This female desire was implicit in Antigone, not only in her call to Ismene and in the latter's belated attempts to help her but also in Antigone's death, as it echoes Jocasta's death. Nicole Loraux noted that Antigone does not die like a virgin, sacrificed with a sword, but rather, like a mother or a wife—hanged.[9]

---

[8] See García (1997), Miranda Cancela (2008), and Bátiz Zuk (2013). Miranda Cancela sees the play as a metatheatrical reflection about marriage and about the institution of theater as reproducing blindly imported conventions. I concur with Miranda Cancela and Bátiz Zuk that the choice of a comedy may be read in terms of what Benítez Rojo said in his famous *The Repeating Island* (1996): "The notion of apocalypse does not occupy an important position in [this] culture" (quoted by Bátiz Zuk 2013: 126).

[9] See Loraux (1986, 1991). See Honig (2013) on Ismene and Antigone, whereby their bond is of love, care, and rivalry; I agree with Goldhill's opinion of a fraught sister bond (see 2012: 247).

244 THE DYNAMICS OF THE CORPUS IN LESSER-KNOWN PLAYS

Goldhill (2012) concludes that tragedy introduces sisters, absent from the Homeric tradition preceding the advent of Athenian democracy.

From the mid-twentieth century onward, Antígona's desire for other women translates to the formation of female collectives, not to act in the name of "woman," but as women-in-relation. Their key word is exchange, almost as the inverse of patriarchal systems of exchange. In the latter, women are exchanged as gifts to secure the bonds of reciprocity among men.[10] In *Antígona* plays, the unburied corpses become the exchanged gifts that allow for reciprocity among women. In Western myths of the patriarchal bond, the death of the father is imagined as solidifying ties among brothers. But Antígona plays show the necro–neocolony pact: the death of the child preserves the dominance of the father. Antigone cares for the dying Oedipus; Antígona gathers with others around the dying children. I have called the dramatic imagination of women's exchange in the neocolony the Antígonal paradigm of politics. We may contrast it, as one of the subtexts of the neocolonial social bond, to the Oedipal paradigm of the (European) republican imagination about the social bond (the son killing the father; the pact among brothers; the daughter tending to the dying father). Consider European mythical accounts wherein society is attained through the elimination of one all-mighty sovereign. In the neocolony, the Roman father who decides his children's fate remains present behind the façade of the republican brothers' contract. The filicidal, instead of patricidal, city denies these Antígonas the bodily product through which they entered the brothers' political pact. Their children will die before them. Antígona can be neither woman nor properly a mother in the new patriarchal nation. If she is to remain, as mother or as woman, she must change the structure of the political sphere.

The first playwright to stage a female system of exchange was Argentine David Cureses (1935–2006) in his *La cabeza en la jaula* (The head in the cage, 1963). Until then, there was merely a glimmer of female bonding onstage. Argia comes to meet her *compañera* Antígona, only to find her dead. The women at La Postrera are too busy with their men to understand Antígona Vélez, who only finds solace in the moon, a nonhuman, mythological mother. Antígona Vélez bonds with a female entourage only unknowingly, when three witches predict and suffer for her fate. In scene 1, they "know" what Antígona will do: "Antígona Vélez will not sleep. Her

---

[10] I do not aim here beyond a general frame of reference, such as twentieth-century anthropological accounts (Lévi-Strauss [1958] 1963) and the feminist literature that grew out of them.

THE DYNAMICS OF THE CORPUS IN LESSER-KNOWN PLAYS   245

heart is outside!"; in scene 2, they predict her death; and, at the end of the play, they are the only ones who recognize her death (and Lisandro's) as unnecessary. Antigòn is "wild": a strangely magical, autonomous woman, always protected by another woman—the godmother Marraine—until the final scene, in which she is unsurprisingly inscribed back into marriage in eternal life. Pedreira's women support Mariana, but she remains alone in the end. Marta carries her dead son with the help of his lover Quitéria, but she is seen mourning alone when Martiniano shows up.

Cureses' play has been almost lost to critics, its performance history difficult to trace. It is a quilting point in the corpus itself: it brings together previous minor engagements with sisterhood and foreshadows what will come fifty years later. It is the first play where Antígona shares her heroism with other women and where the debiologization of motherhood becomes also the deprivatization of love. The national universal expressed in the form of a utopia in Antígonas Pérez and Vélez, Antigòn, Mariana and Marta, finds for the first time its formulation as a utopian universal embodied by the female collective. Up until now, the national utopias of previous Antígonas were "negatively" realized, as Max Dominique qualified Antigòn's world (2002): Pérez, Vélez, and Antigòn produce children in heaven; Mariana may produce children in the future, but we cannot yet know; Argia's son has been saved by her father, not by her; Marta has obtained what she wanted, but it is Martiniano who will make history—and that, we cannot know either.

The only Antígona in the corpus to dramatize events in a nation other than hers, Cureses' heroine acts during Colombia's nineteenth-century independence wars.[11] Like Zavalía, Cureses opted for a beheaded hero, Colombian independence fighter José Antonio Galán (1749–82), juxtaposing his assassination with the life of Colombian national heroine Policarpa Salavarrieta (1795–1817).[12] Like Zavalía, Cureses only mentions Antigone in the epigraph.[13] But, unlike all his predecessors, Cureses multiplies

---

[11] The play premiered on June 12, 1963, in Buenos Aires at the T.E.G.E. (Teatro El Gorro Escarlata), directed by Cureses himself. I thank Nathalie Yankelevich and Cureses' life companion, Horacio Bermúdez, for giving me access to Cureses' archive, which remains in the house where he lived in Buenos Aires Province, under Bermúdez's care. There is practically no critical engagement with this play; see a brief summary of the play in Bañuls Oller and Crespo Alcalá (2008: 445–8) and Pianacci (2008: 93–5).

[12] For a portrait of Policarpa Salavarrieta, see Arciniegas (1986).

[13] Taken from the Sophoclean lines 583–5, the epigraph reads: "They are happy those who go through life without misfortune! Because for those whose house receives a jolt from the gods, there is no calamity that does not fall on their descendants... Nothing happens in human

Antígona by six, paying homage to each and every republican woman who "could be identified with the legendary Antigone" (Cureses, *Diario de Rauch*, July 8, 1979).

Galán was beheaded in a 1782 rebellion; his head was exhibited in the city of Guadas inside a wooden cage in the central plaza. "La Pola," as she was known during the war of independence between 1811 and 1820, was also born in Guadas, the town where Cureses set the play's action. A contemporary of Simón Bolívar, La Pola defied the Spaniards as a spy. The first young woman to face execution by the Spaniards, she was honored all over America and across the Atlantic.

Cureses imagined La Pola burying the head aided by five other women: we can still identify her as a leader, but she depends on her female friends (women are alleged to have started the historical 1782 rebellion).[14] The five American women and one Amerindian servant live at the Galán family's colonial house (Figure 5.3). The women are initially identified in relation to

Figure 5.3 *La cabeza en la jaula.* The six women at the colonial house. Directed by David Cureses. T.E.G.E. (Teatro El Gorro Escarlata), Buenos Aires, Argentina, June 12, 1963. Cureses' personal archive. Photo by Horacio Bermúdez. Courtesy of the photographer.

---

life that is exempt from pain" (*La cabeza en la jaula*, 1987: 14; my translation). Cureses does not indicate which Spanish translation he used.

[14] In 2010, a local museum memorialized fighty-eight women martyrs. See Germán Arciniegas, *Las mujeres y las horas* 74 and Alfredo Escobar's report about the museum in http://www.eltiempo.com/archivo/documento/MAM-361615.

THE DYNAMICS OF THE CORPUS IN LESSER-KNOWN PLAYS   247

their men, but this identification will fade away as their bond strengthens. The matron, Andrea, is José Antonio Galán's mother; Magdalena is his wife; Mariana is Andrea's sister-in-law, who has lost her husband, son, and brother; Mariana's two daughters, La Pola and Isabel, have remained in the house. And the indigenous servant Rosario collaborates because, in so doing, she has "buried my father and my brother" (109).

Cureses' women all sacrifice their lives for "America," which represents equality and freedom, for even Rosario becomes "an American." La Pola whispers to her, "Yes, we are all equals"; Rosario proudly answers, "Americans" (109). They speak the language of patriotism and republicanism. Like their predecessors, they fulfill their republican maternal role in death, giving birth not to one American man but to millions. Lieutenant Morillo, La Pola's lover, is horrified at the actions of his father—the real-life General Morillo—and flings his uniform medals onto the floor: "I am not a Spanish soldier anymore. I am a man of America. For each one of those women that you have killed, a hundred, a thousand, a million patriots have been born" (145).

The surprising twist in Cureses' play, though, is the female bonding: not only stronger than biological motherhood but also than heterosexual monogamy. On this stage, a universal beyond the national appears for the first time: the women refashion themselves as mothers and lovers of all. When Andrea sighs for "her own" son, La Pola is quick: "he was the son of all mothers" (36). When Mariana remembers José Antonio as "like *my* brother," La Pola replies: "like all our men" (37). The socialization of love is most dramatic when José's wife Magdalena agonizes, imagining the "vultures tearing his eyes apart and devouring his flesh [...] His eyes must look at me" (38). La Pola sternly retorts: "José Antonio belongs to all" (38).

Cureses' heroines go further: they thematize the gendered violence suffered by women, rather than just by (unburied) men. For La Pola, "We are only one body and only one will before pain and vengeance" (75). As women, they become gendered "soldiers" in this war. La Pola enlists Rosario: "don't be short of means to make them drunk [...] you are a woman, and beautiful, and young…and they like the forbidden" (76). Magdalena's role is to stage a female war strategy by offering her body to the Captain's lust while the others seek the martyr's body parts. She is convinced by the others that "you must do it *for all the American women* who suffer [...] think of *all the virgin women* sacrificed to Spaniard appetites, you will avenge them! Think of all the children stabbed with Spanish swords, you will avenge them!" (78–81; my emphasis).

248 THE DYNAMICS OF THE CORPUS IN LESSER-KNOWN PLAYS

Cureses' women are unique in identifying with the sexual pain of other women. As Mariana says to Magdalena: "all these lands are full of women who suffer [...] All! Women like you, like us, fearless women" (81). La Pola forgoes her love for Lieutenant Morillo, "small sentiments of man and woman," and focuses on the bond that matters: "four men [are being tortured] so that they speak and accuse a woman of this house [...] one woman or all women [of this house]" (103). In the end, the socialization of motherhood and love is complete. When Rosario confesses that she "buried the head" (136), in an "I am Spartacus" move, all of them, one by one, confess their part in the burial so as not to leave Rosario alone.[15]

Cureses' play foreshadows the gender turn that will take the stage by storm in the twenty-first century. Two other lesser-known twentieth-century plays announce the "gender turn." Sexual abuse against Antígona appears explicitly for the first time in the corpus, in Peruvian Sarina Helfgott's (1928–) one-act Antígona (1964). Also almost lost to critics, Helfgott's play was inspired by the Peruvian left-wing peasant movements who, in the 1960s, claimed land for indigenous peoples, echoing Marechal's Indian drama.[16] As in Marechal's play, land is the conflict; like Antígona Vélez, Helfgott's Antígona cannot sleep at the Peruvian hacienda; her gaze echoes that of Antígona Vélez, out of the hacienda, toward the tree where her brother Javier, leader of the guerrillas, hangs dead. Javier joined the "Indians" and returned to reclaim indigenous land, like Marechal's Ignacio. But the uncle in question, Mr. Ramón, wants sex with Antígona rather than death: he forces a kiss. Antígona, in self-defense, pulls out the knife given to her by sister Elena, but Ramón overpowers and kills Antígona with the knife, just like Haiti's Creon "killed" Antigòn in the water vase. Elena's sisterhood is her suffering: she shouts in despair that she will never sleep again.[17]

Twenty years later, Olga Harmony wrote La ley de Creón (1982), the second play in the twentieth-century corpus to invoke women's pain as a unifying political force—this time the biological pain of birth.[18] Summoning events of the 1910 Mexican Revolution, Harmony almost recreates Cureses'

---

[15] I owe the recollection of the Spartacus figure to a generous anonymous reader.

[16] See the entry for "Peru" in *The World Encyclopedia of Contemporary Theater*, edited by Don Rubin, Carlos Solórzano. Volume 2: The Americas (London: Routledge), 1996: 369 Helfgott's play pays homage to the revolutionary poet Javier Heraud, who was killed in 1963, age twenty-one.

[17] See *Antígona*, by Sarina Helfgott, in *Latin American Women Writers* (2007). The Spanish text was published in *Sarina Helfgott: Teatro* (1967). The play premiered in 1964 at the Club de Teatro in Lima. See Bañuls Oller and Crespo Alcalá (2008: 449–50).

[18] See Appendix (no. 20), the text was published in *Tramoya* (2001). The play premiered on March 30, 1988, at the Teatro Milán and won the "Juan Ruiz de Alarcón" award for the best national play.

THE DYNAMICS OF THE CORPUS IN LESSER-KNOWN PLAYS   249

female collective. But Harmony grants the heroine, Cristina, a new sense of commonality among women, beyond class and ethnicity: motherly physical and emotional pain. Two indigenous brothers, Lorenzo and Francisco, have led a revolt against rich landowner Mr. Marcos; Lorenzo hangs unburied from a tree, just like Helfgott's Javier. Francisco has escaped, in search of more weapons. At the Mexican hacienda, a multiplicity of suppliant, landless, peasant women, whose men have been killed or have gone to fight, approach with their demands. Cristina relates to these women with intensifying desire, listening to her indigenous nanny's stories about their stolen lands. Cristina, like La Pola confronting her love, is anxious about getting married "when there are so many women out there who are hungry, lacking shelter?" (9).

Gender lines, as in many preceding and succeeding plays, distinguish two projects of modernity. The chorus of "Gentlemen" praise progress, roads, and schools, while the chorus of "Women" acknowledge the cost of that progress: they have neither land nor food, and the road to progress "does not lead anywhere, cropped with crosses, a giant cemetery" (15). For the Women, Cristina is "from another country or world" (20) of wealth. But Cristina seeks a gendered coalition: "we are women; we must have something in common"; "someday I will give birth, and the pain will be the same" (21). The Women reply, "Yes, but you will have a doctor" (21). Cristina begins to think of the "lifestyle" of the rich as being "at the expense of the poor" (23). She repeats twice that Lorenzo's burial has become "secondary" (33) compared to the importance of ending injustice. By the end, just like Andrade's Mariana, Cristina admits that she "can't let them kill Francisco" (36), the living brother who has escaped. Gradually, the cause of burial transforms into a bond among the women who unite as mothers—even the nanny, who recognizes: "I have my chain, that between any mother and her children. I am no different than the women in the town" (35).

Like Marechal, Morisseau-Leroy, and Núñez, Harmony prefers that the lovers die together while escaping. They are married in death, lying "close to each other, almost together" (45). Gender dynamics prevail to the end: while the chorus of Women recognizes Cristina (and Ignacio) as their own dead, the chorus of men does not acknowledge the "confused sacrifice" that Cristina made. But the women know something different about sacrifices: they have all given their lives for the lives of others. They have given birth. Harmony's play is the story of a multiplicity of mothers and sisters in communion. And unions of women become the new rumination for Antígona plays from here onward, dominating the twenty-first-century stage.[19]

---

[19] Another lesser-known play with a female collective in the twentieth century is Puerto Rican García del Toro's 1990 *La primera dama* (The first lady), staging a rebellion led by a

250 THE DYNAMICS OF THE CORPUS IN LESSER-KNOWN PLAYS

First Disappearing Bodies: Impossible Burials, Impossible Universals

The second unprecedented shift brought by the 1960s is of paramount importance for the development of this book's corpus. While there was no place for woman in the patriarchal nation—not even the mother, for her child was taken—there was room, at least, for the male corpse and, possibly, its burial. The elements for the ritual were available. The corpse existed, was locatable, and was countable. The corpse was the condition for a certain type of politics and was the vehicle for a lesson, in sight or at hand: in the plaza for everyone to see, abandoned in the desert for Antígona to find, or hanging from a tree at the hacienda. For dramatic purposes, this location guided Antígona to perform the rite: Antígona Vélez walks into the desert at night; Antigòn appears magically near her brother's corpse; Fortunata goes to the plaza at night; Mariana confronts the sight of her brother's death; Marta exposes the body of her son; Helfgott's Antígona goes to the tree from which the corpse hangs; Cureses' women go for the decapitated head. Polynices, Ignacio Vélez, Marco Antonio Avellaneda, José Antonio Galán, Lisandro, José, Martiniano, and the Tavárez brothers have all had their Antígonas—women who were able to imagine the age-old ritual.

By the 1980s, the corpse will have disappeared in a surprising number of vernacular plays. Ritual will have gone awry. And Antígona's political struggle will have to surpass the aims of her predecessors. Historically, the Cold War in South America was implemented through a systematic politics of forced disappearance and displacement (of both the living and the dead). Antígona will now be assigned an extra task onstage: the body must be found. Antígona must develop the desire to know, the persistence to search, the patience to wait, and the strength for the possibility that the corpse will not be found. In its disappearance, the body also becomes uncountable. Bodies in unknown locations, disappearing and reappearing in unexpected places, or never to be found or found to be unrecognizable due to torture, start haunting the stage. The Antígonal paradigm of politics, initiated

heroine, just like Cureses' La Pola. In an unreachable colonial convent, secluded in the middle of a Central American jungle with no possible escape, opponents to the regime have been locked up for twenty years. One of them is the very first lady, sent to the convent after a fit of madness, when her husband assassinated their son and she tried to bury him. Thanks to a writer who visits the convent to investigate, the first lady recovers the memory needed to encourage all other women to accompany her to the palace where she will pull a gun and shoot the president.

THE DYNAMICS OF THE CORPUS IN LESSER-KNOWN PLAYS   251

around the killing of the child, now adjusts to the lack of—and need to create—evidence. Antígonas radicalize; their relationality thickens. If the Antígonas demand burials, they understand that they demand something that may be impossible. If the one corpse they look for cannot be found, then there may be many more. The fight morphs into a search for all the missing and thus the formulation of what I have called an "impossible universal": a demand that cannot be met if the political bond in which it is formulated remains the same.

We may think here of a singular development of an ancient fragment. The ancient prohibition of burial made Polynices' name, not only his body, disappear. Antigone's ritual restored Polynices' name to the decomposed body, and thus his belonging to the community. Simultaneously ancient and modern, the Latin American politically unburied will disappear from the community forever, for there will be no engraved tomb. The corpse's location, in its final decomposition, will not coincide with any naming on a tomb in its honor. Its natural tomb, the place of decomposition, may be a place with "No Name" (NN). Or the corpse may decompose outside the city; or a symbolic tomb may be built without the body, inside the community. From the 1980s onward, Latin American Antígonas restore the names of the disappeared by inventing tombs, bodies, and names. Politically, their actions must render the complete disappearance of the corpse impossible. Antígona's socialization of motherhood and love—the non-correspondence of a mother with one son, or of a wife with one husband—acquires one more expression: the possibility of a non-correspondence between one tomb and one corpse.

Arguably, strange things had already begun to happen to the corpse in 1957: Andrade's Mariana (and later Marta) exposes the corpse. In 1968, Antígona Pérez hides the brothers. While these burials are performed to a certain extent, the ritual has been dislocated. Antígona Pérez's rebels will be forever hidden: no name is attached to their tomb. And before the 1980s, two plays, lost to critics, foreshadow the disarray of ritual that will lead to Antígona's radicalization in that decade. In Nicaraguan Rolando Steiner's 1958 Antígona en el infierno (Antígona in hell) and Venezuelan César Rengifo's 1966 La fiesta de los moribundos (The party of the living dead), the corpse goes missing.

Rolando Steiner (1936–87) wrote against the backdrop of both the dictatorial dynasty of the three Somozas, who governed Nicaragua from 1937 to 1979, and the 1958–63 formative period of the Sandinista National Liberation Front (FSLN), an armed guerrilla group that successfully

252 THE DYNAMICS OF THE CORPUS IN LESSER-KNOWN PLAYS

deposed the Somoza dynasty in 1979.[20] Steiner's Antígona must undertake the strange and new—in the corpus—task of searching for and unburying the brother from a mass grave. Antígona speaks of many bodies rather than just one: "give me back my dead [*mis muertos*, plural in the original], Creon!" (10). Other mourning mothers are present, too: Antígona yells at Creon, "you hide them as war trophies and you deny mourning to the mothers!" (11). When a whistleblower tells Antígona that Polínice's body was hidden beneath a broken column in the palace gardens (12), the stranger and Antígona dig into the earth. Like Andrade's Marta and Mariana, Antígona's strategy is to expose the corpse: "the stench of his crime will go through the roads, the houses of the city and the people will feel nausea and will rebel against the poison of this stench!" (16). Before Cureses' female collective, Steiner grants the preoccupation with gendered violence to Ismena, who is the first courageous one in the corpus. Rebels are successful in reaching the city, and Ismena warns Creon: "from hell *have the dead come*, with their raped daughters, with the cry of the mothers, burning as melted fire to throw it onto your body!" (23; my emphasis). The end is not death: as Antígona says to Creon, "you send me to the myth, and not to death" (19). Steiner condenses themes past and themes to come: the disappeared are many; mothers are deprived of mourning; sisters unite; violence has a gender. The impossibility of the disappearance of the dead could not be clearer: they "return" to oust Creon from power.

Eight years later, César Rengifo (1915–80) staged the first disappearance of a sister rather than a brother, foreshadowing the shift away from the male corpse that will predominate in twenty-first-century plays. Rengifo's play is the most sinister exposure of the economic plan behind the neocolonial militarized politics of forced disappearances of the 1970s. Writing from Venezuela, Rengifo did not need to portray the military on stage: Venezuela's oil boom filled in for that role. Rengifo viewed oil as the evil bringing quick and easy money to foreign hands, just as Andrade had portrayed gold and coffee exploitation in colonial Brazil for foreign markets. In no other play in the corpus is the machinery of political disappearances linked to capitalist exploitation of raw materials so explicitly as in Rengifo's quilting of the tragedy with the grotesque. Casting Antígona as an eighty-year-old virgin, Ms. Antígona Sellers, the tragicomic search for the corpse turns out to be for her virgin twin sister, Ismene.[21]

---

[20] I have not been able to find criticism about this play.
[21] See Rengifo (1981, 2015). The play premiered in Caracas. I quote from Rengifo (1970), see Appendix (no. 12).

THE DYNAMICS OF THE CORPUS IN LESSER-KNOWN PLAYS   253

The tight economic connection between Venezuela and the United States is exploited in the chosen dramatic setting: the corpse has disappeared in the city of Sapulpa, Oklahoma, an oil-producing state with a complex colonial history, given its large indigenous population. Antígona Sellers—the only Antígona in the corpus with an Anglophone surname—comes from Missouri, north of Oklahoma, the site of Monsanto, the giant agrochemical company that produced DDT in the 1950s. The play's action unfolds at the office of the CEO of a company called "Compañía Suministros Biológicos S. A. Limitada" (Biological Supplies, S.A. Ltd.). The CEO, Mr. Blazer, serves "science," selling corpses and organs for scientific experimentation (135). At home, the idea of a company in an oil-producing US state selling body parts suited Rengifo's attack on Venezuela's dependence on oil exportation.[22] Mr. Blazer's grotesque factory is a symbol for the cost of the economic plan enforced under the guise of free-market ideologies by Cold War military–civic pacts.

Mr. Blazer competes with the funerary industry. Doing without burial, after all, is the essence of the politics of forced disappearances. He creates commercials that present the death of relatives as an investment. Running short of corpses, Mr. Blazer suggests a look into places where funerals are not of import, "the news about catastrophes in some country […] Have there been revolts in Bolivia, has the infant mortality increased in Chile or Ecuador […] and as usual keep an eye on India!" (136). The necropolitics of the Global South produces this raw material, too, beyond traditional raw materials like bananas and oil. As the CEO suggests to one of his employees, "please don't write the word corpse in the purchase forms […] just write down […] 'product.'" (170). But because neoliberalism also produces pockets of poverty in the North, the CEO receives an offer from a drunken vagabond, Peter Flinck, who plans to commit suicide and comes to sell his soon-to-be-dead body. He has wasted his life "working for others" (141). This gives the employees the idea for a new commercial: "Everyone will be able to sell their corpse in advance, and start charging their quotas and enjoy life!" (147). After all, expanding free-market economies mean the total commodification of life: that includes freshly dead flesh.

Enter eighty-year-old Antígona Sellers, who shows up at the CEO's office. According to her friend, seventy-year-old virgin Miss Peggy, Ismene's virgin corpse was taken by the company's staff to be sold for experiments. Antígona

---

[22] Most comments about this play belong in larger works about Rengifo's theater in general. See Melo Mendoza (2012), Suárez Randillo (1972), Pianacci (2008: 165–7), Orlando Rodríguez (in volume 1 of Rengifo 1989: 26) and Rafael Salazar (in volume 3 of Rengifo 1989: 20).

254 THE DYNAMICS OF THE CORPUS IN LESSER-KNOWN PLAYS

wants to recover the body; the CEO thinks she is crazy.[23] Soon enough, the disappeared Ismene begins to "return": when the employee who embalmed Ismene sees Antígona, he thinks that Ismene has risen from the dead. The staff searches for the file of the eighty-year-old corpse just embalmed, but on paper she is "NN": "there is no family name, no address [...], unforgivable!" (169). Ismene foreshadows the many unidentifiable, disappeared corpses in the South.

Ismene's fragmented corpse will be found later in Australia: another uncanny reference to the reappearing disappeared in real life, as scattered bones. Only Ismene's torso returns. The CEO offers Antígona cash, but she throws it on the floor in front of the press. The press thinks she is ridiculous. Indeed, this episode only makes business soar. The CEO addresses the audience as "mister stock holders" (stage directions): "we foster science [...] our company will soon control the global market [...] will dispose of all the living human bodies" (196). Letters from all over the world arrive: one Mr. Hoffman wants to buy two hundred thousand "units" (215). He represents the Consortium of Energetic Compost and Food, which processes "from the products like those you sell [...] compost of the best quality; special food for chickens and pigs, and something revolutionary, human brain energy that once injected in monkeys improves their sexual behavior! We also extract from the products lotions, soap for children and new vitamins" (215). An urgent cable asks for "a special product" to make lamps with human skin (229). The sound of military marches begins to play when Mr. Blazer asks the stockholders to raise their cups for a toast: "Long Live Suministros Biológicos SA, an organization with which a new era is inaugurated. The era of man without death [...] Long Live!!" (231).

While the notion of "lamps with human skin" makes Nazism equivalent to the Latin American military and to the nascent neoliberal market economy of unregulated capitalism, "man without death" is an ominous, if farcical, reference to the unburied men who rebelled against its implementation. In Rengifo's play, the disappeared corpses become useful compost; burial is not necessary anymore.

As for Ismene, Antígona suspects gendered violence to have occurred. After all, her bottom half is missing. The four elderly ladies involved (two dead and two alive) are all virgins: they echo other Antígonas in having

---

[23] Rojas Ajmad (2007) speculates about parallels with the ancient text and asks "why in the United States?," venturing that this kind of manipulation with bodies could only be imagined in that country at that time.

THE DYNAMICS OF THE CORPUS IN LESSER-KNOWN PLAYS 255

removed themselves from male exchange and instead bonded with other women. Stage directions have Antígona always carry (and wave) an umbrella, which she uses to reject what she sees as "advances" or lewd gazes from male employees in the company. To the secretary Evangeline she talks "woman to woman": "now, here, between us, [...] she is exactly like she was brought here, right?" (187). Evangeline responds: "our company absolutely respects the integrity of our products [...]" Antígona is horrified: "of the what?"; and Evangeline corrects herself: "of the bodies [...] don't worry, your sister is intact" (187). Of course, having only her torso, the word "intact" has uncertain meaning—just as with corpses found after dictatorship, it will be difficult to assess. The age-old focus on the brother recedes.

Rengifo's play lacks a redemptive scene. His Antígona Sellers cannot stop the company from selling corpses. Recall how previous Antígonas are redemptive: Argia's son is saved and the tyrant killed; Antigòn will live forever as a goddess; Antígona Vélez will "fertilize" the land; the peasant rebellion in Cristina's hacienda gains momentum; Helfgott's Antígona is revived in her sister, Elena; Mariana has let Gabriel live to lead the exodus; Marta transmits her story to the young Martiniano, who will continue her teachings; Steiner has the rebels win the palace; Fuentes Mares' young Antígona teaches a lesson to her comrades; La Pola and her women have transformed a Spaniard into an American.

But what can redeem the lack of a body to bury? The only redemption for postdictatorial Antígonas is a negative utopia—though formulated in life, not realized in death, as in previous cases. A negative utopia in life proposes to imagine what is not yet in existence. Antígona's entrance into the political pact now bears the injunction to reinstate politics after its military destruction. The only hope resides in a female collective that refuses to engage with the reproduction of the patriarchal nation or with the attempt to redress the evils of tyranny. Now that corpses have become unrecognizable or uncountable, the only way for Antígona to remain faithful to her politics is to reclaim politics as a practice of antagonism, non-negotiation, absolute indeterminacy, and thus, permanent contention. After the 1980s, the Antígonas want a different humanity, one not yet in sight.

This is why Antígonas of the 1980s onwards will intensify the impossible demand whose glimmer appeared in 1963 with Cureses' collective of women universalizing their statements about the decapitated head: biological motherhood is rendered meaningless, for he "was the son of *all* mothers" (36); individual love loses meaning, for "José Antonio belongs *to all* of us" (38). The Antígonas of the 1980s effect the passage from the

256 THE DYNAMICS OF THE CORPUS IN LESSER-KNOWN PLAYS

formulation of a national universal to that of an "impossible universal," adding the figure of the unburied: a "corpse that belongs to *all*" will shape plays to come. As the core of politics proper, an impossible universal rejects transactions that transform politics into a version of market economy. There is no end to the search for the disappeared because some bodies are not and will not be anywhere localizable: the exit from this predicament is systemic social change. The Antígonas of the 1980s must keep the bodies "appearing" in the struggle with the formulation that *all* need to appear. More often than not, the new task onstage will be represented as matching an appearing corpse with a name, a name that at times needs to be invented so that the corpse is claimed back and prevented from becoming twice disappeared. This is the case in a lesser-known play of the 1980s: Chilean Ariel Dorfman's 1987 *Widows*. I have engaged with the play elsewhere; suffice here to note its dialogue with this book's corpus.[24]

While for Steiner's and Rengifo's Antígonas the corpse reappears recognizable as Polínice or Ismena, for Dorfman's widows the situation is new in the corpus: the disappeared "appear" but in such decomposed state that they are unrecognizable. Only by restoring the sphere of political action can one make visible the impossibility of complete disappearance. Marechal had suggested that modern genocidal tides fail: he marked the presence of those targeted with extermination—the "Indians"—in Antígona's offspring. Dorfman represents the genocidal failure as the return of the disappeared, even if only as rotten flesh.

Widows is set in the peasant town of Camacho, which has lost practically all its men after an eight-year-long armed conflict, symbolized by two families: the Fuentes family, landless peasants of indigenous descent, and the Kastorias, local landowners who represent colonial theft. As the local Lieutenant tells the newly arrived Captain, the land has circulated among Camacho's "fourteen Families: for four hundred years [...]. There is a deep and inevitable structure in the world, a Holy Structure, if you will" (14). The new Captain arrives wanting to "bring your sorrow and great solitude to an end"[25] with the promise of "modernity": "democracy and technology" (9).

---

[24] See Fradinger (2013). In Spanish, *Viudas* (1996: 89–191); in English, *Widows*, translated by Kessler (Dorfman 1983). The theatrical version came out of the novel *Widows* and took final shape in collaboration with US writer Tony Kushner in 1989. It had premiered a year earlier at the Hip Pocket Theatre in Fort Worth, Texas. It has toured internationally prolifically. Information about all performances can be found in the Afterword to *Widows*, published in Dorfman's *The Resistance Trilogy* (1998).

[25] The Spanish version preserves the word "solitude," which echoes Gabriel García Márquez's *One Hundred Years of Solitude* (1967); the English version uses the word "loneliness."

THE DYNAMICS OF THE CORPUS IN LESSER-KNOWN PLAYS   257

With fertilizer plants and libraries (9), the Captain plans to drag the town "into the twentieth century" (54). The cost is the army's version of politics: the army forgets the people's "disobedience" and asks them to forget its "terrible" response (8).[26] But the local Lieutenant knows the history lesson from the Global South better than the Captain. The modernity of the twentieth century that the Captain seeks depends on the violent expropriation of land in such places like the fictional Camacho. He warns the Captain: "The twentieth century? I thought we were already there [...] What would the twentieth century be without countries like ours?" (54).

The Captain soon learns that the town's peasant women gather by the river washing clothes, and among them, Grandmother Sofía Fuentes sits immobile like a rock, waiting for the waters to bring her disappeared husband, father, and sons back. Suddenly, the river washes up an unrecognizable corpse. Chile's historical backdrop is clear—and chilling: just weeks after General Augusto Pinochet's (1915–2006) military coup toppled socialist President Salvador Allende (1908–73) on September 11, 1973, mutilated corpses started to float in the Mapocho River, which crosses the capital city of Santiago east to west. Women gathered on bridges, waiting to see if their missing ones washed ashore; this was repeated in other landscapes throughout the country.[27]

As in all cases in this book's corpus, the Greek fragment was a point of arrival. Dorfman quilted history with the ancient tragedies that inspired him—*Antigone* and *The Trojan Women*.[28] And, as Marechal had quilted

---

[26] When Dorfman started his novel *Widows* in 1978 while in exile, the Chilean military junta declared self-amnesty (Amnesty Law No. 2,191/1978). Pinochet's statement on September 21, 1995 summarized the military's position: "the only solution that exists for the problem of human rights is to forget," Agencia DPA Deutsche Presse Agentur (German Press Agency). See Loveman and Lira (1999).

[27] On September 27, 1973, the body of Spanish priest Joan Alsina washed ashore on the Mapocho; in November, peasants crossing the Ñuble River in the country's south noticed several headless corpses floating. See Comisión Chilena de Derechos Humanos, *Nunca Más en Chile: Síntesis corregida y actualizada del informe Rettig* (1999); see also Winn (2010: 239–76), Nona Fernández's novel (2002), and http://www.derechoschile.com/english/victims.htm.

[28] Dorfman's inspiration for Sofía's character comes from "the real women who searched for real bodies in a real world" (1997: afterword). See McClennen (2010), Kim (2003), Wallace (2003), and Spargo (2008). Spargo's kind of criticism has also been deployed in the case of Gambaro's *Antígona Furiosa*, which I treat in Chapter 6. Spargo, like critics of Gambaro's play, misses real historical analysis by equating Antigone with Antígona and with real-life mothers searching for their missing, all of whom he sees entering into politics with "family values," read through a Hegelian lens as "apolitical." I explain in Chapter 6 how the militarization of politics implied that of the home in the guise of a "defense" of the family and thus, how women, rather than using apolitical language, shared the language of the military who invaded their homes. In the case of Chile, Chileans had just undergone three years of massive popular revolutionary

258 THE DYNAMICS OF THE CORPUS IN LESSER-KNOWN PLAYS

Christian redemption with an Indian drama at a historical frontier marked by a river (the Salado in the Pampas), Dorfman quilted a historical drama of resistance with myth on the riverbanks in Camacho's fictional world: the quilting point is the unrecognizable corpse floating back for the widows to claim. Dorfman's Sofía, a figure of rumination par excellence in this book's corpus, belongs in a long line of mothers, as it could not be otherwise: she mulls over the disappeared, sitting by the river for months, but also over 400 years of indigenous struggle. On the banks of the same river, their indigenous ancestors died at the hands of the Spanish (16). As she says to her grandchildren, her "fierce" resistance goes back to her "great-great-great grandfather and his wife" (16): according to the Spanish, the latter "ate the eyeballs of her enemies" (16).

The play begins and ends with a motherly parallel between Sofía's daughter-in-law, who cradles her unnamed baby, and Camacho's women, who cradle a corpse out of the river. The mothers who carried the embryonic body of hope in their wombs for nine months are the same women who carry the dead body toward another hope: the hope of a name. The country where the plot unfolds is unnamed too, equivalent to the corpses and the baby. Naming is a gendered act, and it either gives death or life. Some men in captivity have given out names under torture: those names are death sentences. Sofía, and gradually all the women of Camacho, will bring the unrecognizable dead back to "life" by inventing their names.

When the first corpse floats up the river, Sofía names it after her father, Carlos Fuentes. Sofía has found her desire to "locate" her father: as she says, she "knew" (25) it was his corpse. Other women first feel hesitation: "How could I be sure? How could I *want* this to be *my* brother?" (22; my emphasis). Sofía "knows" from the beginning what the women of Camacho will have to learn to want and do: decide on the body's identiy with only fiction as evidence. The Captain's order of a legal and scientific investigation is out of the question, for the bodies have been disfigured. Reclaiming them takes on a different urgency when the first corpse is made to disappear a second time: the Lieutenant burns it.

Sofía likewise "knows" that the second corpse to be cast ashore is her husband, Miguel. An attempt at disappearing the corpse a second time fails. When a fake burial is made for the second corpse, Camacho's women mobilize. They eat bread together at dawn by the tomb. Gradually they all

---

participation in Allende's socialist experiment, where women (both in the left and in the right wing) were hypervisible.

THE DYNAMICS OF THE CORPUS IN LESSER-KNOWN PLAYS   259

recognize the buried man as their own. One of them says "Impossible. It can't belong to all of us […]," but each and every woman then asserts: "It's mine" (49). Not legally, but politically, a body *can* belong to everyone, just as for Cureses' collective José was the "son of all."

The Captain ends up receiving thirty-six petitions from widows asking to bury "their" man. The Lieutenant understands them: "They want all their men back. Not just one. Not just some. All." For the Captain, this is absurd: "All? That's impossible." The Lieutenant repeats "Impossible. No more" (*nunca más*, "never again," in the Spanish version; 65). In Spanish, it is a wordplay pregnant with meaning. The Lieutenant articulates in the words "Impossible. No more," both the meeting and the diverging point of the Captain's and the women's visions. The word that they share—"impossible"— is the premise that reinstates the antagonism of the political as opposed to all politics of negotiation, such as the amnesty sought by the military in fiction and in real life. The "never again" preceded by the "impossible" suggests that the term "never again" also participates in the fictional dynamic of the impossible utopia. In the "no more," Latin American spectators recognize the impossible universals of human rights movements across the region— Gambaro's *Antígona Furiosa* in Chapter 6 will pronounce them onstage, too.

The Captain expects the women to understand that what they want is impossible; the women present the impossible as the utopian horizon of the possible. As they socialize widowhood, they leave behind the liberal legal institutions—of motherhood, of widowhood, of accountability—based on the individual ratio of one-to-one: a son only has one mother; a wife only has one husband; a murder victim has only one murderer (or one identifiable group). Camacho's women stage the process by which each individual demand (one burial) yields to the formulation of a universal demand (*all* burials must be performed). Without the universal premise, there would simply be individual petitions characteristic of all contractual negotiations. Only when the widows' petition becomes a demand for "all" can it be political. Paradoxically, the petition can only be political insofar as it implies its very impossibility: this is the core of antagonism that defines the radicalization of the Antígonas in the second half of the twentieth century and thereafter.

Like Varela's 1824 Argia, like Zavalía's 1959 Fortunata, Sofía is offered the choice to save her grandchild, who has been taken prisoner, if she gives up. Sofía does not negotiate; the Captain kills them both. In response, the women confront the armed soldiers by the river when another corpse floats up. They cradle it in their arms together and advance "perhaps dancing,

260 THE DYNAMICS OF THE CORPUS IN LESSER-KNOWN PLAYS

perhaps singing, perhaps only moving forward" (74; stage directions) toward the soldiers who "draw their rifle bolts, assume positions" (74) ready to fire.

Echoing the 200-year-old political imaginary of the Southern Cone Creole elites,[29] the Captain envisions a nation of immigrants without "Indians." In the final scene, the Captain observes the women congregating by the river and says to the Lieutenant: "This country's hopeless. They'll have to depopulate it, the whole country, and bring in other people, people from outside, people with some other kind of mind" (74). Whereas the military have repeated the cyclical passing on of the land among fourteen families, killing not only peasants but also the possibility of politics, Sofía has reinstated the type of politics that will not concede. Sofía's female collective had socialized motherhood, sisterhood, and widowhood. This radical politics will dominate the *Antígona* plays to come.

---

[29] Southern Cone refers to the tip of the South American territory, formed by Argentina, Chile, and Uruguay. Sometimes Paraguay and Bolivia are included in the designation.

6

The Incorruptible

Griselda Gambaro's 1986 *Antígona Furiosa*

I knew […] I would speak with the voice of a Latin American woman and with the voices of so many women who, in my country, have done what Antígona did […] Antígona is every one of the Mothers of the Plaza de Mayo who has paid with her life for her disobedience.

(Griselda Gambaro)[1]

Antígona Furiosa (*Furious Antígona*) is a one-act play composed of fragments from the Greek source and a myriad of other intertexts. It opens and closes with a quotation from Shakespeare's *Hamlet*. There are three actors: Antígona and two men from the chorus, Corifeo and Antinoo. Corifeo at times delivers Creon's lines from behind a movable polyester shell; the two men, alternating roles, utter the lines of ancient characters. The setting is a modern café in Buenos Aires. The events are narrated in multiple temporalities, as past, present, or future. The play begins when Antígona returns to life. It comes full circle when she kills herself again. The two men constantly mock her. After the dialogues anticipate the fratricide, Antígona performs a paroxysmal dance to represent the battle. After the story of the fratricide is narrated, Antígona stumbles as she walks among dead bodies. More information about Creon's edict is given, and Antígona trips over Polinices' body, represented by a shroud, and performs a funeral rite with stones and dance. The classic confrontations follow, first between Antígona and Creon, then between Creon and Hemon. Antígona's last speech ends with the sinister sound of bird cries. Vast wings touch Antígona's body, and filth representing the plague's arrival falls on the tables. Creon's trip to the cave and Hemon's death are narrated. The two men tell Antígona that Creon pardons her. Antígona still wants to bury her brother.

---

[1] Translations from Spanish are mine unless otherwise specified. See the interview with J. Navarro Benítez (2001).

Antígonas: Writing from Latin America. Moira Fradinger, Oxford University Press. © Moira Fradinger 2023.
DOI: 10.1093/oso/9780192897091.003.0008

262 GRISELDA GAMBARO'S 1986 *ANTÍGONA FURIOSA*

She rejects the bowl of water in the cave and furiously kills herself after saying her last line: "hate rules. The rest is silence."[2]

Historical Returns

Antígona Furiosa premiered at the Goethe Institute in Buenos Aires on September 24, 1986. It ran for ten nights. Director Laura Yusem placed Antígona (actress Bettina Muraña) inside a pyramidal cage near the audience. Wearing a crown of flowers on her head, a white dress fashioned from rags, and bloody bandages over her feet and arms, the actress moved up and down the cage ecstatically, often reenacting the narrated violence. At the beginning, when she came back "alive," she left the cage only to reenter it through a back door and remain there for the play's duration. For Yusem, it was "dance-theater."[3] For reviewers, the actress' gestures were those of "a ferocious wounded beast."[4] Nora Lía Jabif's review for the 1987 restaging of the play noted the actress moved with "epileptic spasms, stretching, contracting [...] climbing the walls of the jail that marks the limits of power [...] the image of a crazy woman protected only by a blood-stained kerchief [...] who does not tremble when confronting power" (*Página 12*, June 2, 1987).

Three café tables surrounded the caged "wounded beast" located at the center of the theater (Figures 6.1 and 6.2). The two-man chorus wearing modern clothes sat at one of those tables, moving to other tables while speaking, drinking coffee, embodying spectatorship, and breaking the fourth wall. To deliver some of Creon's lines, one of the men hid behind the shell—a half-torso of medieval, warrior-like armor originally constructed by sculptor Juan Carlos Distéfano (1933–)—which is eventually abandoned in a corner.[5] The men represented quintessential Buenos Aires urban life: everyday politics, culture, and business that happen in vivid discussions, day and night, in cafés on practically every city block. Osvaldo Quiroga described the men as "careless about justice" and compared Sophocles' and Gambaro's message to Brecht's: "he who knows the truth and hides it, is a

---

[2] I use Marguerite Feitlowitz's translation into English (1991). When I modify the translation I add "Sp" indicating the page number in the Spanish edition of Gambaro's *Teatro 3* (1992: 191–217).

[3] *Clarín*, September 24, 1986.   [4] *La Prensa*, September 29, 1986.

[5] Interview with Laura Yusem, *La Nación*, September 25, 1986. See details of the torso's construction in Puga (2008: 179).

Figure 6.1 *Antígona Furiosa*, Director Laura Yusem. Premiere, Goethe Institute, Buenos Aires, September 24, 1986. The audience surrounds the stage. Courtesy of Susana Arenz at the INET (Archivo Documental del Instituto Nacional de Estudios de Teatro), Buenos Aires, Argentina.

murderer."[6] In 1987 in Córdoba, another reviewer wrote: "[Antígona's unburied brother] is a synthesis of all our own unburied dead ones […] in the end, all of us are at stake."[7]

The press was quick to catch the allusion to middle-class complicity in the 1976–83 military dictatorship and to Gambaro's dedication to the Mothers and Grandmothers of the Plaza de Mayo (hereafter, the Mothers), who still search for their missing and still circle the historic pyramid located at the center of the Plaza de Mayo in Buenos Aires every Thursday at 3:30 p.m., just as they did back when they first gathered there on April 30, 1977.[8] A pyramidal jail on stage, a haunting tortured living dead woman stained with blood inside it, two indifferent middle-class men looking on: for Argentines, this was the ghostly condensation of images of the Mothers, the

---

[6] *La Nación*, September 25, 1986.
[7] "Nuestros muertos insepultos," *La Voz del Interior*, Córdoba, October 25, 1987.
[8] For an introduction to the Mothers of the Plaza de Mayo see Fisher (1989) and Gorini (2006). The Mothers have split into two groups (*Asociación* and *Línea Fundadora*). See https://madres.org/ and http://madresfundadoras.blogspot.com/.

Figure 6.2 Review of Gambaro's *Antígona Furiosa*: "Nuestros muertos insepultos," *La Voz del Interior*, Córdoba, Argentina, October 25, 1987. Courtesy of Argentores Archive, Buenos Aires, Argentina.

Plaza's pyramid, the complicit middle class, and those who disappeared, tortured clandestinely and then disposed of in secret.[9]

Of the dramas studied in this book, *Antígona Furiosa* has received by far the most critical interest. Because the play's historical background has attracted so much international attention, Anglophone critics have used their reading of *Antigone*—and of *Antígona Furiosa*—to explain it to

---

[9] In June 1987, the play was staged in the traditional Cervantes theater, which had hosted *Antígona Vélez* in 1953. In October 1987, the play went to Córdoba and in September 1988 to the Teatro San Martín in Buenos Aires, where Yusem had spectators sit around the cage on the large stage. In 1987, the play was read in English at the Apple Corps Theater in New York. In a 1999 production at Vassar College, director Erin Mee situated spectators around the stage in movable chairs facing outward, forcing them to choose whether or not to face the stage. See Mee and Foley 2011: 19. Marla Carlson produced the play in 2000 at the CUNY Graduate Center, eliminating the cage and adding a fourth actor (2003: 381–403).

GRISELDA GAMBARO'S 1986 *ANTÍGONA FURIOSA*   265

themselves and their audiences. Thus, my purpose in this chapter is twofold. I engage both the play and the fragments of history that Anglophone readers have missed as they tried to understand the Mothers' role during the dictatorship. My aim here is not to write Argentine history, but to draw attention to the odd recurrence of inaccurate historicization affecting criticism on Gambaro's play.[10] Critics focus on dictatorship, but the play was written three years into the transition to democracy. The detail of an Argentine Antígona who rejects pardon is thus lost.

Antígona Furiosa is a palimpsest of international literary references, as well as a mix of literary genres (tragedy, comedy, parody), temporalities (ancient and modern), and linguistic registers, including street slang. As the author said, she was "listening to Sophocles but from very far away."[11] But, for all its postdramatic features, Gambaro's *Antígona* was as embedded in national history as its predecessors. At its core was also an homage to sisterhood and collective motherhood, following in the steps of timid sisterhoods from 1824 onward, the desire of Argia to connect with Antigone, the support Andrade's Mariana had from her friends in Pedreira, the love between Andrade's Marta and Quiteria, the collectives that Cureses' La Pola leads and Dorfman's Sofía inspires, and of course the sisterhood between the fictional Antígona, Gambaro, the Mothers, and the two female friends to whom she dedicated the play: director Laura Yusem and actress Bettina Muraña. Echoing the headline of an Argentine review of the play that read "Antígona: An Argentine Tragedy," Gambaro insisted: "Antígona belonged to us because we had painfully earned the right to it. Antígona lived and still lives in Argentina."[12] In the 1986 program notes, Gambaro wrote: "a new Antígona out of time, that she might paradoxically tell us her story in her time and in ours."

In "our time," *Antígona Furiosa* uncannily spoke to 1986 and literarily ruminated on her Argentine predecessors: Varela's 1824 mother of a kidnapped child and Marechal's 1951 "disappearing" Indians. The crown of flowers on Antígona Furiosa's head symbolizes circular repetitions—not only the circular frame of the play but also the circularity of national history: the full historical circle between the genocidal wave against "Indians" represented in Marechal's play and the genocidal wave against Creole sons during the 1976–83 dictatorship, now represented in *Antígona Furiosa*.

---

[10] As I explained in Chapter 5, this also happened with the scant criticism on Dorfman's *Widows*.
[11] See http://web.uchile.cl/publicaciones/cyber/20/entrev1.html.
[12] See the interview "New Stories from Old" (Gambaro 1995: 58).

266 GRISELDA GAMBARO'S 1986 *ANTÍGONA FURIOSA*

In the final scene of Marechal's play, Antígona Vélez bleeds to make the desert blossom with flowers. In the first scene of Gambaro's play, Antígona awakens by undoing the noose of her veil, crowned with wilting white flowers. The flowers may refer both to Hamlet and Ophelia and to the flowers of civilization that Antígona Vélez planted in Marechal's 1820 desert, which now wither on Antígona Furiosa's head. In Gambaro's opening scene, Corifeo sits in the café, playing with a small branch and tearing a paper napkin into pieces "in the manner of flowers" (Sp 197). The flowers reappear at the end when Antígona places the crown of flowers back on her head and prepares her body for death with a twist of her neck (stage directions).

Marechal's Facundo represents the landowning classes of the nineteenth century. The inheritors of that land stand now on Gambaro's stage, representing the civilians who, even if they do not own the land, had called in the military a decade prior to help preserve, as it was said, "tradition, family, property" against "socialism."[13] Marechal's Antígona makes concessions to power. But the form in which Argentina's state-sponsored politics of extermination returned in the 1970s left Gambaro no option but to ruminate on the figure of Antígona as she who concedes nothing, not even accepting a pardon. In fact, and just like Dorfman's Sofía, Antígona represents the insistence that characterizes the act of rumination: she will "*always* want to bury Polinices. Even if *born* a thousand times, and *he* dies a thousand times" (Sp 217; my emphasis).[14] Marechal's Facundo blessed Captain Rojas for his decision to "wipe out the Indians of these plains" (*Antígona Vélez*, 29). On October 23, 1975, a century after that genocide, the soon-to-be dictator, Lieutenant General Jorge Rafael Videla (1925–2013), declared: "as many people as necessary must die, in order to achieve peace in Argentina."[15] Marechal's critique was directed at what Argentine national historiography had named "National Organization": the consolidation of the nation-state from approximately 1852 to 1880, ending with the "Conquest of the Desert." In 1976, the military coup named itself the "Process of National

---

[13] "Tradición, Familia y Propiedad" is the Catholic right-wing organization founded in 1960 in Brazil.

[14] In Spanish, the conjugation of the verb "to be born" appears in the present subjunctive (*que nazca*) and can indicate both the first- and the third-person singular. The Spanish phrase only determines a pronoun for the verb "to die." It is Polinices who will die; she/he/it will *be born*. The English translation stabilizes meaning: "Though I a thousand times will live, and he a thousand times will die" (158): "I will live"; "he will die." The Spanish reads: " 'Siempre' querré enterrar a Polinices. Aunque nazca mil veces y él muera mil veces" (Sp 217).

[15] Videla at the XI Conferencia de Ejércitos Americanos, Montevideo. See Celso (1999: 345).

Reorganization": a new nation aimed at wiping out, once and for all, the peoples, the books, and the ideas that the (landowning) elites had always perceived as a threat to the "Western Christian values" that had guided the extermination of indigenous peoples a century earlier—for some Argentines, a painful circularity.

Historically, Argentine elites had never welcomed the successive waves of heightened politicization of secular democracy—the anarchosyndicalism and the rise of middle classes at the beginning of the century, then the first Peronist government and the political voice of workers. The elites had supported military coups first in 1930, then in 1943, 1955, 1962, and 1966. The military's "messianic Catholicism" of the 1970s would launch a genocidal tide best summarized in the infamous statement of Brigadier General Ibérico Saint-Jean (1922–2012), de facto governor of Buenos Aires from 1976 to 1981, in 1977: "First we will kill all the subversives; then we will kill their collaborators; then [...] their sympathizers. Then [...] those who remain indifferent; and finally we will kill the timid."[16] In 1990, Sergio Tomasella, a former peasant turned secretary general of the Agrarian Leagues, encapsulated two centuries of this politics of extermination in his testimony to the Tribunal Against Impunity in Buenos Aires: "the line is continuous—those who took the land from the Indians, continue to oppress us."[17] Consider here the parallel with Dorfman's fictional town of Camacho. With the return of the politics of extermination, the Antígona Vélez who had buried her "Indian" brother woke up from death—furious.[18]

---

[16] See his speech in the *International Herald Tribune*, Paris, May 26, 1977.

[17] Quoted in Feitlowitz (1999: 113).

[18] Antígona continues to haunt the Argentine stage to this day. Two highlights of the twentieth century are worthy of note here. In 1989, theater director Alberto Ure staged an *Antígona* faithful to the Greek source—using the translations of Jebb, Hölderlin, and Elisa Carnelli—but having his Antígona wear a crown of thorns and military attire. Ure's notes for rehearsals are worth a chapter of their own: "it has to start with the intolerable [...] the first scene is a banquet with Ismena drugged [...] then the two sisters are at a hair salon [...] they are two Evitas, Antígona wearing a pret-a-porter suit, Ismena an evening gown [...] the chorus is violent [...]" (Carnelli and Ure 2016: 86–7). In 1991, two Argentine musicians composed operas based on Marechal and Gambaro's plays: Juan Carlos Zorzi (1936–99) worked on Marechal, while Jorge Mario Liderman (1957–2008) on Gambaro. Fittingly perhaps, following the footsteps of their respective plays, Zorzi's opera premiered in Buenos Aires at *Teatro Colón*, the paragon of national "high" culture, and Liderman's opera premiered in 1992 in Germany, where it won the 1992 BMW International Music Theater Prize in the Third Munich Biennale. Zorzi's interview with the press was telling: he understood Marechal's question to have been whether "progress" required the sacrifice of war or the fraternal ethics of *Antigone*. See Zorzi in *Clarín*, Buenos Aires, December 8, 1991, p. 3; see also Paz (1998: 91–8). For the array of versions appearing in the twenty-first century, see the Appendix to this book.

268 GRISELDA GAMBARO'S 1986 *ANTÍGONA FURIOSA*

Critics have reduced the play's context mostly to dictatorship or focus on what Pierre Nora has called *"un lieu de mémoire"*[19] in honor of the disappeared, the resistance to military power, and a performance of "memory": in Silvia Pellarolo's words, "an act of mourning" (1992: 82).[20] Indeed, the spectators see an act of burial: like Antigòn, this Antígona blurs the lines between theater and ritual. Puga (2008) and Carlson (2003) point out that the dance-theater recalls the torture undergone by political prisoners. Others have seen the play as a parody of the canon.

Nonetheless, the real stakes for Gambaro and her audience in 1986 were neither the denunciation of dictatorship nor the performance of mourning. Gambaro intervened in a heated postdictatorship debate. The "post" indicates the ghostly presence of dictatorship in the absence of a ruling military junta. The troubled mid-1980s were invested in questioning the meaning of justice and politics after the world-famous 1985 Trials of the Generals. Democratically elected president Raúl Alfonsín (1927–2009) organized the civilian trials in the wake of the 1984 National Truth Commission report on crimes against humanity during the dictatorship (titled *Nunca Más*/Never Again). As the entire world watched, the military staged an uprising on Easter 1987. Military pressure led the Congress to pass two impunity laws after the trials ended: the Full Stop Law in December 1986, setting a deadline for prosecutions, and the Law of Due Obedience in June 1987, exonerating subordinates.[21]

The political anxiety caused by the constraints faced by liberal legal institutions on their ability to judge crimes against humanity increased. The 1986 political debate was about who should be judged and how the legal institutions would cope with the magnitude of the catastrophe left by the dictatorship. At a time of negotiation in Buenos Aires, Gambaro's play presented the field of politics as structured by an incorruptible antagonism rather than negotiation. As it turns out, this was the hard line of one of the two groups into which the Mothers split in January of that very same year: 1986. For the hardliners, as well as for Gambaro's fictional Antígona, the other side had made unacceptable concessions to Alfonsín's government.

Rather than the condemnation of dictatorship or, for that matter, its civilian–military pacts, the play was framed by the 1986 political indictment

---

[19] See Nora (1984).

[20] Resistance to power appears in almost all criticism; for a Foucauldian analysis, see Valdivieso (2009: 285–93).

[21] The report and the trials were a turning point for the global human rights movement. See Sikkink (2008) and Sikkink and Walling (2006: 301–24), Nino (1997) and Malamud Goti (1996).

GRISELDA GAMBARO'S 1986 *ANTÍGONA FURIOSA*

of the liberal justice system and by the debates within the human rights movement. The Mothers were active in these debates. While Antígona Furiosa responds literarily to her sister Antígona Vélez for having negotiated with Facundo, she enters politically the debates over negotiations during the transition to democracy after 1983. Just like Dorfman's Sofía, Antígona Furiosa embodies an incorruptible principle to restore politics—that is, an antagonistic space organized by an "impossible universal": the utopian vector of a dissenting demand that puts the limits of the entire system in crisis.

The Mothers' hardline slogan—*"aparición con vida"* ("back alive")—is one such impossible universal. At times, the Mothers' opponents read the slogan literally as the Mothers' denial of death: why would they want them to appear alive if they knew the disappeared were dead? However, the slogan stressed a political principle of non-negotiation, aiming at the radical trial of society as a whole. *Antígona Furiosa* embodies this type of universal utopian demand.

Following the above, I read the uncanny presence of *Hamlet*, quilting every fragment of the play from beginning to end, as illuminating the epistemological, legal, and political questions of Gambaro's play as it responds to its times. Like Hamlet, to "catch the conscience" of the audience, Antígona performs a play-within-a-play, akin to Hamlet's "Mousetrap." Mobilizing Ophelia in surprising ways, Gambaro gives us also an occasion to reread the Shakespearean character as more than a helpless victim. Like Hamlet, Gambaro's characters, and audience, engage in a "detective" exercise, not knowing who speaks or who lives, conjuring up the political uncertainty of the 1986 Argentine debate: How to know whom to punish? What did justice mean at that time? Antígona answers with the total rejection of negotiations: nobody is innocent.

Gambaro's Rebellions

Named an Honorary Citizen of Buenos Aires by its town council and considered one of Argentina's major dramatists, Gambaro was born to working-class Italian immigrants. She began her theatrical career adapting her first two short novels for the stage in 1965 at the legendary avant-garde Instituto Di Tella, generating a rabid polemic over their alleged "disconnection" from national reality.[22] But Gambaro asserts that "everything is political, even the

---

[22] See Pellettieri (2001: 336–80). For the absurd in Gambaro's theater, see Holzapfel (1970: 5–11).

270 GRISELDA GAMBARO'S 1986 *ANTÍGONA FURIOSA*

most private act, even how you behave with your family."[23] The publication of her novel *Ganarse la muerte* (To earn one's own death, 1976) forced her into exile when the military censors caught the allegory of the story of an abused woman. A report affirmed that the novel was an attack—of the "subversive, not simple" kind—on the family, Argentine nationality, and the armed forces.[24]

Back home in 1986, Gambaro entered a phase of metatheatrical writing. *Antígona Furiosa* belongs to this phase. Critic Osvaldo Pellettieri divides Gambaro's phases as neo-avant-garde in the 1960s; human-rights-focused in the 1970s (with plays such as *Fear* [1972], *Information for Foreigners* [1978], and *To Say Yes* [1981]); and concerned with the metatheatrical question of how to write after dictatorship in the 1980s (with plays such as *Bitter Blood* [1982], *The Rising Sun* [1984], *The Stripping* [1985], and of course, *Antígona*).[25] Victims and victimizers in abusive relations permeate Gambaro's theater and novels. Women are often central characters, with Gambaro gradually engaging more explicitly with the condition of women. Her literary craft displays elements of the absurd and the grotesque. She uses corrosive humor, irony, parody, allegory, and Artaudian concepts of the theater of cruelty, including performing psychological cruelty and physical violence, fragmented dramatic structures, depersonalization, and even scenes bordering on the representation of torture.

Critics tend to analyze Gambaro's work in relation to European authors in circulation in 1960s Argentina: Ionesco, Grotowski, Sartre, Camus, and Beckett. But Gambaro refers to her intertextual style as her commitment to justice: "I deal with real facts; it's just that my form of expression isn't realistic."[26] To the critics who identify European influences in her career, she responds, "If there were elements of the absurd, these did not refer to the European absurd, which is more metaphysical. My first works always started with a social situation."[27] In an interview with *Clarín*, she remarked: "I had never read Pinter, and I don't think I had read Ionesco. Looking for relations with European authors is part of the colonial spirit they have imposed on us" (January 13, 2004). She prefers to point at a very local influence:

---

[23] *Clarín*, January 31, 2004.

[24] The report originally appeared in the magazine *Xul* (see an online version at *Feminaria Literaria*, https://tierra-violeta.com.ar/biblioteca-feminaria/revista-feminaria/). See the interview with Gambaro published in Betsko and Koening (1987: 194). Gambaro first thought of Argentina when she wrote the novel, but when it was published in France by a feminist press, she realized it also spoke of the situation of real-life women.

[25] See Pellettieri (2001) and Martini (1989).   [26] Quoted in Picón Garfield (1985: 63).

[27] Interview with Castro and Jurovietzky (1996).

GRISELDA GAMBARO'S 1986 *ANTÍGONA FURIOSA* 271

Argentine Armando Discépolo, who gave shape to the *grotesco criollo* ("the Creole grotesque"), a theater depicting the life of impoverished immigrants (mostly Italians) at the turn of the century.[28] Gambaro describes her work as a response "to a cultural *mestizaje* produced by colonization and European immigration after the almost total erasure of indigenous cultures [...] this *mestiza* culture is what allows us to be open to all sources, to receive them and transform them."[29]

In 2010, Gambaro opened the International Annual Book Fair in Frankfurt by telling the audience that she considered giving a "normal" speech about something folkloric, such as "Argentine" literature. But she opted for something more "akin to literature": its relation to power. Mentioning Argentine writers who had disappeared, she declared that the writer is always in dissidence.[30] For Gambaro, "drama presupposes not only a very frank, but also a very definitive, commitment to the social environment [...] Every play is a settling of scores, an immediate confrontation with society."[31]

The Greek Source, Parody, Intertext, and Argentine History: Missed Encounters

Marguerite Feitlowitz's English translation was decisive for the play's critical reception in the Anglophone academy. Two main critical gestures prevail: the expected comparison with the Greek source and a historical (mis)reading with reference to dictatorship, rather than postdictatorship.[32]

---

[28] Armando was the brother of Enrique Santos Discépolo, the "man of tango" who directed *Antígona Vélez* in 1951. The "creole grotesque" is a mix of the Italian grotesque, the Spanish "sainete," and the Spanish "theater for hours." For an introduction to these types of Southern Cone theatre, see Pellettieri (2008) and V. Smith (1997: 792–7).

[29] In Navarro Benítez (2001).

[30] See her speech in the collection of Gambaro's opinion articles *Al pie de página* (2011).

[31] Cited in Catena (2011: 18).

[32] Werth (2010: 25–48) mentions the legal limitation of the 1985 trials, though she returns to a focus on mourning. Fleming speaks of the 1980s, and though he points at the empty figure of power represented in the polyester shell, he understands that "Gambaro uses the chorus to condemn life under authoritarian rule" (1995: 77). Scott starts her meditation on Gambaro's refutation of Hegel's vision of tragedy by referring to the political context, but assuming the use of Greek tragedy is a strategy against "the fear of the government censuring artistic engagement" (1993: 99), as if the play had been written during dictatorship; Taylor believes that Gambaro chose the play "to represent the atrocities of the Dirty War" (1997: 209).

272 GRISELDA GAMBARO'S 1986 *ANTÍGONA FURIOSA*

Proximity: Comparison and Parody

With their tendency to impose European readings of Greek classics on Latin American texts, Anglophone critics paradoxically overlook unexpected aspects of the ancient myth foregrounded in Gambaro's play as well as specificities of Argentine history. Anna Krajewska-Wieczorek pigeonholes Gambaro's Antígona as a Sophoclean "archetype" on the mission of love (1994: 327).[33] By contrast, Gambaro's Antígona Furiosa attributes love to Ismena: "we wanted justice. I, for justice itself, she for love" (Sp 206). Antígona hates: "I want for [my persecutors] the same harm for them that they unjustly do to me! The same harm!" (153). Diana Taylor's two often-cited articles—"Rewriting the Classics: Antígona Furiosa and the Madres of the Plaza de Mayo" (1996) and "Trapped in Bad Scripts: The Mothers of Plaza de Mayo" (1997)—begin by comparing the ancient Creon to the modern one: the problems in the *Antigone* "were as urgent during the Dirty War as they were in 441 BC" (1997: 209).[34] For Taylor, Creon mimics the military junta; he appears initially reasonable before revealing his tyranny. However, the Argentine military sought the restoration of authority (rather than peace).[35] Gambaro's text does not portray the military as reasonable or tyrannical. It avoids personifying the military: Creon is an empty polyester shell behind which the two men (civilian forces) hide, indicating the "void" of power that only survived with the support of the upper classes and sectors of the middle classes.

Nancy Kason Poulson seeks "the parallels between the biological fratricide in Sophocles' *Antigone* and the metaphorical fratricide in Gambaro's play" (2012: 48), situating a "fratricidal animosity" between Perón's followers and opponents and considering the 1976 military as a continued "fratricide" between Peronism and its opposition (53). Reading the dictatorship as "fratricide" (or the dictatorship as a conflict between Perón's followers and opponents, or even Perón's opponents in 1946 as "metaphorical fratricide") is, at best, a historical oversight. It not only is historically inaccurate but also reproduces the ideological narrative ("the dirty war") obliterating the state-sponsored terrorism in the 1970s that aimed to reorganize an

---

[33] See also Valdivieso (2009) and Borrachero Mendíbil (2007) for a comparison between the ancient and modern plays.

[34] In Argentina, the discourse of the "dirty war" belongs to a specific ideological narrative about the dictatorship. For those opposed to dictatorship there was no "war," only state terrorism.

[35] See Rafael Videla's 1977 discourses in *Mensajes Presidenciales: Proceso de Reorganización Nacional*.

GRISELDA GAMBARO'S 1986 *ANTÍGONA FURIOSA* 273

entire nation and operated approximately 340 clandestine concentration camps. Argentines have long debated the assignation of "equal violence" to supposedly "two sides," because it leaves a massive number of deaths unexplained. The guerrillas (estimated at two thousand members) were decimated by 1977. The Army officially numbers the killings committed by guerrillas in the 1970s at 697 people; the estimated number of those disappeared by the dictatorship hovers over the tens of thousands.[36] "Fratricide" is not central to Gambaro's text because it simply does not fit the Argentine historical equation.

To be sure, Sophocles' lines appear in Gambaro's text. But they appear dislocated in time, fragmented, voiced by characters not clearly identifiable, revealing "Latin" American heterogeneity throughout. While Sophocles inserts the clause on friendship in Creon's initial pronouncement, Gambaro fragments this speech into selected lines delivered by different characters. The line Taylor quotes comes not at the beginning of the play but right after Antígona's funeral rite, voiced by Corifeo without using the shell that represents Creon: "who holds a loved one dearer than his country is despicable!" (142). Here, any beloved (not necessarily blood relatives) falls into this category, and any citizen (Corifeo, the chorus) upholds this ideology: the line indicts the spectators, not Creon.

These dislocations have led critics who seek the ancient text in Gambaro's play to view the latter as a parody of Sophocles. But this approach does not interrogate why Gambaro (and her audience) would need to parody *Sophocles* in 1986 in order to stage the drama of the Mothers.[37] Which text is really being parodied?[38] The parodied phrases come both from the ancient source and from contemporary political speeches. Would Gambaro's target audience have recognized the Sophoclean lines in fragmentation? Most certainly not. But they would have recognized contemporary parodies of political discourse that may be opaque for critics. Thus, the question of parody merits caution.[39]

---

[36] For an introduction, see Andersen (1993), Gasparini (1999), Calveiro (2004), and Crenzel (2010).

[37] To this effect, compare Mogliani (1997) and Castellvi DeMoor (1992); see also Croce (2003), Pellarolo (1992), and del Rosario Moreno (1997). See also Brunn's dissertation: the play "rework[s] a classical tragedy in the form of parody" (2009: 143).

[38] Irmtrud König (2002) associates the play's parodic elements with an "anthropophagic appropriation" of the myth. In an unpublished work, Garay Tapia (2009; see http://repositorio. uchile.cl/handle/2250/109866) studies the play "with respect to a parodied original".

[39] I concur with Cecilia González (2010) (https://lecturesdugenre.fr/category/numero-07-genre-canon-et-monstruosites/) that this is not "a parody of the classical work" (8), but rather a play about the juridical thought of the city, following what for Vernant was the gist of tragedy.

274   GRISELDA GAMBARO'S 1986 *ANTÍGONA FURIOSA*

Perhaps the best example of the limits of parody emerges as Antígona laments her fate. Corifeo and Antinoo demystify any sense of "the tragic":

ANTINOO: The world approves of you!
CORIFEO: No illness, no suffering!
ANTINOO: No sickliness from old age!
CORIFEO: Of all of us, only you [...] will descend, of your own volition, free and alive to death. It is not so tragic!

(SP 210)

Antígona says that they "laugh at her" (Sp 210), and the two men continue: "It was a joke, don't be offended!" (Sp 210). The mockery soon turns sour as Antígona immediately utters the first reference in the play to the disappeared, urging "citizens" to "bear witness" (152): "I will be separated from both humans and those who died, uncounted among the living and among the dead. I will disappear from the world, alive" (152).

The Greek fragments stand in for official political discourse, and the target of parody is the latter, rather than the former. In fact, we could think this was, at least to some extent, Gambaro's strategic classicism: to mock local political cynicism via the solemnity of a classic. Though, as everything in her text, the classic fragment had also an opposite function: granting solemnity to the Mothers' radicalization. After Antígona says she "will disappear," Corifeo and Antinoo continue to mock her. For the audience, their phrases now resonate somberly, for they are emblematic of the worldview of the middle classes that supported the coup. Corifeo says, "There are no innocents. [...] And if punishment comes down on you, you did something you should not have done" (152). Of course, the ancient Antigone did "something." But in Spanish Gambaro uses the future perfect phrase heard in Buenos Aires during the escalation of disappearances: "*something—you must have done something*" ("*algo habrás hecho*"). It refers both to an action that may have happened, or that may happen in the future before another one—in this case, before detention. For the military, if you had not done something already, you would have done it eventually. The phrase has taken on a life of its own and it even generated a 2005 TV history program that ironized it by alluding to prominent contributions to the nation: "*They must have done something—for the history of the nation.*"[40]

---

[40] Created by historian Felipe Pigna, the program aired in November 2005. The title in Spanish was *Algo habrán hecho (por la historia argentina).*

GRISELDA GAMBARO'S 1986 *ANTÍGONA FURIOSA*   275

The political parody is pervasive, even present in an example Poulson uses as historical background in her 2012 article. To personify a historical dispute between political fathers and sons, Gambaro renders the ancient dialogue where Hemon advises Creon that to rule alone would be "to rule in a desert land" (Sp 206), inserting two words in sequential order that echo an internal fight within the Peronist ranks three years before the military coup. Corifeo says: "And they insulted each other. Creon called his son *stupid* and Hemon said his father spoke like a *beardless* youth" (149; Sp "*imberbe*," 208). Perón called the Peronist Youth "stupid and beardless" in his May 1, 1974 speech before a massive demonstration at the Plaza de Mayo. For many Argentines, this revealed the old leader's disconnection from the youth after his twenty years of exile. The massive columns of the Peronist Youth turned around and left the Plaza. Gambaro turns this into metatheater, producing a "masterly phrase" that can be parodied too. The dispute recurs four text pages later when Corifeo calls Antinoo "stupid." Antinoo echoes the youth historically leaving the Plaza: "They insult me: I leave" (154). But Antinoo only wants to return home because the bird plague has arrived. The previous dispute between Hemon and Creon is preceded by Hemon's phrase "alone, you could rule well only in a desert land" (Sp 208). The phrase is repeated twice and both times framed by a metatheatrical comment by Corifeo: "There it is! The phrase" (Sp 208) and "He will make use of a masterly saying" (147). Thus, the youth mocks the elderly (Hemon calling Creon "beardless"), but the chorus also mocks the youth. The "masterly phrase" is a phrase that anyone can utter.

But for an Argentine audience, just as the reference to Antígona's disappearance, the "masterly phrase" creates a semantic reference that expands to another desert, turning mockery into a painful memory. Gambaro's choice of words—"a desert land" (not a city)—takes us to that mythical foundational "desert" in the nineteenth century, the site of the "disappeared Indians." The question of land emerges in two instances. The first Spanish occurrence is delivered by Corifeo and rendered in English, according to Feitlowitz's (1992) translation, as "one can rule a desert beautifully alone" (147).[41] Antígona repeats Corifeos' sentence later, but in the conditional tense: "*solo*, podrías *mandar bien en una tierra desierta*" (Sp 208), "alone, you *could* rule well in a desert land" (149; my translation). Corifeo delivers a fact: one can rule. Antígona's repetition implies that one could rule alone, if one were alone. In Spanish "alone" and "only" are the same

---

[41] In Spanish it reads: "solo, se puede mandar bien en una tierra desierta" (Sp 206).

276 GRISELDA GAMBARO'S 1986 *ANTÍGONA FURIOSA*

word: "*solo*." Rendered orally, the performer could use intonation to transform the phrase "alone, you can rule well in a desert land" into "you can only rule well" in a land that politics has rendered a barren desert. The repeated "masterly phrase" parodies the modern characters, though Antígona never lends herself to parody except by the two observers, who are, in turn, parodied.

The poetic function of textual fragmentation and iteration of words overrides that of parody. The decomposition of words in Spanish impacts the ear like music. In English, Antígona's line reads: "Creon forbade it. Creon, decree-on, decree, you will kill me" (141). In Spanish it reads: "*Creon te te creo te creo Creon te que me matarás*" (20). This line plays with the Spanish spelling of Creon ("Creonte") decomposing it into the words "te" (reflexive second-person singular) and "creo" (first-person simple present indicative of "to believe"). She thus repeats the phrase "te creo": "I believe you." Depending on the performative rendition, the line could be a playful game or the stuttering prophecy that Creon will indeed kill her.

The above fragmentations reflect Gambaro's penchant for the Artaudian theater of cruelty, albeit in the humorous light with which she "touches" the audience, as she says of her work.[42] The verbal fragmentation provides musical rhythm. For example, I translate literally (not literarily) a fragment delivered by Corifeo as he walks forward with hypnotic emphasis: "Creon. Creon applies the law. Creon. Creon applies the law *en lo tocante* [in what touches]. Creon applies the law *en lo tocante* [in what touches] the dead. Creon. And. The living. The same law" (Sp 200; punctuation modified).[43] I have literalized the Spanish expression "en lo tocante," which in English should be "in what concerns," as "in what touches." Creon's power "touches" (*toca*) the body, as much as the verbal repetition "touches" our ears and enters our defenseless body. Likewise, in clear reference to the Mothers circling the Plaza de Mayo, and in the same speech, we cannot escape the physical rhythm of the following phrase (translated literally to convey the "sound" not the signified): "let no one turn—dare—turn turn like the mad woman turning around the unburied unburied unburied corpse" (Sp 201).[44]

---

[42] Interview, Guthmann (1988).

[43] Feitlowitz translates: "Creon. Creon applies the law. Creon. Creon applies the law, in the matter of the traitor and the true. Creon applies the law touching on the dead and the living. The same law" (1992: 140). The edition in Spanish with which I work does not include the phrase "in the matter of the traitor and the true."

[44] Feitlowitz translates: "let no one come near—dare—to come near, like the mad girl circling, circling, the unburied, unburied unburied corpse" (1992: 141).

GRISELDA GAMBARO'S 1986 *ANTÍGONA FURIOSA* 277

Distance: Fragmentation as Palimpsest

Parody for Gambaro lies in her poetry and politics, not closeness to the Greek source. Should we not focus then on Gambaro's distance from Sophocles? For Patrick Dove, Gambaro's play shows the inadequacy of the tragic genre to account for postdictatorial memory.[45] Carlson (2003) and Forsyth (2009) concur in viewing Gambaro's aesthetics as foregrounding violence and pain. Mogliani (1997) isolates all of Gambaro's distancing strategies: "stylization," "condensation," "temporality," "narration," "denial," "transgression," and "contextualization." Nelli (2009) identifies elements alien to the Greek source—such as the conflict between fear and duty in Antígona.[46] Scabuzzo (2000) concludes that the only presence of the Greek source is Antigone's lament and suffering. She inscribes Gambaro in the tradition of Cocteau's 1922 "contraction" of the classic. Romina Turchi (2008) considers the text's ideas of tragic, circular, and female temporality. For Nieves Martínez de Olcoz (1995), Antígona's object is the legal body, and the play meditates on female resistance.

Gambaro wanted an autonomous text. As she said in 1986: "At first we thought of following the original. Until I was able to break the spell [...]. I forgot about that Antígona and I threw myself into a different project" (in Catena 2011: 88). She did not research ancient Greek culture nor read other versions of the tragedy, save for one in French.[47] She did not consider her play as "a version" of the ancient tragedy, since "some works of art do not allow for that without falling into arrogance."[48] She gave up: "I would not adapt *Antigone*. I needed to produce an independent play [...]. The method consisted of extracting from *Antigone*, despite the profound respect I felt, the fear of using quotations and the fear of comparisons" (1995: 57). History made Gambaro feel a deep "separation from Sophocles": "not only by my lack of knowledge of the culture of his times, but also by my own history and by my gender. I would write with the voice of a Latin American and Argentine woman and with the voices of other women who had tried to do, in Argentina, what Antígona did" (1995: 57).[49]

---

[45] Dove (2013) follows Derrida's and Copjec's meditations on Antigone as unsubsumable into any universality.

[46] Nelli's second article (2010) associates Antigone with Agamben's concept of "bare life."

[47] Gambaro mentions an 1840 translation; Adolphe Regnier translated *Antigone* that year.

[48] See Luongo (1999: 424).

[49] In 1992, Jorge Liderman presented the Munich premiere of his operatic version by saying that "it is the attempt of two men to tell the story of their people by way of commenting on Sophocles' Antigone"; see "Antigona Furiosa: Oper in einem Akt für Sänger, Pianisten und

278 GRISELDA GAMBARO'S 1986 *ANTÍGONA FURIOSA*

Extractivism could be a name for Gambaro's cannibalization of the ancient text. She fragmented, extracted, and quilted back together ancient fragments to modern texts and genres as well as to different temporal frames. In doing so, she played with Spanish language as much as with Western philosophical and theatrical traditions. For Gambaro, her influences allowed "the intrusion of other historical moments into the story, and [...] a frame within which all time periods might fit" (1995: 57). Temporally, the first scene already launches a disconcerting spectator experience, switching from contemporary Argentina to Elizabethan England to Ancient Greece and back. Then there are sporadic itineraries through the nineteenth century on both sides of the Atlantic. The nonlinear temporality, framed by the circularity of the same beginning and end (Antígona's birth/death), weaves together a dense palimpsest of texts across disciplines.

As to antiquity, it is not exhausted with Antigone's lines. Antinoo echoes the grandfather of antiquity, Homer, and his *Odyssey*. Antinoo adds to the disconcerting spectator experience the presence of an ambiguous mythical memory. Antinous is not only Penelope's violent and arrogant leading suitor but also the faithful favorite (and lover) of the Roman emperor Hadrian.[50] He is both active and passive, pursuer and persecuted, victimizer and victimized. In the play, he reflects this ambiguity, shifting positions according to Corifeos' opinions. He is mocked but is also capable of mockery. He defends Creon's lines but also mediates between the main antagonists. While Corifeo appears ferocious, threatening, or even smiling in stage directions, Antinoo is complex. He expresses emotional uncertainty—timid, fearful, exaggerated, parodic, disturbed, and happy.

The Renaissance weighs heavily as the first modern temporal frame, with Gambaro's title echoing Ludovico Ariosto's *Orlando Furioso* and, of course, the overlap between Antígona and Hamlet's Ophelia.[51] The nineteenth

---

Schlagzeuger," at http://archive.muenchener-biennale.de/en/archive/1992/programm/events/event/detail/antigona-furiosa/.

[50] In Argentina in 1999, Daniel Herrendorf wrote a parallel memoir after reading Marguerite Yourcenar's *Memoirs of Hadrian* (1951), this time from Antinoos' point of view, titled *Memorias de Antínoo* (2000). Carlos Cossio wrote a poem to Antinoo (1967). Scabuzzo (2000) related that Gambaro told her the name Antinoo sounded "beautiful."

[51] I concur with Dove's suggestion (2013) that the title echoes antiquity too (the Greek Erinyes of terror and vengeance). Pianacci (2008) adds a modern temporality referring to Woolf's *Orlando* (91).

GRISELDA GAMBARO'S 1986 *ANTÍGONA FURIOSA* 279

century appears with lines from Nicaraguan poet Rubén Darío's (1867–1916) "Sonatina" (1893) and from philosopher Søren Kierkegaard's (1813–55) 1843 meditation on faith, *Fear and Trembling*. The twentieth century makes a fleeting presence with echoes of two Latin American writers of silence: Alejandra Pizarnik (1936–72) and Augusto Monterroso (1921–2003).

These four temporal frames quilt the epistemological, legal, and ethical concerns that Gambaro sets forth to her audience. The last phrase of Shakespeare's Hamlet, "the rest is silence," grants Gambaro the firmest quilting point connecting the ancient Antigone with her contemporary heroines, the Mothers, and an unlikely sister, Ophelia. For all these women, first was justice, fury, vengeance—the rest was silence. As Gambaro's memory of the Greek sister receded, that of the Danish and the Argentine ones emerged. Ophelia's song provides *Antígona Furiosa*'s first words, as she sings while she unties her noose (in quotation marks in print), as if quoting Ophelia, from act 4, scene 5 of the play. The two men at the café fail to recognize her identity at first sight:

CORIFEO: Who is that? Ophelia? (*they laugh*. Antígona *looks at them*). Waiter! Another coffee!

ANTÍGONA (*SINGS*): "He is dead and gone, Lady. He is dead and gone. At his head a grass-green turf. At his heels a stone."

CORIFEO: There should be, but there are no stones. Do you see grass? Do you see stone? Do you see tomb?

ANTINOO: Nothing!

ANTÍGONA (*SINGS*): Larded with all sweet flowers, which bewept to the grave did not go with true-love showers (*she looks at the cups with curiosity*) What are you drinking?

CORIFEO: Coffee.

ANTÍGONA: What is that? Coffee.

CORIFEO: Try it.

ANTÍGONA: No. (*she points*). Dark as poison.

(137; SP 197)

The unsettled temporal frames that this scene reveals weave the epistemological questions embedded in the play and in the Argentine debate about justice for the unburied "dead and gone." Taylor reads in this opening scene a "failure of witnessing," following her concept of a "percepticide" that the dictatorship would have produced by teaching the population "not to see"

280   GRISELDA GAMBARO'S 1986 *ANTÍGONA FURIOSA*

violence as it happened.[52] For Taylor, Gambaro's two men fail "to see this tragedy as their own" (1997: 213). But "percepticide" is not an accurate description of what people saw or did not see: in turning the entire population into victims, the concept bypasses the reality that the military coup only succeeded because vast sectors of civil society saw and approved of what was happening. And the latter is Gambaro's concern.

The men at the café recognize a woman. Theirs is the perception of a problem: who are they in fact seeing? *Hamlet's* very first line is "Who is there?" and the palace guards are uncertain of their perception; Antígona herself has a problem of perception. She asks what she is, in fact, seeing: coffee? Gambaro stages not a failure of witnessing but an engagement with witnessing: how to interpret what one sees? The "What is that? Who is there?" is the mystery that Gambaro poses for the audience, who will have to exercise detection in nonlinear temporality.

The Mothers inhabit a zone of uncertainty, both as subjects and as objects: they ask, where are the disappeared? Is it possible to know the complete list of those who disappeared? Citizens also ask of the Mothers: who are they? The question also provides a metonymy for a more disturbing puzzle that permeates both the play and also the real-life citizens' perception of the Mothers' insistence during and after dictatorship: what do they want? As Corifeo says after Antígona acts out the fratricidal battle: "what does this mad woman pretend to do? Breed grief over grief?" (Sp 199). The English version translates "girl" for woman and "try" for pretend. The English translation connotes an effort, the Spanish "pretend" preserves a polysemy implying desire: to "want" (or lay claim to) something that we think we deserve but also to "court" someone for love. It is also a theatrical verb: to "act as if." The "who is that" is Gambaro's male spectators' question about the mad woman's desire: what do all these women—the Mothers, Antígona, Ophelia—really want?

---

[52] In both her study of Gambaro's and of Watanabe's Antígonas, as well as in her assessment of cultural politics in the aftermath of violence in the region at large, Taylor uses European frameworks stemming from the experience of Nazism. The applicability of this framework is debatable, though this exceeds the scope of this book. Suffice here to quote Huyssen: "While the Holocaust as universal trope of traumatic history has migrated into other, unrelated contexts, one must always ask whether and how the trope enhances or hinders local memory practices and struggles" (2000: 26). Two elements should be a starting point for debate: this region is not fully industrialized and, thus, Hitler's "machinery" does not translate easily as the paramount form of state violence; and the collective memory of genocidal "histories of violence" in this region dates back to the 1500s.

GRISELDA GAMBARO'S 1986 *ANTÍGONA FURIOSA*   281

Gambaro's insertion of Darío's lines, in which the princess is sad because there is no prince for her in sight, also refers to the mystery of women's desire. The two men speak of Antígona's lament that she will not have her beloved, as follows:

ANTINOO: Yes! Daughter of Oedipus and Yocasta. A princess.
CORIFEO: *She is sad/what ails the Princess?/nothing but sighs escape from her strawberry lips*
ANTINOO: *her mouth that does not beg nor kiss*
CORIFEO: if only she could have kept quiet and the corpse of her brother not buried/to Hemon she could have married![53]

Both Darío's lines and Gambaro's chorus answer the question of the princess's desire with a corresponding male fantasy: she wants a prince—what else? Gambaro has Corifeo liken the poem's prince to Hemon. Antígona momentarily asks Creon to let her marry Hemon. But soon enough, she "cries out her name, summoning pride" (stage directions)—"Antígona!"— and snaps out of the romantic rant that she fell into: "she stands up, firm, defiantly" and shouts: "I did it! I did it!" (144). For Corifeo, she is "mad!" (144): what else to call a woman who snaps out of that romantic fantasy?

Antígona wants burial, not marriage, like her ancient sister (and unlike many of her Latin American sisters who want both burial and marriage). For all their hesitation in the first scene, the men at the table discern a presence and utter an ethical judgment. The presence is ghostly, like Hamlet's father; Antígona's speech is of uncertain coherence, like Ophelia's "reason." But the men are certain of the ethicopolitical judgment in her first lines: they "see" the absence of tombs, and Corifeo thinks there "should be" tombs. Immediately after this dialogue, we learn of the unburied Polinices. Epistemological uncertainty is thus coupled with ethical certainty: they don't know who she is, but they recognize the right to burial. Nevertheless, they willfully do not care about it. Acknowledging what is right, they proceed with what is convenient. The spectacle for

---

[53] My italics indicate Darío's lines and isolated words with which Gambaro plays. The standard translation of this poem is Kemp's (not used in Feilowitz's translation of Gambaro's play). I have modified both Feilowitz's English translation and, slightly, Kemp's translation of the poem, approximating the wordplay in Spanish and following Gambaro's modification of Darío's lines. "Corifeo: Está triste,/ ¿Qué tendrá la princesa? / Los suspiros se escapan de su boca de fresa. Antinoo: Que no ruega ni besa." (204)

282 GRISELDA GAMBARO'S 1986 *ANTÍGONA FURIOSA*

Gambaro's audience at this historical time is one of complicity—or "cynical reason."[54]

Antígona's second reference to *Hamlet* in the first scene is poison. Right after this, back in ancient temporal frame, the "plague" (and its corresponding ghosts) is mentioned. For Antígona–Ophelia, coffee looks like poison. Corifeo uses the verb "poison" to speak as if he is dead: "Yes, we poison ourselves," and laughs, "I am dead!" (Sp 198). The Spanish rendition of the verb "poison" is temporally ambiguous: the first-person plural of the indicative simple present and the indefinite past have the same spelling (*"nos envenenamos"*). Thus, we poison—but also we "poisoned"—ourselves: Corifeo speaks from death. Once poisoned, is he Hamlet's father? Antinoo turns historical time yet again: "Forbidden! His plague is contagious!"—back to Greece to Polynices' corpse. Antígona asks "Forbidden?" and breaks Corifeos' crown: there is no king on this stage. Corifeo mocks Polinices, shouting "nobody will bury me! [...] Dogs will eat me!" and laughs (138). Corifeo seems dead on many levels: he is Hamlet senior, perhaps, the dead king, and the dead Polynices. Who will care for the corpse of Corifeo–Polinices–Hamlet? Who is responsible for these crimes?

Gambaro's theater of ambiguity dramatizes the epistemological uncertainty that drove the Mothers to the Plaza, as well as the ethical certainty that possessed them. The intense contemporary public debate about who, besides the Generals, deserved trial after dictatorship encompassed both the uncertainty of what had happened and the certainty of what should have happened and should then happen.

Gambaro's ethical certainty makes a second appearance when Corifeo alludes to Antígona in Kierkegaardian terms: she suffers "fear and trembling" (143).[55] Antígona repeats the phrase before confessing to having blurred the limits between ritual and theater by performing burial on stage. Kierkegaard's reference condenses Antígona's silence and universal ethical commitment. He published under the pseudonym "John the Silent" his essay *Fear and Trembling*, meditating on the tragic, by shifting focus from his earlier 1843 text *Either/Or*. While before he had thought of the tragic in the aesthetic realm, in *Fear* Kierkegaard placed the tragic in relation to the

---

[54] See Sloterdijk's cynic formula: "'they know very well what they are doing, but still, they are doing it'" ([1983] 1987: 28).

[55] The Spanish translation of Kierkegaard's text is *Temor y temblor* (see, for instance, Jaime Gringberg's translation, Buenos Aires: Losada, 1958). Gambaro uses these words.

GRISELDA GAMBARO'S 1986 *ANTÍGONA FURIOSA* 283

ethical: a conflict between a subjective ethical commitment—the love for a child—and a universal ethical commitment—the love for all. The tragic entails the sacrifice of the subjective commitment for a higher version of that same ethical commitment. In Kierkegaard's text about the Greek legend of Agamemnon, the hero ceases to be the father of a child and becomes the father of his people. He thus articulates—though for Kierkegaard this is only possible on stage and not in real life—the ethical command to universality.

But it is precisely an ethical command to universality that Antígona represents—in contrast to Ismena—and that transformed the Mothers in 1986 in real life, when half of them abandoned the search for their own children and, instead, lifted the banner "back alive" for all the disappeared of the nation. Antígona's commitment to eternal return represents this universal. This commitment may appear tragic in its "Kierkegaardian silence": it has no prospect of success within the confines of the system where it is proposed. The Mothers' universal demand was systemic change: How to find *all* the dead? How to judge *all* those responsible? The realization of this universal lies beyond available social conventions, beyond the limits of known language. It is to be related to only negatively, in fear and trembling. What would such justice look like? Antígona remains silent in the end: a new justice has not yet been imagined, in a world where hate commands. In the stage directions, we read twice of Antígona's "fury" at this hatred: "But hate rules. (*Furious*). The rest is silence! (*She kills herself. With fury*)" (159).[56]

The epistemic impossibility—how to know where the disappeared are, where to find them—matches the ethical certainty which has been revealed as an impossible universal. "Silence"—Hamlet's, Antígona's—expresses all uncertainties: all possibilities not yet here.[57] Silence voids politics of content and confronts us with the force of politics as antagonism—as always demanding the impossible. But the hope brought about by art lies in Antígona's and Hamlet's last phrase "the rest is silence," as the rest is both "everything" and the "remainder."

---

[56] Hamlet's phrase "the rest is silence" was first translated as "para mí, solo queda ya...silencio eterno" ("for me, only eternal silence remains now") by Leandro Fernández de Moratín in 1798. See http://www.cervantesvirtual.com/portales/biblioteca_traducciones_espanolas/obra-visor/hamlet-tragedia--0/html/ffc3d04c-82b1-11df-acc7-002185ce6064_244.html. Modern translations are more literal: "el resto es silencio." The most recent in Argentina (to my knowledge) is Eduardo Rinesi's 2016 translation published by Ediciones UNGS, Buenos Aires.

[57] See Pellettieri (1992) and Lusnich (2001) for Gambaro's intracorpus references to the metaphor of silence.

284 GRISELDA GAMBARO'S 1986 *ANTÍGONA FURIOSA*

In *Hamlet*, silence is absolute for him but not for others: the last word is Horatio's, who remains alive to narrate Hamlet's life. Before collapsing into silence, Hamlet has given his vote to the king, Fortinbras, who may set Denmark right. Both kings are led by the same motive: revenge through justice, granted by their "rights of memory," as Fortinbras says (act 5, scene 2). In Kierkegaard's meditation on the tragic in aesthetics, ethics, and religiosity, silence is not realizable but foundational. After all, is John the Silent not a "Horatio figure"? He tells the story of Abraham's silence, articulating the experience that exists within the realm of ethics, but not in the language of rational ethics. In *Antígona* there are two men—the audience—who will need to account for her suicide.

Gambaro's dramatic palimpsest would not be complete without mentioning two writers of her generation. Both left their poetic testament with the idea of silence "beyond language." In 1978, Guatemalan short story writer Augusto Monterroso wrote his only novel, *Lo demás es silencio: la vida y obra de Eduardo Torres* (The rest is silence: the life and work of Eduardo Torres), about the life of a fictional writer.[58] A relentless parody of authorship and intertextuality, Monterroso's novel, like Gambaro's theater, cites clichés and fragments that deconstruct linearity, originality, and authorial control. All is silence, but Monterroso writes his parody.

In 1972, Argentine "poète maudite" Alejandra Pizarnik, whose poetry hovers over the idea of silence, took her own life. Obsessed with language's failure, with solitude, absence, and fear, she searched the eternal promise of language to exorcise and repair. In 1971, Pizarnik dedicated a poem titled "On This Night and In This World" to her friend Martha Isabel Moia. Its first stanza ends with "nothing is promise, within the sayable, which is equivalent to lying (all that is sayable is a lie), the rest is silence; only, silence does not exist."[59] To Moia, she talked of this poem in an interview: "I believe silence does not exist." In 1969, Pizarnik wrote to Antonio Beneyto: "I don't like that there is silence where there should be language."[60] In the poem, silence is truth's promise, but insofar as it does not exist, the truth cannot be distinguished from lies. There is no "rest" outside the house of language: what remains is to speak about not speaking.

---

[58] See Monterroso (2003).
[59] Pizarnik (1990). The Spanish reads: "y nada es promesa/ entre lo decible/ que equivale a mentir (todo lo que se puede decir es mentira)/ el resto es silencio/ sólo que el silencio no existe" (63).
[60] Pizarnik (2003: 53).

GRISELDA GAMBARO'S 1986 *ANTÍGONA FURIOSA*   285

Only lies for Pizarnik, only hatred for Antígona, only parody for Monterroso. Like Hamlet and Fortinbras, nobody negotiates. With their "Kierkegaardian" air, the three references—to Hamlet, Pizarnik, Monterroso—condense in the famous phrase "the rest is silence" no degree of negotiation: nothing counts, save what they seek, be it justice, truth, parody, or language itself. There should be language, there should be tombs, there should be justice around universal ethical commitments.

For Gambaro's audience, the signifier "silence" haunted the stage with the all-too-recent sound of history. During the dictatorship, just a few years before 1986, the phrase "silence is health" appeared in publicity campaigns: the military wanted to combat automobile "urban noise." As the leader of the 1976 coup Lieutenant General Videla said in 1977, "it is a time for silence."[61] But noise for the military was equivalent to citizen's speech. And speech could mean death. Except that, confronting the military, those "crazy" mothers broke silence and shouted desperately at the Plaza. Just as Antígona did, they shouted louder in 1986.

The Mothers: Missed Encounters with Theater Criticism

Gambaro frequently clarified that her characters tell the story of the Mothers:

> [...] when I had finished telling the story, I could see, not so much that Antígona who has been present in so many pages, but rather those Antígonas who every Thursday, during the most difficult days of military rule [...] carrying photos of their children, walked [in circles] around the square, shaking with fear. [...] Most of them were threatened or suffered jail, and some, like Antígona, paid for their disobedience with their lives.
>
> (1995: 58)

For Gambaro, Antígona is one of those Mothers, who act amid riveting fear but are stronger than it. For Antígona, Ismena's courage out of fear is better than Antígona's, which comes out of principles (146). The Mothers' movement, its universal principles, its fear, and its love, compose each sister's

---

[61] The two phrases in Spanish were "el silencio es salud" and "Es un tiempo para el silencio." For the latter, see Videla's declarations in *Clarín*, Buenos Aires, March 7, 1977.

286   GRISELDA GAMBARO'S 1986 *ANTÍGONA FURIOSA*

character on stage. Antígona says: she wants justice "because of justice itself"; Ismena "because of love" (Sp 206).[62]

The history that inspired Gambaro prompts critics to extend the analogy between the Mothers and Gambaro's Antígona. The ancient Antigone figures prominently also among public intellectuals in Buenos Aires to account for the Mothers' appearance in the public sphere. But Anglophone critics have paid little attention to history when projecting the analogy between Antigone and Antígona Furiosa onto the Mothers in order to assess not just the play but the Mothers themselves.[63] Critics have tended to mechanically apply Hegelian readings of the ancient Antigone to the Mothers: just as Hegel's Antigone represented family values, the Mothers embraced the ideology of the family; their political life would have been doomed from the start, for they would have been trapped in a patriarchal script about motherhood. Taylor paved the way for these critical equivalences in her oft-cited articles about Antígona and the Mothers (1996 and 1997). My historical comments here aim at dislocating these mechanical associations, reading history very closely.

Working within a performance studies frame, Taylor concludes that Gambaro's Antígona represents the Mothers under military rule.[64] For Taylor, the Mothers' politics during dictatorship bear the same kind of performative analysis that the play does. The Mothers followed a "script," and state terrorism was "theatrical." Within the play, Gambaro's Antígona remains caged, embodying the dilemma of whether women can be empowered by appropriating patriarchal roles and language (1997: 216). Outside the theater, Taylor sees the Mothers' circular walks around the Plaza as a symbolic caging. Gambaro's Antígona encapsulates the Mothers' "contradictions": they "showed how motherhood was a social [...] construct," but ended up "trapped in a bad script" (185): patriarchal notions of motherhood, which prevented the Mothers from challenging women's position in patriarchy. The Mothers "did not (at least initially) challenge the social system nor women's positions within it. They simply wanted their children back" (219). In brief, they "[were] not feminists, if by feminists one means the politicization of the female subordinate status [...]" (195) and "their

---

[62] For allusions to the Mothers, see also Holledge and Tompkins (2000), Werth (2010), Brunn (2009), Pianacci (2008: 90–2), Forsyth (2009), Nelli (2009, 2010), Wannamaker (2000–1), and Taylor (1997).

[63] As I mentioned in Chapter 5, this is also the case with Spargo's comments on Dorfman's *Widows*. See Fradinger (2013).

[64] Taylor discusses Pellarolo's view that Antígona is "the people" (1997: 216); see Pellarolo (1992).

GRISELDA GAMBARO'S 1986 *ANTÍGONA FURIOSA* 287

decision was a conscious political choice. They could have [...] performed as women, wives, sisters, or human rights activists. The Women in Black, from the Gaza Strip, include, but do not focus on motherhood" (1994: 300). In the "long term" they changed "little" in Argentina, having been locked in "identity politics" and "their use of performance" (1997: 202).[65]

When Taylor focused on some historical contingencies, she could only conclude ambiguously: "On one level [...] the military and the Madres enacted a collective fantasy, a *paso de dos*, that reaffirmed the negativity of the female partner [...] Looking beyond the maternal level, however, [they] redefined the meaning of mothers, family, and home in a patriarchal society" (1997: 205). According to Taylor, the performance of motherhood was "restrictive" but also "freed" them from the "socially restrictive role of motherhood" (1997: 206). That "they could not do everything, that is, *seriously* challenge patriarchal authority, does not mean they could do nothing" (1997: 207; my emphasis). But what could be more serious than knowingly risking one's life to challenge the armed institution that monopolizes violence in a patriarchal society?

The above assignment of traditional women's roles to the Mothers, and to Antígona, reappears in much criticism of this play. Brunn assesses that Antígona's ritual does not "envision a possibility of change" due to its circularity (2009: 135) and asks, citing Taylor, "if the Madres have been reenacting their drama within the deadly constraints of the patriarchal narrative, how are their limitations translated within the vicious circles of repetition from which Antígona cannot break through?" (164). Brunn provides no historical evidence to assess the Mothers: "their movement has never embraced all of Argentine society. Even the participation of the male

---

[65] Taylor's interviews with the Mothers did not convince her that the Mothers were following strategy rather than belief in adopting the role of the sacrificial Mater Dolorosa; the Mothers' opinions about Evita Perón as a model were not enough for Taylor either. Nonetheless, everything was historical contingency at the time. The Mothers' iconic symbol, white kerchiefs over their heads (initially cloth diapers), was thought the best way not to lose track of each other among the multitude when, in 1977, they decided to walk with the massive religious Youth Procession to the sanctuary of the Virgin of Luján. As to Evita, Taylor did not grant her a performative analysis but read her biography literally, concluding Evita's was part of the "bad script" into which the Mothers were trapped (1997: 186). But for the Mothers, Evita meant freedom. For the massive mobilization of women under Evita's leadership, see Barry, Ramacciotti, and Valobra 2008. Although Peronist women are seen as "patriarchal," the only four Peronist women who remained as legislators in the late 1950s proposed one of the most radically feminist labor laws imaginable: wages for domestic work. The Mothers have also been vocal about how politics made them feminists (see the interview with Mother Nora Cortiñas in Bolles 2006).

288 GRISELDA GAMBARO'S 1986 *ANTÍGONA FURIOSA*

relatives of the victims of persecution has been limited [...] it came to highlight the role of women as custodians of the national memory of trauma" (167).

Rather than seriously engaging history, this criticism projects and performs its own cultural assumptions and ironically ends by being another performance of patriarchal discourse. The Mothers, and Antígona, appear to bear a strange form of "lack" that corresponds more to age-old patriarchal notions of women as insufficient or incomplete than to their historical reality: they should have embraced "all" of Argentine society, they should have been more feminist, found nonpatriarchal language, advanced women's rights, presented a "serious" challenge to patriarchy, and so on. But what does it mean to view the women, who actually had their children kidnapped, as "enacting a collective fantasy that reaffirmed the negativity of the female partner"? On what grounds can one forget the tragic predicament of someone searching for the missing, who if they renounce the possibility of saving a still-living person, risks becoming like a killer themselves? The Mothers had the wisdom to translate this possibility into political speech: everyone "back alive." As Tilda Albani put it, "if they took them alive they should be returned alive; if they are dead, then someone has to take responsibility, but we will not be the ones who say they are dead."[66] Why would a mother whose son has been kidnapped want to leave her home to fight for women's rights? Why would fighting for a son to reappear alive not represent a woman's right to politics—for the return of politics, law, and justice?

The above criticism misses the encounter with history: Gambaro's text is used to assess a historical movement ahistorically. An essential trait of political action is lost: its situated contingency. The Mothers are blamed for submitting to patriarchy, but critics only understand the Mothers (and motherhood) through a patriarchal lens—and Antígona through a Hegelian lens. Motherhood becomes a universal, essentialized phenomenon of oppression, rather than a situated, polysemic practice in need of historical analysis. In Gambaro's theater, it is actually the men who are lacking: they are buffoons, and, as Puga well notes, Creon is not "even granted a full-time actor" (2008: 185). Forsyth describes Gambaro's two men as a "denigration of Argentine machismo," reducing "dictatorial patriarchy to little more than an 'act' in costume" (2009: 35).[67] Historically, those who lacked the means to deal with the Mothers were military men.

---

[66] See the documentary *Memorias de la memoria* about the organization Relatives of the Disappeared at Memoria Abierta's website: http://www.memoriaabierta.org.ar/wp/.

[67] Critics such as Scott (1993) and Fleming (1995, 1999) concur on this point; see also Wannamaker (2000–1).

GRISELDA GAMBARO'S 1986 *ANTÍGONA FURIOSA*   289

To assert that the Mothers brought "little change" in the "long term" has uncertain value in an article not written within the discipline of history.[68] To compare the Mothers to Women in Black misses that the latter do not present themselves as fighting for "women's" rights but rather as women against militarization—and they cite the inspiration of the Mothers at that. To consider that any other category—women, wives, sisters—would be better than that of "mother" misses that all these categories are strategic: they have all been "constructed" by patriarchy, especially that of "women." The idea that the Mothers who defied the military did not "seriously" challenge patriarchy reveals only ignorance about life under dictatorship and culturally specific assumptions about how to challenge patriarchy, what the term "feminism" means, or what it means to become political, as the Mothers did. To assume that males were not part of this movement overlooks the complexity of human rights in Argentina.

There is a reason, after all, why Gambaro could say: "the non-impunity is one of the things for which I am proud of Argentina because I believe that it is the country that has most defended its memory."[69] The multilateral Argentine human rights movement, which started before the military coup, set unprecedented standards internationally with the civilian trials of the military and the double rejection of amnesty laws—the second time by annulling presidential pardons granted in the 1990s (also a unique case internationally).[70] The Mothers are only part of this vast movement—no doubt a crucial part. As Nora Cortiñas reminds us, fathers were always there too: "when they detained us [...] the fathers would be in charge of looking for the lawyers to get us out."[71] In 1994, the younger generations moved the legacy forward by founding H.I.J.O.S. (Sons and Daughters for Identity and Justice Against Oblivion and Silence). For Gambaro, "the ideal

---

[68] President Néstor Kirchner (1950–2010) who declared himself to be the "son of the Mothers" in 2003, overturned the presidential pardons to the military; military trials restarted in 2006.

[69] Catena (2011: 171).

[70] For an introduction to human rights in the country, see Sikkink (2008) and Leis (1989). See also the current website coordinated by five organizations, *Memoria Abierta* (Open Memory): http://www.memoriaabierta.org.ar/eng/; and Mother Laura Bonaparte's testimony: *Laura Bonaparte, una Madre de Plaza de Mayo contra el olvido* (2010). In an interview, she said: "Relatives, husbands, brothers, sisters, colleagues, they were all on our side [...] there were people, brave lawyers, foreign journalists, ready to give testimony [...] and without the Truth Commission and the report, Never Again, maybe we would not have resisted to this day" (*Página 12*, November 22, 2010). For a historical view, consider that today human rights are taught in primary school (universities have offered courses on ethics and human rights since the 1990s). In 2006, a law declared March 24 (the day of the coup) a national holiday.

[71] See interview with Graciela di Marco in Bolles (2006).

290 GRISELDA GAMBARO'S 1986 *ANTÍGONA FURIOSA*

would be to construct an unheard of space in politics, such as the one the Mothers built, for instance" (in Catena 2011: 212).

My critical gesture in the search for historical specificity follows in the steps of John Fleming's review of Jill Scott's 1993 reading of *Antígona Furiosa*. Scott reads the play as a critique of Hegel's interpretation of Antigone. For Fleming, Scott's critique suits the desires of the Anglophone academy but says nothing of Gambaro's community (1999). Likewise, the laments that the Mothers are "not feminists" (whatever this might mean) may be a projection of the need of certain academics to reconsider their own "feminist" struggles after joining the patriarchal institution of the university.

Scott's exciting analysis of Gambaro's Antígona as figuring Derrida's feminization of "ça" into "sa," and representing "unlimited semiosis" challenging the "logocentric" Hegelian dialectical oppositions of "family/state," "dissolving patriarchal discourse" through her own gendered version of desire (1993: 106), takes up Luce Irigaray's critique of masculine modernity. Scott concludes that Antígona's "lack of position" and her "no home" show "more a freedom than a hindrance to her political influence" (106). Scott quotes only one line from the text. It happens to be a line that Gambaro carefully chose for her target audience: "who will I share my house with? [...] I will not be counted among the dead or the living. I will disappear from the world alive" (Sp 210). In an interview for *Clarín* on December 14, 1979, Junta leader Videla defined the disappeared: "they are an enigma [...] they are not there, they are neither dead nor alive, they are *desaparecidos*." Antígona's "neither dead nor alive" presented little "unlimited semiosis" for Argentines who saw in her the figure of their own disappeared. When considering Scott's analysis, we must ask: for whom does Antígona's lack of home mean freedom?

Performance studies approaches to the Mothers' visible political language also have limits. Taylor's (1997) analysis uses Richard Schechner's concept of performance: "twice-behaved behavior" or "restored behavior." Schechner defines performance as "actions or scripts that can be stored, transmitted, manipulated, and transformed [...] performance means 'never for the first time'" (1985: 35). And yet, this concept falls short for a study of the Mothers' actions. For the Mothers, it *was* about a "first" time: though there are heroic scripts to inhabit when facing the risk of death (or in the case of motherhood, in the event of biological birth, always a risk to the mother's life), there is hardly a script that will match the event of actual violence. The stakes are the irreversible risk of death. A contingent strategy for a violent

GRISELDA GAMBARO'S 1986 *ANTÍGONA FURIOSA* 291

situation in its specific novelty needs to prevail—and, as we know, any strategy will fail in some cases. Consider the example of "performing femininity" to survive a rape attack, its successes and its failures. Schechner needed to ponder this detail. He asked what, if anything in real life, might fall out of his category of "twice-behaved behavior" (performance) and gave only one example: a patient undergoing surgery. Even if the doctors are "performing" their profession (learned behaviors), Schechner notes, for the patient the stakes fall outside of the purview of his analysis: it is about life or death (2013).[72]

When the Mothers first went to the Plaza, there was no script in the order of "twice-performed" behavior. Like Schechner's doctors, they knew how to perform as "mothers." But they were not just mothers. The Mothers were new mother-figures: "mothers of a politically disappeared person," created by the military, who resignified motherhood by stripping mothers of motherhood. Like Schechner's patient in surgery, they constituted a group under threat of death, in the outlawed "theater" of a public space in a state of siege. Instead, Gambaro's play was the twice-performed space of the ritualized, normative, urban "spectacle."

The stakes involved in the Mothers' case allow us to shift focus. A performance studies point of view, rather than asking whether they performed "patriarchal motherhood," should be asking a real, historical, question: what was it in their improvised "performance" that allowed them to survive? And how was this performance for survival possible? The Mothers' task was to survive because they transgressed physically a forbidden space. Their bodies were at stake, more than their symbols. Some of their performances failed: some Mothers were assassinated. While the possibility of failure is integral to the bodily event of performance, in this case it meant death.[73]

Ironically, the military rightly applied a performance studies model to the Mothers, and they saw them as "performing" a dangerous political script, rather than a "familial," patriarchal, one. The Mothers were actually the opposite of the family. Even more than political, the military viewed their script as military: the Mothers were labeled "terrorist mothers," and their public display of emotions was seen as "emotional terrorism." The military initially suspected that the Mothers were "acting" apolitically in order to hide their association with what the military called "solidarity

---

[72] See Schechner (2013).
[73] Failure might well be at the core of what allows for spectator identification with the actors. See Power (2010).

292   GRISELDA GAMBARO'S 1986 *ANTÍGONA FURIOSA*

organizations" working with the "terrorist" armed left-wing groups. Thus, the Mothers needed to be infiltrated. This was the performative interlocution in which they needed to improvise; they needed to be seen "as mothers" by those who saw them as "terrorists." Soon after the Mothers started gathering at the Plaza, Marine Captain Alfredo Astiz was sent to infiltrate them.[74] In December 1977, the military disappeared three Mothers along with two French nuns and seven human rights activists. Soon after, twelve more Mothers disappeared. The stakes for the Mothers changed; now they searched not only for their children but also for their *compañeras*. They had become their children.

Among the first disappeared was Azucena Villaflor, the Mother who first advocated seizing the Plaza, "so that they see us," as Nora Cortiñas narrates.[75] Azucena came from a well-known family of Peronist activists and had been militant in a union. Another founder who disappeared was Paraguayan Esther Ballestrino, who recovered her daughter but had the (fatal) political determination to return to the Plaza socializing motherhood: "all the others [were] missing."[76] Among the founders, some of them were not "just mothers": there was also the daughter of an anarchist, the daughter of Holocaust survivors, and a young member of the Communist Party.

The real challenge is analyzing what performance—defined as twice-behaved behavior in performance studies—cannot: contingency. We may even see the extremely fragmented and heterogeneous subtexts of Gambaro's play as a result of the novelty brought about by the Mothers, who were forced to create under threat of death, rather than simply reproduce given scripts. For the Mothers, at stake were not only the meaning but also the possibility of political action. Lack of attention to historical contingency obliterates the array of invisible actions that the Mothers carried out to produce their scripted tactic of visible "performance." To survive, the Mothers avoided being seen; they entered a house one at a time so as not to raise suspicion that they were gathering; they raised money for "charity" that in reality paid for their trips; they said they were meeting at a café named "Las Rosas," while actually meeting at "Las Violetas."

Any notion of the Mothers' "choice" in this context must be detached from the association between choice and freedom that determines the sphere of politics as negotiation in "free" market-driven political spaces. If there was a "choice" for these women, it was to stay indoors or go out. Once

---

[74] For Astiz's story, see Goñi (1996). For the military discourse on mothers, see Filc (1997).
[75] Silvia Chejter's 2002 interview with Nora Cortiñas.   [76] Arrosagaray (1997).

GRISELDA GAMBARO'S 1986 *ANTÍGONA FURIOSA*   293

outside, "the rest was silence." Only a minority of mothers left their homes.[77] The "choice" was to let the contingent event of military politics constitute them as political subjects—as Antigone let herself be caught in the political event of Creon's edict. The Mothers responded to the military attack on (and simultaneous defense of) motherhood using the military's language. Grandmother Estela de Carlotto succinctly explains: "the call to action came from the military dictatorship; it did not come from us."[78] Their language was military; their desire was justice, truth, and accountability. Theirs was a political identity the military produced: they were "mothers-who-would-not" negotiate accountability—"mothers who," rather than "mothers of." This formula accounts for Gambaro's association between them and her Antígona Furiosa.

How to respond to the military's reinvention of motherhood? The Mothers' "faithfulness to politics" allowed them to tap into national political scripts and a long-established culture of "political maternalism." Villaflor's idea to occupy the Plaza linked the Mothers forever to the Plaza's symbolism since May 25, 1810, when the people shouted: "The people want to know what this is all about"—as I mentioned in my analysis of *Antígona Vélez*. In this Plaza, instruments of torture were burnt in 1813. Strikingly, performative studies have paid little attention to the meaning of this real-life stage. When the Association of Relatives of the Disappeared issued its first newspaper petition, the slogan read: "We only demand the truth."[79] The Mothers' political maternalism drew from the symbol of Evita and from the political memory of female leadership at the turn of the twentieth century in what became the largest anarchist-unionist movement in the continent.[80] Argentine political culture was well registered in Europe as one of the explanations for the emergence of the Mothers.[81]

What determined the Mothers' success? Recall the strategic obedience of Andrade's Brazilian Antígonas, Marta and Mariana. Like the latter, the Argentine Mothers obeyed to the letter the order that came from the military and thus confused them. The military order was to care for the nation's children. The Mothers took it at face value. They entered the Plaza neither

---

[77] Gorini (2006: 24).

[78] Graciela Di Marco's interview with Nora Cortiñas and Estela de Carlotto, in Leblon and Maier (2006: 133).

[79] *La Prensa*, May 10, 1977.

[80] The first decades of the twentieth century saw intense feminist mobilization. See Nari (2004), Lobato (2007), Bellucci (n.d.), and Suriano (2001).

[81] Gorini (2006: 570).

294 GRISELDA GAMBARO'S 1986 *ANTÍGONA FURIOSA*

as (military) men nor as the negative of men (their assigned patriarchal place). Rather than a performance of patriarchal motherhood, this was a political strategy of citation to unveil the contradictions in the military discourse about motherhood.

The militarization of politics erased so thoroughly the limits between private and public that mothers had become military soldiers at home. Parents were instructed to recognize the vocabulary that "indicated subversive elements in the education of their children: words such as 'bourgeoisie,' 'dialogue,' 'proletariat,' 'América Latina,' 'exploitation,' 'capitalism,' [...] or in the religious courses [...] 'ecumenism,' 'liberation,' 'commitment.'"[82] The nation's mothers were to prevent their children from becoming the "leftist enemy." Parenthood was politically vital for the military; slogans in public campaigns addressed parents with questions such as "Do you know where your child is?" "Letters" to parents appeared in the newspapers. In *La Nación*, a now famous "Letter from the Mother of a 'Subversive'" (September 24, 1976) explained how she had behaved like a "sister" to her son, which might have turned the son into a "subversive" and led to his assassination. The "Letter to Mothers" in the women's magazine *Para Tí* (July 5, 1976) and the "Letter to Parents" published by an "Anonymous Friend" in the popular magazine *Gente* (December 16, 1976) were straightforward. From the latter:

> Understand this once and for all. This war is not somebody else's. It is also yours. [...] it might happen that one day your child [...] is hypnotized by the enemy [...] If this happens and you have to go to the morgue to recognize your child's corpse, you can't blame misfortune. You could have avoided it. For example, do you know what your child reads? [...] Find out and control it. It is not enough to just wash the school uniforms and buy copybooks.[83]

In 1977, a graphic pamphlet titled "How to Recognize Marxist Infiltration in Schools" was distributed in schools. The pamphlet asked teachers to become "custodians of our ideological sovereignty," giving them tools to "fulfill their duty" and identify "the enemy of the Nation."[84] Indeed, the military called mothers to action, as Carlotto later said.

---

[82] Dussel, Finocchio, and Gojman (1997: 30–1).
[83] My translation. See comments on the first example in Bravo (2003). See a reproduction of the letters in the series *Memoria*, Vannucchi (2007).
[84] See part of the text in Almirón (1999).

It was not enough to be just a (patriarchal) mother. A mother had to be ideologically and politically educated and ready to act. The enemy of the nation was at home. Alongside this ideological "penetration" of the home was its actual military invasion: 62 percent of the kidnapping cases registered by the 1984 Truth Commission took place inside homes. Mothers testifying before the Truth Commission reported cases such as a son first being kidnapped at work, taken to his home and presented before his mother and father, and then taken away to become disappeared, or cases of mothers taken away from their homes as they were breastfeeding their babies, with the babies then relocated to "better Christian" families.[85] Insofar as being "good mothers" at this time meant to "recognize" the subversive enemy in their children, the Mothers went knocking on the doors of military headquarters to find those who had not returned from work, from university, from a party, in (ironic) "obedience" of military ideology.

The Mothers dismantled the family discourse of the military by becoming its literal readers. Even the most basic "performative" gesture with which the Mothers are consistently associated—to "walk every Thursday in circles around the plaza," evoked in Gambaro's play—stemmed from political contingency and an "obedient" strategy of citation. The military police who noticed the first fourteen women sitting and knitting on the benches in the plaza yelled at them: "Walk, circulate, circulate, you can't stay here" ("*Circulen!*" in Spanish). Public gatherings were forbidden. The order in Spanish usually means "to clear the way," to move on. The Mothers did "circulate"—they had no "choice" other than to circulate, but they took the word literally and moved in circles, around the plaza, rather than leaving the plaza.

In the end, what gesture could be more "feminist" than showing what a politics of motherhood can accomplish, unveiling motherhood as a political construction that in itself has neither an oppressive nor a liberating essence? For these women, the deconstruction of individual motherhood paved the way to their politics of antagonism. By the time Gambaro wrote her play, the Mothers had long dismantled traditional motherhood and party politics by becoming mothers of all the disappeared.[86]

---

[85] The 1984 Truth Commission report, *Nunca Más* is online at http://www.derechoshumanos.net/lesahumanidad/informes/argentina/informe-de-la-CONADEP-Nunca-mas-Indice. htm#C1. The reports I refer to are from August 10, 1976, and July 13, 1976.

[86] Today, their slogans are internationalist and anticapitalist.

296   GRISELDA GAMBARO'S 1986 *ANTÍGONA FURIOSA*

Antígona, for Gambaro, is each disappeared Mother and every Mother who returned alive.[87] Tellingly, Ulises Gorini's 2006 exhaustive history of the Mothers opens by comparing the Mothers to Antigone: "Antigone's myth seems to re-incarnate in the first steps of the Mothers of the Plaza de Mayo [...] both Antigone's purpose and that of the Mothers of the Plaza de Mayo turned out to be 'non-negotiable' for the forces in power." But for Gorini, the Mothers were trapped in a bad military script: "Antigone will be condemned to death and the Mothers will be threatened with elimination by the dictatorship. But while the protagonist of the myth dies a victim, the Mothers manage to avoid annihilation" (22). In Gambaro's proposal, the Mothers and Antígona succeed: they return "back alive."

1986:   Times of Trouble

Gambaro responded to her own historical contingency, a specific postdictatorial moment to which also the Mothers had to respond: 1986, less than a year after the world-famous 1985 civil trial of the military, when the Mothers split in two groups. The Mothers radicalized after two impunity laws were passed to appease the military: the Full Stop Law (December 24, 1986) and the Law of Due Obedience (June 4, 1987). The Full Stop Law gave lawyers a deadline of sixty days to finish the remaining prosecutions and stopped all future ones. Military unrest culminated in a rebellion at Easter 1987. Gambaro's play was restaged on June 2, 1987, two days before the confirmation of the Due Obedience law, which put an end to all trials of military and police subordinates. Postdictatorial civilian justice appeared to have reached a limit. Three subsequent years of intense social debate consumed the nation, before executive pardons in 1989 and 1990 were given to approximately 1,200 people, including military commanders who had been sentenced in 1985, military officers who staged the 1987 rebellion, officials accused of economic crimes, and left-wing guerrilla leaders serving prison time or in exile.

In 1986, the question of whether or not to negotiate with the government forced a split in the Mothers into the Línea Fundadora (Founding Line) and Asociación de Madres (Mothers' Association). Gambaro's Antígona represents on stage the latter's position. The first point of contention between

---

[87] See the interview with Navarro Benítez (2001).

the two groups was the acceptance of individual corpses. What were the Mothers looking for—one body or all bodies? They first disagreed on whether to accept exhumations, which might provide knowledge about the cause of death but would radically alter the possibility for justice by preventing trials for crimes against humanity, instead switching the charges to individual homicides. The most radical Mothers thought that bringing individual cases to a close would cancel their collective politics of justice.

The Asociación de Madres wanted prosecutions for genocide, not for homicides. The military had made bodies disappear to avoid prosecution. These Mothers, once again, took the military literally: if the military would not make the disappeared bodies appear, then the Asociación would not ask for bodies; if the lack of bodies made prosecutions impossible for bourgeois law, then the Asociación would not want bourgeois law. The Asociación's "socializing motherhood" was now posing a challenge to the liberal legal institution. The two groups disagreed further on whether to accept economic compensation, monuments, and plaques representing the dead. The Asociación opted against any negotiation, standing behind the slogan "*aparición con vida*" ("back alive"). The debate was over what kind of justice, and therefore what kind of society, was at stake. The military had called them "terrorists"; now civilians and even politicians called the Asociación "enemies of democracy."

In reality, the non-negotiation that was now dividing the Mothers had been present all along since the slogan "back alive" took definite shape in 1980. While at a meeting in the OAS (Organization of American States) in Washington, DC, one of the Mothers said to a journalist: "we feel terrible in these corridors where we see how human beings are sold for wheat, for money, for oil" (Gorini 2006: 412). As Mother Mercedes de Meroño put it: "We learned how to do politics—what one calls true politics [...] The politics of not selling out."[88] Gorini adds to the 1980 crisis the documents of a secret challenge the Mothers faced in March 1980, foreshadowing the division to come (2015: 351–64). The twenty Mothers of the movement's organizing committee were presented with a "choice"—think of all the choices Antígonas have had to face on stage since Argia's child was kidnapped by the state in 1824. The Mothers had to list twenty names for the military to release alive. If they negotiated, they thought, the disappeared would be forgotten; if they did not negotiate, they would lose the chance to save their

---

[88] The quote appeared on the website of the Mothers' Asociación; accessed August 20, 2016. https://madres.org/

own children. Six mothers submitted their names. No Mother felt anyone could choose "the right" answer, since there was no right answer. One said: "what if they select our 20 names to kill them?" After six mothers presented their list, no disappeared were released alive.

The seeds of the 1986 schism had been planted. After Washington, the Mothers went to Sweden. They heard some human rights activists say that the disappeared "were dead." Some Mothers spent a night awake crafting a declaration against accepting death. Recall here the fictional Sofía and Camacho's women at dawn, breaking bread at the tomb, refusing to accept an individual burial rather than all burials. For the Mothers, accepting the death of individuals would have meant an end to their plight; this gave birth to the slogan "back alive" that took a life of its own and serves human rights campaigns across the region.

Back Alive in Six Acts: Antígona's Return, with the Help of Ophelia

Gambaro crafted Antígona "back alive" in an eternal return. Blurring the lines between theater, dance, and ritual, Antígona's return reenacts the battle, the funeral, and her death. She comes to life inside the cage, leaves, and then returns inside the no-home space of the cage between life and death. Meanwhile, the two men look forward; as Corifeo says, "It happened. Now on to something else!" (149).

Gambaro's construction of Antígona's arrival "hand in hand" with Ophelia, singing her songs, invites a literary sisterhood between Ophelia and Antigone. Might Antígona have understood Ophelia's desire in ways Hamlet did not? Usually read as representing innocence and victimhood, Renaissance Ophelia was deprived of a ritual in two senses. Polonius was buried under mysterious circumstances, unmourned. Before dying, Ophelia handed out rue flowers: the flower of regret, but also of poison, the killer weapon of the play and, coincidentally, the major method of abortion in its day.[89] Was her love for Hamlet that "honorable"? The only flower she hands herself is rue. As a woman unable to take revenge on others, Ophelia carries out revenge on her own body. Gone "mad," Ophelia drowns in the river. Like her father, Ophelia is but half-honored, her religious rites incomplete

---

[89] See studies on Shakespeare's flowers, such as Kerr (1969).

GRISELDA GAMBARO'S 1986 *ANTÍGONA FURIOSA*   299

due to her alleged suicide. Lacking proof of his father's murder, Hamlet goes "mad," just as Ophelia. But Hamlet's own gendered "madness" instead allows him to kill. His true madness is memory, those "rights of memory" that Fortinbras carries heavily in his heart—a father's command "not to forget."

Gambaro's literary sisterhood allows us to imagine that Antígona and Ophelia teach each other—or perhaps desire each other. Did Antígona teach Ophelia how to feign madness? Did Ophelia train Antígona to play a theater of madness? Gambaro's Antígona "plays" Ophelia, following Hamlet's example, "to catch the conscience of the King" (act 2, scene 2). The framing device of a "play-within-the-play" helped Gambaro to "settle the scores" on the power of theater with her audience in 1986. The play-within-the-play can be viewed in six acts: Antígona comes back alive; she reenacts the battle on her body; she performs the circular march (of the Mothers); she attempts the burial; she rejects her pardon; and finally, she kills herself. The male audience remains somewhere between indifferent and puzzled throughout.

The first act is Antígona's arrival as Ophelia. The men pretend they "believe" her act, they see and mock her as Ophelia. Here, the first antagonistic "No" is posed. The men warn Ophelia–Antígona that there is no tomb. They offer her instead a modern "coffee." Emblematic of modern urban Buenos Aires, coffee was a new beverage in Europe in Ophelia's times, thought to be the devil's drink (as people complained to Pope Clement VIII).[90] Antígona–Ophelia refuses the trade, just as she will disregard the prohibition uttered by Antinoo, who brings up Polinices' memory: "No one touch him! Forbidden! His plague is contagious. It will contaminate the city!" (138). Antígona responds: "Forbidden? Forbidden?" (138) and smashes Corifeos' crown (stage directions). Once decrowned, Corifeo embodies Polinices: "No one will bury me!" (138). Antígona is now modern, as there are no kings in this play. Corifeo mockingly confuses king with citizen: "Forbidden, forbidden! The king prohibited it! 'I' prohibited it!" (Sp 198). Corifeo voices Polinices', the citizens', and Creon's thoughts simultaneously: he will not be buried, for this has been prohibited, and he was the one who prohibited it. Corifeo is at once a "disappeared" body, a contemporary citizen favoring the new negotiations with the military, and the military itself. This is the audience who will watch Antígona–Ophelia's

[90] Allen (1999).

300 GRISELDA GAMBARO'S 1986 *ANTÍGONA FURIOSA*

play; they can put on the crown according to circumstance, as Corifeo will do with the mask-helmet on stage. Gambaro's intentional confusion of the agent who decreed the prohibition—"the king did it; I did it"—is a concise formula for what is known as the "civic-military" pact, whose origins trace back to three 1975 decrees, signed during democracy, to annihilate subversion in all national territory.

Antígona's second act to "catch the conscience of the king" starts when she declares that "the battle" is taking place as they speak. Antígona resurrects a past battle; the dialogue with the men forecasts what will happen. A sound of metal, cries, screams, and horses accompany Antígona's paroxysmal movements. She falls down and performs "as if" the battle were happening on her flesh (stage directions).[91] Corifeo says: "Such grieving can only come to grief. What is this crazy girl trying to do?" (139). Antinoo knows it all too well: "Burying Polinices" (139). Their dialogue allows for ambiguity in interpretation—might the battle that Antígona forced them to watch have "caught their conscience"? Corifeo is tired: "Remembering the dead is like grinding water with a mortar and pestle, useless. Waiter, another coffee" (140). But Antinoo hesitates: "It did not happen long ago" (140). When Antinoo suggests that they celebrate, Corifeo hesitates "darkly asking" (stage directions): "What should we celebrate?" (140). They decide to toast the "peace that has arrived" (140). The time is ambiguous: ancient time; the military bringing "order" in 1976; democracy returning in 1983; wanting to stop the military trials after 1985. They decide to celebrate not with "poison" (140) as they say, mocking Antígona, but with wine.

Antígona interrupts with a third act just as they are about to "celebrate," that is, to "forget" with the new drink. Here, the references to the Mothers crystallize in Antígona's movements. She "marches" among her dead "in a strange gait in which she falls and stands up, she falls and stands up" (Sp 200).[92] The "battle" appears to have ended. She shouts, "Corpses! I step on dead bodies! I am surrounded by the dead! They caress me…they ask me…what?" (Sp 200). The two men respond to Antígona's "embodiment" with the proclamation of Creon's edict. In stage directions, the Spanish for

---

[91] See Taylor (1996) for the argument that the nation is constructed as "woman," which is dramatized in this scene as Antígona "mediates between men" with her body. See Dove (2013) for a criticism of Taylor's view, arguing that Taylor reads too literally the "as if" clause included in the text. See Carlson (2003) for a criticism of Taylor's view that the physicality of Antigone puts torture on stage.

[92] Translation modified: the English version omits the word "marches" and uses "walks"; it also uses "recovers for "se incorpora," which in Spanish refers to the movement of standing back up again. ' "Incorporarse" also means to join, in Antígona's burial, it would be to join the dead.

GRISELDA GAMBARO'S 1986 *ANTÍGONA FURIOSA* 301

"standing up" is the reflexive "*se incorpora*," which contains the polysemy of "body" and its negative: body = *cuerpo* but also not-having-a-body = *incorpórea*. This polysemy presages the end: after embodying the battle, Antígona will become body-less, disappeared. Corifeo is almost hypnotized by her movements: standing up, he moves forward while repeating words that echo the circularity of Antígona's repeated falling down and standing up. He speaks of the edict, the order to "circulate," the madwoman's circular movements around "the unburied unburied unburied corpse" (Sp 201).

After the performance alludes to the Mothers, Antígona prepares her fourth act: burial. Antígona seeks the men's attention: "Do you see me Creon? I cry! Do you hear me, Creon? (she laments)" (141). Corifeo shouts "I did not hear!" and sings "there are no laments" (141). Antígona insists: "do you see me, Creon, I will bury him, with these arms, with these hands!" (141). Antígona suddenly "discovers Polinices" (stage directions) represented by a shroud. His body is not there. Antígona covers the shroud in a motherly way (stage directions). She sprinkles earth on the body and rhythmically clashes two stones together: "she throws herself on him with her body covering him from head to toe" (141). Ophelia–Antígona's song, "At his head grass, at his feet stone" now becomes Antígona's phrase: "Polinices, I will be grass and stone" (142). Echoing the Greek sister, she continues: "Neither dogs nor birds of prey will touch you (with a maternal gesture, stage directions), I will clean your body, I will comb your hair" (142). As he watches, Corifeo advises, "better not to see acts that should not be performed," but Antinoo keeps looking: "She did not manage to bury him" (142).

Corifeo, behind the helmet, speaks Creon's ancient lines. The classic confrontation between Creon and Antigone emerges in the temporal registers of past and present, as the narration of the confrontations between Antígona and Ismena and between Hemon and Creon. She partly answers her previous question—what do the dead want of her?—by saying: "The dead demand earth, not water or scorn" (205). For the Argentine audience, water connoted the river of Buenos Aires into which many "disappeared" bodies were thrown from airplanes. We may recall Ophelia again: the "mad" sister who "flew up" to the willow tree and then "was thrown" down to the river to drown—an act whose invisible hand was the king's, who refused to bury her father with honors.

If Ophelia's fate resembles that of the disappeared—she mysteriously drowns and is buried without ritual—Antígona becomes a disappeared

302 GRISELDA GAMBARO'S 1986 *ANTÍGONA FURIOSA*

when she is taken to the cave: "I will be separated from both humans and those who die, uncounted among the living and among the dead. I will disappear from the world, alive" (152). She will not "die," like the ancient sister, but rather "disappear" in the cave. Corifeo rescues the ancient line by Creon: "If she wishes to die there, let her die. If she wishes to live hidden under this roof, let her live. We will be cleared of her death and she will have no contact with the living" (153). But Antinoo interprets Corifeos' phrase as referring to a disappeared: "What wisdom! She is here and she is not here, we kill and killed her and we do not and did not kill her" (Sp 211). The English translation misses, necessarily, two details. It reads: "what is, is not, we kill her and do not kill her" (153). The form of the verb "to be" in Spanish in this sentence is *estar*, not *ser*. *Estar* mostly refers to the temporality of being, not to its essence: it refers to changes in being, not to permanence. Antígona is not "what is or is not," rather "está y no está": she is (and is not) in a specific place, space, and time. She is what "there is" at a given time. The conjugation of the verb "to kill" in the first-person plural for the present indicative is spelled the same as the (indefinite) past: "*la matamos.*" The sentence thus contains an ambiguous temporality, as if suspending time, conveying perfectly the temporality for a disappeared life: she is, and she is not here and now; we kill her now, and we killed her yesterday; she is alive, and she is not, enhancing the sense that she is at once not killed and killed permanently. Thus, she can be back or not (alive), permanently.

Might this be the mode in which Ophelia enacts Hamlet's existential "to be or not to be"? "To be here or not to be here," in the Spanish mode of *estar*, in the here and now in this space with us, connects Antígona to all the ghosts in *Hamlet* and in Gambaro's play too. She acts as the drowned Ophelia, as the Mother who performs the ritual at the Plaza, as the Mother who was disappeared sharing the fate of her children, and as one of the thousands of uncounted disappeared.

In her fifth act, Antígona will "be Ophelia" again for the last time before her death. The plague has arrived in the city: per stage directions, there is a sound of birds. The wings of a bird touch Antígona, and she pushes them away. "Filth" (per stage directions) falls from above onto the tables and the men's clothes. Creon has pardoned her due to Tiresias' warning, but unaware of her pardon, Antígona begins to twist her neck: "Death arrived, wife, mother, sister" (Sp 215). But when Corifeo delivers the pardon, Antígona acts out "Ophelia's madness." Just as she began by rejecting his coffee, now, with Ophelia's help, she rejects Corifeos' shouts:

CORIFEO: I pardon them! I am the one to be condemned, I who made a holocaust on my son, on my wife. Antígona, who brought so much harm on my head and heritage, I pardon you!

ANTÍGONA (SINGS): "They bore him barefaced on the bier and in his grave rained many a tear."

(158)

Antígona repeats her quotation of Ophelia's song, this time with the last stanza of the same song with which she began her play-within-the-play. The song alludes to burial. Corifeo, using Creon's armor, weeps at the loss of his son—"sincerely" per stage directions—though he does not perform any burial. He is "ashamed" to still have the throne. Antinoo implores Antígona: "The harshest hearts can soften 'at the last moment.' He pardoned you!" (158). Antinoo quotes from Antígona's previous phrase: "I feared [...] at the last moment, crawl and beg" (158). The "last moment" is polysemic: for the men, it is a humanizing pity; for Antígona, it is an inhumane capitulation. Antígona fears this capitulation. She refuses to hear: "No. I still want to bury Polinices" (158).

Ophelia has accompanied Antígona until the end, when Hamlet's fury appears in Antígona's last line. But this last line might have belonged to Ophelia's madness as well, as she falls into the river and embodies "the rest is silence." It is, after all, the phrase of that other woman, Alejandra Pizarnik, who did not yield to the lies of language and killed herself. Antígona's "mad" paroxysm—leaning over her brother's dead body, walking among her dead, and finally killing herself—might have caught the conscience of the king. All the citizens implied in the Corifeo–Antinoo duo pardoned her. Had she accepted the pardon, she would be back alive, from her disappearance, either "returned" to the city or buried properly. But was this what she wanted—*just* to be back alive? Likewise: did Ophelia want to drown or rather to hand out poisoned flowers? What does Antígona—the woman, the Mother, the Disappeared—want? What do Antígona's dead want?

Antígona or the Incorruptible: The Sixth Act, Against the Disappearance of the Political

While the play opens with the absence of tombs, the final moments broach the thorny issue that society was debating in 1986: pardons. The play does

304   GRISELDA GAMBARO'S 1986 *ANTÍGONA FURIOSA*

not question whether there should be tombs. Rather it interrogates the two dramas condensed in the signifier "pardon": on the one hand, the "pardon" granted to a complicit society at large, and on the other, the political meaning of the pardon that Antígona rejects. The Mothers did not want pardon, but rather punishment, for the military. But what did it mean to judge only the generals in 1985? Was the rest of society to be pardoned?

Antígona does not want pardon for having "done something" that made her disappear—and here Antígona condenses the figures of the Mothers and their disappeared children. In the final moments, Antígona considers that Corifeo pardons her because of "fear of the plague" (156), not because of principle. Antinoo tells her "He has a big heart that easily pardons!" but Antígona qualifies: "His own crimes" (Sp 216).[93] Corifeo, in turn, voices Creon's suffering after imprisonment in an ambiguous reference to the 1985 trials: "In this prison, bread and water! [...] I will suffer until they understand;" "I pardon them! They don't know what they do! They intend to condemn me" (Sp 216). Antinoo does not perceive Creon's prison: "What prison? What does he call a prison? Bread and water and delicacies and wine?" (Sp 206). The trials in Buenos Aires had sentenced high officials, but the impunity laws immediately left many to savor "delicacies and wine" at home.

Corifeo has been judged and now pardons his judges. But Corifeo signifies everyone: he is King Creon, Polinices, and a common citizen. Corifeos' pardon is a blanket statement about the innocence of all: Antinoo knows that prison for all the characters allegorized in Corifeo is difficult to imagine: "What prison? What does he call a prison?" What was the meaning of "prison" after thirty thousand had disappeared?

Antígona wants justice, not pardons: "Even if I am born a thousand times and he dies a thousand times," to which Antinoo shouts, "Then Creon will always punish you!" and Corifeo adds "And you a thousand times will die" (158). But she will return "always": "I will always want to bury Polinices" (Sp 217). A thousand times is repeated thrice; "always" is repeated twice. Always, always, a thousand, a thousand, a thousand times: a mythical time, perhaps an echo of the often-used regional political slogan quoting the words that legendary Aymara rebel Túpac Katari is said to have uttered before being quartered in 1781 by the Spaniards: "I will return and I will be

---

[93] The English translation of this phrase—"you have a big heart that easily pardons" (157)—reads as if Antinoo were talking to Corifeo.

millions."[94] Antígona can do just that: a permanent act of rebirth, always, "back alive."

Lifting the banner "back alive" in search of justice, when the culprit is Corifeo, who represents vast sectors of society, if not everyone, interrogates responsibility and punishment in radical terms. If everyone is to blame, then institutions at large must change. Antígona's eternal return insists on this question: back alive until when? Coded in the enigma that persists throughout the play and is voiced from the perspective of men, the question is that of Antígona's true desire. Why does she return? Does she simply want to bury her brother? Does she just want to live? What kind of society would her stance imply?

Antinoo and Corifeo keep wondering about Antígona's desire to insist on her goal throughout the play. Listening to Antígona from her cave, Antinoo asks Corifeo: "If we know already that she dies, why doesn't she die?" (154). Metatheatrically: why tell the story, if we know it already? Likewise, in the Mothers' case, why seek the disappeared—and we can imagine any Antinoo-citizen of Gambaro's times adding: if "we know" they are dead? But Antinoos' question is the play's statement: she does not die. For the men, her survival is the enigma of her desire. For civilians, the Mothers' survival was the enigma of their desire too. The men begin by asking: Who is this woman? After her enacting the battle, Corifeo asks, "what does [she] pretend?" (Sp 199). When she tells the story of her parents, Corifeo pronounces Darío's verse "what ails the princess?" (Sp 204). Corifeo reprimands her after the deed: "What did you expect?" (Sp 211). He asks Antinoo, "how could she think of opposing?" (Sp 211). When Corifeo laments Hemon's desire, he says, "Where are the laws of this world?"; Antinoo replies, "Yes, yes, but what do the laws have to do with Antígona?" (Sp 209).

The men return in circles to the mystery of Antígona's insatiable desire. Why not just accept a pardon? In the cave, she makes clear that life in this society will not be enough for her: "hate rules." For Antígona, a politics of negotiation means the disappearance of politics. When she brings the bowl of water to her lips, she says, "No. I refuse this bowl of mercy that masks their cruelty" (159). The water that "masks their cruelty" symbolizes the

---

[94] This phrase may resonate for Anglophone speakers who recall Howard Fast's 1951 novel *Spartacus*. In Argentina, Evita is said to have pronounced it before dying: "volveré y seré millones." The real writer of this line was the poet José María Castiñeira de Dios.

306 GRISELDA GAMBARO'S 1986 *ANTÍGONA FURIOSA*

river into which so many disappeared from history. Her word in Spanish for "bowl" is "cuenco," which like the feminine,"cuenca," refers to the river basin. Many of those decomposing bodies returned from the river basin to shore in real life. Antígona returns, like the disappeared returned, rejecting the river basin and all it signifies. The politics of extermination fails—it corresponds to the attempt at disappearing politics *tout court*. In the ancient play, Polynices "returns" as the plague when Creon attempts to "disappear" his name; in Marechal's play, the Indians "return" in the arrows that kill Antígona Vélez. Arguably, in *Hamlet*, too, those unjustly killed return.

Antígona returns as a structuring principle for politics: an "impossible universal" whose function is to demand a different society. She differs from Ismena's feelings of love and fear (Sp 206): she is the pure negativity of the principle. We may even say that between the two sisters on stage there is an echo of the 1986 split that radicalized some Mothers. Antígona represents the Asociación's position: not one more burial unless all burials become "possible." Ismena represents the Línea Fundadora: accepting the negotiation of individual burials, out of maternal love. Corifeo wonders if Antígona will "realize how superfluous it is to petition death for life" (159). Antígona herself is unsure; she thinks Ismena's motives are "truer" (146). In Spanish Antígona's *"peticiones de vida"* (208) echo the Asociación's slogan against all negotiation: *aparición con vida*. Unrealizable in the political context in which it is formulated, the slogan does not restore the life of the disappeared but rather "true politics," as the Mothers would say. That is, politics understood as a practice of antagonism and not of consensus: the rejection of the social structure that produced the necropolitics of forced disappearance. Antígona ruminates in her return what we need to recall: the antagonism needed for true politics—radical democracy.

7
Revolutionary Shame in the Year 2000
Yuyachkani's and Watanabe's Peruvian Ismene

Shame is already a revolution of a kind […] if a whole nation really experienced a sense of shame it would be like a lion, crouching ready to spring.

(Karl Marx)[1]

This synopsis is based on Yuyachkani's eighty-minute-long production of José Watanabe's play-poem *Antígona: Versión libre de la tragedia de Sófocles* (Antígona: Free version of Sophocles' tragedy). A single actress plays, without masks, every character in this monologue of twenty-two poems. Accompanied by shifts in music and lighting, she uses only a chair, her tunic, and handclapping, altering her voice and gestures to change characters. The "narrator-character" introduces the characters in every scene, except when Antígona is about to die, at which point the audience hears from her directly. As the play opens, the "narrator-character" enters the stage, glancing fearfully back at the door, carrying a wooden box containing Polinices' mortuary mask. She begins to tell the story: It is the first day of peace. Polinices' corpse lies unburied on the arid land. Creonte delivers his famous speech about order. A fragile Antígona addresses the dead Polinices ("a dead man belonging to us all"), asking what she should do. After Antígona covers Polinices' corpse with dust, an innocent madman is accused of the deed. At night, Creonte is tormented by thoughts of saboteurs, uncertain about who has stolen Polinices' death mask. When Antígona is captured on her second attempt to cover the body, she delivers a warning: "Remember my name, because one day, everybody will say that I was the sister who did not fail her brother: my name is Antígona." As Antígona, sentenced to death, languishes in the cave, Hemón fearlessly confronts his father. While Tiresias attempts to convince Creonte to rescind his decree, Antígona plays with a silk ribbon

---

[1] Letter from Marx to his friend Arnold Ruge, March 1843.

Antígonas: Writing from Latin America. Moira Fradinger, Oxford University Press. © Moira Fradinger 2023.
DOI: 10.1093/oso/9780192897091.003.0009

308 YUYACHKANI'S AND WATANABE'S PERUVIAN ISMENE

she has untied from her waist, using it to hang herself. Creonte rescinds his decree but arrives at the cave too late. In the final poem, the narrator reveals that she is Ismene, the sister who "was handcuffed by fear" and now is overcome by guilt and shame. She takes Polinices' mask from the box, covers it with a shroud, and pours sand over it. As she leaves the stage, the lights dim to illuminate only her hands, arms stretched and palms opened toward the audience. Of the eighty minutes, approximately forty are devoted to Ismene's narration, with no indication of her identity until the final scene.[2]

Ismene, Not Antígona

The curtain rises at Casa Yuyachkani in Lima, on February 24, 2000, for the one-woman show based on the poem-play cowritten by Peruvian poet laureate José Watanabe (1946–2007) and Peruvian theater collective Yuyachkani. A capital city mostly populated by people of Spanish descent, Lima is the home of a cosmopolitan population: Peru's ruling elites, who historically turned their backs on the Andean highlands, preferring to look outward toward Europe.

The urban press praised the monologue, performed by renowned actress Teresa Ralli under Miguel Rubio Zapata's direction. Ralli remembers that during the first two years, the Lima audience would cry. Watanabe recalled that people encouraged him to take this performance to the Government Palace, as "they knew that it was a direct allusion to the problem of the disappeared."[3] Yuyachkani was politically ahead of the game: the commission to investigate crimes against humanity during the nation's internal armed conflict (1980–2000) would only emerge more than a year later.

In 2001, Antígona performed before a different audience: the forgotten Andean highlands in the South. As Morisseau-Leroy's Antigòn had done in Haiti, Yuyachkani's Antígona traveled to southern indigenous peasant villages, the heirs of pre-Columbian cultures, and blurred the differences between theater and ritual, performing in the open air: public plazas, streets,

---

[2] See the abridged online version at the NYU Hemispheric Institute for Performance and Politics Video library: https://hemisphericinstitute.org/en/hidvl-collections/item/2159-nwt-intersection.html. This chapter is based on Yuyachkani's 2005 performance at Yale University, the online video archived at the NYU Hemispheric Institute of Performance and Politics, Watanabe's text (2000), and personal interviews with Teresa Ralli. Together with Anamaría Lascano, I have translated the play into English (forthcoming). All quotations in this chapter are our translations.

[3] See the interview with Martínez Tabares (2007: 9).

YUYACHKANI'S AND WATANABE'S PERUVIAN ISMENE   309

markets, churches, and schools. The Amerindian audience was for the most part either Quechua-speaking or bilingual; rarely was Spanish their primary language.[4]

The Andean communities Antígona first reached were those most affected by the armed conflict between the national armed forces and armed organizations such as Sendero Luminoso (Shining Path) and the MRTA (Movimiento Revolucionario Túpac Amaru/Túpac Amaru Revolutionary Movement). Yuyachkani's mission was to prepare peasant communities for public hearings to be conducted by the newly created human rights Comisión de la Verdad y la Reconciliación (Truth and Reconciliation Commission, CVR hereafter, often transcribed in English as TRC). The *testimonios* of peasant survivors would be heard in a televised, political (ritualized) event of vast proportions.[5] The hearings would seek political justice. Yuyachkani lived up to its name: *yuya-chka-ni* in Quechua means "I am thinking, I am remembering."[6]

In August and September 2001, the show toured nine cities in the south-central region of Ayacucho: Tingo María, Huánuco, Ayaviri, Sicuani, Abancay, Chalhuanca, Vilcashuamán, Huanta, and Huancayo. The show preceded the actual openings of the hearings on April 8, 2002, in the city of Huamanga, and on April 11, in the city of Huanta, both in Ayacucho. The choice of place was not incidental: the armed conflict had begun in Ayacucho and, more precisely, at the University of San Cristóbal de Huamanga, where Sendero Luminoso was created in May 1980. A full-scale armed conflict ensued in the Andes. Peasants were forced to take sides, while distant Lima remained relatively unaffected for nearly a decade.

Antígona traveled extensively with the CVR through the Andes, to Sicuani (in Cuzco), to Abancay (in Apurímac), and to the coast, to Trujillo (in La Libertad) and Chimbote (in Ancash). Yuyachkani witnessed an outpouring of popular emotion: people would approach them to recount personal stories of violence, as if they were members of the CVR; or they would describe how they related to certain scenes in the play.[7] Yuyachkani had

---

[4] In Peru, 75 percent of the population self-identifies as indigenous or of indigenous descent (see the UN Demographic reports or the UNICEF sociolinguistic reports for the last decade). Peru is officially multilingual. A left-wing dictatorship made Quechua official in 1975.

[5] The first public audience was televised on April 4, 2002 on national television.

[6] The suffix "chka" indicates the continuous tense and "ni" is the first person singular; I thank Peruvian scholar José Cárdenas Bunsen for this information.

[7] I thank Ursula León for her assistance and her interviewing Teresa Ralli about the tour to the South, in Lima in November 2011.

managed to blur divisions not only between theater and ritual but also between theater and politics.

As in all previous cases in this book, the ancient heroine was a point of arrival for Yuyachkani and Watanabe. Without knowing it, Andean peasant women were saying what the fictional Antigone had said for thousands of years: "Who will return my relatives to me, who have been eaten by dogs and not even their bones are left to me?" (Andean peasant testimony).[8] Watanabe wrote in one poem: "Such punishment, and even worse, suffers my brother as he also lies prey to ravenous vermin, vultures and dogs" (*Antígona*, 28). Yuyachkani dedicated the play to those Andean women. Ralli's performance of a woman's *testimonio*, though based on a fictional story and theatrical conventions foreign to the peasants' own Andean theatrical traditions, aroused emotions in Andean audiences. What explained the play's success in the Andes? Was it the ancient story alone, or was something else also at work? In Peru, two distinct communities of actors and spectators were at stake: Lima gave birth to the play, but the Andean peasants—those most victimized by the armed conflict—provided Lima with the imaginative horizon.

Shift for a moment to the world: the third community of spectators. In 2000, Yuyachkani and Watanabe's *Antígona* was staged in Puerto Rico, New York, Bogotá, Amherst (US), Cádiz, Málaga, and Madrid. It premiered in Hartford (US) in 2001, in La Habana in 2002, and in Denmark in 2003. In 2004, it opened the Third Annual Latino Theater festival in Los Angeles with a textual translation by Aleida Montejo projected on screen.[9] It opened the XI Festival del Monólogo in Nicaragua in 2005 and was also produced in New Haven (US). New performances were continuing in 2017.

The Peruvian Ismene even generated an Argentine sister: in June 2006, Teatro Celcit (Centro Latinoamericano de Creación y Investigación Teatral) in Buenos Aires ruminated on Yuyachkani's and Watanabe's rumination on *Antigone*. Directed by Carlos Ianni, the production twisted the ending: Ismene does not have Polinices' mortuary mask, nor does she perform the belated ritual. Actress Ana Jovino stands against a brick wall throughout the performance, only using three white ropes hanging from the ceiling as props. Her physical gestures are more restricted than those of her Peruvian

---

[8] A peasant woman's scream before the public hearings of the Truth and Reconciliation Commission in the Department of Ayacucho, quoted in Miguel Rubio Zapata's notes "La Persistencia de la memoria," available online at http://hemi.nyu.edu/esp/newsletter/issue8/pages/rubio2.shtml.

[9] *Los Angeles Times*, October 23, 2004.

counterpart, which Ralli constructed through Andean gestures. With movements recognizable to her Buenos Aires audience, Jovino fashions a rope swing from which she dangles and twirls. Once inside the cave, she swings lifelessly from one of the ropes. By the end, she asks for forgiveness, her arms extended and palms upward in a gesture of supplication toward the audience.[10] In 2013, Argentine theater group Fratacho (from the Province of Buenos Aires) ruminated on Ianni's rumination of Watanabe's *Antígona*: instead of offering her palms to the audience in an act of forgiveness, Ismene curls down on the floor, almost in a fetal position, expressing her grief for acting the way she did.[11]

Like the 2001 production in Peru, the Argentine Ismene premiered in the context of a parallel legal ritual. In 2006, the case for public trials was reopened after a twenty-year-long hiatus following the annulment of the 1986 impunity laws; Commissioner General of Police Miguel Etchecolatz was accused of crimes against humanity during the dictatorship. Cuban theater critic Magaly Muguercia wrote in the theater program: "Not being Argentine myself, I can only speculate about the meaning that the audience in Buenos Aires will glean from these verses of Watanabe's 'Antígona': 'I want every death to have a funeral, and then, then, then, oblivion.'"[12] Those are Antígona's words in Watanabe's text after being caught, but for Argentines, it was a time for judgment, not "oblivion." This Ismene did not engage in symbolic burials.

Though Yuyachkani's Antígona travels easily, the choices made in the Argentine version return us to an analysis of the local. In Peru, Ismene had performed a ritual both in Lima and in the Andes; in Buenos Aires, the only offering was guilt. Peru saw two versions of Ismene, not one: though seemingly identical, Ismene's ritual offering meant something different in Lima than in the Andes. Nonetheless, with the notable exception of Peruvians Ximena Briceño and Gino Luque Bedregal, critics inspired by Ismene's international travels have seen the play as universal because of its minimalist production.[13]

---

[10] The performance premiered at the Celcit theater on June 21, 2006; in January of that year, it went to the Mexican Centro Cultural Olimpo, during the II Festival Internacional de las Artes. Jovino had previously performed in two different productions of Antigone (Anouilh's and Marechal's).

[11] See a version of Fratacho's production here: https://www.youtube.com/watch?v=FoDqh-JPd_tA. Yet another version is Luis Sarlinga's *Antígona narración en rojo y negro* (Antígona narrated in red and black) staged in Chiapas (San Cristóbal de Las Casas, http://antigonanarra-cionenrojoynegro.blogspot.com/), Mexico.

[12] See the text online at https://www.celcit.org.ar/espectaculos/12/antigona/.

[13] Briceño wrote an essay contextualizing the play as a "screen memory" allowing Peruvians to confront the past violence of the armed conflict (2004; unpublished manuscript given to me

312 YUYACHKANI'S AND WATANABE'S PERUVIAN ISMENE

Ralli only needs a chair, a wooden box, a white mask, a cloth, and a bit of sand; the stage merely features two torches and a back door. Ralli's attire appears neutral to a Western audience: a beige top tightly fitted to her chest, loose midcalf pants, and a tunic of the same color, which she uses to change her appearance. As Luque Bedregal observes, for most critics, an apparent absence of "Peruvian" referents onstage would indicate that the story "could happen anywhere" (2010; 83). Critics view the Peruvian performance as a culturally unspecific story of a sister asking for forgiveness and calling for responsible witnessing and remembrance in the face of catastrophe. For Francine A'Ness, the lack of Peruvian markers allows spectators to "complete the story with their own referents" (2004: 406). María Silvina Persino calls the stage an "escena despojada" ("stripped stage" or "scene," 2007: 94) that endows the production with a "universal character," while Brunn considers "universality" in that "obvious ethnic or racial markers are absent as well" (2009: 218), as if Ralli's whiteness were not a marker of race or ethnicity. Recall that Ralli does not perform with a mask.

But as the Buenos Aires audience reminds us, the duality of the Peruvian audience points toward the local. Ismene performs a truth-telling act akin to the "production of truth" demanded by the CVR in those first collections of testimonials. More importantly, though, Ismene's confession performs the desire to reconstitute the broken bonds between Lima and the Andes. To be sure, Ismene is a sister. But she is also a sister from Lima establishing a bond with her Andean sisters. I explore below the local connection between Ismene's revelation of her guilt and her feelings of shame; the dialectics of masking and unmasking in the Andes; the play's Peruvian politics of memory; and Antígona's resignification of sisterhood.

The dual nature of the Peruvian audience allows us to discern the dual aesthetic strategies at stake in the performances. The conflict between two sisters (not between two brothers, nor between Antigone and Creon) haunts this stage. The blending of artistic conventions with ritual, as well as the shift of focus in the main conflict, spoke to the country's multiethnic reality. The limits between tragedy and testimony, ritual and theater, and theater and politics were blurred, as were the limits between the two ancient storylines onstage: Antigone's story (the drama of the unburied) and Ismene's story

---

by the author); Luque Bedregal wrote the longest essay currently available (to my knowledge) on this play: *Ismene Redimida* (2010).

YUYACHKANI'S AND WATANABE'S PERUVIAN ISMENE   313

(the drama of the lone survivor).[14] The tragic form came from the cosmopolitan modern city, but the plot—the story of Antigone in dialogue with the story of the survivor—recalled the fate of the Andean peasant women searching for their dead.

We could venture to label this Peruvian Antígona as "tragic testimony," or "testimonial tragedy"—a hybrid genre born of the classics in the urban setting and the testimonies in the rural communities, quilted by Ismene's shame. This Peruvian Ismene bridges genres and stories through a surprising narrative twist, as the narrator transforms into the forgotten sister, taking center stage when unveiling her identity in shame. Ismene is revealed as the "truth" of the play.

The "strategic classicism" in Yuyachkani's *Antígona* forged a connection between the group's work—otherwise highly localized and referential (to Peru)—and the international stage. This classicism may have helped tell an unsavory story to the sophisticated audience in Lima. *Antígona* is exceptional in Yuyachkani's history: it is the only play that they did not author and that does not directly belong to a Peruvian tradition. *Antígona*'s Western theatrical lingua franca readily opened touring possibilities outside of Peru. But, for an indigenous audience, this was neither a lingua franca nor "universal"; rather, it was the unfamiliar language of the middle-class cosmopolitanism with which the group had begun their journey forty years earlier, inspired by Peter Weiss' documentary theater, Augusto Boal's "joker" system,[15] and Brecht's epic theater.

Just as its language was unfamiliar for indigenous peasants, the performance was uniquely Peruvian to the "world" audience: before then, no other country in Latin America (or Europe, to my knowledge) had produced a version of Ismene's testimony. Anchoring Ismene's narration in a movement from anonymity (concealing her identity) to personhood (revealing her identity) was a novel choice. As Luque Bedregal puts it, in Ismene, the Peruvian nation was at stake: the need to "re-imagine the nation as a unified community

---

[14] There is documentation on cases of one survivor in the Comisión de la Verdad y Reconciliación's final report (CVR 2003). See, for example, the case of the Andean community of Socos, in Volume VII: 2.7, at http://cverdad.org.pe/ifinal/pdf/TOMO%20VII/Casos%20Ilustrativos-UIE/2.7.%20SOCOS.pdf.

[15] Boal's "coringa or joker" model for dramatic production consisted of: delinking the actor from the character (the mask allows an actor to represent any character); unifying narration; using different genres and styles in each scene (thus the impression of a collage); and using music as a fusional element. The "joker" is an omniscient character that introduces perspective and distance. The protagonist is usually one actor opposed to the joker.

314   YUYACHKANI'S AND WATANABE'S PERUVIAN ISMENE

[…] to reinvent collective identity and revise, or even redefine the national project" (2010: 64).

By the late 1990s, the previously invisible Andean women in search of their missing had become too visible for the progressive sectors of Lima's middle class to ignore. When Ralli was asked "Why Antígona?," she first recalled a photo of a peasant woman dressed in black running below the arches of the Plaza de Armas in the city of Ayacucho, searching, Ralli believed, for her disappeared: "she appeared as a figure in flight, an exhalation beneath the shadow created by the sun at its peak. She was dressed in mourning." Ralli then recalled the turning point, on December 17, 1996, when the armed conflict finally hit Lima hard. The MRTA took diplomats at the Japanese Embassy in Lima hostage, right across from Ralli's house. The controversial military raid to liberate the hostages, later investigated for human rights violations, left Yuyachkani's members with the haunting knowledge that a general of the Peruvian army was buried with full honors while the bodies of MRTA members were disappeared. Antigone, Polynices, and Eteocles helped them process these events.[16]

The question in Peru was not *why Antigone?* It was *why Ismene?* By Ralli's account, the answer was far from obvious. Had they staged the tragedy in the 1980s, they might have focused on Antigone. However, in the aftermath of the armed conflict, Ismene seemed much more relevant.[17] If Yuyachkani's Antígona honored so many real-life women fighting for burial, whom did Ismene honor in the national political scene? Why place Ismene, a character emblematic of disloyalty, dishonor, shame, at the center?

Not that Ismene had been completely forgotten in the twentieth century, but she had not been remembered as guilty and dishonorable. Greek exile Yannis Ritsos (1909–90) wrote a long poetic monologue, "Ismene," between 1966 and 1971,[18] in which Ismene, at the end of her life, revisits her memories while talking to her only visitor, a young officer of the palace guard. She pities her sister Antigone, settling "all questions with *It's either right or it isn't*" (196; italics in the original). For Ismene, Antigone was like Polynices: "uncompromising, wrong-headed" (203). After the war ended, everything had been committed to oblivion: everything was just a "gluttonous taste for glory" (205), "a denial of life" (205). Once the young officer has left, Ismene

---

[16] See interviews with the Yuyachkani group as well as documentation in the Hemispheric Institute of Performance and Politics in New York at https://hemisphericinstitute.org.

[17] Interview with Ralli, carried out in Lima by Ursula León, November 2011.

[18] See Ritsos (1993: 192–215); adapted for the theater in 2006 by Nirupama Nityanandan and for the opera by the Greek Georges Aperghis, in 2008.

prepares for bed, ready to take her own life. She creates a plaster mask of her face and puts on one of her sister's dresses, as if she could only confront death in the heroic guise of Antigone, or perhaps as if she meant to kill Antigone or her heroism. Ismene washes down what looks like aspirin, then rests with her eyes closed. Ismene's death seems the least heroic, occurring in the solitude of a palace at night—not shedding blood but rather fulfilling what she has surmised throughout the poem: we are born only to be cut off in death.

Poet David Slavitt (United States, 1935–) also imagined Ismene's quotidian life in a short 1988 poem. "Nothing heroic here," the poem declares. Ismene grows old with "the three plays every night in her dreams"; she suffers "like anyone would"; she is "ordinary"; "How can she appear onstage," the poem asks, "when we have just passed her out on the street, on our way to the theater?" (1994: 25). Peruvian poet Jorge Wiesse Rebagliati (1954–) remembered Ismene in 2005 as choosing to live, albeit sadly, contemplating the "serenity" of her sister and her "eternal gesture." Ismene returns to "kneading the dark bread of life," to her "role," to "the anonymous" (2005: 19). Neither guilt nor shame burdens these Ismenes. Though their memories are sorrowful, they do not believe they acted wrongly. They remove heroism from the battlefield and return it to the challenges of daily life. And occasionally, Ismene has even been courageous, as in Rolando Steiner's 1958 Antígona, where Ismene storms Creon's palace.

Watanabe and Yuyachkani's Ismene is radically different and inaugurates an unprecedented curiosity about the character in the twenty-first century. Antígona's heroism was mysteriously monstrous in the twentieth century, but it will become part of every woman's life in the twenty-first century, as I comment in the final chapter of this book. Ismene's absence of heroism will gradually become mysteriously problematic. While Ralli embodies Antígona as fragile, we can still discern the heroine we have learned to associate with Antigone. She remains the "eternal gesture" that Rebagliati's Ismene imagines; she still represents the glory of which Ritsos' Ismene complains; she is still the frail but heroic Antígona in Sarina Helfgott's 1964 play.[19] And she—like Dorfman's widows, like Gambaro's Antígona—bears an "impossible universal." For her, Polinices is "Brother mine, no longer

---

[19] The Antígona that Peruvian poet Eduardo Eielson (1924–2006) envisioned in his 1945 poem "Antígona" was also frail and heroic as a nurse caring for the dead and the wounded at the end of World War II.

family, but a dead man belonging to all of us" (22).[20] Ismene, by contrast, is the sister who was "handcuffed by fear," who remembers Antígona's "gesture every day, which tortures and shames me" (64). Fear, guilt, and shame: this is the emotional language with which Ismene attempts to build the bridge between the sisters in Lima and the sisters of the Andes.

Political Violence and the CVR: 40,000 Unclaimed Corpses in the Andean Highlands

To interpret Yuyachkani and Watanabe's Antígona without universalizing gestures that empty testimony, witnessing, and community of their historical determinations, we must recall that any cultural analysis in Peru must remain attentive to the territory's profound divisions along three demographic and geographic regions: the coast, the *sierra* (the Andean highlands), and the *selva* (the Amazon rainforest). The stark differences among these regions constitute three nations in one, reflecting how the Creole republic, founded in 1821, never integrated the indigenous descendants of the Inca Empire— the majority population of the country—or those in the Amazon.

Peruvians Briceño and Luque Bedregal consider the country's structural divisions when addressing "the differences between these two audiences with respect to the position they occupied during the armed conflict" (Luque Bedregal 2010: 122). On the one hand, Luque Bedregal accounts for the aesthetic and political distance between Lima and the Andes. A show coming from Lima has symbolic capital dating back to colonial times— "and surely in most cases this was about the first contact [of the peasant audience] with the classic story" (115). The relationship between fiction and reality in Andean communities accustomed to expressing their daily life in music, folk legends, and dance endows the theatrical spectacle with a unique status. Songs, for instance, are so important that in some isolated communities, they are still used daily as the privileged (if not the only) way to express grief or joy: songs replace oral narrations.[21] As Luque Bedregal notes, Andean communities are less prone to separating fiction from reality; thus, fictional characters on stage may appear no less real to them.

---

[20] The Spanish sentence reads: "hermano mío, pero ya no pariente mío sino muerto de todos."

[21] For example, see the folk songs of the Q'eros community in the Andes, the so-called *último ayllu Inka*, "last Inka community." In Peru, they are considered as a national, living cultural heritage. See Holly Wissler's documentary *Kusisqa Waqashayku— "From Grief and Joy We Sing,"* at http://qerosmusic.com/documentary.php.

The ritual roots of theater still live in the Andes, where actors and audience are not clearly differentiated: they merely have different ways of participating in the performance. Miguel Rubio Zapata comments that at the sight of fireworks in one of their shows, the peasants left running (quoted in Luque Bedregal 2010: 120).

On the other hand, both Briceño and Luque Bedregal remind us that this conflict had not ended by the time of Yuyachkani's performance: legal and economic justice was not achieved. The conflict was too fresh. Some testimonials given to the CVR expressed a wish to forget in order to continue with life—a significant warning to remember when reading Antígona's "oblivion." The CVR also had to mount elaborate security operations for the victims who testified. Overcoming the distrust peasants have of any Lima-sponsored initiative to "remember" was a daunting task. Since independence from Spain, Lima had almost always forgotten the Andes—if not flat out denied and excluded them.

The armed conflict that began in 1980 is considered the most violent episode in Peru's republican history, with 28 percent of the fatalities registered in the Andes in 1983–4 alone.[22] The conflict reached Lima in the late 1980s and waned after the 1992 capture of Shining Path leader Abimael Guzmán. Nonetheless, that same year, then-president Fujimori closed the national Congress with a "self-coup" and ruled with exceptional powers until 2000. This meant that, on the one hand, while the conflict had unfolded for over a decade in the *sierra*, Lima experienced its severity for fewer years than the Andes did; and on the other hand, the country would live under quasi-military rule for another eight years.

From the beginning, the epicenter of the armed conflict was the Andean region that had seen intense peasant uprisings aimed at recovering land ownership as well as guerrilla movements during the 1950s and 1960s (consider the Conferación Campesina del Perú [Peasant Confederation of Peru] led by Hugo Blanco (1934–), the Ejército de Liberación Nacional [National Liberation Army] and the Movimiento de Izquierda Revolucionario [Revolutionary Left Movement]). Their objective was to eliminate *gamonalismo*, one of the most atavistic systems of land ownership still in place in

---

[22] For statistics, see the CVR's nine volumes available online at http://www.cverdad.org.pe/. They include national and international human rights reports, CIA documents, expert testimonies, and private and public testimonies. See also *The Findings of Peru's Truth and Reconciliation Commission* (2004); Taylor (2006), Rochlin (2003), and Stern (1998); for a history of insurgency in the late colonial period that shaped indigenous insurgency after Peru's independence, see Thomson (2002).

318   YUYACHKANI'S AND WATANABE'S PERUVIAN ISMENE

Latin America, whereby landowners had absolute power over peasants' lives. Left-leaning General Velasco Alvarado (1910–77) practically dismantled the power of *gamonales* with his agrarian reform during his 1968–75 regime. Velasco Alvarado's experiment was short-lived, and peasants and leftist groups mobilized again.

The CVR was an initiative of a transitional government in cooperation with some seventy nongovernmental human rights groups, which investigated crimes against humanity from 2001 to 2003. The bulk of the CVR evidence comes from the testimonial accounts of approximately 17,000 Peruvians. Peasants, not neatly allied with one group or another, were caught in the crossfire. Many of them shared the long history of autonomous political uprising in the region, or were trained and armed by the military. They were crucial in defeating the Shining Path and MRTA, having formed committees and *ronderos* (peasant self-defense patrols) early in the conflict. In many communities, the participation of women was decisive.[23] "Home" ceased to exist as anything other than one more battlefront. Family members turned against each other.

According to the CVR, 75 percent of the victims were native speakers of Quechua or other indigenous languages; 80 percent of the victims were men; 56 percent were peasants; and 68 percent were illiterate or only had elementary education. The total number of victims was set at 69,280 dead, surpassing the combined totals in all of the country's armed conflicts in the 200 years since independence. The CVR reports that 40,000 dead Peruvians remain unclaimed. If the majority of the victims were the most marginalized members of Peruvian society, then these unclaimed corpses were the marginalized among the marginalized: nobody was left to bury them.

As the representative of a state that had always ignored the highlands, the CVR had to bridge the political chasm between Lima's human rights activists and the indigenous peasants, as well as overcoming Lima's poor credibility. To cite Salomón Lerner Febres, former president of the CVR: "Nearly 70,000 Peruvians have died and [...] this seems not to have affected the rest of Peruvians, and why not? Because they were never recognized as subjects."[24] The CVR report indicates, especially in its "General Conclusions," that in

---

[23] See the film *Mujeres en la guerra*, by Felipe Degregori in 2005 (Centro de Promoción y Desarrollo Poblacional).

[24] See CVR (2003), at http://www.cverdad.org.pe/informacion/discursos/en_ceremonias. php. See also the interview posted by Cendoc, Exclusión Social y Comisión de la Verdad y Reconciliación, September 5, 2006, at http://www.youtube.com/watch?v=dtvwrMJgbJA& feature=related.

the eyes of Lima and from the perspective of all the major actors in the conflict, the peasantry is not composed of "citizens," but rather "inferior Indians" (this is true not only for the armed forces but also for the Shining Path and the urban populations).

During one televised hearing of the CVR in Lima, Juan Mendoza, indigenous coordinator for the National Board for Displaced Persons (who number approximately 600,000) spoke of a "culture of exclusion": "in this country, the laws end where the peasant community begins."[25] Commissioner Carlos Iván Degregori tried to understand how even human rights organizations struggled to imagine the total number of dead as 40,000 more than expected. He rejected the common explanation of the most affected regions' "geographic" distance from Lima, referring instead to "an emotional distance" and "a structure of feelings"—that is, the practical consciousness, thoughts, values, and perceptions shared by a generation.[26] For Degregori "[the] structure of feelings in our societies [...] is of such a nature that [...] many urbanites are sentimentally closer to Miami than to Puerto Copa."[27] For David Sulmont, the Commission's information coordinator, "All of this is like giving a blast of reality to the people who live in Lima, in the cities [...]."[28] The public hearings show peasants repeating what one of them summarized in a single question: "Can you tell me why we are not Peruvians?" During the hearings in Ayacucho, peasant witness Primitivo Quispe Pulido expressed it as follows: "So, my country was a foreign country inside of Peru."[29] In Huamanga, a peasant woman declared, "I was happy, I was even happier when I found out that in *other countries*, for example *in Lima*, I was seen on television" (my emphasis).[30] She provided perhaps the most concise formulation: Lima was not her country.

The contemporary political and emotional distances between Lima and the Andean region must be understood as five long centuries of political "distances." Félix Reátegui Carillo, recalling experiences at the public hearings, describes a peasant woman approaching a Commissioner in Huancavelica, looking at him fearfully and asking: "Who are you? Are you with the

---

[25] CVR, Video: Audiencias Públicas. Lima, December 12, 2002.
[26] Raymond Williams (1977: 128–36) develops the concept of a "structure of feelings."
[27] See video testimony of June 10, 2003 in Lima at https://lum.cultura.pe/cdi/video/entrevista-carlos-iv%C3%A1n-degregori-sobre-la-comisi%C3%B3n-de-la-verdad-y-reconciliaci%C3%B3n.
[28] See video posted by Cendoc, *Mensajes del Informe Final de la CVR: Victimas*, September 27, 2006, at http://www.youtube.com/watch?v=HE_Fu_x5FZ8&feature=related.
[29] Public Hearing, Ayacucho, Huamanga, April 8, 2002.
[30] Anexo 10, Audiencias de Huamanga CVR (2003: 8).

320 YUYACHKANI'S AND WATANABE'S PERUVIAN ISMENE

Royalist army?"[31] The "Royalist" army (*ejército realista*) was the colonial Spanish army, not the Peruvian national army. There are no ironies here. A member of the CVR who was listening to the testimonies of the peasants of Cayara recalled:

The peasants and the Commission looked at each other and recognized their otherness. A difference, the impossibility of saying "we," was very present that day. The peasants watched us anxiously. I thought that the Commission would become the "object of investigation": their gaze was demanding and the music and the dances with which the meeting began were a challenge for all of us because they signified a radical juxtaposition of their cultural identity and their criticism of the State. "We have sung and we have danced," one of them said, "because this is our way of beginning a dialogue."[32]

If Andean communities opened dialogues through dance and song performance, nothing could be more appropriate than another performance to accompany the political and emotional ritual that was to come from Lima with the CVR. The ritual that the CVR established granted political legitimacy to peasants. At the end of each testimonial, the lawyers gave the witness a certificate of participation, thus performing an attempt at community reconstruction.

The editorial in the CVR's *Boletín* No. 1 asks readers to join the work of the twelve commissioners and their collaborators, to be "responsible": "If we wonder, where was I when they killed my compatriots, when this mother lost her son? We will discover that yes, we were there, but reading a newspaper, nothing more. [...] Now we have a second chance" (2002: 4). Like Yuyachkani's Ismene, Peruvians watching the televised spectacle of the testimonies had a second chance. Lerner Febres, in the same *Boletín* No. 1, spoke also of a "second chance" for Lima and referred to his final report to the government: "No period deserves to be marked so soundly with the stamp of shame and dishonor as the fragment of history [...] in the report we deliver today to the nation. The two final decades of the twentieth

---

[31] I quote Félix Reátegui Carrillo, Research Coordinator at Instituto de Democracia y Derechos Humanos de la Pontificia Universidad Católica del Peru, from his conference "Memories of Violence in Peru: Truth-Seeking, Denial and Victims' Collective Remembering," organized by Julia Urrunaga at Yale University on October 30, 2008.

[32] Cayara is the site of a peasant massacre in May, 1988, for which the government denied responsibility. The CVR confirmed the government was responsible.

century are [...] a mark of horror and dishonor for the State and Peruvian society" (7). Lerner refers to the last quarter of a century with shame. Yuyachkani's task was to alleviate deep-seated peasant distrust of Lima authorities: Ismene ends her speech with shame.

Critical Dialogues

Given the above, critics rightly focus on memory and gender in interpreting the play, though they often do so without full consideration for the specific Peruvian conjuncture. Like Dorfman's widows and Gambaro's Antígona, the Peruvian Ismene is almost automatically seen as "the female subversion" of traditional gender roles and is deployed to account for the real-life political conflict in which Andean women were caught. The reading of the Mothers of the Plaza de Mayo as bringing the family into politics is invoked time and again. For Luque Bedregal, the play encourages "the female audience to formulate their political demands starting from their family identities [...] but in unheard-of spaces for the exercise of such roles" (141). Lane comments: "This view need not essentialize or romanticize women as maternal defenders of the family against the state—far from it. It simply describes the facts on the ground: when, for example, the Argentine or Chilean state relentlessly eliminated opposition from the public sphere [...] the formerly 'private' sphere of home or convent could and did offer refuge and generated crucial forms of opposition" (2007: 520). And yet, the Peruvian Andes are not in Argentina or Chile—and, as I have argued in previous chapters, "the facts on the ground" in those countries have little to do with domestic private spheres entering politics. Recall that the Peruvian Antígona does not bury the dead as a sister. Her brother is not "hers," but belongs "to all."

Surprising as it is, critics continue to use the division between the public and the private to understand both fictional and real women in Latin American armed conflicts. As indicated in the previous chapter, there is little explanatory value in the notion that the actions of fictional and real-life women searching for their missing are tantamount to the entrance of "private concerns" into the "male public realm." Even classicists have long—and rightly—debated this (Hegelian) interpretation of the figure of the ancient Antigone. The mechanical association between a political Antigone on an ancient stage and one on a modern stage speaks little of modern women's trajectory into politics. It speaks even less of the context of Southern post-independence nations, where "private and public" spheres have different

322 YUYACHKANI'S AND WATANABE'S PERUVIAN ISMENE

ideological value from that of industrial societies. And in what concerns gender, the Andean communities are at the crossroads of Western and millenary indigenous gender arrangements. For any analysis of Andean indigenous women, rather than the "private nuclear family," we should consider the Andean traditional form of communal property and its main unit, the extended family of the *ayllu*, in which gender roles have been historically more complementary than hierarchical.[33] How can we understand the critical gesture that insists on the private/public ideological division that characterizes modern industrial societies as a key to illuminating the organization of the private and public spheres of the *ayllu* in the Andes? This insistence becomes even less useful in the context of the militarization of politics. The play indeed quotes the famous ancient line with which Ismene warns her sister: "the gods willed that you should be born a woman [...] you can do little but obey laws" (23). But Antígona is not the protagonist of this story. So, how does Ismene fit into the heroic female transgression of entering the public space?

Compared with the ancient Ismene, this Ismene breaches gender roles through testimony. But in the Peruvian context, when Ismene goes to the Andean highlands, her testimony is a sign of obedience rather than transgression. Ismene performs the CVR's state-sponsored demand for women survivors to publicly expose their feelings. While this may appear an entrance of the feminine (typically associated with intimacy and feelings) into the public, thus transforming emotions into a political force, it in fact exposes the affect that the CVR mandated. This command to become public is encapsulated in the real feeling Ismene wants to expose on stage: shame, which collapses all boundaries between the private and the public, manifesting itself externally, dependent on the other's gaze.

Rather than "female transgression," this play follows a thread identified as a subtext in previous Antígonas in this book: the desire for female relationality. Gender analysis provides a prism through which to examine the play's shift from fratricidal war to sisterly abandonment, and the fate of the reconstruction of a female bond. For Ralli, one reason why the tragedy resonated in the Andes was the frequent intrafamilial aspect of the armed conflict.

Concerning the larger question of memory, critics unanimously see this play as an ethico-political staging of the discourses of postmemory—that is,

---

[33] See Rivera Cusicanqui (2010) for a critique of the imposition of Western gender categories onto indigenous communities.

the recovery of the disappeared in memorials—and the refutation of official discourses on forgetting and legal institutionalizations of oblivion, such as amnesty. For Luque Bedregal, the play is "transgressive of a social mandate: that of forgetting the national tragedy" (2010: 132). For Lane, it is also a play against forgetting, since no clear models for political action derive from the play—Creonte is a tyrant, Antígona dies, and Ismene arrives too late. Luque Bedregal and Lane may refer here only to audiences in Lima, for in the Andes, Ismene was obliging the state.

Transitions to "political peace" (always of uncertain meaning in the context of uneven economic distribution) are fraught with debate over what to remember and why. Official discourses that favor forgetting are pervasive; the effort against them is tireless and heroic, to the point of risking death.[34] But as with Gambaro's Antígona and Dorfman's Sofía, at stake is not just memory (bringing back what the official discourses erase). The problem is which politics of memory the present allows. The 2009 controversy over a Peruvian "museum" of memory with German government funding is illuminating. The "museum" would grant a permanent home to the photographic exhibition Yuyanapaq, one of several indigenous-based memorial efforts by Andean artists creating online "museums of memory."[35] The minister of defense, Antero Flores Aráoz, argued that the German funds should go to combatting poverty.[36] The concept of "a museum" is not part of memorializing traditions among Andean peasants. The Peruvian government assigned the mission to Mario Vargas Llosa, renowned Nobel Laureate and political candidate representing the center-right neoliberal coalition Frente Democrático (Democratic Front): the museum should "represent with objectivity and ample spirit the tragedy that Peru lived through due to the subversive actions of the Shining Path and the MRTA."[37] For the

---

[34] A thorough treatment of the subject can be found in Cohen (2001).

[35] Paradoxical as it is to assign the function of memory to such an unstable space as the Internet, these projects are democratic in that peasants' artistic homages are made more accessible. See the project "Yuyarisun: Estamos recordando" ("Let's begin to remember: We are remembering"). In 2005, this project won the award for Marginal Museums "Infolac: Mejores museos en línea"; see http://yuyarisun.rcp.net.pe/. See also http://www.pnud.org.pe/yuyana-paq/yuyanapaq.html. Yuyarisun is a Quechua word compounded with the verb remember, the invocative ri, and the first-person plural sun. Yuyanapaq is composed of na (a nominalizer) and paq, which means "to" ("to remember"). I thank José Cárdenas Bunsen for this clarification.

[36] See https://www.verdadyreconciliacionperu.com/secciones/museo-memoria.aspx

[37] See "Vargas Llosa presidirá comisión para el Museo de la Memoria en Perú," El Universal, March 31, 2009, at http://www.eluniversal.com.mx/notas/587923.html; see the many articles related to this controversy at http://www.aprodeh.org.pe/memoria2009/index1.html. The museum was inaugurated in 2015 with a different name: "Lugar de la Memoria."

324 YUYACHKANI'S AND WATANABE'S PERUVIAN ISMENE

government, "objectivity" meant assigning "enemy groups" the burden of responsibility for the "tragedy." Lima's responsibility was taken off the table. If Yuyachkani's play stages postmemory, *post* must mean the reconstruction of the political sphere as such—that is, of the conditions of possibility for a politics of memory to emerge. At stake are not the monuments, but the debates. On stage, the sisters display a complex dialectics of memory and forgetting: while Ismene's memory is "torturing" her (64), Antígona merely wants the rituals performed and "then" the remembrance of her name. She could have said her "cousin" Antígona Pérez's words—"my truth starts with my name." She does not want museums, but rather—after a funeral, and in due time—oblivion (33). Ismene remembers too much; she needs to disclose in order to forget. Hers is the "narración de urgencia" ("urgent narration") that René Jara assigns to testimonial narratives.[38]

With the exception of Briceño and Luque Bedregal, critics have tended to relate Ismene's torturous memory to an "ethics of witnessing." Ismene would be the witness who lost her "ethical capacity" in the face of overwhelming fear and thus would encourage spectators, albeit mysteriously, to recover ethics.[39] In "ethical" readings of the play, the spectators presumably identify with Ismene's guilt, critically reexamining past behaviors. Taylor describes Yuyachkani's work as a call for "communities of witnesses": they "create a critical distance for 'claiming' experience and enabling, as opposed to 'collapsing,' witnessing" (2003b: 210). For Taylor, Ismene stages "unclaimed" experience and a "collapse" of witnessing.[40] The theoretical model invoked here builds on debates around witnessing in Europe after World War II and conceives of trauma as the erasure of an event's mnemonic traces on account of the subject's inability to grasp its excessive nature. The witness is subjectively "absent" from an event due to its magnitude: the witness's ability to give testimony has "collapsed." For Taylor, Antígona offers hope for the witnesses "who were unable to respond heroically in the face of atrocity. Ismene promises to remember every day, as she reenacts her story again and again" (207). What kind of hope does she offer? That the spectator, "like Ismene, will say 'I' [...] accept the dangers and responsibilities of seeing and acting

---

[38] See Jara's "Prologue" to Jara and Vidal (1986: 3).

[39] See A'Ness (2004: 395–414), Lane (2007: 517–31), and Taylor (2000, 2003b).

[40] Taylor builds on "trauma theory" as it is conceived in the US academy and cites in particular Dori Laub's concept of "the collapse of witnessing" (Laub and Felman 1992: 75–93), which emerged out of debates about the Nazi concentration camps.

on what one has seen [...] Yuyachkani [...] teach communities not to look away" (2003b: 211).

Ismene thus becomes a survivor who has forgotten but now promises to remember, who did not accept or act upon what she saw, who lost her ethics, who would or could not act, who was absent from the events due to their magnitude, who looked away from atrocity out of fear. The ethics to be recovered here would be sacrificial: in other words, Antigone's tragic heroism.

But Ismene's actions on stage convey something different. Just as Ismene does not easily fit into the category of "heroic female transgression," neither does she qualify as an "absent witness," nor as a witness who lacks ethics. Ismene's predicament is not her inability to witness, but the decision she made because she was, in fact, able to witness. She remembers every detail of what happened. Her narration and gestures reveal that she is tormented by what she has seen and its consequences. She was not "absent" from an event whose memory would return, as in the case of trauma, unconsciously, inadvertently, fragmentarily, unarticulated, and abruptly. At no point does Ismene stumble as she articulates what she saw, and there is only one moment where we don't see her as the narrator in the scene, to which I return later.

Ismene does not reject the danger of seeing: rather, she speaks of making a decision based on her perception of the danger she would risk by acting like Antígona. The play acknowledges the complexity of fear: Ismene is fearful, not anxious. Fear, unlike anxiety, orients us to perceive real, not imagined, threats to our survival. Echoing her ancient sister, the modern Ismene says: "let us better beg the dead to forgive us and abide by the orders of the powerful living" (64). As Ritsos imagined her in the 1960s, this Ismene rejects sacrificial ethics, saving her own life. Again, context is determinant: here, a surviving Ismene performing in Lima is different from a surviving Ismene performing for communities that were wiped out, in some cases leaving very few survivors.

In the above criticism of Ismene, the ethics of sacrifice and the ethics of testimony seem to be at odds: her acting "unheroically" yesterday becomes her heroic "witnessing" of today. If Ismene encourages acting upon what one has seen, this makes her unheroic act of survival the basis for her heroic witnessing. Are Ismene's fearful actions the cornerstone for an ethics of witnessing? What code of ethics ensues from a testimony based not on chance survival, but on the fear that led to survival while betraying a sister? There is no ethical ground in the play's proposal that one should choose death (Antígona's option) over survival. Briceño captures this complexity well when she sees Ismene as a

326 YUYACHKANI'S AND WATANABE'S PERUVIAN ISMENE

survivor, suggesting her guilt may be also "survivor's guilt": surviving out of fear lacks the allure of surviving heroically.[41] Ismene's memory—a product of yesterday's fear—is today her torture and paralysis.

Leaving aside the lens of "ethical witnessing," Briceño, Luque Bedregal, and A'Ness see in Ismene's mnemonic suffering a psychic trauma in need of a cure, rather than an ethical imperative. They point to the uneasy distinction between guilt and innocence, which does not allow for a simple reading of Ismene (and, by extension, Andean spectators acting during the armed conflict) as an accomplice to violence. For these critics, Ismene's guilt is a sign of traumatic excess, rather than of ethics.

While A'Ness considers Ismene's final act a "cleansing" of her guilt (406), Briceño and Luque Bedregal both hesitate in understanding Ismene's rite as a cure. For them, Ismene is possessed by the memory of her actions in comparison to her sister's.[42] That the play is a one-woman show does not make things easier: the tortured narrator is a body bearing the same voices that do not grant her any distance from her memories. Ismene not only remembers but also becomes the characters in her memory.[43] Briceño wisely mentions gender: the narrator tells the story of others before telling her own—just like the peasant women would testify before the CVR about their husbands or sons rather than about themselves. Luque Bedregal spins this positively: the one-woman show would indicate equal treatment and "equal respect" (2010: 82) for all the characters, no matter which side they took; Brunn similarly sees in it a tool to "facilitate [...] the assertion of commonalities" (2009: 218). And yet, the characters are not treated equally, for Ismene dominates for half the show's duration.

The above debates reveal Ismene's paradoxical complexities. Her story is indeed a sign of excess that seems to dodge all interpretations. How is Ismene a victim of memory, unable to heal, but simultaneously a figure for an ethics of witnessing? What ethics of witnessing can ensue from guilt—or, alternatively, from the trauma of guilt? If the element of traumatic guilt is introduced, then reading Ismene's ethics of witnessing suddenly means reading an ethics of the cure, one could say, for memory. Is the play about

---

[41] Briceño's unpublished manuscript. Lane identifies this problem as the "ambiguous politics" of the play, though she only refers to Antigone's model as "to die in the attempt," and Ismene's as to "arrive too late" (2004: 529).

[42] Brunn, like A'Ness, sees Ismene's inability to "escape the nightmare of past events" (2009: 199) as positive, with her witnessing becoming "a source of empowerment for the survivor" (204).

[43] See Anne Lambright (2001) for a comment on Antígona's body as the female body of the nation.

curing memory or preserving memory? Critics ascribe an ethical message to Ismene, but it remains unclear where the ethics is grounded.

The crucial problem with the above is that ethical readings risk equating all survivors. Ismene would then stand in, both for the witness who lived in Lima during the armed conflict and the witness in the Andes who was caught in the crossfire. But which spectator, among those political and social actors in the aftermath of the Peruvian armed conflict, would actually identify with Ismene? Need we recall that 75 percent of this armed conflict's dead are not in Lima but in the Andes? The Andean survivors whom the CVR addressed, and to whom the performance was addressed and dedicated, were immersed in a radically different experience of witnessing. The death toll in this armed conflict compels us to situate the question of bystanders and survivors historically. Ismene's trip to the Andes compels us to do the same. No umbrella category can account for the experience of describing what was seen. Lima, Ismene's "birthplace," remained at a distance for almost a decade, until it, too, was hit by the violence. To view the play as "responsible witnessing" bypasses the question of why large numbers of people who allowed for (or fostered) this armed conflict—those who "looked away" or were complicit—would now want to acknowledge themselves as witnesses. It also bypasses what it would really mean for people from Lima to step in, postconflict, and "instruct" indigenous peoples in how to "responsibly witness" the violence that the Creole republic itself fostered: a colonial discourse, as the memory of Spanish conquerors "telling" indigenous peoples what civilization was about would doubtlessly emerge as its subtext.

Applying abstract categories of witnessing or "universality" to this performance strips the play of what is unique to theatrical performance: its presentation to a live audience. Ignoring the specificity of the Andean audience risks constructing a "universal" that excludes Andean populations. Witnessing is not an ahistorical act; nor are the acts of memory and testimony. If we agree that "trauma" signals that which cannot be fully symbolized—a name for the Lacanian "real" often cited in literary criticism—it is useful to recall that the concept of the "real" for Lacan possesses explanatory power in that it does not point to an impossibility in a vacuum, an impossibility per se. Rather, it signals that which cannot be symbolized within a given system of symbols. What counts as trauma depends on the specific events that cannot be inscribed in a concrete set of linguistic, social, or cultural rules (historical, local, memory threads). Thus, "traumatic" means something different in the Andes from that which might have been "traumatic" in

Lima. What could it have meant for witnessing to "collapse" amid the armed conflict in the Andes, in contrast to the witnessing's "collapse" in the distant Creole city? Who looked away? Who did not respond heroically to atrocity? Who had the luxury of living this history as not their own? Luque Bedregal's interrogation is pointed: "Who does the audience of Huanta *really* identify with?" (2010: 123; my emphasis). For Luque Bedregal, Huanta—with the highest number of deaths in both decades of the conflict—epitomizes the "victim itself" (123). Escape was impossible: the population that did not die had to act, by force or by its own will. It is not surprising that the peasants who approached Yuyachkani after the show inquired about Antígona, rather than Ismene.

Ismene's testimony pivots on a process of truth revelation, culminating in the feeling of shame. This realization unveils a lack of integrity vis-à-vis her self, a difference "within," an unwanted self-knowledge in the face of loss. Such knowledge prompts the questioning of the self, rather than the questioning of a deed. While the tragic past cannot be repaired— Antígona's corpse will not be collected, Ismene will not reconstitute that bond—Ismene's shameful testimony is future-oriented in its production of truth. Shame exists at the limit between the tragic and the redemptive. Shame could be a tragic element in the testimony's production of truth in an almost Kierkegaardian sense of the modern tragic: the manifestation of the tension between an objective and a subjective determinant of action that replaces the ancient figure of fate. Shame is a subjective limit parallel to the physical limit where shame usually manifests itself: on the skin, through blushing or other signs of visible anxiety. Shame marks both the internal and the external in that it depends on the community's watchful eyes.

Rather than "responsible witnessing," Ismene's witnessing is the radical promise of subjective change arising from shame. As to testimony, Ismene's words can hardly be considered "in the name of the subaltern community," the way these regional testimonial forms are generally viewed. But her words can be seen as a testimonial voice for a community grounded in the liberal value of the individual—her testimony articulates the consciousness of Lima's middle-class audience confronted with the Andean audience. Ismene mobilizes the affect of guilt for an audience in Lima—an audience that turned a blind eye to the Andes. But showing her shame, she makes a radical shift in the Andes, granting the agency of approval to the other—the indigenous South. Shame can only cease by reconnecting with the community that shows us the difference between how the community sees us and how we see ourselves. But a few more words about Yuyachkani's locality are due before I proceed.

Yuyachkani, Watanabe, Antígona: Made in Peru

During Yuyachkani's fortieth anniversary celebration at Lima's central square in 2011, the group's director, Rubio Zapata, stated: "If there is something that characterizes what we have learned these 40 years, it is to do theater 'imagined from a Peruvian perspective' [*pensado desde Peru*]."[44] Recipient of the highest human rights award in Peru, Yuyachkani is also legendary among Latin American popular theater collectives. The latter have had a greater impact on the region's theater development than individual authors: consider El Galpón (Uruguay); Rajatabla (Venezuela); Teatro del Pueblo (Argentina); Teatro Experimental de Cali and La Candelaria (Colombia); Teatro Arena, Teatro Oficina, and Teatro Macunaima (Brazil); and Malayerba (Ecuador). In Peru, Rubio Zapata traces the beginning of "street theater" to the mythical event of November 1968, when actor Jorge Acuña stood in the plaza San Martín (Lima) with a bench, scant make-up, and chalk, with which he marked a space on the ground (2001: 30). This arrangement was emulated in many public plazas throughout the nation.

Performing in the Andean *sierra* brought the group their first revelation of what committed theater away from Lima meant. The group's very first show, *Puño de cobre* (Fist of copper, 1971), was staged in solidarity with the miners in Cerro de Pasco, in central Andean Peru. The Mining Federation workers had gone on strike against the foreign Cerro de Pasco Corporation. The strike concluded with the massacre of twenty-five workers. Yuyachkani contacted the strikers and compiled testimonies from the prisoners in Huancavelica. Taking inspiration from Peter Weiss' documentary theater, Agusto Boal's "theater of the oppressed," and Teatro Arena, their stage was austere. When they finished the performance, a miner of Allpamina addressed the actors: "*Compañeros*, very good show, it's just too bad that you forgot your costumes." Of course, from their avant-garde, Western perspective, they had forgotten nothing. But as Rubio Zapata puts it, the group had forgotten the identity of their audience and its performance traditions (2001: 2). Soon thereafter, Yuyachkani became involved with the peasant

---

[44] See http://www.limaenescena.com/2011/07/yuyachkani-celebra-sus-40-años-en-la.html. See also Rubio Zapata (2001: p. xvi).

330   YUYACHKANI'S AND WATANABE'S PERUVIAN ISMENE

movement for the recovery of land, which, by the late 1960s and early 1970s, had been organized into Commando groups in response to the failures of agrarian reform. The group accompanied this process with their second show entitled *Allpa Rayku* (Por la tierra/For the land, 1978). Most of the group's shows engage cultural multiplicity in Peru and disseminate the Andean mythical worlds.[45] They incorporate dance, music, and customs, aiming at "a multiple actor," trained in numerous disciplines and aesthetic regimes and able to work with diverse public spaces and objects—plazas, schools, doors, fences, mountains, valleys. Everyone in the group has learned Quechua and plays Andean musical instruments.[46] Inspired by renowned Peruvian writer and anthropologist José María Arguedas (1911–69), who incorporated the Hispanic and Quechua worlds in his work, Yuyachkani culturally mediates between the worlds of the coastal region and the Andean and Amazonian indigenous peasant regions. The group focuses on memory, forced displacements, violence, injustice, corruption, authoritarianism, and human rights. While they are Peruvian, they also feel vehemently "Latin American."[47] Rubio Zapata insists on recovering the Latin American theatrical experimentation of, for instance, Atahualpa del Cioppo (Uruguay), Augusto Boal and Antúnes Filho (Brazil), and Enrique Buenaventura and Santiago García (Colombia).

Amid the Peruvian/Latin American productions, Yuyachkani's *Antígona* stands out as an exception. The composition of Yuyachkani's *Antígona* dates back to the early 1980s. In "Notes about our Antígona" (2000), Ralli and Rubio Zapata write a familiar story about the urban-educated Latin American practitioners of popular theater who read Antigone early in their education. Ralli recalls:

Turning to Antígona is a way of appealing to universal historical memory in order to seek in her the signs that may help us to understand our own tragedy [...] The burial of an event or a person implies evaluating, knowing its significance and giving it a name so as not to forget it [...]. It [the

---

[45] Among the most famous are *Los músicos ambulantes* (1983), *Encuentro de zorros* (1985), *Contraelviento* (1989), *No me toquen ese valse* (1990), *Adiós Ayacucho* (1990), *Hasta cuando, corazón* (1994), *Retorno* (1996), *Antígona* (2000), *Santiago* (2001), *Rosa Cuchillo* (2004), *El último ensayo* (2008), and *Concierto olvido* (2010).

[46] See the group's video *Persistencia de la Memoria* (1998); and the collection of documents online at http://www.yuyachkani.org/and at http://www.youtube.com/user/yuyachkani.

[47] Rubio Zapata has written on the mixed traditions of Latin American theater (2001, 2006, and 2011).

YUYACHKANI'S AND WATANABE'S PERUVIAN ISMENE   331

event or person] should be there, as someone who occupies space, available for a dialogue with us, now or in the future.[48]

Peruvian theater critic Antonio A. Daneri assesses that Antígona "never stopped being the lighthouse that guided" Yuyachkani.[49] He cites Rubio Zapata's assessment that the spirit of the Greeks animates the group because their theater is as local as Greek tragedy was for the ancient Greeks. In Rubio Zapata's words, "The classics were not written to be classics, they recreated their time" (quoted by Daneri, n.d.). *Antígona* emerged when the group invited Watanabe to collaborate with them, after they had read Watanabe's *Cosas del cuerpo* (Bodily things, 1999).

Watanabe, the son of a Japanese immigrant and a northern peasant woman, became a poet of the quotidian: nature and, above all, the body, which he considered the only real possession. Like the members of Yuyachkani, he embraced his generation's dreams for social change. He wrote long, poetic sentences, translatable for the stage. Honoring his success in writing scripts for successful Peruvian films, he decided to compose cue cards for each scene. He edited the most important episodes of the ancient plot so as to convey succinct messages. Each scene is a highly lyrical narrative poem. The sudden revelation at the end performs what Watanabe considered his "cinematic technique."[50]

Watanabe used Ignacio Errandonea's famous Spanish translation of Sophocles, respecting the phrases that he considered "universal." Feeling, much like Gambaro did, that it would have been too "arrogant" on his part to rewrite them, Watanabe inserted them as ancient fragments in his poems.[51] To the ancient story, he added Ismene's theft of a mortuary mask; the innocent madman who is presumed guilty; Antígona's fragility and her thoughts as she approaches death; and Ismene's funerary ritual at the end. Unlike her Greek counterpart, this Ismene does not appear at the moment of Antígona's confrontation with Creonte, but Watanabe did offer a gradual "softening" of the relationship between the sisters.[52] Antígona is more

---

[48] See Ralli and Rubio Zapata (2009).

[49] See his review, "So Classic, So Close," at http://www.yuyachkani.org/obras/antigona/antigona.html.

[50] Watanabe worked extensively in film after he successfully adapted Mario Vargas Llosa's famous novel, *La ciudad y los perros* (1963) for a film directed in 1985 by Peruvian Francisco Lombardi.

[51] Martínez Tabares (2007).

[52] In Poem 5, the "narrator" closely echoes Ismene's ancient lines about Antigone's "hot mind over chilly things" (l. 88) by saying: "Your heart harbors fiery thoughts and the desire to

332   YUYACHKANI'S AND WATANABE'S PERUVIAN ISMENE

fragile than Antigone: "Tell me what I must do!" (22), she beseeches Polinices in Poem 4. As she performs her second dusting of the corpse in Poem 8, she thinks: "Will I have the courage to defy the redoubled guards yet again, or should I resign myself? [...] No, answer me not. Today, every word and whisper enters my nightmare" (28).[53]

As in previous Antígonas, this Creonte is wrong from the beginning. After Creonte's first speech (19–20), Antígona echoes his ancient line that no man can be fully known until he rules (l. 176): "Oh! Sire, it took little for you to speak with the voice of a tyrant [...] No one knows a man's true heart until he is seen with power" (22).[54] In Poem 9, an innocent man is accused of performing the burial. Creonte sends the guards to capture the mad beggar on the hill, but awakens at night, fearful and worried (30). As the narrator qualifies this decision as laughable (26), we assume that Creonte cannot sleep because he has not proven the madman's guilt.

Tiresias' ancient warnings demonstrate certain translation difficulties. The ancient Tiresias places the world of the dead "below": Creon has wrongly kept Polynices "above." The Peruvian Tiresias conveys the perils of re-killing a dead body, but Watanabe had to invert the notion of space in order to address his audience: "You hold Polinices in the world below but he belongs to the world above, as do all the dead. [...] you play a perverse game by keeping Antígona inside a cave, which is a tomb for the dead, for even as she languishes, she lives" (55). Watanabe situates the place of the dead as either "above" (as in the popular Christian imagination) or "in a cave" (as in Andean ancient funerary rites whereby the dead were placed in small towers or caves in the mountains).

Ralli added her own "corporeal poems" to Watanabe's text. Enhanced by lighting hues and musical effects on stage, these gestures, Ralli and Rubio

---

disobey, which would make others freeze" (23). But unlike the ancient sister, Ismene addresses her sister, gently asking her to rest: "let sleep be a peaceful truce through the long night. Sleep" (23). Antígona is also gentle with Ismene before Creonte: Antígona tells him that Ismene's "daring thoughts go no further than her timid forehead" (37).

[53] We also see a difference from the ancient Antigone in that her Peruvian sister utters the famous line, "I was born to love, not to share hatred" (37) but does not claim she would not have buried a husband or a son.

[54] Nonetheless, the Peruvian Creonte is not as harsh as the ancient one. To Hemón, Creonte utters the age-old lines of the father to the son, "let her find a lover in Hades, and you, my son, search among other maidens, there are other fields to plow" (45), but he cannot address his son (and instead only speaks to himself) when it comes to thinking of his son as "bewitched by a vile woman" (52). Ismene, in a moment of hesitation, humanizes Creonte: "Let us not assume that the king's heart is as hard as it seems. He certainly overcame a thousand doubts before condemning the youthful girl" (39).

YUYACHKANI'S AND WATANABE'S PERUVIAN ISMENE   333

Zapata believe, constituted a matrix of identification for Andean audiences. Ralli composed these corporeal poems by recalling the episode of the Japanese Embassy hostage crisis in front of her house, Watanabe's comments as they rehearsed the play, Rubio Zapata's ideas, and, most important, the gestures and stories obtained from interviews with Andean peasant women victims. As she told them the story of the ancient Antigone, the women would say in surprise, "That's exactly what happened to us, we lived through the same thing."[55] The CVR recorded many testimonies from women that portray extraordinary courage and resolve in the face of brutal violence. While Yuyachkani's Ismenes were in Lima, the women Ralli interviewed were the true Antígonas in Peru.

For Rubio Zapata and Ralli, the play is indeed an act of memory, which began as part of a larger project originally titled "La Danza del Olvido" ("The dance of forgetting"), then became "Memoria" ("Memory").[56] However, the discourse of guilt, indifference, and emotional distance that urban citizens felt vis-à-vis the violence became central for their interpretation of Ismene, who became an allegorical figure for "all Peruvians" and, as they often clarify in interviews, "especially those in Lima." Ralli describes: "We had to recognize, all of us, as citizens, that we had maintained a 'despicable silence' before thousands of corpses spread throughout all of Peru […]. We Peruvians were all Ismene […] For almost twenty years, half the country lived in that reality" (quoted in A'Ness 2004: 407). Rubio Zapata asserts that "we Peruvians […] had and we still have much guilt […] rather than Antígonas in Peru, there have been Ismenes. And I believe we certainly identify more with Ismene than with Antígona because of that gesture we could not make in time." Watanabe expresses himself similarly in an interview with Vivian Martínez Tabares (2007): "The idea was that […] the audience feel that in some way the character of Ismene was alluding to them, and I believe that the public really did understand it in this way. Really, the majority of us Peruvians didn't do much."

But in terms of "the pain of others," to recall Susan Sontag's famous title (2003), no "we" can be taken for granted. The real question is from where the "despicable silence" emanated and where the "thousands of corpses" were found. How do we equate the Andean mother who carried her child in

---

[55] Ralli calls this process "sensitive accumulation" (see Lane 2007: 517–31).
[56] Interview with Rubio and Ralli during the First Annual Conference of the Hemispheric Institute of Performance and Politics—Brazil 2000. See Taylor (2000).

334 YUYACHKANI'S AND WATANABE'S PERUVIAN ISMENE

her arms and was forced to decide between killing the child herself or letting the armed man who aimed his gun at her do it (as in an example extracted from the public hearings of the CVR) with the Lima dweller who read about her in the newspapers? In the context of the "impossibility of saying we," of the "emotional distance" between the Andes and Lima, of those unclaimed 40,000 corpses: what was Yuyachkani's Ismene "thinking, remembering" in Huanta? Yuyachkani's task was to create "structures of emotional *closeness*" to counter the "emotional distance" between the capital city and the Andean South. What can the stage tell us about Ismene's "closeness" with the Andean audience?

Ismene's Voyage to the Andean Highlands: The Unmasking Act

The two sisters perform a similar act at different moments in the play: they reveal their identity. Theirs is a "drama of revelation" that transcends the identification of proper names to unveil identity as constituted by a web of relations, thus placing the community at center stage. In Poem 10, Antígona is caught and, lifting her head defiantly, declares: "*everyone will say* that I was the sister who did not fail her brother: my name is Antígona" (34; my emphasis). When Tiresias asks Creonte to reverse his action, he places the king in the eyes of others: "Let *people say* that you were brave" (51; my emphasis). The production highlights Antígona's revelation, as Ralli's line is followed by a moment of stillness: hands as if tied behind her back, head tilted backward as if her hair were being pulled, she gazes silently at the audience. Music and light focus on her body for several seconds. We don't just know her name; we also know how the community will see (and speak of) her. Antígona's second revelatory moment comes in Poem 13: Watanabe breaks the pattern of narrating characters' entrances as Ralli enters the stage as Antígona with no introduction. As she dies, she conceals her face behind the chair and recalls her family's curse: "I am the curse, the odd wave that crashes and dies inside this cave" (42). This is her only unmediated appearance, the sole instance where a prop, rather than narration, guides how the audience understands her. These two departures from the play's rules indicate that Antígona's death cannot be narrated in simple terms but must be framed by the audience (the chair arms form a perfect square, framing her face). The narrator remains silent. Her death is the only excess that Ismene cannot—or has decided not to—put into words, the torturous image that reminds her of the contrast between her actions and Antígona's. Antígona's death is the absent center of Ismene's narration, the unnamed driving force of her speech. It has to be seen, before being narrated. Ismene did not witness it, just as Lima did not witness the death of the Andean peasants.

The divergence in the two sisters' self-definitions is illuminated in this moment. Though both define themselves in terms of their actions, Antígona includes the community in her self-perception, worrying about what "everyone will say" about her burial. Ismene is a testament to the transformative power of action, what Boal ([1979] 1983) called "essential theater": the act of seeing oneself acting. Ismene moves from inaction to action: remembering, reliving, reenacting, and retelling her story changes her, so that, by the end of the play, she can remove her veil of anonymity. Briceño (2004) well notes that she does not name herself, as Antígona does. She is not "Ismene" but "the sister"—a sister, simply. Or not so simply: being a "sister" defines her in relational terms. What "everyone will say" about her is what she realizes about herself: "I am that sister who was handcuffed by fear" (63). Ismene wants her audience to remember her identity-in-relation and gradual self-revelation. Contrast this with what we should remember of Antígona: her name.

The play's performance of truth revelation shares in the veritable "engineering" of truth mounted by the CVR. This national moment attempted to reconstruct a politics of memory through dialectics of revelation and concealment, which required a performance of emotions and truth revelation from peasants and commissioners. The play shared the spirit of the times by positioning the characters as part of the community, just as the peasants who testified in front of the CVR positioned themselves within their own communities. The *zeitgeist* behind the international emergence of Truth Commissions in recent decades equates access to "the truth" (of hidden complicities, betrayals, and perpetrator identities) with political peace. Ismene performed Peru's official national moment by yearning for "unveiling."

I will not try to comment on the possibility (or even existence) of eliciting the "truth" other than in political terms—that is, attending to the demands of specific actors involved in political struggles. Rather, I suggest that we look at the question of "truth" here in light of the local dynamics of disguise characteristic of internal armed conflicts—a sort of theater of truth that we might call "armed performance tactics." *Senderistas* (members of the Shining Path) would often appear disguised as military soldiers, rounding up peasant villagers; conversely, military soldiers, when rounding up villagers whom they suspected were *Senderistas*, would disguise themselves as

336 YUYACHKANI'S AND WATANABE'S PERUVIAN ISMENE

Senderistas to give villagers the impression of conflicts within the rebel group.[57] These tactics differ from military camouflage and the use of hooded masks to conceal face features. They aimed at being seen—but as someone else. This situation further complicates the dynamics of revelation and concealment within Andean peasant communities, especially considering that in these cultures, the boundaries between dreams and reality, visibility and invisibility, truth and lies, and the living and the dead are more difficult to discern than in secular Western contexts.

"Public secrets" pervade communal visions of what happened during what peasants, mixing Spanish and Quechua, call *manchay tiempo* ("the time of fear"). Unveiling events was complicated by villagers' agreements "to remember to forget" everyone's involvement in the conflict. Anthropologist Olga González's ethnography in the Andean village of Sarhua provides an example: to break agreed-upon silences, González showed peasants a variety of local paintings about violence (2011). In her account, stories from both before and during the "times of danger" involve spirit apparitions, people's bewitchment, condemned souls who have not confessed their sins, and people with two faces. The latter are known as the *qarqachas* and are particularly deceitful: they have both a human and an animal face. They can only become human again if they repent to the community. In González's case study, villagers who were *Senderistas*, or killed in obedience to military orders, were often called *qarqachas* (2011: 155–208).

In the context of so much secrecy, the CVR provided a platform for saying who was who, who was where, or who was with whom. Of course, the "production of truth" meant something different to the Lima commissioners than it did to the peasants, but the structure of unveiling is common to both. The testimonies reveal how deeply peasants felt the need to correct Lima's perceptions about the Andes. For all that Ismene's guilt resonated with urban audiences, the reigning sentiment in peasant testimonies is not guilt, but pride at finally being considered part of the Peruvian state. This pride resonates with Antígona's truth. In the hearings in Huamanga, for instance, almost all the testimonies refer to an ethical obligation to maintain unity in the community. Multiple testimonies resemble a version of Antígona's phrase at the moment she is caught: like Antígona, peasants were extremely conscious about how the community would remember them, how everyone would know who they really were and what they had done.

---

[57] See accounts of Senderista strategies in Gorriti (1990); see also Thomson (2002).

YUYACHKANI'S AND WATANABE'S PERUVIAN ISMENE 337

There are striking parallels between Watanabe's play and the testimonies before the commission. Ismene expresses pride for her sister, describing her as a "hunted animal" surrounded by guards, although "in fact, she is the only princess of this land" (35). Peasants reported that they felt like "hunted animals," but were also proud of "having spoken well," of not having "failed" their community.[58] Almost all felt acknowledged as "subjects," or "citizens," rather than "dying like dogs without owners" caught in the crossfire. There were also those who felt proud of being seen by others—their families—on television, and being approved of while giving testimony. Some testified to their innocence after false accusations that they belonged to a certain group. There were peasant *ronderos* who asked their companions for forgiveness for excesses committed as they defended themselves. One woman summarized their long resistance: leaning over the microphone, she clarified that she did not come to "give voice to those without voice," because the peasants "have always had a voice"; she had only come to "give louder voice," to turn up "the volume" so that everyone could hear.[59] There was also a fear of testifying and the weariness stemming from a long history of violence. One peasant told Rubio Zapata: "What good does it do to remember? [...] nothing ever changes"; another one recalled: "When I was a boy I would play on the mountain, looking for the most destroyed corpses."[60]

This was the peasant audience for which Yuyachkani's Ismene performed. In the Andes, nobody could afford the luxury of indifference. Fear drove the peasants to arm themselves—to conceal their daughters, to obey the command to witness the torture of their loved ones. We are obliged to ask under what circumstances Ismene could perform the task of (theatrical) community building before the audience that inspired the play, given the discrepancy between Ismene's feelings and the peasants' testimonies. Ismene does not tell her Andean audience that she is proud to speak, nor does she feel she must establish her innocence in the face of false accusations.

Feelings of guilt such as Ismene's might have remained culturally more difficult for peasants to report. When Luque Bedregal responds to critics who read Ismene's guilt, he assesses Lima's discourse of guilt. He does not think the peasants could have felt guilt for "not having acted on time, or having kept oneself at the margins of violent actions—the basis for the guilt

---

[58] I extract and paraphrase from the hearings of Huamanga, but I have kept quotation marks in for those words that I do not paraphrase. Annex 10 of the CVR's reports summarizes the common themes of the testimonies.

[59] Public Hearing, Ayacucho, Huamanga, April 8, 2002. [60] Rubio Zapata (2006: 64).

338   YUYACHKANI'S AND WATANABE'S PERUVIAN ISMENE

of Lima audiences could not have been valid or possible options in the context of Ayacucho...the guilt is more perverse and asphyxiating in that it lacks a real basis that could originate and justify such feeling" (2010: 125). Luque Bedregal remains uncertain as to the complexity of the Huanta audience's identification with the characters of the play and understands guilt as closer to what I see as shame. For him, it may be difficult for peasants to find emotional tools to overcome their anguish, and guilt may result from community dynamics such as accusations about being on the wrong side of the conflict, not from internalized feelings of failure to follow normative ethical principles. Ralli, in turn, speaks of a complex, shame-ridden guilt among peasant women who blame themselves or are blamed by members of the community for having become victims, for example, of rape.

There remains yet one more dynamic of guilt and innocence to consider as we parse out the differences between the two audiences. In peasant testimonies, the discursive appearances of guilt often refer to assigning innocence. Peasants advocated for mitigating circumstances (of self-defense) to explain their actions. Their urgency was to assert their innocence, as the nature of this armed conflict had eliminated the possibility of innocence for peasants. Both the military and the armed organizations assigned guilt to everyone without the benefit of the doubt; every peasant, including children, became "suspects" of participating in either one or the other side of the conflict. "To be a peasant" during "the times of fear" meant "to be guilty."[61] There was also no room for uncontested fields of "innocence" in the intracommunal assignation of guilt among peasants. Yuyachkani intervenes at this juncture: while the peasants hoped to reveal their innocence, Yuyachkani's Ismene highlighted Lima's reticence to acknowledge its own role in perpetuating the conflict.

In this light, we better understand Poem 7: the scene of the innocent man, found lurking around Polinices' body, who is accused of the crime. The narrator tells that in his madness "there are no kings, nor heroes or traitors, only a dog" (26). Not only is this man considered guilty by the guards and the community despite his "claims" (26) of innocence, he is also a man for whom, as was the case for many real-life peasants, the

---

[61] The CVR's public hearings are filled with cases of arbitrary torture on the accusation of "suspected" alliances. For women, rape was the norm. In the hearings of Trujillo (September 25–6, 2002), Graciela Espinoza Monteza testified of being raped by the military as a high-school teenager and then sentenced to serve twenty years in prison; Magdalena Monteza was kidnapped at the university, forced to give birth in prison, and sentenced to life—neither woman had any relation with any of the groups involved in the conflict.

YUYACHKANI'S AND WATANABE'S PERUVIAN ISMENE   339

terms "hero" and "traitor" are not particularly meaningful. The communal perception that he is guilty is wrong, says the narrator. But the play also suggests that the only innocent man imaginable is one who has gone mad, the one whose "judgment is impaired" (26).

Among the Andean peasant audiences, Ismene would seem not to belong: at this historical moment, the audience is full of real-life Antígonas, survivors trying to establish a discourse of innocence, proud to finally be recognized as citizens with the right to reveal their own truths. It is as if Ismene came from afar, using testimonial forms that the CVR would encourage but expressing a different subjective experience of the armed conflict than that of her peasant sisters. A sense of distance was built into the play from the start: Rubio Zapata first imagined Ismene speaking at a conference. Later, the idea emerged that Ralli could be a radio host inside a sound booth, receiving news from the distant land of Thebes. The host would then leave the booth and speak.[62] In the final version, the distance is temporal: Ismene reports, just as the radio host would have done, but after Antígona has died.

Progressing from the hidden narrator to the unveiling of Ismene's identity, a dialectics of masking and unmasking adds another sign of distance to the drama of revelation: Ismene comes to the Andean highlands wearing no indigenous mask. Critics want to see a "stripped stage," judging it against European conventions. But in the Andes, if this stage was stripped of anything, it was stripped of indigenous performance conventions. Ismene enters the stage carrying a stolen mask inside a wooden box, but she does not wear it: she "wears" the narrative mask when embodying the narrator or the other characters. She has no mask of her own.

Contrast this with the two other plays with which Yuyachkani's tour in the Andes executed its information campaign (named "Para que no vuelva a suceder"/"So it will not happen again"). Antígona was accompanied by two "Peruvian" plays, Adiós Ayacucho (composed in 1990) and Rosa Cuchillo (2002). Both plays incorporate indigenous myths, customs, funeral rituals, and festivity masks—or, alternatively, "white-face." There were also installations in the main plazas featuring Peruvian flags and Andean ritual elements such as candles, sacred vases, and traditional skirts, hats, and masks. One actor played a bombo bass drum while wearing the mask of the Huacón, which, in pre-Hispanic Andean communities of central Peru, translates roughly as

---

[62] Ralli and Rubio Zapata (2000): "Notas sobre nuestra Antígona," see www.geocities.com/antigona_yuyachkani/.

340 YUYACHKANI'S AND WATANABE'S PERUVIAN ISMENE

"mask" and refers to the wooden masks for ritual dances related to the agricultural cycles and the ancestors' cult.[63] As A'Ness points out, the "white-face" helps Yuyachkani avoid a racialized performance whereby they would be clearly identified as urban, uncritically "performing Indian" (2004: 412).

Adiós Ayacucho was a one-man performance that told the story of Alfonso Cánepa, a disappeared peasant leader who travels from the land of the dead to Lima to ask the president to help him recover his bones and have a proper funeral. His bones, he claims, have been stolen and sent to Lima by his killers. The actor is masked, and he wears a traditional Andean belt made of vicuña fur around his waist. The dead man writes a letter to the president and mentions that one of his ancestors once wrote a letter to the King of Spain.[64] Peruvian historian Ponciano del Pino observes that since colonial times, indigenous communities have addressed the supreme leader as guarantor of their rights—perhaps related to ancient memories of addressing the Inca as ruler of the Empire.[65]

In turn, *Rosa Cuchillo* is a one-woman performance staged in Andean plazas, streets, and markets, featuring a white-faced mother who searches for her disappeared son after her own death.[66] Based on Óscar Colchado's novel of the same title, it honors the life of Angélica Mendoza—known as "mamá Angélica"—founder of the Asociación de Familiares y Desaparecidos de Ayacucho (Association of Relatives and Disappeared Persons of Ayacucho). The play incorporates Angélica's real-life declarations about her son, Arquímedes Ascarsa, who was kidnapped by the armed forces in 1983. Actress Ana Correa has spoken of the two-way emotional identification she experienced in Huanta playing Rosa: walking with white-face make-up through the streets and seeing mothers break into tears when they heard her story, she too could not stop crying (in Luque Bedregal 2010: 120).

Antígona was the only non-indigenous show, though the group originally entertained the idea of incorporating the myth of the *Huacón* to produce an

---

[63] See Barraza Lescano's anthropological research (2009).

[64] The reference here is to Felipe Guamán Poma de Ayala (1535?–1616?), who lived in Huamanga and wrote a letter to King Philip III of Spain (February 14, 1615), explaining the history of his people, the Incas, meant as a plea for the King to improve the colonial government. See *The Guaman Poma Website*: http://www.kb.dk/permalink/2006/poma/info/en/frontpage.htm.

[65] I thank Ponciano del Pino for offering me his unpublished article, "In the Name of the Government: Community Politics, Violence and Memory in Modern Peru," presented at Yale University in 2009. See also del Pino (2017).

[66] See http://www.yuyachkani.org/obras/rosacuchillo/rosa.html (accessed May 25, 2010).

"Antígona Huanca."[67] Ismene was the only character speaking in the (dramatic) present, rather than from beyond the grave, and the only one not searching for someone or something. Whereas Cánepa searches for his bones and Angélica for her son, Ismene has already found what she is looking for. She enters the stage having stolen the white mortuary mask that Creonte made for her brother. Wearing neither a mask nor white-face, Ismene is the only character who breaks Andean performance conventions and Yuyachkani's own recourse to white-face as a performance strategy.

The stage that appeared "universal" to critics is, in reality, stripped of an indigenous mask. For an indigenous audience, the lack of a mask conveyed the racialized locality of Lima, where theatrical traditions merge with the "stripped stages" of the twentieth-century European and Latin American avant-garde.[68] We may see in the unmasked performance an allegory for the group itself and, by extension, for the Lima theater-going urbanites willing to transform their "structures of feeling" by engaging with the Andean highlands.

Ismene's unmasked face in Ayacucho is one of the bodily signs in the dialectics of proximity and distance with which she communicates with her audience. If the unmasked Ismene is the sister from afar, Ralli's impersonation of Ismene with the expressions of Andean women reaches out to Ismene's sisters in their language. Ismene's guilt and shame is foreign to her Andean sisters, but her drama of revelation resonates with that audience's urgencies. Masking and unmasking reconstitutes the broken bond between Lima and the Andes.

There is yet one more dialectics of masking onstage: Ismene carries a mask in her box, breaks it, and "buries it." Here, Watanabe's text and Yuyachkani's performance diverge. Ismene does not use the mask to conceal or reveal her appearance, but rather, to perform a funeral ritual as she remains unmasked and non-indigenous. As critics have noted, at first glance it seems that Ismene has stolen the mask after Antígona's death, once Ismene resolved to perform the belated libations. But upon closer scrutiny of the text, we find that this is not the case. Poem 9 suggests that the theft happened right after Antígona finished covering the corpse with dust

---

[67] The reference to the Huacón appears in the announcement at http://www.caretas.com.pe/1998/1506/culturales/culturales.htm (accessed May 1 2010).

[68] Pianacci (2008: 152) notes a line that for him refers to Lima as a location: the presence of "alamedas" (a public walkway surrounded by poplars), which are famous in Lima and celebrated in songs and literature (for instance, the Alameda de los Descalzos). As interesting as the suggestion is, I do not readily concur since there are famous "alamedas" in Ayacucho too—consider the Alameda of Huamanga, the city where the Shining Path began.

342 YUYACHKANI'S AND WATANABE'S PERUVIAN ISMENE

during her first nighttime excursion. Having spoken to the guard who first brought the news of the corpse's burial, Creonte, alone at night, mumbles: "The day I first assumed power I saw my first felony: Polinices' death mask disappeared, the one I had made so that the enemy would have a face, before his features were lost, as I ordered, beneath the sun's rays" (31). Pre-Hispanic Andean funeral traditions used masks to cover the faces of the dead so they would be identified as human despite having decomposed. Creonte's intention was to identify the body as a human enemy. In Poem 8, Antígona expresses anguish over Polinices' putrefaction. She speaks to the gods, protesting the lack of cover for her brother: "How shameful, how obscene it is, to end life unburied; soft, viscous matter exposed to the eyes of the living" (28).

Creonte and Antígona both worried about covering the corpse, though for different reasons. Ismene was in a great rush to find the mask, having stolen it either in the midst of Antígona's attempts or straight afterward. Three types of funeral emerge here, rather than the classical two. First, we have a modified version of Creon's classical funeral rite, with the addition of the mask that identifies Polinices as the enemy. Antígona's funeral in defense of the "equal rights" (37) of both corpses in the world of the dead adds to the classical ritual three libations of wine, which she spits out as she declares them to be "in the name of all the others" (33). Ismene, in contrast, wants to use the mask to perform her own kind of funeral rite. Is this her way of disobeying Creonte and honoring her brother, adhering to the Andean indigenous tradition of using the clothes (in this case, the mask) when a corpse is missing? The text only indicates Ismene's failure: we see her performing the rite after Antígona's death, accompanied by her plea for forgiveness. The unmasked sister lifts Polinices' mask, spits out her own three libations, and says to Antígona: "this is the face of our brother before he was attacked by dogs, vultures, and decay" (64; Figures 7.1 and 7.2).

We can read—literally—this rite as part of Yuyachkani's Andean repertoire in the highlands. Recall Cánepa, the disappeared peasant in *Adiós Ayachucho*. While Cánepa's bones were stolen and sent to Lima, Ismene returns to Huanta from Lima with the indigenous mask she has stolen from power (represented by Creonte, the central government, the presidential house where Cánepa goes to demand his bones) and places it where it belongs—in the Andes, in an indigenous funerary rite—thus (allegorically) placing Cánepa's body where it belongs. This city-dweller has made Cánepa's bones and mask her own. Her gesture honors Cánepa's plea and tradition. Rubio Zapata wrote in a diary about his experience with the shows in

Figure 7.1 Ismene and the mask. Teresa Ralli as Ismene, *Antígona*, Yuyachkani. Courtesy of photographer Elsa Estremadoyro and Teresa Ralli.

Ayacucho that in the Andes, life and fiction mix, and thus, "Alfonso Cánepa could be Antígona's dead brother and Rosa Huanca could be his mother who reunites with him after her own death in an endless dance that defies oblivion" (2006: 63).

Embodied by the Lima dweller Teresa Ralli, the unmasked Ismene goes further. The text does not describe Ismene throwing the mask to the ground and smashing it to pieces in fury. But Ralli does so, performing the "funerary rite" with only the broken pieces of the mask, which she covers with a white translucent shroud and sand. Breaking the mask is polysemic: it might multiply the brother into many. The mask represents indigenous traditions, but also, from Creonte's point of view, the enemy. In Ralli's act, the annihilation may be seen as destroying the symbol of enmity constructed by Creonte's power. If we place this detail in the context of the trilogy once more, we can see Cánepa-Polinices representing a rebel peasant in the troubled thoughts of military leader Creonte.

Figure 7.2 Ismene (Teresa Ralli) grabs the mask and speaks to Antígona, *Antígona*, Yuyachkani. Courtesy of photographer Elsa Estremadoyro and Teresa Ralli.

Recall here the dance of the *Huacón*, which featured in the original plans for the play. Pre-Hispanic communities in the Andes believed death occurred only once the body was no longer there, hence the emphasis on materializing the ancestors through masks, mummification (especially for royalty), and funerary bundles placed in sacred caves (*Huacas*) along with objects. According to Barraza Lescano (2009), the origins of the dance of the *Huacón* lie in masks representing the deceased, sometimes made with the skin and bones of the dead. In some localities, the dance referred instead to foundational wars, and these masks represented the dead enemies. With the masked representation of the enemy, the community appropriated his energy and strength—a cultural act of cannibalism, here not referring to the colonial heritage. Creonte's masking of Polinices preserves Polinices as an enemy. If Polinices is Cánepa, or any peasant enemy of the military who has long demanded inclusion in the nation, Ismene stealing this mask and smashing it on the ground prior to her funerary libations may indicate the

YUYACHKANI'S AND WATANABE'S PERUVIAN ISMENE 345

end of the enmity between Lima and the Andean peasantry. Ismene arrives with the peasant enemy mask to transform it, through a funeral rite, into a friend, as she returns it to where it belongs in the Andes.

A Tale of Two Sisters: The Gaze on Shame

If Watanabe sought to shock the audience with the final revelation of the narrator's identity, a critic could focus on the narrator's final word, "shame," rather than guilt. Shame is the end-point of Ismene's appeal for emotional proximity with the indigenous audience. Ismene's last line addresses Antígona, and, indirectly, Polinices: "And tell him that I already suffer a dreadful punishment: to remember every day your gesture that tortures and shames me" (65). Luque Bedregal emphasizes the word *castigo* (punishment): "the word 'punishment' [...] situates us in the realm of the law" (2010: 78). Nonetheless, if the final scene gives meaning to the poem-play and the final word gives meaning to Ismene's punishment, this punishing remembrance results in her shame. Shame is the quilting point between two genres: testimony and tragedy. It bridges two audiences: urban and peasant. It bonds two sisters.

The focus on guilt only registers Ismene's deeds. Ismene testifies that she did not do what Antígona did. But a discourse about action—on which common law, rather than Roman law, is based—does not fully account for how this Ismene articulates her connection with an audience such as the Andean one.[69] Few emotions imply more intimacy than the "nudity" of shame—an emotion known to cause involuntary physical reactions. The discussion about how to distinguish between guilt and shame exceeds the scope of this chapter, but for the purpose of my reading of Ismene, I note the following.[70]

Guilt seems to relate to ideals internalized as individual, ethical imperatives that can be broken. It refers to actions, thus carrying a discourse of accountability codified by civil and religious institutions, with ritualized mechanisms of atonement, expiation, and forgiveness. If correctly performed, guilt is expiated. But the atonement of guilt is separate from the gaze of

---

[69] Common law prevails in Anglophone America; Roman law, based on consciousness of one's actions, prevails in "Latin" America.

[70] See Lacan (1992), de La Taille (2004), and de Gaulejac (1996). For a distinction between "shame culture" and "guilt culture," see the classic work on the Greeks by Dodds (1951).

346 YUYACHKANI'S AND WATANABE'S PERUVIAN ISMENE

others. It happens in the secluded space of the church or the court. It does not necessarily entail the approval of the community, nor is it guaranteed to prevent future legal transgressions. Like all legal discourses, the discourse of guilt repairs a damage already done, but does not intervene in the future. Guilt is past-oriented.

Instead, shame is a "revolutionary" feeling, to recall the epigraph of this chapter. Shame is a self-conscious feeling structured around the other's vision. I surmise that shame marks the meeting point among aesthetic, political, and ethical feelings. Shame is the rupture at this meeting point: the breaking of any link between aesthetics, politics, and ethics. It is a feeling of discrepancy between one's own image and the image (whether internalized or not) that the community imposes on us. Shame is essentially "theatrical" in its manifestation and is essentially an act of witnessing: we see ourselves being seen by the other. We witness doubly, or perhaps triply: we witness how the other sees us, how we see ourselves, how we see ourselves when the other sees our most intimate self. To recall Sartre's famous line, we feel the shock of the other watching: "I wish you to suffer, like me, the shock of being seen."[71]

Whereas guilt builds on the internalized voices of the bearers of the law, shame is a fundamentally relational feeling. Hinging upon the logic of the image—that is, upon a *Gestalt*—shame can be translated into the language of consciousness as a disturbance in one's feeling of integrity, in one's consistency with one's own words or actions. In shame, we find a splitting between our deeds and our words—or between deeds and words, and our self-image—before the eyes of the other. We are not whole. While, in the West, we tend to think of subjective splitting, after Freud, as a result of our "being in language," Ismene reveals for us the visible aspect of the latter: "being in the gaze" of others, not only in the discourse of others. We may assume that shame is oriented to the relation with the other in ways that guilt is oriented to tasks. Guilt is repaired with a set of coded actions; shame is repaired with the community's approval. A guilty person might be punished (and pardoned) by law, but never accepted by society; a shameful act may be disapproved of by society, but never punished by law. Shame grants agency to the other.

We may understand that Ismene goes naked to Huanta, exposing an image of herself that contradicts the image she has of herself: she suffers not

---

[71] My translation of Sartre's phrase in his preface to "Orphée Noir" (1948).

YUYACHKANI'S AND WATANABE'S PERUVIAN ISMENE   347

for what she did not do, but for realizing that she is not the image she had projected to others. In the final scene, Ismene recounts her last dialogue with Antígona. Her sister tells her: "I trust that having been born noble, villainy has not overpowered you" (63). Nobility is Ismene's self-image, and the image Antígona has of her. Now Ismene witnesses how her self-image differs in the eyes of others. She does not tell her audience that she is guilty of "looking away," as critics contend. Ralli's gestures are telling: she looks away only after staring at her sister. The way Ismene fixes her eyes on her sister does not coincide with how her sister (and the community) expected her to look, nor with how Ismene thought of herself, or perhaps how she thought she would be able to look at her sister. Briceño's idea that Ismene's real "trauma" becomes the sister Antígona may be complemented with the trauma of self-image. Antígona acts according to her beliefs; Ismene does not. She has not only failed to act nobly, feeling like "a small cowering animal," but also tells Antígona something untrue to her own thoughts: "Knowing that she was right, I told her she was delirious, that she had been possessed by an air of madness" (63).

With Briceño, I note that the end is not the only moment in Yuyachkani's *Antígona* in which a communal gaze plays a role. Thebans have been subject to an all-controlling gaze in Creonte's city: he has sent "eyes into all parts of the city [which] have seen people shaking their heads behind [his] back" (30). In Ralli's rendition, as Ismene enters the stage, we sense her fear of being perceived. She arrives as if escaping from afar, casting frantic glances in all directions, turning her head around, panicked. Once calm, she settles on a chair and begins her narration: "Let us thank life today and the sun and peace like limpid air, and let us begin to forget" (16). As she completes her first speech, however, she glances fearfully behind her at the door through which she entered, from which a frightening noise emanates; with her hand, she gestures toward the wooden box she has brought with her, but decides to resume her seat and continue her speech. We sense her fear of being seen even as she asks the audience (in Poem 2): "Do you see that corpse on the arid land stretched out in perfect profile?" (17). She has seen, and because she has seen, she now covers her face with her hands in despair.

Ismene first refers to guilt as an inner feeling. She describes Antígona's gaze as she walks: "The guilt we feel is *in ourselves*, people of Thebes, not in the intention of her gaze" (21; my emphasis). Antígona does not judge others but refers instead to her own vision as the site of her consciousness. While everyone is at the party of peace, she asks how she can erase "with my eyes

348   YUYACHKANI'S AND WATANABE'S PERUVIAN ISMENE

what they do not see but which most certainly is there?" (22; in the Spanish version "they" here can refer to her eyes and to the people).[72]

The communal gaze is so omnipresent that even the trees are watching. In Poem 8, Ismene describes Antígona walking beneath the pines and leaning her cheek against the bark of the trees while the "gods of the poplars watch her pass by" (27). Antígona asks the pine trees, "can you see" that the wind "[has] blown away the fine dust with which I covered his nakedness at dawn?" (28). At the thought of the exposed Polinices, Ralli—in the role of Antígona—covers her face with her hands, mimicking Ismene's gesture when she first mentioned Polinices at the beginning of the play. The light focuses on her. She speaks of the shame caused by the corpse's exposure "to the eyes of the living" (28). All of nature, in this instance, joins the community of watchers.

In Poem 11, the community's eyes are on Antígona. Ismene asks the Thebans, who "watch and hide like inquisitive monkeys," to look closely at how Antígona, treated as "an animal," goes to the palace handcuffed to confront the tyrant (35). In Poem 16, before introducing Tiresias, Ismene imagines how a foreigner would see her land: "He would not see the turbulence beneath the calm waters" (49). To "see" is the responsibility of all Thebans, as Tiresias now reminds the king. The Theban people look, but unlike Ismene, they are blind. As the condemned Antígona is taken to the cave, she sees the Thebans: "faces behind the windows, trees, sidewalks [...]" (39). Hemón, anxiously wandering, is the only one who turns his gaze toward the mountain where Antígona languishes (43). He has "seen" himself suddenly dead in a senseless dream (43) and goes to the palace to reprove his father with a disdainful gaze (60). Ismene asks what has happened to her land that "such young eyes should gaze with such bitterness?" (43), but once Antígona enters the cave not even "the sacred eye of day" penetrates its interior (47).

Surrounded by gazes, yet alone, Antígona imagines a future community where "everyone will say" that she did not fail her brother (34). Ralli's performance emphasizes Ismene's eye gestures. While half covering her eyes, she recalls how Antígona walked away, imitating her own gesture at the beginning of the play as she spoke of Polinices. Antígona's departure, like that of the corpse, needed to be noted. Ismene's final ritual is framed by

---

[72] "They" in the Spanish original is ambiguous because conjugated verbs can omit the subject: the third-person plural in "borrando de mis ojos lo que no ven" allows us to think both of her eyes as the subject (the immediate reference in the sentence) or the people who rejoice with Creonte at peace.

the sister's plea for Antígona to watch her: "Do you see the world below? [...] Sister mine, behold: this is the face of our brother" (63). Ismene's call for her sister's gaze is a call for her approval. As Ismene bears witness to her own being, she asks her sister to do the same. She becomes both spectator and actor: "essential theater," as Boal would have it. Her sister's gaze and her own shame could perform a communion for the restoration of sisterhood implied in her yearning for approval.

Antígona's Political Roadmap in Peruvian Thebes

"There is no worse torture for the mind than one's own imagination, and Antígona does not cease to inhabit mine" (57), Ismene says in Poem 19. She imagines her sister "waiting for an impossible drop of water to form on the dry stone," searching for "a bitter herb with which to mitigate her infinite hunger," talking to herself in order to "keep her company" (57). Just as he crafted an enemy mask for Polinices, Creonte has engineered this torture: "Creonte has chosen for [Antígona's] death to be remembered by everyone" (39). Poem 9 indicts the State.

Antígona "inhabits" Ismene's imagination in a singular way, which Ismene now offers to the public. This singularity is heightened by the percussion music and blow of dust and light that precedes the revelation of her truth (Figure 7.3): "The deaths in this story now *come to me*, not because I want to tell the misfortunes of other people but rather they *come to me*, so vividly, because they are *my own* misfortune: I am that sister who was handcuffed by fear" (63; my emphasis).

The phrase "come to me" is repeated twice: a multiplicity of deaths return to transform her, personally and insistently, as if it were Antígona's wave that returns, a return that Antígona warns shall be Thebes' curse (41). Ismene's dead interpellate her, constituting her as a new subject. We could even rephrase it thus: "they come to take me." Not everyone in Peru has been Ismene in this way. Ismene has given the audience the emotional language that has allowed her to make Peru's story her story. Instead of generalized mourning and memory, Ismene offers an irreducibly individual story. It is the story of a sister transformed by another sister, and other sisters in plural: "the deaths"—*las muertes*.

The two sisters embody the nation's curse. Ismene's curse is Lima's emotional distance that allowed Antígona's Andean curse to return. Antígona's curse is the violence that leaves corpses unburied. Ismene offers her shame

Figure 7.3 Light and dust right before Ismene (Teresa Ralli) reveals her truth, *Antígona*, Yuyachkani. Courtesy of photographer Elenize Dezgeniski and Teresa Ralli.

to the Andean Antígonas. If her gesture is caught by those sisters' eyes, it may contain an embryonic collectivity. The sister's shame is a collective gesture *in potentia*: what would reconciliation look like if all Ismenes felt not the burden of guilt and the urgency of its atonement, but rather the disturbing, burning distance between the projected image and the image that others see? This is a distance from the self that can only be repaired through the agency of the other. Collective shame could mean a revolutionary leap in a different direction than the two hundred years during which Lima looked away, unable to recognize the history of the Andes, or the Amazon, as its own. Lima would feel the shock of being seen by, and would therefore seek the approval of, the Andes. Indeed, we may venture to see in this specific performance of sisterhood not (or not only) the need to bury the dead, but rather, the need for Lima to accept the Andes as part of the nation.

In place of a monument to memory, Antígona offers a dialectics of remembrance and forgetting. After the three libations at the site of the corpse, Antígona wishes only for her name to be remembered. As to the deaths, she says: "I want every death to have a funeral, and then, then, then, oblivion" (33). The word "then" is uttered three times, rhythmically repeating the three libations: ritual is paramount for oblivion.

Antígona knows what still needs to be remembered, even after oblivion: the socialized sisterhood she experiences at the burial site. There, Antígona ceases to be a blood relative and becomes a communal sister. The play provides only a flickering allusion to the maternal ways Antígona has been imagined over the course of the twentieth century in Latin America: we encounter here finally the veritable shift from political motherhood to political sisterhood insinuated in many previous plays where sisterhood was accompanied by central mother figures. At the burial site, Antígona speaks to the guard: "Let me finish opening the earth so that she may be a mother to receive Polinices, as she received Eteocles" (33). English eliminates the ambiguity in Spanish: the sentence uses the present subjunctive for the verbs to be ("para que sea") and to receive ("para que acoja"), whose conjugation in Spanish allows for confusion between the third- and first-person singular. For a moment, we hear that either Antígona ("so that I") or the earth ("so that the earth") could be the mother. We cannot be certain that the subject is "the earth" until the end of the sentence: the second "received" (*acogió*) is unambiguously in the third person.

Not a mother, nor a biological sister, Antígona instead becomes a communal sister. She offers the three libations "in the name of all the others" (33). Polinices, as she has previously stated, is "no longer family" (22): he belongs "to all of us" (22). By changing the meaning of kinship, Antígona not only follows in the steps of her Latin American predecessors but also changes the meaning of memory in her native Peru. She wants her name to be remembered, not because of her heroism, but because it resignifies kinship: no longer a one-to-one relation among brothers or sisters, but a civic kinship whereby all brothers and sisters belong to everybody.

Whereas Cureses, Gambaro, and Dorfman debiologized motherhood to have their Antígonas bear the impossible universal of change, Watanabe resignifies siblinghood to have his Peruvian Antígona bear the "impossible universal" that all siblings have siblings, breaking the equation between kinship and blood.[73] In Poem 13, when we hear Antígona speak directly without the narrator's introduction, she reminds the Thebans that she is "the odd wave that crashes and dies inside this cave," the "curse" to that "great

---

[73] I opted for "siblinghood" for the nongendered Spanish word "hermandad."

event" that is peace (42). The "wave" appears a few lines prior as a repetition of the past: "misfortunes, like the waves of the sea, will be repeated from one generation to the next" (42). Antígona will return like the waves of the sea should Polinices not become "the brother of all," and until the meaning of her name is understood. In the Andean highlands, there are 40,000 siblings who still need to be claimed.

8

Finale

We Are All Antígonas on the
Twenty-First-Century Stage

#VivasNosQueremos (#WeWantUsAlive)

The Effervescence of the Twenty-First Century:
New Dialogues in the Corpus

On the threshold of the twenty-first century, Ismene's 2000 "tragic testimony" in Peru, along with Daniel Fermani's short first-person narrative "Trans Antígona Sexual" (Argentina, 2000) and Jorge Huertas' *AntígonaS: Linaje de hembras* (Lineage of women; Argentina, 2001), condense a series of innovations that shape the current unprecedented flood of *Antígona* plays feeding the corpus constructed in this book. Fermani's "trans Antígona" announces that rather than born to love, "I was born to live" (1–2). She rejects the violence to which patriarchy has submitted her and questions the category "woman/mother" that the twentieth century assigned her: "being woman, mother, wife, daughter of horror" (1) is the root of her tragedy.[1] No change in sight for Creonte, who, like all Creontes of the twentieth century, remains "a tyrant" (2). Ismena also rejects heroic glory: "I am not a tragedy [...] Not a heroine. Martyr. None of that. Human" (4). Antígona tries to shirk her fate: "I am not Antígona" (3); "I am not going to bury myself alive [...] I *was* Antígona" (3; my emphasis); "Woman, they did not let me be. Man. Nauseous. I am. I will be. The only thing. That can be here. A hybrid" (6). She is the hybrid that all ruminations of Antigone are in this book. But there is more: she is a hybrid gender and a hybrid heroism. Now Antígona does without the motherly sacrifice for the nation. Her heroism, as we will see, lies elsewhere.

---

[1] My translation. I thank Daniel Fermani for sharing the unpublished manuscript with me. Fermani also wrote *Antígona Fantasma* (2013; see http://3.bp.blogspot.com/-g4trEac9nF8/UvE2Pb8YgWI/AAAAAAAAAFA/WG8RWd4EIfo/s1600/Antigone+fantasma.jpg).

Antígonas: Writing from Latin America. Moira Fradinger, Oxford University Press. © Moira Fradinger 2023.
DOI: 10.1093/oso/9780192897091.003.0010

Like Fermani's, Huertas' Antígona indicts gender violence. The first twenty-first-century play structured around a female multitude, underscored by the title's capital "S" in the plural *AntígonaS*, multiplies Antígona with six actresses, wearing identical long and ample tunics, each with different embroideries on the chest.[2] All women are equal and each preserves her individuality, at times stepping out of the chorus to play a specific role. Exuding anger in every line with a relentless discourse about the nation's history of violence, the six women identify themselves in the chorus as: "We, Antígonas, brides of filth, mothers of stench, the stained, the dirty ones, the barbarians. I know what my wound is called: females, mares, witches, mad women, whores, always Antígonas, of ill-fated porteño parents [...]" (62; Figure 8.1).[3]

In a radical move, Huertas has Antígona align her fate with modern women, rather than the other way round, whereby modern women are

Figure 8.1 *AntígonaS: Linaje de hembras*. Directed by Roberto Aguirre. Teatro Repertorio del Norte. La Plata, Argentina, 2002. Courtesy of photographer Martín Hoffmann and Jorge Huertas.

---

[2] I have engaged this play elsewhere (Fradinger 2011b: 84–8). See also Sanchez Toranzo and Rocha (2005), Scabuzzo (2012: 509–16), and Louis (2019). I have translated the play into English (forthcoming). Here I use the first edition by Editorial Biblios, 2002.

[3] "Porteño" is slang for a dweller of the port of Buenos Aires.

WE ARE ALL ANTÍGONAS IN THE TWENTY-FIRST-CENTURY   355

identified with their predecessor Antígona/Antigone. Hovering over the entire play is a document of history: the real story of the mistreated corpse of first lady Evita Perón. Recall how, in 1951, Evita had wanted Marechal's *Antígona Vélez* to celebrate the nation. Huertas mentions Marechal twice, as one of the poets who understand Buenos Aires' enigma—a city at once so violent and so cultured (66). Huertas' fictional Evita now names "the national" not after Antígona Vélez but after what the twentieth-century Antígonas in this book have shown: female sacrificial politics—"We are always offerings to the fatherland's phallus that demands women for the sacrifice" (58). Antígona tries to bury Polinices at the intersection of two streets in Buenos Aires where Evita's corpse was displayed for two days after her twelve-day wake in 1952. Antígona wonders if her corpse's fate will be that of Evita's: "will I be a pilgrim? Will [my body] be cut, urinated upon?" (61).

Evita, here named "the Embalmed Pilgrim," condenses the history of the country's women, epitomized in the violation of her corpse: "Yes, my body is the map of the Argentine soul" (48).[4] Her lines in the play honor a "lineage of women": "we, who fight day after day to feed our children without fathers, we who open the doors of the schools and raise the flag, we the badly born, we the badly paid, we the badly fucked, we the girls from Catamarca, raped round and round on the altar to the fatherland's phallus. Hitchhikers, prostitutes, girls drowned by men. There will always be a little female and her open body thrown at the altar of the fatherland's phallus" (58–9).[5] Evita and Antígona unify a heroic collectivity of women from all walks of life. In this play, the fraternal pact has killed too many: it is time for a female pact.

It is impossible to account, in one final chapter, for the avalanche of new Antígonas adding to the corpus either new themes or the full development of those commented on in previous chapters. The incredible number of recent plays merits a book on its own: I have documented more than thirty up until 2016, most of them unpublished (not counting new productions of previous plays). It is as difficult to assess whether the archives hold greater

---

[4] Evita's name here honors her embalmed corpse's fated "pilgrimage," kidnapped by the military in 1955, sent to Italy, disgraced with cuts and urine, and only returned to Argentina in 1971.

[5] "Girls from Catamarca" refers to the case of María Soledad Morales. She was raped and killed in the province of Catamarca in 1990. Throughout the country, every Thursday like the Mothers, the "Marches of Silence" (*Marchas del Silencio*) demanded justice. The culprits were condemned thanks to these national protests.

356 WE ARE ALL ANTÍGONAS IN THE TWENTY-FIRST-CENTURY

numbers of twentieth-century plays than I have collected as it is to keep pace with the flurry of new vernacular Antígonas.[6] Some places where I did not find a preceding tradition cannibalizing Antígona, like Paraguay and Ecuador, have now also produced vernaculars.[7] Restagings of twentieth-century versions crop up everywhere. After briefly introducing the new dominant trends, this final chapter zooms into examples from Mexico and Colombia that encapsulate them.

In this book's Overture, Antigone was killed as Antígona was born, in 1824. In this book's closure, the twenty-first-century stage unfolds the "killing" of Antígona. We have come full circle with the Antígonal paradigm of politics: the twentieth century dramatized the neocolony's killing of its children, but the twenty-first century puts the women who died in focus. The heroic narrative of "motherland or death" has shifted to highlight either the violence of sacrificial politics or the ordinary heroism of women in the quotidian, never before thought of as heroic but indispensable for women's survival in patriarchal social bonds. The new Antígonas demand that the patriarchal nation for which they had to sacrifice give them back their lives. Like Fermani's character, the new Antígonas will not undergo the torture of self-sacrifice. Like Huertas' collective, they bring to the stage the consciousness that the label "woman" makes them prey to violence. Reshaping Antígona's desires, quilting documentary and testimony, and multiplying her on stage, the new plays craft hybrids that erase the difference, so dear to the twentieth century, between the national heroic and the personal unheroic: heroism does not so much disappear but rather transfers to the female heroes of the everyday. They testify and perform a heroic politics of survival: they neither wish to die nor do they die for the nation. In 1972, Haitian Morisseau-Leroy expressed in his poem "Antigone" the wish for "Tigone" not to die again, for

---

[6] Even the Argentine Forensic Anthropologists named their 2002 documentary *Tras los pasos de Antígona* (translated as *Following Antigone*). See https://eaaf.typepad.com/following_antigone_forens/.

[7] Accessing older archives in Paraguay and Ecuador for this book proved impossible. In 2004, Paraguayan Víctor Sosa (1980–) wrote *Antígona Guaraní*, honoring victims of the deadly fire inside the supermarket Ycuá Bolaños (Asunción, Paraguay) on August 1: 400 were killed and 500 more wounded as the market owners shut the exits so that people would not loot. The chorus has the task of identifying burnt bodies, echoing a familiar problem for Antígonas in the corpus. See the press kit: https://www.columbia.edu.py/ycuabolanos/descargar/AntigonaGuarani.pdf and an excerpt on YouTube: https://www.youtube.com/watch?v=1U-fYgE_at2I. In 2013, Casandra Sabag Hillen and the Sindicato Audiovisual (Audiovisual Union) in Quito, Ecuador, produced a multimedia painting where eight ordinary women were photographed as "Antígonas" to convey how they survive everyday life. See online at http://www.antigonaenquito.com/.

WE ARE ALL ANTÍGONAS IN THE TWENTY-FIRST-CENTURY 357

Kreon to die instead. In 2002, Chilean Daniela Cápona Pérez's Antígona (*Antígona. Historia de objetos perdidos* [A history of lost objects]) speaks to her lover, after surviving torture without giving out his name and on the brink of becoming the eternal Antigone by choosing not to go into exile: "I don't feel like dying today. Let's get out of here" (182).[8]

The dramatic exercise of killing Antígona (both killing the twentieth-century dramatic heroine and showing how Antígona undergoes violence on stage) is so prevalent that it even appears in unexpected texts. In 2002, Chilean Juan Carlos Villavicencio, following the ancient text closer than any of this book's vernaculars, rewrote (and broke away from) Chilean Genaro Godoy's 1951 Spanish translation, making the violence on the female corpse visible by adding a shadow in the suicide scene inside the cave. Villavicencio writes: "Creonte approached her happily, and when Antígona […] began to speak, something, something like a shadow, swiftly came out running from one side, and when passing in front of the young woman, lifted the arm, and continued, while from Antígona's open neck, blood silenced her and took away her breath, distancing her from this world" (99).[9] Antígona's violated body emerges from the shadows under which the spectacle of a male body, rotted by the elements, has kept it for millennia.

Formally, the new plays cast Antígona as plural and quilt tragedy with testimony and documentary records. We may recall that the twentieth century did not lack testimony as dramatic strategy, nor plural Antígonas, nor violence upon Antígona's body. Sánchez's 1968 Antígona Pérez addresses her audience in the first person: "Yes, I want to speak" (14). She is also "raped" with a bottle on stage by Creon Molina's guards. Cureses' 1963 La Pola leads a female collective to act, reminding them of the violence suffered by women: "think of all the virgin women sacrificed to Spaniard appetites, you will avenge them!" (78). Harmony's Cristina joins the collective of peasant women, forgetting the unburied male body; Dorfman's widows confront the military united in one front. The 2000s dramatically expand these experiments: Antígona's multiplication leaves behind the clearly distinguishable heroine of the twentieth century. As the twenty-first century

---

[8] See Chapter 2 for Morisseau-Leroy's poem "Antigone." Cápona Pérez's Antígona is in exile; Fernández-Biggs and García-Huidobro (2013) and Pianacci (2008: 179–81) only comment on this aspect of the play.

[9] I thank Villavicencio for providing me with his manuscript. See Fernández-Biggs and García-Huidobro (2013: 231–64).

358   WE ARE ALL ANTÍGONAS IN THE TWENTY-FIRST-CENTURY

seems to recover what the twentieth century dismissed, the choral aspect of tragedy, Antígona ceases to lead and becomes one more in the multitude.[10] Avenge the new Antígonas will do, for theirs is an all-out indictment of patriarchal violence. Dramatic strategies involving textual repetition, scene replication, and multicasting of characters add to character multiplicity. Antígona appears among many, part of a chorus, a pair, a threesome, or exchangeable with other women. The construction of female collectives focused on women's fates reshapes the meaning of solidarity: it does not solely depend on the search for the disappeared corpse. When Argentine Alberto Muñoz's 2009 Antígona staged four scenes of intimate dialogues between two actresses, one of these echoing the ancient sister pair, Olga Cosentino's review asked the telling question: "What is the historical or psychological thread between the mythical Antígona and a cosmetologist in the barrio?" (Revista Noticias, 2010). The twenty-first-century stage equates Antígona with the mundane "woman" in the barrio: Muñoz's cast of a cosmetologist, a teacher, and a kinesiologist share with the mythical Antigone a world of intuitions predating patriarchal laws.

The formal innovations above show a shift from the twentieth-century "redemptive tragic" to the "tragic testimony" of survivors, whether of the past armed conflicts or of the dangers of the feminized quotidian. In terms of "tragic testimonies," as the Peruvian Ismene established, the multiplication of Antígona on stage has produced political events in their own right, often using real-life documentary records and nonprofessional actors. Personal stories of survival can transform the stage into a political arena for nonprofessional actors to find a platform, using mixed media, photos, interviews, and legal documents, for the denunciation that the judicial system has denied them. This contemporary theater becomes "biodrama," a term coined by Argentine theater director Vivi Tellas to capture the theatricality present in fragments of ordinary people's biographies.[11]

Marianella Morena's and Volker Lösch's Antígona Oriental (2012), about which I have written elsewhere, became a history-making event when nineteen women (or daughters of) survivors of the Uruguayan 1973–85 dictatorship indicted on stage their torturers by reading aloud their real

---

[10] See a parallel in Anglophone America: the 2003 play by the Alliance Theater Company in Atlanta (Georgia), We Are Antigone (http://www.playscripts.com/play?playid=2220).
[11] For documentary theater, see Martin (2010). It includes an interview with Vivi Tellas (246–58).

WE ARE ALL ANTÍGONAS IN THE TWENTY-FIRST-CENTURY 359

names and addresses.[12] The professional actress who plays Antígona blends her story with the testimonies of the survivors, whose stylized scripts and ritualized performance theatricalize the world where their theater (of everyday life, of the self) was dismantled, that is, the world of real-life torture. This staging offered victimized women the audience the courts denied them. Antígona's story is made equal to the stories of all women who survived "doing small things" but "did not have photos or press," as the chorus chants.[13] Below, I analyze the similar case of Colombian Carlos Satizábal's 2014 *Antígonas: Tribunal de Mujeres* (A women's tribunal).[14]

To a certain extent, we can think of the quilt between tragedy and testimony also quilting Antígona's/Antigone's heroism and Ismena's/Ismene's domesticity. If Antígona's heroism was mysteriously monstrous in the twentieth century, Ismena's uniqueness is the new mystery. Playwrights either endow her with Antígona's courage and dilemmas or else need to account for her shame: when heroism is assigned to every woman, theater explores its absence. This explains the number of ruminations on Watanabe's 2000 Ismene.[15] Morena's and Lösch's Ismena rebels after being "raped" on stage by the military; Lucía de la Maza's Ismene (2006) finds herself in the predicament of previous Antígonas, with misinformation about the corpses of Franco's dictatorship in Spain.[16]

---

[12] I quote from the unpublished manuscript that Marianella Morena kindly shared with me. See Fradinger (2014).

[13] In 2014, Mexican Lila Avilés' mixed-media performance *Antígona Unipersonal* took testimonies of survivors of the 1994 Rwandan genocide from the report in the news magazine *Proceso* entitled, fittingly, "Anonymous Heroines." See https://www.proceso.com.mx/category/especial-heroinas-anonimas; and see brilliant photos here: https://cargocollective.com/LILAVILES/ANTIGONA.

[14] The documentary aspect of the new plays appears also in those that follow the twentieth-century pattern, whereby Antígona leads and finds herself in similar situations to those this book has described, such as not having the body or being offered "a deal" to stop her quest. Consider Argentine Yamila Grandi's 2003 *Antígona No!*: Ismena goes to the fake funeral of the brother, made mandatory by the government, and Antígona refuses the order because she thinks there is no body. The two sisters do not know their brother's whereabouts because, like many real-life women detained in the concentration camps of the 1976–83 dictatorship, their mother gave birth in captivity, and the child was stolen. Antígona refuses to sign an official funerary act that would confirm her brother's death. State employees start discovering many funerary acts without signature. We can see the construction of an impossible universal here. See http://aniogitna.blogspot.com/2010/11/antigona-no-de-yamila-grandi.html. In Hebe Campanella's 2003 Argentine *Antígona…con amor*, the heroine is offered a "deal" to save her life: she is asked to give information about her brother's militant group, active during the 1973 shootings when Perón arrived at Buenos Aires' airport after his Spanish exile.

[15] See Chapter 7.

[16] See Lucía de la Maza's *Ismene o el dilema moral* at http://ismeneoeldilemamoral.blogspot.com/. Similar developments are happening in the USA: in 2008, Jeremy Menekseoglou produced a version that premiered in Chicago; see http://www.theismeneproject.webs.com/.

360   WE ARE ALL ANTÍGONAS IN THE TWENTY-FIRST-CENTURY

The strategy of multiplication is so dominant that it appears even in monologues or in restagings of twentieth-century Antígonas. Yamila Grandi's monologue *Una mujer llamada Antígona* (A woman named Antígona, 2010), has "Anogítna" tell her story as she looks at the mirror (a large, empty frame, per stage directions) and first thinks: "I will bury my brother alone."[17] But looking "through" the mirror—as the author explains, an allusion to Lewis Carroll—she "can intuit hundreds, thousands, of women doing what I am doing [...] finding and burying their dead." After she is caught, we hear voices "in off," and one of them is Antigone's: "through the mirror I can see another woman, some place, who also buries her brother. [...] if my name is Antígona [...] then hers is...Anogítna...[...] She is my shadow and my guide: my repetition and my starting point. If an Anogítna exists, I am not alone."

When Argentines Sylvia Torlucci and Teresa Sarrail restaged Gambaro's 1986 play in 2011, they multiplied Antígona Furiosa with three actresses of different ages (the youngest was fourteen years old; Figure 8.2).

As the directors put it, "we could all be Antígona."[18] The documentary aspect of the production included films and TV newsreels of the Mothers of the Plaza, military repression in the 1960s and 1970s, and Spain's *indignados* revolt in 2011, as well as clips from Kurosawa's *Ran* (1985) and Coppola's *Apocalypse Now* (1979). Speeches of real-life mothers are multiplied here too.[19] In 2016, a choral version of Marechal's *Antígona Vélez* was staged in the city of Rosario, Argentina. The directors Cielo Pignatta and Hernán Peña intended the main character to be an "Antígona who could be all of us."[20]

It is worth noting that the deheroizing of Antígona has also yielded what seemed implausible: "tragic humor," we may say, combining the comedic, the grotesque, and metatheatrical techniques that break the fourth wall.[21] The experiment that started with Domínguez's 1961 *Antígona Humor* and that was turned into the grotesque by Rengifo's 1966 "feast of the dead" is

---

[17] The short text can be found at https://studylib.es/doc/6876250/una-mujer-llamada-ant%C3%ADgona-por-yamila-grandi-para-mi-quer.

[18] See Soto (2011).

[19] Speeches extracted from Estela Carlotto (1930–), president of the Asociación de Abuelas de Plaza de Mayo (Association of Grandmothers of the Plaza de Mayo); Andrea Romero Rendón, ex-director of the Fundación para la Lucha contra la Trata de Personas (Association against Human Trafficking); and Isabel Vázquez, president of the Asociación de Madres contra el Paco y por la Vida (Mothers Against Drugs and For Life).

[20] Cejas (2016).

[21] The Appendix to this book includes all comedic, grotesque, and metatheatrical versions of the last decade and a half.

Figure 8.2 Gambaro's *Antígona Furiosa*. Mónica Driollet, Uki Capellari, and Sofía Tizón. Directed by Sandra Torlucci and Teresa Sarrail. September 2011. Delborde Espacio Teatral. Buenos Aires, Argentina. Courtesy of photographer Pablo Stubrin.

taken to the next level in Chilean Ana Montaner's *El thriller de Antígona y Hnos. S.A.* (The thriller of Antígona and Brothers S.A., 2006), which centers on the Labdacids' ownership of a transnational organ-selling business. Hiphop, rock, cabaret, and clown techniques mix with melodrama and irony in many productions addressing younger audiences. Adrián Giampani's 2012 cabaret *Antígona en sintonía: tragedia comediada* (Antígona in tune: tragedy made comedy), broadcasts a "reality show" with announcements of traffic jams, the weather, and, of course, the program for the following week—the story of Medea—because "around these times, tragedies are what we have in surplus, ain't it so, citizens?"[22] Metatheatrical strategies in Brazilian director José Alves Antunes Filho's (1929–2019) *Antígona* (2005) "resuscitated" the ancients, who come "alive" out of their tombs (niches on the walls). Antunes Filho invited spectators to "come see Antígona in the theater on Friday, Saturday and Sunday and in TV news every day of the week."[23]

---

[22] See trailers at https://www.youtube.com/watch?v=0V4TDKRAs_M; https://www.youtube.com/watch?v=pH_zkyk3UX0.
[23] Interview in Nespoli (2017). See the review by Mariangela Alves de Lima in *O Estado de São Paulo*, "A visão aterradora de 'Antígona'" (June 10, 2005). In 2010, Antunes Filho staged a

The most daring experiment to date must be Cuban Rogelio Orizondo's 2012 *Antigonón: un contingente épico* (an epic contingent).[24] It condenses all the features mentioned above: the deheroizing of Antígona, the multiplication of heroines of the quotidian, and the final reverence to the right burial (and the right to burial) that follows the steps of Antigone's millenary tradition, only redrawing the stakes of what/who needs burial. An explosion of colors, music, erotic dance, drag cabaret, "exotically absurd costumes"[25] (hairdos made of soda cans, dresses cut out in half), the performance criticizes the mythical heroic discourses of the 1959 Revolution that must be buried—fittingly, the director Carlos Díaz had asked the actresses to "bury" some polyfoam before the rehearsals, telling them they had already performed Antigone and buried her brother (Figure 8.3).

Figure 8.3 *Antigonón: un contingente épico.* Giselda Calero, Linnett Hernández, and Dayse Focade. Directed by Carlos Diaz. Teatro El Público, La Habana, Cuba, 2012. Costume designs by Celia Lendón Acosta. Photo by Lessy Montes de Oca. Courtesy of the photographer.

---

second version: *RockAntygona*. Along these lines, Belo Horizonte's Grupo Mayombe's show *KláSSIco (com K)* also "revived" the classics for a conversation with the actors.

[24] I thank Rogelio Orizondo, who provided me with a video and his manuscript, and the production assistant director, Martha Luisa Hernández.

[25] See a glimpse here: https://www.redcat.org/event/teatro-el-p-blico-antigon-n-un-contingente-pico; see Martha Luisa Hernández's 2014 review.

WE ARE ALL ANTÍGONAS IN THE TWENTY-FIRST-CENTURY 363

Now they needed to read one of the nation's independence heroes: José Martí. Orizondo rescues other heroes, especially women, unsurprisingly in this book's corpus, mothers—more so those who fought for Cuba's independence, and especially the *mambisas* forgotten by official historiography.[26] And Orizondo's found history grants an Antígona to the second-in-command of the Army of Independence against Spain, *mambí* General Antonio Maceo, just like the Haitian Dessalines, in Chapter 2, had found his Antigòn, Defilée-La-Folle. Orizondo honors the young Lieutenant Francisco Gómez (1876–96), who dies by suicide to prevent Maceo's corpse from being defiled.

The title of Orizondo's play follows the continental spirit for female heroic collectivity. "Antigonón" is an augmentative in Spanish, but it is also the name of an "epic contingent," not only contingent as conditional to political conjunctures but also a "*contingente*," in the sense of a brigade assigned special tasks by the Revolution's institutions (in rural areas or in other countries) such as literacy campaigns. The irony that permeates the play asks: were these "contingent" brigades necessary? But we also sense the respect: historically these contingents granted women the previously unheard-of opportunity to leave behind housework. At one point, an actress says that there are other female contingents: "*the ELECTRÓN, the MEDEÓN, the CASANDRÓN, the IFIGENIÓN, the ISMENÓN,*" Greek-inspired heroic names for heroic women, which the fatherland has not given "photos or press"—to recall *Antígona Oriental* again.

There is no doubt that the twenty-first-century Antígonas bring to bear a "glocal" zeitgeist: a volcanic gendered solidarity in social movements across the region and the world has erupted. The indictment of the violence on Antígona's body, the female collectives gathering around gender, placing the male dead body further and further away from center, echo movements such as #NiUnaMenos (#NotOneLess); #VivasNosQueremos (#WeWantUsAlive); #PrimaveraVioleta (#VioletSpring); #MeuPrimeiroAbuso (#MyFirstHarassment), featured even in blogs by UNWomen.[27] After 1989, the mobilization for gender justice has gradually taken planetary dimensions. The United Nations has called the twenty-first century the "century of gender." In 1985, the Nairobi UN World Conference on Women named the end of the twentieth century "the birth of global feminism." In the region, 1994 marks a shift: the Organization of American States (OAS) signed in

---

[26] "Mambises" were guerrilla volunteer men and women, most of them Afrodescendants, during the wars against Spain, who were crucial to winning the battles.

[27] See https://www.unwomen.org/en/news/stories/2017/11/op-ed-ed-phumzile-16days-day5.

Brazil the historic Convention of Belém do Pará, demanding that states ensure a life free of violence against women.

Gender justice is at the center of global politics, and this includes the violence of unprecedented forms of economic precarity, with an ever-widening gender gap in poverty, or what is known as "the feminization of poverty" in United Nations inequality and development indexes. Given the region's incongruent industrial development, the introduction of free-market policies during the Cold War meant the acceleration of extractivist and unregulated forms of capitalist investment and exploitation, triggering new armed conflicts, human displacements from land (Colombia being an extreme case), the creation of precarious low-cost workforce and free-trade zones (such as the *maquilas* at the border between Mexico and the USA), the fight for water, and an unheard-of capital accumulation.[28] In South America, there are areas where towns have been destroyed and widows forced to leave in search of displaced corpses so that multinational companies can move in to extract raw materials. Saskia Sassen's research (2014) shows how previously excluded peoples are now expelled from the market. In her view, our statistical indexes for inequality cannot capture expelled peoples: they become invisible. As does land, which has been exhausted by toxicity. It is as if Rengifo's 1966 "feast of the living dead" had been a prediction of the twenty-first-century factory of unburied corpses expanding through the region.

The locality of the new Antígonas, which has been at the center of this book's approach, highlights the continuation of the twentieth-century Antígonal paradigm aimed at the recovery of politics *tout court*—politics as the antagonism of dissent and not commercial transactions (or fantasized utopian harmony). The twenty-first-century neoliberal political space has embraced politics as commerce: with testimonials and documentary records, the new Antígonas deepen their political work by transforming the stage into the very space of denunciation against real-life politics of amnesty or transactions. The twentieth-century sisters dramatized the disappearance of those who fought for social and economic inclusion. In the twenty-first century, Antígona articulates new forms of economic expulsion with new threats of political expulsion: the human rights activists who keep looking for the disappeared are now also threatened with disappearing themselves.

---

[28] For capital accumulation analysis, see Piketty (2013). In 2018, the UNHCR singled out Colombia as the country with the highest number of internally displaced peoples in the world. For information about working conditions in *maquilas*, see https://www.maquilasolidarity.org/.

But perhaps the most striking aspect of the new internal dialogues in this book's corpus is the rounding off of what I have called the Antígonal paradigm of politics by highlighting the violence against women upon which the brother's neocolonial pact is predicated. This violence—on the corpse of Antígona-the-mother, of Antígona-the-bride, and of course of the ancient virgin—was always a prerequisite for the community of male citizens. In the colonial, neocolonial, necroliberal pact, that violence was paramount, starting with rape as a tool for colonization, as I mentioned in the Introduction to this book. The twenty-first-century stage illuminates that violence, and it is not just due to the sacrificial role of women for the nation, but also due to the simple fact of having been born female.

Mexican Survivors: Precarious Life

The frantic twenty-first-century production of Mexican Antígonas follows the above characteristics and responds to the effects of drug cartel violence ravaging the country. The very first twenty-first-century Antígona, Ricardo Andrade Jardi's 2000 *Los motivos de Antígona* (Antígona's reasons), is a brief reflection on this internal armed conflict, as Antígona suffers in the cave, wanting to live, but realizing her country is a "common grave" becoming larger every day. Antígona is not alone but feels loss, despair, and hatred. These, rather than any ethical principles, are her motives for suicide.

The reader may recall Mexico made two entrances in this book's twentieth-century corpus: Fuentes Mares' young maternal *guerrillera* and Harmony's Cristina, who desired the female peasant rebellion rather than the burial of the male corpse. Fuentes Mares' character betrays a male guerrilla group; Harmony's Cristina "betrays" the male burial. It may be the case that during the twentieth century what Jean Franco called the "anti-Antígona" Mexican literary tradition diminished an appropriation of the classic figure—unless the archives have yet to be discovered. Franco believes that the latter is the result of a national discourse of "woman as traitor" (and woman as the colonial raped mother) constructed by the post-independence official myths around the historical figure of Doña Marina or La Malinche/Malintzin, an indigenous woman who was sold to conqueror Hernán Cortés, bore him a child, and acted as his translator. Nineteenth-century official lore interpreted her role in the conquest as betraying her "race." Franco asks

366 WE ARE ALL ANTÍGONAS IN THE TWENTY-FIRST-CENTURY

how Mexican women could write without speaking from a devalued position or rendering their voices more masculine.[29]

Since the 1970s, feminist groups have resignifed La Malinche as the first Mexican feminist and have called themselves La Malinche's "daughters." In what can be seen as a strategic classicism in dialogue with this tradition, the twenty-first century brings to the stage an avalanche of Mexican Antígonas, mobilized precisely against the rape and killing of women in the context of an unprecedented escalation of drug-related violence since 2006, claiming an estimated 120,000 lives by 2013. This escalation responds, among other factors, to the shift from local drug cartels as vehicles of Colombian cartels to the creation of independent drug cartels after the formation of the Guadalajara Cartel in 1980.[30]

Mexican Perla de la Rosa's *Antígona, las voces que incendian el desierto* (the voices that set the desert on fire, 2004) must be the clearest and most successful multiplication of Antígona to indict gender violence in Mexico. It has toured widely in the country and was invited to Berlin in 2006 to commemorate the International Day Against Violence Against Women (November 25). As Huertas did in his title, de la Rosa's title multiplies the character, placing Antígona in a series, *las voces* (the voices), to dramatize the violent production of female corpses. Particular neither to any one border town nor to Mexico at large, *feminicidio* emerged to typify gender violence at the border city of Juárez where, since the 1990s, female corpses have systematically appeared mutilated, raped, and thrown out into the desert.[31] Juárez, like many towns across the border between the USA and Mexico, was strongly impacted by the uneven development brought about by the North American Free Trade Agreement (NAFTA) and the establishment of multinational assembly plants (*maquilas*), which created precarious jobs for young vulnerable women in towns that had no previous market economy.

---

[29] Franco's analysis of Mexican literature is based on Octavio Paz's thesis in *El Laberinto de la Soledad* (1950) that Mexican identity is constructed as masculine in rejection to the raped "mother" Doña Marina. See Franco (1993: 160–88). See Messinger (1991) for the myth of La Malinche in literature. See Romero and Harris (1993) for feminist readings of Malinche.

[30] See statistics for Mexico's violence at https://justiceinmexico.org/.

[31] In 1993, the term was first applied to the case of thirteen-year-old Alma Chavira, found strangled by her uncle in Juárez. See *Regeneración* (2018). In 1994, Mexican anthropologist Marcela Lagarde borrowed from the term "femicide" (coined by scholars Diana Russell and Jill Radford) and expanded it into *feminicidio* to account for murders as a violation of women's rights and, for this reason, a responsibility of the state. See Russell and Radford (1992), Lagarde (2006), Wright (2011), and Bowden (1998).

WE ARE ALL ANTÍGONAS IN THE TWENTY-FIRST-CENTURY   367

De la Rosa wrote the play in Ciudad Juárez as if it were a "modern Thebes." The allegory of Juárez is made clear as Woman One starts the Prologue with: "I am a woman in this city, where everything is sand. We have been at war for many years. To be a woman here is to be in danger. This is why we decided to construct shelters under the sand…some are courageous, like Clara, and go to work in the factory" (187).[32] Woman One walks alone at midnight, after leaving her job at the *maquila*. There are few cars passing by; she is anguished. She reappears in scene 10, titled "Anecdote." She "unravels her hand bandage, just as life is unraveled day after day" (211). The "anecdote" she narrates is how she survived a street shooting while waiting for the bus after work: "in this city it is difficult to know one is alive…I heard more than thirty shots…Then the second shooting came and I felt it over my head…By the way, I am still alive" (211–12). By scene 12, Woman One decides to enter the shelter below the sand, where she listens to the radio report on a shooting between two gangs of traffickers. She is in fear: "I wanted to escape […] But where?" (213).

The eighteen scenes present the story of any woman living at the border. The story of Antígona and Ismene, who look for their disappeared sister Polinice, is just like Woman One's "anecdote" in the normalized violence of the town at war. There are two more pairs of women: sisters Elena and Isabel, who have lost their sister Clara; and two mothers looking for their daughters. The mothers One and Two do not have names: they could be any mother joining the Antígonal paradigm of politics—they search the assassinated child, this time the female child. While every pair of women looks for a missing woman, in every scene a "politics of disappearance" is made "the new normal" in the town.

In scene 1, titled "One, among many stories," sisters Elena and Isabel, wearing *maquila* workers' clothes, reconstruct at home the events of the previous night. Clara had disappeared for five days. They heard shouting at their door, but fear overwhelmed them. They later discovered the tortured body of Clara in front of their door. A man opening the door yells at them: "this very idiot, disobeying security laws. Going out at night alone, without the company of a man, not a good idea" (191). Isabel, breaking the fourth wall and looking at the audience, recounts: "Clara only wanted to live" (191).

---

[32] Quotations from de la Rosa (2005: 185–228). I have translated the play into English (forthcoming). See the introduction by G. de la Mora where the play is "a distortion" from "the original meaning of the myth in replacing Polynices […] with a murdered woman" (174) in Ciudad Juárez (this same paragraph appears in Pianacci [2010: 167]). See also Wiener (2015).

For Creon, the city is at war with other cities. For the three pairs of women protagonists the war is against women. Antígona shouts at Creon: "you are responsible for the impunity under which this genocide is committed" (217). Antígona has heard that Creon's "edict" denies that there are hundreds of unburied dead women in the city: "There are no bodies to identify. They don't exist. [...] The women reported missing are alive [...] three of [them] were at the beach in the Mediterranean [...]."

Vulnerable women move around the city but risk death. When they cross the frontier, they die. Scenes of the wandering ancient sister are recovered here: de la Rosa's Antígona walks in the desert just like the real-life mothers who look for their daughters there (Figure 8.4). Antígona in fact has returned to Thebes with a suitcase after being exiled. Wandering are the women who appear as a background in scene 4, in the desert, looking for human remains (stage directions).

Ismene has wandered in the desert for Polinice and now just wants to live. Antígona insists on going to the morgue where there are 200 unidentified

Figure 8.4 *Antígona: las voces que incendian el desierto*. Women look for their missing wandering in the desert. Photo taken in Samalayuca, Chihuahua desert, Mexico, by photographer Adrián Valverde Porras in 2004. Courtesy of the photographer and Perla de la Rosa.

WE ARE ALL ANTÍGONAS IN THE TWENTY-FIRST-CENTURY   369

bodies, which Creon wants to ditch in the desert. Ismene begs: "you won't stop until the only thing that remains of us will be a shoe [...] Let's go far from here, let's forget" (201).

The documentary aspect of the play becomes stronger in scene 5. Euridice goes to a religious ceremony at the historic site of the "Campo algodonero" (an open site called "cotton field"), where (per stage directions) one week earlier they found eight female corpses. In real life, eight women (ranging from fifteen to nineteen years old) were found dead there in 2001. Three mothers took the case to the Inter-American Courts of Human Rights, which for the first time recognized the term *feminicidio*. Mexico lost the case and had to compensate the families. When a memorial was inaugurated on the site, mothers interrupted government officials by chanting an impossible universal demand, just like Mothers in previous social movements, dramatized in previous Antígonas in this book: "We don't want a monument, we want our daughters. They were taken alive, we want them back alive."[33]

Perla de la Rosa's Woman One and Two are mothers who yell at Euridice as she tries to console families. Euridice speaks as a mother, but this may be the one mother who has been missing in the Antígona corpus: a wealthy mother, whose children run no risk. Euridice reproduces here the actual discourse of officials speaking to real-life mothers: blaming them for not taking good care of their disappeared daughters.[34] But Woman Two complains as the real-life mothers complained—"there are first and fifth class dead...They buried my daughter so far from Thebes that I can never go visit her" (208). In Thebes, there are disposable bodies left to rot in border places—wastelands, drains, deserts—and properly buried bodies. Euridice's is not the only competing notion of motherhood. In scene 6, another mother, also thus far missing in the Latin American corpus, receives her son covered in blood (his back to the audience) and cleans him while she prays (she is not Woman One or Two, but just Woman). This is the mother of a killer. She cares for her son and just asks: "is everything alright?" (206). The tapestry of the female collective gains complexity in this play: complicity is as much present as rebellion (Figure 8.5).

---

[33] In Spanish: "No queremos un monumento, las queremos a ellas [...] Vivas las llevaron, vivas las queremos." See Fregoso (2012).

[34] On May 10, 2002, while mothers were protesting against the authorities of Chihuahua, they were told they were guilty because they work outside the home and "do not take care of their daughters." Stay-at-home mothers received a discourse of guilt "because they over protect their daughters" Nava Castillo (2002).

370 WE ARE ALL ANTÍGONAS IN THE TWENTY-FIRST-CENTURY

Figure 8.5 *Antígona: las voces que incendian el desierto*. A mother caring for her killer son. Directed by Perla de la Rosa, Telón de Arena AC. Teatro de la Nación, Ciudad Juárez, Chihuahua, Mexico, September 29, 2004. Courtesy of photographer Adrián Valverde Porras and Perla de la Rosa.

Antígona gets into the morgue twice, with Hemón's help, only to find indeed "the 200" hidden corpses and, among them, a beautiful young woman who is not Polinice but whom she wants to bury.[35] Because the scandal has reached the international press, Creon establishes a tribunal to deal with the mothers' claim, though he proceeds with Antígona's execution. The scene takes place in the desert, to which Antígona has returned in search of her sister. However, in a reversal of luck, Creon ends up killing Hemón, not Antígona.

Like other twenty-first-century Antígonas, this one lives to leave and leaves to live. She walks out in the last scene, titled "Hopelessness and Question," leaving her shoes onstage. She addresses the audience, echoing the entire lineage of Latin American Antígonas: governors "want the blood of their sons and daughters" (227). And like her predecessors, Antígona ends the play with an impossible universal: "There won't be justice until all,

---

[35] In June 2005, the case of Minerva Teresa Torres Abeldaño's remains found resolution. She disappeared in 2001 going to a job interview in the city. Her corpse was kept hidden in the morgue by authorities; her identity was determined by the Argentine Team of Forensic Anthropology. See María de la Luz González (2002).

all—do you hear?—all your citizens cleanse the guilt of these crimes. Until all your sons cry the bitter tears of the dead women of the desert" (228). All women and any woman is in danger in the city; each and every citizen must change (Figure 8.6).

Mexicans Gabriela Ynclán, Bárbara Colio, and Sara Uribe follow de la Rosa's penchant for documenting the Mexican uncounted dead. Their characters need to find—and count—the missing bodies. In 2009, for her play *Usted está aquí* (You are here), Colio based the character of mother Ana García on Isabel Miranda Wallace, whose son was kidnapped in 2005 and never reappeared. Ana's words echo her fictional predecessors': she is "a simple mother who searches for her son." [36] Ynclán's 2009 *Podrías llamarte Antígona* (Your name could be Antígona) documents the real-life, and fully

Figure 8.6 *Antígona: las voces que incendian el desierto*. Antígona looks into the desert. Photo taken in Samalayuca, Chihuahua desert, Mexico, by photographer Adrián Valverde Porras in 2004. Courtesy of the photographer and Perla de la Rosa.

---

[36] See Nelli (2012) and Vargas (2013).

372 WE ARE ALL ANTÍGONAS IN THE TWENTY-FIRST-CENTURY

preventable, explosion in the coal mine Pasta de Conchos (Coahuila, Mexico), on February 19, 2006, burying alive sixty-five workers. The chorus of dead miners (on a lower level of the stage) encourages Analía to search for her brother, telling her "you could be Antígona." The two sisters, Analía and Jimena, are shoeless; the miners wear shredded, burnt rags (in the premiere, they wore the real helmets of the dead, loaned to Ynclán and Pedro Linares by the widows).[37] Analía "finds" the brother in a dream-like scene and to the "Tyrant," who challenges her with "it is the body of someone else that you pretend is yours," she retorts that there are things "that one knows before they happen" (14), just like Dorfman's Sofía "knew." Analía finally buries the body, accompanied by a multitude of women and miners who start to inquire about their own dead.

While Ynclán's Analía "could be named Antígona," Sara Uribe borrows from Colombian activist Diana Gómez's blog to write the line "I did not want to be Antígona but I had to" (15). Uribe accepted the commission to write her 2012 poem-essay, *Antígona González*, after the discovery of 196 disappeared bodies in Tamaulipas.[38] David Buuck interviewed Uribe, and he noted that Sophocles was not a "fetishized source" but what he called a "jumping off point" for her text. But Sophocles in reality is a point of arrival for Uribe, as I have argued is the case for all vernacular Latin American Antígonas in this book. Uribe tells Buuck: "the specific event that sparked the writing of *Antígona González* was the discovery, on April 6, 2011, of mass graves in San Fernando."[39] Tamaulipas is reportedly the state with the highest number of missing persons due to drug trafficking.

Uribe's "I did not want to be Antígona" is preceded by the connection between Antígona and real-life women: "who is Antígona González and what shall we do with all the other Antígonas?" (15). Eerily, there is one real-life Antígona González listed as a volunteer who counts the dead for the online project *Menos días aquí* (Fewer days here), one of Uribe's sources for her poem. The real-life González appears to have counted 340 deaths in the week of January 17–23, 2011.[40] In Tamaulipas, the questions begin with

---

[37] See an interview with Linares and Ynclán in González Vaquerizo (2014: 95–106).

[38] Spanish edition: *Antígona González* (2012), translated by John Pluecker in 2016.

[39] See Buuck (2016).

[40] See http://menosdiasaqui.blogspot.com/. Lolita Bosch created the "virtual cemetery" and collective blog project *Menos días aquí*, where volunteer citizens count the dead by offering three hours daily during a week to do research. In six years, the blog has counted 58,000 dead. See also the collective project, *Colectivo Fuentes Rojas* (women who embroider cloth with the names of the dead): http://nuestraaparenterendicion.com/index.php/com-gmapfp-css/comunidad/bordados-de-paz-memoria-y-justicia-un-proceso-de-visibilizacion.

WE ARE ALL ANTÍGONAS IN THE TWENTY-FIRST-CENTURY   373

how to count, name, and identify. Fittingly, the first section of Uribe's poem is titled "Instructions to count the dead" and quotes lines from *Menos días aquí*: "Count all of them. […] Count human beings […] Do not take sides, do not impose a moral frame," to which Uribe adds: "Count them all to say: this body could be mine. The body of one of my own" (13).

Uribe's text epitomizes multiplicity in more than one sense. González is one more woman looking for her missing among many. Uribe's lyric "I" is a nonauthorial voice, the voice of the many with no press: "A woman tells the story of the disappearance of her younger brother. This case did not appear in the news" (20). But González is also all the fictional Antígonas/Antigones that Latin Americans ruminate upon and that Uribe has read about: she quotes lines from Marechal, Gambaro, Yourcenar, Zambrano, and Satizábal. Seven pages of notes indicate the latter and other sources, such as contemporary newspaper articles; real-life testimonies; texts by Cristina Rivera Garza and Harold Pinter; fragments from contemporary websites and blogs, such as the online project *72 migrantes*; and, of course, a few ancient lines. In the first note, Uribe writes the four lines she extracted from Sophocles: "not a sign of beasts or dogs"; "I was born not to share hatred but love"; "I consider, today as yesterday, a bad ruler…"; "would you help me lift the corpse?"[41]

Just as Uribe quotes from the Antígona archive that this book has made visible, she also revisits practically every aspect of burial and search for bodies that have appeared in previous Antígonas: unburying to bury again, recognizing an unrecognizable body; waiting to hear the news; joining with others waiting in line; fainting at the possibility of identifying one's own missing; and many other real-life horror scenarios. Unsurprisingly, at the beginning of the text, the narrator uses the word "impossible": "they are going to kill us all, Antígona. Don't pursue the impossible" (23). By the middle of the poem, Antígona says, "What I desire is the impossible: that the war stops, that we build together […] dignified forms of living" (59). By the end, she announces the impossible universal: "I will always want to bury Tadeo. Even if born a thousand times, and he dies a thousand times" (99; my translation)—echoing Gambaro's famous phrase. The last lines are

---

[41] My translation from Uribe's quotes (there is no indication of the translation she used). On September 23, 2010, seventy-two migrants crossing Mexico toward the United States were found dead and mutilated in Tamaulipas. One survived to tell the story. Guillermoprieto (2011) gathered seventy-two writers to be the voice for each dead person and edited the collection *72 migrantes*. Uribe also has lines from Rivera Garza's poem "La reclamante" ("The claimant") in *Dolerse. Textos desde un país herido* (2011).

374   WE ARE ALL ANTÍGONAS IN THE TWENTY-FIRST-CENTURY

questions borrowed from Pinter's 1997 poem "Death," answered by the many voices Uribe's lyric "I" represents: "How did you know the dead body was dead? They never arrived at their destiny. They were 47" (91); "Did you wash the corpse? We are many. Did you close both its eyes? We are many. Did you bury the body? We are many. Did you abandon the body? We are many" (92–3). Like many Antígonas before her, Antígona González ends by addressing the audience in the second-person singular, so that they act: "Will you join me in lifting the corpse?" (101).

Colombian Tribunals of Female Survivors

Recall for a moment how, in the 1930s, Buarque de Holanda mobilized Antigone to explain Brazil's roots. In the twenty-first century, anthropologist Roland Anrup wrote *Una tragedia a la colombiana* (A tragedy Colombian style, 2009) and *Antígona y Creonte, rebeldía y estado en Colombia* (Rebellion and the state in Colombia, 2014), coining the words "Colombiantígona" and "Colombiacreonte" to account for the longest armed conflict in South America. Unlike his Brazilian peer, Anrup represents Antígona as a figure of rebellion. Colombian human rights lawyers have used Antigone's myth in their arguments. A university collective published a journal with the title *Antígona* in 2006, with articles about the peasant struggles in rural areas in the country.[42] Colombian blogger Diana Gómez writes as Antígona Gómez (mentioned above): "from Greek tragedy, back alive time and again, thousands of Antígonas appear, reappear and disappear in Colombia. They go on stage again."[43]

Colombia had seen some adaptations of the ancient play before the 1990s.[44] But just as in Mexico, the twenty-first century has accelerated the production of vernacular Antígonas, using the strategy of multiplication to document the displaced and disappeared peoples; the military disposal of corpses far away from their land; the concession of "emptied" lands to multinational corporations; the rivers as natural graves for the disappeared;

---

[42] See the journal here: https://en.calameo.com/accounts/1052911.

[43] See http://antigonagomez.blogspot.com/.

[44] See Romero Rey (2015), which includes details about *Antígona fugaz* (directed by Carlos Araque and Vendimia Teatro, 2001) and *Antígona* (adapted from Bertolt Brecht, Enrique Buenaventura, and Fernando González Cajiao, directed by Álvaro Arcos, *c.*1970). See the work of legendary Colombian writer Andrés Caicedo (b. 1951; dead by suicide in 1977) mentioned in the Introduction to this book.

WE ARE ALL ANTÍGONAS IN THE TWENTY-FIRST-CENTURY 375

and military strategies to "make corpses appear," such as the so-called "false positive" cases, in which the military kill innocent people to present their corpses as "fallen guerrilleros" and thus publicize (fake) success in handling this conflict. Patricia Ariza's 2006 *Antígona* features a scene where Antígona, multiplied by three, performs a curious move: instead of sprinkling earth on the body, the actresses drag the body out of sight. The Guard says the corpse "disappeared." In 2013, artist Juan Manuel Echevarría produced a film about peasants who "adopt" corpses that float up in rivers: they bury them with fictional names, just as previous Antígonas name corpses on stage.[45] That same year in Cali, Gabriel Uribe transformed the stage into a river with corpses floating to the surface in his *El grito de Antígona vs. La nuda vida* (Antígona's cry vs. bare life). The scenes go from colorful tourist advertisements about Colombia to an underworld of plastic bags with dead bodies. One of the dead moves inside the bag; a girl stands up soaked in water and spits out rocks, telling the audience how the military said that the Cauca River is "magic": all kinds of beings float in it. She is the ghost of one of the corpses that floats.[46]

Perhaps the best scene epitomizing the twenty-first-century insistence on "strategic classicism" appears in Carlos Satizábal's *Antígona y actriz* (2005): as I commented in this book's Introduction, the play is a dialogue between two migrant peasant women who sit in front of the urban audience and tell the story "of that other woman"—Antigone—so that the audience may listen to their plight. Satizábal captures the articulation of plurality that makes the ancient Antigone the "equalizer" among peasant women in the play's subtitle, "A monologue for two actresses." All is double, different, and the same in this play: two peasant women, two languages (Spanish and Mixteco, an indigenous language from the south of Mexico), two countries (Mexico and Colombia), two temporal frames (antiquity and modern Colombia), and one story unifying them all.

Patricia Ariza and Carlos Satizábal, working within legendary theater groups such as La Candelaria and the Corporación Colombiana de Teatro (operating since the 1960s), train nonprofessional actors, among them homeless persons and peasant women survivors. In November 2006, Ariza coorganized the annual festival of the international Magdalena Project that took place in Bogotá, named "Magdalena Antígona" that year. Five Antígona plays were staged: Satizábal's *Antígona y actriz*, César Castaño's *Antígona*

---

[45] Juan Manuel Echavarría, *Réquiem NN*; see https://jmechavarria.com/en/work/requiem-nn/.
[46] Watch the trailer at https://www.youtube.com/watch?v=0o7swhLbjLs.

376　WE ARE ALL ANTÍGONAS IN THE TWENTY-FIRST-CENTURY

incorpórea, Ariza's two plays *Antígona* and *Antigonías*, Augusto Cubillán's *Antígona factotum* (Venezuela), and *La Pasión de Antígona*, produced by Teatro La Máscara from Cali, Colombia.[47]

Satizábal's *Antígona y actriz* and Ariza's *Antígona*, like the cases mentioned above, build on multiplication and repetitions onstage, dismantling the character of Antígona as an individual and documenting the plight of women victims of the armed conflict.[48] Interestingly, just as de la Rosa recovers a wandering Antígona in the desert, Ariza recalled the ancient heroine while traveling to the northern province of Urabá and encountering wandering women burying their missing in hiding at night.[49] In Ariza's *Antígona*, multiplication is achieved with choral versions of the ancient characters: three actresses play the role of Antígona, two play Ismene, and three play the Erinias (Erinyes). Each Antígona, Ismene, and Erinia makes distinct statements, but sometimes they have a unified message and are slight variations on the same theme. The performance increases the multiplying effect: lines are split in two and spoken by different actresses (Antígonas) or repeated by one of the Antígonas addressing two different Ismenes. Sometimes the actresses speak simultaneously. Sometimes Ismene's three consecutive lines are not addressed to the same Antígona but each to a different one. Each group wears dresses of the same color but different shape. The Erinias emphasize proliferation: not only Antígona's story returns, but her story will be "narrated by us, one and one thousand times" (my literal, not literary, translation, 258).

As Morena and Lösch did in Uruguay in 2012, in Colombia playwrights combine character multiplication with testimonies narrated by real-life victimized peoples, thus transforming the stage into a public tribunal of sorts. In 2013, José Félix Londoño staged in Medellín *El insepulto, o yo veré qué hago con mis muertos* (The unburied, or I will see what I do with my dead), using testimonies of peasant survivors of the armed conflict as well as his own personal loss, as he has a disappeared brother. In 2014, and also in Medellín, Jesús Eduardo Domínguez Vargas staged *Río arriba, río abajo*: *Antígona en el puente cantando* (Up the river, down the river: Antígona singing on the bridge) with the story of massacres in his own hometown (Urrao, Antioquia) and testimonies of women victims. The playwright

---

[47] See the website: https://themagdalenaproject.org/en/content/magdalena-antigona-2006. The Magdalena Project goes back to 1986 and is a global network.

[48] I have engaged these plays in Fradinger (2015). See also Botía Mena (2016).

[49] Personal conversation in Bogotá in 2010.

invited the famous Mothers of La Candelaria (Medellín), who since 1999 have followed the example of the Argentine Mothers. They create an altar onstage using the photos of their relatives. The play incorporates funeral rituals from different communities across the country: the "Gualí" or burial for children, the Wayuu second burial, the *alabaos* sung for nine days for the deceased's soul to depart.[50]

But it was Satizábal again, this time working with the company Tramaluna Teatro, who doubled the stakes, composing *Tribunal de Mujeres* (A women's tribunal) in 2014 with four professional actresses and six women survivors of violence, who testify onstage, intermingled with a few appearances of an actress in Antigone's role. The survivors play "themselves" before the "tribunal" (the audience).[51] They are members of the Reiniciar association (which demands justice for the killing of members of the opposition party, Unión Patriótica [UP]), members of the Lawyers' Collective José Alvear Restrepo, mothers from the Association of Mothers of Soacha, and also one politically persecuted student leader. Like the Argentines, the Mothers of Soacha refuse to concede that their sons' deaths were homicides. In 2008, nineteen youths from the cities of Soacha and Ciudad Bolívar were tricked by the military into working in the countryside. Their corpses appeared dressed as *guerrilleros*, with weapons in their hands, in the north of the country. As founding member Luz Marina Bernal explains: "The ex-president [...] had closed all our access to mass media but a new door opened for us, the theater where we could tell our stories without censorship."[52]

Satizábal's play became a political rite of its own. Critic Nereo Ortegsa Daza reviewed the play in 2015 with the title: "Women victims of the armed conflict become Antígonas." Colombian theater director and playwright Sandro Romero Rey commented: "After seeing *Antígonas: Tribunal de mujeres* many of the reasons why we go to the theater, or do theater, enter into crisis. When you know that those on stage are not 'pretending' but rather expressing the pain that comes from deeper than any of the limits of any scene, the way we meditate about the task of representation shakes."[53]

---

[50] An *alabao* is an Afro-Colombian funeral dirge from the Pacific Chocó state; in 2014, the songs became part of Colombia's official cultural heritage. In Bernardo Rey's *Antígona genealogía de un sacrificio* (2016), produced by the group Cenit as a hybrid between Sophocles' and Maria Zambrano's versions, there is a chorus of sixteen people singing *alabaos* for Antígona's soul.

[51] I thank Satizábal for sharing the script with me; I have translated it into English (forthcoming). See the premiere at https://www.youtube.com/watch?v=OPR5UC17At0.

[52] Ortegsa Daza (2015).

[53] Quoted in Satizábal (2015: 260).

378 WE ARE ALL ANTÍGONAS IN THE TWENTY-FIRST-CENTURY

The stage is minimalist and framed with eight curtains (four on the left and four on the right, placed diagonally pointing at the center). The women enter and exit the stage passing in between curtains, on which images are projected, varying according to the scene. We see the rocky textures of pre-Columbian pyramids when the mothers tell their stories of missing children: it is an old colonial story, the image suggests. We see still or moving images of urban political protests when the UP's or the student's stories are heard. The women survivors present their cases one by one, in different scenes, using their real names and real documentation about their missing. As an equalizing sign of mourning, they wear the same long black dress, with a burgundy ribbon belt at the waist (Figure 8.7).

With little or no music, with no other props than children's belongings, singing a song or shouting a phrase, each woman comes to the proscenium and at some point shows an object or a photo narrating her child's murder and their dreams while alive. Lucero presents her case with her son's shirt; María includes cosmetics that were a gift from her son (Figure 8.8).

Figure 8.7 *Antígonas: Tribunal de Mujeres.* Female collective with the same attire. Directed by Carlos Sátizabal. Tramaluna Teatro, Corporación Colombiana de Teatro. Poster for the 2014 premiere; photo by Juan Domingo Guzmán. Courtesy of Carlos Sátizabal.

WE ARE ALL ANTÍGONAS IN THE TWENTY-FIRST-CENTURY 379

Figure 8.8 *Antígonas: Tribunal de Mujeres.* "He liked to see me with make up on," says the mother about her disappeared son. Directed by Carlos Sátizabal. Tramaluna Teatro, University of British Columbia, 2017. Photo by Felipe Castaño. Courtesy of Carlos Sátizabal.

Fanny brings a body-sized picture of her murdered father (a member of the UP); Orceni brings the photos of assassinated UP members. Marina carries her mentally disabled son's clothes and a teddy bear; in a later scene, she brings the suit her son was wearing the day he disappeared and tells the audience she was given only half his body back (Figures 8.9 and 8.10). The student Mayra speaks of her imprisonment and the disappearance of a fellow student. Altogether, the women perform the choreographed transition from scene to scene, sometimes a dance, detailed to the minutiae in stage directions. Just as in *Antígona Oriental*, the bodily movements of the victims are highly synchronized and stylized to make them look one and the same.

In the first scene, when the women introduce themselves to the audience one by one, the woman who carries her brother's shoe says: "my name is Antígona and I have been trying to bury my brother Polinices for three thousand years." Another woman pronounces the impossible universal that we have heard from previous Antígonas: "this tribunal of women seeks that this country may arrive at the day of Never Again." The chorus of women repeats, gradually raising its voice: "never again death, never again false positives, never again massacres, never again our unburied children,

Figure 8.9 *Antígonas: Tribunal de Mujeres.* Body-sized photo of Fany's murdered father. Directed by Carlos Sátizabal. Tramaluna Teatro. Teatro Seki Sano, Bogotá, Colombia, 2014. Courtesy of photographer Viviana Peretti.

never again rapes." Throughout the play, Antígona wears the same costumes as all others.

Antígona and Ismene are just two more women on stage. They appear together only in scene 2, with a choreographed dance to music for strings and melismas. They hold hands, touching back to back, as if they were one and the same, separating and reuniting: they wear the same dress, they mirror their movements. We can only know they think differently when they speak: Ismene fears death. Antígona will reappear in scene 12 with the news of the edict. But soon thereafter, Marina continues with her son's case, which she sees as equivalent to all: she speaks for the "5,700 clandestine executions, for the rapes of women, girls and boys, for the tortures and forced disappearance, for the genocides."

Figure 8.10 *Antígonas: Tribunal de Mujeres*. Objects of the missing: the teddy bear. Directed by Carlos Sátizabal. Tramaluna Teatro. Casa Ensamble, Bogotá, Colombia, November 2014. Courtesy of photographer Viviana Peretti.

Halfway through, the case of the UP is presented with statistics and the names of officers who shot them dead. As different women come onstage telling the history of the UP's political success, they hang photos with clothes hangers, as if they were the shirt, the skirt, the trouser left behind, now on a rope that crosses the stage diagonally. The women demand justice for the 515 still-missing corpses and for the 5,528 murdered members, as they hold up photos on placards.

Gendered violence becomes more explicit near the end, with a scene that stands out from among the previous ones. A masked torturer wearing a man's overcoat and military boots enters the stage, and a scene of torture is acted out to the sound of frightening electronic music. The image projected on the panels is a big doll. The masked actress takes out of a wooden box a doll and proceeds to tear it apart, first an arm, then the other, then the legs, then the head. At the back of the stage, an actress mimics the doll's breaking. At the moment of decapitation, the actress in the back falls down. Not a man but a woman is tortured—the doll and the actress (Figure 8.11).

Once the scene ends, two women dressed in white and gray urban attire enter, each showing the audience a glass box with an identical bloodied and dismembered doll inside it. One of the women clarifies: while men were "humiliated in public," "Soraya, as a woman, got this doll in the mail, why?" (Figure 8.12).

The women give the two glass boxes to people in the audience. The actresses narrate the minutiae of the political spying on human rights lawyer Soraya

Figure 8.11 *Antígonas: Tribunal de Mujeres*. A doll, depicting a woman, is tortured and killed. Directed by Carlos Sátizabal. Tramaluna Teatro. Teatro Seki Sano, Bogotá, Colombia, November 2014. Courtesy of photographer Viviana Peretti.

Figure 8.12 *Antígonas: Tribunal de Mujeres*. Dismembered doll representing the one that lawyer Soraya received by mail. Directed by Carlos Sátizabal. Tramaluna Teatro; Casa Ensamble, Bogotá, Colombia, November 2014. Photo by Viviana Peretti. Courtesy of the photographer and Carlos Sátizabal.

Gutiérrez and her family (which even included information about their underwear sizes).

In the end, Antígona is just one of them. In the last scene (14), the women enter the stage for a joint choreography with Antígona, who carries out a one-woman ritual in front of the others. As if marking a tomb for the disappeared, she places roses in a circle occupying much of the stage. With a bundle of herbs in her hand, she beats her body to "cleanse" her aura, following indigenous traditions and the rhythm of drums. Each time she beats herself, she names a well-known massacre carried out by right-wing paramilitaries: "I am Antígona […] and I come from the massacres […] of Bahía Portete, of Macayepo, of Mapiripán, of San José, San Rafael, Santa Rosa, of Chinú, of Salao, of Salao, of Salao, of Puerto Bello, Puerto Claver, of Buenaventura, of Buenaventura, of Buenaventura, of Aro, of Sopetrán, of Segovia, of Segovia, of Segovia, of Suarez, of Morales, of Catatumbo[…]" "El Salado" repeated thrice as "Salao" is the name of a peaceful peasant town besieged by 400 paramilitary troops in 2000. They orchestrated an orgy of killings in its central plaza during five days with such brutality that the government had to ask its people for forgiveness. A book about this case has

384 WE ARE ALL ANTÍGONAS IN THE TWENTY-FIRST-CENTURY

the subtitle "esa guerra no era nuestra" ("that war was not ours"),[54] encapsulating the sentiment of the women onstage.

Antígona mentions not only all the death she sees around but also "the barren lands, crops of immense oil palm plantations and a rain of blood on the oil palms." The women perform the same gestures and movements, praying together, as Antígona says, to Saint Mary, to the Pachamama (Mother Earth), and to Lord Jesus. Just as in many twenty-first-century plays, in this play, all women are Antígona, and Antígona is all women.

By Way of a Coda: Classic Fragments for "Our" Heterogeneous Neocoloniality

In April 2016, Chilean Rubén Morgado and the Bandurrias theater company staged *Antígona Insomne* in Santiago de Chile. An insomniac Antígona has been traveling in Hades for three millennia on a boat led by Sisyphus, pointlessly rowing in circles. Onstage, the audience sees a disassemblable metal boat, three trunks, twenty burnt books about world history, Chile, Thebes, and Antigone (Figure 8.13).[55] Three characters are in dialogue. The reader will not be surprised that the third character is a child, placing Antígona again in a motherly relation. A female child desiring knowledge—"I have a lot of questions [...] I am courageous" (9)—she joins the many female heroes of the quotidian on the twenty-first-century stage. No character for Creon, other than just the metaphor of an eternal turning in circles: the eternal military men in so many Antígona plays, the eternal colony, the neocolony, the neoliberal, and the necroliberal colony.

The play allows for a capture, by way of a coda, of many methodological, theoretical, and content-specific issues that have emerged interconnected throughout the chapters in this book, as I argued that an understanding of

---

[54] The Centro Nacional por la Memoria histórica (which documents all massacres) published in 2014 *El Salado: esa guerra no era nuestra* (http://www.centrodememoriahistorica.gov.co/2014-01-29-15-08-26/el-salado-esa-guerra-no-era-nuestra). See also Ruiz (2018). Buenaventura is often described as the most violent city in the country, and Segovia was the site of a massacre against the UP.

[55] My quotes are from the unpublished manuscript that Morgado kindly offered me. The text is, like Gambaro's, highly palimpsestic, with references to several Greek tragedies, German and French modern tragedies, Heiner Müller's *Hamlet Machine*, Albert Camus and José Saramago, Juan Radrigán's *Hechos consumados* (*Children of Fate*), among many other works and authors. Morgado thought of his play as a living memorial commemorating the deaths of women who lost their lives while defending human rights, such as Chilean Gladys Marín (1938–2005) and Sola Sierra (1935–99).

Figure 8.13 *Antígona Insomne*. Antígona and Child. Directed by Rubén Morgado. Compañía Teatro Bandurrias, April 2016, Santiago de Chile, Chile. Photo by Catalina Jara and Grupo Hormiga ONG. Courtesy of Morgado.

the cannibalization, hybridization, and rumination of Greek fragments composing motley Antígonas can only be rigorous from the vantage point of the construction of a vernacular transnational corpus and its internal dialogues. The corpus allows us to see in the imagination around Antígona a continental *dispositif* of narratives about womanhood, motherhood, sisterhood, and, to a certain extent, burials—recall that at times the burial recedes in importance if compared to Antígona's utopian political mission in the face of the destruction of the political sphere.

Morgado's text has a subtitle: "o la versión de la niña" ("or the girl's point of view") Each play in the corpus allows us to see how local agents have historically transferred onto fragments of antiquity their present conjunctures from their point of view. Morgado's Sisyphus and Antígona encounter a schoolgirl who likes to read the burnt history books that her city, Tebas, likes to incinerate. With Brechtian technique, the girl asks the audience about the impossibility of moving forward if the past is forgotten. She only finds fragments of the burnt books to "remember what needs to be forgotten" (1). In these ancient fragments, she learns "serious words" such as "ruins"

386   WE ARE ALL ANTÍGONAS IN THE TWENTY-FIRST-CENTURY

and "insomnia" (3). She does not know the meaning of the latter yet, but she feels her head is made of ruins (3). Ruins: traces of local history that she puts together with traces of words that come from ancient Greece. Just as playwrights have done cannibalizing and ruminating on fragments they found while at the school of history, the girl realizes she likes "the old Greeks [but] we only know the titles [...] their pages were torn away [...] we only have little phrases here and there [...]" (2). Like many Latin American playwrights, the girl stumbles upon the burnt book of *Antigone*. Like many Antígonas on stage, the girl desires to meet Antigone: "who is she? I would like to know her" (3). Like many Antígonas of the twenty-first century, the girl thinks: "She must be another girl *like me*. How would it be to play with Antígona?" (3; my emphasis).

"Play with Antigone": one more metaphor describing the Latin American ruminations of ancient fragments that this book has examined. Morgado's girl stands in for the playwright who finds the ancient Antigone dead: either killed at the beginning of the play or lost in torn-away pages. In "our" America, the ancients can only fragmentarily emerge quilted in local Christian dramas, Vodou rituals, political utopias, testimonial narratives, postdramatic strategies, or biodramas. As Latin Americans play with Antigone, "serious words" appear in the fragments, like burial—or dead alive—or mother. Motley texts appear when the words of history seem serious: motherhood, disappeared, sisterhood, colony, neocolony, necroliberal colony. Some serious patterns can be discerned in this book's corpus, though the latter also follows America's pattern: its homogeneity is its heterogeneity.

When Morgado's girl meets Antígona, she tells her she wants to learn about Thebes, but the books say nothing. Antígona responds that books narrate what happened "to people": if the books do not say anything, then the girl will need "to learn how to read people" (9). Vernacular Antígonas tell us what hurts for their peoples, rather than what can revive a classic. About to narrate Tebas' "history" to Morgado's girl, Antígona says: "these are neither stories nor games" (9). When she tells the girl the history that cannot be found in burnt books, she does not refer to the mythical ancient war between brothers but to the neocolonial one close to home—Chile, a stand-in for "our" America. Echoing the post-Cold War regional human rights movements, Antígona tells the girl that between Polinices and Eteocles there was "no war: war has rules [...] there was no tie here, for one Eteocles there were thirty dead Polinices. What happened here is called [...] an extermination, or some other word that has yet to be invented" (11). The defeat of "thirty dead Polinices" is polyvalent. It refers to the colonial war

WE ARE ALL ANTÍGONAS IN THE TWENTY-FIRST-CENTURY   387

against indigenous peoples, the nineteenth-century nation-building wars against indigenous peoples all over again, and the state terrorism implemented in the Cold War years throughout South America. In every chapter in this book, out of each play, the minutiae of the history close to home have been teased out: Antígona's story is part of the social and political texts available for playwrights to make sense of their times.

The girl wants to "play history," to have an adult "role in the drama" (11) and asks Antígona if she can role-play Ismena. By the twenty-first century, Ismena is a figure that must be explored: Antígona is a girl like all other girls. Like Watanabe's Ismene, this impersonation first speaks to Antígona of shame (17). She now needs to be courageous: the girl tells Antígona that she will find the brother so that Antígona can rest (18). But that search proves too tiring. Experimenting with Ismena did not solve her questions. The girl goes back to her readings. For her, there is something more mysterious: what she perceives as a continuum of violence. Wearing her school uniform, she reads about "more people" (19) in the manner of a soccer match. She learns that Tebas is a "carnivorous beast, needing blood to continue living" (24): the Greeks playing against the Spanish colony, Chile winning over the Spaniards, Creoles winning a never-definite victory, the match that she imagines concatenates world catastrophes and associates Creons with Nero, Hitler, and Videla, who "erased history but most of all erased peoples" (23–5).

Surely enough, in the midst of continuous violence, we should expect at least one scene of American redemption. The girl helps Antígona when Sisyphus almost tortures her so as to bring her back to the boat "to continue moving." Right after that, Polinices' ghost appears, and they embrace: a utopian line, just as in many preceding plays, will close the play. The three characters all turn toward "the south," while the girl points at the tragic redemption: "the character I represent does not exist […] it is still to come" (37). Because the utopia is still to come, it is an impossible universal: Antígona thinks there should not be a new Polinices, there should not be any more Creons (35).

Antígona is insomniac because she is utopian. Latin Americans ruminate time and again on Antígona embodying a project to come—the "never again" necropolitics. Inside Morgado's boat, Antígona wears a mortuary shawl and appears tired. She will remain sleepless, she says, until she finds the unburied body, which is nowhere to be seen. Just as Watanabe's Antígona wishes to bury the brother and then, "only then, oblivion," Morgado's Antígona wants to find the brother and "only then… sleep" (6). Sisyphus keeps reminding

388 WE ARE ALL ANTÍGONAS IN THE TWENTY-FIRST-CENTURY

her that all societies have been built on their forgotten dead. Antígona gets more tired: "we have spent millennia together and you have not said any new word since I met you" (7).

In Morgado's play, Antígona has been on the boat for millennia. In "Our America," Antígona has been on stage for at least 200 years and enters world cultural history with American insomnia. In this region, in the twenty-first century, she does not desire death. She wants sleep—so that she can live. While the earliest plays imagined the need of Antígona's sacrifice for the new republics, this redemption gradually shifts toward a radical reimagination of the social bond as Antígona becomes multiple. The corpus's arc goes from imagining the salvation of the patriarchal nation, to imagining the survival of politics, to imagining the survival of every woman—and the latter tasks can only happen once American heterogeneity becomes the foundation for a different social bond. In the twenty-first century, the sacrificial Antígona of the nineteenth century demands back the life of all disappeared for the nation, but most importantly her life, for which the necropolitical pact of the neocolony cannot continue.

And how could we miss that Antígona again, on Morgado's stage, talks to a child? Motherly imagery follows the American Antígona wherever she goes. She is a figure for relation: she acts politically because she is a mother, or mother-to-be, and as such at least always two. We may even say that the corpus invites us to think that to be an American mother in the colony/neocolony is to "risk" becoming a vernacular version of the mythical Antigone. Rather than the mourning of the father, which would allow for the ideology of the teleological progress of modernity, this mother mourns the corpse of the future. The texts studied in this book stage a specific claim: it is not the father's corpse but the child's corpse that initiates secular politics in the postindependence nation. The ruminated dramatic scene of socialized motherhood around mourning for children is the corpus's meditation on the coexistence of two heterogeneous paradigms of modern politics at war: what I have called an *Antígonal* political paradigm and the paradigm of teleological progress ("development") to which the neocolonial Creole elites subscribed after independence. Morgado's Sisyphus and Antígona represent this political tension once again: going in neocolonial circles or going forward to give birth to a different world, unnamed as yet, and able to unveil the hidden murders of the former.

Antígona does not just resist—like her ancient sister—a tyrannical order in order to restore the laws that nobody can trespass because nobody knows where they came from. Antígona's yearning for a new order is the formulation of "an impossible universal" whose realization demands thinking of a new humanity. Antígona, multiplied by every ordinary woman, embodies a horizontal solidarity of fellow travelers that inverts the traditional arrangement whereby women are exchanged, into the assembly whereby women are the subjects who exchange visions of a world where the condition of possibility for politics ceases to be a corpse. That world, never again filicidal, may be the world where Antígona is able to sleep, to live, or just to rest in peace.

And then, only then, may we not need to knife her on stage again.

APPENDIX

List and Diagram of Plays: Earliest Bibliographic Information Available

1. 1824. *Argia*. Juan Cruz Varela. Argentina (Buenos Aires: Imprenta de Hallet, 1824).
2. 1951. *Antígona Vélez*. Leopoldo Marechal. Argentina (Buenos Aires: Ediciones Citerea, 1965).
3. 1953. *Antigòn an Kreyòl*. Félix Morisseau-Leroy. Haiti (Nendeln, Liechtenstein: Kraus Reprint, 1970).
4. 1957. *Pedreira das Almas*. Jorge Andrade. Brazil (São Paulo: Editôra Anhambi, 1958).
5. 1958. *El límite*. Alberto de Zavalía. Argentina (Buenos Aires: Teatro de Buenos Aires, 1959).
6. 1958. *Antígona en el infierno*. Rolando Steiner. Nicaragua (Nicaragua: Universidad Nacional, 1958).
7. 1961. *Antígona-humor*. Franklin Domínguez. Dominican Republic (Santo Domingo: Sociedad de Autores y Compositores Dramáticos, 1968).
8. 1962. *Odale's Choice*. Kamau Brathwaite. Barbados/Ghana (London: Evans Bros. Ltd., 1967).
9. 1962. *Antígona-América*. Carlos Henrique de Escobar Fagundes. Brazil (São Paulo: Editora Decisão, 1962).
10. 1963. *La cabeza en la jaula*. David Cureses. Argentina (Buenos Aires: Ediciones T.E.G.E., 1986).
11. 1964. *Antígona*. Sarina Helfgott. Peru (in *Sarina Helfgott: Teatro*. Lima: Ediciones del Teatro de la Universidad Católica, 1967).
12. 1966. *La fiesta de los moribundos*. César Rengifo. Venezuela (in *Cuadernos Literarios de la Asociación de Escritores Venezolano*s 132. Caracas: Asociación de Escritores Venezolanos, 1970: 118–235).
13. 1967. *La tumba de Antígona*. María Zambrano. Mexico/Spain (Mexico: Siglo XXI, 1967).
14. 1968. *La pasión según Antígona Pérez*. Luis Rafael Sánchez. Puerto Rico (Hato Rey, PR: Ediciones Lugar, 1968).
15. 1968. *La Joven Antígona Va a la Guerra*. José Fuentes Mares. Mexico (Mexico: Editorial Jus, 1969).
16. 1968. *Detrás Queda el Polvo*. José Triana. Cuba (unpublished).
17. 1969. *As Confrarias*. Jorge Andrade. Brazil (São Paulo: Editôra Perspectiva, 1970).
18. 1975. *Une Manière d'Antigone*. Patrick Chamoiseau. Martinique (unpublished).
19. 1978. *Antígona*. José Gabriel Núñez. Venezuela (Venezuela: Revista *Escena* del CONAC, 1978).
20. 1982. *La ley de Creón*. Olga Harmony. Mexico (in *Tramoya*, January–March 2001: 66, 5–45).
21. 1983. *Soñar con Ceci trae cola*. Carlos Denis. Uruguay (unpublished).

392   APPENDIX

22. 1983. *Golpes a mi puert*a. Juan Carlos Gené. Argentina/Venezuela (Caracas: Ediciones Centro Gumilla, 1984).
23. 1986. *Antígona Furiosa.* Griselda Gambaro, Argentina (in *Teatro 3.* Buenos Aires: Ediciones La Flor, 1989: 195–217; translated into English by Margaret Feilowitz. *(in Information for Foreigners, trans. Evanston, IL: Northwestern University Press).*
24. 1987. *Viudas.* Ariel Dorfman. Chile/USA (in *Teatro 2.* Buenos Aires: Ediciones La Flor, 1992).
25. 1989. *Antígona.* Alberto Ure. Argentina (Cristina Banegas, ed. Buenos Aires: Editorial Leviatán, 2016).
26. 1989. *El viaje en círculo.* Tomás González Pérez. Cuba (in *El bello arte de ser y otras obras.* La Habana: Letras Cubanas, 2005).
27. 1990. *La primera dama.* Antonio García del Toro. Puerto Rico (Coral Gables, FL: University of Miami, 1992).
28. 1990. *Antígona Ritos de paixão e morte.* Brazil (in Ói Nóis Aqui Traveiz and Gilmar Rodrigues, eds., *Caminho para um teatro popular. Associação dos Amigos da Terreira da Tribo de Atuadores Ói Nóis Aqui Traveiz,* Porto Alegre, 1993).
29. 1994. *Antígona.* Joel Sáez. Cuba (online version in *La Jiribilla. Revista de cultura cubana.* Año VIII La Habana, January 16–22, 2010).
30. 1994. *Antígona Antígona.* Héctor Santiago. Cuba/NYC (unpublished).
31. 1997. *Antígona paralelo 76.* Daniel Zaballa. Argentina (unpublished).
32. 1998. *Antígona la necia.* Valeria Folini. Salta. Argentina (in Folini, *Resistencia trágica, la construcción de la embriaguez y el ensueño.* Buenos Aires: Asociación Civil Del Bardo, 2019).
33. 1999. *In memoriam Antigonae.* Rómulo Pianacci. Argentina (unpublished).
34. 2000. *Antígona. Versión libre de la tragedia de Sófloces.* José Watanabe/ Yuyachkani. Perú (Lima: Comisión de Derechos Humanos, 2000).
35. 2000. *Los motivos de Antígona.* Ricardo Andrade Jardi. Mexico (unpublished).
36. 2000. *Trans Antígona sexual.* Daniel Fermani. Argentina (unpublished).
37. 2001. *AntígonaS: Linaje de Hembras.* Jorge Huertas. Argentina (Buenos Aires: Editorial Biblios, 2002).
38. 2002. *Antígona, historia de objetos perdidos.* Daniela Cápona Pérez. Chile (Santiago de Chile: Lenguaje IV, Educación media, Editorial Santillana, 2002).
39. 2002. *Antígona en el espejo.* Juan Carlos Villavicencio. Chile (Santiago de Chile: Descontexto Editores, 2020).
40. 2003. *Antígona…con amor.* Hebe Campanella. Argentina (in *Teatro breve x5.* Buenos Aires: Fundación el libro, 2003: 79–131).
41. 2003. *Antígona No!* Yamila Grandi. Argentina (Online: http://aniogitna.blog-spot.com).
42. 2004. *Antígona; las voces que incendian el desierto.* Perla de la Rosa. Mexico (in G. de la Mora, ed., *Cinco Dramaturgos Chihuahueses.* Mexico: Fondo Municipal Editorial Revolvente—Municipio de Juárez, 2005: 185–228).
43. 2004. *Anti-Antígona.* Habey Hechavarría Prado (*Tablas,* 2004: 3–4: 22–3).
44. 2004. *El rey Creón: tragedia al estilo griego.* Alejandro Carrillo. Mexico (Mexico: A. Carrillo Castro, Edición privada, 2004).
45. 2004. *Contraantígona.* Pepe Santos Marrero. Cuba (unpublished).

APPENDIX 393

46. 2004. *Antígona Guaraní*. Víctor Sosa. Paraguay (unpublished).
47. 2005. *Antígona*. Yuyachkani/Watanabe. Versión Carlos Ianni. Argentina (unpublished).
48. 2005. *Antígona*. Antunes Filho. Brazil (unpublished).
49. 2006. *Antígona*. Patricia Ariza. Colombia (in *Obras del teatro La Candelaria, Vol. 4*. Bogotá: Teatro La Candelaria, 2008: 213–62).
50. 2006. *Antígona y actriz*. Carlos Satizábal. Colombia(in *Revista Colombiana de las artes escénicas*, February 2, 2008: 63–70).
51. 2006. *El thriller de Antígona*. Ana Montaner. Chile (in M. L. Hurtado and V. T. Martínez, eds., *Antología. Dramaturgia chilena del 2000: Nuevas Escrituras*. Santiago: Editorial Cuarto Propio, 2009).
52. 2006. *Ismene*. Lucía de la Maza. Chile (unpublished).
53. 2006–10. *Antígona, tragedia hoy*. Reinaldo Montero. Cuba (in *Ritos I. Mitos y otras actualidades*. La Habana: Editorial Letras Cubanas, 2009).
54. 2007. *Antígona*. Yerandi Fleites Pérez. Cuba (in *Teatro cubano actual. Novísimos dramaturgos*. La Habana: Ediciones Alarcos, 2008).
55. 2009. *Usted esta aquí*. Bárbara Colio. Mexico (Monterrey, Nuevo León: Conarte, 2010).
56. 2009. *Podrías llamarte Antígona*. Gabriela Ynclán. Mexico (unpublished).
57. 2009. *Antígona, narración en rojo y negro*. Luis Sarlinga. Mexico (unpublished).
58. 2009. *Antígona Hot*. Antonio Célico and Manuel Longueira. Argentina. Cabaret (unpublished).
59. 2009. *Antígonas*. Alberto Muñoz. Argentina (in Jorge Dubatti, ed., *Panorama teatral: nuevo teatro argentino*. Buenos Aires: Interzona, 2014).
60. 2010. *RockAntygona*. Antunes Filho. Brazil (unpublished).
61. 2011. *Antígona Furiosa–La Re-Vuelta*. Sandra Torlucci. Argentina (unpublished).
62. 2012. *Antígona Oriental*. Marianella Morena/Volker Lösh. Uruguay (unpublished).
63. 2012. *Antigonón: un contingente épico*. Rogelio Orizondo. Cuba (unpublished).
64. 2012. *Antígona en Vuelvezuela*. León Febres Cordero. Venezuela/Spain (in *Dos comedias: La toma de la pastilla y Antígona en Vuelvezuela*. Madrid: Editorial Verbum, 2016: 67–101).
65. 2012. *Antígona, rápida y furiosa*. Julia Arnaut. Mexico (unpublished).
66. 2012. *Antígona en sintonía*. Adrián Giampani. Grupo teatral AH! Academia del humor. Rosario Argentina (unpublished).
67. 2012. *Antígona González*. Sara Uribe. Mexico (Oaxaca: sur+ ediciones, 2012).
68. 2013. *KláSSIco (com K)*. Grupo Mayombe. Belo Horizonte, Brazil (in Marcos Antonio Alexandre, ed., *KláSSIco (com K). Pesquisa, dramaturgia e espetáculo teatral*. Belo Horizonte: Fale/UFMG, 2015).
69. 2013. *Antígona fantasma*. Daniel Fermani. Argentina (unpublished).
70. 2013. *Antígona*. Yuyachkani/Watanabe. Versión: Grupo Fratacho. Argentina (unpublished).
71. 2013. *El insepulto, o ya veré que hago con mis muertos*. José Félix Londoño. Colombia (unpublished).
72. 2013. *Antígona genealogía de un sacrificio*. Grupo Teatral Cenit. Nube Sandoval. Colombia (unpublished).

394   APPENDIX

73. 2013. *Antígona recortada: cuentos que cantan sobre aterrizajes de pájaros.* Claudia Schapira, Núcleo Bartolomeu de Depoimentos de São Paulo, Brazil (unpublished).
74. 2014. *Río arriba, río abajo: Antígona en el puente cantando.* Jesús Eduardo Domínguez Vargas. Colombia (unpublished).
75. 2014. *Antígona Unipersonal.* Lila Avilés. Mexico (unpublished).
76. 2014. *Antígona 1-11-14 del Bajo Flores.* Marcelo Marán. Argentina (available online at http://marcelomaran.com/antigona-1-11-14-del-bajo-flores-2).
77. 2015. *Antígona.* David Gaitán. Mexico (UNAM Theater, unpublished).
78. 2015. *Antígona Insomne.* Rubén Morgado SJ y Cía Bandurrias. Chile (unpublished).

List and Diagram of Antígona Plays Arranged by Antígona's Characterization

1. Mother/s/Grandmothers/Homage to Mothers/Mothers-to-be
2. Sisters
3. Female collectives
- 1824. *Argia.* Varela. Argentina (1)
- 1951. *Antígona Vélez.* Marechal. Argentina (1, 2)
- 1953. *Antigòn an Kreyòl.* Morisseau-Leroy. Haiti (1)
- 1957. *Pedreira das Almas.* Andrade. Brazil (1, 2)
- 1958. *El límite.* de Zavalía. Argentina (1)
- 1958. *Antígona en el infierno.* Steiner. Nicaragua (1, 2)
- 1962. *Odale's Choice.* Brathwaite. Barbados/Ghana (1)
- 1963. *La cabeza en la jaula.* Cureses. Argentina (1, 2, 3)
- 1964. *Antígona.* Helfgott. Peru (1, 2, 3)
- 1966. *La fiesta de los moribundos.* Rengifo. Venezuela (2)
- 1968. *La Joven Antígona Va a la Guerra.* Fuentes Mares. Mexico (1)
- 1968. *La Pasión según Antígona Pérez.* Rafael Sánchez. Puerto Rico (1)
- 1969. *As Confrarias.* Andrade. Brazil (1)
- 1978. *Antígona.* Núñez. Venezuela (1)
- 1982. *La ley de Creon.* Harmony. Mexico (1, 3)
- 1983. *Soñar con Ceci trae cola.* Denis. Uruguay (1)
- 1986. *Golpes a mi puerta.* Gené. Argentina/Venezuela (1, 2)
- 1986. *Antígona Furiosa.* Gambaro, Argentina (1)
- 1987. *Viudas.* Dorfman. Chile/USA (1, 3)
- 1990. *La primera dama.* García del Toro. Puerto Rico (1, 3)
- 2000. *Antígona. Versión libre de la tragedia de Sófloces.* Watanabe/Yuyachkani. Peru (1, 2)
- 2001. *Antígonas: Linaje de Hembras.* Huertas. Argentina (1, 3)
- 2003. *Antígona... Con amor.* Campanella. Argentina (2)
- 2003. *Antígona No!* Grandi Argentina (2)
- 2004. *Antígona. Las voces que incendian el desierto.* de la Rosa. Mexico (1, 2, 3)
- 2005. *Antígona.* Yuyachkani/Watanabe. Version Ianni. Argentina (1, 2)

APPENDIX 395

- 2006. *Ismene.* de la Maza. Chile (2)
- 2006. *Antígona.* Ariza. Colombia (1, 2, 3)
- 2006. *Antígona y actriz.* Satizábal. Colombia (1, 2, 3)
- 2006. *Festival Magdalena Antígona.* Colombia (3)
- 2007. *Antígona.* Fleites. Cuba (2)
- 2009. *Podrías llamarte Antígona.* Ynclán. Mexico (3)
- 2009. *Antígonas.* Muñoz. Argentina (3)
- 2009. *Usted esta aquí.* Colio. Mexico (1, 2)
- 2009. *Antígona, narración en rojo y negro.* Sarlinga. Mexico (1, 2)
- 2011. *Antígona Furiosa–La Re-Vuelta.* Torlucci. Argentina (1, 2, 3)
- 2012. *Antígona Oriental.* Morena/Lösh. Uruguay (1, 2, 3)
- 2012. *Antígona González.* Uribe. Mexico (1, 2, 3)
- 2012. *Antigonón: un contingente épico.* Orizondo. Cuba (1, 3)
- 2013. *Antígona.* Yuyachkani/Watanabe. Grupo Fratacho. Argentina (1, 2)
- 2013. *El insepulto, o ya veré que hago con mis muertos.* Londoño. Colombia (3)
- 2013. *El grito de Antígona vs. La nuda vida.* Uribe. Colombia (3)
- 2013. *Antígona genealogía de un sacrificio.* Grupo Cenit. Sandoval. Colombia (1, 3)
- 2014. *Antigona Unipersonal.* Avilés. Mexico (2)
- 2014. *Río arriba, río abajo: Antígona en el puente cantando.* Domínguez Vargas. Colombia (3)
- 2015. *Antígona Insomne.* Morgado SJ y Cía Bandurrias. Chile (2)

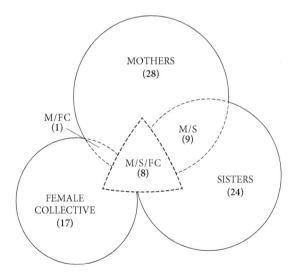

Figure A.1 Intersections of Mothers (M), Sisters (S), and Female Collectives (FC) in the corpus. Grafted by Mark Saba, Senior Designer and Illustrator at Yale University's Information Technology Services.

396 APPENDIX

List of Cabaret/Comedy/Tragicomedy/Farce Vernaculars

- 1961. *Antígona-humor.* Domínguez. Dominican Republic.
- 1966. *La fiesta de los moribundos.* Rengifo. Venezuela.
- 2005. *Antígona* and 2010 *RockAntygona.* Antunes Filho. Brazil.
- 2006. *El thriller de Antígona.* Montaner. Chile.
- 2009. *Antígona Hot.* Célico and Longueira. Argentina.
- 2012. *Antígona en Vuelvezuela.* Febres Cordero. Venezuela/Spain.
- 2012. *Antígona, rápida y furiosa.* Arnaut. Mexico.
- 2012. *Antígona en sintonía.* Giampani. Grupo teatral AH! Academia del humor. Rosario. Argentina.
- 2012. *Antigonón: un contingente épico.* Orizondo. Cuba.
- 2013. *Antígona Recortada.* Schapira, Brazil.
- 2013. *KláSSIco (com K).* Grupo Mayombe. Brazil.
- 2014. *Antígona 1-11-14 del Bajo Flores.* Marán. Argentina.

Bibliography

Adsuar, María Dolores (2004), "Muerte y transfiguración de Antígona Vélez," *Revista Electrónica de Estudios Filológicos* 8, https://www.um.es/tonosdigital/znum8/Resenas/3-libro_antigona.htm.

Aisemberg, Alicia (1997), "Dido y Argia: Las primeras tragedias sudamericanas," in Osvaldo Pellettieri, ed., *De Esquilo a Gambaro* (Buenos Aires: Editorial Galerna), 13–24.

Alberdi, Juan Bautista ([1852] 1923), *Bases y puntos de partida para la organización política de la República Argentina* (Buenos Aires: La Cultura Argentina).

Albrecht, Monika (2013), "Comparative Literature and Postcolonial Studies Revisited: Reflections in Light of Recent Transitions in the Fields of Postcolonial Studies," *Comparative Critical Studies* 10/1: 47–65.

Albrecht, Monika, ed. (2020), "From Cuzco to Constantinople. Rethinking Postcolonialism," in *Post-Colonialism Cross-Examined* (London: Routledge): 197–216.

Alemany, Luis (2016), "Puerto Rico: Crisis y soberanismo en el país del 'mantengo,'" *El Mundo*, March 4, 2016, http://www.elmundo.es/internacional/2016/04/03/570005a6268e3ed9718b45fb.html.

Alencastro, Luiz Felipe de (2000), *O trato dos viventes: Formação do Brasil no Atlântico Sul, séculos XVI e XVII* (São Paulo: Companhia das Letras).

Allen, Stewart Lee (1999), *The Devil's Cup: Coffee, the Driving Force in History* (London: Random House).

Almeida Prado, Décio de (1964), *Teatro em progresso: Crítica teatral 1955–1964* (São Paulo: Martins).

Almeida Prado, Décio de (1998), "Teatro Brasileiro de Comédia rêve os seus 50 anos," *O Estado de S. Paulo*, October 10.

Almirón, Fernando (1999), *Campo Santo: Testimonios del ex sargento Víctor Ibáñez* (Buenos Aires: Editorial 21).

Alonso, Laura (2009), "Antígona Vélez: La tragedia clásica de Antígona releída como rito fundacional del espacio argentino," *Neophilologus* 93: 439–52.

Alvarez Morán, María Consuelo and Rosa María Iglesias Montiel, eds. (1999), *Contemporaneidad de los clásicos en el umbral del tercer milenio (Proceedings of the Congress in La Habana, Cuba, Dec. 1998 Contemporaneidad de los Clásicos: La tradición greco-latina ante el siglo XXI)* (Murcia: Universidad de Murcia).

Amin, Samir (1988), *Eurocentrism* (London: Monthly Review Press).

Andersen, Martin E. (1993), *Dossier Secreto: Argentina's Desaparecidos and the Myth of the "Dirty War."* (Boulder, CO: Westview Press).

Andrade, Jorge (1966), Interview with *Visão*, August 5.

Andrade, Jorge ([1970] 1986), *Marta, a árvore e o relógio*, 2nd ed. (São Paulo: Perspectiva).

398 BIBLIOGRAPHY

Andrade, Jorge ([1978] 2009), *Labirinto* (São Paulo: Manole).

Andrade, Oswald de (1928), "Manifesto Antropófago"; with introduction by Leslie Bary, http://www.corner-college.com/udb/cproK3mKYQAndrade_Cannibalistic_ Manifesto.pdf.

A'Ness, Francine (2004), "Resisting Amnesia: Yuyachkani, Performance, and the Postwar Reconstruction of Peru," *Theatre Journal* 56/3: 395–414.

Anrup, Roland (2009), *Una tragedia a la colombiana* (Bogotá: Mondadori).

Anrup, Roland (2011), *Antígona y Creonte. Rebeldía y estado en Colombia*. Bogotá: Ediciones B. Colección Crónica.

Ansaldi, Waldo, ed. (1984), *Rosas y su tiempo* (Buenos Aires: Centro Editor de América Latina).

Apollodorus and Hyginus (2007), *Apollodorus Library and Hyginus' Fabulae: Two Handbooks of Greek Mythology*, trans. R. Scott Smith and Stephen Trzaskoma (Indianapolis, IN: Hackett Publishing Company).

Apter, Emily (2013), *Against World Literature: On the Politics of Untranslatability* (London: Verso).

Arantes, Luis Humberto Martins (2001), *Teatro da Memória: História e ficção na dramaturgia de Jorge Andrade* (São Paulo: AnnaBlume/Fapesp).

Arantes, Luis Humberto Martins (2009), "*Pedreira das Almas* de Jorge Andrade e Alberto D'Aversa: Cinqüenta anos de criação dramatúgica e transposição cênica," *OPSIS, Catalão* 9/12, January–June: 82–93.

Arciniegas, Germán (1986), *Las Mujeres y las horas* (Santiago: Editorial Andrés Bello).

Ardao, Arturo (1980), *Génesis de la idea y el nombre de América Latina* (Caracas: Centro de Estudios Latinoamericanos Rómulo Gallegos).

Arguedas, José María (1965), *Formación de una cultura nacional indoamericana* (México: Siglo XXI).

Arlt, Mirta (1998), "El mito griego: Permanencia y relatividad en Antígona Vélez de Leopoldo Marechal," in Osvaldo Pellettieri, ed., *El Teatro y su crítica* (Buenos Aires: Galerna), 201–12.

Arriví, Francisco (1967), *Conciencia Puertorriqueña del teatro contemporáneo, 1937–1956* (San Juan: Instituto de Cultura Puertorriqueña).

Arriví, Francisco (1972), *La generación del treinta: Ciclo de conferencias sobre la literatura de Puerto Rico* (San Juan: Instituto de Cultura Puertorriqueña).

Arrosagaray, Enrique (1997), *Azucena Villafor: Creadora del movimiento de Madres de Plaza de Mayo* (Buenos Aires: Catálogos).

Ashcroft, Bill, Gareth Griffiths, and Helen Tiffin (1989), *The Empire Writes Back: Theory and Practice in Post-Colonial Literatures* (New York: Routledge).

Ashcroft, Bill, Gareth Griffiths, and Helen Tiffin (1995), *The Post-Colonial Studies Reader* (London: Routledge).

Asquini, Pedro (1990), *El teatro que hicimos* (Buenos Aires: Editorial Rescate).

Assié-Lumumba, N'Dri Thérèse (2006), *Higher Education in Africa: Crises, Reforms and Transformations* (Dakar, Senegal: Council for the Development of Social Science Research in Africa).

Augoustakis, Antony (2010), *Motherhood and the Other: Fashioning Female Power in Flavian Epic* (Oxford: Oxford University Press).

BIBLIOGRAPHY 399

Avena, Sergio, Alicia Goicoechea, Jorge Rey, Jean Dugoujon, Cristina Dejean, and Francisco Carnese (2006), "Mezcla génica en una muestra poblacional de la Ciudad de Buenos Aires," *Medicina* 66: 113–18.

Avila, Affonso (1967), *Resíduos Seiscentistas em Minas* (Belo Horizonte: Belo Horizonte Centro de Estudos Mineiros/UFMG).

Azevedo, Elizabeth (2014), *Recursos estilísticos na dramaturgia de Jorge Andrade* (São Paulo: EDUSP).

Azevedo, Elizabeth, F. Martins, L de O. Nevers, and F. Viana (2012), *Jorge Andrade: 90 anos (re)leituras. Volume I: A voz de Jorge* (São Paulo: Fapesp).

Badiou, Alain (2001), *Ethics: An Essay on the Understanding of Evil* (London: Verso).

Baigorria, Manuel (1975), *Memorias [1830–1850]* (Buenos Aires: Solar/Hachette).

Balibar, Étienne (2007), "Ambiguous Universality," in *Politics and the Other Scene*, trans. Christine Jones, James Swenson, and Chris Turner (London and New York: Verso), 146–76.

Ballent, Anahí (2004), "Perón en la ciudad sin esperanza" and "La política y las políticas urbanas en Buenos Aires," in Patricia Berrotarán, Aníbal Jáuregui and Marcelo Rougier, eds., *Sueños de bienestar en la Nueva Argentina* (Buenos Aires: Imago Mundi), 301–25.

Bañuls Oller, José Vicente and Patricia Crespo Alcalá (2008), *Antígona(s): Mito y personaje, un recorrido desde los orígenes* (Bari: Levante).

Bañuls Oller, José Vicente, Francesco de Martino, and Carmen Morenilla, eds. (2005), *Teatro clásico en el marco de la cultura griega y su pervivencia en la cultura occidental, IX–X: El teatro greco-latino y su recepción en la tradición occidental*, Universitat de València, Mayo 4–7 (Bari: Levante).

Bañuls Oller, José Vicente, J. Sánchez Méndez, and J. Sanmartín Sáez, eds. (1999), *Literatura iberoamericana y tradición clásica* (Valencia: Universitat Autònoma de Barcelona/Universitat de València).

Barnet, Miguel (1966), *Biografía de un cimarrón* (La Habana: Instituto de Etnología y Folklore).

Barradas, Efraín (1979), "*La pasión según Antígona Pérez*: Mito latinoamericano y realidad puertorriqueña," *Sin Nombre* 10/1: 10–22.

Barrancos, Dora (2002), *Inclusión/Exclusión. Historia con mujeres* (Buenos Aires: Fondo de Cultura Económica).

Barraza Lescano, Sergio (2009), "Apuntes histórico-arqueológicos de la danza del Huacón," *Anthropológica* 27: 93–121.

Barry, Carolina, Karina Ramacciotti, and Adriana Valobra, eds. (2008), *La Fundación Eva Perón y las mujeres: Entre la provocación y la inclusión* (Buenos Aires: Biblos).

Bátiz Zuk, Martha (2013), "Social and Political Criticism: The Reformulation of the Myth of Antigone, in Franklin Domínguez, Antígona-Humor," in Jennifer Duprey, ed., *Whose Voice is This? Iberian and Latin American Antigones, Special Issue of Hispanic Issues Online* 13: 114–29.

Bauduy, Robert (1974), "Un second souffle pour le théatre haïtien," *Conjonction* 124: 55–71.

Bauduy, Robert (1990), "El teatro haitiano contemporáneo," *Conjunto* 82: 43–8.

Bauduy, Robert (2002), "Théâtre. Démocratie. Identité culturelle," *Conjonction* 207: 26–7.

400 BIBLIOGRAPHY

Bayeux, Jean-Claude (1999), *Anthologie de la littérature créole haïtienne* (Port au Prince: Éditions Antilia).

Beauvoir, Simone de ([1947] 1972), *The Second Sex*, trans. H. M. Parshley (New York: Penguin).

Belaval, Emilio S. (1948), "Lo que podría ser el Teatro Puertorriqueño," in *Areyto* (México: Biblioteca de Autores Puertorriqueños), 9–24.

Bellucci, Mabel (n.d.), "Anarquismo y feminismo," *El libertario, año 21, n° 67*, 2006.

Beltrán Valencia, Gina (2014), "Antígona Pérez y el sensacionalismo: la desarticulación de un sistema totalitario," *452°F. Revista electrónica de teoría de la literatura y literatura comparada* 10: 35–49.

Benjamin, Walter ([1940] 2007), "Thesis on the Philosophy of History," in Hannah Arendt, ed., *Illuminations* (New York: Schocken), 253–64.

Ben-Ur, Lorraine (1975), "Myth Montage in a Puerto Rican Tragedy: 'La pasión según Antígona Pérez,'" *Latin American Literary Review* 4/7: 15–21.

Bernal, Irma (1997), *Rosas y los indios* (Buenos Aires: Búsqueda).

Betances, Ramón Emeterio (1867), *Proclama de los Diez Mandamientos de los Hombres Libres*. https://ventanasur.wordpress.com/2011/04/08/los-diez-mandamientos-de-los-hombres-libres-i867/

Betsko, Kathleen and Rachael Koening, eds. (1987), *Interviews with Contemporary Women Playwrights* (New York: Beech Tree).

Bettaglio, Marina (2012), "*Surveiller, faire croire et punir*: The Body in Evidence in Luis Rafael Sánchez's *La pasión según Antígona Pérez*," *Latin American Theatre Review* 45/2: 45–55.

Beverley, John (1993), *Against Literature* (Minneapolis, MN: University of Minnesota).

Beverley, John (1999), *Subalternity and Representation: Arguments in Cultural Theory* (Durham, NC: Duke University Press).

Beverley, John (2004), *Testimonio: On the Politics of Truth* (Minneapolis, MN: University of Minnesota Press).

Beverley, John, José Oviedo, and Michael Aronna, eds. (1993), *The Postmodernism Debate in Latin America* (Durham, NC: Duke University Press).

Bhabha, Homi (1994), *The Location of Culture* (New York: Routledge).

Biglieri, A. Aníbal (2009), "La Argentina de Antígona Vélez," in Aurora López and Andrés Pociña, eds., *En Recuerdo de Beatriz Rabasa: Comedias, tragedias y leyendas grecorromanas en el teatro del siglo XX* (Granada: Universidad de Granada), 110–22.

Biglieri, A. Aníbal (2016), "Antigone, Medea and Civilization and Barbarism in Spanish American History," in Betine Van Zyl Smit, ed., *The Handbook to the Reception of Greek Drama* (Oxford: Wiley-Blackwell), 348–64.

Boal, Augusto ([1979] 1983), *Theater of the Oppressed* (New York: Theater Communications Group).

Bochetti, Carla (2010), *La influencia clásica en América Latina* (Bogotá: Ediciones Universidad Nacional de Colombia).

Boletín No. 1 (2002), Editorial and interview with Salomon Lerner. http://www.cverdad.org.pe/informacion/boletines/pdfs/boletin1.pdf.

BIBLIOGRAPHY 401

Boling, Becky (2013), "Intertextual Uses of Antigone and Liberation Theology: The Passion of Ana in Juan Carlos Gené's Golpes a mi puerta," *Hispanic Issues Online Special Issue*, 13: 220–40.

Bolívar, Simón (1815), *Reply of a South American to a Gentleman of This Island*, September 6, https://library.brown.edu/create/modernlatinamerica/chapters/chapter-2-the-colonial-foundations/primary-documents-with-accompanying-discussion-questions/document-2-simon-bolivar-letter-from-jamaica-september-6-1815.

Bolles, Lynn (2006), "Di Marco Graciela. Interview: Testimonio de Nora Cortiñas," in *De lo privado a lo público: 30 años de lucha ciudadana de las mujeres en América Latina Mexico: Siglo XXI*: 125–32.

Bonaparte, Laura (2010), *Laura Bonaparte, una Madre de Plaza de Mayo contra el olvido* (Buenos Aires: Marea Editorial).

Borges, Jorge Luis ([1951] 1997), "El escritor argentino y la tradición," in Jorge Luis Borges, *Discusión* (Madrid: Alianza), 151–62.

Borrachero Mendíbil, Aránzazu (2007), "Dos Antígonas," *CIEHL: Cuaderno Internacional de Estudios Humanísticos y Literatura* 7: 7–25.

Bosch, Juan ([1960] 2009), *Trujillo: Causas de una tiranía sin ejemplo*, 8th ed. (Santo Domingo: Alfa & Omega).

Bosch, María del Carmen (1999), "Antígona en Iberoamérica," in María Consuelo Álvarez Morán and Rosa María Iglesias, eds., *Contemporaneidad de los clásicos en el umbral del tercer milenio: Actas del congreso internacional Contemporaneidad de los clásicos, la tradición greco-latina ante el siglo XXI* (Havana, Cuba: Editum), 271–80.

Boschi, Caio César (1986), *Os leigos e o poder: Irmandades leigas e política coloniza-dora em Minas Gerais* (São Paulo: Ática).

Bosher Kathryn, Fiona Macintosh, Justine McConnell, and Patrice Rankine, eds. (2015), *The Oxford Handbook of Greek Drama in the Americas* (Oxford: Oxford University Press).

Botelho, Tarcísio Rodrigues et al. (2001), *História quantitativa e serial no Brasil: Um balanço* (Goiânia: Anpuh-MG).

Botía Mena, Juan (2016), "La Antígona de Sófocles como símbolo en el conflicto armado en Colombia," https://www.academia.edu/35042698/La_Ant%C3%ADgona_de_S%C3%B3focles_como_s%C3%ADmbolo_de_protesta_social_frente_al_conflicto_armado_en_Colombia.

Bowden, Charles (1998), *Juárez: The Laboratory of our Future* (New York: Aperture).

Boyce Davis, Carol, ed. (2008), *Encyclopedia of the African Diaspora* (Santa Barbara, CA: ABC-Clio).

Braithwaite, L. (1958), "The Development of Higher Education in the British West Indies," *Social and Economic Studies* 7/1: 1–64.

Braudel, Fernand (1992), *The Perspective of the World. Civilization and Capitalism 15th–18th Century* (Berkeley, CA: University of California Press).

Bravo, Nazareno (2003), "El discurso de la dictadura militar argentina. Definición del opositor político y confinamiento—'valorización' del papel de la mujer en el espacio privado," *Utopía y Praxis Latinoamericana* 8/22: 107–23.

402 BIBLIOGRAPHY

Bravo Elizondo, Pedro (1975), *"La pasión según Antígona Pérez:* Radiografía de la dictadura," *Teatro hispanoamericano de crítica social* (Madrid: Playor), 95–108.

Braziel, Jana Evans (2005), "Re-membering Défilée," *Small Axe* 9/2: 57–85.

Briceño, Ximena (2004), *Ismena, desde la culpa.* Unpublished Paper.

Briones, Claudia (2005), *Cartografías argentinas: Políticas indígenas y formaciones provinciales de alteridad* (Buenos Aires: Editorial Antropofagia).

Brunn, Victoria (2009), "From Tragedy to Ritual: Latin American Adaptations of Sophocles' *Antigone*," Dissertation, Columbia University.

Brunn, Victoria (2012), "Revolutionizing *Antigone*: A Puerto Rican Adaptation of Sophocles' Tragedy," *Romance Quarterly* 59/1: 36–47.

Brutt-Griffler, J. (2002), *World English. A Study of its Development.* Clevedon: Multilingual Matters.

Buarque de Holanda, Sérgio ([1936] 1973), *Raízes do Brasil* (Rio de Janeiro: Olympio).

Bueno Chávez, Ch. (2004) *Antonio Cornejo Polar y los avatares de la cultura latinoamericana* (Lima: Fondo Editorial de la Universidad Nacional Mayor de San Marcos).

Buck-Morss, Susan (2009), *Hegel, Haiti, and Universal History* (Pittsburgh, PA: University of Pittsburgh Press).

Burness, Donald, ed. (1985), "Interview with O. Rotimi," in *Wana Sema: Conversations with African Writers* (Athens, OH: Ohio University Center for International Studies), 11–18.

Butler, Judith (2000), *Antigone's Claim: Kinship between Life and Death* (New York: Columbia University Press).

Buuck, David (2016), "'The Silence…Is Our Most Unyielding Creon': Five Questions for Sara Uribe & John Pluecker about Antígona González," *Queen Mobster House*, June 13, trans. John Pluecker, https://queenmobs.com/2016/06/the-silence-is-our-most-unyielding-creon-five-questions-for-sara-uribe-john-pluecker-about-antigona-gonzalez/.

Caicedo, Andrés ([1976] 2009), *Noche sin fortuna* (Bogotá: Norma).

Calaf de Agüera, Helen (1979), "Luis Rafael Sánchez," *Hispamérica* 23–4: 71–80.

Calveiro, Pilar (2004), *Poder y desaparición* (Buenos Aires, Colihue).

Camacho Rojo, José María (2004), *La tradición clásica en las literaturas iberoamericanas del siglo XX* (Granada: Universidad de Granada).

Camus, Albert ([1974] 1976), *The Plague* (New York: Belmont Tower Books).

Candido, Antonio (1958), *"De a Moratória* a *Pedreira das Almas*," in *Teatro Brasileiro de Comédia 10 aniversário apresenta Pedreira das Almas de Jorge Andrade* (São Paulo/Rio de Janeiro) [Programa n° 1 19.].

Candido, Antonio ([1959] 2000), *Formação da Literatura Brasileira* (Belo Horizonte: Editora Itatiaia).

Cañizares-Esguerra, Jorge (2001), *How to Write the History of the New World: Histories, Epistemologies, and Identities in the Eighteenth-Century Atlantic World* (Palo Alto, CA: Stanford University Press).

Cañizares-Esguerra, Jorge (2006), *Puritan Conquistadors: Iberianizing the Atlantic, 1550–1700* (Stanford, CA: Stanford University Press).

Cañizares-Esguerra, Jorge (2018), "Envoi: Whose Classical Traditions," in Andrew Laird and Nicola Miller, eds., *Antiquities and Classical Traditions in Latin America* (Chichester: Wiley-Blackwell), 196–200.

BIBLIOGRAPHY   403

Cardoso, F. H. and Faletto, E. (1979), *Dependency and Development in Latin América* (Berkeley, CA: University of California Press).

Cardullo, Robert (2010), *Antigone Adapted: Sophocles' Antigone in Classic Drama and Modern Adaptation, Translation and Transformation* (Betsheda: Academica Press).

Carlson, Marla (2003), "Antigone's Bodies: Performing Torture," *Modern Drama* 46/3: 381–403.

Carnelli, Elisa and Alberto Ure (2016), *Antígona por Ure* (Buenos Aires: Leviatán).

Carpentier, Alejo (1949), *El reino de este mundo* (La Habana: Organización Continental de los Festivales del Libro).

Carpentier, Alejo (1959), *Letra y Solfa. Vol. 4, Teatro* (La Habana: Editorial Letras Cubanas).

Casanova, Pascale (2004), *The World Republic of Letters* (Cambridge, MA: Harvard University Press).

Castellvi DeMoor, Magda (1992), "La parodia en el teatro de Griselda Gambaro: interdiscursividad y voluntad de estilo," in Osvaldo Pellettieri, ed., *Teatro y Teatristas* (Buenos Aires: Editorial Galerna), 147–57.

Castro, Alves (1867), *Gonzaga ou a Revolução de Minas* (Rio de Janeiro: Various).

Castro, Marcela and Silvia Jurovietzky (1996), "Interview with Griselda Gambaro," *Feminaria Literaria* IX/17–18: 41–5.

Castro-Gómez, Santiago and Eduardo Mendieta, eds. (1998), *Teorías sin disciplina. Latinoamericanismo, postcolonialidad y globalización en debate* (Mexico City: Miguel Ángel Porrúa).

Catelli, Nora (2017), "Asymmetry: Specters of Comparativism in the Circulation of Theory," *Journal of World Literature* 2/1: 11–26.

Catena, Alberto (2011), *La Flecha y la luciérnaga: Itinerarios de un viaje por la obra de Griselda Gambaro* (Buenos Aires: Capital Intelectual).

Cejas, Julio (2016), "El fantasma de Antígona persiste," *Página 12*, August 21, https://www.pagina12.com.ar/diario/suplementos/rosario/12-56068-2016-08-21.html.

Celso, Ramón Lorenzo (1999), *Manual de historia constitucional argentina, Tomo 3* (Rosario: Editorial Juris).

Cendoc (2006), "Exclusión Social y Comisión de la Verdad y Reconciliación," September 5, http://www.youtube.com/watch?v=dtvwrMJgbJA&feature=related.

Césaire, Aimé ([1963] 1970), *La tragédie du Roi Christophe* (Paris: Présence Africaine).

Chamosa, Oscar and Matthew Karush, eds. (2010), *The New Cultural History of Peronism, 1930–1966* (Durham, NC: Duke University Press).

Chanlatte, Juste ([1818] 1918), "L'Entrée du roi dans sa capital," *Le Nouveau Monde*, August 19, 6–12.

Chanter, Tina (2011), *Whose Antigone? The Tragic Marginalization of Slavery* (Albany, NY: SUNY Press).

Charles, Christopher P. (1984), "Les pionniers de la littérature haïtienne d'expression créole," *Conjonction: Revue Franco-Haïtienne* 161–2: 152–7.

Chejter, Silvia (2002), "Entrevista a Nora Cortiñas. Madre de Plaza de Mayo Línea Fundadora," in Ediciones Cecym, ed., *Travesías. Temas del Debate Feminista Contemporaneo*, Vol. 11 (Buenos Aires: Ediciones Cecym), 149–51.

Chiaramonte, José Carlos (2001), "La cuestión de la soberanía en la génesis y constitución del estado argentino," *Historia constitucional* 2: 107–33. http://www.historiaconstitucional.com/index.php/historiaconstitucional/article/view/122

404 BIBLIOGRAPHY

Cicchini, Susana (1982), "Antígona Vélez: Reinterpretación del mito," *Teatro*. Buenos Aires, Getea.

Clark, Fred M. (1981), "Tragedy and the Tragic: Andrade's *Pedreira das Almas*," *Latin American Theater Review* 15/1: 21–30.

Clark, Vèvè (1983), "Contemporary Forms of Popular Theatre in Haiti," *Ufahamu: Journal of the African Activist Association* 12/2: 93–100.

Clark, Vèvè (1986), "Campesinos actores en Haití: el peso de la tradición," *Conjunto* 70: 14–22.

Clark, Vèvè (1992a), "Haiti's Tragic Overture": (Mis) Representations of the Haitian Revolution in World Drama (1796–1975)," in James Hefferman, ed., *Representing the French Revolution* (Hanover, NH: University Press of New England), 237–60.

Clark, Vèvè (1992b), "When Womb Waters Break: The Emergence of Haitian New Theater (1953–1987)," *Callaloo* 15/3: 778–86.

Clifford, James and George G. Marcus, eds. (1986), *Writing Culture: The Poetics and Politics of Ethnography* (Berkeley, CA: University of California Press).

Coates, Carol F. (1996), "Dessalines: History in Theater," *Journal of Haitian Studies* 2/2: 167–78.

Cohen, Stanley (2001), *States of Denial: Knowing about Atrocities and Suffering* (Cambridge: Polity).

Coicou, Masillon ([1907] 1988), *L'empereur Dessalines; drame en deux actes en vers* (Port-au-Prince: Imp. E. Chenet).

Collins, J. A. (1982), *Contemporary Theater in Puerto Rico: The Decade of the Seventies* (Rio Piedras, Puerto Rico: Editorial Universitaria).

Colón Zayas, Eliseo (1985), *El teatro de Luis Rafael Sánchez: códigos, ideología y lenguaje* (Madrid: Playor).

Comhaire, Jean Louis Léopold (1955), "The Haitian 'Chef de Section,'" *American Anthropologist* 57/3: 620–4.

Comisión Chilena de Derechos Humanos (1999), *Nunca más en Chile: Síntesis corregida y actualizada del informe Rettig* (Santiago: Lom Ediciones).

Comisión de la Verdad y Reconciliación, Perú (CVR) (2002), *Audiencias Públicas. Public Hearings (Lima December 12)* (Peru: CVR).

Comisión de la Verdad y Reconciliación, Perú (CVR) (2003), "Final Report, *Las ejecuciones extrajudiciales en Socos*," http://www.cverdad.org.pe/ifinal/pdf/TOMO%20VII/Casos%20Ilustrativos-UIE/2.7.%20SOCOS.pdf.

Comisión de la Verdad y Reconciliación, Perú (CVR) (2006), "Mensajes del Informe Final de la CVR: Víctimas," http://www.youtube.com/watch?v=HE_Fu_x5FZ8&feature=related.

Comisión Nacional de Verdad y Reconciliación, Chile (1993), *Report of the Chilean National Commission on Truth and Reconciliation*, trans. Phillip Berryman (Notre Dame: University of Notre Dame Press).

Comisión Nacional sobre la Desaparición de Personas, Argentina (1984), *Truth Commission report, Nunca Más* (Buenos Aires: Eudeba), http://www.derechoshumanos.net/lesahumanidad/informes/argentina/informe-de-la-CONADEP-Nunca-mas-Indice.htm#C1.

Conklin, Beth (2001), *Consuming Grief: Compassionate Cannibalism in an Amazonian Society* (Austin, TX: University of Texas).

BIBLIOGRAPHY 405

Contreras, Marta (1994), *Las obras dramáticas de Griselda Gambaro. Teatro de la descomposición* (Concepción: Universidad de la Concepción).

Corbella, Walter, trans. (2008), "Antígona Vélez," *Mosaic* 41: 97–102.

Cornejo Polar, Antonio (1982), *Sobre literatura y crítica latinoamericanas* (Caracas: UCV), 67–85.

Cornejo Polar, Antonio (1998), "Mestizaje e hibridez: los riesgos de las metáforas. Apuntes," *Revista de crítica literaria latinoamericana* 47: 7–11.

Cornejo Polar, Antonio (2004), "*Mestizaje*, Transculturation, Heterogeneity," in Ana Del Sarto, Alicia Ríos, and Abril Trigo, eds., *Latin American Cultural Studies Reader* (Durham, NC: Duke University Press), 116–19.

Cornevin, Robert (1973), *Le théâtre Haïtien des origins à nos jours* (Ottawa: Leméac).

Coronil, Fernando (1992), "Can Postcoloniality Be Decolonized? Imperial Banality and Postcolonial Power," *Public Culture* 5/1: 89–108.

Coronil, Fernando (1996), "Beyond Occidentalism. Toward Nonimperial Geohistorical Categories," *Cultural Anthropology* 11/1: 51–87.

Coronil, Fernando (2000), "Naturaleza del poscolonialismo: del eurocentrismo al globocentrismo," in Edgardo Lander, ed., *La colonialidad del saber: eucrocentrismo y ciencias sociales. Perspectivas Latinoamericanas* (Buenos Aires: CLASCO), 246–56.

Coronil, Fernando (2001), *Postcolonialism: A Historical Introduction* (Cambridge: Blackwell).

Coronil, Fernando (2004), "Latin American Postcolonial Studies and Global Decolonization," in Neil Lazarus, ed., *The Cambridge Companion to Postcolonial Literary Studies* (Cambridge: Cambridge University Press), 221–40.

Correia, Viriato (1941), *Tiradentes: Comédia histórica em 3 atos e 7 quadros* (1939) (Rio de Janeiro: Ministério da Educação, Serviço Nacional de Teatro).

Cortés, Eladio and Mirta Barrea, eds. (2003), *Encyclopedia of Latin American Theater* (London: Greenwood Press).

Cossio, Carlos (1967), "Antinous," in *Agua Herrada* (Buenos Aires: Emecé).

Crenzel, Emilio, ed. (2010), *Los desaparecidos en la Argentina: Memorias, representaciones e ideas: 1983–2008* (Buenos Aires: Biblios.)

Croce, María Victoria (2003), "La muerte en las Antígonas de Sófocles y Griselda Gambaro: intertextualidad y parodia," in *Boletín del Instituto de Investigaciones en Historia del Arte, Vol. 1* (Buenos Aires: El instituto), 39–54.

Crochetti, Silvia, Norma Medus, M. Inés Poduje, Evar O. (Ch) Amieva, Cazenave Héctor, José C. Depetris, Myriam Lucero, and Edgar Morisoli (1997), *Pampas del Sud. Recopilación de textos que hacen a las raíces autóctonas de la provincia de La Pampa* (Santa Rosa: Asociación Pampeana de Escritores y Subsecretaría de Cultura de La Pampa).

Cuitiño, Luis Martínez (1982), "La ley de la llanura y el mito de Antígona," *Boletín del Instituto de Teatro* 3: 38–9.

Curtius, Ernst Robert ([1952] 1990), *European Literature and the Latin Middle Ages* (Princeton, NJ: Princeton University Press).

Dainotto, Roberto M. (2007), *Europe (in Theory)* (Durham, NC: Duke University Press).

Damrosch, David (2004), *The Longman Anthology of World Literature*, 2nd ed. (New York: Longman).

406 BIBLIOGRAPHY

Damrosch, David (2014), "World Literature as Figure and Ground," *American Comparative Literature Association*, website, https://stateofthediscipline.acla.org/entry/world-literature-figure-and-ground-0.

Damrosch, David and David Pike (2009), *Instructor's Manual to Accompany The Longman Anthology of World Literature*, 2nd ed. (New York: Pearson Education).

Daneri, Antonio A. (n.d.), "So Classic, So Close," http://www.yuyachkani.org/obras/antigona/antigona.html.

Daumec, Lucien (1954), "Odyssée d'une langue," *Optique*: 38–40.

Dauster, Frank (1971), "La pasión según Antígona Pérez," *Sin Nombre*, San Juan, I. 4, April–June: 85–6.

Dauster, Frank ed. (1996), *Perspectives on Contemporary Spanish American Theatre* (Lewisburg, PA: Bucknell University Press).

Dávila-López, Grace (1989), "Diversidad y pluralidad en el teatro puertorriqueño contemporáneo: 1965–1985," Dissertation, University of California at Irvine.

Dávila-López, Grace (1992), "Meta-representación teatral en la puesta en escena de *La pasión según Antígona Pérez*," *Gestos* 7/13: 152–8.

Dayan, Joan (1998), *Haiti, History, and the Gods* (Berkeley, CA: University of California Press).

De Cecco, Sergio (1963), *El reñidero* (Buenos Aires: Editorial Talia).

de Gaulejac, Vincent (1996), *Les sources de la honte* (Paris: Desclée de Brouwer).

Degregori, Felipe (2005), *Mujeres en la guerra* (Lima: Centro de Desarrollo Poblacional).

de la Campa, Román (1999), "The Lettered City: Power and Writing in Latin America," in *Latin Americanism* (Minneapolis, MN: University of Minnesota Press), 121–48.

de La Roche, Elisa (1995), *Teatro Hispano! Three Major New York Companies* (Orono, ME: University of Maine).

de La Taille, Yves (2004), *Vergonha, a ferida moral* (Petrópolis: Editora Vozes).

del Pino, Ponciano (2009), "In the Name of the Government: Community Politics, Violence and Memory in Modern Peru," Unpublished paper presented at Yale University.

del Pino, Ponciano (2017), *En nombre del Gobierno. El Perú y Uchuraccay: un siglo de política campesina* (Lima and Juliaca: La Siniestra Ensayos and Universidad Nacional de Juliaca).

Deren, Maya (1983), *Divine Horsemen: The Living Gods of Haiti* (New York: McPherson & Co.).

Desmangles, Leslie (1992), *The Faces of the Gods* (Chapel Hill, NC: University of North Carolina Press).

de Toro, Alfonso and Fernando de Toro, eds. (1999), *El debate de la postcolonialidad en Latinoamérica* (Madrid: Iberoamericana Vervuert).

Dodds, E. R. (1951), *The Greeks and the Irrational* (Berkeley, CA: University of California Press).

Domínguez, Jose Mauricio (2009), "Modernity and Modernizing Moves: Latin America in Comparative Perspective," *Theory, Culture Society* 26/7–8: 208–29.

Dominique, Max (2002), "Kite'm ak Antigòn," *Conjonction* 207: 43–50.

Dorfman, Ariel (1981–7), *Viudas*. México: Siglo XXI Editores.

Dorfman, Ariel (1983), *Widows*, tr. Stephen Kessler (New York: Pantheon Books).

Dorfman, Ariel (1997), "Afterword," in *Widows*, https://scholars.duke.edu/person/adorfman.

BIBLIOGRAPHY 407

Dorfman, Ariel (1998), *The Resistance Trilogy* (London: Nick Hern Books).

Dornheim, Nicolás Jorge (2000), "The Relation between System and Literary Translation in 19th Century Argentina," in *Reconstructing Cultural Memory: Translation, Scripts, Literacy 7*, Proceedings of the XVth Congress of the International Comparative Literature Association.

Dove, Patrick (2004), *The Catastrophe of Modernity: Tragedy and the Nation in Latin American Literature* (Lewisburg, PA: Bucknell University Press).

Dove, Patrick (2013), "In the Wake of Tragedy: Citation, Gesture and Theatricality in Antígona Furiosa," *Hispanic Issues Online* 13: 42–62.

Dubatti, Jorge (2001), "Concepción de la obra dramática," in Osvaldo Pellettieri, ed., *Historia del Teatro Argentino en Buenos Aires* (Buenos Aires, Galerna), 171–81.

Dubois, Laurent (2004a), *Avengers of the New World* (Cambridge, MA: Harvard University Press).

Dubois, Laurent (2004b), *A Colony of Citizens* (Chapel Hill, NC: University of North Carolina Press).

Dubois, Laurent and John Garrigus (2006), *Slave Revolution in the Caribbean: 1789–1804, A Brief History with Documents* (Bedford: St Martin's Press).

Dubois, Laurent and John Garrigus, trans. (n.d.), *The Haitian Declaration of Independence 1804*, https://today.duke.edu/showcase/haitideclaration/declarations text.html.

Dumas, Pierre-Raymond (1985), "Panorama de la littérature haïtienne de la diaspora," *Conjonction 167* (Port-au-Prince: Institut français d'Haïti): 65–7.

Dumas, Pierre-Raymond (2000), *Panorama de la Littérature Haïtienne de la Diaspora* (Port-au-Prince, Häiti : L'Imprimeur II).

Duprey, Jennifer, ed. (2013), *Whose Voice is This? Iberian and Latin American Antigones, Special Issue of Hispanic Issues Online* 13, https://cla.umn.edu/hispanic-issues/online/volume-13-whose-voice-iberian-and-latin-american-antigones.

Dussel, Enrique (1995), *The Invention of the Americas: Eclipse of "the Other" and the Myth of Modernity* (New York: Continuum).

Dussel, Inés, Silvia Finocchio, and Silvia Gojman (1997), *Haciendo memoria en el país del Nunca Más* (Buenos Aires: Eudeba).

Echeverría, Esteban (1981), *Antología de prosa y verso*, ed. Osvaldo Pellettieri (Buenos Aires: Editorial del Belgrano).

Eisenstadt, Shmuel (2003), *Comparative Civilizations and Multiple Modernities* (Leiden: Brill).

Eliot, T. S. ([1921] 1951), "Tradition and the Individual Writer," in *Selected Essays* (London: Faber & Faber), 13–22.

Escobar, Arturo (2004), "Beyond the Third World: Imperial Globality, Global Coloniality and Anti-Globalisation Social Movements," *Third World Quarterly* 25/1: 207–30.

Fanon, Frantz ([1952] 2008), *Black Skin, White Masks* (London: Pluto Press).

Fanon, Frantz (1959), "The Reciprocal Basis of National Cultures and the Struggles for Liberation," *Presence Africaine* 24–5: 89–98.

Feitlowitz, Marguerite (1992), "Antigona Furiosa," in *Information for Foreigners: Three Plays*. Edited, translated, and with an introduction by Marguerite Feitlowitz (Evanston, IL: Northwestern University Press).

408 BIBLIOGRAPHY

Feitlowitz, Marguerite (1999), *Lexicon of Terror: Argentina and the Legacies of Torture* (Oxford: Oxford University Press).

Fernandes Toledo, Plinio (2016), *A Jornada dos inconfidentes: Um ensaio de historiografia filosófica* (São Paulo: Editora LiberArs).

Fernández, Nona (2002), *Mapocho* (Santiago: Planeta).

Fernández-Biggs, Braulio and Joaquín García-Huidobro (2013), "Antígona in the Southern Cone of Latin America," *Ágora. Estudos Clássicos em Debate* 15: 231–64.

Ferreira de Andrade, Marcos (1998–9), "Rebeliões escravas na Comarca do Rio das Mortes, Minas Gerais: O caso Carrancas," *Afro-Ásia* 21–2: 45–82.

Ferreira de Andrade, Marcos (2008), *Elites regionais e a formação do Estado Imperial Brasileiro. Minas Gerais—Campanha da Princesa (1799–1850)* (Rio de Janeiro: Arquivo Nacional).

Fick, Carolyn (1990), *The Making of Haiti: The Revolution from Below* (Knoxville, TN: University of Tennessee Press).

Fiet, Lowell (2004), *El Teatro puertorriqueño reimaginado: notas críticas sobre la creación dramática y el performance* (San Juan: Ediciones Callejón).

Filc, Judith (1997), *Entre el parentesco y la política: Familia y dictadura* (Buenos Aires: Biblos).

Fisher, Jo (1989), *Mothers of the Disappeared* (Boston, MA: South End Press).

Fleming, John (1995), *Argentina on Stage: Griselda Gambaro's* Information For Foreigners *and* Antígona Furiosa, Proceedings of the Louisiana Conference on Hispanic Language and Literatures 1995, 71–82.

Fleming, John (1999), "Antigone in Argentina: Griselda Gambaro's *Antígona Furiosa*," *Text and Performance Quarterly* 19/1: 74–90.

Foley, Helene (2012), *Reimagining Greek Tragedy on the American Stage* (Berkeley, CA: University of California Press).

Font-Guzmán, Jacqueline N. (2015), *Experiencing Puerto Rican Citizenship and Cultural Nationalism* (New York: Palgrave Macmillan).

Font-Guzmán, Jacqueline N. and Yanira Alemán (2010), "Human Rights Violations in Puerto Rico: Agency from the Margins," *Journal of Law and Social Challenges* 12: 107–49.

Ford, Katherine (2013), "Archiving Antigone on the Puerto Rican Stage: Luis Rafael Sánchez's *La pasión según Antígona Pérez*," *Hispanic Issues Online* 13: 82–98.

Forsyth, Alison (2009), "Pacifist Antigones," in Michelle MacArthur, Lydia Wilkinson, and Keren Zaiontz, eds., *Performing Adaptations: Essays and Conversations on the Theory and Practice of Adaptation* (Cambridge: Cambridge Scholars Publishing), 25–41.

Foucault, Michel (2010), *The Birth of Biopolitics: Lectures at the College de France (1978–1979)* (New York: Palgrave MacMillan).

Fouchard, Jean (1981), *The Haitian Maroons: Liberty or Death* (New York: Edward W. Blyden Press).

Fouché, Franck (1955), "Pour présenter Yerma créole," *Optique* 21: 30–4.

Fouché, Franck (1956), "Transes et plaisirs de l'auteur dramatique haïtien," *Optique* 29: 25–31.

Fouché, Franck (1964), *Guide pour l'étude de la littérature haïtienne* (Port-au-Prince: Éditions Panorama).

BIBLIOGRAPHY   409

Fouché, Franck (1976), *Vodou et Théâtre* (Montréal: Éditions Nouvelle).

Fradinger, Moira (2010), *Binding Violence: Literary Visions of Political Origins* (Palo Alto, CA: Stanford University Press).

Fradinger, Moira (2010),"Prologue" in Söderbäck, Fanny, ed. *Feminist Readings of Antigone* (Albany, NY: SUNY Press). (15–23).

Fradinger, Moira (2011a), "Danbala's Daughter: Félix Morisseau-Leroy's *Antigòn*," in Erin Mee and Helene Foley, eds., *Antigone on the Contemporary World Stage* (Oxford: Oxford University Press), 127–47.

Fradinger, Moira (2011b), "An Argentine Tradition," in Erin Mee and Helene Foley, eds., *Antigone on the Contemporary World Stage* (Oxford: Oxford University Press), 67–90.

Fradinger, Moira (2013), "Demanding the Political: Widows or Ariel Dorfman's Antigones," in Jennifer Duprey, ed., *Whose Voice Is This? Iberian and Latin American Antigones, Special Issue of Hispanic Issues Online* 13: 63–81.

Fradinger, Moira (2014), "Tragedy Shakes Hands with Testimony: Uruguay's Survivors Act in Morena's and Lösch's *Antígona Oriental*," *PMLA* 129/4: 731–62.

Fradinger, Moira (2015), "Making Women Visible: Multiple Antigones on the Colombian Twenty-First Century Stage," in Kathryn Bosher, Fiona Macintosh, Justine McConnell, and Patrice Rankine, eds., *The Oxford Handbook of Greek Drama in the Americas* (Oxford: Oxford University Press), 556–75.

Fradinger, Moira (2020), "*Medea* in Argentina," in Andreas Markantonatos, ed., *The Brill Companion on Euripides* (Leiden; Boston: Brill), 1110–28.

Franco, Jean (1993), "Sobre la imposibilidad de Antígona y la inevitabilidad de La Malinche: la reescritura de la alegoría nacional," in *Las conspiradoras. La representación de la mujer en México* (Mexico City: Fondo de Cultura Económica), 160–88.

Franco, Jean (2002), *The Decline and Fall of the Lettered City* (Cambridge, MA: Harvard University Press).

Fregoso, Rosa Linda (2012), "For the Women of Ciudad Juárez," *The Feminist Wire*, December 3, 2012, https://thefeministwire.com/2012/12/for-the-women-of-ciudad-juarez/.

Freire, Paulo ([1968] 2000), *Pedagogy of the Oppressed* (New York: Continuum).

Freyre, Gilberto ([1933] 2002), *Casa Grande & Senzala* (Madrid: Allca XX).

Galich, Manuel (1975), "Boceto puertorriqueño," *Conjunto* 25: 3–21.

Galindo, María (2013), *No se puede Descolonizar sin Despatriarcalizar* (La Paz, Bolivia: Mujeres Creando).

Gálvez, Manuel (1974), *Vida de Don Juan Manuel de Rosas* (Buenos Aires: Centro Literario Americano S.A. y Ediciones Río de la Plata).

Gambaro, Griselda (1995), "New Stories from Old," *Australian Feminist Studies* 21: 55–8.

Gambaro, Griselda (2011), *Al pie de página* (Buenos Aires: Grupo Editorial Norma).

Garavello Martins, Andréia (2012), "Os mitos e a condição humana: *As confrarias*, de Jorge Andrade e *Antígona*, de Sófocles," in Aurora López and Andrés Pociña, eds., *De ayer a hoy* (Coimbra: Centro de Estudos Clássicos e Humanísticos), 305–13.

García, Graciela P. and Hector Cavallari (1995), "Antígona Vélez: Justicialismo y estructura dramática," *Gestos* 10/20: 75–90.

Garcia, Silvana (1991), *O Teatro da militância* (São Paulo: Perspectiva).

410 BIBLIOGRAPHY

García, W. (1997), "Sabotaje textual/teatral contra el modelo canónico: *Antígona-Humor* de Franklin Domínguez," *Latin American Theatre Review* Fall 31/1: 15–29.

García, William (1996), "Subversión y reelaboración de mitos griegos en el teatro latinoamericano contemporáneo," Dissertation, Rutgers University.

García Canclini, Nestor (1995), *Hybrid Cultures: Strategies for Entering and Leaving Modernity* (Minneapolis, MN: University of Minnesota Press).

García Jurado, Francisco (2005), "Borges, las lenguas clásicas y la cultura europea," *Variaciones Borges* 20, 231–49.

García Márquez, Gabriel (1967), *Cien años de soledad* (Buenos Aires: Editorial Sudamericana).

Gasparini, Juan (1999), *Montoneros: Final de las cuentas* (La Plata: Edición de la campana).

Geggus, David, ed. (2001), *The Impact of the Haitian Revolution in the Atlantic World* (Columbia, SC: University of South Carolina Press).

Geggus, David (2002a), *Haitian Revolutionary Studies* (Bloomington, IN: Indiana University Press).

Geggus, David (2002b), "The Seeds of Revolt: The Bois-Caïman Ceremony," in David Geggus, ed., *Haitian Revolutionary Studies* (Bloomington, IN: Indiana University Press), 81–99.

Geggus, David and Norman Fiering, eds. (2009), *The World of the Haitian Revolution* (Bloomington, IN: Indiana University Press).

George, David (2014), *The Modern Brazilian Stage* (Austin, TX: University of Texas Press).

Gerbi, Antonello (1955), *La disputa del Nuovo Mondo. Storia di una polemica* (Milan: Riccardo Ricciardi Editori).

Gilbert, Helen and Joanne Tompkins (1996), *Post-colonial Drama: Theory, Practice, Politics* (London: Routledge).

Glissant, Édouard ([1961] 1986), *Monsieur Toussaint* (Guadalupe, Paris: Seuil).

Goff, Barbara, ed. (2005), *Classics and Colonialism* (London: Duckworth).

Goff, Barbara (2006), "Dionysiac Triangles: The Politics of Culture in Wole Soyinka's *The Bacchae of Euripides*," in Victoria Pedrick and Steven Oberhelman, eds., *The Soul of Tragedy* (Chicago, IL: University of Chicago), 73–88.

Goff, Barbara (2007), "Antigone's Boat: the Colonial and the Postcolonial in Tegonni: An African Antigone by Femi Osofisan," in Lorna Hardwick and Carol Gillespie, eds., *Classics in Post-Colonial Worlds* (Oxford: Oxford University Press), 40–53.

Goff, Barbara (2014), "Postcolonial Translation: Theory and Practice," in Georgios K. Giannakis, ed., *Encyclopedia of Ancient Greek Language and Linguistics* (Brill: Leiden), 122–5.

Goff, Barbara and Michael Simpson (2007), *Crossroads in the Black Aegean* (Oxford: Oxford University Press).

Goff, Barbara and Michael Simpson (2015), "New Worlds, Old Dreams? Postcolonial Theory and Reception of Greek Drama," in Kathryn Bosher, Fiona Macintosh, Justine McConnell, and Patrice Rankine, eds., *The Oxford Handbook of Greek Drama in the Americas* (Oxford: Oxford University Press), 30–50.

Gold, Herbert (1954), "…Et pourquoi nous les traduirons," *Optique* 5: 59–62.

BIBLIOGRAPHY 411

Goldberg, David Theo and Ato Quayson, eds. (2002), *Relocating Postcolonialism* (Malden, MA: Blackwell).

Goldhill, Simon (1986), *Reading Greek Tragedy* (Cambridge: Cambridge University Press).

Goldhill, Simon (2002), *Who Needs Greek? Contests in the Cultural History of Hellenism* (Cambridge: Cambridge University Press).

Goldhill, Simon (2004), "Literary History without Literature: Reading Practices in the Ancient World," in Christopher Prendergast, ed., *Debating World Literature* (London: Verso), 175–97.

Goldhill, Simon (2012), *Sophocles and the Language of Tragedy* (Oxford: Oxford University Press).

Gómez Aponte, José Félix (2012), *La puesta en escena del teatro puertoriqueño 1950–2000* (San Juan: Instituto de Cultura Puertorriquena), 123–8.

Goñi, Uki (1996), *El infiltrado: la verdadera historia de Alfredo Astiz* (Buenos Aires: Sudamericana).

González, Cecilia (2010), "De cómo tres escritoras latinoamericanas reescriben a los clásicos y conversan con ellos," *Lectures du genre* 7, https://lecturesdugenre. fr/2010/12/20/numero-07-genre-canon-et-monstruosites/.

González, María de la Luz (2002), "Castigo a los asesinos de Juárez, claman madres de víctimas," *Cimacnoticias*, November 5, https://www.cimacnoticias.com.mx/ noticia/castigo-los-asesinos-de-ju-rez-claman-madres-de-v-ctimas.

González, Olga (2011), *Unveiling Secrets of War in the Peruvian Andes* (Chicago, IL: University of Chicago Press).

González Barja, José (1972), "Reseña Literaria: La pasión según Antígona Pérez," *Surcos* II/2: 42–4.

González Betancur, Juan David (2010), "Antígona y el Teatro Latinoamericano," *Calle 14* 4/4: 72–85.

González Casanova, Pablo (1963), "Sociedad plural, colonialismo interno y desarrollo," *América Latina, revista del Centro Latinoamericano de Ciencias Sociales* 6/3 (July–September): 15–32.

González Casanova, Pablo (2003), "Colonialismo Interno (una redefinición)," *Revista Rebeldía* 12, http://www.revistarebeldia.org/revistas/012/art06.html.

González Cruz, Michael (2006), *Nacionalismo Revolucionario Puertorriqueño 1956–2005: la lucha armada, intelectuales y prisioneros políticos y de guerra* (San Juan: Isla Negra).

González de Díaz Araujo, María Graciela (1983), "Una tragedia cristiana en la obra de Leopoldo Marechal," *Criterio*, June 26, 225–8.

González Delgado, Ramiro (2015), "Panorama de la literatura griega en Iberoamérica (1767–1850), *Synthesis* 22. http://www.synthesis.fahce.unlp.edu.ar/.

González Vaquerizo, Helena (2014), "Podrías llamarte Antígona: Un drama mexicano contemporáneo," *Aletria: revista de estudos de literatura* 24/1: 95–107.

Gorini, Ulises (2006), *La rebelión de las madres* (Buenos Aires: Editorial Norma).

Gorini, Ulises (2015), *La Otra Lucha: Historia de las Madres de Plaza de Mayo* (Buenos Aires: Biblioteca Nacional).

412 BIBLIOGRAPHY

Gorman Malone, Cora (2010), "Epistemology and The Lettered City: Ángel Rama, Michel Foucault and Ibn Khaldun," *Mester* 39/1, https://escholarship.org/uc/item/1pk1q7xk.

Gorriti, Gustavo (1990), *The Shining Path: A History of the Millenarian War in Peru*, trans. Robin Kirk (Chapel Hill, NC: University of North Carolina Press).

Grammatico, Giuseppina, Antonio Arbea, and María Edwards Luz (2003), *América Latina y lo clásico*, 2 vols (Santiago: Sociedad Chilena de Estudios Clásicos, Universidad Metropolitana de Ciencias de la Educación).

Gramsci, Antonio (1971), *Selections from the Prison Notebooks* (New York: International Publishers).

Gramuglia, Pablo (2007), "Mito, política y usos políticos del mito: Antígona Vélez," *Cuadernos del CILHA* 8/9: 41–50.

Greenwood, Emily (2010), *Afro-Greeks* (Oxford: Oxford University Press).

Greenwood, Emily (2013), "Afterword: Omni-Local Classical Receptions," *Classical Receptions* 5/3: 354–61.

Grünewald, José Lino, ed. (1989), *Os Poetas da Inconfidência* (Rio de Janeiro: Fundação Biblioteca Nacional e Editora Nova Fronteira).

Guidarini, Mário (1992), *Jorge Andrade na contramão da História* (Florianópolis-SC: UFSC).

Guillermoprieto, Alma (2011), *72 migrantes* (Mexico: Editorial Almadia).

Guthmann, Gerardo (1988), *Interview with Griselda Gambaro*. Buenos Aires: Blakman Video no Convencional S.A.

Gutiérrez, Gustavo ([1971] 1988), *A Theology of Liberation: History, Politics, and Salvation* (New York: Orbis Books).

Gutiérrez, Juan María (1893), *Juan Cruz Varela: Su vida, sus obras, su época* (Buenos Aires: Talleres Gráficos Argentinos).

Gutiérrez, Juan María (1941), *Los poetas de la revolución* (Buenos Aires: Academia Argentina de Letras).

Gutiérrez Estévez, Manuel (2004), "El amor a la patria y a la tribu: Las retóricas de la memoria incómoda," *Revista de Antropología* 47/2: 345–77.

Guzik, Alberto (1986), *TBC: crônica de um sonho* (São Paulo: Perspectiva).

Guzmán Bouvard, Marguerite (1994), *Revolutionizing Motherhood: The Mothers of the Plaza de Mayo* (Wilmington, NC: Scholarly Resources).

Hall, Edith (2005), "Antigone with Consequences," in Edith Hall and Fiona Macintosh, *Greek Tragedy and The British Theatre 1660–1914* (Oxford: Oxford University Press), 316–50.

Halperín Donghi, Tulio (1963), "La Expansión Ganadera en la Campaña de Buenos Aires (1810–1852)," *Desarrollo Económico* 3/1–2: 57–110.

Halperín Donghi, Tulio (1965), "El surgimiento de los caudillos en el marco de la sociedad rioplatense postrevolucionaria," in *Estudios de historia social*, Vol. 1 (Buenos Aires: UBA), 121–49.

Halperín Donghi, Tulio (1987), "Imagen argentina de Bolívar: de Funes a Mitre," in *El espejo de la historia: problemas argentinos y perspectivas hispanoamericanas* (Buenos Aires: Editorial Sudamericana), 165–208.

BIBLIOGRAPHY 413

Halperín Donghi, Tulio (1996), "El revisionismo histórico argentino como visión decadentista de la historia nacional," in *Ensayos de historiografía* (Buenos Aires: El Cielo por Asalto).

Hardwick, Lorna (2003), *The Role of Greek Drama and Poetry in Crossing and Redefining Cultural Boundaries* (Milton Keynes: The Open University).

Hardwick, Lorna (2004), *Translating Words, Translating Cultures* (London: Duckworth).

Hardwick, Lorna (2007), "Shades of Multi-Lingualism and Multi-Vocalism in Modern Performances of Greek Tragedy in Post Colonial Contexts," in Lorna Hardwick and Carol Gillespie, eds., *Classics in Post-Colonial Worlds* (Oxford: Oxford University Press), 305–28.

Hardwick, Lorna (2009), "Editorial," *Classical Receptions Journal* 1/1: 1–3.

Hardwick, Lorna and Carol Gillespie, eds. (2007), *Classics in Post-Colonial Worlds* (Oxford: Oxford University Press).

Hardwick, Lorna and Christopher Stray, eds. (2008), *A Companion to Classical Receptions* (Oxford: Blackwell).

Hartigan, Karelisa (1995), *Greek Tragedy on the American Stage* (New York: Greenwood Press).

Harvey, David (2005), *A Brief History of Neoliberalism* (New York: Oxford University Press).

Hegel, Georg Wilhelm Friedrich (1962), *Hegel on Tragedy*, trans. Anne Paolucci (New York: Doubleday).

Hegel, Georg Wilhelm Friedrich (1975), *Aesthetics: Lectures on Fine Arts*, trans. T. M. Knox (Oxford: Clarendon Press).

Hegel, Georg Wilhelm Friedrich (2018), *Phenomenology of the Spirit*, trans. Terry Pinkard (Cambridge: Cambridge University Press).

Helfgott, Sarina (2007), "Antigone" in *Latin American Women Writers* (Alexandria, VA: Alexander Street Press, 2007). http://lit.alexanderstreet.com/laww/view/1002761609

Henríquez Ureña, Pedro (1936), *La cultura y las letras coloniales en Santo Domingo* (Buenos Aires: UBA).

Hernández, Martha Luisa (2014), "Una mirada al fenómeno teatral Antigonón," *El caimán barbudo*, August 14, http://www.caimanbarbudo.cu/artes-escenicas/2014 /08/una-mirada-al-fenomeno-teatral-antigonon-un-contingente-epico/.

Herrendorf, Daniel (2000), *Memorias de Antínoo* (Buenos Aires Editorial Sudamericana).

Herskovits, Melville (1971), *Life in a Haitian Valley* (Garden City: Anchor Books).

Hilton, John and Anne Gosling, eds. (2007), *Alma Parens Originalis? The Receptions of Classical Literature and Thought in Africa, Europe, the United States* (Bern: Peter Lang).

Hoffman, Léon-François (1992), *Haiti: letters et l'être* (Toronto: Éditions du Gref).

Holledge, Julie and Joanne Tompkins (2000), *Women's Intercultural Performance* (London: Routledge).

Holzapfel, Támara (1970), "Griselda Gambaro's Theatre of the Absurd," *Latin American Theatre Review* 4/1: 5–11.

Honig, Bonnie (2013), *Antigone Interrupted* (Cambridge: Cambridge University Press).

Hualde Pascual, Pilar (2012), "Mito y tragedia griega en la literatura iberoamericana," *CFC: Estudios griegos e indoeuropeos* 22: 185–222.

414   BIBLIOGRAPHY

Huber, Elena (1974), "Sófocles y la Antígona Vélez de Leopoldo Marechal," *Románica* 7: 149–56.

Hulme, Peter (1995), "Including America," *Ariel: A Review of International English Literature* 26: 117–23.

Hulme, Peter (1989), "La teoría postcolonial y la representación de la cultura en las Américas," *La Habana: Casa de las Américas* 36/202: 3–8.

Hurbon, Laënnec (1993), *Les mystères du Vaudou* (Paris: Gallimard).

Hurbon, Laënnec (1995), *Voodoo, Search for the Spirits* (New York: Harry N. Abrams).

Huyssen, Andreas (2000), "Present Pasts: Media, Politics, Amnesia," *Public Culture* 12/1: 21–38.

Ibarguren, Carlos (1933), *Juan Manuel de Rosas. Su vida, su drama, su tiempo* (Buenos Aires: Roldán Editor).

Imbert, Julio (1963), *Los navegantes del génesis y Electra* (Buenos Aires: Editorial Talia).

Innocent, Claude (2002), "La SNAD de 1956," *Conjonction* 207: 22–4.

Irigaray, Luce (1985), *Speculum of the Other Woman* (Ithaca, NY: Cornell University Press).

Irizarry, Lucila (2010), *CAL: Una historia clandestina (1968–1972)* (San Juan: Isla Negra).

Iser, Wolfgang ([1976] 1994), *Der Akt des Lesens. Theorie ästhetischer Wirkung*, 4th ed. (Stuttgart: UTB).

Jacobs, Carol (1996), "Dusting Antigone," *Modern Language Notes* 111/5: 889–917.

James, Cyril Lionel Robert ([1934] 2013), *Toussaint Louverture: The Story of the Only Successful Slave Revolt in History; A Play in Three Acts* (Durham, NC: Duke University Press).

James, Cyril Lionel Robert ([1938] 1963), *The Black Jacobins: Toussaint L'Ouverture and the San Domingo Revolution* (New York: Vintage Books).

Jara, René and Hernán Vidal (1986), *Testimonio y literatura* (Minneapolis, MN: Institute for the Study of Ideologies and Literature).

Jáuregui, Carlos (2008), *Canibalia. Canibalismo, calibanismo, antropofagia cultural y consumo en América Latina*, 2nd ed. (Madrid, Frankfurt: Iberoamericana, Vervuert).

Jáuregui, Carlos (2012), "Anthropophagy," in Robert McKee Irwin and Mónica Szurmuk, eds., *The Dictionary of Latin American Studies* (Gainesville, FL: University Press of Florida), 22–7.

Jauss, Hans (1982), *Toward an Aesthetic of Reception* (Minneapolis, MN: University of Minnesota Press).

Kallendorf, Craig W., ed. (2007), *A Companion to the Classical Tradition* (Malden, MA: Blackwell).

Kerr, Jessica (1969), *Shakespeare's Flowers* (New York: Thomas Y. Crowell Company).

Kesteloot, Lilyan and B. Kotchy (1973), *Aimé Césaire, l'homme et l'oeuvre* (Paris: Présence africaine).

Kierkegaard, Søren Aabye (1958), *Temor y temblor*, trans. Jaime Gringberg (Buenos Aires: Losada).

Kim, Euisuk (2003), *Una reconstrucción alternativa del pretérito: Una aproximación psicoanalítica a la obra de Ariel Dorfman* (New Orleans: University Press of the South).

BIBLIOGRAPHY 415

Klor de Alva, Jorge J. (1995), "The Postcolonization of the (Latin) American Experience: A Reconsideration of 'Colonialism,' 'Postcolonialism,' and 'Mestizaje,'" in G. Prakash, ed., *After Colonialism: Imperial Histories and Postcolonial Displacements* (Princeton, NJ: Princeton University Press), 240–75.

Kohn, Margaret and Keally McBride (2011), *Postcolonial Theories of Decolonization* (Oxford: Oxford University Press).

König, Irmtrud (2002), "Parodia y transculturación en Antígona furiosa de Griselda Gambaro," *Revista Chilena de Literatura* 61: 5–20.

Krajewska-Wieczorek, Anna (1994), "Contemporary Antigones," *New Theatre Quarterly* 10/40: 327–30.

Kremser, Manfred, ed. (1990), *Ay Bobo, Afro-Karibische Religionen, Vol. 2* (Vienna: Institut für Völkerkunde der Universität Wien).

Kristal, Efraín (2002), "Considering Coldly...: A Response to Franco Moretti," *New Left Review* 15: 61–74.

Kuehne, Alyce de (1970), "The Antigone Theme in Anouilh, Marechal and Luis Rafael Sánchez," *MLA, Seminar* 17: 50–70.

Kuehne, Alyce de (1975), "Marechal's Antígona: More Greek than French," *Latin American Theater Review* 9: 19–27.

Künstler (1955), "Le Mouvement Théâtral Haitien Gagne du Terrain," *Optique* 21: 63–71.

Lacan, Jacques (1992), *El Seminario XVII "El reverso del psicoanálisis"* (Buenos Aires: Paidós).

Laferrière, Dany, Louis-Philippe Dalembert, Edwige Danticat, Évelyne Trouillot, and Michael J. Dash, Moderator (2005), "Roundtable: Writing, History, and Revolution," *Small Axe* 18: 189–201.

Lagarde, Marcela (2006), "Del femicidio al feminicidio," *Desde jardín de Freud* 6: 216–25.

Lagmanovich, David (1996), "Tebas en el Caribe: La Antígona Pérez de Luis Rafael Sánchez," in Osvaldo Pelletieri, ed., *El teatro y sus claves: estudios sobre teatro argentino e iberoamericano* (Buenos Aires: Editorial Galerna/UBA).

Lahav, Pnina (1975), "The Chef de Section: Structure & Functions of Haiti's Basic Administrative Institution," in Sydney Mintz, ed., *Working Papers in Haitian Society & Culture.* Paper No. 4. (New Haven, CT: Yale University Press), 51–84.

Laird, Andrew (2006), *The Epic of America: An Introduction to Rafael Saldívar and the Rusticatio Mexicana* (London: Duckworth).

Laird, Andrew (2007), "Latin America," in Craig W. Kallendorf, ed., *A Companion to the Classical Tradition* (Malden, MA: Blackwell), 222–36.

Laird, Andrew (2010), "Soltar las cadenas de las cosas: las tradiciones clásicas en Latinoamérica," in Carla Bochetti, ed., *La influencia clásica en América Latina* (Bogotá: Ediciones Universidad Nacional de Colombia), 11–31.

Laird, Andrew (2012), "Patriotism and the rise of Latin in eighteenth-century New Spain: Disputes of the New World and the Jesuit construction of a Mexican legacy," in *Latin Linguistic Identity and Nationalism Renæssanceforum*, 8. http://www.renaessanceforum.dk/rf_8_2012.htm

Laird, Andrew (2015), "Colonial Spanish America and Brazil," in Sarah Knight and Stefan Tilg, eds., *Oxford Handbook of Neo-Latin* (OUP), 525–40.

416 BIBLIOGRAPHY

Laird, Andrew and Nicola Miller, eds. (2018), *Antiquities and Classical Traditions in Latin America* (Chichester: Wiley-Blackwell).

Lambright, Anne (2001), "Woman, Body and Memory: Yuyachkani´s Peruvian Antigone," *Feminist Scholarship Review* 11/1, https://digitalrepository.trincoll.edu/cgi/viewcontent.cgi?article=1006&context=femreview.

Lambruschini, Beatriz de (1995), *Antígona revive en Antígona Vélez* (Paraná: Editorial de Entre Ríos).

Lander, Edgardo, ed. (2000), *La colonialidad del saber: eucrocentrismo y ciencias sociales. Perspectivas Latinoamericanas* (Buenos Aires: CLASCO).

Lane, Jill (2007), "Antígona and the Modernity of the Dead," *Modern Drama* 50/4: 517–31.

Lang, George (1997), "Islands, Enclaves, Continua: Notes Toward a Comparative History of Caribbean Creole Literatures," in Albert J. Arnold, Julio Rodríguez-Luis, J. Michael Dash, eds., *A History of Literature in the Caribbean: Cross Cultural Studies, Vol. 3* (Amsterdam/Philadelphia, PA: John Benjamin), 29–56.

Lanuza, Cacilda (1977a), "Os últimos dias desta Pedreira das almas," *Folha da Tarde*, July 21.

Lanuza, Cacilda (1977b), "Um desafio para mim," *Popular da Tarde*, July 11.

Lanuza, Cacilda (1977c), "Um personagem bem marcante para a atriz Cacilda Lanuza," *A Gazeta*, July 19.

Laroche, Maximilien (1978), *L'image comme écho: Essais sur la littérature et la culture haïtiennes* (Port-au-Prince: Éditions Nouvelle Optique).

Laroche, Maximilien (2005), "The Founding Myths of the Haitian Nation," *Small Axe* 18: 1–15.

Laub, Dori and Shoshana Felman (1992), *Testimony: Crisis of Witnessing in Literature, Psychoanalysis and History* (London: Routledge).

Leblon, Nathalie and Elizabeth Maier (2006), *De lo privado a lo público: 30 años de lucha ciudadana de las mujeres de América Latina* (México: Siglo XXI).

Leconte, Vergniaud ([1901] 1931), *Le Roi Christophe* (Paris: Berger-Levrault).

Leiris, Michel (1958), *La possession et ses aspects théatraux chez les Ethïopiens de Gondar* (Paris: Plon).

Leis, Héctor Ricardo (1989), *El movimiento por los derechos humanos y la política argentina* (Buenos Aires: CEAL).

Lenton, Diana (2008), "La frontera, la guerra y la nostalgia: Construcciones de la Argentina moderna como 'país sin indios,'" in Susana Villavicencio and María Inés Pacecca, eds., *Representaciones de la nación, estado y ciudadanía: hiatos y fisuras en la historia política de los conceptos* (Buenos Aires: Ed. del Puerto), 131–52.

Lenton, Diana (2010), "The Malón de la Paz of 1946: Indigenous Descamisados at the Dawn of Peronism," in Oscar Chamosa and Matthew Karush, eds., *The New Cultural History of Peronism, 1930–1966* (Durham, NC: Duke University Press), 85–113.

Leonard, Miriam (2005), *Athens in Paris: Ancient Greece and the Political in Post-War French Thought* (Oxford: Oxford University Press, 2005).

Leonard, Miriam (2015), *Tragic Modernities* (Cambridge, MA: Harvard University Press).

Leonardi, Yanina, "Espectáculos y figuras populares en el circuito teatral oficial durante los años peronistas," http://www.unsam.edu.ar/home/material/Leonardi.pdf/.

BIBLIOGRAPHY 417

León-Portilla, Miguel (1975), "Trauma cultural, mestizaje e indigenismo en Mesoamérica," *Cuadernos Americanos* 4: 113–34.

León-Portilla, Miguel (1979), "Etnias indígenas y cultura nacional mestiza," *América Indígena* 3: 601–21.

Lévi-Strauss, Claude ([1958] 1963), *Structural Anthropology* (New York: Basic Books).

Lobato, Mirta (2007), *Historia de las trabajadoras en la Argentina: 1869–1960* (Buenos Aires: Edhasa).

López, Aurora, Andrés Pociña, and María de Fátima Silva, eds. (2012), *De ayer a hoy: Influencias clásicas en la literatura* (Coimbra: Universidad de Coimbra).

López, Liliana (2001), "Concepción del texto espectacular," in Osvaldo Pellettieri, *Historia del Teatro Argentino en Buenos Aires, Vol. 4s* (Buenos Aires: Editorial Galerna).

López Baralt, Luce (2016), "La embajada letrada de Luis Rafael Sánchez," in *El Nuevo Día*, December 3, http://www.elnuevodia.com/opinion/columnas/laembajadaletradadeluisrafaelSánchez-columna-2173162/.

López Carmona, J. (1986), "El mito de Antígona en dos piezas de teatro y una novela latinoamericanas," *Conjunto* 67: 36–42.

López Férez, Juan Antonio and Carlos Roura Roig, eds. (1998), *Influencias de la mitología clásica en la literatura española e hispanoamericana del s. XX: guía didáctica* (Madrid: UNED).

López Rojas, Luis (2004), *La mafia en Puerto Rico: Las caras ocultas del desarrollo* (San Juan: Editorial Isla Negra).

Loraux, Nicole (1986), "La Main d'Antigone," *Mètis. Anthropologie des mondes grecs anciens* 1/2: 165–96.

Loraux, Nicole (1991), *Tragic Ways of Killing a Woman* (Cambridge, MA: Harvard University Press).

Louis, Annick (2019), "Justice transitionnelle et justice civile dans *AntígonaS. Linaje de Hembras* (2001) de Jorge Huertas," in Mohamed-Salah Omri and Philippe Roussin, eds., *Literature, Democracy and Transitional Justice: Comparative World Perspectives* (Oxford: Legenda Books).

Louis-Jean, Antonio (1970), *La crise de possession et la possession dramatique* (Montréal: Leméac).

Loveman, Brian and Elizabeth Lira (1999), *Las suaves cenizas del olvido: Vía chilena de la reconciliación política 1814–193* (Santiago: Lom ediciones).

Luongo, Gilda (1999), "El gesto posible: Antígona furiosa de Griselda Gambaro," *Anuario de postgrado* Universidad de Chile, Facultad de Filosofía y Humanidades 3: 409–26.

Lupher, David A. (2003), *Romans in a New World: Classical Models in Sixteenth-Century Spanish America* (Ann Arbor, MI: University of Michigan Press).

Luque Bedregal, Gino (2010), *Ismene Redimida* (Buenos Aires: Celcit).

Lusnich, Ana Laura (2001), "Cambio y continuidad en el realismo crítico de Griselda Gambaro," in Osvaldo Pellettieri, ed., *Historia del teatro argentino en Buenos Aires, Vol. 5* (Buenos Aires: Galerna), 341–52.

Maciel, Diógenes Vieira (2005), "Dossiê em homenagem a Jorge Andrade," *Fênix— Revista de História e Estudos Culturais* 2/4.

Magaldi, Sábato and María Thereza Vargas (2001), *100 anos de teatro em São Paulo, 1875–1974* (São Paulo: SENAC).

418 BIBLIOGRAPHY

Maingot, Anthony ([1994] 2018), "Haiti: Intractable Problems," in *The United States and the Caribbean: Challenges of an Asymmetrical Relation* (New York: Routledge), 204–27.

Malagodi, Stephen and Jeffery Knapp (2008), "Felix Moriso-Lewa, A Portrait of the Poet," http://www.archive.org/details/FelixMoriso-lewaAPortraitOfThePoet.

Malamud Goti, Jaime (1996), *Game Without End: State Terror and the Politics of Justice* (Norman, OK: Oklahoma University Press).

Mandrini, Raúl (2006), *Vivir entre dos mundos. Las fronteras del sur de la Argentina, siglos XVIII y XIX* (Buenos Aires: Taurus).

Mandrini, Raúl and Carlos D. Paz (2002), *Las fronteras hispanocriollas del mundo indígena latinoamericano en los siglos XVIII y XIX. Un análisis comparativo* (Tandil: UNCPBA, UN Comahue).

Manguel, Alberto (2011), "Translation: A Miracle" (conference at Flagey, Brussels, December 1st 2011, as part of the PETRA congress), http://www.passaporta.be/assets/upload/auteursteksten/Manguel_Miracle_EN.pdf.

Mansilla, Lucio V. ([1870] 2016), *Una excursión a los indios ranqueles* (Buenos Aires: Académico Argentina de Leras).

Maquieira, Helena and Claudia Fernández, eds. (2012), *Tradición y traducción clásicas en América Latina* (La Plata: Universidad Nacional de La Plata).

Maranghello, César and Andrés Insaurralde (1997), *Fanny Navarro o un melodrama argentino* (Buenos Aires: Ediciones del Jilguero).

Marcelin, Milo (1995), "Le Vodou: Religion populaire," *Optique* 15: 39–49.

Marchant, Patricio (1984), *Sobre árboles y madres* (Santiago: Ediciones Gato Murr).

Marchant, Patricio (1994), "Desolación," in *Escritura y temblor* (Santiago: Universidad de Chile), 114–20.

Marechal, Leopoldo (1948), *Adán Buenosayres* (Buenos Aires: Editorial Sudamericana).

Marechal, Leopoldo (1984), *Poesía (1924–1950)*, ed. Pedro Luis Barcia (Buenos Aires: Ediciones del 80).

Marechal, Leopoldo ([1966] 1998), "Heptamerón," in *Obras Completas, Vol. 1.* (Buenos Aires: Perfil Libros), 267–395.

Marechal, Leopoldo ([1970] 2008), "El poeta depuesto," in *Cuaderno de navegación* (Buenos Aires: Seix Barral), 147–65.

Mariátegui, José Carlos ([1928] 1971), *Seven Interpretive Essays on Peruvian Reality*, trans. Marjory Urquidi (Austin, TX: University of Texas Press).

Marinho, José Antônio ([1844] 2015), *História da Revolução Liberal de 1842* (Belo Horizonte: Assembleia Legislativa do Estado de Minas Gerais).

Marquese, Rafael, Parron Tâmis, and Berbel Márcia (2016), *Slavery and Politics: Brazil and Cuba 1790–1850* (Albuquerque, NM: University of New Mexico).

Márquez, Rosa Luisa (1979), "Cuarenta años después de 'Lo que podría ser un teatro puertorriqueño' (1939–1979)," *Revista/Review Interamericana* 9/2: 300–6.

Martí, José (1891), "Nuestra América," *La Revista Ilustrada*, January 1.

Martí, José ([1877] 2003), *Política de nuestra América*, 8th ed. (Mexico: Siglo XXI).

Martin, Carol (2009), "The Political Is Personal: Feminism, Democracy and Antigone Project," in Sharon Friedman, ed., *Feminist Theatrical Revisions of Classic Works: Critical Essays* (Jefferson, NC: McFarland), 79–94.

BIBLIOGRAPHY 419

Martin, Carol, ed. (2010), *Dramaturgy of the Real on the World Stage* (London: Palgrave Macmillan).

Martindale, Charles (1993), *Redeeming the Text: Latin Poetry and the Hermeneutics of Reception* (Cambridge: Cambridge University Press).

Martindale, Charles (2006), "Introduction: Thinking through Reception," in Charles Martindale and Richard F. Thomas, eds., *Classics and the Uses of Reception* (Oxford: Blackwell), 1–13.

Martindale, Charles (2013), *Redeeming the Text: Latin Poetry and the Hermeneutics of Reception* (Cambridge: Cambridge University Press).

Martindale, Charles and Richard F. Thomas, eds. (2006), *Classics and the Uses of Reception* (Oxford: Blackwell).

Martínez, Tomás Eloy (1999), "Tombs of Unrest," *Transition* 80: 72–84.

Martínez de Olcoz, Nieves (1995), "Cuerpo y resistencia en el reciente teatro de Griselda Gambaro," *Latin American Theater Review* 28/2: 7–17.

Martínez Estrada, Ezequiel (1974), *Los invariantes históricos en el Facundo* (Buenos Aires: Casa Pardo).

Martínez Tabares, Vivian (2001), "Ariel Dorfman: si supiera quién soy no lo diría," *Conjunto* 120: 82–8.

Martínez Tabares, Vivian (2007), *Antígona: disolverse en la luz* (La Habana: La Ventana, portal informativo de la Casa de las Américas), http://laventana.casa. cult.cu/modules.php?name=News&file=print&sid=3679.

Martini, Maris (1989), "La comedia humana según Gambaro," in N. Mazziotti, ed., *Poder, Deseo y Marginación: Aproximaciones a la obra de Griselda Gambaro* (Buenos Aires: Teatro Puntosur), 25–41.

Mases, Enrique (2002), *Estado y cuestión indígena. El destino final de los indios sometidos en el fin del territorio (1878–1910)* (Buenos Aires: Prometeo).

Masiello, Francine (1997), *Entre civilización y barbarie: Mujeres, nación y cultura literaria en la Argentina moderna* (Buenos Aires: Beatriz Viterbo).

Mattoso, Katia (1969), *La presencia francesa en el movimiento democrático Baiano de 1798* (Salvador: Itapua).

Maturo, Graciela (1999), *Marechal: El camino de la belleza* (Buenos Aires: Editorial Biblos).

Mazzara, Richard A. (1997), "The Theater of Jorge Andrade," *Latin American Theater Review* 3/1: 3–16.

Mbembe, Achille (2003), "Necropolitics," *Public Culture* 15/1: 11–40.

McAlister, Elizabeth (2002), *Rara: Vodou, Power and Performance in Haiti and its Diaspora* (Berkeley, CA: University of California Press).

McClennen, Sophia (2004), "Comparative Literature and Latin American Studies: From Disarticulation to Dialogue," in Sophia McClennen and Earl Fitz, eds., *Comparative Cultural Studies and Latin America* (West Lafayette, IN: Purdue University Press), 220–66.

McClennen, Sophia (2010), *Ariel Dorfman: An Aesthetics of Hope* (Durham, NC: Duke University Press).

McClennen, Sophia and Earl Fitz, eds. (2004), *Comparative Cultural Studies and Latin America* (West Lafayette, IN: Purdue University Press).

420 BIBLIOGRAPHY

Medeiros da Silva Pereira, Júlio César (2014), *À flor da terra: cemitério dos pretos novos no Rio de Janeiro* (Rio de Janeiro: Garamond).

Mee, Erin and Helene Foley, eds. (2011), *Antigone on the Contemporary World Stage* (Oxford: Oxford University Press).

Meireles, Cecília ([1953] 2005), *O Romanceiro da Inconfidência Mineira* (Rio de Janeiro: Nova Fronteira).

Meléndez, Priscilla (1992), "Teoría teatral y teatro puertorriqueño de los 80," *Latin American Theater Review* 25/2: 151–67.

Melo Mendoza, Doris (2012), *Mito y tragedia en el teatro hispanoamericano y dominicano del siglo XX* (San Juan: Biblio Services).

Mennesson-Rigaud, Odette (1958), "Le rôle du Vaudou dans l'indépendance d'Haïti," *Présence Africaine* 17–18: 43.

Messinger, Sandra (1991), *La Malinche in Mexican Literature: From History to Myth* (Austin, TX: University of Texas Press).

Métellus, Jean (1991), *Pont-Rouge* (Ivry-sur-Seine, Haiti: Editions Nouvelles du Sud).

Métellus, Jean (2004), *Toussaint Louverture, le précurseur: roman* (Paris: Le Temps de Cerise).

Métraux, Alfred (1958), *Le Vaudou Haïtien* (Paris: Gallimard).

Michel, Claudine and Patrick Bellegarde-Smith (2006), *Vodou in Haitian Life and Culture* (New York: Palgrave).

Mimoso-Ruiz, Duarte (2002), "La *Médée* d'Euripide et *Gota d'Agua* de Paulo Pontes et Chico Buarque (1975)," in Aurora López and Andrés Pociña, eds., *MEDEAS: Versiones de un mito desde Grecia hasta hoy, Granada: Universidad de Granada* (Granada: Universidad de Granada), 1045–59.

Miola, Robert S. (2014), "Early Modern Antigones: Receptions, Refractions, Replays," *Classical Receptions Journal* 6/2: 221–44.

Miranda Cancela, Elina (1998), "La importancia de llamarse Antígona en la obra de Luis Rafael Sánchez," in José Vincente Bañuls Oller, Francesco de Martino, and Carmen M. Jordi Redondo, eds., *El teatre clàssic al marc de la cultura grega i la seua pervivència dins la cultura occidental* (Bari: Levante), 391–404.

Miranda Cancela, Elina (2001), "Carpentier, Antígona y la recepción de los clásicos," in Francesco de Martino and Carmen Morenilla, eds., *El fil d'Ariadna. Personages femenins a escena* (Valencia: Universidad de Valencia).

Miranda Cancela, Elina (2003), *La tradición helénica en Cuba* (La Habana: Ediciones Arte y Literatura).

Miranda Cancela, Elina (2005), "Medea y la voz del otro en el teatro latinoamericano contemporáneo," *Revista La Ventana* 3/22: 69–90.

Miranda Cancela, Elina (2006), *Calzar el coturno americano* (La Habana: Ediciones Alarcos).

Miranda Cancela, Elina (2008), "Antígona y su primera versión en el Caribe hispano," *Letras Clásicas* 12: 237–50.

Miranda Cancela, Elina (2012b), "Dos Antígonas cubanas en el nuevo milenio," in Aurora López, Andrés Pociña, and María de Fátima Silva, eds., *De ayer a hoy: Influencias clásicas en la literatura* (Coimbra: Universidad de Coimbra), 313–18.

Miranda Cancela, Elina (2015), "Antígona en las Antillas," in *Ianua Classicorum. Temas y formas del mundo antiguo.* Madrid, Sociedad Española de Estudios Clásicos 3: 529–40.

BIBLIOGRAPHY 421

Miranda Cancela, Elina and G. Herrera, eds. (2010), *Actualidad de los clásicos. Actas del III Congreso Internacional de Filología y Tradición Clásicas Vicentina Antuña in memoriam* (La Habana: Editorial U.H, Grupo de Estudios Helénicos).

Mogliani, Laura (1997), "Antígona Furiosa de Griselda Gambaro y su intertexto Griego," in Osvaldo Pellettieri, ed., *De Esquilo a Gambaro* (Buenos Aires: Editorial Galerna), 97–109.

Mogliani, Laura (2005a), "La política cultural del peronismo (1946–1955)," *Revista Teatro XXI, Revista del GETEA* 11/20: 25–8.

Mogliani, Laura (2005b), "Teatro y propaganda: Una dramaturgia peronista," in Osvaldo Pellettieri, ed., *Teatro, Memoria y Ficción* (Buenos Aires: Galerna), 201–8.

Mogliani, Laura (2006), "Principales objetivos de la política cultural teatral del Peronismo (1946–1955): Hegemonía y difusión cultural," http://www.unsam.edu.ar/home/material/Mogliani.pdf.

Montas, Lucien (1955), "Morisseau-Leroy construit un théâtre d'essai," *Optique* 21: 73–5.

Monterroso, Augusto, ed. Jorge Ruffinelli (1986), *Lo demás es silencio: la vida y obra de Eduardo Torres* (Madrid: Cátedra).

Montes Huidobro, Matías (1986), "La pasión según Antígona Pérez," in *Persona, vida y máscara en el teatro puertorriqueño* (San Juan: Centro de Estudios Avanzados de Puerto Rico y el Caribe), 566–79.

Morais, Carlos (2015), "Sob o signo de Antígona: da guerra civil à luta contra a tirania, em *El Límite* de Alberto de Zavalía," in *Caim e Abel: conto e recontos* 12: 359–69.

Morales, Ernesto (1944), *Historia del teatro Argentino* (Buenos Aires: Lautaro).

Morales-Valentín, Magda (2005), "La caracterización de Antígona Pérez," in Miriam González Hérnandez, ed., *Reflexiones literarias: de la creación al estudio* (Puerto Rico: Cepa), 70–8.

Moraña, Mabel (1997), "De *La ciudad letrada* al imaginario nacionalista: Contribuciones de Ángel Rama a la invención de América," in *Políticas de la escritura en América Latina. De la colonia a la modernidad* (Caracas: eXcultura), 165–73.

Moraña, Mabel, Enrique Dussel, and Carlos Jáuregui, eds. (2008), *Coloniality at Large: Latin America and the Postcolonial Debate* (Durham, NC: Duke University Press).

Moreiras, Alberto (2004), "The Conflict in Transculturation," in M. Valdés and D. Kadir, eds., *Literary Cultures of Latin America: A Contemporary History, Vol. 3* (Oxford: Oxford University Press), 129–37.

Morejón Flores, Guillermo (2016), "Armando la 'nueva lucha': Continuidades y rupturas de la lucha armada," in *Puerto Rico en los años setenta*, http://www.cedema.org/ver.php?id=7116.

Morfi, Angelina (1980), *Historia crítica de un siglo de teatro puertorriqueño* (San Juan: Instituto de Cultura Puertorriqueña).

Morfi, Angelina (1982), "El teatro de Luis Rafael Sánchez," *Revista Canadiense de Estudios Hispánicos* 7/1: 189–204.

Morisseau-Leroy, Félix (1953), "Une interview de Morisseau-Leroy, L'auteur d'Antigone en Creole," *Le Matin*, July 24. Port-au-Prince.

Morisseau-Leroy, Félix (1954), "Pourquoi ils écrivent en créole," *Optique* 5: 48–58.

Morisseau-Leroy, Félix (1955a), "À propos des problèmes de la poésie nationale," *Optique* 21: 75.

422 BIBLIOGRAPHY

Morisseau-Leroy, Félix (1955b), "Plaidoyer pour un théâtre en créole," *Panorama* 4: 129–32.

Morisseau-Leroy, Félix (1955c), "Ca'm di nan ça, Depestre," *Optique* 19: 7.

Morisseau-Leroy, Félix (1972), "Antigone," *Diacoute 2. Nouvelle Optique*, Montreal: 13.

Morisseau-Leroy, Félix (1983), "The Awakening of the Creole Consciousness," *The Unesco Courier* 19; reprinted as "L'espace de la conscience créole," *Sapriphage 22/* Nanterre, 1994: 85–7.

Morisseau-Leroy, Félix (1986), "Por el Creole." Speech at the "Segundo Encuentro de Intelectuales por la Soberanía de los Pueblos de Nuestra América," *Conjunto* 70: 57–60.

Morisseau-Leroy, Félix (1991), *Haitiad & Oddities*, trans. Marie-Marcell Buteau Racine (Miami, FL: Pantaléon Guilbaud).

Morisseau-Leroy, Félix (1992), "Interview," *Callaloo* 15/3: 667–70.

Morisseau-Leroy, Félix (1994), "L'espace de la conscience créole," *Sapriphage* 22, Montreal: 85–7.

Mossetto, Anna Paola (2003), "Scene da un 'Antigone' Creola," in Bernardelli Giuseppe and Enrica Galazzi, eds., *Lingua, cultura e testo: miscellanea di studi francesi in onore di Sergio Cigada Vol. 2* (Milan: Vita Pensiero), 875–88.

Mostaco, Edelcio (1982), *Teatro e política: Arena, oficina e opinião* (São Paulo: Proposta).

Mota, Aurea (2015), "Eisenstadt: Brazil and the Multiple Modernities Framework," *Journal of Classical Sociology* 15/1: 39–57.

Movimiento Pro Independencia (1969), *Presente y futuro de Puerto Rico: Segunda tesis política del MPI* (Río Piedras: Editorial Claridad).

Müller, Gesine and Dunia Gras Miravet, eds. (2015), *América Latina y la literatura mundial* (Madrid: Iberoamericana, Vervuert).

Munro, Martin and Elizabeth Walcott-Hackshaw (2006), *Reinterpreting the Haitian Revolution and its Cultural Aftershock* (Kingston: University of the West Indies Press).

Munro, Martin and Elizabeth Walcott-Hackshaw, eds. (2009), *Echoes of the Haitian Revolution 1804–2004* (Kingston: University of the West Indies Press).

Myers, Jorge (1995), *Orden y virtud: El discurso republicano en el régimen rosista* (Buenos Aires: Universidad Nacional de Quilmes).

Nari, Marcela (2004), *Políticas de maternidad y maternalismo político* (Buenos Aires: Editorial Biblios).

Nava Castillo, Juana María (2002), "Castigo a los asesinos de Juárez, claman madres de víctimas," *Cimacnoticias*, November 5, https://www.cimacnoticias.com.mx/noticia/castigo-los-asesinos-de-ju-rez-claman-madres-de-v-ctimas.

Navarro, Marysa (2005), *Evita* (Buenos Aires: Edhasa).

Navarro Benítez, Joaquín (2001), "La transparencia del tiempo. Entrevista a Griselda Gambaro," *Cyber Humanitatis* 20, http://web.uchile.cl/publicaciones/cyber/20/entrev1.html.

Negro Tua, Sandra and Manuel María Marsal, eds. (2000), *Un reino en la frontera: las misiones Jesuítas en la América colonial* (Quito: Pontífica Universidad Católica del Perú y Ediciones Abya Yala).

Neils, Jan, ed. (2011), *Receptions of Antiquity* (Gent: Academia Press).

BIBLIOGRAPHY 423

Nelli, María Florencia (2009), "Identity, Dignity and Memory: Performing/Re-writing Antigone in Post-1976 Argentina," in *New Voices in Classical Reception Studies* 4, http://www2.open.ac.uk/ClassicalStudies/GreekPlays/newvoices/issue%20 4/4Nelli.pdf.

Nelli, María Florencia (2010), "From Ancient Greek Drama to Argentina's 'Dirty War': Antígona Furiosa: On Bodies and the State," in S. E. Wilmer and Audrone Žukauskaite, eds., *Interrogating Antigone in Postmodern Philosophy and Criticism* (Oxford: Oxford University Press), 353–65.

Nelli, María Florencia (2012), "*Usted está aquí*: Antigone against the Standardization of Violence in Contemporary Mexico," *Romance Quarterly* 59/1: 55–65.

Nelli, María Florencia (2015), "Oedipus Tyrannus in South America," in Kathryn Bosher, Fiona Macintosh, Justine McConnell, and Patrice Rankine, eds., *The Oxford Handbook of Greek Drama in the Americas* (Oxford: Oxford University Press), chapter 35.

Nesbit, Nick (2008), *Universal Emancipation: The Haitian Revolution and the Radical Enlightenment* (Charlottesville, VA: University of Virginia Press).

Nespoli, Beth (2017), "Memórias do teatro: leituras de Antígona," *RevLet—Revista Virtual de Letras* 9/1: 281–94.

Newlands, Carole (2006), "Mothers in Statius' Poetry: Sorrows and Surrogates," *Helios* 33/2: 203–23.

Nicholls, David (1985), "Rural Protest and Peasant Revolt," in *Haiti in Caribbean Context: Ethnicity, Economy, and Revolt* (New York: St. Martin's Press), 167–85.

Nicholls, David (1988), *From Dessalines to Duvalier: Race, Colour and National Independence in Haiti* (New Brunswick, NJ: Rutgers University Press).

Nieves-Falcón, Luis (2009), *Un siglo de represión política en Puerto Rico* (San Juan: Optimática).

Nikoloutsos, Konstantinos, ed. (2012), "Reception of Greek and Roman Drama in Latin America," *Romance Quarterly* 59 (special issue).

Nino, Carlos (1997), *Juicio al mal absoluto* (Buenos Aires: Emecé).

Nora, Pierre (1984), *Les lieux de mémoire* (Paris: Gallimard).

Nosella, Berilo Luigi Deiró (2012), "Jorge Andrade e a metateatralidade da conciência histórica," *O Percevejo* 4: 1–26, http://www.repositorio.ufop.br/bitstream/ 123456789/5645/1/ARTIGO_JorgeAndradeMetateatralidade.pdf.

Novais, Fernando (1979), *Portugal e Brasil na Crise do Antigo Sistema Colonial (1777–1808)* (São Paulo: Hucitec).

Novais, Fernando (2008), "Interview," *Revista Brasileira de Psicanálise* 42/2: 15–38.

Nuñez, Carlinda F. P. (1986), "O universo trágico da 'Antígona' de Sófocles e suas relações com 'Pedreira das almas' de Jorge Andrade," Master's thesis, UFRJ, Rio de Janeiro.

Obregón, Osvaldo (1998), *Le théâtre latino-américain contemporain: 1940–1990 (Anthologie)* (Arles: Unesco/Actes Sud Papiers).

Odnell, David (1955), "Le créole: Langage nationale du peuple haïtien," *Panorama* August: 221–6.

O'Gorman, Edmundo ([1958] 1961), *La invención de América [The Invention of America]* (Bloomington, IN: Indiana University Press).

424 BIBLIOGRAPHY

Oliveira, Sírley Cristina (2003), "A Ditadura Militar (1964–1985) à Luz da Inconfidência Mineira nos Palcos Brasileiros: Em Cena *Arena Conta Tiradentes* (1967) e *As Confrarias* (1969)," Dissertation, Uberlândia/MG, Universidade Federal de Uberlândia.

Oliveira, Sírley Cristina (2005), "As Confrarias: A Presença de Jorge de Andrade nos Debates Políticos e Estéticos da Década de 1960." *Revista de História e Estudos Culturais, Uberlândia* 2: 1–19.

O'Neill, Eugene ([1920] 1988), *The Emperor Jones* in *Complete Plays: 1913–1943* (New York: Viking Press).

Operé, Fernando (2001), *Historias de la frontera: El cautiverio en la América Hispánica* (Buenos Aires: Fondo de Cultura Económica).

Orsini, Francesca (2015), "The Multilingual Local in World Literature," *Comparative Literature* 67/4: 345–74.

Ortegsa Daza, Nereo (2015), "Mujeres víctimas se convierten en antígonas," *Las 2 orillas*, August 3, https://www.las2orillas.co/mujeres-victimas-del-conflicto-se-convierten-en-antigonas.

Ortiz, Fernando ([1940] 2000), *Contrapunteo cubano del tabaco y el azúcar* (Madrid: Cátedra).

Oviedo, A. (2014), *Buen Vivir vs Sumak Kawsay* (Tercera Edición) (Buenos Aires: CICCUS).

Pagán, Carlos (1976), "La voz del lector," *El Mundo* 17–18: 6.

Paralitici, Ché (2011), *La represión contra el independentismo puertorriqueño: 1960–2010* (San Juan: Ediciones Gaviota).

Pascoal, Isaias (2008), "Em Carranças, sujeitos se encontraram e se desencontraram," *Fênix—Revista de História e Estudos Culturais* 5/V/4, http://www.revistafenix.pro.br.

Patriota, Rosangela (1992), "O teatro como Objeto de Pesquisa Historiográfica," *Revista História e Debate*.

Patriota, Rosangela (1996), "As Confrarias de Jorge Andrade: Uma interpretação da sociedade mineira do século XVIII," *Anais do X encontro regional de História, ANPUH—MG, Minas trezentos anos: Um balanço historiográfico* 26, Mariana, UFOP, July 22–6.

Paz, Marta Lena (1998), "Antígona Vélez: Del teatro a la tragedia lírica," in Fundación Leopoldo Marechal, ed., *Cincuentenario de Adán Buenosayres* (Buenos Aires: Fundación Leopoldo Marechal), 91–8.

Pellarolo, Silvia (1992), "Revisando el canon/ la historia oficial: Griselda Gambaro y el heroismo de Antígona," *Gestos* 13: 79–85.

Pellettieri, Osvaldo (1992), "El sonido y la furia. Panorama del teatro de los '80 en la Argentina," *Latin American Theatre Review* 25/2: 3–12.

Pellettieri, Osvaldo (2001), *Historia del teatro argentino en Buenos Aires: La segunda modernidad, Vol. 4* (Buenos Aires: Galerna).

Pellettieri, Osvaldo (2008), *El sainete y el grotesco criollo: Del autor al actor* (Buenos Aires: Galerna).

Peña-Jordán, Teresa (2003), "The Multitude," in Luis Rafael Sánchez, "La pasión según Antígona Pérez: A Genealogy of a Future Unknown," *Journal of Latin American Cultural Studies* 12/3: 377–88.

Pérez Asensio, Magdalena (2009), "El mito en el teatro cubano actual, tesis doctoral," Dissertation, Universidad de Murcia.

BIBLIOGRAPHY 425

Pérez Blanco, Lucrecio (1984), "Antígona Vélez: Apropiación y trueque del mensaje sofocleo," *Cuadernos Americanos* 6: 143–72.

Pérez Blanco, Lucrecio (1985), "Antígona y el drama humano en dos textos literarios hispano-americanos contemporáneos," *La Ciudad de Dios*, 197/1 (January–April) El Escorial: 71–101.

Pérez Blanco, Lucrecio (1997), "El puertorriqueño Luis Rafael Sánchez ante dos concepciones del teatro," *Anales de Literatura Hispanoamericana* 26/1, UCM, Madrid: 119–41.

Pérez Martín, Norma (1993), "Antígona Vélez de Leopoldo Marechal: Trágica fusión de culturas," *Alba de América* 11: 233–9.

Persino, María Silvina (2007), "Cuerpo y memoria en el Teatro de los Andes y Yuyachkani," *Gestos* 43: 87–103.

Pianacci, Rómulo (2008), *Antígona: Una tragedia latinoamericana* (Buenos Aires: Ediciones Gestos).

Pianacci, Rómulo (2010), "¡Ni una más! El compromiso del arte frente al feminicidio en Ciudad Juárez," *La Escalera* 20: 159–74.

Picón Garfield, Evelyn (1985), "Griselda Gambaro: Interview," in *Women's Voices from Latin America* (Detroit, MI: Wayne State University), 55–71.

Piketty, Thomas (2013), *Capital in the Twenty-First Century* (Cambridge, MA: Harvard University Press).

Pinto, J. P. (1998), *Uma memória do mundo—ficção, memória e história em Jorge Luis Borges* (São Paulo: Estação da Liberdade).

Pizarnik, Alejandra (1990), *Poesía y Prosa* (Buenos Aires: Corregidor).

Pizarnik, Alejandra (2003), *Dos Letras* (Barcelona: March Editor).

Placoly, Vincent (1983), *Dessalines ou la passion de l'indépendance* (Martinique; Cuba: Casa de las Américas).

Pociña, Andrés and Aurora López (2010), "La eterna pervivencia de Antígona," *Florentia Iliberritana* 21: 345–70.

Poignault, Rémy, ed. (2002), *Présence de l'antiquité grecque et romaine au XXe siècle: Actes du colloque tenu à Tours, 30 novembre–2 décembre 2000* (Tours: Centre de Recherches A. Piganio).

Pollack, Sarah (2009), "Latin America Translated (Again): Roberto Bolaño's *The Savage Detectives* in the United States," *Comparative Literature* 61/3: 346–65.

Pontes, Heloisa and Sérgio Miceli (2012), "Memória e utopia na cena teatral," *Sociologia & Antropologia* 2/4: 241–63.

Porter, James (2010a), "Reception Studies: Future Prospects," in Lorna Hardwick and Christopher Stray, eds., *A Companion to Classical Receptions* (Oxford: Blackwell), 469–80.

Porter, James (2010b), "Why Art Has Never Been Autonomous," *Arethusa* 43/2: 165–80.

Poulson, Nancy Kason (2012), "In Defense of the Dead: Antígona Furiosa, by Griselda Gambaro," *Romance Quarterly* 59/1: 48–54.

Power, Cormac (2010), "Performing to Fail: Perspectives on Failure and Performance in Philosophy," in Daniel Meyer-Dinkgräfe and Daniel Watt, eds., *Ethical Encounters: Boundaries of Theatre, Performance and Philosophy* (Newcastle: CSP).

Prado Júnior, Caio ([1942] 1965), *Formação do Brasil Contemporâneo* (São Paulo: Editora Brasiliense).

426 BIBLIOGRAPHY

Prado Júnior, Caio (1985), *Evolução política do Brasil: Colônia e Império* (São Paulo: Brasiliense).

Prashad, Viyay (2007), *The Darker Nations: A People's History of the Third World* (New York: The New Press).

Preyer, G. and M. Sussman (2016), *Varieties of Multiple Modernities* (Leiden: Brill).

Price Mars, Jean ([1928] 1973), *Ainsi parla l'oncle. So Spoke the Uncle* (Hoboken, NJ: Prentice Hall).

Price Mars, Louis (1946), *La crise de possession, essais de psychiatrie comparée* (Port-au-Prince: Imprimerie de l'état).

Price Mars, Louis (1966), *Témoignages 1 (essai ethnopsychologique)* (Port-au-Prince: Imprimerie de l'état).

Price Mars, Louis (1981), "Ethnodrama: The Dramatic Religion in Haiti," *Quilt* 1: 183–9.

Price Mars, Louis (1982), *Les maîtres de l'aube* (Port-au-Prince: Imprimerie de l'état).

Puga, Ana (2008), *Memory, Allegory and Testimony in South American Theater* (London: Routledge).

Quijano, Aníbal (2000), "Coloniality of Power, Eurocentrism, and Latin America," *Nepantla: Views from the South* 1/3: 533–80.

Quintana de Rubero, Hilda E. (1983), "Myth and Reality in Luis Rafael Sánchez's *La pasión según Antígona Pérez*," Dissertation, State University of New York at Binghamton.

Rabasa, José (1993), *Inventing America: Spanish Historiography and the Formation of Eurocentrism* (Norman, OK: University of Oklahoma Press).

Ralli, Teresa and Miguel Rubio Zapata (2000), "Notas sobre nuestra Antígona," http://www.geocities.com/antigona_yuyachkani/Nuestra.html.

Ralli, Teresa and Miguel Rubio Zapata (2009), "Antígona de Yuyachkani," *Zona del Escribidor*, April 24, http://zonadelescribidor.blogspot.com/2009/04/antigona-de-yuyachkani.html.

Rama, Ángel (1982), *Transculturación narrativa en América Latina* (Buenos Aires: Editora Nómada).

Rama, Ángel ([1984] 1996), *The Lettered City*, trans. John Charles Chasteen (Durham, NC: Duke University Press).

Ramírez, Marta María (2013a), "Cuba tiene su propia Antígona," *On Cuba News*, September 29, https://oncubanews.com/cultura/cine/cuba-tiene-su-propia-antigona/.

Ramírez, Marta María (2013b), "En el pueblo hay muchas Antígonas," *On Cuba News*, October 11, http://oncubamagazine.com/cultura/en-el-pueblo-hay-muchas-antigonas/.

Ramos, Julio (2001), *Divergent Modernities* (Durham, NC: Duke University Press).

Ramos, Julio (2003), *Desencuentros de la modernidad en América Latina: literatura y política en el siglo XIX* (Chile: Editorial Cuarto Propio).

Ramos Escobar, José Luis (2012), "Huyendo del insularismo teatral: La pasión según Antígona Pérez," in Aurora López, Andrés Pociña, and María de Fátima Silva, eds., *De ayer a hoy: Influencias clásicas en la literatura* (Coimbra: Universidad de Coimbra) 429–35.

Ramos-Perea, Roberto (1989), *Perspectiva de la nueva dramaturgia puertorriqueña: Ensayos sobre el nuevo teatro nacional* (San Juan: Ateneo Puertorriqueño).

BIBLIOGRAPHY   427

Rancière, Jacques (1999), *Disagreements: Politics and Philosophy*, trans. J. Rose (Minneapolis, MN: University of Minnesota Press).

Rancière, Jacques (2004a), *The Politics of Aesthetics* (London: Bloomsbury).

Reátegui Carrillo, Félix (2008), "Memories of Violence in Peru: Truth-Seeking, Denial and Victims' Collective Remembering," Unpublished paper presented at Yale University, October 30.

Regeneración (2018), "A 25 años del primer feminicidio en Juárez, nada ha cambiado en el país," January 23, https://regeneracion.mx/a-25-anos-del-primer-feminicidio-en-juarez-nada-ha-cambiado-en-el-pais/.

Rehm, Rush (2003), *Greek Tragic Theatre* (New York: Routledge).

Rengifo, César (1981), "La dramaturgia y la crítica como testimonio histórico y reflexión estética," *Tramoya* 21–2: 129–32.

Rengifo, César (1989), *Obras Completas* (Caracas: Universidad de los Andes).

Rengifo, César (2015), *Teatro. Ensayos* (Caracas: Colección Biblioteca Ayacucho).

Reyes, Alfonso (1959), "Comentario a la 'Ifigenia Cruel'" *Obras completas*, X (México: Fondo de Cultura Económica): 351–59.

Ribeiro, Darcy (1995), *O Povo Brasileiro, A formação e o sentido do Brasil* (São Paulo: Companhia das Letras).

Ricci, Clemente (1923), *Francisco Ramos Mexía: Un heterodoxo argentino como hombre de genio y como precursor* (Buenos Aires: Imprenta Juan H. Kidd y Cía).

Rigaud, Milo (1974), *Diagrammes rituels du Voudou* (New York: French and European Publications).

Rigaud, Milo (2001), *Secrets of Voodoo* (New York: City Light Publishers).

Ritsos, Yannis (1993), "Ismene," in *The Fourth Dimension* (London: Anvil Poetry), 192–215.

Rivera Cusicanqui, Silvia (2010), "The Notion of 'Rights' and the Paradoxes of Postcolonial Modernity: Indigenous Peoples and Women in Bolivia," *Qui Parle* 18/2: 29–54.

Rivera Cusicanqui, Silvia (2014), *Un mundo ch'ixi es posible* (Buenos Aires: Tinta Limón).

Rochlin, James F. (2003), *Vanguard Revolutionaries in Latin America: Peru, Colombia, Mexico* (London: Rienner).

Rodríguez, Ileana, ed. (2001), *The Latin American Subaltern Studies Reader* (Durham, NC: Duke University Press).

Rodríguez, Martín ([1823] 1969), *Diario de la expedición al desierto* (Buenos Aires: Editorial Sudestada).

Rojas, Jorge Enrique (2015), *Tradición clásica: Propuestas e interpretaciones* (México: UNAM).

Rojas, Ricardo (1960), *Historia de la literatura Argentina*, 8 vols (Buenos Aires: Editorial Guillermo Kraft Limitada).

Rojas Ajmad, Diego (2007), "Antígona de nuestro tiempo," *Sarapanda*, June 2, http://saparapanda.blogspot.com/2007/06/antgona-de-nuestro-tiempo.html.

Romane, Jean-Jacques (1823), *La mort de Christophe*.

Romero, Luis Alberto and José Luis Romero (1988), *Pensamiento Político de la Emancipación, tomo I and II: 1790–1825* (Caracas: Fundación Biblioteca Ayacucho).

428 BIBLIOGRAPHY

Romero, Rolando and Amanda Nolacea Harris, eds. (1993), *Feminism, Nation and Myth: La Malinche* (Houston, TX: Arte Público Press).

Romero, Silvia (1981), "Aproximación a la Antígona Vélez de Leopoldo Marechal," *Interamerican Review of Bibliography* 31: 232.

Romero Rey, Sandro (2015), *Género y destino. La tragedia griega en Colombia* (Bogotá: Ediciones Universidad Distrital).

Rosa, José María (1970), *Rosas, nuestro contemporáneo: Sus veinte años de gobierno* (Buenos Aires: Editorial La Candelaria).

Rosario Moreno, Ianni del (1997), "La recontextualización de Antígona en el teatro argentino y brasilero a partir de 1968," *Latin American Theater Review* 30/2: 115–29.

Rosenfeld, Anatol (1962), *Panorama do Teatro Brasileiro* (São Paulo: Difusão Europeia do Livro).

Rosenfeld, Anatol (1986), "Visão do ciclo," in Jorge Andrade, ed., *Marta, a árvore e o relógio*, 2nd ed. (São Paulo: Perspectiva), 559–617.

Rosenfeld, Anatol (1996), "Visão," in *O mito e o herói no moderno teatro brasileiro*, 2nd ed. (São Paulo: Perspectiva), 101–22.

Rotker, Susana (1999), *Cautivas: Olvidos y memoria en la Argentina* (Buenos Aires: Ariel).

Rubio Zapata, Miguel (2001), *Notas de Teatro* (Lima: Grupo Cultural Yuyachkani).

Rubio Zapata, Miguel (2006), "Informe final," in *El Cuerpo Ausente* (Lima: Didi de Arteta, S.A.).

Rubio Zapata, Miguel (2011), *Raíces y semillas: Maestros y Caminos del Teatro en América Latina* (Lima: Grupo Cultural Yuyachkani).

Rubio Zapata, Miguel and Grupo Cultural Yuyachkani (n.d.), "La Persistencia de la memoria," http://hemi.nyu.edu/esp/newsletter/issue8/pages/rubio2.shtml

Ruiz, Marta (2018), "Fiesta de sangre: así fue la masacre de El Salado," *Semana*, August 30, https://www.semana.com/nacion/articulo/masacre-de-el-salado-como-la-planearon-y-ejecutaron-los-paramilitares/557580.

Russell, Diana and Jill Radford (1992), *Femicide: The Politics of Woman Killing* (New York: Twayne Publishers).

Ruy, Affonso (1942), *A Primeira Revolução Social Brasileira (1798)* (São Paulo: Companhia Editora Nacional).

Sáenz Quesada, María (2001), "La Atenas del Plata," in *La Argentina: Historia del país y de su gente* (Buenos Aires: Editorial Sudamericana), 271–3.

Saguier, Eduardo R. and Joaquín Meabe (2007), "Una Antígona americana en el Río de la Plata (1817–1821)," http://www.er-saguier.org.

Said, Edward (1993), *Culture and Imperialism* (London: Chatto & Windus).

Saint-Lot, Marie José Alcide (2003), *Vodou: A Sacred Theater* (Pompano Beach, FL: Educa Vision).

Sala-Molins, Louis (2006), *The Dark Side of the Light: Slavery and The French Enlightenment* (Minneapolis, MN: University of Minnesota Press).

Sánchez Prado, Ignacio, ed. (2006), *América Latina en la "literatura mundial"* (Pittsburgh, PA: Instituto Internacional de Literatura Iberoamericana).

Sánchez Prado, Ignacio (2009), *Naciones Intelectuales: las fundaciones de la modernidad literaria mexicana (1917–1959)* (Indiana: Purdue University Press).

BIBLIOGRAPHY 429

Sánchez Prado, Ignacio (2019), *Intermitencias alfonsinas. Estudios y otros textos* (Monterrey: Universidad Iberoamericana Torreón, Universidad Autónoma de Nuevo León).

Sanchez Toranzo, José and Rolando Jesús Rocha (2005), "Reescritura de la *Antígona* de Sófocles: *AntígonaS, linaje de hembras*, de Jorge Huertas," Universidad Nacional de Tucumán, XIII Congreso Nacional de Literatura Argentina, San Miguel de Tucumán, August 15.

Sant'Anna, Catarina (1997), *Metalinguagem e Teatro* (Cuiabá: EdUFMT).

Santos Silva, Loreina (1981), "La pasión según Antígona Pérez: La mujer como reafirmadora de la dignidad política," *Revista/review Interamericana* 11/3: 438.

Sarlo, Beatriz (1993), *Borges: A Writer on the Edge* (London: Verso).

Sarmiento, Domingo Faustino ([1845] 2003), *Facundo. Civilización y barbarie en las pampas argentinas* (Buenos Aires: Stockcero).

Sarmiento, Domingo Faustino ([1848] 2001), "De la educación de las mujeres," in *Educación popular* in *Obras completas, Vol. 11* (Buenos Aires: Universidad Nacional de la Matanza).

Sassen, Saskia (2014), *Expulsions: Brutality and Complexity in the Global Economy* (Cambridge, MA: Harvard University Press).

Satizábal, C. (2015), "Memoria poética y conflicto en Colombia—a propósito de *Antígonas: tribunal de mujeres*, de Tramaluna Teatro," *Revista Colombiana de las Artes Escénicas* 9: 250–68.

Scabuzzo, Susana (2000), "*Antígona Furiosa* de G. Gambaro: Entre traducción y deconstrucción," *Argos: Revista Argentina de Estudios Clásicos* 24: 145–55.

Scabuzzo Susana (2012), "Antígona se vuelve plural en la Argentina: AntígonaS, linaje de hembras de Jorge Huertas," in Aurora López, Andrés Pociña, and María de Fátima Silva, eds., *De ayer a hoy: Influencias clásicas en la literatura* (Coimbra: Universidad de Coimbra), 509–16.

Schechner, Richard (1985), *Between Theater and Anthropology* (Philadelphia, PA: University of Pennsylvania).

Schechner, Richard (2013), *Performance Studies: An Introduction* (London: Routledge).

Schoo Lastra, Dionisio (1937), *El Indio del desierto 1535–1879* (Buenos Aires: Círculo Militar).

Schumaher, Schuma and Érico Vital (2000), *Dicionário Mulheres do Brasil: de 1500 até a atualidade (biográfico e ilustrado)* (Brasil: Editora Zahar).

Schwarz, Roberto (2007), "Competing Readings in World Literature," *New Left Review* 48: 85–107.

Schwarz, Roberto (2014), *As idéias fora do lugar* (São Paulo: Companhia das Letras).

Scott, David (2004), *Conscripts of Modernity: The Tragedy of Colonial Enlightenment* (Durham, NC: Duke University Press).

Scott, Jill (1993), "Griselda Gambaro's *Antígona Furiosa*: Loco(ex)centrism for 'jouissan(SA)," *Gestos* 15: 99–110.

Shankar, S. (2012), *Flesh and Fish Blood: Postcolonialism, Translation, and the Vernacular* (Berkeley, CA: University of California Press).

Shelton, Marie-Denise (2000), "Le défi théâtral dans *Antigone* de Félix Moriso-Leroy et *La Tragédie du roi Christophe* d'Aimé Césaire," *Boutures* 1/2: 27–30.

430 BIBLIOGRAPHY

Shumway, Nicolas (1991), *The Invention of Argentina* (Berkeley, CA: University of California Press).

Sikkink, Kathryn (2008), "From Pariah State to Global Protagonist: Argentina and the Struggle for International Human Rights," *Latin American Politics and Society* 50/1: 1–29.

Sikkink, Kathryn and Carrie Booth Walling (2006), "Argentina's Contribution to Global Trends in Transitional Justice," in Naomi Roht-Arriaza and Javier Mariezcurrena, eds., *Beyond Truth and Justice: Transitional Justice in the New Millennium* (Cambridge: Cambridge University Press), 301–24.

Silva, María de Fátima Sousa, María do Céu Grácio Zambujo Fialho, and José Luís Lopes Brandão, eds. (2016), *O Livro do Tempo: Escritas e reescritas. Teatro Greco-Latino e sua recepção II* (São Paulo: Universidade de Coimbra, Coimbra Portugal and Annablume Editora).

Silva, Wlamir (1998), "Usos da fumaça: A revolta do Ano da Fumaça e a afirmação moderada na Província de Minas," *Locus: Revista de História* 4/1: 105–18.

Sivonen, Seppo (1995), *White-Collar or Hoe Handle?: African Education under British Colonial Policy 1920–1945*. Bibliotheca Historica 4 (Helsinki: Suomen Historiallienen Seura).

Sjöholm, Cecilia (2004), *The Antigone Complex: Ethics and The Intervention of Feminine Desire* (Palo Alto, CA: Stanford University Press).

Slavitt, David (1994), "Ismene," in *Crossroads* (Baton Rouge, LA: Louisiana State University Press), 23–5.

Smith, Matthew (2009), *Red and Black in Haiti: Radicalism, Conflict and Political Change, 1934–1957* (Chapel Hill, NC: University of New Carolina Press).

Smith, Verity, ed. (1997), *Encyclopedia of Latin American Literature* (Chicago, IL: Fitzroy Dearborn Publishers).

Söderbäck, Fanny, ed. (2010), *Feminist Readings of Antigone* (Albany, NY: SUNY Press).

Sommer, Doris (1991), *Foundational Fictions: The National Romances of Latin America* (Berkeley, CA: University of California Press).

Sontag, Susan (2003), *Regarding the Pain of Others* (London: Penguin Books).

Sophocles, trans. Andrew Brown (1987), *Antigone* (Wiltshire: Aris and Phillips).

Sorrah, Renata (2015), "Antígona, Tragédia Clássica nos Anos de Chumbo— Ocupação João das Neves," *ItaúCultural*, September 29, http://www.itaucultural. org.br/explore/canal/detalhe/renata-sorrah-antigona-tragedia-classica-nos-anos-de-chumbo-ocupacao-joao-das-neves.

Soto, Moira (2011), Entrevista con Torlucci y Sarrail. *Página 12* Buenos Aires, September 16.

Sousa e Silva, María de Fátima, María do Céu Grácio Zambujo Fialho, and José Luís Lopes Brandão, eds. (2016), *O Livro do Tempo: Escritas e reescritas. Teatro Greco-Latino e sua recepção II* (São Paulo: Universidade de Coimbra, Coimbra Portugal and Annablume Editora).

Spargo, Clifton (2008), "The Apolitics of Antigone's Lament (from Sophocles to Ariel Dorfman)," *Mosaic* 41/3: 117–37.

Spivak, Gayatri (1987), "Subaltern Studies: Deconstructing Historiography," in *In Other Worlds: Essays in Cultural Politics* (New York: Methuen), 270–305.

BIBLIOGRAPHY 431

Steiner, George (1984), *Antigones: How the Antigone Legend Has Endured in Western Literature, Art, and Thought* (Oxford: Oxford University Press).

Stephens, Susan A. and Phiroze Vasunia (2010), *Classics and National Cultures* (Oxford: Oxford University Press).

Stern, Steve (1998), *Shining and Other Paths: War and Society in Peru, 1980–1995* (Durham, NC; London: Duke University Press).

Suárez Randillo, Miguel (1972), "Vigencia de la realidad venezolana en el teatro de César Rengifo," *Latin America Theater Review* 5/2: 51–61.

Suriano, Juan (2001), *Anarquistas. Cultura y política libertaria en Buenos Aires, 1890–1910* (Buenos Aires: Manantial).

Svampa, Maristela (1994), *El dilema argentino: Civilización o barbarie* (Buenos Aires: El Cielo por Asalto).

Taboada, Hernán G. H. (2007), "Romas y Hélades criollas: una trayectoria decimonónica," in Leticia Romero Chumacero, ed., *Voces antiguas, voces nuevas* (Mexico: UNAM), 229–41.

Taboada, Hernán G. H. (2012), "Los clásicos entre el vulgo latinoamericano," *Nova Tellus* 30/2: 205–19.

Taboada, Hernán G. H. (2014), "Centauros y eruditos: los clásicos en la Independencia," *Latinaomerica. Revista de Estudios Latinoamericanos* 59: 193–221.

Taylor, Diana (1994), "Las madres de la plaza," in Diana Taylor and Juan Villegas, eds., *Negotiating Performance* (Durham, NC: Duke University Press), 275–305.

Taylor, Diana (1996), "Rewriting the Classics: Antígona Furiosa and the Madres of the Plaza de Mayo," *Bucknell Review* 40/2: 77–93.

Taylor, Diana (1997), "Trapped in Bad Scripts: The Mothers of Plaza de Mayo," in *Disappearing Acts. Spectacles of Gender and Nationalism in Argentina's "Dirty War"* (Durham, NC: Duke University Press), 183–222.

Taylor, Diana (2000), "Interview with Rubio and Ralli," at the First Annual Conference of the Hemispheric Institute of Performance and Politics—Brazil 2000, http://hemi.nyu.edu/cuaderno/holyterrorsweb/teresa/interview2.html.

Taylor, Diana (2003a), *The Archive and The Repertoire* (Durham, NC: Duke University Press).

Taylor, Diana (2003b), "Staging Social Memory: Yuyachkani," in Patrick Campbell and Adrian Kerr, eds., *Psychoanalysis and Performance* (London: Routledge), 218–35.

Taylor, Lewis (2006), *Guerrilla War in Peru's Northern Highlands, 1980–1997* (Liverpool: Liverpool University Press).

The Findings of Peru's Truth and Reconciliation Commission (2004) (London: Peru Support Group).

Thompson, Howard (1972), "Theater: Street Festival: Antígona Perez and Chants Presented," *The New York Times*, May 20, 20.

Thompson, Howard (1972), "Antígona Pérez," *The New York Times*, May 25, 17.

Thomson, Sinclair (2002), *We Alone Will Rule: Native Andean Politics in the Age of Insurgency* (Madison, WI: University of Wisconsin Press).

Thornton, John (1991), "African Soldiers in the Haitian Revolution," *Journal of Caribbean History* 25/12: 59–80.

432 BIBLIOGRAPHY

Thornton, John (1992), *Africa and Africans in the Making of the Atlantic World, 1400–1650* (Cambridge: Cambridge University Press).

Thornton, John (1993), "I Am the Subject of the King of Kongo: African Ideology and the Haitian Revolution," *Journal of World History* 4/2: 181–214.

Thornton, John and Linda Heywood (2007), *Central Africans, Atlantic Creoles and the Foundation of the Americas, 1585–1660* (New York: Cambridge University Press).

Trigo, Benigno (2016), "Psyche, History, Language and Body in Antígona Pérez by Luis Rafael Sánchez," in *Malady and Genius: Self Sacrifice in Puerto Rican Literature* (Albany, NY: SUNY Press), 15–37.

Trouillot, Hénock (1962), *Les origines sociales de la littérature haïtienne* (Port-au-Prince: Imprimerie N. A. Theodore), 372–3.

Trouillot, Hénock (1966), *Dessalines ou la tragédie postcoloniale* (Port-au-Prince: Éditions Panorama).

Trouillot, Hénock (1967), *Dessalines ou le sang du Pont-Rouge* (Port-au-Prince: Imprimerie des Antilles).

Trouillot, Hénock (1970), *Introduction à une histoire du vodou* (Port-au-Prince: Imprimerie des Antilles).

Trouillot, Michel-Rolph (1995), *Silencing the Past: Power and the Production of History* (Boston, MA: Beacon Press).

Turchi, Romina María (2008), "Las experiencias del tiempo en Antígona Furiosa de Griselda Gambaro," Dissertation, Université de Montreal, Montreal.

Turner, Victor (1988), *The Anthropology of Performance* (New York: PAJ Publications).

Valdivieso, L. Teresa (2009), "Exégesis de la tragedia: *Antígona furiosa* de Griselda Gambaro," *Hispanic Journal* 30/1–2: 285–93.

Valko, Marcelo (2007), *Los indios invisibles del Malón de la Paz* (Buenos Aires: Editorial de las Madres de Plaza de Mayo).

Vannucchi, Edgardo, ed. (2007), *Recordar y Entender: carta abierta a los padres: la última dictadura militar, 1976–83* (Buenos Aires, Ministerio de Educación).

Varela, Juan Cruz ([1824] 1915), *Tragedias* (Buenos Aires: Librería La Facultad).

Vargas, Margarita (2013), "The Possibility of Justice: Bárbara Colio's Antigone in *Usted está aquí*," *Mediterranean Studies* 21/1: 67–78.

Vasconcelos, José ([1925] 1997), *The Cosmic Race*, trans. Didier T. Jaen (Baltimore, MD: Johns Hopkins University Press).

Veloz Maggiolo, Marcio (1963), "Creonte," in *Seis cuentos* (Santo Domingo: Arquero).

Venator-Santiago, Charles (2015), *Puerto Rico and the Origins of US Global Empire: The Disembodied Shade* (London: Routledge).

Verde-Amarelismo (1926–9), *Manifesto do Verde-Amarelismo* (São Paulo: Correio Paulistano). 1929.

Verna, Paul (1966), *Robert Sutherland: Un amigo de Bolívar en Haiti* (Caracas: Fundación John Boulton).

Verna, Paul (1969), *Petión y Bolívar* (Caracas: Imprenta Oficial).

Videla, Rafael (1977), *Mensajes Presidenciales: Proceso de Reorganización Nacional, Vol. 1* (Buenos Aires: Presidencia de la Nación).

Vilanova, Ángel Martin (1999a), "*Adán y Antígona* de Leopoldo Marechal: Héroes clásicos y argentinos," in José Vicente Bañuls Oller, J. Sánchez Méndez,

BIBLIOGRAPHY 433

and J. Sanmartín Sáez, eds., *Literatura iberoamericana y tradición clásica* (Barcelona: Universitat Autónoma de Barcelona—Valencia: Universitat de València), 393–7.

Vilanova, Ángel Martin (1999b), "Las Antígonas Iberoamericanas," *Nueva Revista de Filología Hispánica* 47/1: 137–50.

Vilanova, Ángel Martin (1999c), "Las heroínas del drama clásico grecolatino en el teatro iberoamericano: Algunas reflexiones sobre Argia," in José Vicente Bañuls Oller, J. Sánchez Méndez, and J. Sanmartín Sáez, eds., *Literatura iberoamericana y tradición clásica* (Barcelona: Universitat Autónoma de Barcelona—Valencia: Universitat de València), 473–80.

Villar, Daniel, Juan Francisco Jiménez, and Silvia Ratto (1998), *Relaciones inter-étnicas en el sur bonaerense, 1810–1830* (Buenos Aires: Universidad Nacional del Sur UNCPBA).

Villaverde, Edith (1993), "An Intertextual Analysis of the Myth of Antigone in Three Latin American Plays," Dissertation, UMI.

Viñas, David (2003), *Indios, ejército y frontera* (Buenos Aires: Santiago Arcos).

Viveiros de Castro, Eduardo (2014), *Cannibal Metaphysics* (n.p.: Univocal Publishing).

Viveiros de Castro, Eduardo (2015), *The Relative Native: Essays on Indigenous Conceptual Worlds* (Chicago, IL: Hau).

Walcott, Derek ([1950a] 2002), *The Haitian Trilogy* (New York: Farrar, Straus and Giroux).

Walcott, Derek (1950b), *Henri Christophe: A Chronicle in Seven Scenes* (Bridgetown, St Lucia: Advocate CO).

Waldman, Gloria (1988), *Luis Rafael Sánchez: pasión teatral* (San Juan: Institute of Puerto Rican Culture).

Wallace, Jennifer (2003), "We Can't Make More Dirt...': Tragedy and the Excavated Body," *Cambridge Quarterly* 32/2: 103–11.

Wally Waldemar, Juan (2008), *Pensar y amar la patria*, http://www.scribd.com/doc/48704679/Leopoldo-Marechal-Pensar-y-Amar-La-Patria.

Wannamaker, Annette (2000–1), "'Memory Also Makes a Chain': The Performance of Absence in Griselda Gambaro's *Antígona Furiosa*," *Journal of the Midwest Modern Language Association* 33/3: 73–85.

Weaver, Karol Kimberlee (2006), *Medical Revolutionaries: The Enslaved Healers of Eighteenth-Century Saint Domingue* (Urbana, IL: University of Illinois Press).

Weinberg, Félix (1964), "Juan Cruz Varela: Crítico de la literatura nacional," *Boletín de Literatura Argentina* 1/1: 29–65.

Werth, Brenda (2010), *Theatre, Performance, and Memory Politics in Argentina* (New York: Palgrave Macmillan).

Wetmore, Kevin (2001), *The Athenian Sun in an African Sky* (London: McFarland & Company).

Wiener, Jessie (2015), "Antigone in Juarez: Tragedy, Politics, and Public Women on Mexico's Northern Border," *Classical Receptions Journal* 7/2: 276–309.

Wiesse Rebagliati, Jorge (2005), *Vigilia de los sentidos* (Lima: Laberintos).

Williams, Patrick and Laura Chrisman (1993), *Colonial Discourse and Postcolonial Theory* (New York: Columbia University Press).

434 BIBLIOGRAPHY

Williams, Raymond (1977), *Marxism and Literature* (Oxford: Oxford University Press).

Wilmer, S. E. and Audrone Zukauskaite, eds. (2010), *Interrogating Antigone in Postmodern Philosophy and Criticism* (Oxford: Oxford University Press).

Winn, Peter (2010), "The Furies of the Andes: Violence and Terror in the Chilean Revolution and Counter Revolution," in Greg Grandin and Gil Joseph, eds., *A Century of Revolution: Insurgent and Counterinsurgent Violence in Latin America's Long Cold War* (Durham, NC: Duke University Press), 239–76.

Woodyard George (1973), "Toward a Radical Theater in Spanish America," in Harvey Johnson and Philip Taylor, eds., *Contemporary Latin American Theater* (Houston, TX: Latin American Societies Committee).

Wright, Melissa (2011), "Necropolitics, Narcopolitics, and Femicide. Gendered Violence on the Mexico-US Border," *Signs: Journal of Women in Culture and Society* 36/3: 707–31.

Young, Robert (2001), *Postcolonialism: An Historical Introduction* (Oxford: Blackwell).

Yunque, Álvaro (1969), *Hombres en las guerras de las pampas* (Buenos Aires: Ediciones Sílaba).

Zalacaín, Daniel (1981), "La Antígona de Sánchez: Recreación puertorriqueña del mito," *Explicación de textos literarios* 9/2: 111–18.

Zavaleta Mercado, René (1986), *Lo nacional-popular en Bolivia* (Mexico: Siglo XXI Editores).

Zayas de Lima, Perla (1996), *Diccionario de directores y escenógrafos* (Buenos Aires: Editorial Galerna).

Index

Note: Figures are indicated by an italic "*f*" following the page number.

For the benefit of digital users, indexed terms that span two pages (e.g., 52–53) may, on occasion, appear on only one of those pages.

Abya Yala 34
Acuña, Jorge 329
adaptations 5–7
Adsuar, M. Dolores 108
Aguirre, Roberto 354*f*
Albani, Tilda 288
Alberdi, Juan Bautista 64–5, 105
Albizu Campos, Pedro 195–6, 205, 233
Alfaiates Revolt (Inconfidência Baiana) 183, 185
Alfieri, Vittorio 56–7, 60, 62
  Antigone 56
  Philip 59
  Polinice 56
Alfonsín, Raúl 268
Allende, Salvador 257
Almeida Prado, Décio de 153, 161–2
Alonso, Laura 74
Alvarado, Daniel 100*f*
Álvarez, Santiago 224
Améfrica Ladina 34
Amigos del Arte 81
Amphictyonic Congress of Panama 208–9
Andrade Jardi, Ricardo, *Los motivos de Antígona* (Antígona's reasons) 365
Andrade, Jorge 150–92
  and Antigone 161–3
  and Brazilian history 153–4, 158–65, 182–3
  on history 152–3
  on Inconfidência Mineira 183
  Labirinto 161
  on Marta (character) 183–4
  politics of citation 156–8
  on theater and history 161
Andrade, Jorge, *As Confrarias* 151, 182–92
  2013 production 189*f*
  body, use of 187–92
  Marta (character) 182–92

politics of citation 156–8
reviews and reactions 156
Andrade, Jorge, *Pedreira das almas* (Soul quarry) 2, 150–1, 165–81
  1958 production 152–5
  1966 production 154–6
  1975 production 174*f*, 175*f*
  1977 production 155–6
  and Brazilian history 152–8
  enslaved people 167–8, 178–81
  father and son symbolism 165–9
  mothers and motherhood 166–7, 169–78
  politics of citation 156–8
  reviews and reactions 152–6, 165–6, 169
  versions 154
Andrade, Oswald de 1, 5, 37
  O Rei da Vela (The Candle King) 158
A'Ness, Francine 311–12, 326, 339–40
Anouilh, Jean, *Medea* 148–9
Anrup, Roland 374
anthropophagy 36–7, *see also* cannibalization, overview
Antígona (periodical; Colombia) 374
Antígonas, overview
  cannibalism and strategic classicism 32–44
  classics and comparative literature 10–19
  colonialism in Latin America 23–32
  common elements 6*f*, 45–6
  map 6*f*
  postcolonial reception studies 19–23
  rumination 44–9
  vernacular corpus 1–10
  vernacular productions, number of, map 6*f*
Antinous (character), significance 278
Antunes Filho, José Alves, *Antígona* 360–1
Apold, Raúl 68, 71

436 INDEX

Apollodorus of Athens, *Library* 56–7
Arantes, Luis Humberto Martins 158–9
Araxá, Brazil 171
Argentina
  Association of Relatives of the
    Disappeared 293
  Catamarca province 355
  caudillo wars 83–4, 238–9
  Cerro de la Gloria 79
  civic-military pact 299–300
  Conquest of the Desert 64–5, 69, 75, 85–7
  Constitution 64–5, 77
  disappearance and the disappeared 77,
    272–4, 295, 301–2
  Due Obedience law 296
  European immigration 86
  Fratacho (theater group) 310–11
  Full Stop Law 296
  H.I.J.O.S. (Sons and Daughters for Identity
    and Justice Against Oblivion and
    Silence) 289–90
  human rights movement 289–90
  impunity laws 268, 296, 304, 311
  independence 57–8, 82–3, 238–9
  Indian wars 84–5, 92–3, 101
  justice debates after dictatorship 268–9,
    279–80, 282, 296–8, 303–6, 311
  Malvinas Islands 199, 222, 228
  May Revolution 1810 55, 82–3
  national anthem 54n.2, 71
  national literature 55–7, 106
  National Truth Commission report
    (*Nunca Más*/Never Again) 268
  pact of independence 1816 238–9
  Pact of Miraflores 84–5, 92
  Pampas 68–9, 71–2, 79
  presidential pardons 289–90
  Process of National Reorganization
    266–7, 272–3
  revolutionary poets of 1810 55
  Romantics of 1837 55
  Teatro Repertorio del Norte,
    La Plata 354*f*
  Trials of the Generals 1985 268
  Tribunal Against Impunity 267
  Truth Commission 1984 295
  Tucumán 82–3, 238–9
  see also Buenos Aires, Argentina; Mothers
    and Grandmothers of the Plaza de
    Mayo (the Mothers)

Argentine Society of Authors 106–7
Arguedas, José María 330
Ariosto, Ludovico 278–9
Aristotle 186
Ariza, Patricia
  Antígona 374–6
  Antigonías 375–6
Armed Forces of National Liberation of
  Puerto Rico (FALN) 208
Arraial de Santa Rita do Turvo, Revolt of,
  1831 180
Artaud, Antonin 276
Arts, Les (periodical; France) 146–7
Ascarsa, Arquímedes 340
Ashcroft, Bill 21
Asociación de Familiares y Desaparecidos de
  Ayacucho (Association of Relatives and
  Disappeared Persons of Ayacucho;
  Peru) 340
Association of Mothers of Soacha
  (Colombia) 377
Association of Relatives of the Disappeared
  (Argentina) 293
Astiz, Alfredo 291–2
Ateneo de la Juventud (civil association,
  Mexico) 32
audience knowledge 5–7, 40–1, 153–4, 313
Aurore, L' (periodical; Paris) 146–7
Aux Écoutes (periodical; Paris) 147, 147*f*
Avellaneda, Marco 238–9
Ayacucho, Peru 319
  battle of 57–8
Aymara peoples 33–4

"back alive" *(aparición con vida)* slogan
  (Argentina) 269, 283, 298, 305–6
Balaguer, Joaquín 197–8
Balibar, Étienne 42
Ballent, Anahí 106
Ballestrino, Esther 292
Bandurrias theater company
  (Chile) 384–9, 385*f*
Barradas, Efraín 200–1
Barrault, Jean-Louis 128
Batista, Fulgencio 197–8
Baudy, Robert 115
Beauvoir, Simone de 95–6
Bela Cruz massacre, Brazil 165, 178–81
Belaval, Emilio 207–8
Belém do Pará Convention 363–4

INDEX 437

Bellegarde, Dantès 117
Beltrán Valencia, Gina 200–2
Beneficent Society (organization;
Argentina) 59, 65
Benjamin, Walter 41–2
Ben-Ur, Lorraine 200–2
Berenguer Carisomo, Arturo 63–4
Bernal, Luz Marina 377
Betances, Ramón Emeterio 205, 233
Biassou (leader in slave revolt) 125–6
Biglieri, Aníbal 73–4, 87, 104–5
biodrama 358
Blanco, Hugo 317–18
blandengues (militias) 87–8
Boal, Augusto 158–9, 313, 335, 348–9
body, the, uses of 187–92
Bogotá, Colombia
Casa Ensamble 381*f*, 383*f*
Magdalena Project 375–6
Teatro Seki Sano 380*f*, 382*f*
Bois-Caïman Ceremony, Haiti 115,
125–6, 136–8
Bolívar, Simón 8–9, 204, 208–9, 233
Bolivia 33–4, 197, 200n.14, 225, 260n.29
Bondye (Vodou god) 126
Borges, Jorge Luis 17, 38–9
Bosch, Juan 197–8, 225–6
Bosch, María del Carmen 95–6
Bosher, Kathryn 20–1
Bossale people (Haiti) 118–19, 121
Brazil
AI-5 (Ato Institucional/ Institutional
Act) 185
Alfaiates Revolt (Inconfidência
Baiana) 183, 185
Araxá 171
Bela Cruz massacre 165, 178–81
Caramurus revolt 180
Doctrine of National Security 185
economic cycles 160–1, 163–4
Inconfidência Mineira (Minas Gerais
Conspiracy) 1789 151, 164, 182–4
Liberal Revolt 1842 150–1, 164–5, 171
Minas Gerais region 160, 163–4, 171, 180
neocolonialism 30–1
politics of personal relations 162–3, 173–4
and Portuguese empire 25–6
Revolta do Ano da Fumaça 1833 180
Revolt of Arraial de Santa Rita do Turvo
1831 180

Revolt of Vila Rica 1720 164
São Paulo 160, 169
São Tomé das Letras 167–8
sertão region 158–9
slavery 160–1, 178–81
slave trafficking, law against 1831 179
Teatro Alfredo Mesquita, São Paulo 169
Teatro Barreto Júnior, Recife 189*f*
Vila Rica 182–3
Brecht, Bertolt 159–60, 262–3, 313
Brechtian techniques 206, 211–12, 216–19,
241–2, 385–6
Briceño, Ximena 311–12, 316–17, 325–6,
335, 346–7
British Columbia, University of 379*f*
Brunn, Victoria 201–2, 234, 287–8,
311–12, 326
Buarque de Holanda, Sérgio 161–3,
173–4, 186
Buenos Aires, Argentina
as an Athens 57–60
Delborde Espacio Teatral 361*f*
Goethe Institute 262, 263*f*
Instituto Di Tella 269–70
Malón de la Paz (Raid of Peace) 85–6
Plaza de Mayo 82–3, 107–8, 263–4, 293
Saavedra 79–80
Teatro Celcit 310–11
Teatro Cervantes 69*f*, 71, 97*f*, 100*f*
Teatro de Buenos Aires 240*f*, 241*f*
Teatro El Gorro Escarlata (T.E.G.E.) 246*f*
University 58, 106–7
Burda (magazine) 214–15
burial rites
Andean 332, 341–5
Colombian 376–7
Vodou 112–13, 134, 139, 142
burials and the unburied
Andrade's *As Confrarias* 152
Andrade's *Pedreira das almas* (Soul
quarry) 152, 155, 169
Brazil 180, 183
enslaved people 180
European notions 9–10
impossible burials 250–60
Marechal's *Antígona Vélez* 70, 77, 93–4
rumination on 46
Sánchez's *Antígona Pérez* 206, 222
Varela's *Argia* 57, 61
Buuck, David 372

438 INDEX

Cabrera, Pablo 198*f*, 209–18, 210*f*, 212*f*,
   213*f*, 215*f*, 231*f*
Cadengue, Antonio 189*f*
Caicedo, Andrés 40
CAL (Comando Armado de Liberación;
   Puerto Rico) 228–9, 232–3
Calero, Giselda 362*f*
Calfucurá (Mapuche chief) 85, 90–1
Camarano, Marco 174*f*, 175*f*
Camp, André 108
Campo algodonero, Mexico 369
Camus, Albert 200–1, 235
Canales Torresola, Blanca 203
Candido, Antonio 155, 161–2
Cañizares-Esguerra, Jorge 28–9, 33
cannibalization, overview 5, 36–7, 39–41
Capellari, Uki 361*f*
capitalism 9–10, 16–17, 34, 37–8, 42–4, 48,
   183, 192, 226, 252–5, 294, 364
Cápona Pérez, Daniela 356–7
Caracas, Universidad Central 226
Caribbean Creole literatures 116
Carlotto, Estela de 292–3
Carlson, Marla 268, 277
Carneiro de Mendonça, Josefa 171
Carpentier, Alejo 8–9, 148–9
Carrera, José Miguel 84–5
Casa Ensamble, Bogotá 381*f*, 383*f*
Casanova, Pablo 30
Casanova, Pascale 13
Castaño, César, *Antígona incorpórea* 375–6
Castiñeira de Dios, José María 108
Castro, Fidel 197–8
Catamarca province, Argentina 355
Cathedral Church of St. John the Divine,
   New York 215–16
Cathelin, Jean 146
caudillo wars, Argentina 83–4, 238–9
Cayara district, Peru 319–20
censorship 156, 185, 269–70
center/periphery binary 13–15
Centro Sperimentale di Roma 209
Cerro de la Gloria (Argentina) 79
Cerro de Pasco miners' strike, Peru 329–30
Césaire, Aimé 123
Chávez, Fermín 107–8
Chevalier, Michel 34
Chile 230–1, 257
   Bandurrias theater company 384, 385*f*
Christian Democracy 225, 230–1

Christian/indigenous hybridization 101–5
Christianity
   indigenous people and 27–8
   Marechal and 78
   Marechal's *Antígona Vélez* 74–6, 93
   and occidentalism 24–5
   Sánchez's *Antígona Pérez* 202
   Social Doctrine of the Church 230–2
   as universal language 201–2, 207
   see also Roman Catholic Church
Christophe, Henri 119–20, 123, 143
Chronicles of the Indies 221
citation, strategy/politics of 156–8, 187, 192,
   293–5, 297
Ciudad Bolívar, Colombia 377
Ciudad Juárez, Mexico 366
civilization/barbarism binary
   Marechal's *Antígona Vélez* 70, 72–5,
   87–93
   overview 31
   Sarmiento's *Facundo* 58, 73–4, 84, 89–90
   Zavalía's *El límite* (The limit) 238–9
Claridad (periodical; Puerto Rico) 216,
   225–6
Clarín (periodical; Argentina) 270–1, 290
Clark, Fred M. 169
Coicou, Massillon, *L'Empereur Dessalines*
   (Emperor Dessalines) 144
Colchado, Óscar 340
Colio, Bárbara, *Usted está aquí* (You are
   here) 371–2
Coliqueo, Ignacio 91, 107–8
collectives, *see* female bonding and
   collectives
Colombia
   1782 rebellion 246–7
   1957 uprising 197–8
   Ciudad Bolívar 377
   Corporación Colombiana de
   Teatro 375–6, 378*f*
   independence wars 245–6
   massacres 383–4
   Medellín 376–7
   national anthem 54n.1
   Soacha 377
   Unión Patriótica (UP), political
   party 377, 381
   Urabá 376
   Urrao 376–7
   see also Bogotá, Colombia

INDEX 439

Colombian Antígonas 374–84
colonialism
  coloniality of power 25, 30
  critiques 29–32
  internal 30
  in Latin America 23–32
  and property 222–4
Colón, Miriam 215–16
Comando Armado de Liberación (CAL;
    Puerto Rico) 228–9, 232–3
comedic Antígonas 242–3, 360–1
Compañía Teatro Seraphim (Brazil) 189*f*
comparative literature and Latin
    America 10–19
Conferación Campesina del Perú (Peasant
    Confederation of Peru) 317–18
Congo 119, 120, 121, 126, 138
Conquest of the Desert, Argentina 69,
    75, 85–7
Cornejo Polar, Antonio 36–8
Corominas, Joan 195
Coronil, Fernando 21n.38, 23–4
Corporación Colombiana de
    Teatro 375–6, 378*f*
corpses
  "adopted" 374–5
  of children 46–8, 244, 388
  disappeared/missing 237, 250–60,
    372, 381
  dressed as *guerrilleros*, Colombia 377
  as exchanged gifts 244
  female 252, 366, 369
  and necro-neocolonial politics 46–8
  ownership of 169, 206, 218, 226–7, 258–9
  unclaimed, Peru 318
  unrecognizable/unidentified 3, 237,
    256–9
corpses, exposed
  Andrade's *As Confrarias* 152, 156–8,
    185–8, 191
  Andrade's *Pedreira das almas* (Soul
    quarry) 152, 155, 169
  Guevara, Ernesto 197
  Sánchez's *Antígona Pérez* 217
  Steiner's *Antígona en el infierno* (Antígona
    in hell) 251–2
Correa, Ana 340
corrido (musical genre) 10–11
Cortés, Edwin 220
Cortés, Hernán 365–6

Cortiñas, Nora 289–90
Cosentino, Olga 358
costume
  Andean peasant communities and 329–30
  Andrade's *Pedreira das almas* (Soul
    quarry) 154
  Marechal's *Antígona Vélez* 71–2
  masks and "white-face" 339–45, 343*f*, 344*f*
  Orizondo's *Antigonón* 362, 362*f*
  Sánchez's *Antígona Pérez* 195–6, 212–15
  Satizábal's *Tribunal de Mujeres* (A women's
    tribunal) 378–80
  Ynclán's *Podrías llamarte Antígona* (Your
    name could be Antígona) 371–2
  Yuyachkani's and Watanabe's
    Antígona 311–12
Coumbite (periodical; Haiti) 116
countryside, plays performed in, *see* rural
    performances
Creon (character), significance 45–6, 48,
    143, 162–3, 272
Cruz, Zuckie 212–13
Cuba 148–9, 197–8, 225, 362*f*, 363
Cubillán, Augusto, *Antígona factotum* 375–6
Cureses, David, *La cabeza en la jaula* (The
    head in the cage) 4, 244–8, 246*f*
Curtius, Ernst R. 116

Daneri, Antonio A. 331
Darío, Rubén 278–9, 281, 305
Daumec, Lucien 118
Dauster, Frank 218
D'Aversa, Alberto 155
De Cecco, Sergio 40–1
Défilée-La-Folle 143–4, 363
de Gaulle, Charles 197
Degregori, Carlos Iván 319
de la Rosa, Perla, *Antígona, las voces que
    incendian el desierto* (the voices that set
    the desert on fire) 76, 366–71, 368*f*,
    370*f*, 371*f*
Delborde Espacio Teatral, Buenos
    Aires 361*f*
del Pino, Ponciano 340
Democracia (newspaper; Argentina) 71–3
Deren, Maya 126
Derrida, Jacques 290
Descamisados (the shirtless) 225
Dessalines, Jean-Jacques 109, 119–20, 122,
    132–3, 136–7, 143–4

440 INDEX

Diário da noite (periodical; Brazil) 155–6
Díaz, Alba Nidia 216
Díaz, Carlos 362, 362*f*
Díaz Quiñones, Arcadio 195–6
dictatorship, generalization of 199–200
disappearance and the disappeared 3
   Argentina 76–7, 272–4, 301–2
   and capitalism 254
   captive women of Pampas 104–5
   Cold War in South America 250–1
   Colombia 374–7, 379*f*, 380*f*, 381*f*
   disappeared corpses 250–60
   human rights activists 287, 292, 298,
     318, 364
   indigenous people 67, 76, 275–6, 287,
     292, 298, 318
   Marechal and 77
   Mexico 366, 371–2
   Peru 308, 314, 340
   return of 77, 251–2, 254, 256, 306
   Videla on 290
   writers 271
   see also Mothers and Grandmothers of the
     Plaza de Mayo (the Mothers)
Discépolo, Armando 270–1
Distéfano, Juan Carlos 262–3
djab (Vodou spirits) 138
Doctrine of National Security 185
documentary aspect of 21st-c.
   Antígonas 358–60, 364
Domínguez, Franklin, *Antígona*
   Humor 242–3, 360–1
Domínguez Vargas, Jesús Eduardo,
   Río arriba, río abajo (Up the river,
   down the river) 376–7
Dominican Republic 197–8, 202–3, 225–6
   Santo Domingo 28–9, 221–2
Dominique, Max 140–1, 245
Dorfman, Ariel, *Widows* 255–60
Dove, Patrick 277
Driollet, Mónica 361*f*
Drummond de Andrade, Carlos, "Os bens
   e o sangue" ("The goods and the
   blood") 192
Duarte, Juan 71
Dutty, Boukman 125–6
Duvalier, François 131, 142

Echevarría, Juan Manuel 374–5
Echeverría, Esteban 30
   "La Cautiva" (The captive) 104–5

Ecuador 355–6
Efron, Edith 117
Eigsti, Karl 215–16
Ejército de Liberación Nacional
   (National Liberation Army;
   Peru) 317–18
Electra (character), significance 40–1
Eliade, Mircea 73–4
Errandonea, Ignacio 331–2
Estado de S. Paulo, O (periodical;
   Brazil) 165–6, 183–4
Estimé, Dumarsais 114–15
Etchecolatz, Miguel 311
Eurocentrism 16–17
European immigration to Argentina 86
existential readings 200–1
exposed corpses
   Andrade's *As Confrarias* 152, 157,
     185–8, 191
   Andrade's *Pedreira das almas* (Soul
     quarry) 152, 155, 169
   Guevara, Ernesto 197
   Sánchez's *Antígona Pérez* 217

FALN (Armed Forces of National Liberation
   of Puerto Rico) 208
Fanon, Frantz 38–9, 131
fathers 48, 105, 165–9
Fatiman, Cecile 125–6
Fava, Enrique 240*f*, 241*f*
Feitlowitz, Marguerite 271
female bonding and collectives 4
   Andrade's *As Confrarias* 191–2
   Andrade's *Pedreira das almas* (Soul
     quarry) 177–8
   Cureses's *La cabeza en la jaula*
     (The head in the cage) 244–5,
     357–8
   de la Rosa's *Antígona, las voces que
     incendian el desierto* (the voices
     that set the desert on fire) 369
   Dorfman's *Widows* 260
   and gender violence 363–4
   Huertas's *AntígonaS* 355
   instances of, map 6*f*
   lesser-known 20th-c. plays 237–49
   Orizondo's *Antigonón* 363
   overview 46, 220
   Rengifo's *La fiesta de los moribundos*
     (The party of the living dead)
     254–5

INDEX 441

Satizábal's *Tribunal de Mujeres* (A women's tribunal) 378*f*, 379
Varela's *Argia* 62, 66
Yuyachkani's and Watanabe's *Antígona* 322, 351
feminicidio, term 366, 369
feminism in twenty-first century 286–90, 363–4
feminization of poverty 364
Fermani, Daniel, "Trans Antígona Sexual" 353
Fernández, Ani 216–17
Fernández, Piri 212–13
Fernández Unsain, José María 68
Ferré, Luis 199
Fick, Carolyn 121
Fiet, Lowell 209
Figaro, Le (periodical; France) 146–7
Flores Aráoz, Antero 323–4
flowers, symbolism 265–6, 298–9
Focade, Dayse 362*f*
Foley, Helene 20–1
Folha de São Paulo (periodical; Brazil) 154–6
Ford, Katherine 222
Forsyth, Alison 277, 288
Fouché, Frank 112–13, 128–9
fragments of antiquity 5, 40–1, 107, 277–85, 385–6
France 119–20, 122
  French language 110–11, 117–18, 144–5
  French literature 55, 58
France Soir (periodical; France) 146–7
Francia, José Gaspar Rodríguez de 27–8
Franco, Jean 365–6
Fratacho (theater group; Argentina) 310–11
Freyre, Gilberto 161–2
frontiers
  frontier mothers 70, 93–101, 105
  and hybridization 101–5
FSLN (Sandinista National Liberation Front, Nicaragua) 251–2
Fuentes Mares, José, *Young Antígona* 241–2
Fujimori, Alberto 317
funeral rites, *see* burial rites

Galán, José Antonio 245–6
Galeano, Eduardo 204–5
Galván, Cándido 90–1
Galván lakes, Argentina 90–1

Gambaro, Griselda 269–71
  on Argentine history 265
  on facts 270–1
  Ganarse la muerte (To earn one's own death) 269–70
  on justice 271
  on Mothers of the Plaza de Mayo 261, 285
  on the political 269–70
  on Sophocles' *Antigone* 277
Gambaro, Griselda, *Antígona Furiosa* 261–306, 263*f*
  2011 production 361*f*
  comparisons with Sophocles' *Antigone* 272–7
  distance and fragmentation 277–85
  and *Hamlet* 298–303
  historical context 262–9
  Mothers and Grandmothers of the Plaza de Mayo 285–96
  Mothers and Grandmothers of the Plaza de Mayo, schism 296–8
  pardons 303–6
  productions 264n.9
  reviews and reactions 262–4, 264*f*
Gamel, Mary Kay 20–1
gamonalismo (land ownership system; Peru) 317–18
Garcés, Delia 240*f*, 241*f*
García Canclini, Nestor 37–8
García de García, Fortunata 238–9
García, Julio 214*f*
García Lorca, Federico 112, 208
García Márquez, Gabriel 13n.23, 17, 256n.25
Garrett, João Baptista da Silva Leitão de Almeida 190–1
Gatell, Enrique 71
gauchos 67–8, 80, 86–7
Gazeta, A (periodical; Brazil) 169
Gazeta Esportiva (periodical; Brazil) 155–6
gender divisions
  Andrade's *Pedreira das almas* (Soul quarry) 166, 168–9
  global politics 363–4
  Harmony's *La ley de Creón* (Creón's law) 249
  indigenous communities 321–2
  Marechal's *Antígona Vélez* 95, 98, 104
  Sánchez's *Antígona Pérez* 196

442 INDEX

gender divisions (*cont.*)
  twenty-first century Antígonas 353
  Yuyachkani's and Watanabe's
    Antígona 321–2, 326
gender violence
  Cureses's *La cabeza en la jaula* (The head
    in the cage) 247, 357–8
  Helfgott's *Antígonas* 248
  Huertas's *AntígonaS* 355
  Mexico 366, 369
  overview 26–7, 363–5
  Sanchez's *Antígona Pérez* 357–8
  Satizábal's *Tribunal de Mujeres* (A women's
    tribunal) 381–2, 382*f*, 383*f*
  Steiner's *Antígona en el infierno* (Antígona
    in hell) 251–2
Gené, Juan Carlos, *Golpes a mi puerta*
  (Knocks at my door) 242
Gente (magazine; Argentina) 294
Giampani, Adrián, *Antígona en sintonía*
  (Antígona in tune) 360–1
Gilbert, Helen 21
Ginés de Sepúlveda, Juan 29
Godoy, Genaro 357
Goethe Institute, Buenos Aires 262, 263*f*
Goff, Barbara 22–3
Gold, Herbert 118
Goldhill, Simon 15, 32–3, 47–8, 243–4
Golea, Antoine 147–8
Gómez, Diana 372, 374
Gómez, Francisco 363
González, Antígona (real life
  individual) 372–3
González Barja, José 225–6
González Delgado, Ramiro 31
González Lelia 34
González, Olga 336
Gorini, Ulises 296
Grandi, Yamila, *Una mujer llamada Antígona*
  (A woman named Antígona) 360
Greece, nineteenth-century 59n.16
Greek language and culture, teaching of, in
  nineteenth century 31
Greek mythology as universal
  language 200–1, 207
Greenwood, Emily 21–2
gringos (Argentina) 82, 86–7
grotesco criollo (theater form;
  Argentina) 270–1
grotesque genre 252, 360–1
Guadas, Colombia 246

Guánica, Puerto Rico 231–2
Guaraní, Antígona 356
Guaraní people 1, 37, 155
Guevara, Ernesto "Che" 196–7, 220, 234–5
Gutiérrez, Juan María 55–6, 58–60, 65
Gutiérrez, Soraya 382–3, 383*f*
Guzmán, Abimael 317

Haiti
  1804 declaration of independence 115
  Bois-Caïman 115, 125–6, 136–8
  and center/periphery binary 13–14
  College of Agriculture, Damiens,
    Port-au -Prince 110–11
  founding myths 131
  Haitian literature 118
  Institute of Creole Language 118
  and Latin America 8–9
  national anthem 120
  national literature 110–12, 114
  National Society for Dramatic Arts 116
  revolution 33–4, 118–25, 134–6, 142–4
  rural chiefs (chefs de section) 131, 134
  Theater Rex, Port-au-Prince 110–11,
    129n.55
  Théatre d'Haiti, Morne Hercule 129
  US occupation 114–16
  Vodou concept of time 123–4
  see also Vodou
Haitian Creole language
  French reaction to 111, 146–7
  Morisseau-Leroy on 116–17
  national literature in 110–13, 116–18,
    144–5
Haiti-Journal (periodical) 144–5
Hall, Edith 15
Hardwick, Lorna 19–20
Harmony, Olga, *La ley de Creón* (Creón's
  law) 3–4, 248–9
Hegel, Georg Wilhelm Friedrich 47–8, 70,
  75, 88–9, 162–3, 286, 290
Helfgott, Sarina 248–50, 255, 315–16
Hernández, José, *Martín Fierro* 91n.66
Hernández, Linnett 362*f*
Herzog, Vladimir 155–6
Hidalgo de Cisneros, Baltasar 82–3
H.I.J.O.S. (Sons and Daughters for Identity
  and Justice Against Oblivion and
  Silence; Argentina) 289–90
História da Companhia de Jesus (History of
  the Society of Jesus) 182–3

INDEX 443

history vs allegory in Sanchez's *Antígona Perez* 194–204
Hoffman, Léon François 111, 115, 117, 254
Homer, *Odyssey* 278
Huacón mask (Peru) 339–41, 344–5
Huamanga, Peru 309, 319, 336
Huancavelica, Peru 319–20, 329–30
Huanta, Peru 309, 327–8, 337–8, 340
Huertas, Jorge, *AntígonaS: linaje de hembras* (AntígonaS: female lineage) 4, 353–5, 354*f*
human rights movement, Argentina 289–90, *see also* Mothers and Grandmothers of the Plaza de Mayo (the Mothers)
Hurtado, Alberto 230–1
hybridization 37–8, 101–5, 202

Ianni, Carlos 310–11
Imbert, Julio 40–1
impossible universal, *see* utopian/impossible universal
Inca empire 31, 120, 316, 340
independence from Europe 25–6, 76–7
coloniality of power 9–10, 25, 30, 32
Indians, derogatory term 67–8
Indian wars, Argentina 84–5, 92–3, 101
indigenous peoples
civilization/barbarism binary 24–5
hybridization 101–5
as land 104
reparations 85–6
Valladolid Controversy 29
see also Peru, Andean peasant communities
indigenous peoples, violence against
alternatives to 92
Argentina 64–5, 69, 84–5, 88–9, 92–3, 101, 267
Chile and Uruguay 30 n65
Marechal's *Adán Buenosayres* 79–80
Marechal's *Antígona Vélez* 75–6, 101
Morgado's *Antígona Insomne* 386–7
overview 46
rape as colonial weapon 26–7
Instituto Di Tella, Buenos Aires 269–70
Inter-American Courts of Human Rights 369
internal colonialism 9–10, 30
International Club of Commerce 127
International Congress of the Spanish Language (CILE) 208, 224
Internet Archive of Performances of Greek and Roman Drama 21–2

Irigaray, Luce 290
Isella, César 204–5
Ismena/Ismene (character), significance
20th-c. plays 314–15
21st-c. plays 359, 387
European plays 45–6
Gambaro's *Antígona Furiosa* 272, 306
Yuyachkani's and Watanabe's *Antígona* 313–16, 333, 335
Italian immigrants to Argentina 33–4, 86

Jabif, Nora Lía 262
Jamaica, National Theater Festival 149
James, C. L. R. 122
Jara, René 324
Jáuregui, Carlos 36–7
Jeannot (leader in Haitian slave revolt) 125–6
John, Gospel of 168
John XXIII, Pope 201–2
Jornal da Tarde (periodical; Brazil) 155–6
Journal of Classical Receptions (periodical) 20–1
Jovino, Ana 310–11
Joyería Riviera, San Juan 214–15
Julien, A. M. 137*f*
July 26 Movement, Cuba 225
Junín, battle of 57–8
Junqueira family (Brazil) 160, 165, 167, 179
Junqueira, Gabriel Francisco 180
justice debates, Argentina (after dictatorship) 268–9, 279–80, 282, 296–8, 303–6

Kanzo (Vodou term) 123–4
Katari, Túpac 304–5
Kemp, Robert 111
Kennedy, John F. 197, 199
Kierkegaard, Søren 278–9, 282–4, 328
King, Martin Luther 197
Krajewska-Wieczorek, Anna 272
Kristal, Efraín 14
Kuehne, Alyce de 200

Laferrière, Dany 133, 144
Lafforgue, Jorge 78
La Habana
Teatro El Público 362*f*
Tri-Continental Conference 204–5, 234–5
Laird, Andrew 20, 23–4
La Malinche/Malintzin 365–6

444 INDEX

Lane, Jill 321–3
Lang, George 116
Lanuza, Cacilda 169
La Plata, Teatro Repertorio del Norte 354*f*
La Postrera (hacienda) 68–9
Lares Revolt, Puerto Rico 205, 228–9, 231–3
Laroche, Maximilien 120, 123–4, 131, 139
las Casas, Bartolomé de 29
Latin America, continental union
 (1960s) 204–5
Latin American and Caribbean Congress for
 Puerto Rico's Independence 208–9
Latin language, teaching of 31
Lawyers' Collective José Alvear Restrepo
 (Colombia) 377
Leconte de Lisle 113
Lendón Acosta, Celia 362*f*
Lerminier, Georges 146–7
Lerner Febres, Salomón 318–21
lettered cities 28–9, 31
Lettres Françaises (periodical; France) 146–7
Lettres Nouvelles, Les (periodical;
 France) 148
liberation theology 201–2, 230–1, 242
Lima
 and Andean peasant communities 308,
  318–21, 327, 333, 344–5, 349–50
 armed conflict 314, 317, 327–9, 333, 338
 Casa Yuyachkani 308
 discourse of guilt 337–8
 Japanese embassy 314
 Plaza San Martín 329
Linares, Joaquín 72–3
local conditions of cultural
 production 15–16
local differences in theater
 productions 14–15, 310–12, 325
locality and universality 42–4
Londoño, José Félix, *El insepulto, o yo veré
 qué hago con mis muertos* (The
 unburied, or I will see what I do with
 my dead) 376–7
López, Aurora 41–2
López Naguil, Gregorio 71–2
López Rivera, Óscar 208
Loraux, Nicole 243–49
Los Toldos 91, 105–8
love, socialization of 247, 251
Luca, Esteban de 59
Lupher, David A. 31

Luque Bedregal, Gino
 gender roles 321
 Ismene 313–14, 326
 memory and forgetting 322–3
 Peru's two audiences 316–17,
  327–8, 337–8
 shame 345
lwas (Vodou spirits) 125–9

Maceo, Antonio 363
Machado de Assis 17
Magaldi, Sábato 155–6
Magdalena Project, Bogotá 375–6
Magloire, Paul 114–15
Maingot, Anthony 131
Makandal (sorcerer; Haiti) 125, 136–7,
 140–1, 143
malambos (dances; Argentina) 71–2
Malón de la Paz (Raid of Peace;
 Argentina) 85–6
Malón del Salto (Argentina) 84–5
malón, term 68–9
Malvinas Islands 199, 222, 228
mambisas (guerrilla volunteers; Cuba) 363
Manguel, Alberto 31
map of vernacular corpus 6*f*
Mapou, Jan 135*f*, 136*f*
Mapuche nations 33–4, 85
Marchant, Patricio 46–7
Marechal, Leopoldo
 Adán Buenosayres 79–81, 105
 Austral Epitaphs 81
 background and beliefs 78
 Huertas and 354–5
 "El poeta depuesto" 86
 poetry 79
Marechal, Leopoldo, *Antígona Vélez* 67–108
 1951 production, Buenos Aires 69*f*, 84–5,
  97*f*, 100*f*
 1962 production, Paris 99*f*
 caudillo and Indian wars 82–7
 choral version 360
 civilization/barbarism binary 87–93
 colonial hybridization 101–5
 as foundational myth 2–3, 7–8, 68–77
 frontier motherhood 93–101
 lyricism 81–2
 names, use of 89–92
 Peronism 105–8
Maroon societies (Haiti) 125, 136–7

INDEX 445

Marrero, José Luis 231*f*
Martí, José 1, 5–7, 30, 35, 107, 363
Martindale, Charles 19–20
Martínez de Olcoz, Nieves 277
Martínez Estrada, Ezequiel 90
Martín Fierro (Hernández) 91n.66
Martinique 133, 242n.6
Marxism, Haiti 114–15
Marx, Karl 307
  Communist Manifesto 124–5
Mary, Virgin 27–8, 46–7, 64
masculinity 81, 95, 98, 105, 165–9
masks (Peru) 339–45, 343*f*, 344*f*
Maturo, Graciela 73
Mayagüez, Puerto Rico 216
Maza, Lucía de la 359
Medellín, Colombia 376–7
Mee, Erin 20–1
memory and forgetting in Yuyachkani's
  Antígona 322–7, 333, 335, 350–1
Mendonça, Paulo 154
Mendoza, Angélica 340
Mendoza, Juan 319
Mennesson-Rigaud, Odette 115
Menos días aquí (Fewer days here; online
  project; Mexico) 372–3
Mercier, Louis 120, 133
Meroño, Mercedes de 297–8
mestizaje 27–8, 36–8, 196n.7, 270–1
Mexican Antígonas 365–74
Mexico
  1910 Revolution 248–9
  Campo algodonero 369
  Ciudad Juárez 366
  drug cartels 366
  mestizaje 27–8
  Pasta de Conchos coal mine 371–2
  Samalayuca 368*f*, 371*f*
  Tamaulipas 3, 372–3
  Teatro de la Nación, Ciudad Juárez 370*f*
  Telón de Arena AC theater company 370*f*
Miami 149
  Miami Dade Auditorium 129n.55,
    135*f*, 136*f*
  Sosyete Koukouy of Miami, Inc
    135*f*, 136*f*
Minas Gerais region, Brazil 160, 163–4,
  171, 180
Minas Gerais, Teatro em São João
  del-Rei 174*f*, 175*f*

Miola, Robert 45–6
Mirabal sisters 202–3
Miraflores, Pact of (Argentina, nineteenth
  century) 84–5, 92
Mitre, Bartolomé 90–1
Mixteco, language 375
Mogliani, Laura 106–7, 277
Monde, Le (newspaper; France) 111
Montaner, Ana, *El thriller de Antígona y
  Hnos. S.A.* (The thriller of Antígona
  and Brothers S.A.) 360–1
Monterroso, Augusto 278–9, 284
moon imagery 96
Morales, Ernesto 63–4
Morejón Flores, Guillermo 232–3
Morelle, Paul 148
Morena, Marianella and Volker Lösch,
  Antígona Oriental 358–9
Morfi, Angelina 200
Morgado, Rubén, *Antígona
  Insomne* 384–9, 385*f*
Morillo, General 247
Morisseau-Leroy, Félix
  as actor 136, 137*f*
  "Antigone" 141
  on *Antigone* 112, 141
  death 149
  "Defense for a Creole Theater" 118
  "God is good" 133
  on the gods 139–40
  on Haitian Creole 116–17
  and Marxism 116
  "Mèsi Papa Desalin" ("Thank you Papa
    Dessalines") 109, 132
  on peasant audience 146
  political theater 125–9
  "Sa m di nan sa, Depestre" 133
  Théatre d'Haiti 129
  and US occupation 115–16
  "Why Do They Write in Creole?" 118
Morisseau-Leroy, Félix, *Antigòn an Kreyòl*
  (Antigone in Creole) 109–49
  1953 Port-au-Prince production 110,
    129n.55, 136
  1959 Paris production 110–11, 129n.55,
    130, 136, 137*f*, 146–8
  1976 New York production 129n.55
  1998 Miami production 129n.55, 131,
    135*f*, 136*f*, 139n.70
  Creole language 116–18

446 INDEX

Morisseau-Leroy, Félix, *Antigòn an Kreyòl* (Antigone in Creole) (*cont.*)
  gods, use of 140
  overview 2–3, 8–9, 13–14
  prologue and overture scenes 130–3
  reviews and reactions 111–12, 144–9
  and revolution 118–25, 142–4
  rural productions 110–11, 146
  and US occupation 114–16
  Vodou and political theater 125–42
  Vodou ceremony scene 133–42
mothers
  Andrade's *As Confrarias* 182–8
  Andrade's *Pedreira das almas* (Soul quarry) 166–7, 169–78
  Argentine military and 294–5
  bonding between 248–9
  feminism and 286–90
  frontier mothers 70, 93–101, 105
  Harmony's *La ley de Creón* (Creón's law) 248–9
  instances of, map 6*f*
  of killers 369, 370*f*
  Olga Harmony's *La ley de Creón* (Creón's law) 248–9
  Marechal's *Antígona Vélez* 70, 93–101, 105
  motherly bodies 188–9
  Mothers of La Candelaria (Colombia) 376–7
  Mothers of Soacha (Colombia) 377
  overview 6*f*, 46–7, 57, 388
  patriarchal ideology of motherhood 64–5, 235–6
  political mothers 173–8, 185, 235–6, 351
  republican mothers 60–5, 237–43, 247
  Sánchez's *Antígona Pérez* 235–6
  socialization of motherhood 247, 251, 388
  and unnamed corpses in Dorfman's *Widows* 258–9
  Varela's *Argia* 60–3
  wealthy 369
  see also Mothers and Grandmothers of the Plaza de Mayo (the Mothers)
Mothers and Grandmothers of the Plaza de Mayo (the Mothers)
  Asociación de Madres (Mothers' Association) 296–7, 306
  "back alive" slogan 269, 283, 298, 305
  disappearances of 291–2
  feminism and 286–90
  Gambaro on 261

justice debates after dictatorship 268–9
Línea Fundadora (Founding Line) 296–7, 306
and the military 291–6
schism (1986, Argentina) 268, 283, 296–8, 306
theater criticism and 285–91
Mothers of La Candelaria (Colombia) 376–7
motley societies 26n.53, 37–8
Movement for Independence (MPI; Puerto Rico) 228
Movimiento de Izquierda Revolucionario (Revolutionary Left Movement; Peru) 317–18
Movimiento Revolucionario 14 de Junio (Puerto Rico) 202–3
MRTA (Movimiento Revolucionario Túpac Amaru/Túpac Amaru Revolutionary Movement; Peru) 309, 314
Muguercia, Magaly 311
multiplication of Antígona character 357–8, 360, 366–71, 373, 376
Muñoz, Alberto, *Antígona* 358
Muraña, Bettina 262, 265
"museum" of memory, Peru 323–4

Nación, La (newspaper; Argentina) 70, 294
names, use of
  Argentina 89–92
  Puerto Rico 202–3
national anthems 54nn.1–4, 56, 71, 120
national/foreign binary, Argentina 106
nationalism, Puerto Rico 228–33
National, Le (periodical; Haiti) 144–5, 145*f*
National Liberation Army (Ejército de Liberación Nacional; Peru) 317–18
national literature 55–7, 106, 110–11
national myths, argentina 68–81
Nazism 254
necro-neocolonial politics, overview 1–2, 46, 48–9, 76, 244, 388
negritude movement 36n.77, 115
Nelli, María Florencia 277
neocolonialism
  and filicide 244
  overview 30–1, 45–6, 48, 76–7
  and "world literature" 13–14
neoliberalism 9–10, 364–5
Neruda, Pablo 230

INDEX 447

"never again" *(nunca más)*, phrase 45, 259, 379–80, 387–8
Nunca Más/Never Again report 1984 268
New York
    Cathedral Church of St. John the Divine, New York 215–16
    Sacred Heart Auditorium 129n.55
New York Times (newspaper) 215–16
Nicaragua
    Sandinista National Liberation Front (FSLN) 251–2
    Somoza dynasty 251–2
noirisme, Haiti 114–15
Nora, Pierre 268
Nores, Dominique 148
North American Free Trade Agreement (NAFTA) 366
Nouvelliste, Le (periodical; Haiti) 144–5
Novais, Fernando 25
novels, Brazilian north east 158–9
Nueva canción (New song; music movement) 204–5
Nuevo Día, El (periodical; Puerto Rico) 195–6
nun, Antígona as 242
Nunca Más/Never Again report 1984 268
Núñez, José Gabriel, *Antígona* 239–41

OAS (Organization of American States) 297
Occidentalism 24–6, 44
Ogou (Vodou spirit) 125–6
Ophelia (character), significance 279, 298–303
Optique (periodical; Haiti) 117–18
Organization of American States (OAS) 363–4
Oribe, Manuel (Uruguay) 238–9
Orizondo, Rogelio, *Antigonón* 362–3, 362*f*
Orsini, Francesca 13–14
Ortegsa Daza, Nereo 377
Ortiz, Fernando 36–8

palimpsest texts (Gambaro) 277–85, *see also* fragments and minimal references
Pampas, Argentina 68–9, 71–2, 79
Panama 225
    Amphictyonic Congress 208–9
Panama Proclamation 2006 208–9
Panorama (periodical; Haiti) 118
Papillon, Jean-François 125–6, 136–7

Paraguay 27–8, 54n.3, 355–6
Para Tí (magazine; Argentina) 294
pardos, term (in Andrade's plays) 151, 187
Paris
    Sarah Bernhardt Theatre 99*f*, 137*f*, 146, 240*f*, 241*f*
    Theater of Nations (Théâtre des Nations) 99*f*, 108, 111, 129n.55, 136, 137*f*, 146, 240*f*, 241*f*
Parisien Libéré, Le (periodical; France) 146–7
Paris Journal (periodical; France) 111
parody (Gambaro) 273–5, 277
Parrilla Bonilla, Antulio 231–2
Pasta de Conchos coal mine, Mexico 371–2
Patagonia 33–4
Patriota, Rosangela 183–4
peasant audiences, *see* rural performances
Peasant Confederation of Peru (Conferación Campesina del Perú) 317–18
Pedro I, Emperor of Brazil 160–1
Pedro II, Emperor of Brazil 180
Pellarolo, Silvia 268
Pellettieri, Osvaldo 270
Peña, Hernán 360
Pérez Blanco, Lucrecio 199
Pérez Garay, Idalia 214*f*, 216
Pérez Jiménez, Marcos 197–8
performance studies approaches 286–7, 290–2
péristile (Vodou ceremonial space) 127–9
Perón, Evita 68, 71, 79, 107–8, 293, 354–5
Peronism 70, 73–4, 78, 105–8, 225
    National Assembly of the Women's Peronist Party 71
Peronist Youth 275
Perón, Juan Domingo 70, 79, 85–6, 275
Persino, María Silvina 311–12
personal relations, politics of, Brazil 162–3, 173–4
Peru
    Asociación de Familiares y Desaparecidos de Ayacucho (Association of Relatives and Disappeared Persons of Ayacucho) 340
    Ayacucho 309, 314, 319
    Cayara 319–20
    Cerro de Pasco 329–30
    Conferación Campesina del Perú (Peasant Confederation of Peru) 317–18

448 INDEX

Peru (*cont.*)
Ejército de Liberación Nacional (National Liberation Army) 317–18
Huamanga 319, 336
Huancavelica 319–20, 329–30
Huanta 309, 327–8, 340
languages 308–9
Movimiento de Izquierda Revolucionario (Revolutionary Left Movement) 317–18
MRTA (Movimiento Revolucionario Túpac Amaru/Túpac Amaru Revolutionary Movement) 309
"museum" of memory 323–4
National Board for Displaced Persons 319
Sarhua 336
Sendero Luminoso (Shining Path) 309
structural divisions 316–17
University of San Cristóbal de Huamanga 309
see also Lima
Peru, Andean peasant communities
armed conflict 309, 317–21, 327, 333–7
as audience 308–9, 327–8, 337
culture 316–17
funerary rites 332, 341–5
gender roles 321–2
guilt and innocence, discourse of 337–9
Helfgott and 248
Ralli and 314, 332–3
Peru, armed conflict
Andean peasant communities 309, 317–21, 327, 333–7
Lima 314, 317–21, 327–9, 333, 338
Peru, Comisión de la Verdad y la Reconciliación (Truth and Reconciliation Commission, CVR) 309, 318–21
gender 322, 326
performance of truth 335
testimonies 310, 319–20, 332–4, 336–8
Petwo (Vodou pantheon) 126–7
Pianacci, Rómulo 239–41
Piazzolla, Astor 71
Pignatta, Cielo 360
Pinochet, Augusto 257
Pinter, Harold, "Death" 373–4
Pinto, J. P. 177–8
Pizarnik, Alejandra 278–9, 284, 303
Plato 186

Plaza de Mayo, Buenos Aires 82–3, 107–8, 263–4, 293, *see also* Mothers and Grandmothers of the Plaza de Mayo (the Mothers)
Pociña, Andrés 41–2
poetry in theater 154–5, 276
political mothers 173–8, 185, 235–6, 351
political sisterhood, shift to 351
political theater 158–60, 185
Pollín, Yolanda 40
Ponferrada, Oscar 99*f*, 108
Port-au-Prince
College of Agriculture, Damiens 110–11
Theater Rex 110–11, 129n.55
Porter, James 18–19, 33
Portugal 25–7, 160–1
postcolonial classical reception studies 19–23
postcolonialism 18, 23–4
Poulson, Nancy Kason 272–3, 275
Prado Júnior, Caio 161–2
Price Mars, Jean 115, 117
Price Mars, Louis 128
private property, Puerto Rico 222, 226–7, 229
public/private division in the Andes 321–2
Puerto Rico
anticolonial struggle 199, 204, 207–9, 218–27
Armed Forces of National Liberation of Puerto Rico (FALN) 208
Comando Armado de Liberación (CAL) 228–9
Division for Community Education 210
Guánica, 231–2
Jayuya uprising, 1950 203
Lares Revolt 1868 205, 228–9, 231–3
Mayagüez 216
Movement for Independence (MPI) 228
Nationalist Party of Puerto Rico (PNPR) 195–6
Panama Proclamation 208–9
Partido de Acción Cristiana (Christian Action Party) 231–2
Puerto Rican Traveling Theater (PRTT) 215–16
racial labels 196
Sylvia Rexach Theater, San Juan 216
Teatro Tapia, San Juan 194, 198*f*, 210*f*, 212*f*, 213*f*, 215*f*, 231*f*

Teatro UPR, San Juan 214*f*
Theater Festival 194, 198*f*, 210*f*, 212*f*, 213*f*,
  215*f*, 231*f*
theater in Puerto Rico 207–9
University of Puerto Rico 210, 216
Puga, Ana 268, 288

Quechua language 14–15, 308–9, 318,
  330, 336
Quijano, Aníbal 25, 30
quilting points, definition 39
Quiroga, Facundo 83–5, 89–90, 92
Quiroga, Osvaldo 262–3
Quispe Pulido, Primitivo 319

race
  Andes 339–40
  Andrade's plays 186–7
  Puerto Rico 196
Rada (Vodou pantheon) 126–7, 130
Ralli, Teresa 343*f*, 344*f*, 350*f*
  on Andean women 314, 332–3
  audience reaction 308, 310, 322
  gestures 310–11, 332–5, 343, 346–9
  "Notes about our Antígona" 330–1
Rama, Ángel 28
Ramos Escobar, José Luis 200, 206–7,
  216, 225–6
Ramos Mejía, Francisco Hermógenes 92
Rancière, Jacques 110, 186
rape 26–7, 365
Reátegui Carillo, Félix 319–20
reception studies, postcolonial 19–23
Recife, Teatro Barreto Júnior 189*f*
Reiniciar association 377
Rengifo, César, *La fiesta de los moribundos*
  (The party of the living dead)
  251–5, 360–1
republican mothers 60–5, 237–43, 247
Revolta do Ano da Fumaça 1833, Brazil 180
Revolutionary Left Movement (Movimiento
  de Izquierda Revolucionario;
  Peru) 317–18
rewritten vernacular plays, routes of 6*f*
Reyes, Alfonso 38–9, 41–2
Ritsos, Yannis 314–15, 325
ritual and theater 308–9, 316–17
Rivadavia, Bernardino 58–9
Rivero, Antonio 228
Rivollet, André 147–8, 147*f*

Roca, Julio Argentino 85, 92–3
Rodó, José Enrique 32
Rodríguez, Martín 84–5, 92–3
Rojas Pinilla, Gustavo 197–8
Rojas, Ricardo 59, 63–4
Roman Catholic Church 189, 229–33
  liberation theology 201–2, 230–1, 242
  Social Doctrine of the Church 230–2
Romero Rey, Sandro 377
Rosario, Argentina 360
Rosas, Juan Manuel 83–7, 90–3, 108, 238–9
Rosenfeld, Anatol 183–4
Rotimi, Ola 14–15
Rotker, Susana 104–5
Roumain, Jacques 114–15
Royal Academy of Spain (RAE) 208–9
Rubio Zapata, Miguel 308, 316–17,
  329–31, 342–3
rumination, overview 5, 44–9
rural performances
  Haiti 110–11
  map 6*f*
  Peru 308–10, 312–13, 316–17, 329–30,
    337–41
Rusk, Dean 197

Saba, Mark 6*f*
Sacred Heart Auditorium, New York 129n.55
Sáez, Gloria 212–13
sainete (popular Spanish theatre form) 63–4
Saint-Jean, Ibérico 267
Salavarrieta, Policarpa ("La Pola") 245–7,
  255, 265
Saldaña, Rafael Enrique 212–13, 213*f*,
  215*f*, 231*f*
Samalayuca, Mexico 368*f*, 371*f*
Sánchez, Luis Rafael
  *guaracha del macho Camacho, La (Macho
    Camacho's Beat)* 207–8
  and Puerto Rican identity 207–9
  on Puerto Rico 224
Sánchez, Luis Rafael, *La pasión según
    Antígona Pérez: crónica americana en
    dos actos* (The passion according to
    Antígona Pérez: an American chronicle
    in two acts) 193–236
  1968 production 194, 198*f*, 209–18, 210*f*,
    212*f*, 213*f*, 215*f*, 231*f*
  1972 New York production 215–16
  1976 production 216, 225–6

450 INDEX

Sánchez, Luis Rafael (*cont.*)
 1992 production 214*f*, 216
 2011–12 production 216
 context, 1960s 204–7
 history vs allegory 194–204
 nationalism 228–33
 prologue 225
 Puerto Rico's anticolonial struggle 218–27
 reviews and reactions 215–17, 222–3, 225–6
San Cristóbal de Huamanga, University of, Peru 309
Sandinista National Liberation Front (FSLN; Nicaragua) 251–2
San Juan, Puerto Rico
 Joyería Riviera 214–15
 Sylvia Rexach Theater 216
 Teatro Tapia 194, 198*f*, 209, 210*f*, 212*f*, 213*f*, 215*f*, 231*f*
 Teatro UPR 214*f*
San Juan Star (periodical; Puerto Rico) 216–17
San Marcos, University of, Lima 28–9
San Martín, José de 79, 82–3, 91
Sans Souci, Jean-Baptiste 120
Sant'Anna, Catarina 183–4
Santiago de Chile 384, 385*f*
Santo Domingo, Dominican Republic 28–9, 221–2
Santos Discépolo, Enrique 71
Santos Freire, Felipe dos 164
Santos Silva, Loreina 234
Santo Tomás de Aquino University 28–9
São Paulo 160
 Teatro Alfredo Mesquita 169
 University of 155–6
São Tomé das Letras 167–8
Sarah Bernhardt Theatre, Paris 99*f*, 137*f*, 146, 240*f*, 241*f*
Sarhua, Peru 336
Sarlo, Beatriz 17
Sarmiento, Domingo Faustino 65, 88
 Facundo 58, 73–4, 84, 89–90
Sarrail, Teresa 360, 361*f*
Sartre, Jean-Paul 197, 346
Sassen, Saskia 364
Satizábal, Carlos 375–6
 Antígona y actriz (Antígona and actress) 10–12, 375–6
 Tribunal de Mujeres (A women's tribunal) 377–84, 378*f*, 379*f*, 380*f*, 381*f*, 382*f*, 383*f*

Scabuzzo, Susana 277
Schechner, Richard 290–1
Schwarz, Roberto 17
Scott, David 122
Scott, Jill 290
Séclé-Quitté (Vodou spirit) 137–8
self-revelation 235–6
Sendero Luminoso (Shining Path) 309, 317, 335–6
sexual violence, *see* gender violence
Shakespeare, William, *Hamlet* 261–2, 269, 279–80, 282, 284
shame 320–2, 328, 337–8, 345–50
Shelley, Percy Bysshe 56
Shelton, Marie-Denise 140–1
Shumway, Nicolas 63–4
silence 118–19, 283–5, 333–4
Simpson, Michael 22–3
slavery and enslaved people
 Andrade's *Pedreira das almas* (Soul quarry) 167–8, 178–81
 Brazil 160–1, 167, 178–81
 Haiti 118–27, 129–30, 134, 139, 141–2
Slavitt, David 315
Soacha, Colombia 377
Social Doctrine of the Church 230–2
social justice
 and Peronism 106
 Puerto Rico 224–5, 229–32
Society of Good Taste in Theater (Argentina) 58
Society of Jesus 182–3
solitude, Puerto Rico 218–19
songs, importance of, in Andes 316–17
Sons and Daughters for Identity and Justice Against Oblivion and Silence (H.I.J.O.S.; Argentina) 289–90
Sophocles, *Antigone*
 Cureses and 245–6
 Gambaro and 272–3, 277
 Marechal and 81
 Morisseau-Leroy and 111–12
 Uribe and 373
 Watanabe and 331–2
Sophocles, *Oedipus Rex* 112
Sosyete Koukouy of Miami, Inc. 135*f*, 136*f*
Spain
 Chronicles of the Indies 221

literature in Argentina 58
Royal Academy (RAE) 208–9
Spanish language
  continental unity 30, 55
  International Congress of the Spanish
    Language (CILE) 208, 224
  Puerto Rico 224–5
  Varela and 55
staging and props
  Marechal's *Antígona Vélez* 71–2
  Sánchez's *Antígona Pérez* 210–12
  Satizábal's *Tribunal de Mujeres* (A women's
    tribunal) 378
  Yuyachkani's and Watanabe's
    Antígona 311–12, 334–5, 339–40
Statius, *Thebaid* 56–7
Steiner, George 12–13, 74
Steiner, Rolando, *Antígona en el infierno*
  (Antígona in hell) 3, 251–2, 315
strategic classicism
  in 21st c. 366, 375
  Andrade 152–3, 183–4
  Gambaro 274
  Marechal 106
  Morisseau Leroy 112
  overview 41–4
  Sánchez 216–17
  Yuyachkani and Watanabe 313
Stray, Christopher 19–20
Sulmont, David 319
survival, ethics/politics of (Peru) 325–6,
  358, 388
Sylvia Rexach Theater, San Juan 216

Taboada, Hernán 31
Tamaulipas, Mexico 3, 372–3
Tavárez Justo, Manuel Aurelio 202–3
Taylor, Diana 272, 279–80, 286–7,
  324–5
Teatro Alfredo Mesquita, São Paulo 169
Teatro Barreto Júnior, Recife 189*f*
Teatro Brasileiro de Comédia (TBC), São
  Paulo 152–3, 155, 159–60
Teatro Celcit (Centro Latinoamericano de
  Creación y Investigación Teatral),
  Buenos Aires 310–11
Teatro Cervantes, Buenos Aires 68, 69*f*, 71,
  97*f*, 100*f*, 108n.88, 264n.9
Teatro de Arena (São Paulo) 158–60
Teatro de Buenos Aires 240*f*, 241*f*
Teatro de la Nación, Ciudad Juárez 370*f*

Teatro El Gorro Escarlata (T.E.G.E.), Buenos
  Aires 246*f*
Teatro El Público, La Habana 362*f*
Teatro em São João del-Rei, Minas
  Gerais 174*f*, 175*f*
Teatro La Máscara, *La Pasión de
  Antígona* 375–6
Teatro Oficina, Brazil 158
Teatro Repertorio del Norte, La Plata 354*f*
Teatro Seki Sano, Bogotá 380*f*, 382*f*
Teatro Seraphim, Recife 189*f*
Teatro Tapia, San Juan 198*f*, 209, 210*f*, 212*f*,
  213*f*, 215*f*, 231*f*
Teatro UPR, San Juan 214*f*
Tejada Gómez, Armando 204–5
Tellas, Vivi 358
Telón de Arena AC theater company,
  Mexico 370*f*
testimonies from Peru, Comisión de la
  Verdad y la Reconciliación (Truth and
  Reconciliation Commission,
  CVR) 310, 319–20, 332–4, 336–8
testimony genre
  Domínguez Vargas's *Río Arriba, río abajo*
    (Up the river, down the river) 376–7
  Londoño's *El insepulto, o yo veré qué hago
    con mis muertos* (The unburied, or I will
    see what I do with my dead) 376–7
  Morena's and Lösch's *Antígona
    Oriental* 358–9
  Sánchez's *Antígona Pérez* 203–4
  Satizábal's *Tribunal de Mujeres* (A women's
    tribunal) 377–84
  twenty-first century 358, 364
  Yuyachkani's and Watanabe's
    Antígona 313, 322, 324, 328–9
Texas, University of, Hispanic
  theater 215–16
theater
  political theater 158–60, 185
  Puerto Rican 207–9
  and ritual 308–9
  theater of cruelty, Gambaro and 276
  theater of expression 155
  theater of the oppressed, Brazil 158
  Vodou and 125–42
Theater of Nations (Théâtre des Nations),
  Paris 99*f*, 108, 111, 129n.55, 136, 137*f*,
  146, 240*f*, 241*f*
Theater Rex, Port-au-Prince 110–11, 129n.55
Théâtre d'Haiti, Morne Hercule 129

452 INDEX

theory of crisis (Puerto Rican left-wing movement) 228
Thomas, Saint 157, 167–9, 173–4, 181
Thompson, Howard 215–16, 222–3
Tiempo, El (newspaper; Argentina) 55
Time (periodical; USA) 144–5, 145*f*
Tiradentes (Brazilian rebel) 157, 164–5
Tizón, Sofía 361*f*
Tomasella, Sergio 267
Tompkins, Joanne 21
Tonton Macoutes (Haiti) 131
Toriano, Martín, chief, La Pampa 91
Torlucci, Sylvia 360, 361*f*
Toussaint Louverture 119–20, 122
Tramaluna Teatro, theater company, Colombia 377, 378*f*, 379*f*, 380*f*, 381*f*, 382*f*, 383*f*
transculturation 36n.76, 37–8
Tri-Continental Conference, La Habana 204–5, 234–5
Trouillot, Hénock 122
  Dessalines ou le sang du Pont Rouge (Dessalines or the blood of Pont Rouge) 144
Trouillot, Michel-Rolph 118–20, 134–6
Trujillo Molina, Rafael Leónidas 197–9, 202–3, 212–13, 221–2, 226
truth and armed conflict, Peru 335–6
Truth Commissions, emergence 335
Tucumán, Argentina 82–3, 238–9
Turchi, Romina 277

United Nations 196–7, 363–4
United States
  attack on House of Representatives 1954 203
  Commonwealth of Puerto Rico v. Sánchez Valle (Supreme Court decision) 193
  and Dominican Republic 197–8
  Insular Cases (Supreme Court decisions) 223
  occupation of Cuba 199
  occupation of Haiti 114–16
  Platt Amendment 1901 199
  and Puerto Rico 199, 222–3
  Puerto Rico Oversight, Management, and Economic Stability Act 223
  racial segregation 196
  and Venezuela 253

universality 42–4, 107, 148, 282–3, 311–12, 327–8
universities, Spanish and British colonial 28–9, 31, 35
Urabá, Colombia 376
Uribe, Gabriel, *El grito de Antígona vs La nuda vida* (Antígona's cry vs bare life) 374–5
Uribe, Sara, *Antígona González* 3, 372–4
Urrao, Colombia 376–7
Uruguay 54n.4, 358–9
utopian/impossible universal
  de la Rosa's *Antígona, las voces que incendian el desierto* (the voices that set the desert on fire) 370–1
  Dorfman's *Widows* 259
  and female collective 245
  Gambaro's *Antígona Furiosa* 268–9, 283, 306
  Mexico 369
  Morgado's *Antígona Insomne* 387
  overview 43, 237, 250–1, 255–6, 388–9
  Satizábal's *Tribunal de Mujeres* (A women's tribunal) 379–80
  Uribe's *Antígona González* 373–4
  Yuyachkani's and Watanabe's *Antígona* 315–16, 351–2
utopianism
  1960s 199, 204–5
  Andrade 156, 169
  Dessalines 120
  Morisseau-Leroy's *Antigòn an Kreyòl* (Antigone in Creole) 129–30
  overview 42–3, 45–6, 57, 238
  Sánchez's *Antígona Pérez* 236
utopias, conditional, Saint Thomas and 168
utopias, negative 140–1, 245, 255

Valenzuela, Gilberto 216
Valladolid Controversy, colonial Spain 29
Varela, Juan Cruz
  background and career 59
  Dido 56, 59
  "National Literature" 55
  "Oda a la Victoria de Maipú" 59
Varela, Juan Cruz, *Argia* 1–2, 54–66
  Buenos Aires as an Athens 57–60
  critiques 63–4
  national literature 55–7
  republican motherhood 60–6
Vargas Llosa, Mario 323–4
Vásquez, Myrna 212, 213*f*

INDEX 453

Velasco Alvarado, Juan 317–18
Vélez Sarsfield, Dalmacio 92
Venezuela 197–8, 252
Veríssimo, Érico 161–2
Verna, Paul 8–9
Viana, Hilton 155–6
Videla, Jorge Rafael 266–7, 285, 290
Vietnam War 207–8, 224
Vila Rica 182–3
 revolt of, 1720 164
Villaflor, Azucena 292
Villavicencio, Juan Carlos, *Antígona en el
 espejo* 357
Viñas, David 67, 75–6, 86, 102
Viscal Garriga, Olga 203
Vodou
 candomblé (Brazil) 128
 cosmology 126–7, 130, 134, 137–41
 Dessalines and 143
 and independence 115, 142–4
 Marxism and 114–15
 noirisme and 114–15
 and political theater 125–42
 rites and ceremonies 112–13, 125–7,
 139, 142
Voz del Interior, La (periodical;
 Argentina) 264*f*

Waldman, Gloria 225–6, 234
Wallace, Isabel Miranda 371–2
Wally, Juan W. 78
Watanabe, José 14–15, 33–4, 45–6, 331, 333
 Cosas del cuerpo (Bodily things) 331
Watanabe, José and Yuyachkani, *Antígona*
 307–54, 343*f*, 344*f*, 350*f*
 Andean communities' suffering 334–45
 Argentine version 310–11
 creation of Peruvian Antígona 329–34
 critical dialogues 321–9
 dual nature/dual audience 308–13
 performances 308–11
 political roadmap for Peru 349–52
 political violence and the CVR 316–21
 shame and guilt 345–9
 why Ismene? 314–16
Weinberg, Félix 55
Weiss, Peter 313
White, Edward Douglass 223
white-face make-up (Yuyachkani,
 Peru) 339–41
widowhood, socialization of 259

Wiener, Odette 111
Wiesse Rebagliati, Jorge 315–16
Wilde, Eduardo 86
witnessing, ethics of 324–6, 328–9
women
 Andean 310, 314, 321–2, 326, 332–4,
 337–8
 Beneficent Society (Argentina) 59, 65
 Creole women and indigenous
 peoples 104–5
 female body, the 188–9
 feminicidio, term 366, 369
 feminism 286–90, 363–4
 feminization of poverty 364
 "ordinary" heroism of 355–8, 384, 388–9
 Sánchez's *Antígona Pérez* 196, 234–6
 widowhood 259
 Women in Black 286–7, 289
 Women's Peronist Party 71
 see also female bonding and collectives;
 mothers; Mothers and Grandmothers of
 the Plaza de Mayo (the Mothers)
Women in Black 286–7, 289
Women's Peronist Party 71
world literature, subfield 13–15, 17–18

Yanquetruz, chief, La Pampa 84–5
Yanvalou dances, Haiti 130
Ynclán, Gabriela, *Podrías llamarte Antígona*
 (Your name could be Antígona) 371–2
Yrigoyen, Hipólito 85–6
Yucateca language 10–11
Yusem, Laura 262, 263*f*, 265
Yuyachkani, Casa, Lima 308
Yuyachkani theater collective 14–15, 307–8,
 329, 343*f*, 344*f*, 350*f*
 Adiós Ayacucho 339–40, 342–3
 Allpa Rayku (Por la tierra/For the
 land) 329–30
 Puño de cobre (Fist of copper) 329–30
 Rosa Cuchillo 339–40
 see also Watanabe, José and Yuyachkani,
 Antígona
Yuyanapaq (exhibition; Peru) 323–4

Zalacaín, Daniel 206
Zavaleta Mercado, René 26, 33–4, 37–8
Zavalía, Alberto de, *El Límite* (The limit) 2,
 238–9, 240*f*, 241*f*
zombies and zombification, Haiti 112–13,
 123–4, 134, 139